International Human Rights and Hu

How do international human rights and humanitarian law protect vulnerable individuals in times of peace and of war? René Provost analyses systemic similarities and differences in the construction of each body of law, showing how they achieve a similar goal. By detailing the dynamics of human rights and humanitarian law, Provost reveals how each performs a task for which it is better suited than the other, and that the fundamentals of both fields remain partly incompatible. This helps us understand why their norms succeed in some ways and fail, at times spectacularly, in others.

Provost's study represents innovative and in-depth research, covering all relevant materials from the UN, ICTY, ICTR, and regional organisations in Europe, Africa and Latin America. This study will be of interest to academics and graduate students in international law and international relations, as well as to legal practitioners in related fields, and NGOs active in human rights.

RENÉ PROVOST is Associate Professor at the Faculty of Law and the Institute of Comparative Law, McGill University. He has published in the *British Yearbook of International Law*, the *Columbia Journal of Transnational Law* and the *University of Miami Inter-American Law Review*.

CAMBRIDGE STUDIES IN INTERNATIONAL AND COMPARATIVE LAW

This series (established in 1946 by Professors Gutteridge, Hersch Lauterpacht and McNair) is a forum of studies of high quality in the fields of public and private international law and comparative law. Although these are distinct legal subdisciplines, developments since 1946 confirm their interrelationship.

Comparative law is increasingly used as a tool in the making of law at national, regional and international levels. Private international law is increasingly affected by international conventions, and the issues faced by classical conflicts rules are increasingly dealt with by substantive harmonisation of law under international auspices. Mixed international arbitrations, especially those involving state economic activity, raise mixed questions of public and private international law. In many fields (such as the protection of human rights and democratic standards, investment guarantees and international criminal law) international and national systems interact. National constitutional arrangements relating to 'foreign affairs', and to the implementation of international norms, are a focus of attention.

Professor Sir Robert Jennings edited the series from 1981. Following his retirement as General Editor, an editorial board has been created and Cambridge University Press has recommitted itself to the series, affirming its broad scope.

The Board welcomes works of a theoretical or interdisciplinary character, and those focusing on new approaches to international or comparative law or conflicts of law. Studies of particular institutions or problems are equally welcome, as are translations of the best work published in other languages.

General Editors: Professor James Crawford SC FBA
                    Whewell Professor of International Law, Faculty of Law and Director, Lauterpacht Research Centre for International Law, University of Cambridge
                    Professor John S. Bell FBA *Professor of Law, Faculty of Law, University of Cambridge*

Editorial Board: Professor Hilary Charlesworth, *University of Adelaide*
                    Professor Lori Damrosch, *Columbia University Law School*
                    Professor John Dugard, *Universiteit Leiden*
                    Professor Mary-Ann Glendon, *Harvard Law School*
                    Professor Christopher Greenwood, *London School of Economics*
                    Professor David Johnston, *University of Edinburgh*
                    Professor Heinz Kötz, *Max-Planck-Institut, Hamburg*
                    Professor Donald McRae, *University of Ottawa*
                    Professor Onuma Yasuaki, *University of Tokyo*
                    Professor Reinhard Zimmermann, *Universität Regensburg*

Advisory Committee: Professor Sir D. W. Bowett QC
                    Judge Rosalyn Higgins QC
                    Professor Sir Robert Jennings QC
                    Professor J. A. Jolowicz QC
                    Professor Sir Elihu Lauterpacht QC
                    Professor Kurt Lipstein QC
                    Judge Stephen Schwebel

A list of books in the series can be found at the end of this volume

International Human Rights and Humanitarian Law

René Provost

CAMBRIDGE
UNIVERSITY PRESS

CAMBRIDGE UNIVERSITY PRESS
Cambridge, New York, Melbourne, Madrid, Cape Town, Singapore, São Paulo

Cambridge University Press
The Edinburgh Building, Cambridge CB2 2RU, UK

Published in the United States of America by Cambridge University Press, New York

www.cambridge.org
Information on this title: www.cambridge.org/9780521806978

First published 2002
Third printing 2004
This digitally printed first paperback version 2005

A catalogue record for this publication is available from the British Library

Library of Congress Cataloguing in Publication data
Provost, René, 1965–
International human rights and humanitarian law / René Provost.
       p.   cm. – (Cambridge studies in international and comparative law)
Includes bibliographical references and index.
ISBN 0 521 80697 6 (HB)
1. Humanitarian law.   2. Human rights.   I. Title.   II. Cambridge studies in international
and comparative law (Cambridge, England: 1996)
KZ6471.P76   2002
341.4′81 – dc21   2001043248

ISBN-13 978-0-521-80697-8 hardback
ISBN-10 0-521-80697-6 hardback

ISBN-13 978-0-521-01928-6 paperback
ISBN-10 0-521-01928-1 paperback

A mes parents,
pour tout

Contents

Preface to the paperback edition

When the attacks of 11 September 2001 occurred, the original edition of this book was already well into its pre-publication production. As a result, the analysis does not include express references to these events nor to the ensuing reaction of the international community in general. The scale of human and economic devastation caused by the September 11 attacks, the difficult characterisation of the multinational intervention in Afghanistan following the Taliban regime's refusal to stop Al-Qaeda activities on its territory, the troubling legal issues surrounding episodes of the 'war on terror' such as the targeted killing by an unmanned CIA drone inside Yemen in 2002, and the invasion and occupation of Iraq on uncertain grounds in 2003, all deny the possibility of a neat division between war and peace. These events, like many others that preceded them over the last several decades, reinforce the need for a fuller articulation of the relationship between two normative regimes designed to protect fundamental human interests: international humanitarian law and human rights.

This book tackles the broad issue of the interrelationship between human rights and humanitarian law by focussing on three transversal themes: first, the normative frameworks of each regime; second, the place of reciprocity; and third, the challenges posed by normative indeterminacy combined with the need for characterisation of facts and situations. All are systemic traits touching on the very nature of human rights and humanitarian law, destined to evolve gradually over a period of time. Even the globalisation of the threat of terrorism does not fundamentally alter the dynamics of these regimes, although it may give rise to new modes and types of questioning. When terrorists today refuse to adhere to human rights and humanitarian law and, in reaction, states deny the *de jure* applicability of these norms or paint them as the quaint rules of antiquated regimes not suitable for contemporary realities, we hear echoes of Palestine, Vietnam, Algeria and countless other situations. Current debates, then, are variations on painfully familiar themes rather than radically new challenges for international human rights and humanitarian law.

Two international judicial decisions in the last three years have addressed directly the connection between human rights and humanitarian law: the International Court of Justice Advisory Opinion on the Legal Consequences of the Construction of a Wall in the Occupied Palestinian Territory, issued on 9 July 2004, and the Eritrea-Ethiopia Claims Commission Partial Award in Ethiopia's Civilian Claim 5, rendered on 17 December 2004.[1] Both tribunals insisted on the complementarity of the two regimes, made possible by the continuous application of human rights to situations of armed conflicts, save possible derogations authorised by treaties, alongside the *lex specialis* embodied in humanitarian law. Given this dual applicability, as noted by the ICJ, it may be that some matters will be governed exclusively by one or the other regime, or concurrently by both of them. The Eritrea-Ethiopia Commission offered more specifically that human rights norms might be especially helpful *vis-à-vis* situations affecting individuals enjoying a more limited protection than others under humanitarian law. The Commission referred in particular to a state's treatment of its own nationals, traditionally not seen as 'protected persons' under the Fourth Geneva Convention and thus benefiting from much more limited protections under humanitarian law. Human rights, of course, rarely make any distinctions on the basis of nationality, and would in this context supplement in a significant fashion the normative web protecting such individuals in times of war.

It is revealing to note the impact of the non-criminal context of these two decisions, coming in the wake of the phenomenal development of international humanitarian law spearheaded by the work of the International Criminal Tribunals for the Former Yugoslavia and Rwanda. Faced with a similar challenge to strengthen the protection given to individuals sharing the same nationality as their abusers, the ICTY Appeals Chamber in *Tadic* had redefined the concept of nationality used in the Fourth Geneva Convention to enlarge the class of 'protected persons' and thus open the door to criminal responsibility in this context.[2] The rejuvenation of humanitarian law through a criminal process, which began

---

[1] *Legal Consequences of the Construction of a Wall in the Occupied Palestinian Territory,* [2004] ICJ Rep. 1, at 41 para. 106; Eritrea-Ethiopia Claims Commission, *Partial Award in Ethiopia's Civilian Claim 5,* 17 December 2004, at 7 para. 26 (available at www.pca-cpa.org).

[2] *The Prosecutor v. Tadic* (Appeals Judgment), 19 July 1999, Case No. IT-94-1-A (Appeals Chamber, ICTY), paras. 165-68 (published at 124 ILR 61). See below, at pp. 39-40.

with the ICTY-ICTR and was continued by the International Criminal Court Statute, has tended to downplay the interconnection with human rights because of the absence of a general principle of individual responsibility in the latter. The exception to this phenomenon relates to provisions such as Article 75 of the 1977 Additional Protocol I which, as noted by the Eritrea-Ethiopia Commission, incorporate by reference many important human rights into humanitarian law.[3]

The decisions of the ICJ and the Eritrea-Ethiopia Commission raise a host of legal issues of relevance to the articulation of arguments in this book, but which cannot be given full attention in the context of a brief preface. More importantly, they stand as a reminder that there is considerable danger in reducing any field of law to court decisions, especially those in the criminal context. Various strands of critical theories of law over recent decades have taught jurists to look for sites of normativity beyond courts and even formal state institutions. The great promise of human rights and humanitarian law lies more concretely in the everyday relationships among individuals, even when marked by abuse or hostility, than in formal structures of the state. It is this vision of the potential for learning from human experience which informs much of the argument presented in this book.

René Provost
McGill University
March 2005

---

[3] Eritrea-Ethiopia Claims Commission, see note 1 above, at 8 para. 29.

Acknowledgments

Over the course of writing a book, one accumulates many more debts than can be acknowledged in a few lines. I am grateful to Ian Brownlie, who gave me constant support and advice throughout the course of this project, even after I had left Oxford. My thanks go to Louis Henkin at Columbia Law School, with whom I had my first discussions to articulate the topic of this work. David Daube and Stefan Riesenfeld at UC Berkeley provided, in very different ways, inspiring models of what academic pursuit should be about. Christine Gray, Benedict Kingsbury, James Crawford and Stephen Toope gave me helpful comments and advice at various stages.

St Antony's College proved a very warm and hospitable place to spend my time in Oxford, for which I am thankful to the Warden, Fellows and staff. The Faculty of Law of McGill University provided, and continues to provide, a collegial, friendly and stimulating environment. I am indebted to the staff of the Bodleian Law Library and the McGill Law Library for accommodating my frequent requests for esoteric books and articles. I am also grateful for the financial support provided by a number of sources, including the Fonds pour la formation de chercheurs et l'aide à la recherche du Québec, the Centennial Scholarship Fund, the IODE War Memorial Scholarships Fund and the Boulton Trust Fund of McGill University.

With Amanda Dickins, Fabien Gélinas, Carolina Labarta, David Lametti, Susan Law, Hans Meier, David N'dii, Peter Oliver, Sophie Probert Oliver, Diarmuid Rossa Phelan, Nandini Ramanujam, Geneviève Saumier, Stephen Smith and Robert Wintemute, I shared much food, wine, whisky, movies, sports, outings and so many other things essential to the production of a work such as this one. J'ai dédié ce livre à mes

parents, Jean et Denyse, pour tout ce que j'ai appris et continue
d'apprendre d'eux. Finally my greatest debt is owed to Shauna, without whom nothing would have been possible . . . et pour Daniel Sol et
Micah, pour qui rien n'est impossible.

Table of cases

Table of treaties

Bold type indicates that the article is reproduced in whole or in part

Table of other international instruments

Bold type indicates that the article is reproduced in whole or in part

UN General Assembly Resolutions

UN Security Council Resolutions

Miscellaneous

Introduction

Armed conflict and massive violations of fundamental human rights continue to elude the efforts of the international community to prevent them. The shortcomings of international law are more strikingly illustrated with every crisis. Even genocide, the most intolerable assault on humanity, so far has proven impossible to stamp out. To most people, and probably to most jurists, international law appears not merely ill-equipped but broadly impotent in its ability to provide concrete solutions to these blatant violations. While international lawyers may not subscribe completely to this assessment, a real unease must accompany an analysis of theoretical constructs which are supposed to provide solutions to these intractable problems. Clearly, human rights and humanitarian law do not offer easy answers as to how to prevent infringements of the basic dignity and integrity of all people in times of war and peace. They represent rational attempts to articulate standards which ideally will become universally accepted and guide the international community in its evaluation of, and reaction to, such violations.

The international community has succeeded in building a consensus on a large number of standards in the fields of human rights and humanitarian law. We now have a thick code of rules at our disposal, although it clearly does not address every situation nor cover every region. Those rules will be called upon to evolve as the challenges facing the international community take on new shapes. Indeed the adoption of the Statute of the International Criminal Court and the growing jurisprudence of the International Criminal Tribunals for former Yugoslavia and Rwanda, for example, are signals of the speed at which some segments of international law are changing. But adding new rules and creating new institutions, even if they are accepted by a large number of states, does not in itself provide relief to individuals whose interests are being trampled. We must attempt not only to better our understanding of why such violations occur, a task primarily carried out by sociologists and political scientists, but also to investigate what can be achieved with the normative instruments already at our disposal.

Comparative law's promise is that, by examining how two legal systems seek to protect similar interests by way of different norms or institutions, we achieve a greater understanding of each of these systems. A comparison of human rights and humanitarian law thus seems full of potential, as the two systems appear to share, as one of their central goals, the protection of the integrity of the human person. One of the by-products of comparative analysis is the possibility of finding in one system answers which may be borrowed and adapted to solve challenges faced by another legal system. Such cross-pollination between human rights and humanitarian law is also made possible by their similarity. This study undertakes to analyse systemic similarities and differences between human rights and humanitarian law, to assess whether and to what extent the promise of comparative law can indeed be realised in their respect.

The issue of a connection between human rights and humanitarian law surfaced on the legal and political scene in the late 1960s and early 1970s. Links between the two bodies of law had been discussed from the end of the Second World War, following the successive adoptions of the 1948 Universal Declaration of Human Rights and the 1949 Geneva Conventions. By the late 1960s, humanitarian law stood at a standstill following the cool reception by the majority of states to the proposal by the International Committee of the Red Cross for supplementary rules for the protection of civilian populations in times of war, approved by the XIXth International Conference of the Red Cross in New Delhi in 1957.[1] Human rights law, on the other hand, was experiencing a great boom, most strikingly with the adoption in 1966 of the International Covenants on Civil and Political Rights and on Economic, Social and Cultural Rights,[2] which concretised into positive norms the ideals embodied in the Universal Declaration. Given the bleak prospects for a renewed

[1] Draft Rules for the Limitation of the Dangers Incurred by the Civilian Population in Time of War, reprinted in Dietrich Schindler and Jiří Toman, The Laws of Armed Conflict, 3rd edn (Dordrecht: Nijhoff, 1988) 251.
[2] 16 December 1966, (1966) 999 UNTS 1 and 171, reprinted in Ian Brownlie ed., Basic Documents on Human Rights, 3rd edn (Oxford: Clarendon, 1992) 114 and 125.

humanitarian order, the pressing need for increased protection of victims of war caught in the conflicts in Algeria, Nigeria, the Middle East and the Indochinese peninsula, and the more extensive range of treaty human rights norms at the time, a partial fusion of human rights and humanitarian law appeared to be a practical and effective way of increasing protection for individuals affected by armed conflicts.[3]

The rapprochement of human rights and humanitarian law was given a decisive push by the 1968 International Conference on Human Rights, convened by the UN in Tehran to celebrate the International Year for Human Rights. The conference marked the UN's first foray into the development of humanitarian law, a field considered up to then incompatible with the very purpose of the organisation and the prohibition of the use of force in Article 2(4) of the UN Charter.[4] Humanitarian desire to expand the protection afforded the individual by international law in times of war was compounded by the charged political context in which the conference took place. Following the Six Day War, Arab states wanted condemnation of Israeli behaviour in the occupied territories, while Third World and Eastern Bloc states sought to legitimise decolonisation wars.[5] The first resolution of the Conference, entitled 'Respect and Enforcement of Human Rights in the Occupied Territories', combined human rights and humanitarian law in calling on Israel to apply both the Universal Declaration and the 1949 Geneva Conventions in the occupied territories.[6] The Conference then adopted the more general Resolution XXIII entitled 'Respect for Human Rights in Armed Conflicts', which proffered, in a manner rather more vague and general than its title would suggest, that 'peace is the underlying condition of the full observance of human rights and war is their negation', and that 'even during the periods of armed conflicts, humanitarian principles must prevail'. It also called for those fighting racist or colonial regimes to be

---

[3] See G. I. A. D. Draper, 'The Relationship Between the Human Rights Regime and the Law of Armed Conflict', in *Proceedings of the International Conference on Humanitarian Law – San Remo, 24–27 Sept. 1970* (Grassi: Istituto Editoriale Ticinese, 1970) 141, 145; Alessandro Migliazza, 'L'évolution de la réglementation de la guerre à la lumière de la sauvegarde des droits de l'homme', (1972-III) 137 *Recueil des cours* 142, 192; 'Report of the Secretary-General on Respect for Human Rights in Armed Conflicts', UN Doc. A/8052 (1970) 13 para. 28.

[4] 'Report of the Secretary-General on Respect for Human Rights in Armed Conflicts', UN Doc. A/7720 (1969) 11 para. 19.

[5] See Henri Meyrowitz, 'Le droit de la guerre et les droits de l'homme', (1972) 88 *Revue de droit public et de la science politique en France et à l'étranger* 1059, 1061–2.

[6] 12 May 1968, 'Final Act of the International Conference on Human Rights', 22 April–13 May 1968, UN Doc. A/Conf.32/41 (Sales No. 68.XIV.2).

treated as either prisoners of war or political prisoners.[7] Despite the ambiguous reference to 'humanitarian principles', which could reasonably be interpreted to refer to either human rights or humanitarian law, Resolution XXIII has been seen as a turning point, marking a change in attitude in thinking about the relationship between human rights and humanitarian law.[8]

Resolution XXIII was reaffirmed by the UN General Assembly later that year, with the adoption of Resolution 2444 (1968), 'Respect for Human Rights in Armed Conflicts', which called on the Secretary-General to draft a report on measures to be adopted in order to increase the protection given to all individuals in times of armed conflict.[9] No direct linkage of human rights to humanitarian law can be found in the body of the resolution. The only hint of such a connection lies in the title, borrowed from Resolution XXIII. The Secretary-General's two reports issued in 1969 and 1970, likewise entitled 'Respect for Human Rights in Armed Conflicts', represent a significant contribution to the position that no fundamental distinction exists between human rights and humanitarian law.[10] In the wake of these reports, the General Assembly called for the enforcement of human rights in times of armed conflict in the form of Resolution 2675 (1970), which affirmed that '[f]undamental human rights, as accepted in international law and laid down in international instruments, continue to apply fully in situations of armed conflict'.[11] The General Assembly later adopted a number of similar resolutions leading up to the inception of the 1977 Additional Protocols.[12]

The resolutions of the International Conference on Human Rights and the UN General Assembly did not create an entirely novel concept, but rather reflected real and recognised links between human rights and humanitarian law. Although the regulation of the conduct of warfare in international law considerably predates the appearance of human

---

[7] Ibid., reprinted in Schindler and Toman, Laws of Armed Conflict, at 261.

[8] See Meyrowitz, 'Droit de la guerre', at 1060–4; Arthur Henri Robertson, 'Humanitarian Law and Human Rights', in Christophe Swinarski ed., Studies and Essays on International Humanitarian Law and Red Cross Principles in Honour of Jean Pictet (Geneva/The Hague: ICRC/Nijhoff, 1984) 793, 795.

[9] 19 December 1968, UN GAOR, 23rd Sess., Supp. No. 19, at 50–1, reprinted in Schindler and Toman, Laws of Armed Conflict, at 263.

[10] UN Doc. A/7720 (1969); UN Doc. A/8052 (1970).

[11] UN GAOR, 29th Sess., Supp. No. 31, reprinted in Schindler and Toman, Laws of Armed Conflict, at 269.

[12] A partial list of the resolutions adopted by the UN General Assembly can be found in Claude Pilloud et al., Commentary on the Additional Protocols of 8 June 1977 to the Geneva Conventions of 12 August 1949 (Geneva: Nijhoff, 1987) 1571–7.

rights, the two bodies of law share as a basis a fundamental concern for humanity. The transformation in the last century and a half of the ancient law of arms into modern humanitarian law stems from humanitarian values derived from a variety of social, religious, political, moral, military and scientific factors.[13] This humanitarian dimension of the law of war was expressed explicitly in the 'Martens clause', inserted in the preamble of the 1899 Hague Convention II, and later in the 1907 Hague Convention IV, as well as in the 1949 Geneva Conventions and 1977 Additional Protocols.[14] It is commonly remarked that while human rights law is infused with considerations of humanity, humanitarian law is shaped by the tension between concerns for humanity and military necessity.[15] Meyrowitz suggests the further distinction that, while human rights law derives from humanity understood as the defining characteristic of the human race (*menschheit*), humanitarian law is coloured not only by that aspect of humanity, but also by humanity understood as a feeling of compassion towards other human beings (*menschlichkeit*), so that in humanitarian law humanity–*menschheit* is safeguarded through humanity–*menschlichkeit*.[16] It seems in fact possible to discern elements of humanity–*menschlichkeit* in human rights as well, particularly in economic, social, cultural and collective rights.

Apart from sharing this concern for humanity as a basis, human rights and humanitarian law have had some influence on each other's development. On the one hand, human rights law in part grew out of war and humanitarian law, more specifically the experiences of the Second World War and, in particular, the Nuremberg trials. Defendants in those trials were charged not only with crimes against peace and war crimes, but also with 'crimes against humanity', that is crimes committed

---

[13] Draper, 'Relationship', at 141; Theodor Meron, *Human Rights in Internal Strife: Their International Protection* (Cambridge: Grotius, 1987) 12–13; Jean Pictet ed., *The Geneva Conventions of 12 August 1949 – Commentary on the IV Geneva Convention Relative to the Protection of Civilian Persons in Times of War* (Geneva: ICRC, 1958) 77.

[14] The most relevant passage of the Martens clause states that 'in cases not included in the present Regulations ..., populations and belligerents remain under the protection and empire of the principles of international law, as they result from the usages established between civilized nations, from the laws of humanities, and the requirements of the public conscience'. 1899 Hague Convention (II) with Respect to the Laws and Customs of War on Land, 29 July 1899, *reprinted in* Schindler and Toman, *Laws of Armed Conflict*, at 69; 1907 Hague Convention (IV) Respecting the Laws and Customs of War on Land, 18 October 1907, *reprinted in ibid.,* at 77.

[15] See the comments of Judge Koroma in his dissent in the *Advisory Opinion Concerning the Legality of the Use or Threat of Nuclear Weapons,* 8 July 1996, at 15.

[16] Henri Meyrowitz, 'Réflexions sur le fondement du droit de la guerre', in Swinarski, *Mélanges Pictet,* at 419, 426–31.

against any individuals, including a state's own nationals. Hersch Lauterpacht suggested that the acknowledgment by the international community that crimes against humanity existed in customary international law necessarily implied the recognition of corresponding fundamental human rights for the individual.[17] The prohibition of genocide, derived from the concept of wartime crimes against humanity and later enlarged to prohibit similar peacetime behaviour, can perhaps be seen as an example of the intersection of human rights and humanitarian law. On the other hand, the Universal Declaration of Human Rights, drafted in the aftermath of the Nuremberg judgments, had some influence on the development of humanitarian law through the preparation and adoption of the 1949 Geneva Conventions. The influence of the Universal Declaration on the text of the Geneva Conventions may be seen, for instance, in the provisions prohibiting discrimination (Arts. 12/12/16/27). Similar influences can be perceived in other provisions dealing with torture, cruel, unusual and degrading treatment or punishment, arbitrary arrest or detention, and due process.[18] Some parts of the more recent 1977 Additional Protocols bear a strong resemblance to human rights instruments: for instance Article 75 of Protocol I resembles Article 14 of the Covenant on Civil and Political Rights. The progressive rejection of military necessity as a valid justification for disregarding humanitarian law over the course of the last century can also be linked to the development of individual human rights.[19] Thus, as emphasised by UN resolutions in the late 1960s and early 1970s, there has been some degree of cross-pollination in the development of human rights and humanitarian law. This movement continues to this day, most visibly in the work to elaborate minimum humanitarian standards.[20]

Despite the UN's efforts to bring together human rights and humanitarian law, differences between these two areas of international law

---

[17] Hersch Lauterpacht, *International Law and Human Rights* (London: Stevens & Sons, 1950) 35–7; Hersch Lauterpacht, 'The Subjects of the Law of Nations – 2', (1948) 64 *L Quart. Rev.* 97, 104; Johannes Morsink, 'World War Two and the Universal Declaration', (1993) 15 *Hum. Rts Quart.* 357–405.

[18] See Meron, *Human Rights in Internal Strife*, at 13; Migliazza, 'L'évolution', at 191–2; Giuseppe Barile, *'Obligationes erga omnes* e individui nel diritto internazionale umanitario', (1985) 68 *Rivista di diritto internazionale* 5, 12; Claude Pilloud, 'La Déclaration universelle des droits de l'homme et les Conventions internationales protégeant les victimes de la guerre', [1949] *Revue internationale de la Croix-Rouge* 252, 254–7.

[19] Migliazza, 'L'évolution', at 198–201.

[20] See UN Secretary-General, 'Report on Minimum Humanitarian Standards', UN Doc. E/CN.4/1998/87, para. 99.

remain, most clearly with regard to their respective context of application and the types of relationships they regulate. The classic conception of human rights and humanitarian law is that they apply in different situations and to different relationships. That is, human rights are understood to regulate the relationship between states and individuals under their jurisdiction in every aspect of ordinary life, but are largely inapplicable in times of emergencies that threaten the life, independence or security of the nation or state. Humanitarian law, meanwhile, historically has governed the wartime relationship of belligerent states and of states and protected persons, which include enemy persons and neutrals, but not a state's own nationals. Recent developments have narrowed this gap somewhat and have created real examples of crossover between the fields of application of human rights and humanitarian law. In human rights law, a so-called 'third generation' of rights based on global human solidarity and possessing both individual and collective dimensions purports to create rights and obligations between individuals and states other than their own. For instance, the right to peace, the right to development, and the right to food could be claimed by individuals or peoples against other states.[21] In humanitarian law, the ripening into custom of common Article 3 of the 1949 Geneva Conventions, applying basic humanitarian norms to non-international armed conflicts, supplemented by the adoption of Protocols I and II (e.g. Arts. 1(4) and 75, Protocol I; Art. 1(1), Protocol II), has expanded the scope of humanitarian law to cover certain relationships between a state and its own nationals.[22] A measure of overlap can thus be ascertained between the fields of human rights and humanitarian law, although by and large they remain applicable to different situations.

The nature of the relationships envisaged by human rights law and humanitarian law also remains generally and significantly different. Despite humanistic ideas put forward during the Enlightenment to the effect that wars occur between governments and not between peoples, the reality of modern armed conflicts is such that all members of a belligerent state's population are considered enemies, although a clear distinction is drawn between combatants and non-combatants. The

---

[21] See Stephen Marks, 'Emerging Human Rights: A New Generation for the 1980s?', (1981) 33 *Rutgers L Rev*. 435–52; Louis B. Sohn, 'The New International Law: Protecting the Rights of Individuals Rather than States', (1982) 32 *Am. UL Rev*. 1, 48–62.

[22] Part II (Arts. 13–26) of the 1949 Fourth Geneva Convention also contains minimal norms applicable to the populations of all parties to a conflict, including a state's own nationals.

relationship embodied in humanitarian law is resolutely based on hostility. This holds true not only for relations between a belligerent state and
enemy combatants and prisoners of war, but also for relations between
non-combatants of enemy states. For example, according to Article 45 of
the 1907 Hague Regulations, it is a war crime for an occupying power
to attempt to sway the allegiance of the occupied population. Correspondingly, Article 4(A)(2) and (6) of the 1949 Third Geneva Convention
grants prisoner-of-war status to civilians taking up arms against an enemy power – inasmuch as they comply with the specific requirements
of these provisions – which can be construed as a right of resistance of
the population against a hostile force.[23] More generally, humanitarian
law as a whole is coloured by the legality of killing enemy combatants
and – at least collaterally – innocent civilians.

Human rights law, to the contrary, is based on a model fostering a
harmonious relationship between the state and individuals under its
jurisdiction. It focuses on individuals and seeks to protect and support
personal development to the maximum of their potential. Not only must
the state respect individuals by refraining from encroaching on their
protected sphere, but it must also at times actively support personal
development and be representative of its population, as democracy is
an essential condition of freedom and human rights.[24] As such, human
rights can be seen as having a constitutional nature, setting universal
criteria of political legitimacy.[25]

Human rights and humanitarian law appear related but distinct. Because the substantive norms they contain are in many ways similar or
related – for example both provide a protection against torture – there

---

[23] Meyrowitz, 'Droit de la guerre', at 1097–9. Purely private individuals taking up arms
against an occupying power without complying with the command and openness
requirements of the 1949 Third Geneva Convention commit a war crime punishable
by the enemy power: United Kingdom War Office, British Manual of Military Law,
part III – 'The Law of War on Land' (London: HMSO, 1958) para. 634; Art. 5(2), 1949
Third Geneva Convention. See Lassa Oppenheim, International Law, Hersch
Lauterpacht ed., 7th edn (London: Longmans, 1952) II, 574; Julio A. Barberis,
'Nouvelles questions concernant la personnalité juridique internationale', (1983–I) 179
Recueil des cours 145, 210.

[24] H. Lauterpacht, International Law and Human Rights, at 123; CSCE, 'Document of the
Copenhagen Meeting of the Conference on the Human Dimension of the CSCE' (1990)
at I(5), (6) and (7), reprinted in Brownlie, Basic Documents, at 456–9.

[25] Jack Donnelly, Universal Human Rights in Theory and Practice (Ithaca: Cornell UP, 1989)
14; Meyrowitz, 'Droit de la guerre', at 1083.

seems to be fertile ground for comparison and perhaps cross-pollination between the two systems. Indeed, writers analysing specific norms in either human rights or humanitarian law increasingly refer to the corresponding norm in the other system to strengthen their argument.[26] Given that norms will be specific to their context, such exchanges must be undertaken with some degree of caution if they are to be enlightening and positive. There is an observable tendency in the literature inspired primarily by human rights law to consider humanitarian law as merely a subset of human rights. Conversely, some writers in humanitarian law have argued for an overly rigid differentiation between human rights and humanitarian law, as a defence against the perceived threat to subsume the latter into the former.[27] Comparative analysis ought to be grounded in a deep understanding of both legal systems and an awareness of the differences in the nature and structure of human rights and humanitarian law, as well as an openness to meaningful interaction.

The interaction of human rights and humanitarian law is multifaceted, and gives rise to a number of enquiries. Given that they may apply concurrently, not only in the context of internal armed conflicts but also in international conflicts, the relationship between the fields of application of human rights and humanitarian law calls out for an examination. In particular, it seems important to determine whether gaps exist whereby neither set of norms applies. Many studies have concluded that existing norms are deficient and that new ones must be developed, leading to calls for the adoption of the proposed Declaration of Minimum Humanitarian Standards.[28] Another line of enquiry focuses on whether the normative web created by human rights offers substantively superior protection to that offered by humanitarian law, and vice versa. Several studies of this type have been conducted, highlighting the fact that each system offers, in some areas, greater

---

[26] See e.g. René Provost, 'Starvation as a Weapon: Legal Implications of the United Nations Food Blockade Against Iraq and Kuwait', (1992) 30 *Colum. J Transnat'l L* 577, 631–2.

[27] See Christopher Greenwood, 'Rights at the Frontier – Protecting the Individual in Time of War', in *Law at the Centre – The Institute of Advanced Legal Studies at Fifty* (Dordrecht: Kluwer, 1999) 277.

[28] See 'Declaration of Minimum Humanitarian Standards', UN Doc. E/CN.4/1996/80; UN Secretary-General, 'Report on Minimum Humanitarian Standards', UN Doc. E/CN.4/1998/87; Theodor Meron, 'On the Inadequate Reach of Humanitarian and Human Rights Law and the Need for a New Instrument', (1983) 77 *Am. J Int'l L* 589–606.

protection than the other.[29] A further line of enquiry, pursued in this book, calls for a systemic comparison of human rights and humanitarian law, to consider their respective normative dynamic in order to learn more about each and, ultimately, to gain a greater understanding which will inform the interpretation, application and future development of human rights and humanitarian law. There will thus be no attempt here to offer a comprehensive exposition and comparison of all facets, or even of all important facets, of each system. Rather than seek informational exhaustiveness, the analysis highlights selected elements of human rights and humanitarian law in order to bring out significant similarities and differences at structural and substantive levels. As such, the comparative approach adopted here departs from more traditional comparative methodology to provide a fully integrated or transsystemic analysis. While arguments are necessarily grounded in existing law, the integration of human rights and humanitarian law has led to the formulation of themes which up to now were not regarded as 'issues' in either field.

This enquiry is carried out through three transversal themes which correspond to the three parts of this book: the first part sketches the normative frameworks of human rights and humanitarian law, meaning the legal structures used to achieve their related goal of protection of the individual; the second part turns to reciprocity which, while one of the grounding principles of both legal systems, is said to occupy a fundamentally distinct place in human rights and humanitarian law; finally, the third part examines problems related to the translations of these norms into concrete standards to be applied by the various actors of the international community, and more specifically the role of normative indeterminacy and factual characterisation in the application of human rights and humanitarian law.

[29] See Aristidis Calogeropoulos-Stratis, *Droit humanitaire et droits de l'homme: La protection de la personne en conflits armés* (Geneva: Institut universitaire de hautes études internationales, 1980); Mohammed El Kouhene, *Les garanties fondamentales de la personne en droit humanitaire et droits de l'homme* (Dordrecht: Nijhoff, 1986); Paul Urner, *Die Menschenrechte der Zivilperson im Krieg gemäss der Genfer Zivilkonvention von 1949* (Winterthur: Keller, 1956) 55–150; Yoram Dinstein, 'Human Rights in Armed Conflict: International Humanitarian Law', in Theodor Meron ed., *Human Rights in International Law: Legal and Policy Issues* (Oxford: Clarendon, 1984) II, 345–68.

PART I • NORMATIVE FRAMEWORKS

Le devoir et le droit sont frères. Leur mère commune est la liberté. Ils naissent le même jour, ils se développent et périssent ensemble.
Victor Cousin, *Justice et charité* (1848)

The true source of rights is duty. If we all discharge our duties, rights will not be far to seek. If leaving duties unperformed we run after rights, they will escape us like a will-o'-the-wisp. The more we pursue them, the farther they will fly.
Mahatma Gandhi, *All Men Are Brothers* (1958)

Introduction

Part I analyses and compares the normative frameworks of international human rights law and humanitarian law by examining the way in which each is constructed to achieve its purpose, whether, in the first case, the granting of fundamental rights to the individual or, in the second, the alleviation of human suffering in times of armed conflict. This analysis will lead to an assessment of a number of conceptual differences between human rights and humanitarian law. While some have argued that the distinction is one of mere terminology, a convenient way of underlining the different fields of application of these two areas of international law, others have characterised the difference as fundamental and necessary for the development and viability of both human rights and humanitarian law.[1] The discussion will also touch on the nature of the relations between the individual and the state in human rights and humanitarian law and, more generally, on the position of the individual in international law as embodied in these two areas of law.

It will be argued that there exists a real and meaningful difference between the normative frameworks of human rights law and humanitarian law. This difference rests on the fact that human rights law is centred, indeed built, on the granting of rights to the individual, while humanitarian law is focused on the direct imposition of obligations on the individual. Conversely, the granting of rights by humanitarian law and the imposition of obligations by human rights law do not fit easily within the accepted construction of either body of law and imply significant changes to the nature of both.

Studies examining the international legal status of the individual, or of other participants in the international community, have deconstructed the concept of subjecthood into two to four constitutive elements. The more general deconstruction differentiates between the subject of international law as, on the one hand, a subject of rights, and on the other hand, a subject of obligations. These two elements are deconstructed further in the works of some authors, using a great

---

[1] Compare, for instance, R. Quentin-Baxter, 'Human Rights and Humanitarian Law – Confluence or Conflict?', (1985) 9 *Australian YB Int'l L* 94, 96 (arguing for a lack of meaningful distinction between human rights and humanitarian law), and Henri Meyrowitz, 'Le droit de la guerre et les droits de l'homme', (1972) 88 *Revue de droit public et de la science politique en France et à l'étranger* 1059, 1075 (arguing that the fusion of human rights and humanitarian law presents a grave threat to the viability of humanitarian law).

variety of terms to describe basically the same notions. The concept of the subject of rights is subdivided into a subject of interests, meaning that a substantive right has been granted for the benefit of that participant, and a subject of proceedings, that is the procedural capacity to activate mechanisms aimed at enforcing the substantive right. Similarly, the concept of the subject of obligations is subdivided into a subject of duties, that is the requirement imposed by an international norm to act in a certain way, and a subject of responsibilities, referring to the possibility of being held personally responsible for the breach of that duty.[2]

This deconstructive approach will be adopted here given its capacity to highlight the normative frameworks of human rights and humanitarian law, or, in other words, the manner in which each is constructed to achieve its purpose. The aim of the deconstruction in this context differs from that in studies seeking to establish whether the individual is a subject of international law. In the latter, the rights and obligations of the individual are assessed in order to determine the degree of international personality possessed by the individual under international law. Here, however, rights and obligations of the individual will be assessed in order to understand better the nature of international human rights and humanitarian law. Any conclusions as to the international personality of the individual under international law will be purely incidental to this main goal.[3]

The following analysis therefore adopts a structure whereby rights and procedural capacity are addressed prior to obligations and responsibility. There is an inherent difficulty, at one level, in detaching rights and obligations from their enforcement, given the fact that the reality of a right or obligation often lies in its enforcement.[4] There exists a corresponding evidentiary difficulty in that the proof of the existence of a right or obligation can be derived partly from its vindication. Nevertheless, as discussed below, the dissociation of rights and obligations from their enforcement is an accepted notion in international law. Further,

---

[2] See Carl Nørgaard, *The Position of the Individual in International Law* (Copenhagen: Munksgaard, 1962) 27ff., for an extensive discussion of that question.

[3] Indeed, a critique of the necessity of a dichotomy between objects and subjects of international law has been put very forcefully by several writers. See e.g. Rosalyn Higgins, *Problems and Process – International Law and How We Use It* (Oxford: Clarendon, 1994) 50–5.

[4] See e.g. *Gouriet v. Union of Post Office Workers*, [1977] 1 QB 729, 761 (*per* Lord Denning MR); *Ashby v. White*, (1703) 92 ER 126, 136 (KB – Holt CJ, diss.) (referring to 'that vain thing of a right without a remedy').

questions relating to enforcement and, in particular, standing in international proceedings, will be touched on in the context of both rights and obligations. The aim is not to provide a comprehensive list of the various mechanisms available to protect norms of human rights and humanitarian law, but rather to examine salient features of the enforcement of these norms so as to highlight their nature within the normative frameworks of human rights and humanitarian law.

1   Rights and procedural capacity

There is a marked difference between human rights and humanitarian law with respect to the rights and procedural capacity of the individual. The emphasis of human rights law is on granting positive rights to the individual, while humanitarian law protects the interests of the individual through means other than the granting of rights. This difference is reflected in the recognised procedural capacity of individuals to act to enforce their rights under international human rights law and humanitarian law.

As mentioned earlier, the dissociation of rights and enforcement mechanisms can raise conceptual problems going to the very existence of the rights. International law, with its traditional emphasis on the state as the sole international subject, has had to grapple with this difficulty from the moment it recognised international rights of entities other than states. The Permanent Court of International Justice acknowledged the reality of rights even if detached from the capacity to act on them in the *Peter Pázmány University* v. *Czechoslovakia* case, where it noted with respect to that university that 'the capacity to possess civil rights does not necessarily imply the capacity to exercise those rights oneself'.[1] Conversely, the agent's lack of procedural capacity to enforce a given right does not necessarily establish the non-existence of that right. The explanation given to validate a finding that the agent does indeed have a right under international law even in the absence of procedural capacity is that other actors, most often states, can act on behalf of the right-holder at the international level without transforming the nature of that right. Claims presented by states to the United Nations Compensation Commission on behalf of individuals and corporations provide an

---

[1] (1933) PCIJ Reports, Ser. A/B No. 61, at 231.

example.[2] Increased direct access by individuals to international bodies entrusted with the enforcement of international norms tends to undermine this interpretation, however, in creating rights that are more 'full' than others due to the fact that they can be acted on by the individual without the necessary intervention and consent of the state or other international subjects.

Rights

The notion that individuals may hold rights by the direct effect of international law, without any necessary intervention of the state posterior to the creation of the international norm, has been recognised for some time, starting with the 1928 advisory opinion of the Permanent Court of International Justice on the *Jurisdiction of the Courts of Danzig*.[3] Examples of such rights include labour rights contained in ILO conventions, minorities rights under the League of Nations minorities and mandates systems and the UN Trusteeship system.[4] The study now turns to consider whether human rights and humanitarian law similarly create individual rights, and what are the essential characteristics of rights under these two systems.

Before proceeding to that discussion on rights, a word of caution is needed with respect to the meanings of the word 'right'. As Hohefeld demonstrated many years ago, the concept of right can be used to describe a variety of legal relationships: an entitlement to something from the bearer of a corresponding obligation, an immunity against encroachments of certain fundamental interests, a privilege to do something, a

---

[2] See below, at pp. 51–3. Diplomatic protection is cited by some as an example because the state does not have a claim for restitution or compensation until the individual victim has exhausted local remedies. See Hersch Lauterpacht, *International Law and Human Rights* (London: Stevens & Sons, 1950) 27; F. V. García Amador, 'Le sujet passif de la responsabilité et la capacité d'être demandeur en droit international', (1956) 34 *Revue de droit international, des sciences diplomatiques et politiques* 266, 267–9; Rosalyn Higgins, 'Conceptual Thinking About the Individual in International Law', (1978) 24 *New York L School L Rev.* 11, 14. This view challenges the traditional construction of diplomatic protection, seeing the state as exercising its own right: *Mavrommatis Palestine Concession Case (Jurisdiction) (Greece v. UK)*, (1924) PCIJ Reports, Ser. A No. 2, at 12.

[3] (1928) PCIJ Reports, Ser. B No. 15, at 17–18. See also Thomas Buergenthal, 'Self-executing and Non-self-executing Treaties in National and International Law', (1992-IV) 235 *Recueil des cours* 303, 322–5.

[4] See Carl Nørgaard, *The Position of the Individual in International Law* (Copenhagen: Munksgaard, 1962) 96–8.

power to create a legal relationship, and several other variations.[5] It will be taken here as covering claims grounded in the interest of a holder, as opposed to claims grounded in the public or common interest. It would of course be possible to adopt a different meaning of rights which would encompass both types of claims; the argument would simply shift to posit that different kinds of rights are created.[6] The critical point which is made in the following pages is not so much that human rights endow individuals with 'true' rights and humanitarian law does not, which would necessarily rest on an essentialist vision of rights, but rather that there is an important difference in the normative frameworks designed to protect fundamental human interests in human rights and humanitarian law. The labels used to highlight this significant difference are not central to the argument.

HUMAN RIGHTS

Entitlement

There is little doubt that international human rights law was intended to endow individuals directly with basic rights. There is perhaps ground for some debate as to the identity of the holder of rights in the case of rules relating to injuries to aliens, because the offending party is by definition not the state of nationality, which can thus legitimately be presented as possible rights-holder.[7] In the context of human rights, however, the state of nationality is most often the offending party. That state cannot possibly be at the same time the holder of the right and its negator. The individual – and in some cases the group or people – is left as the sole possible holder of rights under human rights law.[8] The rights-based normative focus of human rights law finds confirmation in the frigid reception given to attempts to frame these standards primarily as obligations imposed upon states. The Declaration of the Basic Duties of

[5] Wesley Hohefeld, 'Fundamental Legal Conceptions as Applied in Judicial Reasoning', (1913) 23 *Yale LJ* 16. See also Jeremy Waldron ed., *Theories of Rights* (Oxford: Oxford UP, 1984); Carol Smart, *Feminism and the Power of Law* (London: Routledge, 1989) 138–45; Joseph Raz, 'Legal Rights', (1984) 4 *Ox. J Leg. Stud.* 1; Carl Tushnet, 'An Essay on Rights', (1984) 62 *Tex. L Rev.* 1363.

[6] For a relation of rights theories to international human rights, see Jerome Shestack, 'The Jurisprudence of Human Rights', in Theodor Meron ed., *Human Rights in International Law: Legal and Policy Issues* (Oxford: Clarendon, 1984) II, 69.

[7] See above, at p. 17.

[8] See generally Louis Henkin, 'International Human Rights as "Rights"', (1979) 1 *Cardozo L Rev.* 425–47.

Peoples and Governments adopted by ASEAN in 1983, for example, can be seen more as a challenge to the viability and universality of human rights than as a sound alternative to a construction of human rights as granting individual rights.[9]

Human rights attach to individuals as against any state bound by the international norm. Narrow constructions of the applicability of human rights have been rejected to ensure that, in the words of the UN Secretary-General, they 'apply always and everywhere'.[10] Thus, the provisions of many human rights treaties which restrict their application to 'individuals under the jurisdiction of the state concerned' have been interpreted to ensure the broadest application of these treaties. The European Convention on Human Rights, for example, provides in Article 1 that '[t]he High Contracting Parties shall secure to everyone within their jurisdiction the rights and freedoms defined in Section I of the Convention'.[11] The American Convention on Human Rights contains a similarly drafted applicability provision (Art. 1(1)).[12] The word 'jurisdiction' has been taken to refer to the state's power rather than the geographical or territorial limitation of this power. The question of whether acts taking place outside national territory were covered by the European Convention was raised before the European Commission of Human Rights with respect to the Turkish occupation of part of Cyprus. The Commission, finding support in the French version of the provision speaking of everyone 'relevant de leur juridiction', concluded that states party to the Convention were 'bound to secure the said rights and freedoms to all persons under their actual authority and responsibility, whether that authority is exercised within their own territory or abroad'.[13] This was confirmed by the European Court of Human Rights in *Loizidou* v. *Turkey*, where it found Turkey responsible for acts carried out in the area controlled by its armed forces on Cyprus.[14]

---

[9] The Declaration is reprinted in Albert Blaustein, Roger Clark and Jay Sigler eds., *Human Rights Sourcebook* (New York: Paragon, 1987) 646–57.

[10] 'Report on Human Rights in Armed Conflict', UN Doc. A/8052 (1970) 13 para. 25.

[11] Convention for the Protection of Human Rights and Fundamental Freedoms, 4 November 1950, (1950) 213 UNTS 222, *reprinted in* Ian Brownlie ed., *Basic Documents on Human Rights*, 3rd edn (Oxford: Clarendon, 1992) 326 (hereinafter European Convention on Human Rights).

[12] 22 November 1969, OAS Treaty Series, No. 36, at 1, *reprinted in* Brownlie, *Basic Documents*, at 495.

[13] Appl. 6780/74 and 6950/75, *Cyprus* v. *Turkey*, (1975) 2 Decisions and Reports 125, 136.

[14] *Loizidou* v. *Turkey (Merits)*, Judgment of 18 December 1996, paras. 52–7; *Loizidou* v. *Turkey (Preliminary Objections)*, Judgment of 23 March 1995, Ser. A No. 310, at 23–4 para. 62; *Chrysostomos* v. *Turkey*, Appl. 15299/89, 15300/89, 15318/89, (1991) 12 *Hum. Rts LJ* 113,

The jurisdiction covered by the European Convention on Human Rights would thus cover ships and aircraft registered in the state, as well as actions by its agents abroad.[15] No distinction is made under this provision with respect to the nationality of individuals benefiting from these rights.[16]

The Inter-American Commission on Human Rights has come to a similar conclusion in a series of decisions and reports, finding that the American Convention on Human Rights and the Declaration on the Rights and Duties of Man were applicable to actions of Chile in the United States, Suriname in the Netherlands, and the United States in Panama and Grenada.[17] Indeed in one respect, the jurisprudence of the American Commission goes further than that of the European bodies: whereas the latter have so far applied the European Convention only to extraterritorial acts taking place on the territory of another state party to the Convention (as in Cyprus), the American Commission has found states in breach of their human rights obligations for acts taking place wholly outside the territorial scope of the American instruments (for example, in the Netherlands). The expansive approach would support a conclusion that all military operations abroad remain governed by the relevant human rights treaties, inasmuch as they are not derogated from, so that, for instance, French and British troops in Kuwait and Iraq would have had to comply with the European Convention. Pushed to the extreme, it could lead to the conclusion that an individual injured in Belgrade by a falling British bomb was at that moment under

121 para. 32 (Eur. Com'n Hum. Rts). See Hans-Konrad Ress, 'Die Zulässigkeit territorialer Beschränkungen bei der Anerkennung des Zuständigkeit des europäischen Gerichtshofs für Menschenrechte', (1996) 56 *Zeitschrift für ausländisches öffentliches Recht und Völkerrecht* 427–38.

[15] *Loizidou v. Turkey (Preliminary Objections)*. See also *Cyprus v. Turkey* (1975), at 136; *Cyprus v. Turkey*, Appl. 8007/77, (1979) 13 Decisions and Reports 85, 148–9; J. E. S. Fawcett, *The Application of the European Convention on Human Rights*, 2nd edn (Oxford: Clarendon, 1987) 23; P. van Dijk and G. J. H. van Hoof, *Theory and Practice of the European Convention on Human Rights*, 3rd edn (The Hague: Kluwer, 1998) 9–10.

[16] Note, however, the incongruous exception inserted in the European Convention as a remnant of European colonialism, providing for the optional application of the Convention to 'all or any of the territories for whose international relations it [the state party] is responsible'. See Syméon Karagiannis, 'L'aménagement des droits de l'homme outre-mer: La clause des "nécessités locales" de la Convention européenne', (1995) 1 *Revue belge de droit international* 224.

[17] *Coard v. United States*, Report No. 109/99, Case No. 10,951 (1999), para. 37 (on Grenada); *Salas v. United States*, Report No. 31/93, Case No. 10,573 (1993) (on Panama); 'Report on the Situation of Human Rights in Chile', OAS Doc. OEA/Ser.L/V/II.66, doc. 17 (1985); 'Second Report on the Situation of Human Rights in Suriname', OAS Doc. OEA/Ser.L/V/II.66, doc. 21 rev. 1 (1985).

the 'jurisdiction' of the UK, calling for an examination to determine whether the bombing respected the individual's right to life under the European Convention.[18]

A more restrictive formulation is used in the International Covenant on Civil and Political Rights, where every state party undertakes 'to respect and to ensure to all individuals within its territory and subject to its jurisdiction the rights recognized in the present Covenant' (Art. 2(1)). There is here an added geographic component which would seem to exclude from the reach of the Covenant acts committed outside national territory. According to that interpretation, the population of a territory occupied by another state would not benefit from the rights entrenched in the Covenant, so that it would be inapplicable to situations like the Turkish occupation of Cyprus or the Israeli occupation of Southern Lebanon.[19] More generally, the Covenant would not cover actions of state agents carried out abroad, even against that state's own nationals. Conversely, acts committed on national territory but with respect to individuals not within the jurisdiction of the state would not be covered by the Covenant. Such cases would include areas occupied by a foreign state or effectively controlled by an insurgent group. For example, the Government of Cyprus cannot be held accountable for human rights violations against Cypriot nationals carried out by Turkish soldiers in the portion of its territory occupied by Turkey since 1974.[20] This construction leads to the result that individuals in occupied territories, highly vulnerable to human rights violations, would not be covered under the Covenant, either with respect to the territorial state or with respect to the occupying state. Such an interpretation would appear inconsistent with the direct granting of rights to individuals as against any state exercising power over them.

[18] Such a case has been presented against seventeen NATO states to the European Court of Human Rights: *Banković et al.* v. *17 Member States of the Council of Europe*, Appl. 52207/99 communicated on 26 Sept. 2000. A similar case dealing with the 1982 sinking of the Argentine battleship *General Belgrano* was rejected by the European Court of Human Rights without a discussion of this issue: *Romero de Ibanez* v. *UK*, Appl. 58692/00, Decision on Admissibility, 19 July 2000. See Christopher Greenwood, 'Rights at the Frontier – Protecting the Individual in Time of War', in *Law at the Centre – The Institute of Advanced Legal Studies at Fifty* (Dordrecht: Kluwer, 1999) 277, 286–7.

[19] Meyrowitz, 'Droit de la guerre', at 1087; Dietrich Schindler, 'Human Rights and Humanitarian Law: The Interrelationship of the Laws', (1982) 31 *Am. UL Rev.* 935.

[20] See the list of alleged human rights violations in *Cyprus* v. *Turkey*, Appl. 6780/74 and 6950/75, (1975) 2 Decisions and Reports 125, 128–9. See also the comments by the expert members of the UN Human Rights Committee, *cited in* Dominic McGoldrick, *The Human Rights Committee* (Oxford: Clarendon, 1991) 271 n. 23.

This interpretation of Article 2(1) has been challenged both by writers and by the UN Human Rights Committee. Buergenthal argues that the conjunction 'and' should be read in a disjunctive manner, to indicate that a state must guarantee the rights of individuals within its territory and to individuals under its jurisdiction.[21] Such a construction would conform to the text of Article 1 of the Optional Protocol to the International Covenant on Civil and Political Rights, which refers only to the wider criterion of jurisdiction.[22] Further, some rights recognised by the Covenant necessarily imply that the benefited person be outside national territory, such as the right to enter one's own country (Art. 12(4)). The *travaux préparatoires* reveal that the territorial reference was retained not to limit the Covenant's reach strictly to national territory, but rather for fear that its elimination might allow an interpretation of the undertaking to 'ensure' individual rights that rendered a state responsible for the breach of its nationals' rights by a foreign state taking place outside national territory.[23] The obligation to 'ensure' rights does impose duties on the state which are in excess of the obligation to respect the rights entrenched in the Covenant, lending further support to a wider application of that instrument.

The disjunctive interpretation has been adopted by the UN Human Rights Committee, in its general comment on Article 2 of the Covenant, in individual communications pursuant to the Optional Protocol, and in Concluding Observations upon review of periodic reports by states. In its views on the communication of *López* v. *Uruguay*, the Committee clearly rejected the idea that the Covenant does not cover acts carried out by state agents outside the national territory. That case dealt with the kidnapping of a Uruguayan national by Uruguayan agents on Argentinian territory, apparently with the cooperation of Argentinian officials. Referring to Article 5(1) of the Covenant, according to which it should not be interpreted to permit human rights violations otherwise prohibited, the Committee reasoned that 'it would be unconscionable to so interpret the responsibility under Article 2 of the Covenant as to permit a State party to perpetrate violations of the Covenant on the territory of another State, which violations it could not perpetrate on its own

---

[21] Thomas Buergenthal, 'To Respect and to Ensure: State Obligations and Permissible Derogations', in Louis Henkin ed., *The International Bill of Rights* (New York: Columbia UP, 1981) 72–7.

[22] GA Res. 2200A (1966), (1966) 999 UNTS 302.

[23] Marc Bossuyt, *Guide to the 'Travaux Préparatoires' of the International Covenant on Civil and Political Rights* (Dordrecht: Nijhoff, 1987) 53–5; Buergenthal, 'To Respect and to Ensure', at 74–5.

territory'.[24] The Human Rights Committee reiterated this position in its Concluding Observations on the periodic report by Israel, where it criticised the lack of reference to any acts taking place in foreign territories under Israeli control. The Committee insisted that the Covenant was applicable to Gaza, the West Bank and all areas in Southern Lebanon where Israel exercises effective control.[25]

Individual entitlement to rights under human rights law is corroborated by the direct applicability or self-executing character of many of these norms. Nearly every aspect of the notion of a self-executing or directly applicable norm is fraught with controversy, from the very question of whether it is a principle of international law or merely a rule found in some municipal legal systems.[26] It can generally be described as an internally valid international norm which may be invoked before national jurisdictions without requiring further legislation.[27] The criteria for finding a rule self-executing are commonly presented as including the intent of the parties to the treaty as revealed in the *travaux préparatoires* and the 'completeness' and clarity of the norm.[28] A great many human rights provisions have been found to be directly applicable, especially those of the European Convention on Human Rights and International Covenant on Civil and Political Rights, although there is by no means universal consensus on that point.[29] Not all international

---

[24] Communication No. 52/1979, *reprinted in* 'Human Rights Committee – Selected Decisions Under the Optional Protocol', UN Doc. CCPR/C/OP/1 (1985) (Sales No. E.84.XIV.2), at 91. In an individual opinion appended to the views of the Committee, Mr Christian Tomuschat adds that '[n]ever was it envisaged, however, to grant States parties unfettered discretionary power to carry out wilful and deliberate attacks against the freedoms and personal integrity of their citizens living abroad', *ibid.*, at 92. See Theodor Meron, *Human Rights in Internal Strife: Their International Protection* (Cambridge: Grotius, 1987) 41–3.

[25] Human Rights Committee, 'Concluding Observations', UN Doc. ICCPR/C/79/Add.93 (4 July 1998) para. 10.

[26] See *Restatement (Third) of the Foreign Relations Law of the United States* (St Paul: American Law Institute, 1987) §111 comment h; Buergenthal, 'Self-executing Treaties', at 317–20.

[27] See Jacques Velu, *Les effets directs des instruments internationaux en matière de droits de l'homme* (Brussels: Swinnen, 1981) 11–12; Joe Verhoeven, 'La notion d'applicabilité directe en droit international', (1980) 15 *Revue belge de droit international* 243.

[28] See Buergenthal, 'Self-executing Treaties', at 328–33; Yuji Iwasawa, 'The Doctrine of Self-executing Treaties in the United States: A Critical Analysis', (1986) 26 *Va. J Int'l L* 627, 654–73; Carlos Manuel Vázquez, 'The Four Doctrines of Self-executing Treaties', (1995) 89 *Am. J Int'l L* 695–723.

[29] See for reviews of the relevant case law: Andrew Drzemczewski, *European Human Rights Convention in Domestic Law* (Oxford: Clarendon, 1983); Velu, *Les effets directs*, at 21–53; Marc J. Bossuyt, 'The Direct Applicability of International Instruments on

norms directly creating rights for individuals need be self-executing, and there is a debate as to whether all self-executing norms create rights for individuals. Nevertheless, in the case of human rights, the self-executing character of some of these norms underlines their nature as individual rights because it envisages, within the municipal sphere, the reliance on international rights by individuals.[30]

Individual entitlement, or the direct creation of international rights in the individual by human rights law, does not imply that such are the sole normative effect of the latter. Indeed, human rights standards embody concerns which extend beyond those of the individual right-holder to touch also on public policy. This added dimension is illustrated by the possibility of inter-state petitions under most general human rights conventions, clearly not grounded exclusively in the rights of individual victims. It is further reflected in the possibility, under the European Convention on Human Rights, for the European Court to refuse to stop consideration of a case despite the wish of the petitioner to discontinue proceedings, if this is so demanded by the general interest to ensure respect for human rights (Art. 37(1), European Convention).[31]

Individuals thus enjoy rights against any state bound by the human rights norm by direct effect of law. The main feature of this endowment is its universality, that is the fact that it is generally non-distinctive and unconditional.

Universality

The conditions under which rights are granted to individuals under human rights law highlight the nature of these rights. In customary as

Human Rights', (1980) 15 *Revue belge de droit international* 317; Yuji Iwasawa, 'The Relationship Between International Law and Municipal Law: Japanese Experiences', (1993) 64 *Brit. YB Int'l L* 333, 350; Eduardo Jiménez de Aréchaga, 'La Convención interamericana de derechos humanos como derecho interno', (1989) 7 *Revista del Instituto interamericano de derechos humanos* 25.

[30] It is granted here that because, as put by Brownlie, '[t]he whole subject resists generalization' (Ian Brownlie, *Principles of Public International Law*, 5th edn (Oxford: Clarendon, 1998) 51), the finding that some or all human rights are or should be self-executing is not in itself determining as to the character of human rights as individual rights. This is so because factors other than the intent to create individual rights, such as the completeness or clarity of the norm and the presence of provisions on incorporating legislation, are taken into account in concluding whether an international norm is self-executing. The finding that many human rights are self-executing is nevertheless a further indication that at least some human rights norms do create international individual rights.

[31] See *Tyrer v. UK*, (1978) 2 Eur. Hum. Rts Rep. 1, paras. 24–5 (Eur. Ct Hum. Rts); *Gericke v. FRG*, Appl. 2294, [1965] YB Eur. Com'n Hum. Rts 314, 320–2 (Eur. Com'n Hum. Rts).

well as conventional law, the grant is generally universal and unconditional. That is, rights are given to everyone, including nationals of
states not bound by the same norm and stateless individuals.[32] In this,
individuals are rights-holders in a manner completely disconnected
from their state of nationality.[33]

Exceptions to the universality of enjoyment by individuals of rights
under human rights law are either exclusions from the benefit of some
rights or, correspondingly, the granting of supplementary rights to special classes of persons. These exceptions include the right to enter one's
own country[34] and the right to participate in public affairs and the
democratic process, given only to citizens of the concerned state,[35] special due process guarantees applicable to the deportation of aliens lawfully in the territory of a state,[36] protection against expulsion from the
country of nationality,[37] the prohibition of mass expulsion of aliens,[38]
and, more broadly, the rights of minorities. The 1985 UN Declaration
on the Human Rights of Individuals who are not Nationals of the State
in Which They Live provides rights for aliens which are additional to
general human rights law.[39] In particular, it includes the right to trans-
fer assets abroad (Art. 5(1)(g)), the right to be reunited with one's family
(Art. 5(4)) and the right to communicate with diplomatic representatives
of the state of nationality (Art. 10).[40]

[32] René Cassin, 'L'homme, sujet de droit international, et la protection des droits de
l'homme dans la société universelle', in La technique et les principes du droit
public - Etudes en l'honneur de Georges Scelle (Paris: LGDJ, 1950) I, 67, 71-90.
[33] This recalls the second paragraph of the preamble of the American Convention on
Human Rights ('the essential rights of man are not derived from one's being a
national of a certain state, but are based upon attributes of the human personality').
[34] Art. 13(2), Universal Declaration of Human Rights; Art. 3(2), Protocol 4 to the
European Convention on Human Rights; Art. 12(2), African Charter on Human and
Peoples' Rights.
[35] Art. 21(1), Universal Declaration of Human Rights; Art. 25, International Covenant on
Civil and Political Rights; Art. 16, European Convention on Human Rights; Art. 23,
American Convention on Human Rights; Art. 13, African Charter on Human and
Peoples' Rights.
[36] Art. 13, International Covenant on Civil and Political Rights; Art. 1, Protocol 7 to the
European Convention on Human Rights; Art. 22(6), American Convention on Human
Rights; Art. 12(4), African Charter on Human and Peoples' Rights.
[37] Art. 9, Universal Declaration of Human Rights; Art. 3(1), Protocol 4 to the European
Convention on Human Rights; Art. 22(5), American Convention on Human Rights.
[38] Art. 22(9), American Convention on Human Rights; Art. 12(5), African Charter on
Human and Peoples' Rights.
[39] GA Res. 144(XL), GAOR, 40th Sess., Supp. No. 53, at 253, reprinted in David J. Harris,
Cases and Materials on International Law, 4th edn (London: Sweet & Maxwell, 1991)
520-3.
[40] See generally Francesco Capotorti, 'Incidenza della condizione di straniero sui diritti
dell'uomo internazionalmente protetti', in Studi in onore di Giuseppe Sperduti (Milan:

The key feature of these exceptional exclusions or additions is that they are fully consistent with the universality of individual entitlement to rights under international human rights law. This is so because these exceptional regimes reflect the nature of the protected interests. Thus, only citizens of a given country are given the right to go back home, but the right to leave a country is given to all; the exclusion of non-nationals from the right to participate in the public affairs of the state reflects the representative nature of governments; aliens are given special due process guarantees against expulsion because they are much more susceptible to being victims of such orders, especially under the regimes of the Universal Declaration and European and American Conventions where citizens are protected against exile.

A small number of exclusions do not follow this pattern, and cannot be said to be fully consistent with the nature of the interest protected. These include, most clearly, the general exception inserted in Article 2(3) of the International Covenant on Economic, Social and Cultural Rights, whereby non-nationals are not guaranteed economic rights in developing countries. The interests protected by the right to an adequate standard of living or the right to education seem equally relevant for nationals and aliens. Such an exclusion is 'contrary to the spirit of universality and equality' grounded in international human rights law, which can be explained only as a political concession to economic constraints and states' desire to see to their own citizens' needs before helping non-citizens.[41]

Apart from these extremely limited instances, human rights law embodies a principle of universal enjoyment of rights by all individuals. This universality must be contrasted to the patchwork protection afforded to individuals by humanitarian law.

HUMANITARIAN LAW

The human interests which humanitarian law seeks to protect are largely similar to those safeguarded by human rights law. It does not

---

Giuffrè, 1984) 143; Ugo Villani, 'I diritti degli stranieri negli atti internazionali sui diritti dell'uomo', (1987) 99 *Studi senesi* 105–28; David Weissbrodt, 'Working Paper on the Rights of Non-Citizens', UN Doc. E/CN.4/Sub.2/1999/7.

[41] Myres McDougal, Harold Lassel and Lung-chu Chen, 'The Protection of Aliens from Discrimination and World Public Order: Responsibility of States Conjoined with Human Rights', (1976) 70 *Am. J Int'l L* 432, 458 n. 100. See Matthew Craven, *The International Covenant on Economic, Social and Cultural Rights* (Oxford: Clarendon, 1995) 172–4; Villani, 'I diritti', at 113–14.

necessarily follow, however, that the two systems adopt identical normative frameworks and achieve the protection of such interests by way
of granting rights to individuals. This section examines, first, whether
individuals are rights-holders under humanitarian law, and, secondly,
the general pattern of protection in that legal system.

Entitlement

The normative framework adopted in humanitarian law to alleviate human suffering in times of armed conflict does not emerge as clearly
as it does in human rights law. From the 1864 Geneva Convention on,
the framers sought to 'safeguard the dignity of the human person, in
the profound conviction that imprescriptible and inviolable rights are
attached to it even when hostilities are at their height'.[42] That this goal
does not necessarily involve granting rights to the protected persons is
hinted at by the fact that neither the word 'right' nor any other equivalent is used in the 1864 Convention. No concept of the human rights of
individuals, be they civilians, prisoners of war or combatants, is found
in the 1899 and 1907 Hague Regulations. The notion of 'rights' of protected persons is clearly expressed for the first time in the 1929 Geneva
Convention Relative to the Treatment of Prisoners of War.[43] The 1949
Geneva Conventions, drafted in the aftermath of the proclamation of
the Universal Declaration of Human Rights, contain many references to
the 'rights' of the protected persons.[44] Does that mean that individuals
are granted international rights by the Geneva Conventions?

Two provisions of the 1949 Geneva Conventions, common Articles
6/6/6/7 and 7/7/7/8, have been interpreted as an indication that the
Conventions grant rights to the benefited individuals. Common Articles
6/6/6/7 provide that, although High Contracting Parties are at liberty
to conclude special agreements among them with respect to any matter

---

[42] Jean Pictet ed., *The Geneva Conventions of 12 August 1949 – Commentary on the IV Geneva
Convention Relative to the Protection of Civilian Persons in Times of War* (Geneva: ICRC, 1958)
77.

[43] 27 July 1929, *reprinted in* Dietrich Schindler and Jiří Toman, *The Laws of Armed Conflict*,
3rd edn (Dordrecht: Nijhoff, 1989) 339 (hereinafter 1929 Geneva Convention on
Prisoners of War). These included the right to petition military authorities about the
conditions of detention (Art. 42), the right to counsel in judicial proceedings (Art. 62)
and the right to appeal a sentence (Art. 64).

[44] Pictet, IV, at 77. See also Claude Pilloud, 'La Déclaration universelle des droits de
l'homme et les Conventions de Genève de 1949', [1949] *Revue internationale de la
Croix-Rouge* 252–8.

governed by the Conventions, '[n]o special agreement shall adversely affect the situation of [protected persons] nor restrict the rights which it confers upon them'. Common Articles 7/7/7/8 state that in no circumstances may protected persons validly renounce 'in part or in entirety the rights secured to them by the present Convention'. Some have seen in the interplay of these provisions evidence that the Conventions grant rights of a dual nature, in that they belong to the state at the same time as to the individual protected.[45] As the state is not the sole holder of the rights, it cannot validly waive them for the individual; the same is true for the individual vis-à-vis the state. The practical advantage of this construction of the normative framework of the Conventions, according to Dinstein, is that '[t]he lawful combatant or civilian may stand on his or her right without having to rely on the goodwill of the state of nationality and, by the same token, the state of nationality may stand on its right without depending on a call for help from the individual'.[46] He gives as an example the prohibition of torturing prisoners of war found in the 1949 Third Geneva Convention (Art. 17), whereby, following his interpretation, '[e]ach is entitled to take whatever steps are available and deemed appropriate by virtue of their separate rights'.[47] The reality of these 'rights' is open to question, however, as illustrated by the dearth of effective steps open to the prisoner of war in a detention camp or to the state already at war with the perpetrator of the violation of this right.[48]

---

[45] See Pictet, IV, at 77–8; Georges Abi-Saab, 'The Specificities of Humanitarian Law', in Christophe Swinarski ed., *Studies and Essays on International Humanitarian Law and Red Cross Principles in Honour of Jean Pictet* (Geneva/The Hague: ICRC/Nijhoff, 1984) 265, 269; Yoram Dinstein, 'Human Rights in Armed Conflict: International Humanitarian Law', in Meron, *Human Rights in International Law*, at 345, 354–6; Greenwood, 'Rights at the Frontier', at 282; Theodor Meron, 'The Humanization of Humanitarian Law', (1999) 94 *Am. J Int'l L* 239, 251–3; René-Jean Wilhelm, 'Le caractère des droits accordés à l'individu dans les Conventions de Genève', [1950] *Revue internationale de la Croix-Rouge* 561–2. Maresca takes the same provisions to mean that only states have rights and that no legal relation is created between the detaining state and prisoners of war: Adolfo Maresca, *La protezione internazionale dei combatenti e dei civili* (Milan: Giuffrè, 1965) 37–8.

[46] Dinstein, 'Human Rights in Armed Conflict', at 355.   [47] *Ibid.*

[48] A prisoner of war has a limited right to transmit his 'requests regarding the conditions of captivity' to the detaining power, and to draw the attention of the protecting power to the same (Art. 60, Third Convention). The prisoner of war's state, given the unlikely success of mechanisms for the peaceful settlement of disputes between warring parties, can only act through the protecting power or through belligerent reprisals not directed at its own prisoners of war (Art. 13, Third Convention). See Pictet, IV, at 78.

The use of the word 'rights' in the 1949 Geneva Conventions is not by itself conclusive as to the nature of the norms created by the Conventions or its possible equivalent in customary humanitarian law.[49] Another construction of Articles 6/6/6/7 and 7/7/7/8 suggests that the waiver of protection granted prisoners of war and other protected persons is invalid because the Convention actually sought to decree standards of treatment of individuals rather than 'rights' similar in nature to human rights.

Common Articles 6/6/6/7 are derived from Article 83 of the 1929 Geneva Convention Relative to the Treatment of Prisoners of War, which provided for the possibility of special agreements among belligerents to vary the terms of the Convention. It became clear during the Second World War that this type of provision left prisoners of war too vulnerable, because states in weaker positions might be pressured to agree to waive some of the norms protecting prisoners. For example, Vichy France agreed to 'transform' some prisoners of war held by Germany into civilian workers, who were thus no longer entitled to a range of protections granted by the 1929 Convention.[50] Common Articles 6/6/6/7 of the 1949 Geneva Conventions were intended to prohibit any special agreement trenching on standards written into the Conventions. Seen in this light, the provisions appear not so much as a statement that the rights of protected persons cannot be waived by the state, but rather that the regime instituted by the Geneva Conventions represents a minimum standard from which no derogation is allowed.

As for common Articles 7/7/7/8, the initial Red Cross draft did provide for the validity of a waiver by protected persons, unless undue pressure had been exerted on them. Such a provision would have reinforced a claim that 'rights' were being given to protected persons by the Conventions. At the Geneva Conference, a regime of absolute prohibition was adopted instead, because without such a prohibition, claims of waiver from the state under whose power protected persons find themselves would have been easy to make and hard to disprove.[51] The only way to create a protection regime setting up absolute standards of treatment

---

[49] See Michael Akehurst, *A Modern Introduction to International Law* (London: Routledge, 1987) 73.

[50] The Scapini–Hitler Agreement of 16 November 1940 and the Laval–Sauckel Agreement of April 1943, *cited in* Wilhelm, 'Caractère des droits', at 575–6.

[51] See II-B *Final Record of the Diplomatic Conference of Geneva of 1949* (Berne: Federal Political Dept, 1949) 17–18; Theodor Meron, *Human Rights and Humanitarian Norms as Customary Law* (Oxford: Clarendon, 1989) 223; Pictet, IV, at 74–5; Wilhelm, 'Caractère des droits', at 588.

is to declare these standards unalterable. The ICRC Commentary to the 1949 Geneva Conventions notes in a general way that, because protected persons are not in a position freely to assess what is in their best interest, 'the authors of the Convention have endeavoured to ensure standards of treatment which depend as little as possible, for their application, on the wishes of those concerned'.[52] The rigidity of these standards means, for example, that combatants who have been enlisted against their will by one belligerent and later taken prisoner could not legally decide to fight for the detaining state, even if they desired to do so.[53]

Another element supporting the interpretation of humanitarian law norms as standards of treatment or conduct rather than as rights of protected persons is provided by Article 85 of the 1949 Third Geneva Convention. The Article states that a prisoner of war found to be a war criminal 'shall retain, even if convicted, the benefits of the present Convention'. State practice immediately preceding the adoption of the 1949 Geneva Conventions indicates that this norm was not considered to be generally accepted under international law. Under customary humanitarian law, a person who had committed a war crime was deemed to have renounced the benefit of its protection. This was supported by state practice during the Second World War and by post-war judicial decisions in France, the Netherlands, Italy, Japan, and in particular by the US Supreme Court decision in the *Yamashita* case.[54] Article 85 received little support from the Conference of Government Experts in Geneva in 1947, was opposed by a number of states at the 1949 Diplomatic Conference which adopted the Convention, and was the subject of numerous reservations upon ratification, mostly by Eastern Bloc countries.[55] The Government of North Vietnam officially adopted a similar stance during much of the Vietnam war.[56] The rationale for rejecting the rule embodied in Article 85 is

[52] Pictet, IV, at 75.

[53] Wilhelm, 'Caractère des droits', at 588.

[54] *US v. Yamashita*, (1946) 4 L Rep. Trials War Crim. 1, 44–8 (US Supreme Court). See the cases cited in Jean Pictet ed., *The Geneva Conventions of 12 August 1949 – Commentary on the III Geneva Convention Relative to the Treatment of Prisoners of War* (Geneva: ICRC, 1960), 413; *US v. Dosler*, (1945) 1 L Rep. Trials War Crim. 22, 27–8 (US Mil. Com'n, Rome); *France v. Wagner*, (1946) 3 L Rep. Trials War Crim. 23, 50 (French Permanent Mil. Trib., Strasbourg and Court of Appeals); Jean-Pierre Maunoir, *La répression des crimes de guerre devant les tribunaux français et alliés* (Geneva: Editions Médecine et Hygiène, 1956) 162–82; Charles C. Hyde, 'Japanese Executions of American Aviators', (1943) 27 *Am. J Int'l L* 480–2.

[55] Maunoir, *Répression* at 183–8; Pictet, IV, at 415. The reservations and the objections they generated are reprinted in Schindler and Toman, *Laws of Armed Conflict*, at 563–92.

[56] See Mohammed El Kouhene, *Les garanties fondamentales de la personne en droit humanitaire et droits de l'homme* (Dordrecht: Nijhoff, 1986) 59–61; Henri Meyrowitz, 'Le

that an individual violating humanitarian law rejects that law as a whole, thus waiving any entitlement or right to enjoy the protection afforded by its norms. Opposition to the rule embodied in Article 85 has been waning, however, and it was reiterated in Article 44(2) of the 1977 Protocol I. Detaching the standards of treatment found in humanitarian law from the individual conforms to the continued status of war criminals as prisoners of war, because the protection given is not in the nature of rights held by individuals but of standards existing independently of any action of the benefited persons.

The corresponding provision for civilian protected persons under the 1949 Fourth Geneva Convention is somewhat different. According to Article 5, a protected person suspected of carrying out hostile acts 'shall not be entitled to claim such rights and privileges under the present Convention' and, in particular, shall be deemed to have 'forfeited rights of communication under the present Convention'.[57] The language used in this provision seems to suggest that individual rights had been granted to, and then forfeited by, the protected person. A closer look at the substance of the rule and interplay of norms, however, reveals that even in this provision it is by no means clear that the individual was meant to hold rights directly under the Convention. Despite the wording, the limitations or suspension of the protected person's 'rights' is not justified by their presumed forfeiture, but rather by reference to the security of the state. Throughout the provision, protections benefiting protected persons may be curtailed only to the extent 'absolute military security so requires' (Art. 5(2)), and the full regime must resume its application

droit de la guerre dans le conflit vietnamien', [1967] *Annuaire français de droit international* 153, 195–6.

[57] The full text provides:

'*Article 5*   Where in the territory of a Party to the conflict, the latter is satisfied that an individual protected person is definitely suspected of or engaged in activities hostile to the security of the State, such individual person shall not be entitled to claim such rights and privileges under the present Convention as would, if exercised in the favour of such individual person, be prejudicial to the security of such State.

Where in occupied territory an individual protected person is detained as a spy or saboteur, or as a person under definite suspicion of activity hostile to the security of the Occupying Power, such person shall, in those cases where absolute military security so requires, be regarded as having forfeited rights of communication under the present Convention.

In each case, such persons shall nevertheless be treated with humanity and, in case of trial, shall not be deprived of the rights of fair and regular trial prescribed by the present Convention. They shall also be granted the full rights and privileges of a protected person under the present Convention at the earliest date consistent with the security of the State or Occupying Power, as the case may be.'

as soon as the security of the state allows for it. Suspension of 'rights' thus appears linked not to a presumed renunciation by the individual but strictly to military necessity.

Construing the protection granted by the 1949 Geneva Conventions as standards rather than rights shifts the emphasis from the would-be right-holder to the person in the position of power, on whom an obligation to comply with the standard is imposed directly by public order. This appears more consistent than a rights-based interpretation with the enforcement scheme of humanitarian law generally, which is centred on punitive rather than curative or preventive measures. It further conforms to the concept of war crimes as international crimes as well as to the duty of every state party to the 1949 Geneva Conventions either to punish or to extradite war criminals (Arts. 50/51/130/147), detached from the specific victims whose 'rights' were violated. The invalidity of absolution by a state – and *a fortiori* by an individual – of war crimes (Arts. 51/52/131/148) appears fully consistent with this non-rights-based construction of humanitarian law.

The 1977 Protocols do not fundamentally depart from the normative framework adopted in the 1949 Geneva Conventions. This is so despite the fact that the inspiration for some of their provisions can be traced much more directly to human rights law than was the case under the older Conventions. In particular, the paragraphs providing for the due process guarantees in Article 75 of Protocol I are drawn from Article 14 of the International Covenant on Civil and Political Rights.[58] Other parts of Article 75 prohibiting certain acts such as torture or murder are derived from common Article 3 of the 1949 Geneva Conventions.[59] Each portion borrows the language of its antecedent, making it difficult to characterise the normative framework of the provision as a whole. It is quite possible that due process guarantees will be taken as conferring rights on individuals, given that these guarantees will become applicable only in a judicial context where such rights are more easily conceivable. The rest of Article 75, like most rules found in the Protocols and Conventions, contains norms which are difficult to characterise as 'rights' held by individuals.

In a fashion similar to the characterisation of rights in human rights law as self-executing or directly applicable, the refusal by various tribunals to consider humanitarian treaty law as self-executing

---

[58] Claude Pilloud et al., *Commentary on the Additional Protocols of 8 June 1977 to the Geneva Conventions of 12 August 1949* (Geneva: Nijhoff, 1987) 879 (hereinafter *ICRC Commentary*).
[59] *Ibid.*, at 871–2.

corroborates its nature in representing objective public order standards rather than individual rights. Few cases have touched on this question directly, but they have found that neither the 1907 Hague Convention IV nor the Geneva Conventions and Protocols are self-executing.[60] This is of course not in itself determining as to the creation of individual rights at the international level, but nevertheless it appears consistent with the construction of humanitarian law presented here.[61]

The existence of a right often appears from the capacity either to exercise it or to renounce it.[62] Under the scheme created by humanitarian conventions, the protection granted to individuals cannot be waived either by the protected persons or by their state. Further, a realistic drafting of the Conventions and Protocols, taking into consideration the limitations proper to armed conflict and belligerent relations, has meant that no real avenue exists for protected persons to act individually on the basis of the protection created by the Conventions. There is therefore an incapacity for individuals either to exercise or to waive the 'rights' enacted in their favour. Protection given to individuals thus would not be in the nature of rights, either for the state or the individual, but more in the nature of standards of treatment.[63] It is interesting

---

[60] See *Iwanowa v. Ford Motor Co.*, 67 F.Supp.2d 424, 439 (D. New Jersey, 1999); *Javor v. X*, Cour d'appel de Paris, 24 November 1994, *reprinted in* (1995) 78 *Rivista di diritto internazionale* 826–9 (*discussed in* Flavia Lattanzi, 'La competenze delle jurisdizioni di stati "terzi" a ricercare e processare i responsabili dei crimini nell'ex-Iugoslavia a nel Ruanda', *ibid.*, at 707, 716–22); *Princz v. Federal Republic of Germany*, 26 F.3d 1166, 1175 (DC Cir. 1994); *Siberian Internment Case*, (1993) 811 Hanrei Taimuzu 76 (Tokyo High Court) (*discussed in* Iwasawa, 'Japanese Experiences', at 361–5); *Goldstar (Panama) v. United States*, 967 F.2d 965 (4th Cir. 1992); *Tel-Oren v. Libya*, 726 F.2d 774, 809–10 (DC Cir. 1984) (Bork J conc.); *Huyn Thi Anh v. Levi*, 586 F.2d 625 (6th Cir. 1978); *Handel v. Artukovic̀*, 601 F.Supp. 1421, 1425 (CD Cal. 1985); *In re Medina*, (1988) 19 Imm. & Nat. Dec. 734; David Boling, 'Mass Rape, Enforced Prostitution, and the Japanese Imperial Army: Japan Eschews International Legal Responsibility?', (1995) 32 *Colum. J Transnat'l L* 532, 562–4; Burrus C. Carnahan, '*In re Medina*: Are the 1949 Geneva Conventions Self-Executing?', (1987) 26 *Air Force L Rev.* 123; Felice Morgenstern, 'Validity of the Acts of the Belligerent Occupant', (1951) 28 *Brit. YB Int'l L* 291, 293–4.

[61] See above, at pp. 23–4.

[62] See e.g. Charles Taylor, 'Human Rights: The Legal Culture', in Paul Ricoeur ed., *Philosophical Foundations of Human Rights* (Paris: UNESCO, 1968) 49, 50 ('Granting me the right to live amounts to more than prohibiting others from killing me. This may be seen as a privilege or power in my possession which automatically gives me a margin of liberty in invoking and applying the rule').

[63] See generally on this point: Jean Combacau and Serge Sur, *Droit international public*, 2nd edn (Paris: Domat, 1995) 315; Françoise J. Hampson, 'Human Rights Law and Humanitarian Law: Two Coins or Two Sides of the Same Coin?', (1991) 1 *Bull. Hum. Rts* 46, 49; Henri Meyrowitz, 'Le droit de la guerre et les droits de l'homme' (1972) 88 *Revue de droit public et de la science politique en France et à l'étranger* 1059, 1063 and 1100

to note that in the one human rights convention specifically referring to humanitarian law, the 1989 Convention on the Rights of the Child, the provision affirming the state duty to protect children during armed conflicts does not refer to any 'right' of the child to such a protection (Art. 38); this article stands apart from most other provisions of the Convention which typically proclaim that 'The States Parties recognize the right of every child to...' In this, the Convention on the Rights of the Child echoes the conclusion reached here that humanitarian law standards, although grounded in the principle of humanity, are not directly attached to the human person but instead stem from international public order requirements.

Conditionality

In a manner similar to human rights law, the application pattern of rules protecting individuals under humanitarian law highlights key features of the normative framework of that legal system. Contrary to human rights, where universality is the dominant characteristic, humanitarian law is applied in a highly irregular manner, creating an incomplete and inconsistent patchwork of protections for victims of armed conflicts. This framework is based not on universality but on conditionality, with the benefit of humanitarian law depending on membership in a designated group. In addition, numerous persons are excluded from the benefit of the norms for reasons which do not reflect the nature of the interests protected.

Apart from the obvious factor that individual protection under humanitarian law is conditioned on the existence of an armed conflict,[64] it is further conditioned on membership in a group. This is so despite the fact that the individual is clearly the intended ultimate beneficiary of the norms. The group may be either one of combatants, under one of the limited number of categories provided by humanitarian law, or one of protected persons.

Customary law, as embodied in Hague law and in the 1949 Geneva Conventions, extends the status of combatants to militia, volunteer and resistance groups inasmuch as they comply with four basic conditions:

(who goes so far as to argue that the prohibition of torturing prisoners of war 'to secure from them information' (Art. 17 of the Third Geneva Convention) does not protect so much the integrity of the individual as the military interests and sovereignty of the state).

[64] This condition and the problems it raises are discussed in Part III.

that they have a command structure, wear distinctive markings, carry arms openly, and abide by the laws and customs of war.[65] Protocol I relies on basically the same four criteria in order to recognise belligerent status of the armed forces of a national liberation movement (Arts. 43–4). Unlike the 1949 Geneva Conventions, however, Protocol I differentiates the requirements strictly linked to the group from those linked to the individual. Article 43 contains the group requirements: that the armed forces be organised, under responsible command and subject to an internal disciplinary system charged, *inter alia*, with the enforcement of international humanitarian law applicable in armed conflict. Requirements of a more individual character – the duty to distinguish oneself from the civilian population and to carry arms openly in certain situations – are provided in Article 44. It must be noted that these 'individual' requirements have both individual and group dimensions. The need to wear distinguishing clothing or signs, for instance the distinctive red and white scarf worn by the Khmer Rouge in Cambodia, implies a uniformity among the members of the group. Similarly, the duty to carry arms openly must habitually be obeyed by members of the group if they want to be assured recognition as privileged belligerents.[66] This group

---

[65] Art. 1, 1907 Hague Convention IV; common Arts. 13(3)/13(3)/4(A)(2), 1949 First, Second and Third Geneva Conventions; United Kingdom War Office, *British Manual of Military Law*, part III – 'The Law of War on Land' (London: HMSO, 1958) paras. 91–4 (hereinafter 1958 *British Manual of Military Law*); Art. 25, Legge di guerra italiana del 1938, Regio Decreto 8 luglio 1938-XVI, n. 1415, *reprinted in* Alfred Verdross, 'Das neue italienische Kriegs- und Neutralitätsrecht', (1939) 19 *Zeitschrift für öffentliches Recht* 193–315, amended by Legge 16 dicembre 1940, n. 1902. Resistance groups in occupied territory were originally not considered legitimate combatants under any circumstances, even when they abided by the conditions found in the Hague Conventions. The extension of prisoner-of-war status to resistance fighters in the 1949 Third Geneva Convention thus constituted a change from customary law, which later evolved into customary humanitarian law. Compare: United Kingdom War Office, *British Manual of Military Law*, ch. 14 – 'The Laws and Usages of War on Land', Hugh Godley ed., 7th edn (London: HMSO, 1929) 275–7 paras. 20–8 (hereinafter 1929 *British Manual of Military Law*); Art. 52(2), 'Instruction for the Government of Armies of the United States in the Field', General Order No. 100, 24 April 1863, *reprinted in* Schindler and Toman, *Laws of Armed Conflict*, at 3 (hereinafter 'Lieber Manual'); *Trial of Carl Bauer et al.*, (1945) 8 L Rep. Trials War Crim. 15, 16–19 (French Permanent Military Tribunal); A. Pearce Higgins, *War and the Private Citizen* (London: King & Son, 1912) 42–3; Pictet, III, 58–9; J. M. Spaight, *War Rights on Land* (London: MacMillan, 1911) 53–65; Julius Stone, *Legal Control of International Conflict*, 2nd edn (London: Stevens & Sons, 1959) 564–8; Remigiusz Bierzanek, 'Le statut juridique des partisans et des mouvements de résistance armées: Evolution historique et aspects actuels', in Vladimir Ibler ed., *Mélanges offerts à Juraj Andrassy* (The Hague: Nijhoff, 1968) 54, 60–4.

[66] For example, in *US* v. *Hangobl*, (1945) 14 L Rep. Trials War Crim. 86 (Gen. Mil. Ct, Dachau), the accused was not treated as a lawful combatant although he belonged to

dimension of individual requirements follows from the general requirement that the group abide by humanitarian law (Art. 43(1), Protocol I),
the rules of which include the duty to carry arms openly in certain
situations.

Protection is also granted to the spontaneous *levée en masse* of inhabitants of a non-occupied territory upon the approach of an enemy force,
in so far as they carry weapons openly and comply with the laws of war
(common Arts. 13(6)/13(6)/4(A)(6), 1949 First, Second and Third Geneva
Conventions). This is an exceptional regime in that it subsists only for a
short period of time preceding the occupation of a territory by an enemy
belligerent, after which time such groups must comply with the four
conditions listed above in order to be considered lawful combatants.[67] In
all cases, the existence of, and appurtenance to, an identifiable group is
an absolute condition for application of humanitarian law in favour of
irregular combatants. Isolated *francs-tireurs* are not given any protection
as privileged belligerents and are liable to be tried as war criminals.[68]

Further conditions limit the entitlement to the protection provided
by humanitarian law. They fall into two categories, relating to the conduct of the individual and to his or her nationality. Under the scheme
created by the 1949 Geneva Conventions, informed by the experiences of
the Second World War with organised 'regular' resistance movements,
all members of a group meeting the conditions listed in common
Articles 13/13/4(A) of the First, Second and Third Geneva Conventions
are to be considered prisoners of war. However, just as members of the
military are not protected when captured in enemy territory without
their uniform (Art. 29, 1907 Hague Regulations), members of armed
resistance groups captured in combat while not wearing the distinctive
sign or not openly carrying arms are not considered combatants and
are not entitled to prisoner-of-war status.[69] Because humanitarian law

a German paramilitary unit, the *Gauwehrmannschaft*, and carried his weapon openly
at all relevant times, because the *Gauwehrmannschaft* as a formation did not usually
carry arms openly or wear uniforms.

[67] Art. 2, 1907 Hague Convention IV; Arts. 13(2)/13(2)/4(A)(2) 1949 First, Second and Third
Geneva Conventions; paras. 97–101, 1958 *British Manual of Military Law*; Art. 27, Legge
di guerra italiana del 1938; Pictet, III, at 67–8.

[68] Para. 634, 1958 *British Manual of Military Law*; Art. 29, Legge di guerra italiana del
1938; Art. 85, 'Lieber Manual'; A. Pearce Higgins, *War and the Private Citizen*, at 41–2;
Albéric Rolin, *Le droit moderne de la guerre* (Brussels: Dewit, 1920) I, 275–6 para. 289;
Spaight, *War Rights on Land*, at 34–52 ('the character of belligerent results from the
resistance of a respectable number', *ibid*. at 52, citing Bonfils).

[69] See e.g. *Krofan v. Public Prosecutor*, (1966) 52 Int'l L Rep. 497 (Singapore Fed. Ct); *Public
Prosecutor v. Koi*, [1968] AC 829, 856–8; *Mohamed Ali v. Public Prosecutor*, [1969] AC 430,
452 (Privy Council).

is called to be applied instantly to armed intercourse, membership in a group can produce an effect only if it can be immediately ascertained from afar. In this type of situation, the visibleness of the individual's link to the group will be more significant than the substance of that link, at least for a time. Protocol I, informed by the experiences of the Vietnam war and other post-Second World War conflicts, attempted to address realistically the phenomenon of guerrilla warfare, largely incompatible with the permanent wearing of distinctive signs and the open carrying of arms.[70] Thus, under the conventional regime of Protocol I, combatants are required to differentiate themselves from the civilian population only 'while they are engaged in an attack or in a military operation leading to an attack' (Art. 44(3)). In addition, they are required to carry their arms openly 'during each military engagement' and when visible to the enemy while deploying to prepare an attack. Protocol I specifies that combatants retain their status even if they violate international law applicable in armed conflict (Art. 44(2)) or if they fail to distinguish them-selves from the civilian population (Art. 44(3)). If they are captured while not carrying their arms openly, however, they may be denied prisoner-of-war status, although they nevertheless are entitled to benefit from the protection generally given to such persons (Art. 44(4)), meaning that they may be criminally prosecuted for committing what would otherwise constitute lawful acts of war.[71] A related rule applies with respect to non-combatants engaging in activities hostile to the security of a belligerent state, including *francs-tireurs*, whereby such persons no longer benefit from the full array of protections normally granted to non-combatants under the 1949 Fourth Geneva Convention, but are entitled only to a fair trial and to be treated with humanity (Art. 5, 1949 Fourth Geneva Convention).

Application of the 1949 Geneva Conventions is further limited in many respects according to the nationality of the individuals concerned. The 1949 Geneva Conventions largely do not apply to a state's own nationals,

[70] Pilloud et al., *ICRC Commentary*, 520–1; UN Doc. A/8052 (1970) 56 paras. 177–8. Because the provisions of Protocol I on the status of combatants were the subject of bitter disagreement at the 1977 Geneva Conference, and the text of Articles 43 and 44 the result of a compromise which did not fully satisfy any of the parties present (*ICRC Commentary*, at 522), the possible ripening of these provisions into customary humanitarian law is questionable. See Meron, *Human Rights and Humanitarian Norms*, 66; Frits Kalshoven, 'Reaffirmation and Development of International Humanitarian Law Applicable in Armed Conflict: The Diplomatic Conference, Geneva, 1974–77', (1977) 8 *Netherlands YB Int'l L* 107, 133.

[71] *ICRC Commentary*, at 538; Yoram Dinstein, 'The Distinction Between Unlawful Combatants and War Criminals', in Yoram Dinstein ed., *International Law at a Time of Perplexity – Essays in Honour of Shabtai Rosenne* (Dordrecht: Nijhoff, 1989) 105, 111.

as indicated by Articles 87 and 100 of the Third Convention and Articles 67–8 and 118 of the Fourth Convention, which call on a court to consider as a mitigating circumstance the fact that a prisoner of war or protected person, 'not being a national' of the detaining or occupying power, does not owe it a duty of allegiance. Deserters, for instance, do not enjoy prisoner-of-war status when detained by their state of nationality.[72]

Most importantly, application of a large portion of the 1949 Fourth Geneva Convention is restricted to 'protected persons', as defined in Article 4 of that Convention. Article 4 specifies that protected persons do not include a state's own nationals, nationals of a state which has not ratified or otherwise accepted the Convention, or nationals of neutral or co-belligerent states which maintain diplomatic relations with the state under whose power they find themselves. One section of the Fourth Convention, Part II (Arts. 13–26), enjoys a broader field of application, being applicable to the whole of the population of the belligerent states (Art. 13), therefore including a belligerent's own population and nationals of co-belligerent states. That section includes forms of protection related to sieges and blockades, evacuations of wounded and sick civilians, and special care for children under fifteen.

The most numerous and substantively crucial protections granted the civilian population by the Fourth Convention are to be found in Part III (Arts. 27–78), which applies solely to 'protected persons' as defined in Article 4. The exclusion on the basis of nationality of a significant portion of civilians during wartime thus covers essential protections concerning personal integrity, religious conviction, equality, and the prohibition of torture, medical experiment, mass deportation, forced enlistment in the armed forces, etc.[73] For example, the general internment of American and Canadian citizens of German and Japanese descent in the United States and Canada during the Second World War, including women and children, would not be contrary to the Fourth Geneva Convention.[74] Even more graphically, the extermination policy of Nazi Germany concerning Jewish members of its own population and

---

[72] Marco Sassòli, 'The Status, Treatment, and Repatriation of Deserters under International Humanitarian Law', [1985] YB Int'l Inst. Hum. L 9, 19–21; Public Prosecutor v. Koi, [1968] AC 829 (Privy Council). But see Eric David, Principes de droit des conflits armés (Brussels: Bruylant, 1994) 378–9.

[73] Arts. 27, 32, 49 and 51, 1949 Fourth Geneva Convention.

[74] For background, see Commission on Wartime Relocation and Internment of Civilians, Personal Justice Denied (Washington: US Gov. Printing Office, 1982); Edward G. Hudson, 'The Status of Persons of Japanese Ancestry in the United States and Canada During World War II: A Tragedy in Three Parts', (1977) 18 Cahiers de droit 61–90.

that of co-belligerents would not contravene the 1949 Fourth Geneva Convention (although it is clearly a violation of other international norms, including the customary prohibition of genocide and the customary basic principles of humanity corresponding to the norms found in common Article 3[75]).

In the *Celebici* case, a Trial Chamber of the International Criminal Tribunal for former Yugoslavia (ICTY) concluded that the concept of nationality ought to be interpreted flexibly, given the uncertainties regarding the emergence and disappearance of states in that conflict.[76] The ICTY in that case found it relevant that the victims 'were clearly regarded by the Bosnian authorities as belonging to the opposing party in an armed conflict', underscoring the significance of the individuals' link to a defined group.[77] This was approved and expanded upon in the *Tadić* appeals judgment, where the Appeals Chamber found that the rationale for labelling certain individuals 'protected persons' – their lack of allegiance to the party to the conflict in whose hands they are – should be seen as the fundamental criterion, rather than the formal link of nationality.[78] The Appeals Chamber thus reversed the decision of the Trial Chamber in that case and concluded that the torture, beatings and murder of Croats and Muslims by Serbs in the so-called *Republika Srpska* were grave breaches of the Fourth Convention despite the fact that the perpetrators and victims were of the same nationality because, in that situation, ethnicity led to different allegiances.[79] As noted by the Appeals Chamber in the *Celebici* appeals judgment, the more significant ethnic or religious dimension of contemporary armed conflict must be reflected in a progressive interpretation of the Geneva Conventions.[80] This exercise in creative interpretation by the ICTY ought to be applauded, for it connects the protection granted by the Geneva Conventions to substantive links between an individual and a party to the conflict rather

---

[75] *Military and Paramilitary Activities in and Against Nicaragua (Merits) (USA v. Nicaragua)*, [1986] ICJ Rep. 14, 114.

[76] *The Prosecutor v. Delalić, Mucić, Delić and Landzo* (the *Celebici* case) (Judgment), 16 Nov. 1998, Case No. IT-96-21-T (Trial Chamber, ICTY) at 89–99 paras. 236–66.

[77] *Ibid.*, at 99 para. 265.

[78] *The Prosecutor v. Tadić* (Appeals Judgment), 15 July 1999, Case No. IT-94-1-A (Appeals Chamber, ICTY), paras. 165–8.

[79] *Ibid.*, para. 166; *The Prosecutor v. Tadić* (Opinion and Judgment), 7 May 1997, Case No. IT-94-1-T (Trial Chamber II, ICTY), paras. 577–608; *The Prosecutor v. Blaskić* (Judgment), 3 March 2000, Case No. IT-95-14-T (Trial Chamber, ICTY), paras. 126–7; *The Prosecutor v. Aleksovski* (Appeals Judgment), 24 March 2000, Case No. IT-95-14/1-A (Appeals Chamber, ICTY), paras. 147–52.

[80] *The Prosecutor v. Delalić, Mucić, Delić and Landzo* (the *Celebici* case) (Appeal Judgment), 20 Feb. 2001, Case No. IT-96-21-A (Appeals Chamber, ICTY) 21 para. 73.

than fixing on the rather formal, and at times highly artificial, concept of nationality.

It should further be noted that no restriction based on the nationality of the concerned individual is found in the application provision of the 1949 First and Second Geneva Conventions on wounded, sick or shipwrecked combatants (Arts. 12/12), nor in common Article 3 relative to non-international armed conflicts. It follows that a state's own nationals would be protected under these norms.[81]

There is a move away from application clauses based on nationality in the 1977 Additional Protocols. Protocols I and II are declared to be applicable 'to all those affected by' the international or non-international armed conflict (Art. 9, Protocol I; Art. 2, Protocol II). The very notion of protected person is abandoned in favour of the all-encompassing notion of 'civilian', defined in contradistinction to combatants (Art. 43, Protocol I). Protocol I also contains a general provision creating a net granting basic protections to any individual affected by an international armed conflict as defined in Article 1 of the Protocol (Art. 75). Article 75 affords protection to classes of individuals who were left partly or totally unprotected under the 1949 Fourth Geneva Convention. Benefited persons include, first and foremost, a state's own nationals, but also nationals of neutral and co-belligerent states which still maintain diplomatic relations with the state under whose power they find themselves, individuals suspected of actions hostile to the state (Art. 5, Fourth Geneva Convention), refugees and stateless persons not covered by Article 73 of Protocol I, and individuals not protected by the Conventions and Protocols such as spies and mercenaries (Arts. 46–7, Protocol I), guerrillas not meeting the conditions for prisoner-of-war status (Art. 4(A)(2) and (6), Third Geneva Convention; Arts. 43–4, Protocol I), and, in the practice of some states, combatants guilty of war crimes.[82] The substance of the protection granted by Article 75 contains many of the most important elements found in Part III of the Fourth Geneva Convention. If the normative framework articulated by Article 75 remains difficult to characterise with certainty, that is whether individual rights are meant to be created, the universality of entitlement under this provision represents a real progression from the scheme of the 1949 Geneva Conventions. Article 75 is already considered by some experts and some states – including the United States – as a codification of customary humanitarian law.[83] Like Protocol I as a whole, however, Article 75 merely supplements

[81] *Tadić* (Judgment), para. 615; Meron, *Human Rights in Internal Strife*, at 30–3.
[82] See above, at pp. 30–1.
[83] See Meron, *Human Rights and Humanitarian Norms*, at 65 and 68; Bruce Carnahan,

the 1949 Geneva Conventions, leaving nearly unchanged the patchy protection provided by those instruments.

For the largest part, both numerically and substantively, protection is granted under humanitarian law according to conditions which exclude from the benefit of the norms individuals whose interests call for protection. Exclusions indeed do not reflect the nature of the interests protected. The prohibition against non-therapeutic medical experimentation (Art. 39, Fourth Convention), for example, should extend not only to enemy nationals but also to a state's own population and that of co-belligerent and neutral states who maintain normal diplomatic relations with the occupying power (Art. 4, Fourth Convention). These exclusions make no sense if we try to transpose to humanitarian law the normative framework of human rights law. Only in the wider context of inter-belligerent relations can we see – but not necessarily approve – the rationale for the apparently inconsistent allocation of protection under humanitarian law. Entitlement to protection under humanitarian law is in fact intimately connected to the relation of the state of nationality to the state or group in whose hands the individuals find themselves. As such, the protection found in the Geneva Conventions dovetails with the international standards on treatment of aliens, becoming applicable only in situations where these standards are inapplicable or when diplomatic protection is unavailable.[84] This is confirmed by Article 44 of the Fourth Convention, providing that enemy aliens shall not be treated as such on the simple basis of their nationality if they are 'refugees who do not, in fact, enjoy the protection of any government'.[85] Only when shown in this framework does the protection scheme of the Geneva Conventions seem coherent.

The generality of international human rights seems all the more evident when contrasted to the applicability of humanitarian law. Despite some limitations in conventional law, human rights law constitutes a bundle of rights attaching to the individual as a human being, in most places and situations. Humanitarian law, on the contrary, is a patchwork

---

'Customary Law and Additional Protocol I to the Geneva Conventions for Protection of War Victims: Future Direction in Light of the US Decision not to Ratify', (1989) 81 *ASIL Proc.* 26, 37; Antonio Cassese, 'The Geneva Protocols of 1977 on the Humanitarian Law of Armed Conflict and Customary International Law', (1984) 3 *UCLA Pac. Basin LJ* 55.

[84] *The Prosecutor* v. *Tadić* (Appeals Judgment), 15 July 1999, Case No. IT-94-1-A (Appeals Chamber, ICTY), para. 168; *The Prosecutor* v. *Blaskić* (Judgment), 3 March 2000, Case No. IT-95-14-T (Trial Chamber, ICTY), paras. 144–6.

[85] As noted, this is expanded by Art. 73 of Protocol I, which deems refugees and stateless persons to be protected persons under the 1949 Fourth Geneva Convention.

of variable protections granted individuals in some specific situations, if they meet criteria linked to conduct and nationality or group membership. The difference goes much further than the classic acknowledgment that human rights law applies mostly in peacetime while humanitarian law governs only armed conflict; even within war, within the basic duality of humanitarian law based on the principle of distinction between combatants and non-combatants, individual protection proffered by humanitarian law does not parallel that of human rights law.

Under humanitarian law, as mentioned earlier, the protection granted the individual is generally derived not from human nature, but from membership in a group, be it a resistance group or a nation entertaining a specific kind of relationship with the state under whose power the individuals find themselves. Article 75 of Protocol I stands out as a limited exception to this framework, purporting to detach humanitarian protection from any conditions of nationality or conduct. It is the closest humanitarian law comes to adopting a human rights approach. In human rights, conversely, it is extremely unusual for a right to be granted on the basis of any kind of connection between the individual and a group. There is no distinction to make in this respect between civil and political rights and economic, social and cultural rights. The right to work or to enjoy an adequate standard of living, for example, does not rest on any membership in a group. Some rights, for example the right to education or to form trade unions, will likely be exercised collectively, but again there is no conceptual requirement of a connection to a collectivity as a basis for the individual entitlement to such rights. One exception concerns minority rights, where individual rights are indeed dependent on appurtenance to a given minority. The rationale for such a link is that the human rights standard seeks to protect collective interests over and above those of individuals.[86] It is the closest human rights comes to adopting a humanitarian law approach.

Procedural capacity

The connection between rights and procedural capacity is not necessarily an immediate one. As mentioned earlier, right-holders may be

---

[86] See Human Rights Committee, 'General Comment 23 – The Rights of Minorities (Article 27)', UN Doc. CCPR/C/21/Rev.1/Add.5 (1994). In yet another distinct variation, some rights under human rights law are rights of peoples, implying that the primary holder of the right is the people rather than the individual. See e.g. *Lubicon Lake Band v. Canada*, Communication No. 167/1984 (26 March 1990), UN Doc. Supp. No. 40 (A/45/40) at 1 (1990).

denied the capacity to exercise their rights and, conversely, actors who do not hold a right directly by effect of international law may be recognised some standing to set into motion mechanisms designed to enforce that right. Once again, this aspect of the procedural framework differs markedly between human rights and humanitarian law. Two related aspects of the question of the procedural capacity of the individual will be addressed: first, the existence of a right to a remedy for individual victims under human rights and humanitarian law, and, second, the standing given to individuals in international fora created pursuant to each of these two legal systems.

SUBSTANTIVE RIGHT TO A REMEDY

The existence of an international right to a remedy does not necessarily lead to a corresponding right to an international remedy. Remedies may be internal as well as international, the latter usually playing a role complementary to the former. Whether internal or international remedies are created will depend not only on the specific requirements of human rights and humanitarian law, but also on the manner in which these norms are incorporated into municipal law.

A substantive right to a remedy is clearly created by international human rights law. The tone was set right from the beginning with the Universal Declaration of Human Rights, which stated in Article 8 that 'Everyone has the right to an effective remedy by the competent national tribunal . . . ' Similar provisions affording the individual a substantive right to an effective remedy can be found in all major human rights instruments.[87] Whether there exists a similar right in customary

---

[87] See Art. 2(3), International Covenant on Civil and Political Rights; Art. 13, European Convention on Human Rights; Art. 25, American Convention on Human Rights; Art. 7, African Charter on Human and Peoples' Rights; Art. 14, Convention Against Torture and Other Cruel, Inhuman or Degrading Treatment or Punishment; Art. 6, International Convention on the Elimination of All Forms of Racial Discrimination. See Pierre Mertens, *Le droit de recours effectif devant les instances nationales en cas de violation d'un droit de l'homme* (Brussels: Université Libre de Bruxelles, 1973) 18–46; Oscar Schachter, 'The Obligation to Implement the Covenant in Domestic Law', in Henkin, *International Bill of Rights*, at 311–31. Bodies created under the European Convention have devoted particular attention to the implications and extent of a right to an effective remedy: Fawcett, *Application of the European Convention*, at 291–3; van Dijk and van Hoof, *Theory and Practice*, at 696–710; Jean F. Flauss, 'Le droit à un recours effectif: L'article 13 de la Convention européenne des droits de l'homme dans la jurisprudence de la Commission et de la Cour', in Gérald-A. Beaudoin ed., *Vues canadiennes et européennes des droits de la personne* (Drummondville, Quebec: Yvon Blais, 1989) 258.

law is a question that has received only scant attention. Certainly, in some countries, individuals are permitted to seek redress for violation of their customary human rights. In the United States, in particular, a growing case-law has followed the decision in *Filartiga* v. *Peña-Irala* in which was recognised a victim's right to sue his torturer for violation of the customary international prohibition of torture.[88] If municipal law were to envisage no remedy for racial discrimination, for example, would this breach a right to a remedy distinct from the breach of the customary prohibition of racial discrimination? Attention is usually focused on the state's duty to protect internationally guaranteed human rights as a necessary corollary to these substantive rights, rather than as an application of an independent right to a remedy.[89] As a rule, individuals are not given a right to a remedy under customary international law, even if they hold substantive rights directly.[90] Given the nature of human rights as essentially individual rights, however, a substantive right to a remedy appears as a necessary element of the normative framework of human rights. Without such an element, the danger looms of that 'vain thing' of a right without a remedy threatening the reality of human rights as rights of individuals.[91] Despite the desirable character of such a rule, there is little evidence to suggest that it has evolved into customary law.[92]

---

[88] 630 F.2d 876 (2d Cir. 1980), relying on the Alien Torts Claims Act, 28 USC §1350. See David Kunstle, '*Kadić* v. *Karadzić*: Do Private Individuals Have Enforceable Rights and Obligations Under the Alien Torts Claims Act?', (1996) 6 *Duke J Comp. & Int'l L* 319–46.

[89] See UN Secretary-General, 'Annotation of the Text of the Draft International Covenants on Human Rights', UN Doc. A/2929 (1955) at 52; International Law Association, 'Final Report on the Status of the Universal Declaration of Human Rights in National and International Law', in International Law Association, *Report of the 66th Conference, Buenos Aires, 1994* (London: ILA, 1994), *quoted in* Richard B. Lillich and Hurst Hannum eds., *International Human Rights – Problems of Law, Policy and Practice* (Boston: Little, Brown, 1995) 168; Meron, *Human Rights and Humanitarian Norms*, at 139–40.

[90] *Restatement* §907 comment a; Oscar Schachter, 'International Law in Theory and Practice', (1982-V) 178 *Recueil des cours* 9, 232–3.

[91] The US *Restatement* §703 comment c takes a narrow position and finds that there probably is not a customary right to a remedy, but that lack of remedies could be evidence of a violation by the state of its obligations. See Mertens, *Droit de recours*, at 3–15; Christian Tomuschat, 'Individual Reparations Claims in Instances of Grave Human Rights Violations: The Position Under General International Law', in Albrecht Randelzhofer and Christian Tomuschat eds., *State Responsibility and Human Rights* (The Hague: Nijhoff, 1999) 1–25.

[92] The existence of a substantive right to a remedy is a question distinct from that of whether the international norm is directly applicable or self-executing under international law. For example, the European Court of Human Rights concluded in the *Swedish Engine Drivers' Union* case that the European Convention on Human Rights

International human rights are typically incorporated into municipal laws as guarantees entrenched into constitutional or statutory bills of rights. This is reflected in the type of mechanisms created to give effect to the individual's international right to an effective remedy, which may take the form of judicial orders for the cessation of the violation (injunction, amparo or habeas corpus), compensation through civil litigation or government programmes, restitution, declaratory judgments, truth commissions, resort to an ombudsman or other types of remedies.[93]

The existence of a general right to a remedy under humanitarian law is much more dubious. There is no exact equivalent to the human rights provisions mentioned above in the Geneva Conventions and Protocols or in the earlier Hague Conventions. One provision possibly having a similar effect is Article 3 of the 1907 Hague Convention IV. Article 3 lays down the broad principle, now part of customary law, that a belligerent state shall pay compensation for violations of the laws of war and shall be held responsible for all acts of its armed forces. Application of this rule is not limited to the 1907 Convention but extends to all norms on the conduct of warfare. An identical provision was inserted in Protocol I (Art. 91), expressly extending the rule to cover both the 1949 Conventions and Protocol I. Despite some indications in the *travaux préparatoires* of the 1907 Hague Convention IV that the obligation to compensate imposed by Article 3 could have been intended to benefit individuals as well as states, subsequent practice indicates that the corresponding customary rule has evolved to envisage claims from states only.[94]

was not self-executing despite the presence of Article 13 providing for a right to a remedy: Ser. A No. 20, at 1, 18. See also Inter-American Court of Human Rights, *Enforceability of the Right to Reply or Correction (Arts. 14(1), 1(1) and 2 of the American Convention on Human Rights)*, Adv. Op. OC-7/86 (1986); Buergenthal, 'Self-executing Treaties', at 335–40.

[93] See M. Cherif Bassiouni, 'Final Report of the Independent Expert on the Right to Restitution, Compensation and Rehabilitation for Victims of Grave Violations of Human Rights and Fundamental Freedoms', UN Doc. E/CN.4/2000/62, along with his 'First Report', UN Doc. E/CN.4/1999/65; Theo van Boven, 'Final Report of a Study Concerning the Right to Restitution, Compensation and Rehabilitation for Victims of Gross Violations of Human Rights and Fundamental Freedoms', UN Doc. E/CN.4/Sub.2/1993/8, along with his previous reports, UN Docs. E/CN.4/Sub.2/1990/10, -/1991/7 and -/1992/8.

[94] See Pierre Boissier, *L'épée et la balance* (Geneva: Labor et Fides, 1953) 134; Joseph L. Kunz, *Kriegsrecht und Neutralitätsrecht* (Vienna: Springer, 1935) 34–5; Lassa Oppenheim, *International Law*, Hersch Lauterpacht ed., 7th edn (London: Longmans, 1952) II, 594–5; Frits Kalshoven, 'State Responsibility for Warlike Acts of the Armed Forces', (1991) 40 *Int'l & Comp. L. Quart.* 827, 830–7; Yves Sandoz, 'Les dommages illicites dans les conflits armés et leur réparation dans le cadre du droit international humanitaire', (1982) 228 *Revue internationale de la Croix-rouge* 135, 141.

Attempts by individuals to obtain compensation based on the international responsibility of the enemy state have been rejected after the Second World War, for example by the Italian Court of Cassation in *Soc. Timber, Soc. Zeta, Soc. Obla* v. *Ministeri Esteri e Tesoro*.[95] The difficulties of a right to a remedy for violations of humanitarian law are illustrated more recently by the struggle of 'comfort women' to obtain compensation from Japan for military sexual slavery during the Second World War. While a 1998 decision awarded damages to former Korean 'comfort women' on the basis of a constitutional duty to apologise and compensate for Japan's colonial rule, it refused to recognise a right to compensation for breaches of humanitarian law.[96] At least seven other decisions have denied claims by former Philippine, Chinese, Taiwanese and Dutch comfort women on the same ground. Recent cases brought by former British and Dutch prisoners of war as well as Chinese victims of medical experimentation were also rejected in Japan on the ground that there was no right to compensation accruing to the individual under the laws of war.[97] A claim by former slave labourers based on international law was likewise rejected by a US District Court on the ground that 'under international law claims for compensation by individuals harmed by war-related activities belong exclusively to the state of which the individual is a national'.[98] On the other hand, in *Kadić* v. *Karadzić* the US Second Circuit Court concluded that a suit could be brought pursuant to the Alien Tort Claims Act for violations of common Article 3

[95] (1951) 18 Int'l L Rep. 621 ('But it is clear that its [the Hague Convention's] violation can involve responsibility only on the international plane, that is to say between state and state, and that an inhabitant of an occupied territory acquires thereunder no individual right as against an occupying power failing to observe the limits and conditions imposed upon it', *ibid.*, at 622).

[96] 'Japan Court Rules in Favour of "Comfort Women"', *Reuters News Service*, 27 April 1998 (judgment of 27 April 1998, Yamagushi District Court, Chikashika J); Doug Struck, 'Koreans Press War Claims Suit', *Washington Post*, 1 February 2000, at A12. On the need for compensation, see Radhika Coomaraswamy, 'Report on Violence Against Women, its Causes and Consequences', UN Doc. E/CN.4/1996/53/Add.1 paras. 91–124 (1996); Gay McDougall, 'Systematic Rape, Sexual Slavery and Slave-like Practices During Armed Conflict', UN Doc. E/CN.4/Sub.2/1998/3, Appendix ('An Analysis of the Legal Liability of the Government of Japan for "Comfort Women Stations" Established During the Second World War').

[97] 'Japan Court Rejects WWII Claims', *The National Law Journal* (New York), 14 December 1998 (decisions of the Tokyo District Court of 26 November 1998 (Shigeki Inoue J) and 30 November 1998 (Taichi Kajimura J)); 'Japan Court Rejects War Crimes Suit', *United Press International*, 23 September 1999 (Tokyo District Court, Ko Ito J).

[98] *Burger-Fischer et al.* v. *DeGussa AG*, 65 F.Supp.2d 248, 273 (D. New Jersey, 1999) at 82. See also *Iwanowa* v. *Ford Motor Co.*, 67 F.Supp.2d 424 (D. New Jersey, 1999).

of the Geneva Conventions.[99] While the court conclusively demonstrated that such a violation is a crime under international law, it offered little to justify its conclusion that it is, still under international law, a tort.

Under current international law, compensation rights for violations of humanitarian law norms would thus not accrue to the individual but pass on directly to the victim's state. Conversely, Article 3 of the 1907 Hague Convention IV and customary law impose a clear obligation on the part of the responsible state to provide compensation. These rights have served as the basis for reparation clauses in peace treaties, including the Treaty of Versailles.[100] State claims of this type are still being presented for Second World War violations, including those committed against 'comfort women'.[101] As for individuals, the ICRC Commentary to the 1949 Fourth Geneva Convention states clearly:

The Convention does not give individual men and women the right to claim compensation. The State is answerable to another contracting State and not to the individual . . . It is inconceivable, at least as the law stands today, that claimants should be able to bring a direct action for damages against the State in whose service the person committing the breach was working.[102]

---

[99] Kadić v. Karadžić, 70 F.3d 232, 242–3 (2d Cir., 1995). See also Doe v. Islamic Salvation Front (FIS), 993 F.Supp. 3, 8 (DDC, 1998). Note as well the May 2000 judgment of the Hellenic Supreme Court affirming an earlier decision of the Court of First Instance of Leivadia (Greece), which in 1997 awarded 9,448,105,000 drachmas ($30 million) to claimants as victims of the murder and destruction of private property by German soldiers in 1944; the court apparently denied state immunity to Germany (which did not appear) and relied on Art. 3 of the 1907 Hague Convention IV: Prefecture of Voiotia v. Federal Republic of Germany, Case No. 11/2000, 4 May 2000, noted in (2001) 95 Am. J Int'l L 198–204.

[100] See Civil War Claimants Assoc. Ltd v. R, [1932] AC 14 (House of Lords); Alwyn Freeman, 'Responsibility of States for Unlawful Acts of their Armed Forces', (1955-II) 88 Recueil des cours 267, 333. For other examples in treaty law, see Georg Schwarzenberger, International Law as Applied by International Courts and Tribunals – The Law of Armed Conflict (London: Stevens & Sons, 1968) II, 778–83.

[101] See e.g. Kikuyo Komesu, 'Taiwan Lawmakers Demand Japan Compensate WWII Sex Slaves', 25 May 2000, Japan Economic Newswire.

[102] Pictet, IV, at 211 and 603. This is consistent with the scheme created by the Third Convention (Art. 68) in case of disputes over compensation between prisoners of war and the detaining power: prisoners' claims are to be presented to the power on which they depend, and not to the detaining power (Pictet, III, at 334–8). After the First and Second World Wars, mechanisms were instituted to give back property illegally taken in times of war to its rightful owners (Oppenheim, International Law, II, at 595; Freeman, 'Responsibility'). In such cases, however, the right on which the individual relies need not be the provision of the 1907 Hague Regulation protecting property (Arts. 23(g), 46–8, 52–3), but simply property rights. For a more recent

Article 91 of Protocol I was adopted in the same spirit, aiming to guarantee a right to compensation in favour of parties to the conflict and not individual victims, who are directed to petition their own government to press for an international claim against the offending party.[103] No international right to a remedy is thus envisaged for individual victims of violations of humanitarian law.

The lack of an international right to a remedy is echoed by the form of incorporation of humanitarian law into municipal law. The most common form of incorporation is in the shape of field manuals issued to the armed forces, as required by Articles 48/48/127/144, Article 83 of Protocol I and Article 19 of Protocol II. These field manuals do not spell out rights for the benefit of combatants and civilians but rather constitute professional or *métier* rules of conduct to be followed by the armed forces.[104] Another form of incorporation, mandated by Articles 49/50/129/146 but in practice somewhat more unusual, is the adoption of penal provisions specifically allowing for the prosecution of grave breaches of the Geneva Convention and Protocols and, more broadly, war crimes.[105] Humanitarian law conventions have not been incorporated into municipal law so as to create rights directly invocable by

example, see Hans van Houtte, 'Mass Property Claim Resolution in a Post-War Society: The Commission for Real Property Claims in Bosnia and Herzegovina', (1999) 48 Int'l & Comp. L. Quart 625–38.

[103] See Pilloud et al., *ICRC Commentary*, at 1056.

[104] See for example the contents of: *1992 German Manual on Humanitarian Law in Armed Conflict, DSK VV207320067* (Bonn: German Ministry of Defence, 1992) (hereinafter *1992 German Manual on Humanitarian Law*); *1958 British Manual of Military Law; US Dept of the Army, Field Manual 27–10*, 18 July 1956 (Washington DC: US Gov. Printing Office, 1956); Legge di guerra italiana del 1938.

[105] See e.g. the US War Crimes Act, 18 USC §2401 (1996), the Belgian Law of 16 June 1993 (*Moniteur Belge*, 5 August 1993), the British War Crimes Act 1991 and s. 7(3.71) of the Canadian Criminal Code (Rev. Stat. of Can. 1985, c. C-46). See generally Michael Bothe, Peter Macalister-Smith and Thomas Kurzidem eds., *National Implementation of International Humanitarian Law* (The Hague: Nijhoff, 1990); Michael Bothe, 'The Role of Municipal Law in the Implementation of International Humanitarian Law', in Swinarski, *Mélanges Pictet*, at 301; Georges Levasseur and Roger Merle, 'L'état des législations internes au regard des obligations contenues dans les conventions internationales de droit humanitaire', in *Droit humanitaire et conflits armés – Colloque des 28, 29 et 30 janvier 1970, Université Libre de Bruxelles* (Brussels: Editions de l'Université de Bruxelles, 1976) 219–51; Rafaëlle Maison, 'Les premiers cas d'application des dispositions pénales des Conventions de Genève par les juridictions internes', (1995) 6 Eur. J Int'l L 260–73; Manuel Pérez González, 'Consideraciones sobre la aplicación del derecho internacional humanitario, con especial referencia a su aplicación en el orden interno', in *Héctor Gros Espiell Amicorum Liber* (Brussels: Bruylant, 1997) II, 1087, 1099–113.

individuals in judicial proceedings, with the narrow exception of military codes of justice.[106]

It is critical to note that lack of a right to a remedy under humanitarian law does not prevent all claims for injuries suffered by individuals in times of armed conflict. Human rights also apply during armed conflict, although many rights may be suspended by the state. Most egregious violations of humanitarian law will be coextensive with violations of non-derogable human rights, for which there is undoubtedly a right to a remedy. The complementarity of human rights and humanitarian law thus ensures that victims will not be left without a right to reparation for their injuries.

INTERNATIONAL STANDING

It is interesting to note briefly the standing enjoyed by individuals before international fora in human rights and humanitarian law, as the difference reflects the lack of a right to a remedy in the latter and, more broadly, the normative frameworks of the two systems.

Much has been written on the various mechanisms created by human rights treaties whereby private persons are given the possibility of individually setting into motion procedures designed to protect their basic rights, and there would be little point in rehearsing it all here.[107] There are some significant differences between the various mechanisms as to the position occupied by the individual victim. In some cases, such as before the Inter-American Commission and European Court of Human Rights, the rights-holder is the prime mover and a full participant in the proceedings. In other international fora, for instance the Human Rights Commission or UNESCO, the individual simply acts as a provider of information rather than as a full 'party' to the proceedings. In nearly all

---

[106] A number of countries recently have created national humanitarian law commissions with advisory powers to suggest legislative changes to implement international obligations: Adama Dieng, 'La mise en oeuvre du droit international humanitaire: Les infractions et les sanctions, ou quand la pratique désavoue les textes', in *Law in Humanitarian Crises – How Can International Humanitarian Law be Made Effective in Armed Conflict?* (Luxembourg: European Communities, 1995) I, 311, 370–1; Olivier Dubois, 'Meeting of Experts on Committees or Other Bodies for the National Implementation of International Humanitarian Law, Geneva, 23–25 October 1996', (1997) 317 *Int'l Rev. Red Cross* 187–91.

[107] See e.g. Hurst Hannum ed., *A Guide to Human Rights Practice*, 3rd edn (Philadelphia: U Penn. Press, 1999); Meron, *Human Rights and Humanitarian Norms*, at 140–8; Nørgaard, *Position of the Individual*, at 99–172.

cases where the individual is given full standing, the jurisdiction of the international body is subject to optional acceptance, either directly or indirectly through ratification of the relevant human rights convention, by the state concerned by the alleged violation of human rights.[108] There is no customary or universal mechanism allowing for a person individually to trigger control mechanisms in which he or she has full standing.

The situation in humanitarian law appears dramatically different. There is no international body with jurisdiction to provide redress to individual victims of violations of humanitarian law. No supervising body was envisaged by the 1907 Hague Conventions or by the 1949 Geneva Conventions. Only a rather loose system of enforcement through protecting powers was provided for in the Geneva Conventions, whereby prisoners of war or protected persons could direct petitions or complaints regarding their treatment to the protecting power (Art. 78, Third Convention; Art. 101, Fourth Convention). The protecting power may then lend its good offices to facilitate conciliation between the parties to the conflict as to the proper application of the Conventions (Arts. 11/11/11/12). A party to the conflict may also request an enquiry to be instituted to verify any violation of the Conventions (Arts. 52/53/132/149). These two procedures are not only highly theoretical but also completely disconnected from the individual victim of the violation of the Conventions.

The 1977 Additional Protocol I provided for the creation of a permanent body to oversee the implementation of the Conventions and Protocol I, the International Fact-Finding Commission (Art. 90, Protocol I).[109] The Commission, whose competence is optional, has broad jurisdiction to investigate any allegation of grave breaches or other serious violations of the Conventions or Protocol I. The power to set such an investigation in motion is not given to individuals but is reserved to parties to the conflict (Art. 90(2)(a) and (d), Protocol I). Input by the individual victim is not considered at any stage of the proceedings as described in this long-winded provision, although the Rules adopted in 1992 by the International Fact-Finding Commission do envisage hearing testimonies of witnesses, which would probably include victims.[110]

---

[108] One exception relates to the powers of the Inter-American Commission on Human Rights to apply the American Declaration of the Rights and Duties of Man pursuant to the OAS Charter. See below, p. 65 note 29.

[109] Other aspects of the competence of the International Fact-Finding Commission are discussed in chapter 7, pp. 328–32.

[110] See Rule 27(2), Règlement intérieur de la Commission internationale humanitaire d'établissement des faits, adopted on 8 July 1992, reprinted in [1993] Revue internationale de la Croix-rouge 184–95.

Does the establishment of the UN Compensation Commission, created by Security Council Resolution 687 (1991) to provide compensation for losses suffered by states, nationals and corporations in the wake of the Iraqi invasion and occupation of Kuwait in 1990, indicate a move away from established practice? Claims of nationals are to be submitted by states and not individuals but appear clearly based on the personal rights of individual victims: they are submitted by a state 'on behalf of its own nationals' and must include a signed statement by each individual victim.[111] Persons not in a position to have their claim presented by a state can do so through a person, body or authority designated by the UN Compensation Commission, for example the UN Development Programme for Palestinians in the Occupied Territories.[112]

The legal basis of Iraqi responsibility before the UN Compensation Commission seems to lie essentially in the Security Council's finding of a violation of Article 2(4) of the UN Charter rather than in violations of international humanitarian law. Indeed, because Iraq is deemed responsible for all war damages regardless of whether they issue from violations of or compliance with humanitarian law, or even whether they were caused by Iraq or by the coalition forces, there is little point in seeking to determine whether there have been any breaches of humanitarian law.[113] The Commission is not a purely judicial organ but rather a hybrid body whose function is based on a premiss of Iraqi liability, simply determining the scope of such liability and entitlement of

---

[111] UN Compensation Commission, Decision 1 'Criteria for Expedited Processing of Urgent Claims', 2 August 1991, UN Doc. S/AC.26/Dec.1 (1991) paras. 19–20, reprinted in 30 Int'l Leg. Mat. 1712; Report of the UN Compensation Commission, 1 September 1992, S/24589 para. 33 (1992), reprinted in 31 Int'l Leg. Mat. 1067–8. The reports and various other documents relating to the UNCC can be found at www.uncc.ch.

[112] UN Compensation Commission, Decision 5 'Guidelines Relating to Paragraph 19 of the Criteria for Expedited Processing of Urgent Claims', UN Doc. S/AC.26/Dec.5 (1991). See generally Marco Frigessi di Rattalma, Nazione Unite e danni derivanti dalla guerra del Golfo (Milan: Giuffrè, 1995); John R. Crook, 'The United Nations Compensation Commission: A New Structure to Enforce State Responsibility', (1993) 87 Am. J Int'l L 144; Pierre d'Argent, 'Le fonds et la Commission de compensation des Nations Unies', [1992] 2 Revue belge de droit international 484; Bernard Graefrath, 'Iraqi Reparations and the Security Council', (1995) 55 Zeitschrift für ausländisches öffentliches Recht und Völkerrecht 1–68; Richard B. Lillich et al., 'Claims Against Iraq: The UN Compensation Commission and Other Remedies', (1992) 86 Am. Soc. Int'l L Proc. 477.

[113] UN Compensation Commission, Decision 7 'Criteria for Additional Categories of Claims', UN Doc. S/AC.26/Dec.7/Rev.1 (1991) para. 21; Marco Frigessi di Rattalma, 'Le régime de la responsabilité internationale institué par le Conseil d'administration de la Commission de compensation des Nations Unies', (1997) 101 Revue générale de droit international public 44, 48–54.

claimants.[114] As such, its primary source of law, as set out in Article 31 of the Commission's Rules, is Security Council Resolution 687 (1991) and other relevant Security Council resolutions; other sources of international law, including humanitarian law, are given as merely subsidiary sources of applicable law.[115] The one, narrow exception concerns members of the allied coalition armed forces, who cannot present any claim except for injury suffered as prisoners of war involving a violation of humanitarian law.[116] Very few claims have been presented, but one panel of the Commission has awarded compensation for torture and beatings aimed at extracting information from prisoners of war.[117] One must note, however, that claims for grave breaches of the 1949 Geneva Conventions are accepted only from members of the allied coalition forces, and not from members of the Iraqi armed forces, even if they were not Iraqi nationals.[118] Clearly, the system set up by the Compensation

---

[114] See 'Report of the Secretary-General Pursuant to Paragraph 19 of Security Council Resolution 687', UN Doc. S/22559 (1991) para. 20; 'Report and Recommendations Made by the Panel of Commissioners Concerning the First Instalment of Individual Claims for Damages up to US $100,000 (Category "C" Claims)', 21 December 1994, UN Doc. S/AC.26/1994/3 (1994) at 9, *reprinted in* (1996) 35 Int'l Leg. Mat. 1020. See Felipe Paolillo, 'Reclamaciones colectivas internacionales: El caso de los damnificados por la crisis del Golfo', in Manuel Rama-Montaldo ed., *El derecho internacional en un mundo en transformación – Liber Amicorum en homenaje al profesor Eduardo Jiménez de Aréchaga* (Montevideo: FCU, 1994) 545, 553–6; Brigitte Stern, 'Un système hybride: La procédure de règlement pour la réparation des dommages résultant de l'occupation illicite du Koweit par l'Irak', (1992) 37 *McGill LJ* 625, 634.

[115] UN Compensation Commission, Decision 10 'Provisional Rules for Claims Procedure', UN Doc. S/AC.26/Dec.10 (1992) Art. 31; UN Compensation Commission, 'Panel Decision on "C" Claims'. See also David Berderman, 'Historic Analogues of the UN Compensation Commission', in Richard Lillich ed., *The United Nations Compensation Commission* (Irvington NY: Transnational, 1995) 257, 285; John R. Crook, 'The UNCC and Its Critics: Is Iraq Entitled to Judicial Due Process?', in Lillich, *UNCC* at 77, 80–4.

[116] UN Compensation Commission, Decision 11 'Eligibility for Compensation of Members of the Allied Coalition Armed Forces', UN Doc. S/AC.26/Dec.11 (1991).

[117] 'Report and Recommendations Made by the Panel of Commissioners Concerning Part One of the Second Instalment of Claims for Serious Personal Injury or Death (Category "B" Claims)', 15 December 1994, UN Doc. S/AC.26/1994/4 (1994) para. 14, *reprinted in* (1996) 35 Int'l Leg. Mat. 992. No "C" claims (up to US $100,000) have been presented under this heading.

[118] 'Report and Recommendations Made by the Panel of Commissioners Concerning Part Two of the Second Instalment of Claims for Serious Personal Injury or Death (Category "B" Claims)', 22 March 1995, UN Doc. S/AC.26/1995/1 (1995) para. 4, *reprinted in* (1996) 35 Int'l Leg. Mat. 1002. See Hazel Fox, 'Reparations and State Responsibility: Claims Against Iraq Arising out of the Invasion and Occupation of Kuwait', in Peter Rowe ed., *The Gulf War 1990–1991 in International and English Law* (London: Routledge, 1992) 261, 284.

Commission aims to protect not just individual interests but also some state interests. Because the near totality of the Commission's work relates to claims not involving any alleged violations of humanitarian law, but rather the general compensation of war-related injuries, it seems unlikely that this development will trigger the evolution of a customary right to compensation for victims of violations of the laws and customs of war.

Also in recent practice, the Security Council, in creating the ICTY, specified in Resolution 827 (1993) that the work of the Tribunal would not in any way prejudice the right of victims to seek compensation for damages resulting from violations of humanitarian law.[119] This was articulated in Rule 106 ('Compensation to Victim') of the Rules of Procedure and Evidence of the ICTY, directing the Tribunal's Registrar to transmit to national authorities the decision finding an accused guilty of a crime having caused an injury to a victim (para. A). Paragraph B states that '[p]ursuant to the relevant national legislation, a victim or person claiming through him may bring an action in a national court or other competent body to obtain compensation'.[120] What is apparently set up here is a mechanism to facilitate suits by the victim against the perpetrator in tortious or delictual liability pursuant to national law, rather than the creation or acknowledgment of an individual right to compensation under international humanitarian law.

Indications of international law's receptivity to an eventual right of victims of violations of humanitarian law appear more clearly in the Statute of the International Criminal Court, adopted in Rome in 1998.[121] Article 75 of the ICC Statute goes much further than the ICTY Rules, to provide that the Court may award reparations to the victims of international crimes falling under its jurisdiction, which include a comprehensive list of war crimes (Art. 8, ICC Statute). This is prospective in the sense that the Statute holds that the 'Court *shall establish* principles relating to reparation to, or in respect of, victims' (Art. 75(1), ICC Statute), acknowledging that such principles do not exist yet.[122] This provision is completed by Rules 93–9 of the Rules of Procedure and Evidence, adopted by the Preparatory Commission of the ICC, which detail some

---

[119] S/RES/827 (1993) para. 7.
[120] ICTY, 'Rules of Procedure and Evidence', UN Doc. IT/32/Rev.17 (1999).
[121] UN Doc. A/Conf.183/9 (17 July 1998).
[122] See Preparatory Commission for the International Criminal Court, 'Proceedings of the Preparatory Commission at its Second Session (26 July–13 August 1999)', UN Doc. PCNICC/1999/L.4/Rev.1 at 48–50.

of the conditions for the granting of compensation to victims.[123] The ICC represents the first clear opening in positive international law to the possibility of an individual right to compensation for violations of humanitarian law.

Generally speaking, the breach of a right triggers a derivative right to restitution in kind or restoration to the situation existing before the breach, if possible, or to compensation or indemnification. Breach of humanitarian law norms entails, *de lege lata*, none of these derivative rights for the individual.[124] There are some provisions in conventional and customary law providing for the liability of the state for breaches of humanitarian law. The primary consequence of the violation of humanitarian law, that is the prosecution and punishment of the individual perpetrator, is in no sense derivative of the rights of the victims. On the contrary, it stems from the public order character of the standards embodied in international humanitarian law.

Conclusion

The nature of the norms forming part of humanitarian law is not static. It continually evolves under the pressure of changes both in general international law – including the recognition in the last half-century that some fundamental individual rights are protected by customary law – and in the conduct of warfare – from high-intensity widespread international conflicts such as the Second World War to medium- and low-intensity non-international conflicts sometimes fought through third parties, such as the wars in Vietnam and Afghanistan. The 1977

---

[123] 'Report of the Preparatory Commission for the International Criminal Court', Addendum (Finalised Draft Text of the Rules of Procedure and Evidence), UN Doc. PCNICC/2000/INF/3/Add.1.

[124] Thus, the general right to a remedy for violation of humanitarian law which appeared in Theo van Boven's last report to the UN Sub-Commission on the Prevention of Discrimination and Protection of Minorities seems more *de lege ferenda* than *de lege lata*: Theo van Boven, 'Revised Set of Principles and Basic Guidelines on the Rights to Reparation for Victims of Gross Violations of Human Rights and Humanitarian Law', UN Doc. E/CN.4/Sub.2/1996/17 (1996) Art. 4; 'Report of the Sessional Working Group on the Administration of Justice and the Question of Compensation', UN Doc. E/CN.4/Sub.2/1996/16 (1996) paras. 10–32. This was followed up by resolutions of the Human Rights Commission in which it called upon states to give due attention to 'the right to restitution, compensation and rehabilitation for victims of grave violations of human rights', omitting any reference to such a right under humanitarian law: Human Rights Commission Res. 1997/29, para. 1; Res. 1998/43, para. 1; Res. 1999/33, para. 1; Res. 2000/41, para. 2. See Bassiouni, 'First Report', para. 84.

Additional Protocols are as much the progeny of this new context as the 1949 Geneva Conventions were of the experiences of the Second World War. The language and philosophy of human rights has permeated international law as a whole, and humanitarian law is no exception, as testified by the change in its very name from 'law of war' to 'humanitarian law'. As mentioned in the Introduction, Protocol I arose partly from a movement started in the late 1960s to press for the convergence of human rights and humanitarian law. Several of its provisions can be traced back not to earlier humanitarian conventions or state practice in warfare but to human rights instruments. These provisions include Article 1(4) of Protocol I, defining the field of application of the Protocol as including armed conflict in which a people is fighting a racist, colonial or alien regime. Article 1 echoes the human right of peoples to self-determination, entrenched in Article 1 of the International Covenant on Civil and Political Rights and recognised as having evolved into customary law by the International Court of Justice in the *Namibia*, *Western Sahara* and *East Timor* cases.[125] Another provision directly derived from international human rights law is Article 75 of Protocol I, which borrows from Article 14 of the Political Covenant to establish a basic set of protections afforded to any individual affected by an armed conflict. Further, as mentioned earlier, the universality of the protection granted by Article 75 stands in stark contrast to the patchwork approach adopted in the 1949 Geneva Conventions.

Human rights law has transformed the legal position of individuals as against their own states. With the general acceptance that some human rights are protected by customary law came the notion that such rights might be exercised against the wishes of the state. The demise of the traditional conception that a state's rights over its own nationals are absolute opened the door, albeit slightly, to the idea of valid claims by individuals against a hostile state during an armed conflict. Such claims are different in nature from the traditional humanitarian approach to the protection of individuals, which relied more on means related to diplomatic protection through the offices of protecting powers.

---

[125] *Legal Consequences for States of the Continued Presence of South Africa in Namibia (South West Africa) Notwithstanding Security Council Resolution 276 (1970), Advisory Opinion*, [1971] ICJ Rep. 16; *Western Sahara*, [1975] ICJ Rep. 12; *Case Concerning East Timor (Portugal v. Australia)*, [1995] ICJ Rep. 90. See Meron, *Human Rights and Humanitarian Norms*, at 96, 111–13. The possible ripening of Article 1(4) of Protocol I into customary humanitarian law seems more problematic, however, given the strong opposition it generated from several Western governments, including the United States, and the lack of consistent state practice so far. *Ibid.*, at 66.

As discussed in the Introduction, the relationships embodied in the law of human rights, between a state and its own nationals, and in humanitarian law, between individuals and a hostile state, are profoundly different. The adoption in humanitarian law of a framework granting individuals rights against an occupying state would constitute a significant shift in the nature of humanitarian law and an attempt to reframe the relationship between a state and an enemy people. Such a shift would clearly signal a convergence between human rights and humanitarian law.

The limitations of such a convergence appear rapidly, however, not only because of the distinct relationships embodied in each body of law, but also because of differences in the context in which each legal system is called upon to be applied. Human rights law both presupposes and requires that the interaction between the state and the individual be under constant judicial supervision, even if such supervision is activated only occasionally. Humanitarian law, on the other hand, will become applicable in a hostile context where recourse to judicial supervision is most often impracticable or impossible. Situations combining institutional stability and applicability of humanitarian law are somewhat unusual, consisting mostly of long-term belligerent occupations such as that of the Gaza Strip by Israel. Thus, while the introduction of a rights-based approach in a judicialised context such as that calling for the application of Article 75 of Protocol I seems a positive development, a general reinterpretation of humanitarian law as based on individual rights seems unwarranted and probably undesirable.[126]

---

[126] Another example of such a positive reinterpretation of humanitarian law concerns the right of prisoners of war to be repatriated after the end of active hostilities (Art. 118, Third Convention). The nature of the protected interests as well as the fact that hostilities are over support a rejection of the traditional absolute duty to repatriate in favour of a right of prisoners to elect to be sent back home or not: Christiane Shields Delessert, *Release and Repatriation of Prisoners of War at the End of Active Hostilities* (Zurich: Schulthess Polygraphischer Verlag, 1977); Greenwood, 'Rights at the Frontier', at 283.

2   Obligations and responsibility

Obligations and responsibility of international actors other than states are not inextricably linked. They are related in a way similar to the relationship between rights and procedural capacity noted at the beginning of chapter 1. The fact that an obligation is imposed on individuals does not necessarily lead to the conclusion that they will be held personally accountable for its breach. Conversely, the fact that someone can be ascribed responsibility for the violation of a norm of international law does not necessarily evidence the existence of an obligation imposed on that person. Delictual capacity and responsibility are related but not necessarily attached. An illustration can be found in crimes against peace. The prohibition of the use of force in international relations can be breached only by states but, as demonstrated by the convictions handed down by the International Military Tribunal at Nuremberg and by Article 5 of the ICC Statute, the penal responsibility is borne by the individuals with control over the conduct of the state.[1]

The dissociation of obligation and sanction might be seen as problematic, because of the apparent unfairness of someone being held responsible for the breach of another. There was no such difficulty with respect to rights, where a similar dissociation resulted only in the imposition of restrictions on the exercise of the rights. The justification lies at the levels of both practice and theory. From a practical standpoint, because

---

[1] Wilhelm Wengler, 'La noción de sujeto de derecho internacional público examinada bajo el aspecto de algunos fenómenos políticos actuales', (1951) 3 *Revista española de derecho internacional* 831, 836 (also published in German in (1951-3) 51 *Die Friedens-Warte* 113). See Carl Nørgaard, *The Position of the Individual in International Law* (Copenhagen: Munksgaard, 1962) 83; Julio A. Barberis, 'Nouvelles questions concernant la personnalité juridique internationale', (1983-I) 179 *Recueil des cours* 145, 164-5 and 206-7; Hans Kelsen, 'Collective and Individual Responsibility for Acts of State in International Law', (1948) 1 *Jewish YB Int'l L* 226, 229.

international law traditionally centres on states rather than individuals, most of the obligations created by international law are imposed on states, despite the fact that decisions are made by human beings. Thus, to inflict a sanction on an individual although the obligation nominally rested with the state does not offend any sense of justice.[2] From a theoretical standpoint, the purpose of sanctions in the international legal system is not one of expiation of, or revenge against, the perpetrator, but one of preventing further breaches of the law. As such, the target of the sanction need not necessarily be the perpetrator but rather the person with effective power to breach the rule again. There must be a certain legal or psychological link between the perpetrator and the target of the sanction to justify the dissociation of obligation and responsibility.[3] There is such a link, for instance, between a government and its population hit by countermeasures, and between a head of state and the actions of the state in breaching the prohibition of the use of force.

Obligations

The normative frameworks of human rights law and humanitarian law are diametrically opposed with respect to obligations, as indeed they are with respect to the granting of rights. While human rights law imposes obligations mostly on the state rather than the individual, humanitarian law seeks directly to regulate the conduct of individuals as much as that of the state.

HUMAN RIGHTS

One vision of human rights law contemplates the existence of an individual obligation corresponding to every individual right recognised by general international law. This is contrasted with the generally accepted

---

[2] Hersch Lauterpacht, *International Law and Human Rights* (London: Stevens & Sons, 1950) 40–5 ('The judgment of the Nuremberg Tribunal treated the provisions of the Charter [of the IMT] laying down the individual responsibility of the accused for acts committed on behalf of the state as a self-evident rule of international law, as a matter both of principle and of the effectiveness of the law of nations': *ibid.*, at 45); Nørgaard, *Position of the Individual*, at 86–7.

[3] Hans Kelsen, *Principles of International Law* (New York: Rinehart, 1952) 9–11; Wengler, 'La noción', at 833. It is interesting to note that Wengler sees in the imposition of responsibility the defining characteristic of a subject of international law. *Ibid.*, at 845.

concept in human rights law of a state obligation corresponding to every individual right.[4] The effect of such an individual obligation would be to extend the reach of human rights law to cover interpersonal relations, or what is often referred to as *Drittwirkung* (literally 'effect on third parties'). As such, for example, a private school could be found in breach of a woman's international human right to privacy if she were fired for living with a man while not married.[5] Perhaps more importantly, the activities of non-state groups engaging in terrorist activities could be covered by human rights law.[6] The individual would thus be the bearer of an obligation when acting *qua* individual, and not merely as an agent of the state. As indicated above, the fact that the state is later found responsible for the violation does not necessarily deny the existence of an obligation imposed on the individual personally. Before turning to the issue of individual obligations, however, state duties are briefly examined so as to differentiate them clearly from those of individuals.

State obligations

Individual obligations under human rights law must not be confused with the state obligation to enforce and protect the rights granted to individuals by that law. In many cases, the state has an obligation to adopt measures in municipal law which in turn create obligations for individuals. Such individual obligations, however, are not directly imposed by international law, but only through the operation of municipal law. Several international conventions expressly direct state parties to act at the domestic level to enforce the rights entrenched in the treaties through the creation of domestic obligations. For instance, Article 2(1)(d) of the Convention on the Elimination of All Forms of Racial Discrimination provides that '[e]ach State Party shall prohibit and bring to an end, by all

---

[4] U. Umozurike, 'The African Charter on Human and Peoples' Rights', (1983) 77 *Am. J Int'l L* 902, 907.

[5] Cour de travail de Bruxelles, 24 November 1977, [1978] *Journal des tribunaux du travail* 63–4 (relying on Art. 8 of the European Convention on Human Rights), *cited in* Andrew Drzemczewski, *European Human Rights Convention in Domestic Law* (Oxford: Clarendon, 1983) 208. Other instances could include sexual harassment, wife-battering, employment discrimination, etc.: Patricia F. Marshall, 'Violence Against Women in Canada by Non-State Actors: The State and Women's Human Rights', in Kathleen E. Mahoney and Paul Mahoney eds., *Human Rights in the Twenty-First Century – A Global Challenge* (Dordrecht: Nijhoff, 1993) 319–34.

[6] 'Report of the Secretary-General on Minimum Humanitarian Standards', UN Doc. E/CN.4/1998/87, paras. 62 and 65.

appropriate means, including legislation as required by circumstances, racial discrimination by any persons, group or organization'.[7]

Under general international law, the state has an obligation of due diligence to protect the enjoyment of the rights of individuals which may involve, depending on the circumstances, the imposition of individual obligations through domestic legislation.[8] A general obligation of due diligence also flows from conventional provisions which impose on state parties a duty to respect and secure or ensure respect of the rights guaranteed in the conventions. This type of provision can be found, in related forms, in the American Convention on Human Rights (Art. 1), the European Convention on Human Rights (Art. 1), the African Charter on Human and Peoples' Rights (Art. 1) and the International Covenant on Civil and Political Rights (Art. 2(1)). It was analysed in depth by the Inter-American Court of Human Rights in the *Velásquez Rodríguez* case brought against Honduras, a case involving the involuntary disappearance of students where the involvement of state agents was probable but not established.[9] The Court noted that the duty to 'ensure' full enjoyment of the rights involves a duty to prevent, investigate and punish any violation, through the enactment of appropriate legislation and the reorganisation of the state apparatus. Failing this, the state may be in breach of its international obligation even though the actual violation was not committed by a state agent:

An illegal act which violates human rights and which is directly not imputable to a State (for example, because it is the act of a private person or because the person responsible has not been identified) can lead to international responsibility of the State, not because of the act itself, but because of the lack of due diligence to prevent the violation or to respond to it as required by the Convention.[10]

---

[7] See also Art. 2(b), Convention on the Elimination of All Forms of Discrimination Against Women (CEDAW) (1981) 1249 UNTS 13; Art. 2, Convention Against Torture and Other Cruel, Inhuman or Degrading Treatment or Punishment, 10 December 1984, UN Doc. A/RES/39/46 (1984), *reprinted in* Ian Brownlie ed., *Basic Documents on Human Rights*, 3rd edn (Oxford: Clarendon, 1992) 38.

[8] Ian Brownlie, *System of the Law of Nations: State Responsibility* (Oxford: Clarendon, 1983) I, 161–2; Theodor Meron, *Human Rights and Humanitarian Norms as Customary Law* (Oxford: Clarendon, 1989) 164; Barberis, 'Nouvelles questions', at 208; Alexandre-Charles Kiss, 'La protection des droits de l'homme dans les rapports entre personnes privées en droit international public', in *René Cassin Amicorum Discipulorumque Liber* (Paris: Pedone, 1971) III, 221.

[9] I/A Court HR, Judgment of 28 July 1988, Ser. C No. 4.

[10] *Ibid.*, at 154 para. 172. In the end, the Court found Honduras in breach of Velásquez's right to life, liberty and humane treatment.

Similar reasoning has been adopted by other human rights bodies with respect to other instruments.[11] The state's duty thus is breached if infringements by private individuals are tolerated or condoned by the state, even though it does not specifically endorse the violations. The duty to prevent the infringement of human rights includes an obligation to enact legislation necessary to render the violation illegal under municipal law.[12]

There has been some confusion between obligations of this type imposed on the state with regard to actions in the private sphere and obligations imposed on individuals by the direct effect of international human rights norms. In his discussion of rights and duties imposed by international instruments, for instance, Meron gives as an example of a provision imposing duties on individuals Article 20 of the International Covenant on Civil and Political Rights.[13] That article, stating that '[a]ny propaganda for war shall be prohibited by law', imposes an obligation

---

[11] The Committee on the Elimination of Discrimination against Women, for example, used wording manifestly borrowed from the *Velásquez Rodríguez* decision in describing state parties' duties under CEDAW: Committee on the Elimination of Discrimination against Women, General Recommendation 19, 'Violence against Women', UN Doc. HRI/GEN/1/Rev.1 at 84 (1994). With respect to the International Covenant on Civil and Political Rights, see the views of the Human Rights Committee in *Herrera Rubio v. Colombia*, Comm. 161/1983, UN Doc. A/43/40 (1987) at 198. With respect to the European Convention, see *Young, James and Webster* case (*Closed Shop* case), (1981) 44 Eur. Ct Hum. Rts (Ser. A), 62 Int'l L Rep. 359, 376–7; *Case of X and Y v. The Netherlands*, (1985) 91 Eur. Ct Hum. Rts (Ser. B) 11; *Ahmed v. Austria*, (1996) 24 Eur. Hum. Rts Rep. 278 (Eur. Ct Hum. Rts). With respect to the African Charter on Human and Peoples' Rights, see the decision of the African Commission in *Commission nationale des droits de l'homme et des libertés fondamentales v. Chad*, Comm. 74/92, 11 Oct. 1995, paras. 19–22, reprinted in (1997) 18 Hum. Rts LJ 34–5.

[12] *Velásquez Rodríguez*, at 155 para. 175. See also I/A Court HR, *Compulsory Membership in an Association Prescribed by Law for the Practice of Journalism (Arts. 13 and 29 of the American Convention on Human Rights)*, Advisory Opinion OC-5/85 of 13 November 1985, Ser. A No. 5, at 110–14; Juliane Kokott, 'No Impunity for Human Rights Violations in the Americas', (1993) 14 *Hum. Rts LJ* 153, 154–6; Meron, *Human Rights and Humanitarian Norms*, at 166–8; Thomas Buergenthal, 'To Respect and to Ensure: State Obligations and Permissible Derogations', in Louis Henkin ed., *The International Bill of Rights* (New York: Columbia UP, 1981) 77–8; Andrew Clapham, 'Drittwirkung and the European Convention of Human Rights', in R. St J. Macdonald et al. eds., *The European System for the Protection of Human Rights* (Dordrecht: Nijhoff, 1993) 163–206; M. Forde, 'Non-governmental Interference with Human Rights', (1985) 56 *Brit. YB Int'l L* 253, 278; Guiseppe Sperduti, 'Responsibility of States for Activities of Private Law Persons', in R. Bernhardt ed., [Instalment] 10 *Encyclopedia of Public International Law* (1987) 373, 375.

[13] Theodor Meron, *Human Rights in Internal Strife: Their International Protection* (Cambridge: Grotius, 1987) 34–5.

on the state, whereby the state must enact the appropriate legislation.[14] No individual obligation is created by this provision. Another confusion is the characterisation of the infringement by the individual as a breach of international law, on which is tacked a separate violation by the state for not acting to protect the right. The individual violation is thus seen as the breach of the duty not to trench upon the human rights of others, while the state violation refers to its own international duty.[15] No evidence is given to support the conclusion that there exists an individual obligation. Without such evidence, a better interpretation is to view the individual infringement as the objective condition triggering the breach by the state, and not as an independent violation of international law.[16] Our focus here is not on the private/public dichotomy and whether the state may be held accountable for actions in the private sphere, but rather on the role, if any, played by the imposition of obligations directly on the individual in the protection against violations of human rights.[17]

Individual obligations

The direct imposition of obligations on individuals by customary or conventional human rights law is, of course, not an impossibility. The Permanent Court of International Justice noted in the *Jurisdiction of the Courts of Danzig* case that no principle of international law prevents parties to a treaty from directly granting rights or imposing duties on individuals, if they so desire.[18] There would not seem to be any reason why customary norms could not achieve the same result, given that international law recognises the possibility for rights to be given directly to individuals as a result of customary law. The prohibitions of piracy, slave trade, breach of blockade and war contraband are generally thought to constitute examples of individual obligations imposed directly by customary

[14] Nigel S. Rodley, 'Can Armed Opposition Groups Violate Human Rights?', in Mahoney and Mahoney, *Human Rights*, at 297, 308–9.

[15] Kiss, 'La protection', at 215, 221.

[16] Brownlie, *System*, at 159; 'Commentary on the Draft Articles on State Responsibility', [1975] 2 *YB Int'l L Com'n* 82 ('although the international responsibility of the State is sometimes said to exist in connection with acts of private persons, its sole basis is the internationally wrongful conduct of organs of the State in relation to the acts of the private persons concerned').

[17] On the question of state responsibility for violations of human rights in the private sphere, see generally Andrew Clapham, *Human Rights in the Private Sphere* (Oxford: Oxford UP, 1993) 80–149.

[18] *Jurisdiction of the Courts of Danzig*, (1928) Ser. B No. 15, at 17–18. See [1964] 2 *YB Int'l L Com'n* 115–18 for a debate on that point.

international law.[19] The principle was reaffirmed by the General Assembly in its resolution on the 'Principles of International Law Recognised in the Charter of the Nürnberg Tribunal and in the Judgment of the Tribunal'.[20]

As mentioned earlier, under the *Drittwirkung* theory, every positive individual right entrenched in an international instrument can be construed to imply the existence of an individual obligation.[21] However, the historical sources and the context of international human rights conventions indicate that human rights were intended to stand as bulwarks against intrusions originating in the state rather than in other human beings.[22] This emerges clearly from the preamble of the Universal Declaration, holding the entrenchment of human rights to be essential 'if man is not to be compelled to have recourse, as a last resort, to rebellion against tyranny and oppression'. This is illustrated, for example, by the customary and conventional protection against torture, which covers only acts of torture carried out by or with the consent of the state, and not by individuals acting in a purely private manner.[23] The debate over the appointment of a special rapporteur on human rights and terrorism

---

[19] See Kelsen, *Principles*, at 124–31; Nørgaard, *Position of the Individual*, at 88–95; Dionisio Anzilotti, 'L'azione individuale contraria al diritto internazionale', in *Opere di Dionisio Anzilotti* (Padua: CEDAM, 1956) II:1, 210–41; Kelsen, 'Collective and Individual Responsibility', at 230.

[20] Principle I: 'Any person who commits an act which constitutes a crime under international law is responsible therefor and liable to punishment', General Assembly Resolution 95(I), 11 December 1946. The commentary to Principle I adds that 'the general rule underlying Principle I is that international law may impose duties on individuals directly without any interposition of internal law'.

[21] See Drzemczewski, *European Human Rights Convention*, at 199–228; Evert Albert Alkema, 'The Third-Party Applicability or "Drittwirkung" of the European Convention on Human Rights', in Franz Matscher and Herbert Petzold eds., *Protecting Human Rights: The European Dimension*, 2nd edn (Cologne: Karl Heymanns, 1990) 33–45; Marc-André Eissen, 'La Convention européenne des droits de l'homme et les obligations de l'individu: Une mise à jour', in *René Cassin Amicorum Discipulorumque Liber*, III, at 151–62; Ole Espersen, 'Human Rights and Relations Between Individuals', in *ibid.*, at 177–87; Forde, 'Non-governmental Interference', at 253–80; Kiss, 'La protection'.

[22] See e.g. 'Report of the Secretary-General on Minimum Humanitarian Standards', para. 61. This construction of human rights grounded in rights of individuals, it has been argued, is directly attributable to their mostly Western origins, given that Eastern thought focuses more on obligations of individuals towards the state and towards others: S. S. Rama Rao Pappu, 'Human Rights and Human Obligations: An East–West Perspective', (1982) 8 *Phil. & Soc. Action* 15–27.

[23] See Art. 1(1), Convention Against Torture and Other Cruel, Inhuman or Degrading Treatment or Punishment (1984); Arts. 2–3, Inter-American Convention to Prevent and Punish Torture (1985); *Filartiga v. Peña-Irala*, 630 F.2d 876, 878–85 (2d Cir. 1980); *Tel-Oren v. Libyan Arab Republic*, 726 F.2d 774, 791–3 and 805–6 (DC Cir. 1984); *The Prosecutor v. Furundzija* (Judgment), 10 December 1998, Case No. IT-95-17/1-T (Trial Chamber, ICTY), para. 162.

illustrates the still controversial character of the *Drittwirkung* applica-tion of human rights.[24] A valid conclusion that there exist individual obligations, then, must rely on a clear intention of states expressed in substantive provisions of binding multilateral conventions or by way of customary law.

There are several instances where, in preambular provisions, interna-tional instruments on human rights consider the possibility of individ-uals having duties corresponding to rights. The Covenants on Civil and Political Rights and on Economic, Social and Cultural Rights both state in their preambles that, in principle, the individual has obligations with respect to other individuals: '*Realizing* that the individual, having duties to other individuals and to the community to which he belongs, is under a responsibility to strive for the promotion and observance of the rights recognized in the present Covenant'.[25] Similar declarations of principle can be found in the preambles of the American Declaration of the Rights and Duties of Man[26] and in the African Charter on Human and Peoples' Rights.[27] Indeed, the very title of the American Declaration of the Rights and Duties of Man implies the existence of obligations imposed on the individual.

The non-binding provisions of the body of the Universal Declaration of Human Rights also contain a reference to individual obligations. Article 29(1) of the Universal Declaration proclaims that '[e]veryone has duties to the community in which alone the free and full development of his personality is possible'. The emphasis here is on individual duties towards the community, and the *travaux préparatoires* indicate that the provision was inserted to limit rights and ensure that they would not be used in an abusive and arbitrary manner. Article 29 was not intended to embody obligations from one individual towards another.[28]

---

[24] Kalliopi Koufa, 'Preliminary Report on Terrorism and Human Rights', UN Doc. E/CN.4/Sub.2/1999/27, paras. 44–6.

[25] See Christian Tomuschat, 'Grundpflichten des Individuums nach Völkerrecht', (1983) 21 *Archiv des Völkerrecht* 289, 304–5.

[26] 'Final Act of the Ninth International Conference of American States', Bogotá (Colombia), 1948, *reprinted in* Brownlie, *Basic Documents*, at 488 ('[t]he fulfilment of duty by each individual is a prerequisite to the rights of all').

[27] '*Considering* that the enjoyment of rights and freedoms also implies the performance of duties on the part of everyone'.

[28] See Albert Verdoodt, *Naissance et signification de la Déclaration universelle des droits de l'homme* (Louvain: Nauwelaerts, 1964) 262–71; René Cassin, 'De la place faite aux devoirs de l'individu dans la Déclaration universelle des droits de l'homme', in *Mélanges Poly Modinos – Problèmes des droits de l'homme et de l'unification européenne* (Paris: Pedone, 1968) 479, 483–6; Erica-Irene A. Daes, 'Freedom of the Individual Under Law:

Chapter 2 of the American Declaration (Arts. 29–38) states very generally that '[i]t is the duty of the individual to so conduct himself in relations to others that each and everyone may fully form and develop his personality' (Art. 29), from which might be implied an obligation not to breach the human rights of others, and then gives a list of duties ranging from the duty to educate oneself (Art. 31) to that of paying taxes (Art. 36). Like the Universal Declaration of Human Rights, the American Declaration was originally intended as a non-binding statement of highly desirable principles. The activist stance of the Inter-American Commission on Human Rights, relying on open-textured provisions of its Statute and of the Charter of the Organization of American States (OAS), found that states in ratifying the Charter had undertaken to comply with the provisions of the American Declaration.[29] It is unlikely, for institutional and jurisdictional reasons, that the Inter-American Commission on Human Rights will follow its own path and construe the Declaration as imposing individual duties.[30] More generally, because of the indirect basis of state obligations with respect to the American Declaration, it seems difficult to conclude that binding duties for individuals were also meant to be created by state ratification of the OAS Charter.

Despite the fact that the Universal and American Declarations are not directly binding with respect to individual obligations, they may

The Individual's Duties to the Community and the Limitations on Human Rights and Freedoms Under Article 29 of the Universal Declaration of Human Rights', UN Sales No. E.89.XIV.5 (1990), at 17–64; Karel Vasak, 'Proposition pour une Déclaration universelle des devoirs de l'homme, introduction et texte', (1987) 168 *Le supplément – Revue d'éthique et de théologie morale* 9, 11.

[29] See Statute of the Inter-American Commission on Human Rights, Art. 2(b), OAS Gen. Ass. Res. 447 (1979); *White and Potter* v. *United States* (the '*Baby Boy*' case), Case 2141, OAS Doc. OEA.Ser.L/V/II.54, doc. 9 rev. 1 (1981), (1981) 1 *Hum. Rts LJ* 110, paras. 15–17; *Roach and Pinkerton* v. *United States*, Case 9647, OAS Doc. OEA.Ser.L/V/II.71, doc. 9 rev. 1 (1987), para. 48. This is supported by an expansive construction by the Inter-American Court of Human Rights of its advisory jurisdiction to interpret 'other treaties concerning the protection of human rights', which the Court has taken to include the American Declaration despite the fact that it is not a treaty: '*Other Treaties' Subject to the Advisory Jurisdiction of the Court (Article 64, American Convention on Human Rights)*, Advisory Opinion OC-1/82 (24 Sept. 1982); *Interpretation of the American Declaration on the Rights and Duties of Man in the Context of Article 64 of the American Convention on Human Rights*, Advisory Opinion OC-10/89 (14 July 1989).

[30] Jurisdictional reasons refer to the fact that the Commission may only entertain individual petitions alleging that human rights have been violated by a state (Arts. 44–5, American Convention); institutional reasons refer to the fact that the Article 2(b) of the Statute of the Commission mentions only 'the *rights* set forth in the American Declaration of the Rights and Duties of Man'.

nevertheless serve as tools in the interpretation of other, binding, human rights instruments.

Turning to human rights treaties, there are no substantive provisions indicating an intention to impose obligations directly on individuals in the International Covenant on Economic, Social and Cultural Rights. Some have seen in Article 5(1) of the Civil and Political Rights Covenant and Article 17 of the European Convention the imposition of individual obligations.[31] The provisions are basically interpretation clauses, indicating that the treaties should not be construed as justifying conduct trenching upon or denying human rights guaranteed by the treaty. The absence of a right does not signal the presence of an obligation, however, and there is nothing in these provisions indicating the imposition of an individual duty not to interfere with the rights of others.[32] Article 19(3) of the Civil and Political Rights Covenant and Article 10(2) of the European Convention provide that the exercise of freedom of expression 'carries with it special duties and responsibilities', so that legal restriction may lawfully be imposed by the state. The nature and content of such duties are not articulated, and they seem to have been included essentially as justification for the 'clawback' clause permitting limitation of the right.[33] Nevertheless, they do represent an acknowledgment that human duties may be envisaged within the framework of those two instruments.

The American Convention on Human Rights for its part contains a chapter on 'personal responsibilities'. Its sole article, entitled 'Relationship between duties and rights' (Art. 32), provides very broadly that '[e]very person has responsibilities to his family, his community, and mankind' (para. 1), and that the rights of individuals under the Convention are limited by a number of factors, including the rights of others (para. 2). While the second paragraph imposes no obligation, being merely concerned with the limitation of rights, the first recognises the existence of individual duties, including duties towards other individuals.[34] This acknowledgment, however, is made at a most general

---

[31] Meron, *Human Rights in Internal Strife*, at 34–5; Jordan Paust, 'The Other Side of Rights: Private Duties Under Human Rights Law', (1992) 5 *Harv. Hum. Rts J* 51, 55.

[32] This aspect of Art. 5(1) is discussed by the UN Human Rights Committee in *López v. Uruguay*, Communication No. 52/1979, *reprinted in* 'Human Rights Committee – Selected Decisions Under the Optional Protocol', UN Doc. CCPR/C/OP/1 (1985) (Sales No. E.84.XIV.2), at 91.

[33] See e.g. *Handyside v. United Kingdom*, (1968) Ser. A No. 24, para. 49 (Eur. Ct Hum. Rts).

[34] Héctor Gros Espiell, *La Convención americana y la Convención europea de derechos humanos – Analysis comparativo* (Santiago: Ed. jurídica de Chile, 1991) 133–5. Unlike the

level, with only a broad statement as to the existence of duties, but no hint as to what the implication of such a pronouncement might be within the framework of the American Convention. The Inter-American Commission and Court of Human Rights have yet to examine closely this most interesting provision.

The most recent general multilateral convention on human rights, the African Charter on Human and Peoples' Rights, includes a chapter setting out the duties of individuals much more clearly (Arts. 27–9). This is partly a reflection of the distinct conception of human rights in African culture, centred on the individual not in an atomistic manner but rather as necessarily and dialectically connected with the community, which forms the second and equally significant focus point of the Charter.[35] Thus, Article 27(1) provides that the individual has duties towards various levels of community, including the family, society, the state and the international community. Article 29 articulates in eight paragraphs the nature of these duties, including the preservation of the family's cohesion (para. 1), of the security of the state (para. 3) and of African cultural values (para. 7). Article 27(2), however, directs persons to exercise their rights 'with due regard for the rights of others', which can be construed as a duty not to interfere with the human rights of others. Even clearer is Article 28, stating that '[e]very individual shall have the duty to respect and consider his fellow beings without discrimination'. Despite the collective dimension of the necessity to lessen ethnic or tribal tensions in the African context, as expressed in the prohibition of discrimination, this type of drafting suggests that private persons were intended to be directly obligated towards others by the provision.[36]

English version of the Convention, which uses the somewhat vague word 'responsibilities', the Spanish version refers to 'deberes', clearly implying duties.

[35] See Fatsah Ouguergouz, *La Charte africaine des droits de l'homme et des peuples – une approche juridique des droits de l'homme entre tradition et modernité* (Geneva: Presses Universitaires de France, 1993) 233; Kéba Mbaye, *Les droits de l'homme en Afrique* (Paris: Pedone, 1992) 213–14; Etienne-Richard Mbaya, 'Symétrie entre droits et devoirs dans la Charte africaine des droits de l'homme', (1987) 168 *Le Supplément – Revue d'éthique et de théologie morale* 35, 38; Makau wa Mutua, 'The Banjul Charter and the African Cultural Fingerprint: An Evaluation of the Language of Duties', (1995) 35 *Va. J Int'l L* 339–80.

[36] See Emmanuel Bello, 'The African Charter on Human and Peoples' Rights', (1985-V) 194 *Recueil des cours* 13, 178–9; Ouguergouz, *La Charte africaine*, at 246–54; Oji Umozurike, *The African Charter on Human and Peoples' Rights* (The Hague: Nijhoff, 1997) 65; Umozurike, 'African Charter', at 907. Mbaye, one of the drafters of the Charter, is less inclined to see in the provision a clear intent to generate individual obligations: Mbaye, *Droits de l'homme*, at 216 ('Il est certain que les dispositions relatives aux devoirs ne peuvent avoir qu'une portée limitée. D'ailleurs, la généralité avec laquelle

The imposition of obligations on individuals sometimes takes the form of a criminal-type prohibition whereby an act is proclaimed criminal by the convention itself, not to be confused with an obligation imposed on state parties to enact domestic legislation having the same effect within each state.[37] While the imposition of individual obligations is not necessarily connected to criminal responsibility, the attribution of such a responsibility in most cases indicates that individual obligations do exist. There are no such provisions in general universal or regional conventions on human rights, but only in specialised treaties dealing with specific issues. The International Convention on the Suppression and Punishment of the Crime of Apartheid thus declares that apartheid is a crime under international law (Arts. I(2) and III), instituting a system whereby any state party to the Convention may try persons suspected of this international crime (Art. V). Similarly, the Supplementary Convention on the Abolition of Slavery, the Slave Trade, and Similar Institutions and Practices Similar to Slavery[38] states that slavery and several of its manifestations shall be a crime in the domestic law of every state party to the Convention (Arts. 3(1), 5 and 6). Finally, the Genocide Convention 'confirm[s] that genocide . . . is a crime under international law' (Art. I), and holds anyone taking part in the crime of genocide to be criminally responsible, whether they be state agents or private individuals (Arts. I and IV).[39]

Some could perhaps question whether instruments like the Genocide Convention and the Apartheid Convention can properly be said to fall within international human rights law. It could be suggested that they belong not to human rights but rather to international criminal law, a juridically distinct body of international law. While it is true that the prohibitions of genocide and apartheid seek to protect interests beyond

les devoirs sont spécifiés montre bien que le législateur a voulu plutôt insister sur une philosophie que prescrire des règles strictes qui doivent être appliquées avec rigueur').

[37] The possibility of a convention directly declaring an act to be an international crime is incorporated into Art. 1 of the International Law Commission's Draft Code of Crimes Against the Peace and Security of Mankind: 'Report of the International Law Commission on the Work of its 48th Session', UN Doc. A/51/10 (1996).

[38] 7 September 1956, (1956) 266 UNTS 3, reprinted in Brownlie, Basic Documents, at 58.

[39] See Meron, Human Rights and Humanitarian Norms, at 165. Contra Barberis, 'Nouvelles questions', at 208, who denies that direct obligations are imposed on individuals by the effect of the conventions on slavery and genocide, arguing that only a state obligation to enact domestic legislation is created. An obligation of this type is created by Art. 4(1) of the 1984 Convention against Torture, although the UK House of Lords took an expansive view of its effect in the Pinochet case: see below, note 194 and accompanying text.

those of the individual victims, they are clearly related to human rights. The same is true, *a fortiori*, for the prohibition of slavery which is more squarely centred on the protection of individual interests. Neither human rights law nor international criminal law have clearly delineated borders or fixed meanings, and it seems likely that they overlap to some significant extent.[40] In any event, conventional provisions on apartheid, slavery and genocide are taken here as indications that the protection of interests related to human rights can be achieved by way of individual obligations.

Leaving aside treaty law to turn now to customary law, there is no broad principle of individual obligations corresponding to human rights under general international law. In a limited number of cases in *lex specialis*, duties have come to be recognised as directly attached to private persons as a result of customary international law. As with treaties, some could argue that these norms are properly characterised as belonging to international criminal law rather than to human rights law, bringing the same response as given just above. Thus, for example, the customary individual obligations regarding slavery and participation in the slave trade have been construed as relating to the protection of human rights although they predate the emergence of the latter.[41]

The most important instance of customary individual obligation probably derives from the prohibition of genocide and crimes against humanity. Initially linked to war crimes in the Charter of the International Military Tribunal,[42] where the norm was for the first time expressed in an international document, the prohibition of genocide and crimes against humanity gradually grew to be independent of armed conflict and became applicable in times of peace as well as war.[43] It is now generally accepted that the prohibition of genocide and crimes against humanity forms part of customary law.[44]

---

[40] See Steven Ratner, 'The Schizophrenias of International Criminal Law', (1998) 33 *Tex. Int'l LJ* 237.

[41] See Art. 4, Universal Declaration of Human Rights; Art. 8, International Covenant on Civil and Political Rights; *Restatement (Third) of the Foreign Relations Law of the United States* (St Paul: American Law Institute, 1987) para. 702(b); Meron, *Human Rights and Humanitarian Law*, at 165.

[42] 8 August 1945, *reprinted in* Dietrich Schindler and Jirí Toman, *The Laws of Armed Conflict*, 3rd edn (Dordrecht: Nijhoff, 1989) 911.

[43] *Case Concerning the Application of the Convention on the Prevention and Punishment of the Crime of Genocide (Bosnia-Herzegovina v. Yugoslavia), Preliminary Objections,* [1996] ICJ Rep. para. 31; *The Prosecutor v. Tadić* (Opinion and Judgment), 7 May 1997, Case No. IT-94-1-T (Trial Chamber II, ICTY) para. 627.

[44] See ICJ Advisory Opinion, *Reservations to the Genocide Convention,* [1951] ICJ Rep. 15, 23 ('the principles underlying the [Genocide] Convention are principles which are

There is still some debate as to whether this customary prohibition creates obligations for private individuals or only for state agents, despite the apparent rejection of such a distinction in the Genocide Convention (Arts. I and IV). Thus, while the French Court of Cassation in the *Barbie* case (1985) seemed to require state action, the necessity for state action was rejected explicitly by the US Second Circuit Court of Appeals in *Kadić* v. *Karadzić* (1995).[45] In the definitions of genocide and crimes against humanity in the Statutes of the International Criminal Tribunals for former Yugoslavia and Rwanda, no mention is made of a state action requirement. On the contrary, a broad principle of individual responsibility is incorporated, specifying that any official position held by the accused cannot excuse or mitigate responsibility.[46] Similarly, the definition of genocide in the International Law Commission's 1996 Draft Code of Crimes Against the Peace and Security of Mankind does not include state action, and thus envisages purely individual obligations.[47] As for crimes against humanity, the ILC finds a requirement that they be 'instigated or directed by a Government *or by any organization or group*' (Draft Art. 18), once again rejecting a construction imposing obligations only on the state and its agents.[48] Article 25 of the Statute of the International Criminal Court, in referring to actions of 'a group of persons', broadly reflects the definitions set out in the ICTY and ICTR Statutes, as well as in the 1996 Draft Code of Crimes Against the Peace and Security of Mankind.[49] The Preparatory Commission of the ICC, in defining the elements of the crime of genocide and crimes against humanity, did

recognized by civilized nations as binding on States, even without any conventional obligations'); *Restatement*, at para. 702(a); *The Prosecutor* v. *Akayesu* (Judgment), 2 September 1998, Case No. ICTR-96-4-T (Trial Chamber I, ICTR) para. 495; Ian Brownlie, *Principles of Public International Law*, 5th edn (Oxford: Clarendon, 1998) 563; M. Cherif Bassiouni, *Crimes Against Humanity in International Criminal Law* (The Hague: Nijhoff, 1992) 191; Meron, *Human Rights and Humanitarian Law*, at 10–12, 91 and 111.

[45] Judgment of 20 Dec. 1985, Cass. crim. JCP II G No. 20,655 (*Affaire Barbie*), *reprinted in* [1986] *Journal du droit international* 129–42 (a position softened in the *Papon* case, Judgment of 23 Jan. 1997, Cass. crim., JCP II G No. 22,812); *Kadić* v. *Karadzić*, 70 F.3d 232, 241–2 (2d Cir. 1995). See Bassiouni, *Crimes Against Humanity*, at 247 and 255–7; Jacques Françillon, 'Crimes de guerre, crimes contre l'humanité', (1993) 410 *Juris-Classeurs de droit international* paras. 78–9; Leila Sadat Wexler, 'The Interpretation of the Nuremberg Principles by the French Court of Cassation: From *Touvier* to *Barbie* and Back Again', (1994) 32 *Colum. J Transnat'l L* 289, 360.

[46] See Arts. 2, 3 and 6, ICTR Statute, UN Doc. S/RES/955 (1994) Annex.

[47] ILC Draft Code, at 89–90 (Art. 17, commentary para. 10).

[48] *Ibid.*, at 98 (Art. 18, commentary para. 5).

[49] International Law Commission, 'Report of the International Law Commission on the Work of its 46th Session', Draft Statute of an International Criminal Court, UN Doc. A/49/10 (1994); Mauro Politi, 'The Establishment of an International Criminal Court

not require an element of state action, mentioning instead 'the plan or policy of the State or organization'.[50]

The rejection of a narrow interpretation of crimes against humanity to require state action is confirmed by the judgment of the Trial Chamber of the ICTY in *Prosecutor v. Tadić*, where the Tribunal quoted and adopted the 1996 ILC commentary and concluded that such crimes may reflect the policy of a *de facto* power, or a terrorist group or organisation, and not necessarily that of a state.[51] In that case, the Tribunal concluded that there was an organised policy by the insurgent *Republika Srpska* or its armed forces of targeting a particular group of civilians. The ICTR agreed in the *Akayesu* judgment, finding that there was no requirement of a policy formally adopted by a state.[52]

This conclusion was left untouched by the Appeals Chamber when it issued its judgment on appeal in the *Tadić* case, given its conclusion that the *Republika Srpska* was acting on behalf of a state, the Federal Republic of Yugoslavia.[53] The appeal did, however, raise the related question of whether crimes against humanity could be committed for purely personal motives. The Appeals Chamber disagreed, and found that precedents from post-Second World War cases clearly supported the conclusion that a crime against humanity may be committed for motives wholly unrelated to a campaign against a civilian population, as long as the crime itself was so related and the accused was aware of that relation. Thus a disgruntled husband who denounces his wife to the police in order to be with his mistress, or the tenant who does

at a Crossroad: Issues and Prospects After the First Session of the Preparatory Committee', (1997) 13 *Nouvelles études pénales* 115, 123–5 and 137–41.

[50] 'Report of the Preparatory Commission for the International Criminal Court', Addendum (Finalised Draft Text of the Elements of Crimes), UN Doc. PCNICC/2000/INF/3/Add.2.

[51] *The Prosecutor v. Tadić* (Opinion and Judgment), 7 May 1997, Case No. IT-94-1-T (Trial Chamber II, ICTY) paras. 654–5. See also *The Prosecutor v. Kordić* (Judgment), 26 Feb. 2001, Case No. IT-95-14/2-T (Trial Chamber, ICTY) paras. 181–2; *The Prosecutor v. Blaskić* (Judgment), 3 March 2000, Case No. IT-95-14-T (Trial Chamber, ICTY) para. 205; *The Prosecutor v. Kupreskić* (Judgment), 14 Jan. 2000, Case No. IT-95-16-T (Trial Chamber, ICTY) paras. 551–5; *The Prosecutor v. Kayishema and Ruzindana* (Judgment), 21 May 1999, Case No. ICTR-95-1-T (Trial Chamber, ICTR) paras. 124–6; *The Prosecutor v. Nikolić* (Review of Indictment), 20 Oct. 1995, Case No. IT-94-2-R61 (Trial Chamber I, ICTY) para. 26.

[52] *The Prosecutor v. Akayesu* (Judgment), 2 Sept. 1998, Case No. ICTR-96-4-T (Trial Chamber, ICTR) para. 580; *The Prosecutor v. Rutaganda*, (Judgment), 6 Dec. 1999, Case No. ICTR-96-3-T (Trial Chamber, ICTR) para. 69.

[53] *The Prosecutor v. Tadić* (Appeals Judgment), 15 July 1999, Case No. IT-94-1-A (Appeals Chamber, ICTY) paras. 238–72.

the same to get rid of his landlord, do indeed commit crimes against humanity if in so doing they knowingly participate in a campaign against a civilian population.[54] There is no question here of any agency between the perpetrator and the state (or other group) carrying out the campaign against a civilian population, leading to the conclusion that the obligations not to commit crimes against humanity are imposed directly upon the individual and not only through the state or group. It would thus seem that there is no requirement of state action either for the collective attack on a population or for the individual acts which are related to that attack.[55] The conclusion is important in that it calls for international sanction of crimes against humanity committed by groups which are unrelated to the state, for example insurgents or terrorist groups, or in situations where it is impossible to connect the group to the state apparatus conclusively.

As noted earlier, some have questioned whether the prohibition of genocide and crimes against humanity can properly be characterised as falling squarely within human rights law. More directly, in its 1991 Draft Code of Crimes Against the Peace and Security of Mankind, the ILC had included as one of the crimes the systematic or mass violation of human rights (Art. 21). In its commentary upon the provision, the Commission suggested that such a crime could be committed by individuals acting in a purely private capacity, and not only by state agents.[56] The draft code was sent to governments for comments and observations, generating significant opposition to Draft Article 21:

The view was also expressed that the crimes listed under Article 21 as adopted on first reading had mistakenly attributed to individuals the capacity to violate human rights. It was considered to be widely accepted within the Sixth Committee that States had an obligation to respect and protect human rights and, by implication, that only States could violate such rights. Individuals could only commit crimes in violation of criminal law.[57]

In the version of the draft code adopted by the ILC in 1996, Article 21 relating to systematic or mass violations of human rights has disappeared,

---

[54] *Ibid.*, paras. 257–67. See also *The Prosecutor* v. *Kupreskić* (Judgment), 14 Jan. 2000, Case No. IT-95-16-T (Trial Chamber, ICTY) paras. 551–5.

[55] See Steven Ratner and Jason Abrams, *Accountability for Human Rights Atrocities in International Law* (Oxford: Oxford UP, 1997) 64–7.

[56] [1991] 2 *YB Int'l L Com'n* 103 (Art. 21, commentary para. 5); See also Stanislav Chernichenko, 'Definition of Gross and Large-Scale Violations of Human Rights as an International Crime', UN Doc. E/CN.4/Sub.2/1993/10 (1993) at 9 para. 32.

[57] ILC, 'Report of the International Law Commission on the Work of its 47th Session', UN Doc. A/CN.4/472 (1996) at 33 para. 127.

subsumed into the more familiar concept of crimes against humanity.[58] The ILC takes great pains in its commentary to Draft Article 1 to point out that the omission of crimes from this trimmed down version of the code should not be taken as an indication that the omitted crimes are not crimes against international law calling for criminal responsibility.[59] Despite this statement, the elimination of the crime of systematic or mass violation of human rights along with the more controversial proposed crimes such as colonial domination, use of mercenaries and wilful and severe damage to the environment, seems a clear indication that none of these crimes are yet considered by the international community to be part of customary law or implied in human rights conventions.[60]

Conclusion

The imposition of obligations on the individual by international human rights thus seems exceptional. It remains limited to a very few treaties and, under the broadest interpretation of human rights law, to acts which are spin-offs of collective violations of the prohibition of crimes against humanity. The normative framework of human rights is still geared towards the granting of rights to individuals and the imposition of obligations on the state. This is problematic when infringements of human rights may come from other individuals acting in a purely private capacity, as well as from state agents. In the *United States Diplomatic and Consular Staff in Teheran (United States of America v. Iran)* case, which concerned the hostage-taking of American diplomats initially carried out by students acting without any official knowledge or support, the ICJ noted '[t]he frequency with which at the present time the principles of international law ... are set to naught by individuals or groups of

---

[58] Doudou Thiam, 'Thirteenth Report on the Draft Code of Crimes Against the Peace and Security of Mankind', UN Doc. A/CN.4/466 (1995) at 22 paras. 84–7.

[59] ILC Draft Code, Art. 1, commentary para. 3.

[60] The 1996 Draft Code contains only the crimes of aggression, genocide, crimes against humanity, crimes against United Nations and associated personnel, and war crimes: *ibid.* The criminality of all these acts is well established by either custom or treaties. This list is reflected in the core crimes over which the International Criminal Court has competence: genocide, crimes against humanity, war crimes and aggression (Art. 5, ICC Statute). The ILC had also suggested annexing to the Statute a list of treaty crimes which would also have fallen within the ICC's competence, but the proposal was not taken up by the 1998 Rome Conference on the ICC. See Politi, 'International Criminal Court', at 119–23. See generally the discussion of individual responsibility, below, pp. 102–10.

individuals'.[61] For a variety of social and political reasons, governments are often unable or unwilling to step in to protect persons whose human rights are being violated by other private individuals or groups. Individual rights violations in the form of terrorist acts, performed by groups with no discernible links to any state, for instance, seem to pose an insoluble challenge to human rights law.[62]

Inattention to the phenomenon of individual infringements is amplified by structural elements of human rights law. Universal and regional bodies charged with enforcing human rights norms centre their work exclusively on state breaches. The treaty provisions establishing the jurisdictions of the UN Human Rights Committee, the European Court of Human Rights and the Inter-American Commission on Human Rights all limit receivable complaints to those alleging a violation by a state party to the conventions.[63] These bodies thus are not naturally drawn to examine human rights violations which do not involve the state at some level, and may even resist invitations to expand their work in that direction.[64]

There is no conceptual difficulty in imposing obligations on individuals with respect to human rights, as demonstrated by the experiences of many countries where municipal and even international norms are applied between individuals.[65] If human rights are envisaged not as a limit to the power of the state, but as a barrier effectively protecting the individual from undue interference, to allow all persons to grow and

---

[61] [1980] ICJ Rep. 4, 42.

[62] See Meron, *Human Rights and Humanitarian Norms*, at 162 n. 86. A partial response which does rely upon criminalisation is the 1998 International Convention for the Suppression of Terrorist Bombings, UN Doc. A/52/164 (9 Jan. 1998).

[63] Art. 41 of the International Covenant on Civil and Political Rights; Art. 1 of the Optional Protocol to the International Covenant on Civil and Political Rights, 23 March 1976, *reprinted in* Brownlie, *Basic Documents*, at 144; Arts. 33–4 of the European Convention on Human Rights; Arts. 44–5 of the American Convention on Human Rights. See Meron, *Human Rights and Humanitarian Law*, at 162; Eissen, 'La convention européenne des droits de l'homme' at 157.

[64] See e.g. the invitation by OAS General Assembly Resolution 1043 (XX-0/90) to the Inter-American Commission on Human Rights to focus on violations of human rights by irregular armed groups in its country reports. The Inter-American Commission initially declined to follow up on the invitation: [1990–1] *Ann. Rep. I/A Com'n Hum. Rts* 504–14.

[65] For example in Germany and Belgium: Drzemczewski, *European Human Rights Convention*, 151, at 207–18; Eissen, 'La Convention européenne des droits de l'homme', at 159–61. In Latin America constitutional human rights norms are regularly enforced with respect to interpersonal relationships through the institution of amparo: Enrique Vescovi, *Los recursos judiciales y además medios impugnativos en Iberoamérica* (Buenos Aires: Depalma, 1988) 468 ff.

realise their potential, then a development of human rights obligations is perhaps desirable. On the other hand, there is a danger in moving in that direction: governments have been known to rely upon the actions of private individuals and non-state groups as an excuse for refusal to comply with human rights standards.[66] More generally, the creation of individual obligations may invite abuse by states, focusing exclusively on individual obligations while neglecting human rights.[67]

HUMANITARIAN LAW

Individual responsibility is a basic tenet of humanitarian law, marking the key difference between an analysis of the normative framework of humanitarian law with respect to the imposition of obligations and that of human rights. Although the distinction between a subject of responsibility and a subject of obligations has been clearly stated, there is a tendency to accept the notion that a person punished for an offence has been under a duty all along not to commit that offence. The issue of who is the subject of obligations in the normative framework of humanitarian law is complicated by the fact that most violations of the laws and customs of war are carried out by members of the armed forces, whose character as state organs cannot be denied. It is clear that duties are imposed on states by the effect of humanitarian law. These state obligations are reflected in the principle that the state is responsible for acts of its armed forces and, more generally, of its agents.[68] Because soldiers are state agents and as such are bound indirectly by the laws of war, no pressing need has arisen in the past to determine whether humanitarian

---

[66] This was the rationale given by the Inter-American Commission on Human Rights to decline the invitation to comment on violations of human rights by non-state groups: Inter-American Commission on Human Rights, [1990–1] Ann. Rep. I/A Com'n Hum. Rts at 512. A link between rights and duties of individuals is actually suggested by the title of Art. 32 of the American Convention on Human Rights, which refers to the 'relationship' ('corelación') between duties and rights: Gros Espiell, La Convención americana at 133. This may explain, for example, the reluctance by some states to support an annual resolution presented by Turkey to denounce violations of human rights by terrorist groups: Michael Dennis, 'The Fifty-Fourth Session of the UN Commission on Human Rights', (1999) 93 Am. J Int'l L 246, 248; Michael Dennis, 'The Fifty-Fifth Session of the UN Commission on Human Rights', (2000) 94 Am. J Int'l L 189, 192–3.

[67] See 'Report of the Secretary-General on Minimum Humanitarian Standards', para. 64; Gros Espiell, La Convención americana; Mbaye, Droits de l'homme, at 216; Mbaya, 'Symétrie', at 35; Umozurike, 'African Charter', at 911.

[68] Art. 3, 1907 Hague Convention IV; Art. 29, 1949 Fourth Geneva Convention; Art. 91, Protocol I.

law imposes obligations only on the state, or also on individuals. The question is nevertheless important given that some acts constituting violations of humanitarian law are carried out by individuals in a private capacity. This is especially so in situations of non-international armed conflict, where by definition at least one party, if not all parties, to the conflict are non-state actors. For these persons, a finding that humanitarian law imposes no obligations on the individual *qua* individual would lead to the inapplicability of its norms to their conduct. Private individuals would as a result be shielded from the reach of humanitarian law.

No consensus has been reached on this question, and the opinions of writers span the entire spectrum of possible answers. For some, norms of humanitarian law bind states but not individuals, thus governing only the behaviour of persons acting as state organs. This usually implies an extensive concept of state organs whereby parastatal entities and persons are assimilated to the state for the purposes of applying humanitarian law. Under this construction, the individual remains a passive subject of responsibility, and the ability to commit an international delict rests solely with the state. The individual is thus not a subject of obligations.[69]

A different stance is adopted by Kelsen, for whom there can be no individual responsibility for persons who commit violations of humanitarian law in the performance of their functions as state organs. All state organs are covered by the principle of inter-state immunity, and one state cannot try an individual for war crimes without the express consent of the individual's own state. Past examples of consent to waive immunity include Article 228 of the Treaty of Versailles and the Japanese Instrument of Surrender of 2 September 1945, but not the Charter of the Nuremberg International Military Tribunal.[70] It appears clearly from

---

[69] Constantin Eustathiades, 'Les sujets de droit international et la responsabilité internationale – Nouvelles tendances', (1953-III) 84 *Recueil des cours* 397, 462–3 and 475–81. See also Barberis, 'Nouvelles questions', at 207–8 (although he makes an exception for obligations imposed directly on civilians, such as the duty not to commit hostile acts against the occupying forces).

[70] Kelsen, *Principles*, at 132–9; Kelsen, 'Collective and Individual Responsibility', at 230; Hans Kelsen, 'Collective and Individual Responsibility in International Law with Particular Regard to the Punishment of War Criminals', (1943) 31 *Cal. L Rev.* 530, 539–41 and 561. Universal ratification of the 1949 Geneva Conventions moots this argument, because of the undertaking by all states parties either to try or to extradite individuals guilty of war crimes (Arts. 49/50/129/146), which can be characterised as the waiver required under Kelsen's analysis. It does not, however, decide the wider question of whether humanitarian law imposes obligations directly on individuals or only on states.

Kelsen's analysis that he does not view humanitarian law as imposing obligations directly on individuals *qua* state organs, except in rare cases such as the duty of a commander to give warning and to spare specific buildings during a naval bombardment.[71] Rather, humanitarian law primarily imposes obligations on the state at large. International law also imposes the obligation not to infringe humanitarian law directly on individuals acting in a purely private capacity, as shown by the fact that non-belligerents perpetrating hostile acts enjoy very limited protection under humanitarian law. Under Kelsen's interpretation, the concept of state organs is reduced to a minimum, so that even members of the armed forces of a state act as state organs at some times and as private individuals at other times.[72]

Yet another position interprets international humanitarian law as imposing obligations directly on individuals whether acting in a purely private capacity or as state organs. Thus, for Hersch Lauterpacht, war crimes can be committed by combatants equally when acting under direct orders and for private gains or lust.[73] Obligations attach to the individual regardless of status.

Much uncertainty remains as to this fundamental aspect of the normative framework of humanitarian law, calling for a closer examination of state practice with respect to the existence of obligations to comply with humanitarian law and the punishment of war criminals. The most numerically and substantively significant practice dates from the Second World War and includes the current work of the International Criminal Tribunals for former Yugoslavia and Rwanda.

---

[71] Arts. 5–6, Hague Convention (IX) Concerning Bombardment by Naval Forces in Times of War, 18 October 1907, *reprinted in* Schindler and Toman, *Laws of Armed Conflict*, at 813; Kelsen, *Principles*, at 131; Hans Kelsen, 'Théorie générale du droit international public – problèmes choisis', (1932-IV) 42 *Recueil des cours* 116, 154. War treason and espionage constitute two further exceptions whereby individual responsibility is accepted for acts of state. Kelsen, 'Théorie générale', at 129; Kelsen, Collective and Individual Responsibility in International Law', at 552; *Ex parte Quirin*, 317 US 1, 22 (1942) (US Supreme Ct) (dealing with German agents captured while on a sabotage mission in the United States during the Second World War).

[72] Kelsen, *Principles*, at 128–9 ('Hence general international law imposes upon individuals, *as private persons*, the obligation to refrain from committing war crimes, and establishes individual criminal responsibility for the commission of such crimes *by private persons*' – emphasis added).

[73] H. Lauterpacht, *International Law and Human Rights*, at 10 and 39. See also Nørgaard, *Position of the Individual*, at 82–8 and 197–8 (although Nørgaard limits war crimes to those committed not for private aims); Giuseppe Barile, '*Obligationes erga omnes* e individui nel diritto internazionale umanitario', (1985) 68 *Rivista di diritto internazionale* 5, 17–27.

Going back to the First World War, there was great uncertainty as to the existence in the laws and customs of war of a principle affirming the individual penal responsibility of authors of violations of these international norms. As mentioned earlier, the 1907 Hague Convention IV in Article 3 provided for the responsibility of the state, but not of the individual. There were many war crimes trials during the war, but most writers at the time found the basis for such trials in municipal law and not in international law.[74] In any case, the recorded war crimes trials deal with acts of soldiers, that is of state agents, and not of private individuals.[75] Finally, the feeble post-war attempts by the Entente powers to secure, partly on the basis of the law of nations, prosecution of German war criminals not in their custody met with stiff resistance from Germany and her allies, and were in the end unsuccessful.[76]

The imposition of obligations directly on the individual by humanitarian law appears most clearly in two types of situations where the author of what would be a violation of international norms cannot be viewed as an agent of the state: first, when the act is carried out by a non-combatant during an armed conflict; and second, when the impugned behaviour is that of irregular combatants not linked to the state apparatus, either because they are part of a resistance group fighting independently or because they are part of an insurgent group fighting in a non-international armed conflict.

[74] Elbridge Colby, 'War Crimes', (1924–5) 23 *Mich. L Rev.* 482–511; James Garner, 'Punishment of Offenders Against the Laws and Customs of War', (1920) 14 *Am. J Int'l L* 70–94; A. Mérignhac, 'De la sanction des infractions aux droit des gens commises au cours de la guerre européenne par les empires du centre', (1917) 24 *Revue générale de droit international public* 5, 29–42.

[75] Some German industrialists were prosecuted for war crimes: for example, Herman and Robert Roechling, German industrialists who were found guilty of war crimes by the Court Martial of Amiens in 1919 for the plunder of French property: (1921) 48 *Journal du droit international* 362–3. The convictions eventually were quashed on appeal on technical grounds unrelated to the applicability of the laws of war to private individuals. See Ernst Fraenkel, *Military Occupation and the Rule of Law – Occupation Government in the Rhineland 1918–23* (London: Oxford UP, 1944) 60; Garner, 'Punishment of Offenders', at 79–80.

[76] See Jean-Pierre Maunoir, *La répression des crimes de guerre devant les tribunaux français et alliés* (Geneva: Editions Médecine et Hygiène, 1956) 16. On the Leipzig Trials and other war crimes proceedings during and following the First World War, see James W. Garner, *International Law and the World War* (London: Longmans, Green, 1920) II, 472–80; Claud Mullins, *The Leipzig Trials* (London: Witherby, 1921); United Nations War Crimes Commission, *History of the United Nations War Crimes Commission and the Development of the Laws of War* (London: HMSO, 1948) 32–52; James F. Willis, *Prologue to Nuremberg: The Politics and Diplomacy of Punishing War Criminals of the First World War* (Westport, Conn.: Greenwood, 1982) 126–68.

Violations by non-combatants

Issues surrounding the possible violation of humanitarian law by non-combatants have arisen in the context of the Second World War both in the work of the International Military Tribunal and in the numerous war crimes trials which took place, mostly after the war had ended. These decisions have been actualised only to some degree by the jurisprudence of the International Criminal Tribunals for Rwanda and former Yugoslavia, which rely extensively on cases from that period.

The International Military Tribunal

Under the Charter of the IMT, annexed to the London Agreement between the United States, the United Kingdom, France and the Soviet Union,[77] the Tribunal had 'the power to try and punish persons who, acting in the interest of the European Axis countries, whether as individuals or as members of organizations, committed any of the following crimes', including crimes against peace, war crimes and crimes against humanity (Art. 6). Two elements in this provision can be linked to the status of persons as directly obligated by the laws and customs of war: first, the expression 'acting in the interest of the European Axis countries', and second, the responsibility of persons as 'members of organizations'.

The expression 'in the interest of the European Axis countries' (in the French version 'pour le compte des...') can be interpreted either as a desire to limit the Tribunal's power to the prosecution of European Axis war criminals, and not war criminals from the Far East or from Allied states, or as an indication that the target of the proceedings would be the European Axis states and their agents. Under the first construction, Article 6 sheds no light on the question of whether individuals are directly obligated by the laws and customs of war, while under the second, the provision would seem to indicate that the law of war imposes duties only upon state organs.

Some have gone so far as to suggest that the expression 'in the interest of' limits the definition of war crimes in the IMT Charter such that they can be committed only by public servants.[78] Others propose that both interpretations can be applied to the expression, so that war crimes

---

[77] 8 August 1945, *reprinted in* Schindler and Toman, *Laws of Armed Conflict*, at 911. The Agreement was opened to accession and was eventually acceded to by a further nineteen states: *ibid.*, at 919.

[78] Barberis, 'Nouvelles questions', at 209.

thus defined would exclude not only non-Axis individuals but also individuals acting in a purely private capacity, for private gains or lust.[79] A look at the *travaux préparatoires* of the IMT Charter reveals that the expression embodies a limitation to the jurisdiction of the IMT rather than an element of the definition of war crimes under international law.[80] Consensus on the formulation of the definition of war crimes at the London Conference was long in coming, and other expressions such as 'on behalf of', 'on the part of', 'in the service of', 'in aid of', were suggested by the various participants before agreeing on 'in the interest of'.[81] The aim was to limit clearly the jurisdiction of the IMT while at the same time avoiding the creation of a definition of war crimes covering only actions of Axis powers. It was a recurrent worry of the United States in particular, heeded by the other representatives at the conference, that war crimes thus defined would be illegal for individuals of any nation, and not only for Axis nationals.[82] The tension and vagueness in this portion of the IMT Charter results from the fact that it seeks not to give a general definition of war crimes punishable under international law, but rather to create an *ad hoc* tribunal for the judgment of specific individuals.[83] There was no need to give a definition of war crimes, as the IMT was to rely primarily on the laws and customs of war. As such, and contrary to what some writers have suggested, this passage of Article 6 of the IMT Charter is not indicative of whether the laws and customs of war impose obligations on individuals on a private basis or as state organs.

Another portion of Article 6 *in limine*, holding that the IMT shall have jurisdiction to try and punish persons having committed one of the

---

[79] Nørgaard, *Position of the Individual*, at 198–9.

[80] Robert H. Jackson, *International Conference on Military Trials (London, 1945)* (Washington DC: US Gov. Printing Office, 1949) (hereinafter *London Conference*). The Conference was a meeting of the four original signatories of the London Agreement – France, the Soviet Union, the United Kingdom and the United States – where the principles designed to guide the trials of major German war criminals were hammered out. See Henri Meyrowitz, *La répression par les tribunaux allemands des crimes contre l'humanité et de l'appartenance à une organisation criminelle en application de la loi no. 10 du Conseil de contrôle allié* (Paris: LGDJ, 1960) 28–53.

[81] *London Conference*, at 197, 202, 293, 312, 327, 354, 361, 374 and 392–3.

[82] *Ibid.*, at 330 (Jackson), 333 (Trainin), 361 (Jackson), 394 (Jackson) and 416 (Nikitchenko).

[83] Meyrowitz, *Répression*, at 264 ('L'expression "…acting in the interest of the European Axis countries"…se rapporte à la définition de la *compétence* du tribunal, non pas à la définition des crimes. Elle sert à fonder, sur le plan du droit international, la compétence *ratione materiae* du tribunal militaire international' – emphasis in the original).

listed crimes 'whether as individuals or as members of organizations', provides more insight on the question of who – whether private individual or state organ – is the bearer of obligations under the Nuremberg scheme. The provision was inserted both to arrive at a political declaration that Nazi groups such as the Gestapo, SS and the National Socialist Party were criminal organisations, and to provide a basis for using a legally binding declaration of the criminality of these organisations in order to speed up the trials of the hundreds of thousands of lesser members, whose membership itself could serve as a *prima facie* presumption of guilt.[84]

This segment of Article 6 refers to the capacity in which the individuals were acting at the time of the perpetration of the war crime, *qua* private individuals or *qua* members of organisations, as can be seen more clearly from the authentic French version of the passage ('auront commis, individuellement ou à titre de membres d'organisation'), and from the comments of the drafters of the IMT Charter at the London Conference.[85] Individuals acting in a private capacity are thus seen to possess the faculty of breaching international obligations, implying that they are bearers of such obligations in the first place. In addition, the fact that individuals could have breached international obligations while 'acting as members of organizations' implies that the organisations themselves violated international law through their organs, and thus that they were the bearers of the obligations. This is in fact exactly what the IMT Charter intended, as indicated by Articles 9–11 which give the Tribunal jurisdiction to declare an accused organisation to be a war criminal. At Nuremberg, the leadership of the National Socialist Party, SS, SD, Gestapo, SA, Reich Cabinet and General Staff and High Command of the German armed forces were indicted, and individuals representative of those organisations brought to trial. All but the last three organisations were later found criminal by the IMT.[86] As forcibly

---

[84] *Ibid.*, at 129–30; UN War Crimes Commission, *History*, at 290.

[85] *London Conference*, at 216–18.

[86] International Military Tribunal, *Trial of the Major War Criminals* (IMT: Nuremberg, 1947) I, 255–79 (hereinafter IMT). For instance, Kaltenbrunner was seen as representative of the Gestapo, and the finding of his breaching of international law led to the declaration that the Gestapo itself was a criminal organisation.

    The wider question of whether the criminality of international organisations, implying that they are bearers of obligations under international humanitarian law, conforms to generally accepted principles of international law seems quite debatable. That debate, however, lies beyond the scope of the present discussion. See *London Conference*, at 129–42 and 215–18; UN War Crimes Commission, *History*, at 289–343; Maunoir, *Répression*, at 389–475; Henri Donnedieu de Vabres, 'Le procès de Nuremberg

argued by Kelsen, the position according to which obligations under the law of war attach to individuals only in their capacity as state agents would lead to a finding that the state itself has breached international law. In other words, a conclusion that an individual *qua* state organ has violated the laws and customs of war is one implying that the state is a war criminal. This was not the purpose of the IMT. There was a suggestion by the British prosecution at Nuremberg that the guilt of the individuals accused should reflect the guilt of the German state, but that was not taken up by the Tribunal.[87] On the contrary, referring to the United States Supreme Court's decision in *Ex parte Quirin*, the IMT made a broad statement affirming the existence of individual obligations under international law:

> It was submitted that international law is concerned with the actions of sovereign States, and provides no punishment for individuals; and further, that where the act in question is an act of State, those who carry it out are not personally responsible, but are protected by the doctrine of the sovereignty of the State. In the opinion of the Tribunal, both these submissions must be rejected. *That international law imposes duties and liabilities upon individuals as well as upon States has long been recognized* ... Crimes against international law are committed by men, not by abstract entities ...
>
> *[T]he very essence of the Charter [of the IMT] is that individuals have international duties which transcend the national obligations of obedience imposed by the individual State.* [Emphasis added.][88]

It naturally follows from this construction of international law that the fact that a person acts as a state organ in any position cannot serve to shield him (Art. 7), and that superior orders cannot prevent individual breaches of the individual's obligations under international law (Art. 8).[89] Indeed, it would seem difficult to reconcile a rejection of the defences of state immunity and superior orders with a conclusion that the state is the primary bearer of obligations under the laws and customs

devant les principes modernes du droit pénal international', (1947-I) 70 *Recueil des cours* 477, 543–58; Quincy Wright, 'International Law and Guilt by Association', (1949) 43 *Am. J Int'l L* 746–55.

[87] IMT II, at 104–5; David, *Principes*, at 557; James Crawford, 'First Report on State Responsibility', UN Doc. A/CN.4/490 (1998) para. 61; Eustathiades, 'Les sujets', at 441 n. 3; Wright, 'Guilt by Association', at 753.

[88] IMT I, at 222–3.

[89] These two principles have since ripened into customary norms, and have been incorporated, *inter alia*, in the statutes of the International Criminal Tribunals for Former Yugoslavia and Rwanda as well as that of the International Criminal Court. See Yoram Dinstein, *The Defense of 'Obedience to Superior Order' in International Law* (Leiden: Sijthoff, 1965); Leslie Green, *Superior Orders in National and International Law* (Leiden: Sijthoff, 1976).

of war, as that would result in individual responsibility for a violation completely disconnected from the convicted person.[90] Thus, under the scheme of the IMT Charter, individuals *qua* individuals as well as organisations are the prime bearers of obligations.

Much has been made of the fact that all but one of the twenty-four individual defendants brought to trial before the IMT clearly acted as organs of the state. The one exception, Gustav Krupp von Bolhen und Halbach, was the head of Krupp AG, one of Germany's biggest weapon manufacturers, but he was never tried due to illness at the time of the proceedings from which he never recovered.[91] Prosecution of individuals who were not state organs was not necessarily considered incompatible with the IMT Charter, however, as illustrated not only by the indictment of Krupp – although his position within the German establishment might raise questions about his disconnectedness with the state – but also by the proposal that a second trial before the IMT take place in order to judge a group of industrialists. The proposal eventually was rejected by the IMT for reasons unrelated to the question of the applicability of the laws and customs of war to private individuals, and the industrialists were later tried by US military tribunals.[92] The principles developed by the IMT were affirmed by later war crimes tribunals and, in a general manner, by Resolution 95(I) of the UN General Assembly.[93]

Subsequent war crimes trials

In conformity with the 1943 Moscow Declaration, the IMT was meant as a showcase of individual responsibility for war crimes, crimes against peace and crimes against humanity, and thus its jurisdiction was strictly limited to the trial of *major* war criminals.[94] The vast majority of war criminals were to be, in the words of the Moscow Declaration, 'brought back to the scene of their crimes and judged on the spot by the people they outraged', i.e. by special or regular courts of the Allied and Axis powers. While the fairness and legal soundness of these trials varied

[90] See Bassiouni, *Crimes Against Humanity*, at 218–19; Nørgaard, *Position of the Individual*, at 198; Barile, '*Obligationes erga omnes*', at 23; Eustathiades, 'Les sujets', at 515; Gerry Simpson, 'War Crimes: A Critical Introduction', in Timothy McCormack and Gerry Simpson eds., *The Law of War Crimes* (The Hague: Kluwer, 1997) 1, 15.

[91] IMT I, at 124–47.

[92] Robert H. Jackson, 'Report to the President', 7 Oct. 1946, *reprinted in London Conference*, at 432, 436.

[93] Adopted on 11 Dec. 1946, *reprinted in* Schindler and Toman, *Laws of Armed Conflict*, at 921.

[94] Moscow Conference (United Kingdom, United States, Soviet Union), Declaration on German Atrocities, 1 Nov. 1943, *reprinted in* (1944) 38 Am. J Int'l L Supp. 7.

greatly, they do provide instances of state practice regarding the status of the individual under the laws and customs of war. A number of issues raised in these cases have not been fully or satisfactorily addressed by the ICTY and ICTR, nor in the ICC Statute and 'Elements of Crimes', and so they remain important sources today.

Before turning to the manner in which violations of the laws and customs of war were treated by war crimes tribunals, it is important to note the great disparity in the legal norms administered by these tribunals. In a number of countries, war criminals were tried pursuant to domestic legislation rather than international law. For instance, the *Lex*[95] and *Bommer*[96] trials by French tribunals were based on municipal penal provisions whereby the offence must have been a crime under both domestic and international law in order to be punishable.[97] Cases where war crimes were tried as offences against municipal law nevertheless can provide guidance as to the content of the laws and customs of war, because municipal law often refers to international law to define acceptable defences. For instance, the defence of belligerent reprisals is derived directly from international law, as there is no equivalent under municipal law.[98] In other countries, war crimes were defined with respect to the laws and customs of war. On occasion, a statute incorporated the concept into municipal law without changing its nature. For example, the *Washio Awochi*[99] trial rested on Dutch East Indies statutes

[95] *France v. Lex*, (1946) 7 L Rep. Trials War Crim. 74, 75 (French Permanent Mil. Trib., Nancy). The editor's note argues that although the tribunal mentions only French domestic law, the criminal behaviour (aiding the deportation of French nationals) also constitutes a war crime under international law.

[96] *France v. Alois and Anna Bommer*, (1947) 9 L Rep. Trials War Crim. 62 (French Permanent Mil. Trib., Metz). This case, dealing with the reception of stolen goods, refers both to the Penal Code and to the War Crime Ordinance of 28 August 1944, a statute incorporating international law into domestic law. According to the note by the UNWCC accompanying the text of the judgment, it constitutes 'a confirmation of the principle that laws and customs of war are applicable not only to military personnel, combatants or those acting as members of occupying authorities, or, generally speaking, to organs of the State and other public authorities, but also to any civilian who violates these laws and customs': *ibid.*, at 65–6.

[97] UNWCC, 'Digest of Law and Cases', (1949) 15 L Rep. Trials War Crim. 30–4 (with references to similar provisions in the laws of Norway, Denmark and Luxembourg); 'Annex II on French Law Concerning Trials of War Criminals', (1948) 3 L Rep. Trials War Crim. 93–102; Maunoir, *Répression*, at 53–88.

[98] *Norway v. Gerhard Flesch*, (1948) 6 L Rep. Trials War Crim. 111, 119 (Norwegian Sup. Court).

[99] *The Netherlands v. Washio Awochi*, (1946) 13 L Rep. Trials War Crim. 122 (Dutch Temporary Court-Martial, Batavia), dealing with the enforced prostitution of Dutch women.

which required the tribunal to rely directly on international law.[100] Finally, tribunals acting pursuant to Allied Control Council Law No. 10, which incorporated both the 1943 Moscow Declaration and the 1945 London Agreement, stated that they were not applying their respective municipal laws but rather international law.[101]

The rejection by the IMT of a construction of the laws and customs of war obligating only state agents and not private individuals is unanimously echoed and amplified in the jurisprudence of later war crimes trials. In many cases, persons with no connection to the state whatsoever were found to have breached the law of armed conflict through purely private behaviour. In the *Hadamar* trial, doctors working in a German sanatorium for the mentally insane were found guilty of war crimes for the murder of about 400 Polish and Soviet nationals, killed by lethal injections of drugs.[102] In the *Essen Lynching* case, three British airmen just captured were attacked by a civilian mob and kicked and beaten to death. In addition to convicting the German soldiers under whose guard the prisoners had been, the tribunal found three civilians who had taken part in the lynching guilty of murder under the law of armed conflict.[103] Similar spontaneous killings by private individuals of American prisoners of war and unarmed airmen who had bailed

[100] 'Annex on Netherlands Law Concerning Trials of War Criminals', (1949) 11 L Rep. Trials War Crim. 86–110; UNWCC, 'Digest', at 34–5.

[101] Allied Control Council Law No. 10, Punishment of Persons Guilty of War Crimes, Crimes Against Peace and Against Humanity, 20 Dec. 1945, 3 Official Gazette of the Control Council for Germany 50, 31 Jan. 1946, *reprinted in* M. Cherif Bassiouni ed., *International Criminal Law* (Dobbs Ferry: International Publishers, 1987) I, 129. See *UK v. Heyer and Six Others* (the *Essen Lynching* case), (1945) 1 L Rep. Trials War Crim. 88, 91 (Brit. Mil. Ct, Essen); *US v. Flick*, (1947) 9 L Rep. Trials War Crim. 1, 27 (US Mil. Trib., Nuremberg) ('The Tribunal is not a Court of the United States as that term is used in the Constitution of the United States. It is not a court martial. It is not a military commission. It is an international tribunal established by the International Control Council...The Tribunal administers international law. It is not bound by the general statutes of the United States or even by those parts of its Constitution which relate to courts of the United States'); Meyrowitz, *Répression*, at 198–211. The nature of these tribunals is discussed in *The Prosecutor v. Erdemović* (Judgment), 7 Oct. 1997, Case No. IT-96-22-A (Appeals Chamber, ICTY), Joint Sep. Op. Judges McDonald and Vohrah at paras. 52–5, Sep. and Diss. Op. Judge Cassese at para. 21.

[102] *US v. Klein and Six Others* (the *Hadamar* trial), (1945) 1 L Rep. Trials War Crim. 46 (US Mil. Com'n, Wiesbaden). Eustathiades argues that the sanatorium was a public institution under the jurisdiction of the local government: Eustathiades, 'Les sujets', at 470. The evidence reveals, however, that the state exercised very limited control over the employees of the sanatorium (at 48).

[103] *UK v. Heyer and Six Others* (the *Essen Lynching* case), (1945) 1 L Rep. Trials War Crim. 88 (Brit. Mil. Ct, Essen).

out over Germany were found to constitute war crimes in the cases of *US v. Black*,[104] *US v. Goebel et al.*[105] and *US v. Schosser, Goldbrunner and Wilm*.[106]

Several cases dealt with the actions of German industrialists who, as private citizens engaged in business during the Second World War, committed violations of the laws and customs of war. In the *Zyklon B* case, the owner and the director of a firm which manufactured and supplied poison gases to the SS, with full knowledge of their intended use in extermination camps, were found guilty of war crimes and sentenced to death.[107] There is no trace in the record of any discussion of the applicability of the law of armed conflict to private individuals, which seems to have been taken for granted by the court and by the accused.[108] Similarly in the *Roechling* case, several industrialists were convicted of war crimes relating to plunder of occupied territory and the use of slave labour, apparently without any discussion of whether the accused were personally obligated by the law of war.[109] On the contrary, the question was argued openly in the *Flick* trial, which concerned six industrialists

---

[104] (1945) 3 L Rep. Trials War Crim. 60 (US Mil. Com'n, Ahrweiler).

[105] Case No. 12-489, *Survey of War Crimes Trials Held at Dachau, Germany* (15 Sept. 1948) 2–3, cited in *The Prosecutor v. Tadić* (Opinion and Judgment), 7 May 1997, Case No. IT-94-1-T (Trial Chamber II, ICTY) para. 686.

[106] (1945) 3 L Rep. Trials War Crim. 65 (US Mil. Com'n, Dachau). During the war, Germany tried civilians in the territories it occupied for similar crimes. For instance, three French civilians were sentenced to death by a German Military Court for illegal acts of war for killing the crew of a German plane which crashed near Vimy (6 June 1940, *Bundesarchiv-Militärarchiv* (Military Archive of the Federal Republic of Germany), Freiburg, RW 2/v.65, at 121). In another case, two French farmers were condemned to death by a German Military Court for assaulting downed German airmen near Brest (23 June 1940, *ibid.*, at 116). Both cases are cited in Alfred M. de Zayas, *The Wehrmacht War Crime Bureau 1939–1945* (Lincoln: U Nebraska Press, 1989) 94–5. It remains doubtful, however, whether these proceedings by military courts in the field gave rise to a dependable search for existing rules of international law applicable to such cases.

[107] *UK v. Tesch* (the *Zyklon B* case), (1946) 1 L Rep. Trials War Crim. 93 (Brit. Mil. Ct, Hamburg).

[108] Eustathiades, 'Les sujets', at 467–8.

[109] *In re Roechling*, (1948) 15 Ann. Digest Rep. Pub. Int'l L Cases 398, 14 USMT 1061–143 (Gen. Trib. at Rastadt of the Mil. Gov. for the French Zone of Occ. in Germany; Superior Trib. of the Mil. Gov. for the French Zone of Occ. in Germany). The named accused in this case, Herman Roechling, eventually occupied an official position but the other accused were convicted in their quality as directors and officials of the Roechling Konzern. In this and several of the following cases, industrialists were also accused of crimes against peace and crimes against humanity. As the focus here centres specifically on humanitarian law, a discussion of the character of these norms falls beyond the scope of the present study.

who held powerful positions in the coal, iron and steel industries during the war.[110] They stood accused of, among other things, using enemy civilians as slave labour, using prisoners of war in work directly connected to war operations, and plundering public and private property in occupied territory. These actions were performed in a strictly private capacity as, except for one, 'the accused were not officially connected with the Nazi Government, but were private citizens engaged as business men in the heavy industry of Germany'.[111] Referring to the judgment of the International Military Tribunal, the US Military Tribunal stated:

But the International Military Tribunal was dealing with officials and agencies of the State, and it is argued that individuals holding no public office and not representing the State, do not, and should not, come within the class of persons criminally responsible for a breach of international law. *It is asserted that international law is a matter wholly outside the work, interest and knowledge of private individuals. The distinction is unsound.* International law, as such, binds every citizen just as does ordinary municipal law. *Acts adjudged criminal when done by an officer of the Government are criminal also when done by a private individual.* The guilt differs only in magnitude, not in quality. The offender in either case is charged with personal wrong and punishment falls on the offender *in propria persona*.[112]

This last sentence indicates clearly that, in the opinion of the Tribunal, the law of war binds individuals *qua* individuals, regardless of whether or not they are state agents. This position was quoted and adopted in the *IG Farben* trial, leading to the conviction of another group of German industrialists for war crimes similar to those committed by the accused in the *Flick* case.[113] In the *Krupp* trial, which once again dealt with analogous war crimes committed by German industrialists, a key argument of the defence was that '[n]either obligations nor rights fall to the lot of the private individual under the Terms of International Law', supported by an analysis of several provisions of the 1907 Hague Regulations demonstrating that only states were obligated under its terms.[114]

---

[110] *US v. Flick*, (1947) 9 L Rep. Trials War Crim. 1, 6 USMT 1 (US Mil. Trib., Nuremberg).

[111] *Ibid.*, at L Rep. 17. Eustathiades, 'Les sujets', at 475–7, suggests that state control of every facet of the German economy meant that industrialists acted in a manner accessory to the state, that they were in fact parastatal entities. This reinterpretation of the facts, however interesting, is at odds with their characterisation by war crimes tribunals, on which rested judicial pronouncements holding that private individuals were obligated directly by humanitarian law.

[112] *Ibid.*, at L Rep. 18 (emphasis added).

[113] *US v. Krauch and Twenty-Two Others* (the *IG Farben* trial), (1948) 10 L Rep. Trials War Crim. 1, 47–8, 7 USMT 1 (US Mil. Trib., Nuremberg).

[114] *US v. Alfred Krupp von Bohlen und Halbach and Eleven Others*, (1948) 10 L Rep. Trials War Crim. 69, 168–70, 9 USMT 1 (US Mil. Trib., Nuremberg).

The prosecution answered the argument by relying on the judgment of the US Military Tribunal at Nuremberg in the *Einsatzgruppen* trial, where that court concluded that 'when Germany signed, ratified and promulgated the Hague and Geneva Conventions, she bound each one of her subjects to their observance'.[115] Thus, as envisaged by the Permanent Court of International Justice in the *Danzig* case,[116] states parties to humanitarian conventions intended thereby to create obligations directly binding on individuals. In a manner consistent with this position, the tribunal in the *Krupp* trial rejected the argument of the defence and found the accused personally guilty of war crimes.

Despite some academic opinion to the contrary, the judicial practice generated in the wake of the Second World War does not support a distinction between state agents and private individuals when administering international law norms relating to armed conflict.

Recent developments

The ICTR in the *Akayesu* judgment, referring to some of the cases discussed above, noted in passing that individuals could be found guilty of war crimes even if they are not members of the military or government officials.[117] The Tribunal at one point refers, however, to the need to establish that an accused 'was legitimately mandated and expected, as a public official or agent or person otherwise holding public authority or *de facto* representing the government, to support or fulfil the war effort'.[118] The ICTR, while affirming that civilians may commit war crimes, thus seemed to require some institutional link to the state apparatus. In that case the accused was a bourgmestre, i.e. a local state official, so that this element was not in dispute.[119]

---

[115] *US v. Alfred Krupp*, at 172–3; *US v. Ohlendorf et al.* (the *Einsatzgruppen* trial), (1948) 4 USMT 1, 15 Ann. Digest Rep. Pub. Int'l L Cases 656, 659 (US Mil. Trib., Nuremberg).

[116] *Jurisdiction of the Courts of Danzig* case, (1928) Ser. B No. 15, at 17–18.

[117] *The Prosecutor v. Akayesu* (Judgment), 2 Sept. 1998, Case No. ICTR-96-4-T (Trial Chamber I, ICTR) paras. 630–4. The ICTY also considered civilians as possible authors of war crimes: *The Prosecutor v. Mrksić, Radić, Šljivančanin and Dokmanović* ('*Vukovar Hospital*' case) (Revised Indictment), 3 April 1996, Case No. IT-95-13a, para. 27.

[118] *The Prosecutor v. Akayesu*, at para. 634. The Tribunal included other limitations based on motives, which are discussed below, in the conclusion to the present section.

[119] See also *The Prosecutor v. Kayishema and Ruzindana* (Judgment), 21 May 1999, Case No. ICTR-95-1-T (Trial Chamber, ICTR) paras. 173–6 and 616–23; *The Prosecutor v. Rutaganda* (Judgment), 6 Dec. 1999, Case No. ICTR-96-3-T (Trial Chamber, ICTR) paras. 96–8 and 458–60.

The ICTY touched on the issue in its discussion of the international-isation of internal armed conflict in the *Tadić* appeals judgment.[120] In that decision, the Appeals Chamber noted that private individuals some-times act as *de facto* organs of a state, in which case the state may be held internationally responsible for any breach of humanitarian law carried out by that 'private' person.[121] In referring to cases where such a *de facto* relationship was found to have been established, the Tribunal added in a footnote that '[a]lthough these cases concerned State responsibility, they may be relevant to the question of the criminal responsibility of individ-uals perpetrating grave breaches of the Geneva Conventions, inasmuch as they set out the conditions necessary for individuals to be considered as *de facto* State organs'.[122] While the ICTY does not clearly embrace the position that only state agents may commit grave breaches, which in this case would have been an *obiter*, it does come perilously close to it.

The analysis of earlier cases has shown clearly that individuals acting in a purely private capacity can and do commit acts which fall within the class of belligerent relationships governed by humanitarian law. In-deed the ICTR in *Musema* examines some of the same Second World War cases to come to an identical conclusion, only to introduce the require-ment of a link to a party to the conflict in the form of a *de jure* or *de facto* public mandate, something not found in those older cases.[123] The ICTR and ICTY offer no justification for restricting the application of humanitarian law to the state, and indeed there seems to be no pol-icy or legal reason to do so, quite the contrary. This is buttressed by the principles governing acts of irregulars during international armed conflicts and those of insurgents during internal conflicts, which rest on the premiss that non-state actors are under an obligation to comply with humanitarian law and may be held criminally responsible if they fail to do so. The approach hinted at by the *Akayesu* and *Tadić* cases repre-sents a needless restriction of the scope of humanitarian law and as such should be rejected. The fact that neither Article 8 of the ICC Statute nor the 'Elements of Crimes' adopted by the Preparatory Commission for the ICC make any reference to a requirement of an institutional link should be seen as such an implicit rejection.[124]

---

[120] *The Prosecutor v. Tadić* (Appeals Judgment), 15 July 1999, Case No. IT-94-1-A (Appeals Chamber, ICTY).

[121] *Ibid.*, para. 144.

[122] *Ibid.*, footnote 175.

[123] *The Prosecutor v. Musema* (Judgment), 27 Jan. 2000, ICTR-96-13-T (Trial Chamber, ICTR) paras. 264–75 and 280.

[124] PCNICC, 'Elements of Crimes'.

Violation by irregular armed forces

Application of humanitarian law to combatants belonging to irregular armed forces in international and non-international conflicts further underscores the individual nature of obligations under humanitarian law. Pursuant to general international law, irregular armed forces in an international conflict need not be attached to the armed forces of their country in an organic way. Combatant status is extended to militia, volunteer and resistance corps by Article 1 of the 1907 Hague Regulations and Articles 13(2)/13(2)/4(A)(2) of the 1949 First, Second and Third Geneva Conventions, as long as members of these irregular forces comply with the four conditions listed in these provisions.[125] As noted in identical terms in the 1958 *British Manual of Military Law* and 1956 *US Field Manual 27–10*, express state recognition of these groups is not a prerequisite to them being characterised as lawful combatants.[126] Older practices such as those embodied in the 1902 German *Kriegsbrauch im Landkriege* whereby each irregular must prove state authorisation are inconsistent with modern customary humanitarian law.[127] The requirement that these resistance groups 'belong' to a party to the conflict (common Arts. 13(2)/13(2)/4(A)(2)) means that they must have some factual links with one of the parties to the conflict. A rather loose requirement, this does not imply any degree of formal control over resistance groups by the state but simply that they 'are acknowledged by [a party to the conflict] as fighting on its behalf or in its support'.[128] Indeed, irregular

---

[125] See the discussion in chapter 1, pp. 34–6.

[126] 1958 *British Manual of Military Law*, para. 91; 1956 *US Field Manual 27–10*, para. 64(a) ('State recognition, however, is not essential, and an organisation may be formed spontaneously and elect its own officers'); *Baffico v. Calleri*, (1948) Ann. Digest Rep. Pub. Int'l L Cases 426 (Torino (Italy) Court of App.).

[127] J. H. Morgan, *The War Book of the German General Staff* (Kriegsbrauch im Landkriege) (London: Murray, 1915) 58–60; 1929 *British Manual of Military Law*, at 276 n. 5; Michel Veuthey, *Guérilla et droit humanitaire* (Geneva: Institut Henri-Dunant, 1976) 220.

[128] Canadian Armed Forces, *The Law of Armed Conflict at the Operational and Tactical Level (B-GG-005-027/AF-020)* (Ottawa: Judge Advocate General, 1999) 3-2 para. 12. See also 'Report on Human Rights in Armed Conflict', UN Doc. A/8052 (1970), 55 para. 175; David, *Principes*, at 355; Jean Pictet ed., *The Geneva Conventions of 12 August 1949 – Commentary on the III Geneva Convention Relative to the Treatment of Prisoners of War* (Geneva: ICRC, 1960) 58–9; Angelo Sereni, *Diritto internazionale* (Milan: Giuffrè, 1965) IV, 1877; Henri Meyrowitz, 'Le statut des saboteurs dans le droit de la guerre', (1966) 5 *Revue de droit pénal militaire et de droit de la guerre* 121, 153; Henri Meyrowitz, 'La guérilla et le droit de la guerre, problèmes principaux', in *Droit humanitaire et conflits armés – Actes du colloque du 28 au 30 janvier 1970, Université libre de Bruxelles* (Brussels: Ed. U de Bruxelles, 1970) 185, 188 ('L'"appartenance à une partie au conflit" *ne vise pas un lien de dépendance ou d'allégence au sens du droit public interne ou international, mais plutôt*

groups meeting in every respect the requirements laid out by the laws and customs of war have had aims divergent from those of their 'official' government – in the instances where there was still some form of official government. During the Second World War, many resistance groups, for example Tito's forces in Yugoslavia or the Greek Popular Liberation Army (ELAS), embraced a communist revolutionary ideology which led them to seek the overthrow or at least non-recognition of the pre-war government while they were still fighting the German occupier with the support of states party to the conflict.[129] Such lawful combatants cannot realistically be labelled state agents, given that their activities were often considered illegal under municipal law before the armed conflict, and yet it is accepted that their actions should be governed by humanitarian law.

In the context of a discussion of whether the conflict in Bosnia-Herzegovina had become internationalised because of links between the *Republika Srpska* and the Federal Republic of Yugoslavia, the Appeals Chamber in the *Tadić* case examined common Articles 13(2)/13(2)/4(A)(2).[130] The Tribunal reasoned that if, in any given armed conflict, a group of irregulars was found to 'belong' to a state other than the one they were fighting, then it was a *de jure* or *de facto* organ of a foreign state and the conflict necessarily ought to be characterised as international:

In other words, States have in practice accepted that belligerents may use paramilitary units and other irregulars in the conduct of hostilities only on the condition that those belligerents are prepared to take responsibility for any infringements committed by such forces. In order for irregulars to qualify as lawful combatants, it appears that international rules and State practice therefore require control over them by a Party to an international armed conflict and, by the same token, a relationship of dependence and allegiance of these irregulars vis-à-vis that Party to the conflict. These then may be regarded as the ingredients of the term 'belonging to a Party to the conflict'.[131]

The Tribunal then fleshed out the notion of 'belonging' by referring to general rules on state responsibility and primarily the discussion of the

---

une liaison de fait sur le plan militaire et politique' (emphasis added)); Alessandro Migliazza, 'L'évolution de la réglementation de la guerre à la lumière de la sauvegarde des droits de l'homme', (1972-III) 137 *Recueil des cours* 142, 207–9.

[129] See M. R. D. Foot, *Resistance*, 2nd edn (London: Granada, 1978) 181 and 190–7.

[130] *The Prosecutor* v. *Tadić* (Appeals Judgment), 15 July 1999, Case No. IT-94-1-A (Appeals Chamber, ICTY) paras. 92–7.

[131] *Ibid.*, para. 94.

responsibility of the United States for acts of the *Contras* in the *Nicaragua* case.[132] Criticising the reasoning of the ICJ in that decision, the ICTY concluded that a flexible test of overall control of a group should be applied.[133]

In equating the conditions for the internationalisation of an internal armed conflict with the conditions under which irregulars will be considered lawful combatants, the ICTY pointlessly forces a considerable narrowing of the class of protected combatants in international armed conflict. It confuses the application of common articles 13(2)/13(2)/4(A)(2), defining lawful combatants, with the application of common Article 2, defining an international armed conflict, and Article 3 of the 1907 Hague Convention IV, Article 13 of the Third Geneva Convention, Article 29 of the Fourth Convention and Article 91 of Protocol I, on a state's responsibility for violations of humanitarian law. Locked in the logic of its discussion of the internationalisation of conflicts, the ICTY seemed to have lost sight of the fact that the situation most clearly envisaged by common Articles 13(2)/13(2)/4(A)(2) was that of an existing international armed conflict in which irregulars take up arms, on the model of partisan action during the Second World War.[134] In presenting the rationale for that provision as that of the responsibility of the state for acts of 'its' irregulars, the Appeals Chamber overlooks the fact that humanitarian law creates obligations not only for states but also for individuals, and that state responsibility plays a role clearly secondary to that of individual criminal responsibility. This may have been invited by the argument of the Prosecutor that the loose connection traditionally required under common Articles 13(2)/13(2)/4(A)(2) was sufficient to internationalise the conflict.

There seem to be valid reasons indeed to demand a tighter connection for internationalisation of internal conflicts than for defining lawful irregular combatants in an otherwise clearly international armed conflict. The responses to these two very distinct questions should be equally

---

[132] *Military and Paramilitary Activities in and Against Nicaragua (Nicaragua v. US)*, [1986] ICJ Rep. 14.

[133] *Tadić* (Appeals Judgment) paras. 98–145. See also *The Prosecutor v. Blaskić* (Judgment), 3 March 2000, Case No. IT-95-14-T (Trial Chamber, ICTY) paras. 75–123; *The Prosecutor v. Aleksovski* (Appeals Judgment), 24 March 2000, Case No. IT-95-14/1-A (Appeals Chamber, ICTY) paras. 125–46; *The Prosecutor v. Delalić, Mucić, Delić and Landzo* (the *Celebici* case) (Appeal Judgment), 20 Feb. 2001, Case No. IT-96-21-A (Appeals Chamber, ICTY) paras. 6–51; *The Prosecutor v. Kordić* (Judgment), 26 Feb. 2001, Case No. IT-95-14/2-T (Trial Chamber, ICTY) paras. 111–46.

[134] See Pictet, III, at 49–50 and 59.

distinct. The ICTY offers no authority for its position apart from an Israeli case where it is doubtful that any armed conflict was ongoing,[135] and brushes aside the consistent body of state practice and doctrinal authorities discussed above. The import of formal rules on state responsibility in the interpretation of common Articles 13(2)/13(2)/4(A)(2) can have dire consequences for groups of irregulars which are not found to act as agents of a foreign state, because it will mean that these groups are neither lawful combatants nor peaceful civilians. It seems difficult to see in this decision an incitement to the broadest possible application of international humanitarian law.

A further problem with linking the application of the laws and customs of war to the status of state agent relates to the recognition of the state by an enemy belligerent in an international armed conflict. For instance, Free French Forces fighting under General de Gaulle after 1940, when the official French Government had signed an armistice, claimed that they fought for France. Germany had solid legal grounds for denying this, as the Armistice Agreement between France and Germany specified that French nationals would no longer be entitled to the protection of the laws of war as French combatants.[136] More generally, one of the bases invoked by German forces to deny combatant status to partisans was that they were not fighting on behalf of a recognised government.[137] Articles 13(3)/13(3)/4(A)(3) of the 1949 First, Second and Third Geneva Conventions sought to avoid this difficulty by detaching the status of combatants from that of the recognition of the belligerent state by its enemy.[138] Regular combatants in an international armed conflict are thus considered lawful combatants regardless of whether the state they profess allegiance to actually exists according to the enemy state. This explains why, for example, the non-recognition of Israel by its Arab neighbours did not hinder the application of humanitarian law during the various armed conflicts involving these states. This

[135] Military Prosecutor v. Kassem, (1971) 42 Int'l L Rep. 477–8.
[136] See ICRC, Report of the International Committee of the Red Cross on its Activities During the Second World War (Geneva: ICRC, 1949) I, 519–20; Pictet, III, at 61–2. Germany eventually granted members of the Free French Forces the status of lawful combatants by treating them as belonging to Britain.
[137] Wilhelm Wengler, Völkerrecht (Berlin: Springer, 1964) II, 1408–9; Remigiusz Bierzanek, 'Le statut juridique des partisans et des mouvements de résistance armées: Evolution historique et aspects actuels', in Vladimir Ibler ed., Mélanges offerts à Juraj Andrassy (The Hague: Nijhoff, 1968) 54, 64–5.
[138] The Article states that '[m]embers of regular armed forces who profess allegiance to a government or an authority not recognized' by the enemy belligerent shall be considered as combatants.

illustrates broadly the point that humanitarian law may be applicable to individuals who cannot be considered as agents of a state.

Turning now to the normative framework of humanitarian law as it applies to internal armed conflicts, we find that both international norms and recent practice concur in the articulation of standards. In all norms related to internal conflicts, obligations are imposed on all parties to the conflict, meaning the state (if it is involved) as well as non-state parties.[139] Thus common Article 3 of the 1949 Geneva Conventions states that 'each Party shall be bound to apply, as a minimum, the following provisions'. These elementary considerations of humanity have been found to have ripened into customary law by the International Court of Justice, the ICTY and the ICTR.[140] The two 1977 Additional Protocols incorporate the same principle. Pursuant to Protocol I, 'internal' conflicts by oppressed peoples in pursuance of their right to self-determination are characterised as international armed conflicts (Art. 1(4)). In such a war, if the necessary conditions are met (Arts. 1(4), 43–44, 96(3)), the full array of humanitarian norms applies equally to both sides, despite the fact that there is only one state present in the field. Similarly, under Protocol II, norms additional to common Article 3 of the 1949 Geneva Conventions are articulated in a purely negative manner throughout the treaty, providing for standards opposable to all sides to the conflict. In all these situations, the insurgents can hardly be considered as agents of the state, as they are engaged in hostilities against the state or against one another. The Inter-American Commission on Human Rights came to the same conclusion in its 1999 *Third Report on the Situation of Human Rights in Colombia* when it found that paramilitary groups were bound by humanitarian law by effect of their participation in the conflict, an issue wholly distinct from the possible international responsibility of Colombia should it be found that these groups acted as agents or proxies of the state.[141]

The direct imposition of obligations on the individual during an internal armed conflict is confirmed by the newly emerged principle of international individual criminal responsibility for violations of

[139] See Inter-American Commission on Human Rights, 'Third Report on the Situation of Human Rights in Colombia', OAS Doc. OEA/Ser.L/V/II, doc. 102 (1999), chapter IV paras. 13 and 85.
[140] *Military and Paramilitary Activities in and Against Nicaragua (Nicaragua v. US)*, [1986] ICJ Rep. 14, at 114 para. 218; *The Prosecutor v. Akayesu* (Judgment), 2 Sept. 1998, Case No. ICTR-96-4-T (Trial Chamber I, ICTR) para. 608; *The Prosecutor v. Blaskić* (Judgment), 3 March 2000, Case No. IT-95-14-T (Trial Chamber, ICTY) paras. 164–7.
[141] OAS Doc. OEA/Ser.L/V/II, doc. 102 (1999) para. 234.

humanitarian law during such a conflict. Until very recently, there generally was consensus that 'war crime' was a notion applicable only in the context of international armed conflicts. This was reflected in the fact that serious violations of common Article 3 of the 1949 Geneva Conventions were not included in the list of grave breaches in those conventions (Arts. 50/51/130/147). In a similar fashion, Protocol II makes no mention of either grave breaches or serious violations, as the possibility of incorporating these concepts in the protocol had been considered and then rejected at the 1977 Geneva Conference. Finally, the customary concept of war crimes did not extend to offences committed in internal armed conflicts.[142] Recent practice indicates a shift away from this position to expand the concept of war crimes to non-international armed conflict. First, the Statute of the ICTR, adopted by UN Security Council Resolution 955 (1994), grants the Tribunal jurisdiction for violations of common Article 3 and of Protocol II (Art. 4, ICTR Statute), the only humanitarian law norms applicable to that internal conflict. This provision, complemented by Article 6 providing for individual criminal responsibility for anyone who committed in any way a violation of, among others, common Article 3 and Protocol II, confirms the introduction of the concept of war crimes in the context of internal armed conflict.[143]

A related development occurred in the ICTY in the *Tadić* case.[144] In that case, the defence objected that the Tribunal was partly without jurisdiction because the conflict in the former Yugoslavia was an internal armed conflict and no violations of the laws or customs of war could occur in such a context. Indeed, the ICTY Statute lacks an equivalent to

[142] See 'Final Report of the Commission of Experts Established Pursuant to Security Council Resolution 780 (1992)', UN Doc. S/1994/674 Annex (1994) at 15–16 paras. 52 and 54 ('In particular, there does not appear to be a customary international law applicable to internal armed conflict which includes the concept of war crimes...It must be observed that the violations of the laws or customs of war referred to in article 3 of the statute of the International Tribunal [for former Yugoslavia] are offences when committed in international, but not in internal armed conflicts'); ICRC, 'Preliminary Remarks on the Setting-up of an International Tribunal for Prosecution of Persons Responsible for Serious Violations of International Humanitarian Law Committed in the Territory of the Former Yugoslavia', 15 March 1993, DDM/JUR/442b, para. 4 ('according to humanitarian law as it stands today, the notion of war crimes is limited to situations of international armed conflict'); Denise Plattner, 'The Penal Repression of Violations of International Humanitarian Law Applicable in Non-international Armed Conflicts', (1990) 30 *Int'l Rev. Red Cross* 409, 414.
[143] UN Secretary-General, 'Report to the Security Council Pursuant to Paragraph 5 of Resolution 955 (1994)', UN Doc. S/1995/134 (1995) para. 12.
[144] *The Prosecutor v. Tadić* (Decision on the Defence Motion for Interlocutory Appeal on Jurisdiction), 2 Oct. 1995, Case No. IT-94-1-AR72 (Appeals Chamber, ICTY).

Article 4 of the ICTR Statute, referring to violations of common Article 3 and Protocol II. It provides for jurisdiction of the ICTY in cases of grave breaches of the 1949 Geneva Conventions (Art. 2, ICTY Statute) and for violations of the laws or customs of war (Art. 3, ICTY Statute). In its decision, the Appeals Chamber agreed with the defence that 'grave breaches' referred to the 1949 Geneva Conventions and Protocol I and could occur only in the context of an international armed conflict.[145] On the other hand, the Chamber found that the customary concept of 'violations of the laws or customs of war' had evolved to cover all serious violations of international humanitarian law, including those of common Article 3, of customary rules governing internal armed conflict, and of other agreements binding upon the parties.[146] This reasoning was later adopted by the ICTR in the *Akayesu* case to support the customary nature of penal responsibility for war crimes committed during an internal conflict.[147]

The move by UN organs to expand individual criminal responsibility both rests and has had an effect on state practice in that respect. For example, the *1992 German Manual on Humanitarian Law* and the Belgian penal code provide for criminal responsibility in cases of violations of common Article 3 and Protocol II.[148] More recently, the adoption of the Statute of the International Criminal Court codified the extension of war crimes to include those perpetrated during internal conflicts (Art. 8(2)(c) and (e)). Under such a scheme, persons held criminally responsible can be connected in no way to the state, either because they are acting on behalf

---

[145] *Ibid.*, at 44–8 paras. 79–85.

[146] *Ibid.*, at 48–71 paras. 86–137. The latter class of crimes further covers serious violations of Protocol II, which is not mentioned in the ICTY Statute despite the fact that it was applicable to the conflict: Sep. Op. Judge Sidhwa, *ibid.*, at 68 para. 118; *The Prosecutor v. Kordić and Cerkez* ('*Lasva Valley*' case) (Decision on the Joint Defence Motion to Dismiss the Amended Indictment for Lack of Jurisdiction Based on the Limited Jurisdictional Reach of Articles 2 and 3), 2 March 1999, Case No. IT-95-14/2-PT (Trial Chamber III, ICTY) para. 34. See also *The Prosecutor v. Tadić* (Opinion and Judgment), 7 May 1997, Case No. IT-94-1-T (Trial Chamber II, ICTY) paras. 609–12; *The Prosecutor v. Rajić* (Review of the Indictment Pursuant to Rule 61), 13 Sept. 1996, Case No. IT-95-12-R61 (Trial Chamber II, ICTY) at 23 para. 48; *The Prosecutor v. Martić* (Review of the Indictment Pursuant to Rule 61), 8 March 1996, Case No. IT-95-11-R61 (Trial Chamber I, ICTY) paras. 8–10 and 19–20.

[147] *The Prosecutor v. Akayesu* (Judgment), 2 Sept. 1998, Case No. ICTR-96-4-T (Trial Chamber I, ICTR) paras. 611–17.

[148] *1992 German Manual on Humanitarian Law*, para. 1209; Loi du 16 juin 1993 relative à la répression des infractions graves aux Conventions internationales de Genève du 12 août 1949 et aux Protocoles I et II du 8 juin 1977, additionnels à ces Conventions, *Moniteur Belge*, 5 Aug. 1993. Further examples are available online at www.icrc.org/ihl-nat.

of the insurgents or because they are acting in a purely personal capacity. It is interesting to note that in the *Tadić* judgment, it was neither alleged nor demonstrated that the accused was acting on behalf of the insurgent *Republika Srpska* or its army.[149] That this was not considered a relevant element by the Tribunal confirms that international humanitarian law imposes obligations directly on the individual, and not through the state or other groups.[150]

The fact that humanitarian law imposes obligations on insurgents during an internal armed conflict and also on resistance groups during an international armed conflict has raised the question of how the binding character of such obligations on these groups may be explained. Some writers have suggested that the insurgent group could be considered the eventual successor of the official government in place.[151] As such, the rebel authority would seek to assume all international obligations of the established government, including treaty and customary obligations under humanitarian law, and thereby be bound by such obligations. This is consistent with the law of state responsibility, which provides for the 'retroactive' imputability to the state of acts of an insurrectional movement successful in overthrowing the government.[152] The rebel authority, however, may not be successful or may not enjoy the political development sufficient to enable such a claim to be made realistically. It may well reject all international obligations contracted by the existing state, as did the Vietcong during the Vietnam war, for

[149] *The Prosecutor* v. *Tadić* (Opinion and Judgment), 7 May 1997, Case No. IT-94-1-T (Trial Chamber II, ICTY); *The Prosecutor* v. *Tadić* (Appeals Judgment), 15 July 1999, Case No. IT-94-1-A (Appeals Chamber, ICTY). The question was, rather, whether the *Republika Srpska* acted on behalf of the Federal Republic of Yugoslavia.

[150] The US Second Circuit Court of Appeals implicitly adopted the same reasoning in *Kadić* v. *Karadzić* when it concluded that Karadzić could have committed war crimes by way of violating common Art. 3: 70 F.3d 232, 242–3 (2d Cir. 1995). See also *Iwanowa* v. *Ford Motor Co.*, 67 F.Supp.2d 424, 443–5 (D New Jersey, 1999); *Doe* v. *Islamic Salvation Front (FIS)*, 993 F.Supp. 3, 8 (DDC, 1998); Theodor Meron, 'International Criminalization of Internal Atrocities', (1995) 89 *Am. J Int'l L* 554, 562–3.

[151] See Jean Pictet ed., *The Geneva Conventions of 12 August 1949 – Commentary on the IV Geneva Convention Relative to the Protection of Civilian Persons in Times of War* (Geneva: ICRC, 1958) 36; Heather A. Wilson, *International Law and the Use of Force by National Liberation Movements* (Oxford: Clarendon, 1988) 50–1; Richard Baxter, '*Jus in Bello Interno*: The Present and Future Law', in J. Moore ed., *Law and Civil War in the Modern World* (Baltimore: Johns Hopkins, 1974) 518, 527–8; Shigeki Miyazaki, 'The Application of the New Humanitarian Law', (1980) 217 *Int'l Rev. Red Cross* 184, 187.

[152] See International Law Commission, 'Draft Articles on State Responsibility', [1975] 2 *YB Int'l L Com'n* 91–106 (Arts. 14–15); Hazem Atlam, 'National Liberation Movements and International Responsibility', in Marina Spinedi and Bruno Simma eds., *United Nations Codification of State Responsibility* (New York: Oceana, 1987) 35–57; Crawford, 'First Report', UN Doc. A/CN.4/490 (1998) paras. 263–80.

example.[153] Under common Article 3 of the 1949 Geneva Conventions, there is no formal requirement that the rebel authority be more than an organised military force. Further, in the context of an international armed conflict, resistance groups benefiting from the status of lawful combatants might not want to constitute the new government of the country. Such was the situation of many resistance groups in Europe during the Second World War whose aim was simply the driving out of the occupying forces, with no ulterior political motives.[154] No element of international humanitarian law seems to justify the conditioning of the imposition of humanitarian law obligations on such highly variable characteristics of insurgent and resistance groups. A better construction, equally valid in international and non-international armed conflicts, leads to the conclusion that humanitarian law embodies public order norms which impose obligations directly on individuals as well as on states and groups.[155]

Conclusion

International humanitarian law creates obligations for all individuals in times of armed conflicts. The relationship between an individual and his or her state is irrelevant to that fact. This explains why the defences of acting in an official capacity or under the direct orders of a hierarchical superior do not detract from the individual character of the violation of humanitarian law.

The conclusion that humanitarian law imposes obligations directly on individuals calls for some limiting principle, otherwise that body of law would displace nearly all other penal laws during an armed conflict.

---

[153] In reply to an ICRC appeal to apply the 1949 Geneva Conventions, the National Liberation Front of Vietnam (Vietcong) replied that 'the NLF was not bound by the international treaties to which others besides itself subscribe': (1965) 5 *Int'l Rev. Red Cross* 636. See Wilson, *International Law*, at 50–1; Miyazaki, 'Application', at 187.

[154] See Foot, *Resistance*, at 93–4.

[155] See II-B *Final Record of the Diplomatic Conference of Geneva of 1949* (Berne: Federal Political Dept, 1949) 94; Sydney D. Bailey, *Prohibitions and Restraints in War* (London: Oxford UP, 1972) 88; Geoffrey Best, *War and Law Since 1945* (Oxford: Oxford UP, 1994) 177–9; Morris Greenspan, *The Modern Law of Land Warfare* (Los Angeles: U California Press, 1959) 623–4; Meron, *Human Rights in Internal Strife*, at 39; Baxter, 'Jus in Bello Interno', at 527–8; Miyazaki, 'Application', at 188; Mónica Pinto, 'Responsabilidad internacional por la violación de los derechos humanos y los entes no estatales', in *Héctor Gros Espiell Amicorum Liber* (Brussels: Bruylant, 1997) II, 1155, 1163; Dietrich Schindler, 'The Different Types of Armed Conflicts According to the Geneva Conventions and Protocols', (1979-II) 163 *Recueil des cours* 117, 151–2.

Clearly, some offences committed during a conflict, for instance a simple case of theft or an assault in a bar brawl, do not call for application of international law and even less that of war crimes. Such a limiting principle is quite difficult to articulate, however, given that during an armed conflict, relationships between people of different allegiances are coloured by the belligerency, such that no 'normal' relationship necessarily falling beyond the pale of humanitarian law can be said to exist. Even contacts between civilians can occasion violations of the laws and customs of war, as shown by the *Hadamar* trial where doctors were convicted for killing enemy civilians.[156] State practice generated after the Second World War denied that the motives of the violation could serve as criterion, as war crimes can be committed for personal greed or out of sadism, as well as under strict orders reflecting a well-defined policy.[157] Similarly, the nature of the offence offers no guide, given that a vast number of acts may be characterised as either war crimes or common crimes – sexual assault, for example.

The ICTY in the *Tadić* case has articulated such a requirement based on the necessary nexus of the offence to the conflict.[158] Based on the Appeals Chamber's conclusion that the crimes must be 'closely related to the hostilities', the Trial Chamber stated that in order to meet this test:

It would be sufficient to prove that the crime was committed in the course of or as part of the hostilities in, or occupation of, an area controlled by one of the

---

[156] *US* v. *Klein and Six Others* (the Hadamar trial), (1945) 1 L Rep. Trials War Crim. 46 (US Mil. Com'n, Wiesbaden); Lassa Oppenheim, *International Law*, Hersch Lauterpacht ed., 7th edn (London: Longmans, 1952) II, 204–6; 1958 *British Manual of Military Law*, para. 624 ('The term "war crime" is a technical expression for violations of the laws of warfare, whether committed by members of the armed forces or by civilians'); 1956 *US Field Manual 27–10*, para. 499.

[157] H. Lauterpacht, *International Law and Human Rights*, at 39. For example, the 1958 *British Manual of Military Law* provides in para. 636: 'A special class of war crimes is that sometimes known as "marauding". This consists of ranging over battlefields and following advancing or retreating armies in quest of loot, robbing, maltreating and killing stragglers and wounded and plundering the dead – *all acts done not as means of carrying on the war but for private gains. Nevertheless such acts are treated as violations of the laws of war.* Those who commit them, whether civilians who have never been lawful combatants, or persons who have belonged to a military unit, an organised resistance movement or a *levée en masse*, and have deserted and so ceased to be lawful combatants, are liable to be punished as war criminals' (emphasis added).

[158] *The Prosecutor* v. *Tadić* (Opinion and Judgment), 7 May 1997, Case No. IT-94-1-T (Trial Chamber II, ICTY) para. 573; *The Prosecutor* v. *Tadić* (Decision on the Defence Motion for Interlocutory Appeal on Jurisdiction), 2 Oct. 1995, Case No. IT-94-1-AR72 (Appeals Chamber, ICTY) at 38 para. 70.

parties. It is not, however, necessary to show that armed conflict was occurring at the exact time and place of the proscribed acts alleged to have occurred, as the Appeals Chamber has indicated, *nor is it necessary that the crime alleged takes place during combat, that it be part of a policy or of a practice officially endorsed or tolerated by one of the parties to the conflict, or that the act be in actual furtherance of a policy associated with the conduct of war or in the actual interest of a party to the conflict*; the obligations of individuals under international humanitarian law are independent and apply without prejudice to any questions of the responsibility of States under international law. The only question, to be determined in the circumstances of each individual case, is *whether the offences were closely related to the armed conflict as a whole.* [Emphasis added.][159]

In that case, the Trial Chamber of the ICTY found that the offences – the torture and killing of civilian internees in a camp run by the insurgent *Republika Srpska* – were in fact furthering a general policy of ethnic cleansing, and so should be characterised as violations of the laws and customs of war. The requirement proffered by the ICTY is extremely flexible, and not dissimilar to the standard of persons 'affected by' an armed conflict found in Article 75 of Protocol I.

The ICTR in the *Akayesu* case adopted a position in this respect which stands at odds with the reasoning of the ICTY Trial Chamber in the *Tadić* judgment and, more broadly, with existing international law. The Tribunal concluded that the accused could be found guilty of war crimes only if it was proven beyond reasonable doubt that his actions were carried out in the execution of the conflict objectives of one of the belligerents. It stated that 'the crimes must not be committed by the perpetrator for purely personal motives' but 'to support or fulfil the war effort'.[160] On that basis, the Tribunal acquitted Akayesu on all counts of war crimes given that it had not been proven that the rapes, cruel treatments and murders were part of the war effort. This rigid construction of the nexus requirement has been repeated in later cases, leading the ICTR again to acquit the accused on the charge of war crimes in the *Kayishema and Ruzindana, Rutaganda* and *Musema* cases.[161]

The decisions of the ICTR seem mistakenly to incorporate into war crimes an element of crimes against humanity, where the link between

---

[159] *Tadić* (Opinion and Judgment). This conclusion was left undisturbed by the Appeals Judgment in the same case.

[160] *The Prosecutor* v. *Akayesu* (Judgment), 2 Sept. 1998, Case No. ICTR-96-4-T (Trial Chamber I, ICTR) paras. 640–4.

[161] *The Prosecutor* v. *Kayishema and Ruzindana* (Judgment), 21 May 1999, Case No. ICTR-95-1-T (Trial Chamber, ICTR) paras. 599–615; *The Prosecutor* v. *Rutaganda* (Judgment), 6 Dec. 1999, ICTR-96-3-T (Trial Chamber, ICTR) paras. 461–3; *The Prosecutor* v. *Musema* (Judgment), 27 Jan. 2000, ICTR-96-13-T (Trial Chamber, ICTR) para. 974.

the crime and a broader attack against a civilian population is a defining element of the crime.[162] To seek this element with respect to war crimes would be to limit the protection of humanitarian law only to those whose life or integrity is significant to one of the belligerents, not to mention evidentiary difficulties in establishing individual motives beyond reasonable doubt. The link between an individual and a given group in the context of an armed conflict grounds the protection offered by humanitarian law, but that does not mean that only an offence which primarily focuses on this link will be prohibited. Neither the treaty definition of 'grave breaches' in the Geneva Conventions (Arts. 50/51/130/147) and Protocol I (Art. 85), nor that of war crimes as interpreted in Second World War jurisprudence, discussed above, includes the furtherance of a belligerent's war effort as an element of the crime.

In its judgments in the *Celebici* and *Blaskić* cases, which were issued after the *Akayesu* decision, the ICTY reiterated the nexus test as it had been articulated in the *Tadić* judgment.[163] The ICTY touched on the issue more directly in its discussion of the elements of the crime of plunder. In response to a defence argument which sought to narrow the scope of the crime, the Trial Chamber observed in *Celebici* that

the prohibition against the unjustified appropriation of public and private enemy property is general in scope, and extends to both acts of looting committed by individual soldiers for their private gains, and to the organised seizure of property undertaken within the framework of a systematic economic exploitation of occupied territory. Contrary to the submission of the Defence, the fact that it was acts of the latter category which were made the subject of prosecutions before the International Military Tribunal at Nürnberg and in subsequent proceedings before the Nürnberg Military Tribunals *does not demonstrate the absence of individual criminal liability under international law for individual acts of pillage committed by perpetrators motivated by personal greed. In contrast, when seen in a historical perspective, it is clear that the prohibition against pillage was directed precisely against violations of the latter kind.*[164]

---

[162] *The Prosecutor* v. *Tadić* (Appeals Judgment), 15 July 1999, Case No. IT-94-1-A (Appeals Chamber, ICTY) paras. 270–1.

[163] *The Prosecutor* v. *Delalić, Mucić, Delić and Landzo* (the *Celebici* case) (Judgment), 16 Nov. 1998, Case No. IT-96-21-T (Trial Chamber, ICTY) at 74–5 paras. 193–8 (the Appeals Chamber judgment did not discuss this point); *The Prosecutor* v. *Blaskić* (Judgment), 3 March 2000, Case No. IT-95-14-T (Trial Chamber, ICTY) para. 70. See also *The Prosecutor* v. *Aleksovski* (*Lasva Valley* case) (Judgment), 25 June 1999, Case No. IT-95-14/1-T (Trial Chamber, ICTY) para. 45 ('Il faut nécessairement démontrer que cet acte, qui aurait certes pu être commis en l'absence de conflit, l'a été contre la victime en question en raison de ce conflit' – a holding left untouched by the appeals judgment in that case).

[164] *Celebici*, at 200 para. 590; *Blaskić*, at 61 para. 184. See also *The Prosecutor* v. *Kunarac* (Judgment), 22 Feb. 2001, Cases No. IT-96-23-T and IT-96-23/1-T (Trial Chamber, ICTY)

There is thus no link to be established between the crime of plunder and the general war effort. More generally, the soldier who by pure cruelty tortures prisoners of war, as well as the insurgent who by prurience rapes enemy women, commits acts which, in all likelihood, are closely related to the armed conflict as a whole and which, as found by the ICTY, should be considered violations of humanitarian law. This is the position which seems to be adopted by the Preparatory Commission for the ICC when it defines a war crime as a conduct which 'took place in the context of and was associated with' an international or internal armed conflict.[165]

The individual character of obligations under humanitarian law thus stands in stark contrast to that of obligations flowing from international human rights law. On the one hand, the normative framework of human rights centres obligations firmly on the state and its agents, in a manner consonant with its basic purpose of protecting individuals against abuses by the state. On the other hand, the normative framework of humanitarian law obligates individuals at large, a necessary response to the fact that, in times of armed conflict, it is entire nations, and not only states and their agents, that become enemies.[166]

Responsibility

It was stated at the outset of this chapter that there is no absolute correlation between the existence of an obligation and the imposition of responsibility. States may in some circumstances be held responsible for actions of private individuals, and private persons may sometimes be held responsible for violations committed by the state.[167] It follows that, in itself, the conclusion reached above regarding the existence of obligations imposed directly on the individual by international humanitarian law but not by human rights law does not provide a cogent picture of principles regarding individual responsibility under international law. In fact, however, discussions of the existence of individual obligations generally have been so closely connected to the question of individual responsibility that the analysis in the previous section has brought out

paras. 407 and 568; *The Prosecutor* v. *Jelisić* (Judgment), 14 Dec. 1999, Case No. IT-95-10-T (Trial Chamber, ICTY) para. 48.

[165] PCNICC, 'Elements of Crimes', UN Doc. PCNICC/2000/INF/3/Add.2.

[166] Emer de Vattel, *Le droit des gens ou principes de la loi naturelle*, James Brown Scott ed. (Washington: Carnegie, 1916, 1st edn 1758) III, part V, para. 70.

[167] See above, pp. 57–8.

many of the key features of individual responsibility with respect to violations of human rights and humanitarian law. The purpose of this section will not be to repeat what has been said already, nor to delve into minute details of the articulation of individual responsibility, but rather to examine the role of responsibility in the normative framework of human rights and humanitarian law. This will lead to, first, some general remarks on the accepted character and significance of individual responsibility in the normative framework of each legal system and, secondly, to a discussion of the existence of a state duty to prosecute perpetrators of violations of human rights or humanitarian law, as a reflection of the centrality of individual responsibility in these two systems.

ROLE OF RESPONSIBILITY

Responsibility in the field of international law has traditionally reflected that legal system's focus on inter-state rights and obligations. State responsibility is one of the foundations of international law and, as such, has helped shape both human rights and humanitarian law. In the latter, specific provisions in the 1907 Hague Convention IV (Art. 3), the 1949 Geneva Conventions (Art. 12, Third Convention; Art. 29, Fourth Convention) and Protocol I (Art. 91) provide for a broad principle of state responsibility, now part of customary law.[168] In human rights law, state responsibility is envisaged expressly only in some provisions relating to particular rights; for instance, there is a right to compensation for wrongful arrest or conviction.[169] Despite the absence of a provision stating a general principle of state responsibility in case of breach, the general rule to the effect that 'every internationally wrongful act of a state entails the international responsibility of that state' does apply fully to human rights norms.[170] There is no corresponding principle holding

---

[168] See above, pp. 45-7.

[169] Art. 14(6), International Covenant on Civil and Political Rights; Art. 5(5), European Convention on Human Rights; Art. 10, American Convention on Human Rights.

[170] Art. 1, Draft Articles on State Responsibility, [1973] 2 YB Int'l L Com'n 173-6; Art. 19(3)(c), Draft Articles on State Responsibility, [1976] 2:2 YB Int'l L Com'n 95-122. See generally Felix Ermacora, 'Über die völkerrechtliche Verantwortlichkeit für Menschenrechtsverletzungen', in H. Miehsler ed., Ius Humanitaris: Festschrift für Alfred Verdross (Berlin: Duncker & Humblot, 1980) 357-78; B. G. Ramcharan, 'State Responsibility for Violations of Human Rights', in Edith Brown Weiss ed., Contemporary Problems of International Law: Essays in Honour of Georg Schwarzenberger (London: Stevens & Son, 1988) 246-61; Dinah Shelton, 'State Responsibility for Aiding and Abetting Flagrant Violations of Human Rights', in D. Prémont ed., Essays on the Concept of a 'Right to Life' (Brussels: Bruylant, 1988) 222-32.

that every violation of international law by an individual calls for penal responsibility; that will occur only with respect to such violations which are deemed to be international crimes under public international law.[171] Individual criminal responsibility for violations of the laws and customs of war has been recognised for some time in customary law, and was incorporated into treaty law over the course of the last century. A move is now afoot in human rights law to trigger the development of individual penal responsibility in that field as well.

Why should the international community insist on or reject the idea of individual penal responsibility for violations of certain international norms, and not of others? It is partly a desire to make the reaction to a breach mirror the interests protected by the primary norm. When the protected interest lies essentially in the individual, the proper remedy is usually the granting of rights of action to the victims themselves. When the violation is taken as transcending individual harm to trench upon collective interests, however, a simple individual right of action appears insufficient, and some form of collective reaction must be envisaged, very often in the form of punitive action.[172] The rationale of punishment as an appropriate sanction has been articulated in a variety of theories, which situate it in different places among the three poles of punishment identified as deterrence, rehabilitation and retribution. Although some have tried to adapt these theories specifically to the field of international law, no one theory has emerged as the accepted explanation for patterns of individual responsibility in international criminal law.[173] In examining the rationale for punishment of the crimes under its jurisdiction, the ICTY in the *Erdemović* sentencing judgment concluded that international penal responsibility involves some element of deterrence, that is the prevention of future violation of the same norm, reprobation, that is the expression of societal condemnation of the offence, and retribution, affording some degree of satisfaction of the victim's need

[171] See Michael Reisman and Janet Koven Levit, 'Reflections on the Problem of Individual Responsibility for Violations of Human Rights', in Antonio Cançado Trindade ed., *The Modern World of Human Rights* – *Essays in Honour of Thomas Buergenthal* (San Jose, Costa Rica: Inter-American Institute for Human Rights, 1996) 419, 430.
[172] See Naomi Roht-Arriaza, 'Punishment, Redress, and Pardon: Theoretical and Psychological Approaches', in Naomi Roht-Arriaza ed., *Impunity and Human Rights in International Law and Practice* (New York: Oxford UP, 1995) 13, 18; M. Cherif Bassiouni, 'The Proscribing Function of International Criminal Law in the Process of International Protection of Human Rights', (1982) 9 *Yale J World Public Order* 193–214.
[173] See Farooq Hassan, 'The Theoretical Basis of Punishment in International Criminal Law', (1983) 15 *Case W Res. J Int'l L* 39, 51–60; Reisman and Levit, 'Reflections', at 432–3; Roht-Arriaza, *Impunity*.

for justice.[174] To these can be added secondary functions such as the creation of a historical record of war crimes and, more generally, the education of present and future generations.[175]

The place of individual criminal responsibility within the framework of international humanitarian law has grown to become central. This is a relatively new development. Prior to the First World War, it was accepted that a belligerent could try captured enemy soldiers who had committed crimes against the detaining power.[176] During and after the First World War, there were clear statements of a general principle of international law on individual penal responsibility for war crimes, in particular in the report of the Commission on the Responsibility of the Authors of War and on Enforcement of Penalties and in the Treaty of Versailles.[177] These statements were challenged by Germany and her allies, and had very limited echo in actual practice, so that it can hardly be said that a general principle of individual penal responsibility had been accepted in international law in the aftermath of that conflict.[178] This is reflected in the provisions of the two 1929 Geneva Conventions, which do not make reference to penal responsibility for breaches, except for one small exception.[179]

This was dramatically changed in the wake of the Second World War, when the Nuremberg and Far East International Military Tribunals and other courts rigidly applied criminal responsibility for breaches of the 1907 Hague Convention IV and the 1929 Geneva Conventions, despite the fact that none of these treaties expressly envisaged such an individual responsibility.[180] As noted in the analysis of individual obligations, the

---

[174] *The Prosecutor* v. *Erdemović* (Sentencing Judgment), 29 Nov. 1996, Case No. IT-96-22-T (Trial Chamber I, ICTY) paras. 64–6 (the tribunal clearly rejects rehabilitation as a possible rationale for international criminal law).

[175] See Simpson, 'War Crimes', at 19–21.

[176] See Art. 13, 'Lieber Manual'; Art. 84, 'Oxford Manual' on the Laws of War on Land, (1880) 5 *Annuaire de l'Institut de droit international* 156, both *reprinted in* Schindler and Toman, *Laws of Armed Conflict*, at 6 and 47; Lassa Oppenheim, *International Law*, Ronald Roxburgh ed., 3rd edn (London: Longmans, 1921) II, 342. Whether this was grounded purely in municipal jurisdiction or also in the law of nations is not altogether clear: see above, p. 78.

[177] Art. 218, Treaty of Versailles; Commission on the Responsibility of the Authors of War and on Enforcement of Penalties, Report Presented to the Preliminary Peace Conference, Versailles, 29 March 1919, *reprinted in* (1920) 14 *Am. J Int'l L* 95, 112–24.

[178] See Fraenkel, *Military Occupation*, at 47–68.

[179] Art. 30 of the 1929 Geneva Convention on Wounded and Sick refers to the duty to 'repress' violations.

[180] See *British Manual of Military Law*, Hugh Godley ed., 6th edn (London: HMSO, 1914) 302–4; David, *Principes*, at 550; Oppenheim, *International Law* (1921) II, at 344; G. I. A. D. Draper, 'The Modern Pattern of War Criminality', (1976) 6 *Israel YB Hum. Rts* 9, 16.

repetition and firmness of judicial statements in this respect grounded the criminalisation of breaches of the laws and customs of war, which was then partly codified and partly expanded in the 1949 Geneva Conventions provision on 'grave breaches' (Arts. 50/51/130/147). Also in the aftermath of the Second World War, individual penal responsibility replaced state responsibility as the main sanction for violations of the laws and customs of war, contrary to what had happened after the First World War.

The generality and centrality of individual criminal responsibility was confirmed not only by the more recent 1977 Protocol I, which expanded the list of 'grave breaches' found in the Geneva Conventions (Art. 85, Protocol I), but also by the creation of the International Criminal Tribunals for former Yugoslavia and Rwanda. The Security Council, in creating the ICTR, defined its jurisdiction as including individual responsibility for violations of common Article 3 of the Geneva Conventions and Protocol II (Art. 4, ICTR Statute). More generally, in the *Tadić* decision on jurisdiction, the Appeals Chamber took an even more expansive view of the place of criminal responsibility in the framework of humanitarian law, to conclude that Article 3 of the ICTY Statute referring to violations of the laws or customs of war implied the criminalisation of *all* serious violations of humanitarian law, including customary law, common Article 3 and any other provision of the 1949 Geneva Conventions, Protocol II, and any agreement binding upon the parties to an armed conflict.[181] The *Tadić* decision completes the shift in humanitarian law to a blanket criminal responsibility for all violations of customary and conventional humanitarian law, which has now been codified in the Statute of the International Criminal Court (Art. 8).[182]

---

[181] *The Prosecutor v. Tadić* (Decision on the Defence Motion for Interlocutory Appeal on Jurisdiction), 2 Oct. 1995, Case No. IT-94-1-AR72 (Appeals Chamber, ICTY) 49–52 paras. 87–93. This is echoed in Art. 20 of the International Law Commission's 1996 Draft Code of Crimes Against the Peace and Security of Mankind. See also the 1996 revised text of Art. 14(2) of Protocol II of the 1981 Conventional Weapons Convention, introducing penal responsibility for violation of its provisions: (1996) 35 Int'l Leg. Mat. 1206, 1215.

[182] See also *The Prosecutor v. Delalić, Mucić, Delić and Landzo* (the *Celebici* case) (Appeal Judgment), 20 Feb. 2001, Case No. IT-96-21-A (Appeals Chamber, ICTY) 46–53 paras. 153–81; *The Prosecutor v. Akayesu* (Judgment), 2 Sept. 1998, Case No. ICTR-96-4-T (Trial Chamber I, ICTR) paras. 611–17. It is interesting to note that the establishment of the United Nations Compensation Commission stands out from the general progression away from state responsibility towards individual penal sanctions. As mentioned earlier, the UNCC represents at least in part a return to state responsibility for violations of humanitarian law, although that basis of Iraq's responsibility seems to

We move from the centre to the periphery when looking at the place of individual responsibility in human rights as compared to humanitarian law. A number of specialised treaties related to the protection of human rights provide for criminal responsibility of the individual perpetrator of designated violations. For example, the Genocide Convention (Art. IV), the International Convention on the Suppression and Punishment of the Crime of Apartheid (Art. III), the Convention Against Torture (Arts. 4–7) and the Supplementary Convention on the Abolition of Slavery (Art. 3) all provide for criminal responsibility of the individual.[183] As the *Pinochet* case before British courts graphically illustrates with respect to the Convention Against Torture, such treaty provisions may be used effectively and have a significant political impact.[184] The incorporation of individual penal responsibility in the framework of human rights law, however, remains unusual. In the vast majority of human rights conventions, including all general universal and regional instruments, we find no requirement or power to criminally sanction perpetrators of serious human rights violations similar to what was incorporated in humanitarian law conventions.

Within general international law, the most significant penal norm which can be linked to human rights is the prohibition of genocide and crimes against humanity. As noted earlier, the prohibition of genocide and crimes against humanity has been accepted as customary for quite some time.[185] The customary norm includes not only the prohibition of genocide but also its punishment, that is the penal responsibility of the

have been nearly totally subsumed into responsibility for illegal use of force (see the discussion in chapter 1, pp. 51–3). Despite the large number of Iraqi prisoners of war in the hands of the Coalition Forces, little was done regarding the possibility of an international effort to bring to trial those responsible for the numerous violations of humanitarian law in Kuwait. The Kuwaiti Government has been left to take action alone in that respect, in stark contrast to the massive international compensation effort. See Adam Roberts, 'The Laws of War: Problems of Implementation in Contemporary Conflict', in *Law in Humanitarian Crises – How Can International Humanitarian Law be Made Effective in Armed Conflict?* (Luxembourg: European Communities, 1995) I, 13, 53–5 (also published in (1995) 6 *Duke J Int'l & Comp. L* 11–78).

[183] As for whether these instruments should properly be seen as falling within human rights law, see above, pp. 68–9.

[184] *R v. Bow Street Metropolitan Stipendiary Magistrate, ex parte Pinochet (No. 3)*, (1999) 38 Int'l Leg. Mat. 581.

[185] See Advisory Opinion, *Reservations to the Convention on the Prevention and Punishment of the Crime of Genocide*, [1951] ICJ Rep. 15. Indeed, the prohibition of crimes against humanity was presented as already part of customary law in the work of the Nuremberg International Military Tribunal.

authors of such an international crime.[186] Penal responsibility for genocide and crimes against humanity, however, is grounded only partly in
the sanction of violations of human rights in that there is a critical collective dimension to both the crimes and their repression. As stated by
the Appeals Chamber of the ICTY in the *Erdemović* case, crimes against
humanity 'address the perpetrator's conduct not only towards the immediate victim but also towards the whole of humankind', so that it
is 'the concept of humanity as victim which essentially characterises
crimes against humanity'.[187] The ICTR in the *Akayesu* and other cases
concurred in its conclusion that 'the victim of the crime of genocide
is the group itself and not only the individual'.[188] This last remark seems
more appropriate in relation to the crime of genocide than to crimes
against humanity, in light of a recent trend to lessen the significance
of a clearly identifiable collectivity as victim with respect to the latter.
This can be seen in the judgment of the Appeals Chamber of the ICTY
in the *Tadić* case, where the Tribunal denied that a discriminatory intent
was part of the definition of the crime against humanity.[189] As a result,
random and indiscriminate violence against a civilian population could
constitute a crime against humanity.[190] This is supported by the definition of crimes against humanity found in the Statute of the ICC (Art. 7),
where a discriminatory intent is not a general requirement. There remains a clear collective dimension to the criminalisation of genocide
and crimes against humanity, norms inspired by international human
rights but protecting interests which are broader than those embodied
in human rights norms.[191]

There is no historic equivalent in human rights to the general penal
responsibility for violations of the laws and customs of war, and state
practice in relation to punishment of fundamental rights rarely refers to

[186] See *The Prosecutor v. Tadić* (Opinion and Judgment), 7 May 1997, Case No. IT-94-1-T (Trial
Chamber II, ICTY) paras. 618–23; *Nulyarimma v. Thompson*, [1999] FCA 1192 (Fed. Ct
App., Australia); Bassiouni, *Crimes Against Humanity*.

[187] *The Prosecutor v. Erdemović* (Judgment), 7 Oct. 1997, Case No. IT-96-22-A (Appeals
Chamber, ICTY) para. 21 (Joint Sep. Op. Judges McDonald and Vohrah); *The Prosecutor
v. Erdemović* (Sentencing Judgment), 29 Nov. 1996, Case No. IT-96-22-T (Trial Chamber I,
ICTY) para. 28.

[188] *The Prosecutor v. Akayesu* (Judgment), 2 Sept. 1998, Case No. ICTR-96-4-T (Trial Chamber
I, ICTR) para. 521; *The Prosecutor v. Rutaganda* (Judgment), 6 Dec. 1999, ICTR-96-3-T
(Trial Chamber, ICTR) para. 60; *The Prosecutor v. Musema* (Judgment), 27 Jan. 2000,
ICTR-96-13-T (Trial Chamber, ICTR) para. 165.

[189] *The Prosecutor v. Tadić* (Appeals Judgment), 15 July 1999, Case No. IT-94-1-A (Appeals
Chamber, ICTY) paras. 281–305. Note that a discriminatory intent is explicitly
required by Art. 3 of the ICTR Statute: *Rutaganda*, paras. 73–6.

[190] *Tadić* (Appeals Judgment), para. 285.

[191] *Akayesu*, para. 469.

international standards. The International Law Commission's work on a Draft Code of Crimes Against the Peace and Security of Mankind has provided a forum for exploring the place of individual responsibility as a sanction for serious human rights violations. As was noted, the Commission had proposed in 1991 that the systematic or mass violations of human rights be considered an international crime (Art. 21) calling for the individual criminal responsibility of the perpetrator (Art. 5), but that proposal was withdrawn in the face of opposition by states in the Sixth Committee as well as academic criticism that it did not correspond to customary law.[192]

The adoption of a broad principle of criminal responsibility for perpetrators of serious violations of human rights as proposed by the International Law Commission is of course not unimaginable. It would, however, require a significant reinterpretation of human rights law, a shift of focus in its normative structure, to envision the direct imposition of obligations on all individuals, given that individual responsibility for state and private action is presently found only in some specialised treaties like the Convention on the Prohibition of Torture.[193] Such a shift may well be starting, as signalled by various statements of members of the House of Lords in the *Pinochet* decisions, albeit in *obiter*, that the criminality of torture was not limited to the Convention on the Prohibition of Torture but was also to be found in international customary law.[194] Although little evidence is given in support of such a statement which, unlike the mere illegality of torture, appears indeed difficult to sustain under the canons of customary law, it does signal an interesting opening to international penal responsibility of individuals for violations of human rights without the collective dimension necessarily present in the repression of genocide and crimes against humanity.[195]

---

[192] See above, pp. 72–3; Paul Peters,'Commentary on the Draft Code of Crimes – Article 21', (1993) 11 *Nouvelles études pénales* 249–60; Christian Tomuschat, 'Crimes Against the Peace and Security of Mankind and the Recalcitrant Third State', in Yoram Dinstein and Mala Tabory eds., *War Crimes in International Law* (Dordrecht: Nijhoff, 1996) 41, 48–50.

[193] See Ratner, 'Schizophrenias', at 251–6.

[194] *R v. Bow Street Metropolitan Stipendiary Magistrate, ex parte Pinochet (No. 3)*, (1999) 38 Int'l Leg. Mat. 581, 585 (Lord Browne-Wilkinson), 650 (Lord Millet). See *The Prosecutor* v. *Furundžija* (Judgment), 10 Dec. 1998, Case No. IT-95-17/1-T (Trial Chamber, ICTY) paras. 143–6; Roland Bank, 'Der Fall Pinochet: Aufbruch zu neuen Ufern bei der Verfolgung von Menschenrechtsverletzungen', (1999) 59 *Zeitschrift für auslandisches öffentliches Recht und Völkerrecht* 677, 682–8.

[195] This is specifically underlined by Lord Millet. *Pinochet*'s first progeny was the brief indictment in Senegal in February 2000 of the former Chadian head of state, Issène Habré, for acts of torture committed while in office.

As such, a customary international crime of torture seems a promising candidate for the role of Trojan horse whereby criminality for human rights violations may be introduced in general international law.

DUTY TO PROSECUTE

Given the obstacles remaining to be overcome before the International Criminal Court can enforce the penal responsibility of individuals who have committed crimes against international law, and given the limited and optional jurisdiction of such a court, the reality of individual responsibility rests largely in the existence of a willingness and a duty on the part of states to enforce such a norm. The presence of a duty to prosecute can be taken as a reflection of the centrality of individual penal responsibility in the normative framework of human rights and humanitarian law.

Turning first to humanitarian law, a clear state duty to prosecute or extradite is created in the 1949 Geneva Conventions (Arts. 49/50/129/146) and, by extension, Protocol I (Arts. 85 and 86(1)) with respect to grave breaches (Arts. 50/51/130/147) of the Conventions and Protocol. The rationale of this obligation of *aut dedere aut judicare* is that every state party to the Conventions or Protocol has universal jurisdiction to prosecute perpetrators of grave breaches, but that this obligation is absolute only for the international community as a whole. In other words, no state is under an absolute duty to prosecute. It always has the option of extraditing the suspected war criminal to another High Contracting Party which has made a *prima facie* case against that individual. This implies that the state to which the suspect is extradited is both under a similar obligation to try or extradite, and intends to prosecute the person. Conversely, the detaining state must prosecute if no other state requests extradition and there is sufficient evidence to warrant prosecution.[196] The elements of this system in principle collectively ensure that all perpetrators of grave breaches shall be prosecuted.[197]

The conventional duty to prosecute or extradite attaches only to narrowly defined grave breaches but, as we saw earlier, the criminalisation of violations of humanitarian law now extends far beyond that category to encompass all serious violations of humanitarian law, including the 1949 Geneva Conventions, Protocols I and II, and the laws and customs

---

[196] Pictet, III, at 623; International Law Commission, Draft Code of Crimes Against the Peace and Security of Mankind, at 51–5 (Art. 9 commentary para. 7).

[197] See M. Cherif Bassiouni and Edward Wise, *Aut Dedere Aut Judicare – The Duty to Extradite or Prosecute in International Law* (Dordrecht: Nijhoff, 1995) 26; David, *Principes*, at 643.

of war. Even if it is accepted that universal jurisdiction attaches to 'other' war crimes, which is by no means an undisputed statement, there is very little in either conventional instruments or customary law to suggest that an obligation *aut dedere aut judicare* would extend to such crimes. The Geneva Conventions and Protocol I do provide that states 'shall take measures necessary for the suppression of all acts contrary to the provisions' of the Conventions and Protocol which are not grave breaches (Arts. 49/50/129/146; Art. 86(1), Protocol I). This duty to 'suppress' ('faire cesser') other violations, however, stands in contrast to the duty to 'repress' ('réprimer') grave breaches found in the same provisions.[198] The ICTY Appeals Chamber in the *Celebici* case suggested that the combination of the duty to suppress other violations and the duty to ensure respect of the Geneva Conventions could, arguably, mean that states are required to criminalise non-grave breaches under domestic law.[199] While a number of states have enacted, since 1995, provisions criminalising some non-grave breaches of the Geneva Conventions, in particular common Article 3 and Protocol II, such statutes remains rare, with few actual prosecutions, and practically no *opinio juris* to suggest that states were reacting to a perceived duty to act as such.

The International Law Commission in its 1996 Draft Code of Crimes Against the Peace and Security of Mankind proposed the establishment of a general duty to try or extradite with respect to all listed crimes (Art. 9), including war crimes committed in a systematic manner or on a large scale (Art. 20).[200] There is, again, very little state practice to buffer a claim that a general duty to prosecute or extradite all war criminals has grown to be accepted as a customary norm, and it seems unlikely that such a duty exists today.[201]

---

[198] The ICRC commentaries to the Conventions and Protocol I indicate that the duty to suppress may include the prosecution of perpetrators of non-grave breaches of the convention, as well as other types of measures (e.g. administrative, disciplinary), which would imply a certain discretion of states to appreciate which means are the most appropriate to suppress other violations: Pictet, III, at 624; Claude Pilloud et al., *Commentary on the Additional Protocols of 8 June 1977 to the Geneva Conventions of 12 August 1949* (Geneva: Nijhoff, 1987) 975 para. 3402; Theodor Meron, 'Is International Law Moving Towards Criminalization?', (1998) 9 *Eur. J Int'l L* 18, 23.

[199] *The Prosecutor v. Delalić, Mucić, Delić and Landzo* (the *Celebici* case) (Appeals Judgment), 20 Feb. 2001, Case No. IT-96-21-A (Appeals Chamber, ICTY) 50 paras. 165-7.

[200] UN Doc. A/SI/10 (1996). This is also suggested in General Assembly Resolution 3074 (XXVIII) on Principles of International Cooperation in the Detection, Arrest, Extradition and Punishment of Persons Guilty of War Crimes and Crimes Against Humanity.

[201] This led the Institut de droit international merely to 'urge' states to prosecute or extradite the authors of war crimes, whereas the initial draft of the resolution

Turning to human rights law, it may seem paradoxical to enquire into the existence of a state duty to prosecute given the conclusion reached earlier that there is no general principle of individual criminal responsibility for violations of human rights. Indeed, the only instances of conventional obligations to try or extradite perpetrators of human rights violations are found in treaties which specifically provide for individual penal responsibility, such as the Genocide Convention (Arts. VI–VII), the Convention on Apartheid (Arts. IV and XI) and the Convention Against Torture (Art. 7).[202] Likewise, the 1996 Draft Code of Crimes Against the Peace and Security of Mankind provides for a duty of *aut dedere aut judicare* only in respect of the three core crimes of aggression, genocide and crimes against humanity, in addition to war crimes examined in the previous paragraph (Art. 9). No general duty is suggested in the latest draft vis-à-vis human rights violations.

A series of reports by the Inter-American Commission on Human Rights regarding the validity of amnesty laws passed by newly democratic regimes was seen by some as implying a state duty to prosecute all human rights violations under general human rights instruments. In the reports on amnesty statutes in Argentina, Uruguay, El Salvador and Chile, the Inter-American Commission found that the American Convention on Human Rights imposed a duty to prosecute violations of the Convention on the basis of the right to a remedy (Art. 25), interpreted in conjunction with the rights to life (Art. 4), physical integrity (Art. 5) and due process (Art. 8), and the state's duty to ensure the rights entrenched in the Convention (Art. 1).[203] It must be noted at the outset that, in the

provided that states were bound to do so: 'Resolution on the Application of International Humanitarian Law and Fundamental Human Rights, in Armed Conflicts in which Non-State Entities are Parties', (1999) 68:2 *Annuaire de l'Institut de droit international* 282 and 397. One instance of state practice which does allude to such a duty is the 1995 Dayton Peace Agreement, which specifically refers in Article IX to the 'obligation of all Parties to cooperate in the investigation and prosecution of war crimes and other violations of international humanitarian law'.

[202] To this list could be added: Inter-American Convention to Prevent and Punish Torture (1985), *reprinted in* Brownlie, *Basic Documents*, at 531 (Art. 14); Inter-American Convention on Forced Disappearance of Persons (1994), OAS Doc. OEA/Ser.P.AG/doc.3/114/94 rev.1; Convention on the Safety of United Nations and Associated Personnel, UN Doc. A/RES/49/59 (1994), Art. 14 (although its characterisation as a human rights convention is more debatable). See Naomi Roht-Arriaza, 'Sources in International Treaties of an Obligation to Investigate, Prosecute and Provide Redress', in Roht-Arriaza, *Impunity*, at 24–38.

[203] Inter-American Commission on Human Rights, Report No. 26/92 (El Salvador), OAS Doc. OEA/Ser.L/V/II.82 doc. (1992); Report No. 29/92 (Uruguay), OAS Doc. OEA/Ser.L/V/II.82 doc. 25 (1992); Report No. 24/92 (Argentina), OAS Doc.

case of Argentina and Uruguay, the procedural links between civil and criminal suits meant that the amnesty statutes had the supplementary effect of rendering impossible any civil actions. Some have suggested that it is not clear whether the Inter-American Commission on Human Rights would have reached a similar result had civil redress been available to victims of serious violations of human rights.[204]

The reports of the Inter-American Commission on amnesty laws must be seen in the light of several decisions in the Inter-American and other human rights regimes bearing on the existence of a duty to prosecute. In the *Velásquez Rodríguez* case, in the wake of the Inter-American Court of Human Rights' finding that Honduras had breached its duty to 'prevent, punish and investigate any violations of the rights' in the American Convention, parents of the disappeared asked for an injunction requiring Honduras to prosecute those responsible.[205] The Court noted that 'the objective of international human rights law is not to punish those individuals who are guilty of violations, but rather to protect the victims and to provide for the reparation of damages resulting from the acts of the state responsible'.[206] It declined to issue an injunction, awarding only monetary compensation, a decision which seems irreconcilable with the existence of a general duty to prosecute under the American Convention. The Human Rights Committee was asked more directly in an individual petition, *HCMA* v. *The Netherlands*, whether the victim of a violation of human rights could allege a breach of the International Covenant on Civil and Political Rights if no punitive sanction was brought to bear against the perpetrator.[207] The Committee answered in the negative, finding no duty to prosecute specific violators of human rights. A similar

OEA/Ser.L/V/II.82 doc. 24 (1992) (all three are *reprinted in* (1993) 14 *Hum. Rts LJ* 167); *Hermosilla* v. *Chile*, Case No. 10843, Rep. No. 36/96, OAS Doc. OEA/Ser.L/V/II.95 doc. 7 at 156 (1997). See also 'Report of the Committee Against Torture', *OR, HM and MS* v. *Argentina*, Cases No. 1-3/1988, decision of 23 November 1989, UN Doc. A/45/44 Annex VI; *Bleier* v. *Uruguay*, Case No. 30/1978, UN Doc. CCPR/C/OP/1 (1985); Kai Ambos, 'Impunity and International Criminal Law – A Case Study on Colombia, Peru, Bolivia, Chile and Argentina', (1997) 18 *Hum. Rts LJ* 1–15; Kokott, 'No Impunity', at 153–9; Diane Orentlicher 'Settling Accounts: The Duty to Prosecute Human Rights Violations of a Prior Regime', (1991) 100 *Yale LJ* 2539, 2568.
[204] See Naomi Roht-Arriaza, 'Special Problems of a Duty to Prosecute: Derogations, Amnesties, Statutes of Limitation, and Superior Order', in Roht-Arriaza, *Impunity*, at 57, 62.
[205] *Velásquez-Rodríguez* v. *Honduras*, I/A Court HR, Judgment of 18 July 1988, Ser. C No. 4, para. 166.
[206] *Ibid.*, para. 134.
[207] Comm. No. 213/1986, UN Doc. A/44/40 (1989) para. 11.6. See also *SE* v. *Argentina*, Comm. No. 275/1988, UN Doc. A/45/40 (1990).

conclusion was reached by the European Court of Human Rights in *Ireland v. United Kingdom.*[208]

There is no inconsistency between the positions of the Inter-American Commission on Human Rights and other human rights bodies, as they all reflect both the state's duty to ensure rights and the individual's right to a remedy. Pursuant to the state's duty to ensure rights entrenched in the various human rights instruments, it must adopt means for the protection of fundamental rights, including the sanction of violations of these rights. Amnesty laws represent a blanket and absolute failure of the duty to ensure rights, because they can be seen as encouraging rather than discouraging further violation of basic human rights.[209] As noted by the Inter-American Court of Human Rights in the *Paniagua Morales* case, lack of efficient prosecution coupled with absence of civil remedies creates a climate of impunity which is inconsistent with the state's duty to ensure human rights.[210] The state is left with a margin of appreciation to decide, in individual cases, which is the most appropriate reaction to a violation, whether prosecution, compensation, education, public awareness campaign, truth commission, and so on. For example, the South African Truth and Reconciliation Commission would not contravene that state's duties under human rights instruments despite the fact that the Commission does have power to grant amnesties for political crimes. From the victim's perspective, there is no right to every possible remedy in regard to each violation, but rather a right to some remedy which is appropriate to the violation. Under such a construct, there is no general duty to prosecute each violation of human rights in international human rights instruments, a conclusion consistent with state practice under both conventional and customary law.[211] Even with

---

[208] (1978) Eur. Ct Hum. Rts, Ser. A, vol. 25, at 95 para. 10. See Rosalyn Higgins, *Problems and Process – International Law and How We Use It* (Oxford: Clarendon, 1994) 158.

[209] See Human Rights Committee, General Comment No. 20 (44), UN Doc. CCPR/C/21/Rev.1/Add.3 (1992) para. 15 ('Amnesties are generally incompatible with the duty of States to investigate such acts; to guarantee freedom from such acts within their jurisdiction; and to ensure that they do not occur in the future. States may not deprive individuals of the right to an effective remedy including compensation and such full rehabilitation as may be possible'); Human Rights Committee, 'Annual Report to the General Assembly on the Work of its 57th Session', UN Doc. A/51/40 (1996) para. 347 (Review of Peru's periodic report); Roberto Ago, 'Fourth Report on State Responsibility', [1972] 2 YB Int'l L Com'n 71.

[210] *Paniagua Morales v. Guatemala*, Judgment of 8 March 1998, Ser. C No. 37, paras. 173–4.

[211] See Higgins, *Problems and Process*, at 157–8; Ratner and Abrams, *Accountability*, at 133–4; Christina Cerna, 'The Inter-American Court of Human Rights', in Mark Janis ed., *International Courts for the Twenty-First Century* (Dordrecht: Nijhoff, 1992) 117, 147;

respect to customary crimes against humanity, there seems to be little state practice and only scant *opinio juris* to support the existence of a duty to prosecute.[212] Given the powerful social and political arguments in favour of prosecuting perpetrators of human rights violations in certain cases, the state will often and rightly choose prosecution, but human rights norms seem to leave that choice up to the state.

Despite the uncertainty regarding a general customary duty to prosecute war crimes which are not grave breaches as defined in the 1949 Geneva Conventions and Protocol I, the existence of an obligation *aut dedere aut judicare* with respect to the most egregious violations of the Conventions and Protocol stands in stark contrast to the lack of any equivalent in either treaty or customary human rights law (with genocide, crimes against humanity and torture as distinct exceptions). Individual obligations and penal responsibility emerge as the nucleus of humanitarian law, on which the framework of the entire system is built. Human rights law, on the contrary, was essentially built on the idea that the state would be the menace against individual human rights. As such, individual obligations and responsibility are largely absent and appear as an unsteady addition to the edifice of human rights.

Naomi Roht-Arriaza, 'Nontreaty Sources of the Obligation to Investigate and Prosecute', in Roht-Arriaza, *Impunity*, at 39, 41; Marco Sassòli, 'Mise en oeuvre du droit international humanitaire et du droit international des droits de l'homme', (1987) 43 *Annuaire suisse de droit international* 24, 34; Oscar Schachter, 'The Obligation to Implement the Covenant in Domestic Law', in Louis Henkin ed., *The International Bill of Rights* (New York: Columbia UP, 1981) 311, 326; Michael Scharf, 'The Letter of the Law: The Scope of the International Legal Obligation to Prosecute Human Rights Crimes', (1996) 59 *L & Contemp. Prob.* 41, 48–52. The point is clearly distinct from the question of whether the duty to respect and ensure rights implies an obligation to criminalise certain violations of human rights under municipal law. For instance, in *X and Y v. The Netherlands* ((1985) 91 Eur. Ct Hum. Rts, Ser. A, para. 27), the European Court of Human Rights found that the impossibility of prosecuting the author of a rape was a violation of the victim's rights to privacy. Criminalisation of an offence may indeed constitute a necessary part of deterrence, but in any case it does not imply a duty to prosecute under international law: see above, note 12.

[212] See Scharf, 'Letter of the Law', at 52–9. In *Nulyarimma v. Thompson*, [1999] FCA 1192 (Fed. Ct App., Australia), both Wilcox JA (para. 18) and Merkel JA (para. 141) find a customary duty to extradite or prosecute authors of genocide, but very little support is proffered to substantiate that conclusion.

Conclusion to Part I

The ultimate aims of human rights and humanitarian law may be the protection of the individual, but they are constructed to achieve this goal in significantly different ways. An analysis of the normative frameworks of these two legal systems reveals that each is fundamentally shaped by the place occupied by the individual. In human rights law, the individual is directly given fundamental rights by treaties and customary law, whereas in humanitarian law it is obligations which are imposed on the individual directly by conventional and customary law. Attempts to read individual obligations into the framework of human rights and see rights in humanitarian law norms are unconvincing because they are at odds with the basic thrust of each system. The differences in procedural capacity and responsibility are simply the consequences flowing from the initial emphasis on rights and obligations in human rights and humanitarian law.

The choice of a different nucleus in the two legal systems studied here is not coincidental nor the result of arbitrariness. It is the mirror of the vastly different realities which human rights and humanitarian law norms seek to address. In the context of a relationship between a state and private persons taking place in normal socio-economic conditions, it seems eminently suitable to entrust into the hands of individuals the tools which will enable them to defend the fundamental rights and freedoms necessary for their full development. An array of mechanisms is available to the individual, including judicial proceedings, the media, the political process, etc. That human rights law is posited on such a 'normal' context is reflected in the fact that, in times of emergency threatening the life of the nation, the vast majority of rights may be suspended by the state. Armed conflict is the consummate emergency threatening the life of the nation. Humanitarian law is constructed to apply only in a context where relationships between individuals and authority no longer follow normal patterns. In such a context, it is not suitable to insist on a rights-based approach, because it refers us back to the holders of such rights, the individuals, who are typically powerless and vulnerable whether they be combatants, prisoners of war or civilians. During an armed conflict, individuals need to be protected more than empowered, and that can be done much more effectively through the creation of public order norms addressed to those wielding the power over vulnerable individuals. That is why humanitarian law is constructed around the direct imposition of obligations on individuals who wield some power over others.

Does this fundamental difference between human rights and human-itarian law mean that no constructive cross-pollination can take place at the level of their normative frameworks? That is clearly not the les-son which should be drawn from the analysis in Part I. On the con-trary, each system, in responding to the peculiar demands of its field of application, has generated indigenous concepts which may be bene-ficial to the other. Such cross-pollination, however, must be done with an appreciation of the fundamental differences between the normative frameworks of human rights and humanitarian law. For example, the incorporation into Protocol I of Article 75 granting procedural rights to all those affected by the conflict, clearly inspired by Article 14 of the International Covenant on Civil and Political Rights, is appropriate be-cause Article 75 will become applicable only in the context of judicial proceedings, where the individual is more likely to be capable of holding rights and exercising them. Conversely, the possible extension of indi-vidual penal responsibility for serious state violations of human rights, on the model of the repression of grave breaches of humanitarian law, could help lessen impunity and contribute to greater compliance with human rights in certain categories of situations. The mixed experience of war crimes prosecutions, however, should teach us not to expect a sea change in favour of compliance with human rights norms as a re-sult of this possible development.[1] These are but two examples where cross-pollination seems not only possible but even highly desirable, and it will be left to those overseeing the development of human rights and humanitarian law to assess each time whether any given institution ought to be borrowed from the other system.

Looking at the normative frameworks of the two legal systems, like the study of architectural drawings of a building, reveals much of the structure of the edifice, but by no means provides a complete picture. We must move from a two-dimensional analysis to go deeper into the driving forces behind human rights and humanitarian law. Lon Fuller underscored the connection between the place of duties in a legal system and the principle of reciprocity, finding in the latter the 'pervasive bond' holding together the entire system.[2] On the basis of the findings of Part I on the fundamentally distinct role of duties – and rights – in human rights and humanitarian law, the next part explores the role played by reciprocity in each field to assess to what extent it is central to their creation and stability.

[1] See Gerry Simpson, 'War Crimes: A Critical Introduction', in Timothy McCormack and Gerry Simpson eds., *The Law of War Crimes* (The Hague: Kluwer, 1997) 1 at 29.

[2] Lon Fuller, *The Morality of Law*, rev. edn (New Haven: Yale UP, 1969) 19–22.

PART II • RECIPROCITY

Reciprocity seems to be the most effective strategy for maintaining cooperation among egoists.
Robert Keohane, *After Hegemony: Cooperation and Discord in the World Political Economy* (1984)

As a horizontal system, international law rests upon the logic of reciprocity in its entirety.
Bruno Simma, 'Reciprocity' in *Encyclopedia of Public International Law* (1984)

Introduction

International law, being a system based on the formal equality and sovereignty of states, has arisen largely out of the exchange of reciprocal rights and duties between states.[1] Reciprocity refers to the interdependence of obligations assumed by participants within the schemes created by a legal system.[2] In other words, obligations are reciprocal if their creation, execution and termination depend, in a general manner, on the existence of connected obligations on others. Reciprocity may be fundamental but it is also variable: distinctions must be made according to the type of norms and the kind of relationship they embody. A regional trade treaty and the customary precautionary principle in environmental law, for example, will both imply elements of reciprocity, albeit distinct ones.[3]

Human rights and humanitarian law have been said largely to escape from reciprocity because both essentially aim to protect the interests of individuals rather than states. It would follow that, in the frameworks of human rights and humanitarian law, reciprocity occupies a much smaller place than in the rest of international law. This could provide a rationale for the development of institutions particular to these two areas of law and the unsuitability of some principles of general international law. The ensuing discussion examines various elements of human rights and humanitarian law to determine whether they indicate a relevance for reciprocity markedly more limited than in general international law, and whether similar patterns appear in this respect in both

[1] See Emanuele Calò, *Il principio di reciprocità* (Milan: Giuffrè, 1993); Cristina Campiglio, *Il principio di reciprocità nel diritto dei trattati* (Padua: CEDAM, 1995) 45–56; Emmanuel Decaux, *La réciprocité en droit international* (Paris: LGDJ, 1980); Rosalyn Higgins, *Problems and Process – International Law and How We Use It* (Oxford: Clarendon, 1994) 16; Georg Schwarzenberger, *The Frontiers of International Law* (London: Stevens & Sons, 1962) 15–16 and 29–34; Georges Scelle, 'Règles générales du droit de la paix', (1933-IV) 46 *Recueil des cours* 327, 672; Bruno Simma, *Das Reziprozitätselement im zustandekommen völkerrechtlicher Verträge* (Berlin: Duncker & Humblot, 1972) 43–9; Bruno Simma, 'Reciprocity', in Rudolf Bernhardt ed., [Instalment] 7 *Encyclopedia of Public International Law* (Amsterdam: North-Holland, 1984) 400; Michel Virally, 'Le principe de réciprocité dans le droit international contemporain', (1967-III) 122 *Recueil des cours* 1, 63.

[2] Reciprocity refers here to a general principle underlying many rights and obligations in international law, and not merely to one of its forms termed the 'condition of reciprocity' or *inadimplenti non est adimplendum*, which is a special rule of the law of treaties permitting a state to suspend or terminate provisions of a treaty following a material breach by another party. The condition of reciprocity is discussed in chapter 4, pp. 163–81.

[3] See Lon Fuller, *The Morality of Law*, rev. edn (New Haven: Yale UP, 1969) 20–2. This statement is more fully justified in the following pages.

areas of law. The need to draw on and compare the role of reciprocity in human rights and humanitarian law informs the wider debate as to the degree of similitude of these two systems. Reciprocity has been branded as either supporting or disproving this similitude.[4]

States, like individuals, generally consent to being bound by obligations only if there is *quid pro quo* of some sort, although the existence of a corresponding obligation is not a condition of the binding character of either obligation. Indeed, this need not be expressed in the language of obligations, and sociological and anthropological studies have shown that reciprocity is 'a key intervening variable through which shared social rules are enabled to yield social stability'.[5] Legal systems usually incorporate this basic principle and therefore rely on some form of reciprocity. The presence of such an element of reciprocity is said to lend legal systems an appearance of being grounded in justice, while at the same time obscuring the powers behind and within the systems.[6] Far from being an end in itself, however, reciprocity also has been presented as a middle stage in imperfect legal systems, where the formal equality of all participants is not yet fully entrenched. To ensure that its obligations are not unilateral vis-à-vis certain participants in such systems, a state accepts a duty towards another only in so far as that specific state is similarly obligated. In a system where the equality of participants has been achieved, obligations are no longer synallagmatic and reciprocity is transformed from immediate to systemic.[7] Obligations are not tied to those of other states, but rather to the continued existence of the system. It can be said that reciprocity moves from a bilateral to a systemic level, whereby the state accepts to bear an obligation on the basis of a legitimate expectation that the system will generally ensure the imposition of similar or corresponding obligations on all members of the system. Immediate reciprocity would thus be a transitional stage, a means to enable the attainment of full equality and the exclusive reliance on systemic reciprocity.[8]

---

[4] See the symposium on links between human rights and humanitarian law in (1991) 2 *Human Rights Bulletin* 1–60.

[5] Alvin Gouldner, 'The Norm of Reciprocity: A Preliminary Statement', (1960) 25 *Am. Sociol. Rev.* 161. See also Howard Becker, *Man in Reciprocity* (New York: Prager, 1956).

[6] Georg Schwarzenberger, '*Jus Pacis ac Belli*? Prolegomena to a Sociology of International Law', (1943) 37 *Am. J Int'l L* 460, 478.

[7] This parallels a distinction made by some international relations theorists between 'specific' and 'diffuse' reciprocity: Robert Keohane, 'Reciprocity in International Relations', (1986) 40 *Int'l Org.* 1, 4.

[8] Decaux, *La réciprocité*, at 9 ('Le problème du droit n'est pas tant l'abandon de la réciprocité que son dépassement dans des formes de solidarité plus larges: elle se

In legal systems, the passage from reciprocity to equality goes hand in hand with centralisation. In a decentralised system, obligations are usually created and enforced along bilateral lines, given the lack of a central authority to impose norms. This can be the case even if rights and obligations are contained in multilateral agreements: such agreements can represent the aggregate of bilateralisable relationships formed by the parties. For instance, conventional as well as customary rules on diplomatic privileges and immunities can be construed as creating, on an individual basis, a distinct set of rights and obligations for each state party with respect to each other party. Reciprocity plays an obvious role in this type of relationship.[9] General international law, based on the independent sovereignty of all states, is an example of a decentralised system where reciprocity can be expected to constitute a key element.[10]

In centralised systems, there is a much smaller need to rely on reciprocity, given the presence of a central authority which can act to both impose norms and enforce them. Equality among participants is usually a requirement for this type of system, and immediate reciprocity between participants becomes less essential. Relationships stemming from multilateral agreements which cannot be construed as creating a multiplicity of parallel bilateral relationships tend to lead to the establishment of institutionalised systems.[11] Such non-bilateralisable relationships are not grounded in immediate reciprocity, but in the fashioning of a normative public order, a bundle of shared commitments and values which underlie systemic reciprocity.[12]

dissout dans l'égalité générale. En ce sens, la réciprocité est bien une étape entre l'altérité et l'égalité'); Fuller, *Morality*, at 209; Keohane, 'Reciprocity', at 21 and 25.

[9] See Ian Brownlie, *Principles of Public International Law*, 3rd edn (Oxford: Clarendon, 1979) 340 (in a passage omitted from later editions); Schwarzenberger, *Frontiers*, at 30; D. W. Greig, 'Reciprocity, Proportionality, and the Law of Treaties', (1994) 34 *Va. J Int'l L* 295, 299; Antonio Malintoppi, 'L'elemento della reciprocità nel trattamento delle missioni diplomatiche', (1956) 39 *Rivista di diritto internazionale* 532–45; Art. 47(2)(a), Vienna Convention on Diplomatic Relations, 221 UNTS 500. It is interesting to note that the ICJ described diplomatic relations as a self-contained system where reciprocity is limited to the inter-relations of rules on diplomatic immunities, so that they cannot be suspended in response to the breach of other types of norms, for instance following the interference by one state in the internal affairs of another: *Case Concerning United States Diplomatic and Consular Staff in Teheran (United States v. Iran)*, [1980] ICJ Rep. 3, 39–40; Linos-Alexandre Sicilianos, *Les réactions décentralisées à l'illicite* (Paris: LGDJ, 1990) 344–51.

[10] See Decaux, *La réciprocité*, at 11–13; Oscar Schachter, *International Law in Theory and Practice* (Dordrecht: Nijhoff, 1991) 54.

[11] See Willem Riphagen, 'Preliminary Report on the Content, Form and Degree of State Responsibility', [1980] 2:1 *YB Int'l L Com'n* 107, 119–20.

[12] See Keohane, 'Reciprocity', at 4.

Relationships created pursuant to labour treaties, on the one hand, and labour conventions, on the other hand, all adopted under the aegis of the International Labour Organization, illustrate the difference between bilateral and non-bilateral systems. Labour treaties are synallagmatic agreements according to which states agree to grant a number of rights to workers from other member states. Such agreements are based on immediate reciprocity between states. International labour conventions aim to establish minimum labour standards applicable to all individuals, irrespective of whether their state of origin has accepted these standards, and as such they provide an example of systemic reciprocity.[13]

In international law, reciprocity and the question of whether agreements create bilateralisable obligations are related to the concept of obligations *erga omnes*. The concept was used by the International Court of Justice in the *Barcelona Traction* case to refer to 'obligations of a State towards the international community as a whole', implying that all states have a legal interest in their enforcement.[14] The Court gave as specific examples of *erga omnes* obligations the prohibitions of the use of force, genocide, racial discrimination and slavery, noting that they could stem either from customary law or from widely accepted international instruments.[15] To this list, the Court added the right of peoples to self-determination in the *Case Concerning East Timor*.[16] The concept of obligations *erga omnes* has generated much debate in international law, and there is no consensus yet as to its definition or its relation to related concepts such as *jus cogens* and international crimes.[17] Reciprocity is largely alien to *erga omnes* obligations because they are grounded not in

---

[13] Decaux, *La réciprocité*, at 59–60; Jean Morellet, 'La notion de réciprocité dans les traités de travail et les conventions internationales de travail', [1931] *Revue de droit international privé* 643, 644–5.

[14] *Barcelona Traction, Light and Power Co. Ltd (Belgium v. Spain)*, [1970] ICJ Rep. 3, 32 ('In particular, an essential distinction should be drawn between the obligations of a State towards the international community as a whole, and those arising vis-à-vis another State in the field of diplomatic protection. By their very nature the former are the concern of all States. In view of the importance of the rights involved, all States can be held to have a legal interest in their protection; they are obligations *erga omnes*').

[15] *Ibid.* The Court reiterated its characterisation of genocide as creating obligations *erga omnes* in the *Case Concerning the Application of the Convention on the Prevention and Punishment of the Crime of Genocide*, Preliminary Objections, [1996] ICJ Rep. 115, para. 31.

[16] *Case Concerning East Timor (Portugal v. Australia)*, [1995] ICJ Rep. 90.

[17] See Claudia Annacker, *Die Durchsetzung von erga omnes Verpflichtungen vor dem internationalen Gerichtshof* (Hamburg: Kovac, 1994); André de Hoogh, *Obligations Erga Omnes and International Crimes* (The Hague: Kluwer Law International, 1996); Flavia Lattanzi, *Garanzie dei diritti dell' uomo nel diritto internazionale generale* (Milan: Giuffrè, 1983) 120–48; Theodor Meron, *Human Rights and Humanitarian Norms as Customary Law* (Oxford: Clarendon, 1989) 188–201; Maurizio Ragazzi, *The Concept of International Obligations Erga Omnes* (Oxford: Clarendon, 1997); James Crawford, 'First Report on

an exchange of rights and duties but in the adherence to a normative system. One element central to such obligations is that they imply a corresponding or secondary right of every other state bound by the same customary or conventional norms to react to a violation of the primary norms.[18] In exercising this secondary right, states act not in defence of individual or state interests, but rather in the name of the community as a whole.[19]

In institutionalised systems, the central body will be entrusted with the right to react in the name of the community. A secondary right to react does not appear to derive directly from the theory of non-bilaterisable obligations, although such obligations are certainly compatible with that right. Indeed, it has been suggested that the concepts of non-bilaterisable and *erga omnes* obligations are related, in that all obligations *erga omnes* are non-bilateralisable, while the reverse is not necessarily true.[20] As such, the non-bilaterisable dimension of obligations centres on the legal relationships created by the primary norm, while the *erga omnes* dimension of obligations emphasises the secondary norm governing the individual or collective response of other states to violations.[21]

Reciprocity is at once a social, political and legal phenomenon, the presence of which is so common that it is rarely the object of specific

State Responsibility', UN Doc. A/CN.4/490 (1998) paras. 66–77; Carlo Focarelli, 'Le contromisure pacifiche e la nozione di obblighi *erga omnes*', (1993) 76 *Rivista di diritto internazionale* 52, 64–7; Giorgio Gaja, 'Obligations *Erga Omnes*, International Crimes and *Jus Cogens*: A Tentative Analysis of Three Related Concepts', in Joseph Weiler, Antonio Cassese and Marina Spinedi eds., *International Crimes of States – A Critical Analysis of the ILC's Draft Article 19 on State Responsibility* (Berlin: de Gruyter, 1989) 151–60; Willem Riphagen, 'Fourth Report on the Content, Form and Degree of State Responsibility', [1983] 2:1 *YB Int'l L Com'n* 3, 10–12; Prosper Weil, 'Vers une normativité relative en droit international?', (1982) 86 *Revue générale de droit international public* 5–47 (also published in (1983) 77 *Am. J Int'l L* 413).

[18] See Art. 2(2), 'Resolution on the Protection of Human Rights and the Principle of Non-intervention in Internal Affairs of the State', (1989) 63:2 *Annuaire de l'Institut de droit international* 341–3; Yoram Dinstein, 'The *Erga Omnes* Applicability of Human Rights', (1992) 30 *Archiv des Völkerrecht* 16, 19–20. See the discussion in chapter 5, pp. 202–11.

[19] Gaetano Arangio-Ruiz, 'Fourth Report on State Responsibility', UN Doc. A/CN.4/444/Add.1 (1992) at paras. 140–52; See Giuseppe Barile, '*Obligationes erga omnes* e individui nel diritto internazionale umanitario', (1985) 68 *Rivista di diritto internazionale* 5, 14–15; and especially the substantial contribution made by Paolo Picone, 'Obblighi reciproci e obblighi *erga omnes* degli Stati nel campo della protezione internazionale dell'ambiente marino dall'inquinamento', in Vincenzo Starace ed., *Diritto internazionale e protezione dell'ambiente marino* (Milan: Giuffrè, 1983) 14, 33–93.

[20] See Ragazzi, *Concept*, at 188–91.

[21] See Picone, 'Obblighi reciproci', at 40; Karin Oellers-Frahm, 'Comment: The *Erga Omnes* Applicability of Human Rights', (1992) 30 *Archiv des Völkerrecht* 28–9.

commentary in legal literature.[22] It can be said in a general way that it is present in one form or another in all areas of law, municipal as well as international. There are some areas of law, however, where immediate reciprocity plays a more fundamental role, for example the law of contracts, while in other areas, such as criminal law, which rest to a greater extent on systemic reciprocity, it plays a more limited role. In human rights and humanitarian law, immediate reciprocity has not been discarded completely and does play some role. The purpose of this discussion is to go beyond this observation to an assessment and comparison of the relative importance of immediate and systemic reciprocity in human rights law and humanitarian law. Because of the fundamental role of reciprocity, variations have a significant impact on substantive and procedural rules. The assessment of whether there exists any marked difference in the degree to which human rights and humanitarian law are grounded in reciprocity will be based on an analysis of the reciprocal nature of rules in the formation (chapter 3), application (chapter 4) and sanction (chapter 5) of these norms. This will in turn inform the wider discussion of the similarities and differences between human rights and humanitarian law.

[22] See Campiglio, *Il principio*, at 9–43; Simma, *Das Reziprozitätselement*, at 15–24.

3 Formation

Procedural aspects

In primitive legal systems such as the international legal system, in which there is no centralised legislative body capable of imposing rules, new norms emerge from the concerted or aggregated actions of states. Each state acts primarily in defence of what it perceives as its own best interests. Thus, a necessary give and take, in the form of immediate reciprocity, is generally present in the creation process of international law.[1] Beyond this general observation, there exist clear variations in the degree to which the evolution of new rules depends on immediate reciprocity. Differences emerge in this respect between human rights and humanitarian law both in treaty and customary law, which are treated distinctly here given their particular modes of evolution.

TREATY LAW

With regard to treaties, states give their assent to the development of new human rights and humanitarian law norms through multilateral conventions, usually the fruit of compromise reached during preparatory conferences or the work of international organisations.[2] New rules

---

[1] See Bruno Simma, 'Reciprocity', in Rudolf Bernhardt ed., [Instalment] 7 *Encyclopedia of Public International Law* (Amsterdam: North-Holland, 1984) 400; Richard Thurnwald, *Economics in Primitive Communities* (London: Oxford UP, 1932) 106; Michel Virally, 'Le principe de réciprocité dans le droit international contemporain', (1967-III) 122 *Recueil des cours* 1, 63 (referring to reciprocity as a 'principe dynamique du développement du droit').

[2] See George H. Aldrich, 'Establishing Legal Norms Through Multilateral Negotiations – The Laws of War', (1977) 9 *Case W Res. J Int'l L* 9–16; Richard B. Baxter, 'Humanitarian Law or Humanitarian Politics? The 1974 Diplomatic Conference on Humanitarian Law' (1975) 16 *Harv. Int'l LJ* 1–26. See generally Bruno Simma, *Das Reziprozitätselement*

are jointly proposed by the community of nations, relying on a mixture of collegiality and reciprocity. The presence of reciprocity in the process is clearly illustrated by the fact that multilateral conventions concerning both humanitarian law and human rights usually include a clause conditioning entry into force upon ratification by a certain number of states. The requirement is minimal in the 1949 Geneva Conventions and the 1977 Additional Protocols, which came into force after only two parties deposited an instrument of ratification (Arts. 58/57/138/153; Art. 95(1), Protocol I; Art. 23, Protocol II).[3] By contrast, the most recent humanitarian convention, the 1981 UN Convention on Conventional Weapons,[4] requires twenty ratifications before entering into force (Art. 5(1)). Similar clauses are found in the major human rights instruments, including the Genocide Convention (Art. XIII: twenty ratifications), the European Convention on Human Rights (Art. 59(2): ten ratifications), the International Covenants on Civil and Political Rights (Art. 49(1): thirty-five ratifications) and on Economic, Social and Cultural Rights (Art. 27(1): thirty-five ratifications), the American Convention on Human Rights (Art. 74(2): eleven ratifications) and the African Charter on Human and Peoples' Rights, which entered into force only after a majority of members of the Organization of African Unity had ratified the treaty (Art. 63(3)).

A concern for reciprocity in the creation by way of treaty of new undertakings by states is thus reflected in both areas of international law. This is so even where the obligations have a predominantly internal effect and thereby do not involve substantive relationships with other states party to the same treaty. Such 'internal' obligations include all substantive human rights norms and a limited number of humanitarian norms (e.g. common Art. 3, 1949 Geneva Conventions). Substantive human rights norms, once created, apply to a state's relations with

---

im zustandekommen völkerrechtlicher Verträge (Berlin: Duncker & Humblot, 1972) 73–219.

[3] The same was true of the 1929 Geneva Conventions on Wounded and Sick (Art. 33) and on Prisoners of War (Art. 92), 27 July 1929, while there was no such condition in the 1907 Hague Convention (IV) Respecting the Laws and Customs of War on Land (Art. 7), 10 Oct. 1907, nor in the 1906 (Geneva) Convention for the Amelioration of the Condition of the Wounded and Sick in Armies in the Field (Art. 30), 6 July 1906. The suggestion by one state (Indonesia) that Protocol I enter into force only after a majority of states had become parties was rejected at the 1977 Geneva Conference: CDDH/SR.46 Annex, 6 *1977 Off. Records*, at 375.

[4] Convention on Prohibitions or Restrictions on the Use of Certain Conventional Weapons Which May be Deemed to be Excessively Injurious or to Have Indiscriminate Effects, 10 April 1981, *reprinted in* Dietrich Schindler and Jiří Toman, *The Laws of Armed Conflict*, 3rd edn (Dordrecht: Nijhoff, 1989) 179.

individuals under its control, independent of any element of reciprocity. Very broadly, no interaction with any other state is required, and states by and large act unilaterally in applying human rights. It may therefore seem surprising to find in such conventions a requirement of wide acceptance before they become binding. The need to have at least two ratifications is explained by the fact that the vehicle used is a treaty, which requires at least two parties. The *travaux préparatoires* indicate that states justified the need for broader participation before entry into force of the treaty on the need to give it 'real force' and 'international significance'.[5] The more extensive ratification requirement in many human rights treaties can thus be seen as a reflection of the diffuse reciprocal state interest in the collective creation of a regime imposing non-bilateralisable obligations upon them.[6] This can be contrasted to the minimal participation required under the Geneva Conventions, which is an indication of the prevalence of immediate reciprocity in those treaties.

Clearly then, despite their character as 'internal' obligations, substantive human rights norms do have repercussions on the international sphere which may involve elements of reciprocity. For instance, international minimum standards governing the treatment of aliens have co-opted a number of human rights norms, including the prohibition of racial discrimination, genocide and inhuman or degrading treatment.[7] Although the relationship between international minimum standards and human rights remains ill-defined, it is likely that practice in the field of diplomatic protection relying on human rights norms would have an impact on the development of the latter, in custom as well

[5] See Marc Bossuyt, *Guide to the 'Travaux Préparatoires' of the International Covenant on Civil and Political Rights* (Dordrecht: Nijhoff, 1987) 755–8.
[6] It can, at the same time, be a reflection of other factors such as the need to share the startup cost of treaty-monitoring bodies: Manfred Nowak, *CCPR Commentary* (Kehl: Engel, 1993) 635; Louis-Edmond Pettiti et al. eds., *La Convention européenne des droits de l'homme* (Paris: Economica, 1995) 958.
[7] See e.g. Ian Brownlie, *Principles of Public International Law*, 5th edn (Oxford: Clarendon, 1998) 528–31; *Restatement (Third) of the Foreign Relations Law of the United States* (St Paul: American Law Institute, 1987) para. 711(a); Thomas E. Carbonneau, 'The Convergence of the Law of State Responsibility for Injuries to Aliens and International Human Rights Norms in the Revised Restatement', (1984) 25 *Va. J Int'l L* 99–123; F. V. García Amador, 'Second Report on the Responsibility of the State for Injuries Caused in its Territory to the Person or Property of Aliens', [1957] 2 *YB Int'l L Com'n* 104, 112–16; P. Weiss, 'Diplomatic Protection of Nationals and International Protection of Human Rights', (1971) 2–3 *Revue des droits de l'homme* 645. Other examples could include international norms on refugees and stateless persons and ILO standards on migrant workers.

as treaty law.[8] More generally, once a state undertakes to comply with human rights norms, these are co-opted into international discourse so that that state may be called upon to honour these obligations by any other state for which they are also binding. That process of applying and receiving pressure on the basis of human rights norms is based on the anticipation of reciprocity, and plays a central role in a state's decision to ratify conventions.[9]

CUSTOMARY LAW

In customary law, reciprocity plays a somewhat different role in the creation of humanitarian law than in that of human rights. Humanitarian law follows the general pattern of development of international law, whereby new norms are derived from the aggregate practice and *opinio juris* of states in their relations with one another. Thus, reciprocity is often present in the development of humanitarian norms, given that emerging standards which have not matured into custom are not yet legally binding, and must be freely agreed to by the various parties to an armed conflict, usually on a reciprocal basis.[10] For example, the content of the now customary 1864 Geneva Convention was largely inspired by similar rules found in cartels drafted on an *ad hoc* basis by warring parties.[11] In this sense, then, reciprocity does play some role in the development of customary humanitarian law.

[8] See e.g. the UN Declaration of the Rights of Individuals not Citizens of the Country in Which they Live, UN GA Res. 40/144 (1985), *reprinted in* David J. Harris, *Cases and Materials on International Law*, 4th edn (London: Sweet & Maxwell, 1991) 520–3. See Richard B. Lillich, *The Human Rights of Aliens in Contemporary International Law* (Manchester: Manchester UP, 1984) 51–6; Baroness Elles, 'The Problem of the Applicability of Existing International Provisions for the Protection of Human Rights to Individuals who are not Nationals of the Country in which they Live', UN Doc. E/CN.4/Sub.2/392/Rev.1 (1982).

[9] See Cristina Campiglio, *Il principio di reciprocità nel diritto dei trattati* (Padua: CEDAM, 1995) 124–32; Menno Kamminga, *Inter-State Accountability for Human Rights Violations* (Philadelphia: U Pennsylvania Press, 1992) 136; Simma, *Das Reziprozitätselement*, at 194–212.

[10] H. W. Halleck, *International Law* (New York: Van Nostrand, 1861) 444–5.

[11] P. Bogaïewsky, 'Les secours aux militaires malades et blessés avant le XIXème siècle', (1903) 10 *Revue générale de droit international public* 202–21; Henri Coursier, 'L'évolution du droit international humanitaire', (1960-I) 99 *Recueil des cours* 357, 371 ('En effet, les "cartels" ou arrangements particuliers conclut entre chefs d'armées adverses, en faveur des blessés et des malades avaient pu leur accorder des garanties analogues à celle prévue par la Convention de Genève, mais ces accords n'avaient qu'un caractère occasionnel...Ils n'engageaient d'ailleurs que les parties contractantes selon une

Reciprocity, however, is by no means a necessary element of the development of new customary rules on the conduct of warfare. Some states may unilaterally adopt rules over and above what is required by positive international law, in the hope of being imitated by other states, but without making this a condition. For instance, the French National Convention enacted a decree on 25 May 1793 whereby wounded and sick enemies were to be given the same treatment as the French wounded and sick, with the goal of creating a new standard.[12] Further, states may adopt rules for purely internal purposes, without any intention of generating a new international law norm but nevertheless having that effect. Military manuals are enacted in large part to maintain internal discipline in the armed forces and limit the damage caused by warfare in order to facilitate the return to normality after the end of hostilities. Often, manuals of different countries adopt a consistent stance and eventually result in the creation of generally accepted rules of international law. The now-customary requirement that belligerent reprisals be authorised by a superior officer can be seen as one example of this non-reciprocal law-making process.[13]

In the field of human rights law, on the other hand, norms are derived from practice and *opinio juris* which are essentially of a unilateral character. That is, infra-state practice predominates, given that human rights norms govern the internal relationships between a state and the

---

stricte réciprocité'). A similar pattern inspired the drafting of the 1929 Geneva Prisoners of War Convention, based on agreements made amongst belligerents during the First World War: Jean Pictet ed., *The Geneva Conventions of 12 August 1949 – Commentary on the III Geneva Convention Relative to the Treatment of Prisoners of War* (Geneva: ICRC, 1960) 79.

[12] See Ernest Nys, *Le droit international: les principes, les théories, les faits*, new edn (Brussels: Weissenbruch, 1912) III, 501; D. W. Greig, 'Reciprocity, Proportionality, and the Law of Treaties', (1994) 34 *Va. J Int'l L* 295, 300; Arthur Lenhoff, 'Reciprocity: The Legal Aspect of a Perennial Idea', (1954–5) 49 *Northwestern ULJ* 617, 624–5.

[13] The requirement is not found in any international convention but in several military manuals, e.g. Legge di guerra (Italy), Reggio decreto 8 luglio 1938-XVI, n. 1415, *reprinted in* (1938) *Collezione delle leggi e decreti* 1175–1204, Art. 10; US Dept of the Army, *Field Manual 27–10*, 18 July 1956 (Washington DC: US Gov. Printing Office, 1956) para. 497(e); UK War Office, *Manual of Military Law*, Part III 'The Laws and Usages of War on Land', Hersch Lauterpacht ed. (London: HMSO, 1958) para. 645; Judge Advocate General, *The Law of Armed Conflict at the Operational and Tactical Level B-GG-005-027/AF-020* (Ottawa: Dept Nat'l Defence, 1999) s. 15–13 (hereinafter 1999 *Canadian War Manual*). See W. Michael Reisman and William K. Leitzau, 'Moving International Law from Theory to Practice: The Role of Military Manuals in Effectuating the Law of Armed Conflict', in Horace B. Robertson ed., 64 *US Naval War College International Law Studies, The Law of Naval Operations* (Newport RI: Naval War Coll. Press, 1991) 1, 7–9.

individuals under its control.[14] *Opinio juris* sometimes does take the form of an appeal by one or more states for another to abide by certain standards which do not yet form part of general international law. Such appeals, however, are grounded in a principle of humanity rather than reciprocity. In other related situations, inter-state practice can influence the construction of existing norms the content of which remains vague, and thus import an element of reciprocity to the definition of human rights norms. Decisions and opinions of judicial or advisory bodies entrusted with the task of enforcing or monitoring compliance with human rights are a further influential force in the development of customary norms, yet the work of such bodies is of an institutional rather than reciprocal nature.[15] Finally, the ratification of new international conventions for the protection of human rights, in which reciprocity does appear, has some impact on the development of corresponding customary norms. Internal state practice nevertheless remains the decisive element in the ripening of human rights norms into general international law, thus limiting to a minimum the role of reciprocity in the process.[16]

In the end, no generalisation seems warranted as to the importance of reciprocity in the development of human rights and humanitarian law beyond the statement that reciprocity occupies a more prominent position in the creation of new rules in humanitarian law. The complex nature of the creation process of international law, however, refutes positions that reject any relevance for reciprocity in the evolution of human rights law and, at the other extreme, that suggest

---

[14] The situation would be different with respect to so-called 'third-generation' human rights, involving rights claimable by individuals and states against other states. Reciprocity does play a significant role in the development of this type of human rights.

[15] Georg Schwarzenberger, *The Frontiers of International Law* (London: Stevens & Sons, 1962) 31-2, mentions as an example of a relationship based on reciprocity the actions of the tribunal set up pursuant to the Upper Silesia Convention between Germany and Poland, on the basis that interpretations put forward by one country eventually were applied by the tribunal in the other country. This example illustrates not the creation of rights and obligations for the two states conditioned on reciprocity, but rather the elaboration of norms by the tribunal in the context of either Poland or Germany, and then their institutional application to the other state party to the convention. The end result is the equality of treatment of the two state parties in the system set up by the convention.

[16] See Theodor Meron, *Human Rights and Humanitarian Norms as Customary Law* (Oxford: Clarendon, 1989) 100. For a broader reflection on the role of reciprocity in the formation of customary international law, see Bruno Simma, *Das Reziprozitätselement in der Entstehung des Völkergewohnheitsrecht* (Munich: Fink, 1970) 45-70.

total reliance on reciprocity in the development of humanitarian law, positions which are not infrequently adopted in academic and judicial opinions.

Object and purpose of norms

Both human rights and humanitarian law ultimately aim to protect the individual. Despite this shared purpose, however, the evolution of neither set of norms is entirely insulated from the influence of particular state interests, expressed through negotiations at international conferences or the behaviour of states in their day-to-day affairs. The balance struck in each of human rights and humanitarian law translates into a distinct role for reciprocity in the development of their norms.

HUMAN RIGHTS

Human rights law does not depend on any special relationship between the individual and the state. As such, it may benefit persons with no special relation to the state, for instance nationals of states not party to a given treaty or stateless persons. The International Law Commission has characterised interests embodied in human rights norms as 'extra-state', to underline the fact that the protection afforded by these norms goes beyond that required by an aggregate of state interests.[17] The ICJ expressed this clearly in its classic description of the motives underlying state acceptance of the Genocide Convention:[18]

In such a convention the contracting States do not have any interests of their own; they merely have, one and all, a common interest, namely, the accomplishment of the high purposes which are the raison d'être of the Convention. Consequently, in a convention of this type one cannot speak of individual advantages or disadvantages to the States, or of the maintenance of a perfect contractual balance between rights and duties. The high ideals which inspired the Convention provide, by virtue of the common will of the parties, the foundation and measure of all its provisions. [Emphasis added.]

[17] Willem Riphagen, 'Second Report on the Content, Forms and Degrees of State Responsibility', [1981] 2:1 *YB Int'l L Com'n* 79, 86. See generally Campiglio, *Il principio*, at 102–13.
[18] *Reservations to the Convention on Punishment and Prevention of the Crime of Genocide*, [1951] ICJ Rep. 15, 23. See also the arguments presented by the UK in that case: [1950] ICJ Pleadings 64–8 and 378–88.

The Court accordingly went on to characterise the 'basic rights of the human person' as obligations *erga omnes* in the *Barcelona Traction* case.[19]

The European Commission of Human Rights commented on this aspect of the legal system created by the European Convention on Human Rights in its decision in *Austria v. Italy*, noting that the Convention's purpose was not to create reciprocal obligations and rights in pursuance of national interests, but rather to establish a 'common public order'.[20] Accordingly, the Commission found that Austria could present a petition regarding events which took place at a time when the European Convention was inapplicable to it. This reasoning later prompted the

---

[19] *Barcelona Traction, Light and Power Co. Ltd (Belgium v. Spain)*, [1970] ICJ Rep. 3, 32. See Meron, *Human Rights and Humanitarian Norms*, at 193–200; *Restatement*, 41, at para. 703(2); Article 1, 'Resolution on the Protection of Human Rights and the Principle of Non-Intervention in the Internal Affairs of the State', (1989) 63:2 *Annuaire de l'Institut de droit international* 341.

In a controversial dictum, the Court later added that, in contrast to the European Convention on Human Rights 'which entitles each State which is a party to the Convention to lodge a complaint against any other contracting State for violation of the Convention, irrespective of the nationality of the victim', 'on the universal level, the instruments which embody human rights do not confer on States the capacity to protect the victims irrespective of their nationality' (p. 47). The passage refers strictly to treaty law and the distinct regimes of admissibility of inter-state complaints under the European Convention (Art. 33) and universal instruments such as the International Covenant on Civil and Political Rights (Art. 41). Some have seen in the reference to '*basic* rights of the human person' an indication that, under both customary and treaty law, not all human rights generate *erga omnes* obligations because some rights are more 'basic' than others, but the judgment does not appear to contain such a far-reaching pronouncement, however logical or desirable it might be. See Separate Opinion of Judge Petrén, *Nuclear Tests Case (Australia v. France)* [1974] ICJ Rep. 253, 303; Brigitte Bollecker-Stern, *Le préjudice dans la théorie de la responsabilité internationale* (Paris: Pedone, 1973) 83–90; Flavia Lattanzi, *Garanzie dei diritti dell'uomo nel diritto internazionale generale* (Milan: Giuffrè, 1983) 140–1; Maurizio Ragazzi, *The Concept of International Obligations* Erga Omnes (Oxford: Clarendon, 1997) 131–6 (expressing some uncertainty as to the *erga omnes* character of all human rights); Jochen Frowein, 'Die Verpflichtungen *erga omnes* im Völkerrecht und ihre Durchsetzung', in Rudolf Bernhardt et al. eds., *Völkerrecht als Rechtsordnung, internationale Gerichtsbarkeit, Menschenrechte: Festschrift für Herman Mosler* (Berlin: Springer, 1983) 243–4; José Juste Ruiz, 'Las obligaciones "erga omnes" en derecho internacional público', in *Estudios de derecho internacional: Homenaje al profesor Miaja de la Muela* (Madrid: Tecnos, 1979) I, 219, 231–3; Theodor Meron, 'On a Hierarchy of International Human Rights', (1986) 80 *Am. J Int'l L* 1, 10–11.

[20] Appl. 788/60, [1961] *YB Eur. Conv. Hum. Rts* 116, 138–40 ('The obligations undertaken by the High Contracting Parties in the Convention are essentially of an objective character, being designed rather to protect individual rights . . . than to create subjective and reciprocal rights for the High Contracting Parties themselves'). See also *Ireland v. UK*, (1978) 25 Judgments and Decisions (Ser. A) 5, 90–1 (Eur. Ct Hum. Rts).

Commission to refuse the waiver of claims already presented when they raise public order interests going beyond those of the parties.[21]

Similar views were expressed more recently by the Inter-American Court of Human Rights with respect to the American Convention on Human Rights in its advisory opinion on *The Effect of Reservations on the Entry into Force of the American Convention (Arts. 74 and 75).*[22] In that opinion, the Court noted that, unlike most multilateral conventions, the American Convention on Human Rights did not consist of the reciprocal exchange of state rights and obligations, but instead represented a series of parallel unilateral undertakings by states to abide by certain human rights standards. Such undertakings are directed towards individuals more than towards states, and their effect is not primarily to initiate a contractual relationship between states party to the convention, but rather to create a new legal order whose beneficiaries are not states but individuals.[23] There is also an inter-state component created by human rights conventions, justifying the right of third states to demand compliance with treaty provisions, but that dimension remains clearly secondary.[24] In view of such principles developed in the context of treaties on human rights, the nature and purpose of customary human rights norms *a fortiori* indicates minimal relevance for reciprocity in their creation.[25]

---

[21] See *Gericke v. Fed. Rep. of Germany*, Appl. 2294/64, [1965] YB Eur. Conv. Hum. Rts 314, 320–2; P. van Dijk and G. J. H. van Hoof, *Theory and Practice of the European Convention on Human Rights*, 3rd edn (The Hague: Kluwer, 1998) 190.

[22] OC-2/82 of 24 Sept. 1982, Ser. A No. 2, at 20–3.

[23] *Ibid.*, at 20. The Court reiterated this position in *Bronstein v. Peru*, Jurisdiction, 24 Sept. 1999, Ser. C No. 54, paras. 42–5, and in *Caso del Tribunal constitucional*, Jurisdiction, 24 Sept. 1999, Ser. C No. 55, paras. 41–4. See also Meron, *Human Rights and Humanitarian Norms*, at 100.

[24] Bruno Simma, 'From Bilateralism to Community Interest in International Law', (1994-VI) 250 *Recueil des cours* 217, 371–5.

[25] See, for an early example, Wyndham A. Bewes, 'Reciprocity in the Enjoyment of Civil Rights', (1918) 3 *Transact. Grotius Soc.* 133, 135 (noting that reciprocity does not apply to 'any rights enjoyed by man as a member of a civilised nation, such as family rights, the right to liberty and property, and, generally, the right to dispose of himself and his interests as a free man').

Once again, the situation would be different for so-called third-generation human rights which have an important group dimension, such as the right of peoples to self-determination and the right to development. The direct inter-state dimension of these rights, whereby one state would have to endure economic or political cost for the benefit of another state or its nationals, suggests that states act in furtherance of their individual interests and that some form of reciprocity may be required for states to support the new norms. Decaux suggests that, because of the temporary and remedial nature of these rights, they should be regarded as mere exceptions to the

HUMANITARIAN LAW

The development of humanitarian law norms clearly is less insulated from the influence of state interests. This follows from the very nature of humanitarian law, presented as a compromise between humanitarian ideals and the desire to ensure military effectiveness in warfare. Under human rights law, state claims to valid limitations can rest only on elements of state security and public order.[26] Restrictions on individual rights are thus more limited than under humanitarian law, where reliance on military necessity can ultimately lead to a theory of *Kriegsräson* which could justify the suspension of humanitarian law if so demanded by the situation in the field. While some commentators have denied any role for reciprocity in the formation of humanitarian law,[27] reciprocity is usually present when states actively seek to protect their particular interests in the development of new norms.[28]

Historically, reciprocity occupied a dominant place in the development of the laws of war. Before codification efforts were initiated by the International Committee of the Red Cross in the second half of the nineteenth century, the practice was either to rely on custom or to fix by cartel, on an *ad hoc* basis, the conditions governing warfare.[29] Such cartels bear closer resemblance to the contractual exchange of reciprocal rights and obligations than to the constitution of a new legal order. Alternatively, rules on the conduct of warfare stemmed from directives issued by commanders to their troops, for example the 1643 British Laws and Ordinances of War, which were driven primarily by the goals of military discipline and war readiness and only slightly by humanitarian sentiments.[30]

general rule that reciprocity is irrelevant to the development of human rights law: Emmanuel Decaux, *La réciprocité en droit international* (Paris: LGDJ, 1980) 41.

[26] See chapter 6, pp. 269–76.

[27] René-Jean Wilhelm, 'Le caractère des droits accordés à l'individu dans les Conventions de Genève', [1950] *Revue internationale de la Croix-Rouge* 561, 579 ('la réciprocité est un élément de l'application effective de ces règles conventionnelles, comme il est pour d'autres parties du droit des gens; elle n'en constitue nullement le fondement').

[28] Georg Schwarzenberger, *International Law as Applied by International Courts and Tribunals – The Law of Armed Conflict* (London: Stevens & Sons, 1968) II, 452 ('In other [spheres], the rules of international law which are based on a *basic reciprocity of interests*, derive from this situation a remarkable degree of stability. Actually, the laws of war constitute a typical illustration of the international law of reciprocity'); Simma, *Das Reziprozitätselement*, at 89–97.

[29] See above, note 11.

[30] Montague Bernard, 'The Growth of Law and Usages of War', in *Oxford Essays* (London: Parker, 1856) 88, 89.

There has been a gradual progression in the development of the laws of war towards a greater emphasis on their humanitarian nature. The rejection after 1907 of the *si omnes* clause, whereby humanitarian conventions become wholly inapplicable if one belligerent is not a party to them, can be construed as one illustration of this progression.[31] There are now rules derived mainly from humanitarian ideals which go so far as to restrict military efficacy directly. For instance, Article 54 of Protocol I prohibits the destruction of objects indispensable to the survival of the civilian population, even if the same are also used by enemy soldiers and thus provide a tactical advantage to the enemy.[32] The evolving nature of humanitarian law means that its creation now involves less the defence of state interests and more the establishment of public order standards applicable in warfare, somewhat comparable to those in human rights law. In such a context, the relevance of reciprocity to the development of humanitarian law is likely to diminish, although the inter-state nature of the relationships governed by humanitarian law makes a complete rejection of reciprocity improbable.

A specific break from humanitarian law's reliance on reciprocity for the development of its rules can be found in the imposition of an obligation not only to respect but also to 'ensure respect' of the terms of the 1949 Geneva Conventions and Protocol I (Art. 1). The undertaking is unconditional and unilateral, in that it is not based on any consideration in the form of the creation of similar obligations on behalf of other state parties to the Conventions and Protocol. As noted in the commentary on the Geneva Conventions:

It is not an engagement concluded on a basis of reciprocity, binding each party to the contract in so far as the other party observes its obligations. It is rather a series of unilateral engagements solemnly contracted before the world as represented by the other Contracting Parties. Each State contracts obligations *vis-à-vis* itself and at the same time *vis-à-vis* the others.[33]

---

[31] Article 2 of the 1907 Hague Convention IV provides an example of *si omnes* clauses: 'The provisions . . . do not apply except between contracting Powers, and then only if all belligerents are party to the Convention.' It was abandoned in favour of a regime whereby humanitarian conventions remain in force between states party to them in their mutual relations (e.g. common Art. 2(3), 1949 Geneva Conventions). See Hodos, *Die Allbeteiligungsklausel als eine Erscheinungsform kriegsrechtlicher Gegenseitigkeit* (diss., Innsbruck, 1947); Simma, *Das Reziprozitätselement*, at 91–2.

[32] See René Provost, 'Starvation as a Weapon: Legal Implications of the United Nations Food Blockade Against Iraq and Kuwait', (1992) 30 *Colum. J Transnat'l L* 577, 605.

[33] Jean Pictet ed., *The Geneva Conventions of 12 August 1949 – Commentary on the IV Geneva Convention Relative to the Protection of Civilian Persons in Times of War* (Geneva: ICRC, 1958) 15. Some have seen in the inclusion of this obligation not an exception to the

This provision has attracted growing scholarly attention but has generated little state practice directly traceable to it, and the practical implications of Article 1 remain rather vague. The ICJ in the *Nicaragua* case did find the United States in breach of its obligation to 'ensure respect', based on its encouragement of violations of humanitarian law through the publication of a war manual entitled *Operaciones sicológicas en guerra de guerillas* which advocated the assassination of various protected persons.[34] The obligation would involve a general duty whereby a state must use all means at its disposal, whether formal or informal, to try to foster respect for humanitarian law.[35]

Clearly, some humanitarian law norms impose obligations *erga omnes* on states. This appears not only in the duty to 'ensure respect' described

reciprocal nature of humanitarian law, but an indication that reciprocity is alien to the nature of that law as a whole: Barile, 'Obligationes erga omnes', at 5–6 ('La frase "rispettare e far rispettare in ogni circostanza"... conferma la natura incondizionale (e non sinallagmatica) delle obligazioni di diritto umanitario previste da detti accordi, le quali vanno per l'appunto rispettare in ogni caso, così que non valenei loro confronti la logica della reciprocità e, in paticolare, la logica che sta alla base dell'istituto delle rappresaglie'). This position seems to overlook important differences in the nature of humanitarian law and human rights, discussed above, to identify humanitarian law only with respect to its component protecting the individual.

[34] *Military and Paramilitary Activities in and Against Nicaragua (Nicaragua v. USA)*, [1986] ICJ Rep. 14, 104.

[35] See Paolo Benvenuti, 'Ensuring Observance of International Humanitarian Law: Functions, Extent and Limits of the Obligation of Third States to Ensure Respect of International Humanitarian Law', [1989–90] YB Int'l Inst. Humanitarian L 27, 27–55; Luigi Condorelli and Laurence Boisson de Chazournes, 'Quelques remarques à propos de l'obligation des Etats de "respecter et faire respecter" le droit international humanitaire "en toutes circonstances"', in Christophe Swinarski ed., *Studies and Essays on International Humanitarian Law and Red Cross Principles in Honour of Jean Pictet* (Geneva/The Hague: Nijhoff, 1984) 17–35; Luigi Condorelli and Laurence Boisson de Chazournes, 'Common Article 1 of the Geneva Conventions Revisited: Protecting Collective Interest', (2000) 837 Int'l Rev. Red Cross 67–87; Hans-Peter Gasser, 'Ensuring Respect for the Geneva Conventions and Protocols: The Role of Third States and the United Nations', in Hazel Fox and Michael Meyer eds., *Armed Conflict and the New Law – Effecting Compliance* (London: British Institute of International and Comparative Law, 1993) II, 15–49; Nicolas Levrat, 'Les conséquences de l'engagement pris par les hautes parties contractantes de "faire respecter" les conventions humanitaires', in Frits Kalshoven and Yves Sandoz eds., *Implementation of International Humanitarian Law* (Dordrecht: Nijhoff, 1989) 263–97; Konstantin Obradović, 'Le "conflit yougoslave" et le problème de la responsabilité des Etats parties aux Conventions humanitaires quant à la mise en oeuvre', (1992) *Jugoslenvska revija za medunarodno pravo* 222–37. Other implications would include a duty to bring municipal law in line with the conventions (Condorelli and Chazournes, 'Quelques remarques', at 25), to use informal channels to pressure states to halt breaches (Gasser, 'Ensuring Respect', at 28–30), or to vote against resolutions of international organisations implementing measures contrary to humanitarian law (Provost, 'Starvation', at 600–1).

above, but also in the duty to repress grave breaches regardless of the nationalities of the perpetrator and victim (Arts. 49/50/129/146). The nature of humanitarian law as *erga omnes* was recently highlighted in the judgment of the Appeals Chamber of the International Criminal Tribunal for former Yugoslavia in the *Tadić* case.[36] In its justification of the primacy of the international tribunal over domestic courts in the prosecution of war crimes, the Appeals Chamber quotes and adopts the following dicta from the Italian Supreme Military Tribunal in the *General Wagener* case:

> Crimes against the laws and customs of war cannot be considered political offences, as they do not harm a political interest of a particular state, nor a political right of a particular citizen. They are instead crimes of *lèse-humanité* (*reati di lesa umanità*) and, as previously demonstrated, the norms prohibiting them have a universal character, not simply a territorial one. Such crimes, therefore, due to their very subject-matter and particular nature are precisely of a different and opposite kind from political offences. The latter generally concern only the state against whom they are committed; the former concern all civilised states, and they are to be opposed and punished, in the same way as the crimes of piracy, trade of women and minors, and enslavement are to be opposed and punished, wherever they may have been committed.[37]

Likewise, the fact that High Contracting Parties cannot absolve each other of responsibility for grave breaches of the 1949 Geneva Conventions (Arts. 51/52/131/148) underscores the non-bilateral, *erga omnes* character of some obligations under humanitarian law.[38]

Given the dynamics of the creation of humanitarian law, however, it seems unlikely that it 'does not lay down synallagmatic obligations, i.e. obligations based on reciprocity, but obligations *erga omnes* ... which are designed to safeguard fundamental human values and therefore must be complied with' by each party regardless of the conduct of the other party or parties'.[39] If the blanket statement of the ICTY Trial Chamber is taken to amount to a complete rejection of immediate reciprocity, it would

---

[36] *The Prosecutor v. Tadić* (Decision on the Defence Motion for Interlocutory Appeal on Jurisdiction), 2 Oct. 1995, Case No. IT-94-1-AR72 (Appeals Chamber, ICTY) 30–2.

[37] [1950] *Rivista penale* 753, 757 (Sup. Mil. Trib., Italy), as translated in *Tadić, ibid.*, at 31 para. 57.

[38] See Simma, *Das Reziprozitätselement*, at 173–4; Georges Abi-Saab, 'The Specificities of Humanitarian Law', in Swinarski, *Mélanges Pictet*, at 365, 370; Benvenuti, 'Ensuring Observance', at 30–1; Dietrich Schindler, 'Die erga omnes-Wirkung des humanitären Völkerrecht', in Ulrich Byerlin et al. eds., *Recht zwischen Umbruch und Bewahrung: Völkerrecht, Europarecht, Staatsrecht. Festschrift für Rudolf Bernhardt* (Berlin: Springer, 1995) 199–211.

[39] *The Prosecutor v. Kupreskić* (*Lasva Valley* case) (Decision on Defence Motion to Summon Witness), 8 Feb. 1999, Case No. IT-95-16-T (Trial Chamber, ICTY) at 3.

be warranted only if humanitarian law had become a regime so stable that it could function exclusively on the basis of systemic reciprocity.[40] As the analysis of patterns of application and sanction of humanitarian law will show, such a high degree of stability has unfortunately not been achieved, far from it. That being said, immediate reciprocity need not be seen as the disease to eradicate. It is simply a significant variable in the life of the humanitarian norm which can, to some degree and in some circumstances, play a positive role.

Reservations and reciprocity

States make reservations to treaties as a way of controlling the extent of their obligations while at the same time giving their general assent to the treaties. Reservations thus have the effect of altering the relationship between the reserving state and other states party to the treaty. They are of a fundamentally reciprocal nature, in that the reserving state and the other states will be bound in their mutual relationship by the treaty as amended by the reservation.[41] The reserving state has discretion to decide the nature of its reservations, limited only by the conventional and customary principle of compatibility with the object and purpose of the treaty and, to a point, by objections of other states to the reservations.[42] Some treaties specify which provisions may be reserved and under what conditions. Reservations in full compliance with these conditions can nevertheless generate valid objections by other states. The following analysis focuses on reservations as indicators of the reciprocal or non-reciprocal nature of human rights and humanitarian law.

---

[40] The same ICTY Trial Chamber qualified its position slightly in the final judgment in the case, in which it stated that 'the bulk of [humanitarian law] lays down absolute obligations, namely obligations that are unconditional or in other words not based on reciprocity', thus implying that at least part of humanitarian law is not so based: Kupreškić (Judgment), 14 Jan. 2000, Case No. IT-95-16-T (Trial Chamber, ICTY) para. 517 (emphasis added).

[41] Art. 21(1), Vienna Convention on the Law of Treaties, 23 May 1969, (1969) 155 UNTS 331; Norwegian Loans Case (France v. Norway), [1957] ICJ Rep. 23–7; Interhandel Case (Switzerland v. USA) (Preliminary Objections), [1959] ICJ Rep. 25; Frank Horn, Reservations and Interpretative Declarations to Multilateral Treaties (Amsterdam: North-Holland, 1988) 146; Pierre-Henri Imbert, Les réserves aux traités multilatéraux (Paris: Pedone, 1978) 249; Simma, Das Reziprozitätselement, at 58–64; Alain Pellet, 'First Report on the Law and Practice Relating to Reservations to Treaties', UN Doc. A/CN.4/470 (1995).

[42] Reservations to the Convention on Genocide, [1951] ICJ Rep. 15, 24; Art. 19(c), Vienna Convention on the Law of Treaties.

HUMAN RIGHTS

In the field of human rights, only a few instruments contain express limitations on the availability of reservations. The nature of these limitations varies from a mere reference to either the Vienna Convention on the Law of Treaties (Art. 75, American Convention on Human Rights) or the principle pertaining to the object and purpose of the convention,[43] to more detailed prescriptions like that found in the European Convention on Human Rights, which allows only limited reservations if necessary to validate pre-existing national legislation (Art. 57). Total prohibition of reservations is extremely uncommon in human rights conventions.[44]

Many of the most important human rights conventions, however, do not address the question of reservations at all. In such instruments, which include the Genocide Convention, the Economic and Political Covenants, the Convention Against Torture and the African Charter on Human and Peoples' Rights, the sole restriction to the making of reservations is the customary requirement that they be compatible with the convention's object and purpose. Few standards have emerged to guide the determination of compatibility between reservations and the object and purpose of a human rights convention.[45] The Inter-American Court of Human Rights in the *Restrictions to the Death Penalty (Arts. 4(2) and 4(4) American Convention on Human Rights)* case did provide one such standard by declaring that reservations enabling a state to suspend non-derogable provisions are *per se* incompatible with the object and purpose

---

[43] Art. 51(2), Convention on the Rights of the Child; Art. 20(2), Convention on Racial Discrimination (also providing that the objection to a reservation by two-thirds of states party to the Convention makes it inadmissible, a further limitation unlikely to have a great impact on the availability of reservations under the Convention: Meron, *Human Rights and Humanitarian Norms*, at 21); Art. 28, Convention on Discrimination Against Women.

[44] For example the 1956 Supplementary Convention on the Abolition of Slavery (Art. 9), the 1960 UNESCO Convention Against Discrimination in Education (Art. 9) and the 1987 European Convention Against Torture (Art. 21), *reprinted in* Ian Brownlie ed., *Basic Documents on Human Rights*, 3rd edn (Oxford: Clarendon, 1992) 58, 318 and 383. Likewise, there is a longstanding practice of refusing reservations to ILO conventions: International Law Commission, 'Report to the General Assembly on the Work of its 52nd Session', UN Doc. A/55/10 (2000) para. 663. See Thomas Giegerich, 'Vorbehalte zu Menschenrechtsabkommen: Zulässigkeit, Gultigkeit und Prufungskompetenzen von Vertragsgremien', (1995) 55 *Zeitschrift für ausländisches öffentliches Recht und Völkerrecht* 712, 729–35.

[45] See Liesbeth Lijnzaad, *Reservations to UN Human Rights Treaties – Ratify or Ruin?* (Dordrecht: Nijhoff, 1995) 80–103; Alain Pellet, 'Second Report on the Law and Practice Relating to Reservations to Treaties', UN Doc. A/CN.4/477 (1996) 45–52 paras. 165–76.

of the American Convention on Human Rights.[46] The Court, however, did not go so far as to declare that any reservation to such provisions would be invalid, explicitly leaving open the possibility of licit reservations which 'merely sought to restrict certain aspects of a non-derogable right without depriving the right as a whole of its basic purpose'.[47] The Human Rights Committee adopted a somewhat similar position in its General Comment on Reservations, stating that while reservations to non-derogable rights are not automatically incompatible with the object and purpose of the International Covenant on Civil and Political Rights, a state 'has a very heavy onus to justify such a reservation'.[48] It remains to be seen whether this rule will be followed with respect to other human rights conventions, given that reservations to non-derogable provisions are not uncommon.[49]

In its comment, the Committee further suggested that reservations are invalid if made in relation to *jus cogens* norms or, much more broadly, to *erga omnes* norms which embody customary standards.[50] Both elements seem quite logical: if a state may not contract out of a *jus cogens* norm by way of a treaty with other states, it should not be able to do the same by way of the more unilateral reservation mechanism. As for treaty norms which embody customary law, the international community is usually given a measure of control through the possibility of objecting

---

[46] 8 Sept. 1983, Advisory Opinion OC-3/83, Ser. A No. 3, para. 61.

[47] *Ibid.* The Court in fact found that the impugned Guatemalan reservation merely restricted the non-derogable right to life, and was therefore not incompatible with the object and purpose of the treaty.

[48] Human Rights Committee, General Comment 24 (52), 'General Comment on Issues Relating to Reservations Made Upon Ratification or Accession to the Covenant or the Optional Protocol Thereof, or in Relation to Declarations Under Article 41 of the Covenant', UN Doc. ICCPR/C/21/Rev.1/Add.6 (1994) para. 10.

[49] For instance, reservations have been made by Germany, Liechtenstein, Malta and Portugal to Arts. 2, 4 and 7 of the European Convention on Human Rights, all non-derogable provisions: Dinah Shelton, 'State Practice on Reservations to Human Rights Treaties', (1983) 1 *Can. Hum. Rts YB* 208, 225; similarly, reservations were made to Arts. 6, 7, 11, 15 and 18 of the Political Covenant by Argentina, Congo, Ireland, Italy, Mexico, Norway, Trinidad and Tobago, United Kingdom and United States: Lijnzaad, *Reservations*, at 204–14. See Jaime Oráa, *Human Rights in States of Emergency in International Law* (Oxford: Clarendon, 1992) 127–39; Giegerich, 'Vorbehalte zu Menschenrechtsabkommen', at 772–3.

[50] Human Rights Committee, General Comment 24 (52), para. 8 ('Although treaties that are mere exchanges of obligations between States allow them to reserve *inter se* application of rules of international law, it is otherwise in human rights treaties, which are for the benefit of persons within their jurisdiction. Accordingly, provisions in the Covenant that represent customary international law (and *a fortiori* when they have the character of peremptory norms) may not be the object of reservations').

to the reservation which leaves intact, as between the reserving and objecting state, the customary norm (Art. 21(3), Vienna Convention on the Law of Treaties); however, the ineffective nature of objections to reservations to human rights treaties, discussed below, means that a state would be able to opt out of a customary norm unilaterally with little possibility of international control. This unchecked right to opt out of existing customary human rights norms stands at odds with the rigid limits imposed on persistent objection to such norms.[51] Without such a rule, South Africa under the apartheid regime would have been able to opt out of the customary prohibition of racial discrimination simply by ratifying the Political Covenant and entering a reservation to that effect, a clearly problematic proposition.[52] Despite its logical and probably desirable nature, there seems to be little support in state practice for the rule proposed by the Human Rights Committee, which has also been the object of some criticism in the International Law Commission.[53]

The special nature of human rights conventions has a direct impact on the substantive effect of reservations. As mentioned earlier, these treaties represent not a contractual exchange of substantive rights and obligations but rather a unilateral undertaking by states to respect and enforce a certain set of basic individual rights. The reciprocal component of this undertaking is very limited, and at the substantive level no significant inter-state relationship is created among states party to the same human rights convention.[54] A reservation to a human rights convention alters the substance of the reserving state's obligations towards individuals under its control at the internal level, but has no significant effect at the international level. As such, little consequence attaches to the acceptance of, or objection to, the reservation by other

[51] See Brownlie, *Principles*, at 10. This goes hand in hand with an argument supporting institutional review of the validity of reservation, accepted under the European and American Conventions (see *Belilos* v. *Switzerland*, [1988] 10 Eur. Hum. Rts Rep. 466, 482–3 (Eur. Ct)) but debated in other systems (International Law Commission, 'Report to the General Assembly on the Work of its 49th Session', UN Doc. A/52/10 (1997) paras. 78–87 and 133–56; ILC, 'Report to the General Assembly on the Work of its 50th Session', UN Doc. A/53/10 (1998) paras. 483–5; Françoise Hampson, 'Reservations to Human Rights Treaties', UN Doc. E/CN.4/Sub.2/1999/28, paras. 23–30).
[52] Note that for this particular example, relief can be found if it is agreed that racial discrimination and, even more specifically, the prohibition of apartheid are peremptory norms.
[53] ILC, 'Report on the 49th Session', at 111 para. 106.
[54] *Ibid.*, at 102 para. 69 (Pellet); Matthew Craven, 'Legal Differentiation and the Concept of the Human Rights Treaty in International Law', (2000) 11 *Eur. J Int'l L* 489–519. The reciprocal component of provisions concerned with the application of human rights treaties is discussed in chapter 4.

states, because neither the reservation nor the reaction to it changes the content of the accepting or objecting state's obligations under the human rights treaty.[55] In particular, a state which objects to another's reservation could not thereby justify a refusal to grant the reserving state's nationals more protection than that offered by their own state. Such a refusal would constitute an illegal breach of the human rights convention. Under human rights law, because rights attach primarily to the individual rather than the state, even the unlawful breach of a convention by one state does not justify another's suspension of the application of the convention (Art. 60(5), Vienna Convention on the Law of Treaties).[56] A fortiori, then, a lawful limitation of a state's obligations by means of a reservation clearly cannot justify such a reaction.[57]

One possibly reciprocal effect of reservations is their use as interpretative tools by adjudicatory bodies, even in cases not involving the reserving states. For instance, in the Case of Kjeldsen, Busk, Madsen and Petersen, the European Commission of Human Rights in its report to the Court used reservations made by Sweden and the United Kingdom as evidence that the meaning of the provision as drafted was unclear, noting that '[t]hose reservations are also useful guides to its interpretation'.[58] The element of reciprocity here is very limited, however, as the interpretation given in the reservation is not applied to other states on a reciprocal basis, but solely on the basis of its soundness as a legal interpretation of the treaty.

A further possible reciprocal effect of reservations upon substantive norms is procedural, relating to the ability of the reserving state to bring

---

[55] ILC, 'Report on the 49th Session', at 103 para. 74 (Pellet). The rule adopted in Art. 21 of the Vienna Convention on the Law of Treaties thus has no effect on human rights treaties, apart from the possibility of the objecting state refusing the entry into force of the treaty between itself and the reserving state (Art. 20(4)(b)). Human Rights Committee, General Comment 24 (52), para. 17; Horn, *Reservations*, at 148 and 155; Imbert, *Réserves*, at 255; Massimo Coccia, 'Reservations to Multilateral Treaties on Human Rights', (1985) 15 *Cal. W Int'l LJ* 1, 38; Gérard Cohen-Jonathan, 'Les réserves à la Convention européenne des droits de l'homme (à propos de l'arrêt Bélilos du 29 avril 1988)', [1989] *Revue générale de droit international public* 273, 277–8; Sir Gerald Fitzmaurice, 'Reservations to Multilateral Conventions', [1953] *Int'l & Comp. L Quart.* 1, 13–16; Pellet, 'Second Report', UN Doc. A/CN.4/477 (1996), at 40 para. 155.

[56] See chapter 4.

[57] See Horn, *Reservations*, at 156–7; Imbert, *Réserves*, at 255 (suggesting that a state granting refugees limited rights because they are nationals of a state having made reservations to conventions on the status of refugees would breach at least the spirit of these conventions); Giegerich, 'Vorbehalte zu Menschenrechtsabkommen', at 753–5; Pierre-Henri Imbert, 'Reservations and Human Rights Conventions', (1981) 6 *Hum. Rts Rev.* 28, 33.

[58] Eur. Ct Hum. Rts, Ser. B No. 21, at 45; Imbert, *Réserves*, at 55.

a claim in an international forum asserting a breach of the reserved obligation by another state party. For example, India made a reservation to Article 1(1) of the International Covenant on Civil and Political Rights, stating 'that the words "the right to self-determination"...apply only to the peoples under foreign domination and that these words do not apply to sovereign independent States or to a section of a people or nation – which is the essence of national integrity'.[59] France and a number of other states objected to this reservation. Had both India and France made a declaration pursuant to Article 41 of the Political Covenant recognising the Human Rights Committee's competence to hear inter-state complaints, could India lay a claim against France for the alleged breach of Article 1(1) with respect to, for example, the Basque people, if it appeared clearly that such a conduct would be covered by the Indian reservation? It has been suggested, incorrectly, that despite the fact that obligations under human rights conventions are not reciprocal, a state having made a reservation cannot force compliance with the reserved norm on the part of other states party to the same convention.[60] Following that position, India's claim in the previous example would be rejected by the Human Rights Committee on the basis of reciprocity.

This interpretation disregards the *erga omnes* character of human rights conventions. Given that a state's obligations to comply with certain human rights norms are not conditional on a similar undertaking or compliance by other states, the state in breach of its obligation could not excuse its violation based on the fact that the petitioning state was not similarly obligated. In the field of human rights, a state that acts to force another's compliance with its obligations pursuant to a treaty does not have any national legal interest in the matter (however politically charged its petition may be), but instead acts on behalf of the community of states party to the treaty to enforce public order norms protecting individuals. Thus in the *Barcelona Traction* case, the individualised legal interest which a state must prove in order to bring a claim to enforce 'obligations the performance of which is the subject of diplomatic protection' was contrasted by the ICJ to the general interest of all states in the observance of obligations *erga omnes* such as human rights norms.[61] This position also conforms to the decision of the European Commission of Human Rights in *Austria* v. *Italy*, which allowed a claim brought by

---

[59] Shelton, 'State Practice', at 212.
[60] Horn, *Reservations*, at 158–9; Campiglio, *Il principio*, at 187–9; ILC, 'Report on the Work of its 49th Session', at 117 para. 127.
[61] *Barcelona Traction, Light and Power Co. Ltd (Belgium v. Spain)*, [1970] ICJ Rep. 3, 32.

Austria even though it related to a violation that took place prior to Austria's ratification of the European Convention on Human Rights.[62] If a state can bring a valid claim with respect to a violation committed at a time when it was not at all obligated under a human rights convention, then a state can clearly do the same despite having made a reservation and thus limited its own obligation under the convention. Adherence to the system, rather than to a specific norm, is the requirement to have standing.[63] The European Commission in *France* v. *Turkey* concluded that this extends even to reservations to the jurisdiction of treaty bodies, which cannot be opposed on the basis of reciprocity unless the treaty specifically provides for that possibility.[64] The only tangible effect of rejecting a claim on the basis of a reservation by the petitioning state, by effect of reciprocity, would be to deny individuals the benefit of the human rights convention until another state came along to present the same petition to the enforcement body.

HUMANITARIAN LAW

In the field of humanitarian law, none of the 1907 Hague Conventions, 1949 Geneva Conventions, 1954 Hague Convention on Cultural Property, 1977 Additional Protocols or 1981 UN Convention on Conventional Weapons contains any provision dealing with the admissibility or effect of reservations. States consequently enjoy vast discretion in drafting reservations to humanitarian conventions, limited only – and perhaps only theoretically – by the customary requirement that the reservations be compatible with the object and purpose of the conventions.[65] At a

---

[62] Appl. 788/60, [1961] YB Eur. Conv. Hum. Rts 116, 142 (Eur. Com'n Hum. Rts). See also Meron, *Human Rights and Humanitarian Norms*, at 203–4.

[63] Even that requirement is not an absolute condition for possessing standing under human rights treaties, as exemplified by the American Convention on Human Rights where individuals and groups – which are not party to the Convention – from any member state may present an application to the Inter-American Commission on Human Rights (Art. 44).

[64] *France, Norway, Denmark, Sweden and the Netherlands* v. *Turkey*, Cases Nos. 9940–4/82, (1983) 35 Decisions and Reports 143, 169. Acceptance of supervisory bodies' competence to receive inter-state petitions is most often conditioned on reciprocity by the treaty provision itself. See e.g. Art. 46(2), European Convention (competence of the Court); Art. 41, International Covenant on Civil and Political Rights; Art. 21, Convention Against Torture; Art. 76, International Convention on the Protection of the Rights of All Migrant Workers and their Families, 1990, *reprinted in* Brownlie, *Basic Documents*, at 203; Arts. 45(2) and 62(3), American Convention on Human Rights.

[65] The ICRC had proposed a detailed provision on reservations for Protocol I, specifying which articles were non-reservable and requiring the renewal of reservations every five

minimum, reservations which would undermine the short list of standards found in common Article 3 of the 1949 Geneva Conventions, representing 'elementary considerations of humanity', would surely be considered inconsistent with the object and purpose of these conventions.[66] The distinct nature of obligations created under humanitarian conventions, in contrast to those under human rights treaties, is reflected in the effect of reservations on the relationship between the parties. As noted earlier, there is a significant inter-state component to humanitarian rights and obligations, largely based on immediate reciprocity. According to common Article 2 of the 1949 Geneva Conventions, only state parties are obligated towards one another. Under the Conventions, High Contracting Parties have no obligation towards non-party states. The reciprocity of obligations applies not only to the conventions generally, but also to a certain extent to rules embodied in the conventions. As such, particular bilateral relationships are created between state parties, the content of which varies according to reservations made by each state. For example, several French and British maritime prize court decisions at the start of the First World War found that Germany could not claim the benefit of some provisions of the 1907 Hague Convention VI because it was itself not bound by the Convention's rules as a result of reservations it had made.[67] In other words, Germany's reservations had altered its relationships with France and Britain. The reciprocal nature of reservations to humanitarian treaties was expressly mentioned in the United States' observations upon ratification of the Geneva Conventions.

years. The proposal was not adopted by the 1974–7 Geneva Conference: Claude Pilloud, 'Reservations and the 1949 Geneva Conventions (1)', (1976) 180 Int'l Rev. Red Cross 107, 108. See also Claude Pilloud, 'Les réserves aux Conventions de Genève de 1949', [1957] Revue internationale de la Croix-Rouge 409–37; Claude Pilloud, 'Reservations and the 1949 Geneva Conventions', (1965) Int'l Rev. Red Cross 315–24; Claude Pilloud, 'Reservations and the 1949 Geneva Conventions (2)', (1976) 181 Int'l Rev. Red Cross 163–87.

[66] Military and Paramilitary Activities in and Against Nicaragua (Nicaragua v. USA), [1986] ICJ Rep. 14, 114. See Greig, 'Reciprocity', at 301–4. Some have gone so far as to suggest that all humanitarian norms are jus cogens and therefore non-reservable, but that position appears unsubstantiated by state practice. See Legality of the Threat or Use of Nuclear Weapons, Advisory Opinion, [1996] ICJ Rep. para. 83 (where the Court touches on the question without answering it); Dissenting Opinion of Judge Weeramantry, ibid., at 44 (concluding that 'the rules of humanitarian law of war have clearly acquired the status of ius cogens'); The Prosecutor v. Kupreskić (Lasva Valley case) (Judgment), 14 Jan. 2000, Case No. IT-95-16-T (Trial Chamber, ICTY), para. 520 (noting that most of humanitarian law is jus cogens, but without any supporting analysis); Eric David, Principes de droit des conflits armés (Brussels: Bruylant, 1994) 89.

[67] 1907 Hague Convention VI Relating to the Status of Enemy Merchant Ships at the Outbreak of Hostilities, 18 October 1907, reprinted in Schindler and Toman, Laws of Armed Conflict, at 791; Horn, Reservations, at 145; Imbert, Réserves, at 251.

In rejecting reservations made by other states, the United States declared that it 'accept[ed] treaty relations with all parties to that Convention, except as to the changes proposed by such reservations'.[68] Such a rejection removes norms targeted by the reservations of other states from treaty relations, and leaves them regulated only by custom. Acceptance of reservations by another state, on the other hand, has the effect of creating a distinct regime shaped by the reservations.[69]

The influence of reservations on state practice must be differentiated from that of reprisals. A reserved rule never forms part of the normative relationship between the reserving state and the other states party to the convention. In the case of reprisal, however, a state temporarily suspends compliance with its obligations under a convention in order to force another state party similarly bound to abide by those obligations.[70] This implies that rules in the 1949 Geneva Conventions and 1977 Additional Protocols prohibiting reprisals against various groups of protected persons would be irrelevant if subject to reservation by one of the belligerent states. For instance, a large group of states, including the Democratic Republic of (North) Vietnam and the Provisional Revolutionary Government of the Republic of South Vietnam, made reservations regarding Article 85 of the 1949 Third Geneva Convention, whereby prisoners of war accused and convicted of war crimes would no longer be granted prisoner-of-war status. Other states, including the United States and the United Kingdom, have objected to such reservations.[71] Thus, if there were valid convictions of grave breaches of humanitarian law, the denial of prisoner-of-war status to US airmen held by North Vietnam during the Vietnam war would not have constituted a breach of its obligations under the Third Geneva Convention, nor would identical retaliatory practices of the United States, despite

[68] Reprinted in Schindler and Toman, *Laws of Armed Conflict*, at 590. This is confirmed by a statement of the US Senate Committee on Foreign Relations with respect to this reservation: 'It is the Committee's view that this statement adequately expresses the intention of our Government to enter into treaty relations with the reserving States so that they will be bound toward the United States to carry out reciprocally all the provisions of the Conventions on which no reservations were specifically made', Report of the Committee on Foreign Relations, 48th Congress, 1st session, Washington, 1955, at 29, *reprinted in* Pilloud, 'Reservations (1)', at 113.

[69] Horn, *Reservations*, at 161–2; Imbert, *Réserves*, at 362–6; Jean de Preux, 'The Geneva Conventions and Reciprocity', (1985) 244 *Int'l Rev. Red Cross* 25, 26.

[70] See below, chapter 5, pp. 183–201.

[71] The reservations and objections are reprinted in Schindler and Toman, *Laws of Armed Conflict*, at 588–92.

the prohibition of reprisals against prisoners of war found in Article 13 of that convention.[72]

Reservations have a reciprocal effect even with respect to some provisions in humanitarian conventions which mirror the protection granted individuals under human rights treaties. There have been some attempts in the past to divide humanitarian law into 'Hague law' and 'Geneva law', the first being technical and reciprocal, the second purely humanitarian and unilateral.[73] Apart from the difficulty inherent in such a rigid compartmentalisation of norms which often straddle 'Hague law' and 'Geneva law', even 'purely humanitarian' norms are not free from reciprocity. Such 'humanitarian' norms include, for instance, the protection against physical or moral coercion (Art. 31, 1949 Fourth Geneva Convention) and the prohibition against the torture of prisoners of war (Art. 17, 1949 Third Geneva Convention). Yet the fact that only certain classes of persons are entitled to the protection offered by these norms, excluding for instance a state's own nationals as well as nationals of states not party to the conventions, suggests that they are not unilateral undertakings by states. Rather, these norms supplement international standards on the treatment of aliens and create bilateral obligations between the parties to the conflict. As such, reservations to these provisions would have a reciprocal effect on the parallel obligations of other states in their relations with the reserving state. For example, the United States' reservation to Article 68 of the 1949 Fourth Geneva Convention relating to the imposition of the death penalty by an occupying power could be invoked by its enemy during an armed conflict.[74] The rationale for this reciprocity is that the protection given to individuals under the 1949 Geneva Conventions does not attach to any human being *per se*, but rather derives from membership in a group, be it as nationals of an

---

[72] This is true despite the acceptance by both states, without any reservations, of the provision prohibiting reprisals in the 1949 Third Geneva Convention, because reprisals involve the suspension of binding obligations and, as between North Vietnam and the United States, Article 85 never became binding. See Campiglio, *Il principio*, at 190–2; Imbert, *Réserves*, at 362; Howard S. Levie, 'Maltreatment of Prisoners of War in Vietnam', (1968) 48 *Boston UL Rev.* 323, 344–52; Henri Meyrowitz, 'Le droit de la guerre dans le conflit vietnamien', [1967] *Annuaire français de droit international* 153, 196–7.

[73] See *Legality of the Threat or Use of Nuclear Weapons*, Advisory Opinion, [1996] ICJ Rep. para. 75; *The Prosecutor v. Delalić* (the 'Celebici' case) (Appeals Judgment), 20 Feb. 2001, Case No. IT-96-21-A (Appeals Chamber, ICTY), para. 132; Stanislaw E. Nahlik, 'Droit dit "de Genève" et droit dit "de la Haye": Unicité ou dualité?', [1978] *Annuaire français de droit international* 9–27.

[74] See Pilloud, 'Reservations (1)', at 184.

enemy state or as members of the armed forces.[75] The granting of individual protection under the Geneva Convention is conditionally linked to the behaviour of the group or state, especially its acceptance of obligations under humanitarian conventions.[76]

Not all norms of humanitarian conventions follow this pattern, however, because not all can be considered bilateralisable. As was pointed out earlier, part of humanitarian law embodies *erga omnes* obligations which do not lead to the formation of a series of parallel bilateral links, but rather to duties exercised unilaterally and owed to the international community as a whole. In a fashion similar to human rights law, reservations to conventional provisions which embody this type of norm do not latch on to an international relation and produce no reciprocal effect. For example, the United States made a reservation regarding the duty to control the domestic use of the red cross emblem (Art. 53, First Geneva Convention) and Israel made a reservation to indicate its intention to use the red shield of David rather than the red cross or red crescent (Art. 38, First Geneva Convention).[77] Although there is some international dimension to these rules, they primarily relate to the internal obligations of state parties and produce no significant reciprocal effect.[78] More importantly, a number of crucial provisions of the Geneva Conventions and Protocols also contain non-bilateralisable norms, including common Article 3 of the 1949 Geneva Conventions, Part II of the Fourth Geneva Convention, Articles 73 and 75 of Protocol I, and Protocol II as a whole.[79] Reciprocity plays little role with respect to these norms, so that reservations affecting them would not have any significant impact on relations between High Contracting Parties.

In conclusion, a measure of confusion exists in both human rights law and humanitarian law as to the reciprocal nature of reservations. Broadly speaking, in order for reservations to operate on a reciprocal

---

[75] This is made clear in the case of Art. 31 of the Fourth Convention and Art. 17 of the Third Convention by the fact that both provisions specify the prohibition to apply in particular where the coercion or torture aims at obtaining information from the protected persons. See Henri Meyrowitz, 'Le droit de la guerre et les droits de l'homme', (1972) 88 *Revue de droit public et de la science politique en France et à l'étranger* 1059, 1100.

[76] See above, chapter 1, pp. 34–42.

[77] *Reprinted in* Schindler and Toman, *Laws of Armed Conflict*, at 576.

[78] See Greig, 'Reciprocity', at 333; Pilloud, 'Reservations (1)', at 124.

[79] Claude Pilloud et al., *Commentary on the Additional Protocols of 8 June 1977 to the Geneva Conventions of 12 August 1949* (Geneva: Nijhoff, 1987) 869; Mohammed El Kouhene, *Les garanties fondamentales de la personne en droit humanitaire et droits de l'homme* (Dordrecht: Nijhoff, 1986) 43.

basis, there must be an inter-state component to the relationship created by the treaty whereby substantive rights and obligations are interdependent. This inter-state component is present both in human rights and in humanitarian law, at degrees which vary not only as between these two areas of law, but also within each, thereby making generalisations difficult. It must be acknowledged, however, that with respect to reservations, as with the creation of obligations more broadly, immediate reciprocity plays a much more prominent role in humanitarian law than in human rights, a reflection of the different place of reciprocity in the substantive inter-state relationships created. Human rights norms represent a collective statement of shared values and the converging commitments of states to uphold them. Their very nature sows the seeds of relationships based on trust which can sustain a regime grounded in systemic reciprocity. Shared values are also significant in humanitarian law, more so now than fifty years ago, but there remains in the nature of relationships governed by these norms a pull towards immediate reciprocity which reflects the strong state interests present.

4   Application

The analysis now turns to the role played by reciprocity in the application of obligations contracted under both human rights law and humanitarian law. Its relevance is examined with respect to, first, the conditions of applicability of each system, and secondly, the suspension and termination of treaty human rights and humanitarian law norms.

Initial applicability and reciprocity

Neither human rights nor humanitarian law is grounded in the principle that the benefit of a norm should be given to a certain individual or group only in so far as that individual or group abides by the same obligation. Beyond this general pronouncement, differences arise between the two areas of law with regard to the place of reciprocity in the application of norms.

HUMAN RIGHTS

In human rights law, obligations pertaining to substantive norms are absolute or, in other words, unconditional and *erga omnes*.[1] Human rights are construed liberally to apply 'always, everywhere, and to everyone'.[2] There are, in fact, limitations to the applicability of human rights based on, for example, nationality or membership in a minority group. These limitations, however, incorporate no element of reciprocity based on the

---

[1] Emmanuel Decaux, *La réciprocité en droit international* (Paris: LGDJ, 1980) 58; Pierre-Marie Dupuy, *Droit international public* (Paris: Dalloz, 1996) 135–6; Theodor Meron, *Human Rights and Humanitarian Norms as Customary Law* (Oxford: Clarendon, 1989) 188–201.

[2] See UN Secretary-General, 'Respect for Human Rights in Armed Conflicts', UN Doc. A/8052 (1970) 13 para. 25.

152

behaviour of the benefited person or group.[3] That the latter may lose the right to exercise some human rights fully because of the adverse effect on the rights of others is a question conceptually distinct from initial applicability of these rights to the individual or group. It raises not so much elements of reciprocity but rather limitations on the content and effect of human rights.[4]

HUMANITARIAN LAW

In humanitarian law, two levels of applicability must be differentiated: first, the initial applicability of norms such that an armed conflict is governed by conventional rules, and second, in an armed conflict in which humanitarian rules do govern, the applicability of these norms to specific classes of individuals and groups.

Applicability to armed conflicts

In a broad manner, there must be some reciprocity for humanitarian conventions to become applicable to an international armed conflict. This is most clearly evidenced by common Article 2 of the 1949 Geneva Conventions and Article 96(2) of Protocol I, whereby conventional norms govern belligerent relations among High Contracting Parties but not between a party and a state not party to the Conventions. For example, the 1929 Geneva Convention on Prisoners of War was not directly applicable between the United States and Japan during the Second World War because Japan was not a party. The two states did exchange communications with a view nevertheless to applying the terms of the Convention on the basis of reciprocity.[5] Germany, for her part, complied with the 1929 Convention in its treatment of prisoners of war from treaty parties such as France or the United Kingdom, but refused to grant similar treatment to Soviet prisoners of war because the USSR was not a party and refused to agree to apply the Convention.[6]

---

[3] See above, chapter 1, pp. 18–26.

[4] See e.g. *Kommunistische Partei Deutschland* v. *Federal Republic of Germany*, Appl. 250/57, [1955–7] *YB Eur. Conv. Hum. Rts* 222 (with respect to Art. 17 of the European Convention).

[5] See *Judgment of the International Military Tribunal for the Far East*, 1 November 1948, *reprinted in* B. V. A. Röling and C. F. Rüter eds., *The Tokyo Judgment* (Amsterdam: UP Amsterdam, 1977) I, 422–5.

[6] A distinction graphically illustrated by Marcel Junod, *Le troisième combattant* (Geneva: ICRC, 1989) 262.

Reliance on reciprocity, however, even at that very general level, is by no means absolute. Under paragraph 3 of common Article 2 of the Geneva Conventions and Article 96 of Protocol I, belligerent relations between a party to the Conventions and a non-party will be governed by the Conventions if the latter 'accepts and applies' the provisions of the Conventions, terms which are not devoid of ambiguities. For instance, it is not clear whether the acceptance by the non-party must be express or may be implied from that state's conduct.[7] On the question of reciprocity, there was a debate at the 1949 Geneva Conference as to whether the state party should apply the Conventions until it becomes apparent that the non-party refuses to accept and apply their norms (resolutive approach), or whether the Conventions should remain inapplicable until the non-party makes a declaration and starts applying their provisions (suspensive approach).[8] The text of Article 2(3) eventually adopted does not provide any indication as to which approach was preferred. The uncertainty remained and the debate was repeated at the 1977 Geneva Conference, once again not resulting in any clear choice.[9] In accordance with a party's obligation to 'respect and ensure respect for' the Conventions 'in all circumstances' (common Art. 1), and taking into consideration the fact that any hesitation in declaring the Conventions applicable risks derailing the fragile mechanism provided by common Article 2(3) and Article 96(2) of Protocol I, the resolutive approach seems the more appropriate.[10] The Conventions would thus apply despite a lack of express reciprocity, based on a rebuttable presumption that the non-party

---

[7] The danger is illustrated by the refusal by South Africa to accept the validity of such a declaration by SWAPO in 1976 because it was not formal enough: Edward K. Kwakwa, *The International Law of Armed Conflict: Personal and Material Field of Application* (Dordrecht: Nijhoff, 1992) 71; John Dugard, 'SWAPO: The *Jus ad Bellum* and the *Jus in Bello*', (1976) 93 *S Afr. LJ* 144, 152–7. This was resolved with respect to the 1981 UN Convention on Conventional Weapons by requiring that the non-party send notification of its acceptance to the depositary (Art. 7(2)). The same is required of national liberation movements under Art. 96(3) of Protocol I.

[8] See II-B *Final Record of the Diplomatic Conference of Geneva of 1949* (Berne: Federal Political Dept, 1949) 107–8; Jean Pictet ed., *The Geneva Conventions of 12 August 1949 – Commentary on the III Geneva Convention Relative to the Treatment of Prisoners of War* (Geneva: ICRC, 1960) 21–7.

[9] Compare the positions of the Federal Republic of Germany, for whom only common Art. 3 applies before a declaration by the non-party state that it accepts and applies the Conventions (CDDH/I/SR.78 para. 2, 8 *Off. Records* 369), and of Vietnam, which proposed an amendment whereby the state party is bound by the Protocol until the enemy 'after a reasonable period, declares that it refuses to apply it or does not in fact apply it' (CDDH/I/350/Rev.1 para. 13, 10 *Off. Records* 237).

[10] Pictet, III, at 25–6; Claude Pilloud et al., *Commentary on the Additional Protocols of 8 June 1977 to the Geneva Conventions of 12 August 1949* (Geneva: Nijhoff, 1987) 1087–8. But see

would accept and apply their provisions. Reciprocity is suspended but
not discarded. That is, the Conventions cease to apply if they are refused
or consistently not complied with by the non-party.[11]

The applicability of customary humanitarian law to an international
armed conflict does not raise the same problem, given that all states
are bound by these norms. Every armed conflict is automatically subject to customary humanitarian law, without any condition relating to
reciprocity.[12] Given that customary humanitarian law is a large body of
norms, comprising at least the basic elements of the 1907 Hague Convention IV and Regulations, the 1949 Geneva Conventions and at least
parts of Protocols I and II, this is a significant principle.[13]

In wars of national liberation, characterised as international armed
conflicts under Article 1(4) of Protocol I, the rebel authority must make
an express declaration, communicated to the depositary, of its intention
to apply the Protocol and Conventions (Art. 96(3), Protocol I).[14] Given that

Bruno Simma, *Das Reziprozitätselement in zutstandekommen völkerrechtlicher Verträge*
(Berlin: Duncker & Humblot, 1972) 107–8; Howard S. Levie, 'Maltreatment of
Prisoners of War in Vietnam', (1968) 48 *Boston UL Rev.* 323, 327.

[11] This was made particularly clear in the 1954 Convention for the Protection of
Cultural Property in the Event of Armed Conflict, 14 May 1954, *reprinted in* Dietrich
Schindler and Jiří Toman, *The Laws of Armed Conflict*, 3rd edn (Dordrecht: Nijhoff, 1989)
25, at 745 (hereinafter 1954 Hague Convention on Cultural Property), providing in
Article 18(3) that the Convention shall apply 'so long as it [the non-party] applies [its
provisions]'. See also Arts. 91 and 102, Legge di guerra italiana del 1938. In this
respect, Art. 60(5) of the Vienna Convention on the Law of Treaties represents an
attempt to render unconditional the duty to comply with a humanitarian
convention once it has been agreed to apply it: see below, pp. 178–9.

[12] Israel made a statement with respect to several declarations by Oman, Syria and the
United Arab Emirates regarding the non-recognition of Israel pursuant to accession
to Protocol I. The Israeli statement provides that the declarations 'cannot in any way
affect whatever obligations are binding... under general international law or under
particular conventions', and that it would adopt 'an attitude of complete reciprocity'
(*reprinted in* Schindler and Toman, *Laws of Armed Conflict*, at 711–12). The last part of
this statement referring to 'complete reciprocity' should be taken to refer to
conventional obligations only, and not to customary law.

[13] *Legality of the Threat or Use of Nuclear Weapons*, Advisory Opinion, [1996] ICJ Rep. para.
79.

[14] The idea that a non-state entity is not a 'power' capable of taking advantage of
common Art. 2(3) is still a debated proposition: Georges Abi-Saab, 'Wars of National
Liberation and the Laws of War', (1972) 3 *Annales d'études internationales* 102–7; Georges
Abi-Saab, 'Wars of National Liberation in the Geneva Conventions and Protocols',
(1979-IV) 165 *Recueil des cours* 357; Antonio Cassese ed., *The New Humanitarian Law of
Armed Conflict – Proceedings of the 1976 and 1977 Conferences* (Naples: Ed. Scientifica, 1980)
26 (Cassese); Denise Plattner, 'La portée juridique des déclarations de respect du droit
international humanitaire qui émanent de mouvements en lutte dans un conflit
armé', (1984–5) 18 *Revue belge de droit international* 298–320.

this condition is clear and its fulfilment independently observable, it has been suggested that the state party to Protocol I has no obligation to apply the provisions prior to express acceptance by the national liberation movement.[15] In accordance with the characterisation in Protocol I of national liberation wars as international armed conflicts, the regime is closer to accession than to acceptance by a non-party state under Article 96(2). That is, upon acceptance of the Conventions and Protocol *as a whole* (and no longer 'of [their] provisions', Art. 2(3) of the Conventions), the authority representing a people engaged in a liberation struggle is immediately subject to their force.[16] As in the case of armed conflicts amongst states party to the Conventions and Protocol, the instruments will apply to the conflict without any condition based on reciprocity requiring that the liberation movement 'apply' the provisions.[17]

In internal conflicts, common Article 3 of the 1949 Geneva Conventions sets basic standards which must be complied with by all parties, irrespective of the conduct of enemy combatants. No express or implied acceptance of, nor factual compliance with, conventional rules is required. The ICJ in the *Nicaragua* case found in this provision a customary minimum regime applicable in all circumstances.[18] Common Article 3 and its customary equivalent thereby impose an absolute obligation, completely disconnected from reciprocity, on all parties to an armed conflict.[19] Protocol II, which develops and supplements common

---

[15] Heather A. Wilson, *International Law and the Use of Force by National Liberation Movements* (Oxford: Clarendon, 1988) 169–70.

[16] See W. Thomas Mallison and Sally V. Mallison, 'The Juridical Status of Privileged Combatants Under the Geneva Protocol of 1977 Concerning International Conflicts', (1978) 42:2 *L & Contemp. Problems* 4, 14 (relating that many experts at the 1977 Conference privately expressed misgivings about imposing an obligation to apply the Conventions and Protocol as a whole, which will often prove impossible for national liberation movements).

[17] Pilloud et al., *ICRC Commentary*, at 1089–90. This is also the case for ratification by a state involved in an armed conflict. The normal six-month delay is inapplicable and the Conventions immediately enter into force for the ratifying state (Arts. 62/61/142/157). There is thus no resort to common Art. 2(3) or Art. 96(2) of Protocol I, unless the armed conflict involves another belligerent not party to the Conventions or Protocol. Pictet, III, at 646.

[18] *Military and Paramilitary Activities in and Against Nicaragua (Nicaragua v. USA)*, [1986] ICJ Rep. 14, 114.

[19] II-B *Final Record*, at 94 ('any civilized government should feel bound to apply the principles of the Convention even if the insurgents failed to apply them': Sir Robert Craigie, UK Representative); Jean Pictet ed., *The Geneva Conventions of 12 August 1949 – Commentary on the IV Geneva Convention Relative to the Protection of Civilian Persons in Times of War* (Geneva: ICRC, 1958) 36–7; W. J. Ford, 'Resistance Movements and International Law', (1967–8) 79 *Int'l Rev. Red Cross* 515, 517. It is worth noting that in

Article 3, adds a condition in that the conflict must take place between government forces and dissident armed forces capable of implementing the rules set out in the Protocol (Art. 1(1)) if its norms are to apply. This is more restrictive than common Article 3, but there is no reciprocity requirement, the rather low threshold being that the dissident armed group 'may reasonably be expected to apply the rules developed in the Protocol'.[20] The internal armed conflict in El Salvador offers an example of two unilateral undertakings, one by the insurgents and one by the government, to abide by common Article 3 and Protocol II.[21]

Rejection of reciprocity in the context of internal conflicts may sometimes adversely affect the chances that the state concerned will acknowledge the existence of hostilities intense enough to warrant application of Article 3 or Protocol II. For instance, one of the reasons for France's reluctance to apply Article 3 in Algeria was said to be the fact that the rebels were not similarly obligated.[22] Parties to an internal armed

the initial draft presented by the ICRC at the 1949 Conference, application of the whole of humanitarian law in a non-international armed conflict was expressly conditioned on reciprocity: Pictet, IV, at 29; Jean Siotis, *Le droit de la guerre et les conflits armés d'un caractère non-international* (Paris: LGDJ, 1958) 190–3 and 203–4; Charles Zorgbibe, 'De la théorie classique de la reconnaissance de belligérance à l'Article 3 des Conventions de Genève', in *Droit humanitaire et conflits armés – Actes du colloque du 28 au 30 janvier 1970, Université libre de Bruxelles* (Brussels: Ed. U de Bruxelles, 1976) 91–2.

[20] Pilloud et al., *ICRC Commentary*, at 1353; Abella v. Argentina (*La Tablada* case), Rep. No. 55/97, Case No. 11,137, OAS Doc. OEA/Ser.L/V/II.97 doc. 38 (1997) para. 174 ('the obligation to apply Common Article 3 is absolute for both parties and independent of the obligation of the other'). See e.g. the Swiss Government note of 20 January 1986 regarding the applicability of Protocol II to El Salvador in 1986, where the standard is stated as '[i]l faut donc établir si, compte tenu de la situation de fait, les dissidents peuvent assurer l'application de cet instrument; *peu importe s'ils le font effectivement*': Lucius Caflisch, 'Pratique suisse relative au droit international en 1986', (1987) 43 *Annuaire suisse de droit international* 185–7 (emphasis added). *Contra* Frits Kalshoven, *Constraints on the Waging of War* (Dordrecht: Nijhoff, 1987) 138; Peter Kooijmans, 'In the Shadowland between Civil War and Civil Strife: Some Reflections on the Standard-Setting Process', in Astrid Delissen and Gerard Tanja eds., *Humanitarian Law of Armed Conflict: Challenges Ahead – Essays in Honour of Frits Kalshoven* (Dordrecht: Nijhoff, 1991) 225, 233.

[21] FMLN, *La legitimidad de nuestros métodos de lucha* (El Salvador: Secretaria de promoción y protección de los derechos humanos del FMLN, 1989) 89; El Salvador, *Informe de la Fuerza Armada de El Salvador sobre el respecto y la vigencia de las normas del derecho internacional humanitario durante el período de septiembre de 1986 a agosto de 1987* (1987). Both are cited in *The Prosecutor v. Tadić* (Decision on the Defence Motion for Interlocutory Appeal on Jurisdiction), 2 Oct. 1995, Case No. IT-94-1-AR72 (Appeals Chamber, ICTY) 58–9 para. 107 and 63 para. 117, also referring to similar unilateral undertakings by the Congo in 1964 and Nigeria in 1967.

[22] See Simma, *Das Raziprozitätselement*, at 106–7; Tom J. Farer, 'The Laws of War 25 Years After Nuremberg', (1971) 358 *Int'l Conciliation* 47.

conflict may of course pay heed to the call made in common Article 3 to pass agreements to apply humanitarian norms over and above those provided in that provision and Protocol II. Such agreements have been made in the past, such as the 1994 agreement between the Guatemalan Government and rebels to apply Protocol II despite its legal inapplicability to the conflict, and do entail reliance on reciprocity.[23]

Applicability to individuals and groups

Even when an armed conflict clearly calls for the application of humanitarian law, some rules in both customary and conventional law limit its reach to groups and individuals which themselves comply with humanitarian law.[24] In this sense, all obligations are not unconditional and absolute, but rather depend, in certain circumstances, on the reciprocal behaviour of those who will benefit from the norms in question. This element of reciprocity thus becomes a condition of applicability alongside others such as nationality and, for combatants, responsible command, the open carrying of arms and the wearing of distinctive markings.[25]

A distinction must be made between rules that protect combatants and those protecting non-combatants.[26] That is, rules protecting non-combatants apply independently of the behaviour of protected persons. Individuals may by their actions jeopardise their status as non-combatants, and thus their entitlement to the protection granted by these rules (Art. 5, 1949 Fourth Geneva Convention), but that possibility is conceptually distinct from the question of whether the rules applied to them in the first place. The application of humanitarian law follows in this respect the same pattern as that of human rights.[27]

The rules of the 1949 Geneva Conventions that protect combatants also apply regardless of reciprocity when the combatants form part of the regular forces of two states party to the Conventions engaged in

---

[23] See Adama Dieng, 'La mise en oeuvre du droit international humanitaire: Les infractions et les sanctions, ou quand la pratique désavoue les textes', in *Law in Humanitarian Crises – How Can International Humanitarian Law be Made Effective in Armed Conflict?* (Luxembourg: European Communities, 1995) I, 311, 339–40.

[24] See e.g. Art. 4(A)(2), 1949 Third Geneva Convention, and Art. 43, Protocol I.

[25] On these conditions, see above, chapter 1, pp. 34–7.

[26] This is different from a classification distinguishing between 'Hague law' and 'Geneva law': Yoram Dinstein, 'Human Rights in Armed Conflict: International Humanitarian Law', in Theodor Meron ed., *Human Rights in International Law: Legal and Policy Issues* (Oxford: Clarendon, 1984) II, 345, 348–9.

[27] See above, note 2 and accompanying text.

an international armed conflict. Thus, conventional rules apply with regard to every enemy unit despite its possible disregard for humanitarian law.[28] This is translated in paragraph 121 of the 1958 *British Manual of Military Law* into a clear rejection of a broad principle of reciprocity: 'A belligerent is not justified in declaring himself freed altogether from the obligation to observe the laws of war or any of them on account of their suspected or ascertained violation by his adversary.'[29] Protocol I departs somewhat from this regime in that it defines regular armed forces of a belligerent as those which, among other conditions, comply with rules of humanitarian law (Art. 43(1)). This reflects the definition of international armed conflict, found in Article 1(4) of the Protocol, which includes conflicts between a government and a people in furtherance of its right to self-determination, where the fighting takes place between government and dissident forces. The framework of the Geneva Conventions is thus abandoned in Protocol I, in that reliance on reciprocity is also present at the application stage in a fashion similar to the regime, described below, which applies to international armed conflicts involving irregular combatants.[30]

Application of humanitarian law between regular forces and irregular combatants in an international armed conflict relies on direct reciprocity. This is so under both customary and conventional law, in that

[28] Once again applicability refers here to the initial binding force of humanitarian rules and not their possible suspension or the taking of reprisals following violations by the enemy.

[29] The rejection of reciprocity is not phrased in absolute terms, as indicated by the word 'altogether', leaving open the possibility of temporarily disregarding the laws of war in reprisals against an earlier violation by the enemy (as provided for in paragraphs 642–9 of the Manual). The Manual gives as an example of unlawful reliance on reciprocity the German 'Commissar Order' of 22 June 1941 in which it was declared that the laws of war did not apply to communist commissars in the Soviet army because they would not themselves recognise its validity: para. 121 note 1(a), 1958 *British Manual of Military Law*.

[30] This change in Protocol I, apparently towards greater reliance on reciprocity between all types of armed forces, may explain the relatively open position taken in this respect by the 1992 *German Manual on Humanitarian Law in Armed Conflict*, DSK VV207320067 (Bonn: German Ministry of Defence, 1992) (hereinafter 1992 *German Manual on Humanitarian Law*). The Manual states in para. 1204 that 'People complying with the provisions of international humanitarian law can expect the adversary to observe the dictates of humanity in an armed conflict. No one shall be guided by the suspicion that the soldiers of the other party to the conflict might not observe these rules. Soldiers must treat their opponents in the same manner as they themselves want to be treated.' This provision lends itself much more easily than para. 121 of the 1958 *British Manual* to being construed as permitting a rejection of the binding character of humanitarian norms once they have been violated by the adversary.

humanitarian norms apply only if complied with by the irregular forces. Articles 1(4) and 2 of the 1907 Hague Regulations, as well as Articles 13(2)–(6)/13(2)–(6)/4(A)(2)–(6) of the 1949 First, Second and Third Geneva Conventions, articulate as a condition for the applicability of the laws of war to militia, resistance groups and *levées en masse* that they too 'conduct their operations in accordance with the laws and customs of war'. Clearly, then, the operation of humanitarian norms depends on immediate reciprocity between the regular forces and irregulars. Government forces belonging to a state party to the 1907 Hague Convention IV or 1949 Geneva Conventions, or bound by customary law, are under no duty to treat as privileged belligerents the members of irregular units which consistently disregard humanitarian law.[31] On the other hand, if irregular forces abide by the laws of armed conflict – in addition to complying with the other conditions for privileged irregular belligerency – then regular forces have no discretion to deny their application.[32] Protocol I, as we have seen, rejects the distinction between regular and irregular privileged belligerents, and similarly conditions applicability of humanitarian law on reciprocity in all cases.[33]

In situations of internal armed conflict, no distinction is drawn by common Article 3 or Protocol II between regular and irregular, or privileged and unprivileged combatants. The very notion of privileged belligerency in the context of non-international war has been rejected so far. Given that only one category of privileged belligerents, the armed forces of the state party, is given recognition, there can be no element

[31] See Henri Meyrowitz, 'La guérilla et le droit de la guerre, problèmes principaux', in *Droit humanitaire et conflits armés*, at 185, 197.

[32] For example, during the Second World War, the *Forces françaises de l'intérieur* – which complied with the other conditions on privileged belligerents – stated their intention to apply the terms of the 1929 Geneva Convention on Prisoners of War, but that statement was rejected by the German forces (ICRC, *Report of the International Committee of the Red Cross on its Activities During the Second World War* (Geneva: ICRC, 1949) I, 519–23). The context was somewhat different in that the 1929 Geneva Convention on Prisoners of War (Art. 82) did not envisage its acceptance by a non-party state, to say nothing of acceptance by partisan groups belonging to an unrecognised belligerent, in this case the de Gaulle government.

[33] See Plenary Meeting, 25 May 1977, CDDH/SR.39, Annex, 4 *Off. Records* 113 (remark by Israel); Pilloud et al., *ICRC Commentary*, at 513; Wilson, *International Law*, at 173–4; Mallison and Mallison, 'Juridical Status', at 20.
   Despite the fusion in Protocol I of the legal regimes governing regular and irregular combatants in an international armed conflict, there will probably be a difference in applying the rules to these two classes of protected combatants, in so far as the regular forces of a state party to Protocol I will be presumed to comply with humanitarian law while irregular troops will likely benefit from no such presumption.

of reciprocity in the applicability of humanitarian law. The state thus has a unilateral obligation to apply Protocol II if the situation conforms to Article 1(1), even with respect to individual units – or even *francs-tireurs* – which do not fulfil the conditions listed in that provision.[34] The insurgents are likewise absolutely obligated to comply with humanitarian law, regardless of compliance by the state's armed forces.[35]

The pattern emerging from an analysis of the application of humanitarian law from the point of view of reciprocity is, in the first place, that the initial applicability of treaty norms to an international armed conflict is clearly conditioned on reciprocity of obligations. In noninternational armed conflicts, on the other hand, only one international agent is present, and there is no international relation on which to tag a condition of reciprocity. Humanitarian law there escapes this condition to follow instead the application pattern of human rights, largely free from immediate reciprocity. This is particularly clear for common Article 3, the content of which is very close to human rights standards. At the level of initial applicability, then, there has been no progressive rejection of immediate reciprocity as a condition of the application of humanitarian norms. On the contrary, Protocol II reintroduced a limited reciprocity component by requiring as a condition of application that the rebel party possess the capacity to implement its norms (Art. 1). At the level of initial applicability, then, reciprocity can be seen as a positive force inducing belligerents to accept the application of humanitarian law norms.[36]

The lack of systemic reciprocity benefiting insurgents may explain to some extent the great difficulties encountered in attempting to ensure compliance with humanitarian law by rebel groups. The expansion of the scope of war crimes to cover internal atrocities, committed by

---

[34] For instance, if one dissident group, under responsible command, exercises such control over part of the national territory so as to enable it to carry out sustained and concerted military operations and to implement Protocol II (to paraphrase Art. 1(1)), the state party's armed forces are still under an obligation to apply the Protocol to other groups or individuals which, for example, do not control any significant part of territory or do not implement Protocol II, unless the two armed conflicts are clearly distinct. This occurred in El Salvador, for example, where five distinct rebel groups were fighting the government: Caflisch, 'Pratique suisse', at 186.

[35] On the basis of such an obligation, see above, chapter 2, pp. 90–8. This conclusion still leaves open the possibility of a temporary suspension by either the state or the insurgents of some rules of humanitarian law by way of belligerent reprisals. This is discussed below, in chapter 5, pp. 183–201.

[36] See Cristina Campiglio, *Il principio di reciprocità nel diritto dei trattati* (Padua: CEDAM, 1995) 118; Simma, *Das Reziprozitätselement*, at 96–7.

state or non-state actors, does act as a negative incentive upon insurgents to comply with humanitarian law. One lesson of the events in Kosovo in 1998–9, however, is that the existence of criminal responsibility even when coupled with a functioning international tribunal cannot alone prevent war crimes. Perhaps it is time to envisage, as a complement to this negative inducement and in view of earlier comments on the positive force of reciprocity, the broadening of the concept of privileged combatant to insurgents, with the consequence that they would be granted prisoner-of-war status and immunity from prosecution for lawful acts of war. It seems likely that such a form of systemic reciprocity – which is admittedly far from being *de lege lata* – would generate significantly greater compliance with humanitarian law on the part of insurgents.[37]

As regards the application of humanitarian norms to individuals and groups, this does not depend on reciprocity in relations among states and between the state and persons deemed to be under its control, including rebels during an internal conflict. This suggests that, under humanitarian law, a state's relationship with the civilian population it controls should be viewed in isolation, disconnected from the state's continued belligerency against armed forces drawn from the same population. For example, an occupier's relation with the occupied population is in no way linked to continuing hostilities with the occupied state's armed forces. Irregular forces active in an international conflict stand as an exception to this pattern. The requirement of reciprocity in this case can be explained by the peculiar status of irregulars, neither fully part of the enemy state bound by humanitarian law nor belonging to a civilian population deemed to be controlled by the state fighting the irregulars. Protocol I broke from this pattern by introducing a condition of reciprocity for all 'regular' troops during international armed conflicts, including national liberation armed conflicts. This is probably due to the distrust on the part of states of the ability of liberation movements to apply humanitarian law. Thus, the expansion of humanitarian law to cover actors and situations fitting uneasily in the traditional framework of international law has actually meant a greater role for immediate

---

[37] It should be noted that, under municipal law, insurgents in fact frequently enjoy absolute immunity, for war crimes as well as for acts of war, as a result of peace agreements. Privileged belligerency would at least draw the line between war crimes and lawful acts of war. The introduction of privileged belligerency for insurgents could be balanced against the creation of an international crime of internal aggression, so as not to immunise those who decide to resort to force against a regime which complies with the emerging right to democratic governance and the right of peoples to self-determination.

reciprocity in the application of humanitarian law rather than its gradual rejection.

Further application and reciprocity

ARTICLE 60 OF THE VIENNA CONVENTION ON THE LAW OF TREATIES

Reciprocity may have relevance not only to the initial applicability of norms but also to their continued application. In general, if an exchange of rights and obligations takes place at the creation of an international norm, it must be preserved throughout the life of that norm. Following the rule *inadimplenti non est adimplendum*, a state generally can suspend or terminate its obligations under a treaty if the other contracting party has defaulted on its corresponding or connected obligations.[38] The *inadimplenti* rule is an application of the principle of reciprocity sometimes referred to as the 'condition of reciprocity'. It forms the basis of Article 60 of the Vienna Convention on the Law of Treaties, which provides:

Article 60

1. A material breach of a bilateral treaty by one of the parties entitles the other to invoke the breach as a ground for terminating the treaty or suspending its operation in whole or in part.
2. A material breach of a multilateral treaty by one of the parties entitles:
    (a) the other parties by unanimous agreement to suspend the operation of the treaty in whole or in part or to terminate it either:
        (i) in the relations between themselves and the defaulting State, or
        (ii) as between all the parties;
    (b) a party specially affected by the breach to invoke it as a ground for suspending the operation of the treaty in whole or in part in the relations between itself and the defaulting State;
    (c) any party other than the defaulting State to invoke the breach as a ground for suspending the operation of the treaty in whole or in part with

---

[38] See *Legal Consequences for States of the Continued Presence of South Africa in Namibia (South West Africa) Notwithstanding Security Council Resolution 276*, Advisory Opinion, [1971] ICJ Rep. 16, 47; the *Diversion of Water from the Meuse* case (*Belgium* v. *Denmark*), (1937) 70 PCIJ Ser. A/B No. 4, 50 and 77 (Sep. Op. Judges Anzilotti and Hudson); *Tacna-Arica Arbitration (Chile* v. *Peru*), (1925) 2 Rep. Int'l Arb. Awards 921, 943–4; Decaux, *La réciprocité*, at 266–78; Lord McNair, *The Law of Treaties*, 2nd edn (Oxford: Clarendon, 1961) 570–1; Simma, *Das Reziprozitätselement*, at 64–6; Sir Ian Sinclair, *The Vienna Convention on the Law of Treaties*, 2nd edn (Manchester: Manchester UP, 1984) 188; Bhek Pati Sinha, *Unilateral Denunciation of Treaty Because of Prior Violation of Obligations by Other Party* (The Hague: Nijhoff, 1966) 5–34.

respect to itself if the treaty is of such a character that a material breach of its provisions by one party radically changes the position of every party with respect to the further performance of its obligations under the treaty.

3. A material breach of a treaty, for the purposes of this article, consists in:
(a) a repudiation of the treaty not sanctioned by the present Convention; or
(b) the violation of a provision essential to the accomplishment of the object or purpose of the treaty.

4. The foregoing paragraphs are without prejudice to any provision in the treaty applicable in the event of a breach.

5. Paragraphs 1 to 3 do not apply to provisions relating to the protection of the human person contained in treaties of a humanitarian character, in particular to provisions prohibiting any form of reprisals against persons protected by such treaties.

Apart from the addition of paragraph 5 and other minor changes, Article 60 as adopted by the Vienna Conference is the product of the ILC's preparatory work, including the important reports by the special rapporteurs Waldock and Fitzmaurice.[39] While the principle embodied in the provision can confidently be said to represent general international law, the duality of regimes governing bilateral and multilateral conventions as well as the specific mechanisms limiting the right to suspend or terminate multilateral agreements include a mixture of old and new.[40]

The condition of reciprocity codified in Article 60 must be differentiated from the institution of countermeasures or reprisals. The two are very close and, indeed, often difficult to tell apart. A single measure may constitute, at the same time, a reprisal and a suspension under the *inadimplenti* rule.[41] Both represent embodiments of the principle of reciprocity, but at different stages of the life of a norm. The condition of

[39] On the origins of Article 60 and details of the work of the ILC, see Decaux, *La réciprocité*, at 279–306; Mohammed Gomaa, *Suspension or Termination of Treaties on Ground of Breach* (Dordrecht: Nijhoff, 1996); Riccardo Pisillo Mazzeschi, *Risoluzione e sospensione dei trattati per inadempimento* (Milan: Giuffrè, 1984) 94–111 and 147–54; Bruno Simma, 'Reflections on Article 60 of the Vienna Convention on the Law of Treaties and its Background in General International Law', (1970) 20 *Österreichische Zeitschrift für öffentliches Recht* 5–81.

[40] See the ILC's commentary on Draft Art. 57 (which became Art. 60), 'Report of the International Law Commission on the Work of its Eighteenth Session', [1966] 2 YB *Int'l L Com'n* 172, 253–5; Simma, 'Reflections on Article 60', at 58–9.

[41] Campiglio, *Il principio*, at 248–55; Sinha, *Unilateral Denunciation*, at 206; D. W. Greig, 'Reciprocity, Proportionality, and the Law of Treaties', (1994) 34 *Va. J Int'l L* 295, 370–82; Simma, 'Reflections on Article 60', at 40. See also, finding the two institutions to be distinct: ICJ, *Case Concerning the Gabcíkovo-Nagymaros Project (Hungary v. Slovakia)*, 25 Sept. 1997, para. 106; Laura Forlati Picchio, *La sanzione nel diritto*

reciprocity relates to the continued application of a norm, while counter-measures are properly construed as a sanction of the breach of a norm.[42] Significant differences flow from this distinction. First, while the condi-tion of reciprocity involves the permanent or temporary extinction of the violated norm, countermeasures involve the justified violation of a still-binding norm.[43] A further distinction is that, unlike the case of the condition of reciprocity, countermeasures must be undertaken with the purpose of forcing the state to resume compliance with the violated norm (*Beugezwang*) or provide reparation.[44] In a situation where either resumption of compliance with, or further violations of, the norm are impossible for any reason, and where compensation or reparation has been provided, countermeasures cannot legally be justified.[45] On the contrary, the condition of reciprocity continues to apply such that the norm is no longer binding. Further, countermeasures must be halted as

internazionale (Padua: CEDAM, 1974) 71–97; Andrea de Guttry, *Le rappresaglie non comportanti la coercizione militare nel diritto internazionale* (Milan: Giuffrè, 1985) 39–49; Oscar Schachter, *International Law in Theory and Practice* (Dordrecht: Nijhoff, 1991) 190–1; Elizabeth Zoller, *Peacetime Unilateral Remedies: An Analysis of Countermeasures* (Dobbs Ferry: Transnational Publishers, 1984) 14–44; James Crawford, 'Third Report on State Responsibility', UN Doc. A/CN.4/507 (2000), paras. 324–5 and 364–6; Linos-Alexandre Sicilianos, 'The Relationship Between Reprisals and Denunciation or Suspension of a Treaty', (1993) 4 *Eur. J Int'l L* 341–59. Some authors make no significant distinction between the condition of reciprocity and reprisals. See, for instance, Benedetto Conforti, *Diritto internazionale*, 4th edn (Naples: Ed. Scientifica, 1992) 359; Pisillo Mazzeschi, *Risoluzione*, at 328–44; Frederic L. Kirgis, 'Some Lingering Questions About Article 60 of the Vienna Convention on the Law of Treaties', (1989) 22 *Cornell Int'l L J* 549, 566–7.
[42] See Gaetano Arangio-Ruiz, 'Fourth Report on State Responsibility', UN Doc. A/CN.4/444/Add.1 (1992), para. 3. Sanction is used here broadly to cover instrumental means designed to ensure compliance: Crawford, 'Third Report', para. 287.
[43] Decaux illustrates the distinction by characterising the condition of reciprocity as a *condition résolutoire* and countermeasures as a *condition suspensive*: Decaux, *La réciprocité*, at 233 and 255.
[44] Arangio-Ruiz, 'Fourth Report', para. 3; Willam Riphagen, 'Fourth Report on the Content, Form and Degree of State Responsibility', [1983] 2:1 *YB Int'l L Com'n* 3, para. 51; Simma, 'Reflections on Article 60', at 20 and 55 ('While retaliatory non-performance is exercised as "*Beugezwang*", i.e. with the intention of compelling the defaulting state to return to integral performance on its part and to make reparation of eventual damages caused by the treaty violation, suspension or termination of a treaty in pursuance of the right arising out of the *do ut des* aspect of the reciprocity principle and expressed in the maxim *inadimplenti non est adimplendum* serves more as a remedy than as a coercive measure': *ibid.*, at 20).
[45] For example, an attack on a belligerent's sole nuclear reactor, in violation of Art. 56 of Protocol I, could not justify countermeasures because further violations are factually impossible: Frits Kalshoven, 'Belligerent Reprisals Revisited', (1990) 21 *Nether. YB Int'l L* 43, 57.

soon as compliance resumes, but no such imperative is present under the condition of reciprocity.[46] Yet another distinguishing element is proportionality, which forms an integral part of any countermeasures but has no relevance to the condition of reciprocity, where the inapplicability must concern the norm corresponding to the one initially breached.[47] Finally, the *inadimplenti* rule exists only with respect to conventional obligations, given that one state does not have the power to terminate a customary rule (Art. 43, Vienna Convention on the Law of Treaties).[48] Countermeasures, on the other hand, may authorise the suspension of both customary and conventional norms.[49]

The very fact that Article 60 of the Vienna Convention excludes treaty clauses prohibiting reprisals from the operation of the condition of reciprocity indicates that the two are distinct principles. Violation in the form of countermeasures of a provision that itself prohibits reprisals or countermeasures is inescapably a breach of that provision.[50]

---

[46] Under humanitarian law, expression of regret for the violation and punishment of the guilty individuals by the enemy also stands in the way of lawful countermeasures: 1999 *Canadian War Manual* s.15–17(b).

[47] See *Case Concerning the Gabcíkovo-Nagymaros Project (Hungary v. Slovakia)*, 25 Sept. 1997, paras. 85–7; 1956 *US Field Manual FM 27–10*, para. 649; Erik Castrén, *The Present Law of War and Neutrality* (Helsinki: Suomalaisen Tiedeakatemian Toimituksia, 1954) 69–70; Forlati Picchio, *La sanzione*, at 92; Frits Kalshoven, *Belligerent Reprisals* (Leiden: Sijthoff, 1971) 24–5 and 362–3; Pisillo Mazzeschi, *Risoluzione*, at 318–19 (criticising the distinction); Gaetano Arangio-Ruiz, 'Third Report on State Responsibility', UN Doc. A/CN.4/440 (1991) paras. 69–83; Arangio-Ruiz, 'Fourth Report', paras. 53–6; Simma, 'Reflections on Article 60', at 21–2. An American suggestion at the Vienna Conference to include a proportionality requirement in Art. 60 of the Vienna Convention on the Law of Treaties was rejected: Francesco Capotorti, 'L'extinction et la suspension des traités', (1971-III) 134 *Recueil des cours* 417, at 551 and n. 97.

[48] See Villiger who states with respect to Art. 60 of the Vienna Convention on the Law of Treaties that 'para. 5 concerns conventional rules which are customary', although there seem to exist no grounds for summarily excluding from the breadth of para. 5 conventional rules which have not yet ripened into customary law. Mark E. Villiger, *Customary International Law and Treaties* (Dordrecht: Nijhoff, 1985) 274–5. On the contrary, Art. 60(5) has no impact on customary rules (as indicated by Art. 43) and will have an effect only with respect to norms not yet customary: Giuseppe Barile, 'The Protection of Human Rights in Article 60 Paragraph 5 of the Vienna Convention on the Law of Treaties', in *International Law at the Time of its Codification: Essays in Honour of Roberto Ago* (Milan: Giuffrè, 1987) II, 3, 10–11.

[49] See Fitzmaurice's Draft Art. 18(2), whereby reprisals may be used to suspend a treaty rule following the breach of a customary obligation: Sir Gerald Fitzmaurice, 'Fourth Report on the Law of Treaties', [1959] 2 *YB Int'l L Com'n* 45; Arangio-Ruiz, 'Third Report', at 38–9.

[50] This is now reflected in Art. 50(1)(c) of the 2001 ILC Articles on State Responsibility: UN Doc. A/CN.4/L.602/Rev.1 (2001) 14; Crawford, 'Third Report', para. 341.

Noncompliance, then, must rest on a different legal mechanism, in this case the condition of reciprocity. For instance, the British and Canadian shackling of prisoners of war as a reprisal against a similar German measure in the wake of the 1942 Dieppe raid could never be legally justified in light of the absolute prohibition of reprisals found in the 1929 Geneva Convention on Prisoners of War (Art. 2(3)).[51] Justification based on the condition of reciprocity might be attempted, however, in the form of suspension of the norm following its breach, which is exactly what Article 60(5) seeks to prevent.

In keeping with these differences between the two notions, the ensuing discussion addresses only the question of the condition of reciprocity or *inadimplenti non est adimplendum*, while countermeasures are considered later. In both human rights and humanitarian law, application of the condition of reciprocity is limited by a number of rules restricting the rights of states to suspend or terminate obligations which have been breached by other state parties to the same convention.

HUMAN RIGHTS

In human rights law, the initial question is whether the condition of reciprocity gives a state party to a multilateral convention the right to suspend or terminate compliance with certain human rights norms following their violation by another party. In the work of the International Law Commission, changes were made to the Draft Articles on the Law of Treaties to limit such a right to states which were 'specifically affected' by the breach, and it is this formulation which was eventually adopted as Article 60(2)(b) of the Vienna Convention.[52] Given the internal nature of substantive human rights obligations, a breach by one state normally will not affect any other state in a direct way, even if the latter is a party to the multilateral convention the norms of which were violated: hence the concept that human rights norms found in multilateral conventions constitute obligations *erga omnes* and that their breach has an indirect, universal impact on states.

There are instances where third states legitimately may argue that they are directly and specifically affected by the breach of a treaty human

---

[51] See Kalshoven, *Belligerent Reprisals*, at 178–83.

[52] 'Report of the International Law Commission on the Work of its Seventeenth Session', [1966] 1:1 *YB Int'l L Com'n* 59–66 and 127–8; Egon Schwelb, 'The Law of Treaties and Human Rights', in Michael Reisman and Burns Weston eds., *Toward World Order and Human Dignity – Essays in Honor of Myres S. McDougal* (New York: Macmillan, 1976) 262, 272–4 (also published in (1973) 16 *Archiv des Völkerrecht* 1–27).

rights norm. First, the violation of human rights may be on a scale sufficient to provoke a sudden influx of refugees in neighbouring countries,
such as the exodus of Rwandans to Zaire in 1993–4 following staggering
human rights violations in their own country. Secondly, there may be
a violation of the human rights of individuals who enjoy a special relationship with another state based on national, ethnic, religious or other
bonds.[53] Thirdly, some human rights norms protecting essential human
needs involve the imposition of economic standards. Norms in which
human interests are laced with economic interests include many standards in international labour conventions developed under the aegis of
the ILO, as well as a number of norms found in universal and regional
human rights instruments.[54] Application of these norms by a state may
have an impact not only at an individual level but also in national and
even international spheres, if that state would be adversely affected by
another state's violation of human rights norms.[55] For example, the exploitation of child labour in some countries constitutes an important
element of a national industry, but can also occasion the violation of
several basic human rights standards. Such is the case of the carpet-
weaving industry in India, in which 60 per cent of the workforce is
made up of children under the age of fourteen. Child labourers are often badly paid, if at all, and can easily be denied the most basic work
benefits such as vacations and accident compensation. Enforcement of
human rights norms by the state would, in all likelihood, make that
industry less competitive with respect to similar industries in countries
where child labour goes unchecked.[56] Thus, a strict application of the

---

[53] For example, in *Austria v. Italy*, Appl. 788/60, [1961] *YB Eur. Conv. Hum. Rts* 116, 142
(Eur. Com'n Hum. Rts), Austria intervened because the individuals involved belonged
to the German-speaking minority in Italy. In fact, it seems that a majority of
inter-state applications under the European Convention on Human Rights have been
triggered by such links rather than by the general interest of states in the
application of its norms: Rudolf Bernhardt, 'The International Enforcement of
Human Rights: General Report', in Rudolf Bernhardt and John Anthony Jolowicz eds.,
International Enforcement of Human Rights (Berlin: Springer-Verlag, 1987) 143, 148–9.

[54] Such norms include, among many others, Art. 8 of the International Covenant on
Economic, Social and Cultural Rights (on trade unions) and Art. 11(1)(d) of the
Convention on the Elimination of All Forms of Discrimination Against Women (on
equal pay for work of equal value).

[55] Egon Schwelb, 'Termination or Suspension of the Operation of a Treaty as a
Consequence of its Breach', (1967) 7 *Indian J Int'l L* 309, 324–6.

[56] Human rights standards include Art. 10(3) of the International Covenant on Civil and
Political Rights; the ILO Minimum Age Convention (No. 132), 26 June 1973, *reprinted
in* UK Command Papers 5829; Art. 32 of the Convention on the Rights of the Child,
20 Nov. 1989, *reprinted in* Ian Brownlie ed., *Basic Documents on Human Rights*, 3rd edn

inadimplenti rule might lead a state, in certain circumstances where it is specifically affected, to argue that it should be allowed to suspend human rights norms in response to their breach by another state.[57] It is difficult to reconcile, on the one hand, the possibility that a state might validly suspend or terminate its obligations under a human rights convention because of another state's breach, and, on the other hand, the purpose of human rights law to protect the fundamental rights of all persons at all times and the *erga omnes* nature of human rights obligations.[58] The obvious problems associated with applying the *inadimplenti* rule to human rights conventions were noted by the ILC during its preparation of the Draft Articles on the Law of Treaties.[59] Despite apparent agreement as to the undesirability of suspending human rights conventions in response to a breach, however, the ILC was reluctant to prohibit at large any such action vis-à-vis the defaulting state. The Draft Articles were thus left silent in this respect.[60] At the Vienna Conference on the Law of Treaties, an amendment was put forward by Switzerland to add what is now paragraph 5 of Article 60, excluding 'provisions relating to the protection of human persons contained in treaties of a humanitarian character' from the application of the *inadimplenti* rule embodied in paragraphs 1 to 3 of the same article.[61] Although the Swiss proposal may have originated with the 1949 Geneva Conventions specifically in mind, as indicated by the use of terms such as 'protected persons', 'reprisals' and 'humanitarian' treaties, reference was also made during the conference to 'conventions concerning ... the protection of human rights in

(Oxford: Clarendon, 1992) 182; and the ILO Convention on the Worst Forms of Child Labour (No. 182), 17 June 1999. See Philip Alston, 'Implementing Children's Rights: The Case of Child Labour', (1989) 58 *Nordic J Int'l L* 35–53; Patricia Hyndman, 'The Exploitation of Child Workers in South and South East Asia', (1989) 58 *Nordic J Int'l L* 94–109; 'Slavery and Slavery-Like Practices – Report of the Working Group on Slavery on its Twelfth Session', UN Doc. E/CN.5/Sub.2/1987/25 (1987) 8–9.

[57] Compare with the regime governing the right of states indirectly injured by the violation of human rights norms to adopt countermeasures, below, chapter 5, pp. 202–11.

[58] Flavia Lattanzi, *Garanzie dei diritti dell'uomo nel diritto internazionale generale*, (Milan: Giuffrè, 1983) 294. This point is examined more fully in the discussion of the possible suspension of human rights as a countermeasure, below, chapter 5, pp. 211–27.

[59] Sir Gerald Fitzmaurice, 'Second Report on the Law of Treaties', [1957] 2 *YB Int'l L Com'n* 54; ILC, 'Summary Records of the Second Part of its Seventeenth Session', [1966] 1:1 *YB Int'l L Com'n* 66 (Sir Humphrey Waldock).

[60] See Pisillo Mazzeschi, *Risoluzione*, at 151–2; ILC, 'Summary Records' (Waldock), at 66.

[61] *United Nations Conference on the Law of Treaties* (New York: UN, 1970) I, 354–9; II, 112–15; José Daniel, 'The Vienna Convention of 1969 on the Law of Treaties and Humanitarian Law', (1972) 136 *Int'l Rev. Red Cross* 367, 378–9.

general'[62] which indicates that human rights conventions were meant to be included in the notion of 'treaties of a humanitarian character'. This conforms to the idea expressed in paragraph 6 of the preamble to the Vienna Convention, whereby parties agree to keep 'in mind the principles of international law embodied in the Charter of the United Nations, such as the principle . . . of universal respect for, and compliance with, human rights and fundamental freedoms for all'.[63] The notion of 'provisions relating to the protection of the human person' might encompass not only 'pure' human rights norms such as the prohibitions of genocide and slavery, but also other norms preserving essential human interests, such as economic rights and minimal work conditions.[64]

The 1969 Vienna Convention on the Law of Treaties does not, as a rule, have a retroactive effect (Art. 4), so that many of the most important human rights treaties would not be touched by Article 60(5). However, there have been some suggestions that this provision is a codification of existing law rather than new law developed at the Vienna Conference. The ICJ in its *Namibia* advisory opinion held, in a somewhat imprecise manner, that Article 60 embodied 'in many respects' existing rules of customary law.[65] The Court also mentioned in the same passage: '[T]he

---

[62] *United Nations Conference on the Law of Treaties*, II, at 112 (remark by Switzerland).

[63] Schwelb, 'Law of Treaties', at 278. There is now consensus on this point: Gomaa, *Suspension or Termination*, at 109–12; *Restatement (Third) of the Foreign Relations Law of the United States* (St Paul: American Law Institute, 1987) 41 para. 335 comment (c); Sinclair, *Vienna Convention*, at 190; Villiger, *Customary International Law*, at 369; Barile, 'Protection of Human Rights', at 3; Capotorti, 'L'extinction', at 554.

[64] See Paul Reuter, *Introduction to the Law of Treaties* (London: Pinter, 1989) 154–6; Sir Gerald Fitzmaurice, 'The General Principles of International Law Considered from the Standpoint of the Rule of Law', (1957–II) 92 *Recueil des cours* 125–6; Schwelb, 'Law of Treaties', at 278–81 (arguing that even the right to property would be covered). But see Erik Suy, 'Droit des traités et droits de l'homme', in Rudolf Bernhardt et al. eds., *Völkerrecht als Rechtsordnung, internationale Gerichtsbarkeit, Menschenrechte: Festschrift für Herman Mosler* (Berlin: Springer, 1983) 935, 939–42, who states that the exception in paragraph 5 applies only 'aux dispositions relatives à la protection *physique* de la personne humaine' (*ibid.*, at 942 – emphasis in the original). No justification is offered in support of this statement, and it is difficult to agree with a construction which excludes dimensions of the protection of the human person other than physical well-being (e.g. freedom of expression or right to due process).

[65] *Legal Consequences for States of the Continued Presence of South Africa in Namibia (South West Africa) Notwithstanding Security Council Resolution 276* (Advisory Opinion), [1971] ICJ Rep. 16, 47 ('[t]he rules laid down by the Vienna Convention on the Law of Treaties concerning termination of a treaty relationship on account of breach (adopted without a dissenting vote) may in many respects be considered as a codification of existing customary law on the subject'); *Case Concerning the Gabcíkovo-Nagymaros Project (Hungary v. Slovakia)*, 25 Sept. 1997, paras. 46 and 99; ILC commentary, [1966] 2 *YB Int'l L Com'n* 172, 253–5.

general principle of law that a right of termination on account of breach must be presumed to exist in respect of all treaties, except as regards provisions relating to the protection of the human person contained in treaties of a humanitarian character (as indicated in Art. 60, paragraph 5 of the Vienna Convention).'[66] Some have challenged the generality of this pronouncement, but they usually refer to elements of the first three paragraphs of Article 60 rather than the norm set out in paragraph 5.[67] Indeed, that norm is echoed by an identical provision included in the Vienna Convention on the Law of Treaties Between States and International Organisations or Between International Organisations,[68] and in the work of the ILC on state responsibility.[69] The Court touched on this issue in the *Application of the Genocide Convention* case when it decided that the admissibility of the Yugoslav counter-claim could not be taken as a reflection of any reciprocal link between the obligations of the parties under the Genocide Convention.[70]

The fact that provisions protecting fundamental human rights of individuals are unconditional *erga omnes* norms means that their application cannot be subject to reciprocity. Human rights obligations, conventional as well as customary, represent the adherence of the state to a normative, public order system which is not conditioned on the performance of any parallel obligation by other states.[71] The rule *inadimplenti non est*

---

[66] *Namibia* Opinion, at 47.
[67] See e.g. Shabtai Rosenne, *Breach of Treaty* (Cambridge: Grotius, 1985) 35–44; Zoller, *Peacetime Unilateral Remedies*, at 34; Herbert W. Briggs, 'Unilateral Denunciation of Treaties: The Vienna Convention and the International Court of Justice', (1974) 68 *Am J Int'l L* 51–68.
[68] UN Doc. A/CONF.129/15, Art. 60(5). International organisations are party neither to general or regional human rights treaties nor to humanitarian conventions, but some international agreements such as mandates do contain provisions of a humanitarian character.
[69] Arangio-Ruiz, 'Fourth Report', at paras. 78–83; Riccardo Pisillo Mazzeschi, 'Termination and Suspension of Treaties for Breach in the Work of the ILC', in Marina Spinedi and Bruno Simma eds., *The UN Codification of State Responsibility* (New York: Oceana, 1987) 57–94; Willem Riphagen, 'Sixth Report on the Content, Form and Degree of State Responsibility', [1985] 2:1 *YB Int'l L Com'n* 3, 12–13.
[70] *Case Concerning Application of the Convention on the Prevention and Punishment of the Crime of Genocide (Bosnia & Herzegovina v. Yugoslavia)*, Counterclaims Order, 17 Dec. 1997, para. 35. See also the Separate Opinion of Judge *ad hoc* E. Lauterpacht, at para. 20.
[71] Sinha, *Unilateral Denunciation*, at 91–6; Fitzmaurice, 'General Principles', at 125–6 ('The obligation is, for each State, an absolute obligation of law not dependent on its observance by others. This is because all rules of this particular character are intended not so much for the benefit of the States, as directly for the benefit of the individual concerned, as human beings and on humanitarian grounds. In the same way, a breach by one party of a convention on human rights, a convention providing

adimplendum thus appears structurally incompatible with the legal system created by human rights conventions, and cannot justify suspending the application of substantive norms protecting the individual, even with respect to treaties to which Article 60(5) of the Vienna Convention on the Law of Treaties is inapplicable.

HUMANITARIAN LAW

There has been, during the last century, a general erosion of the role of reciprocity in the further application of humanitarian law. Originally, reciprocity was a fundamental element in the continued application of all rules regulating the conduct of war. One stark example is provided by the 1863 Lieber Code, stating that troops giving no quarter were entitled to receive none (Art. 62), a rule carried over *verbatim* in the 1914 US Rules of Land Warfare (para. 368).[72] During the First World War, courts of various countries found that substantive violations of the 1907 Hague Conventions entitled other belligerents to suspend or terminate compliance with the Conventions.[73] More immediately, the treatment of prisoners of war by one belligerent during the First World War was often expressly a reflection of the treatment its own prisoners of war received from the enemy.[74] This led to the inclusion in the 1929 Geneva Prisoners

for the safety of life at sea, labour conventions regarding hours and conditions of work, etc., would not justify corresponding breaches of the treaty by other parties even vis-à-vis the treaty-breaking State and its nationals, for reasons of a broadly similar character. *Such conventions involve obligations of an absolute and, so to speak, self-existent kind, the duty to perform which, once assumed, is not (as for instance for commercial treaties or such conventions as disarmament conventions) dependent on a reciprocal or correspondent performance by other parties.'* Emphasis added).

[72] US War Dept, *Rules of Land Warfare*, WD Doc. No. 467, Office of the Chief of Staff (1914). See Elbridge Colby, 'War Crimes', (1924–5) 23 *Mich. L Rev.* 482, 495.

[73] See 'Conseil de guerre de Paris (4ᵉ)', 18 June 1919, (1919) 46 *Journal du droit international (Clunet)* 737, 740 ('On ne saurait utilement arguer que la France est tenue d'appliquer vis-à-vis de l'Allemagne les termes de la Convention de la Haye, que cette dernière puissance a elle-même violés depuis le début des hostilités'); *The Blonde*, [1922] 1 App. Cases 313, 329–31 (House of Lords); A. Mérignhac, 'De la sanction des infractions aux droit des gens commises au cours de la guerre européenne par les empires du centre', (1917) 24 *Revue générale de droit international public* 5, 16 ('Les accords, en effet, nationaux ou internationaux, ne sont obligatoires qu'à charge d'exécution réciproque par toutes les parties contractantes; et leur violation systématique par nos ennemis les a rendus caducs').

[74] For example, in a note of 10 January 1915, the French Government protested against the treatment of its soldiers held prisoners of war in Germany, warning that '[t]outes les restrictions dont nos compatriotes ont à se plaindre en Allemagne et dont une protestation officielle n'aura pas réussi à les délivrer sans délais feront de même

of War Convention, and later in the 1949 Conventions and 1977 Protocol
I, of a general prohibition of reprisals against prisoners of war, as well
as the establishment of objective conventional standards applicable by
belligerents at all times.

After the First World War, the further application of the laws of war to
protected persons moved away from a reliance on reciprocity between
belligerents. Not only were reprisals prohibited, and objective standards
adopted, but a regime of 'internal' reciprocity was put into place. In a
fashion similar to the treatment of aliens,[75] protected persons under
the various Geneva Conventions and Protocol I benefit from an equality
of treatment with the nationals of the state under whose power they
find themselves. Thus, under both the 1929 and 1949 Geneva Conventions, prisoners of war are entitled to the same conditions as the detaining state's troops with respect to living quarters, food, work, penal
and disciplinary measures, as well as due process guarantees.[76] Reciprocity is limited by the minimum standards given in the Convention,
which mostly concern the disciplining and punishment of prisoners of
war. Application of norms protecting prisoners of war therefore is still
grounded in reciprocity, but a reciprocity that has shifted, through multilateral conventions, from its historical and, one could say, 'natural'
tendency of one state mirroring its conduct in that of the enemy, to a
reciprocity that in no way involves the conduct of other states. Detaching
the standards protecting prisoners of war from 'external' reciprocity has
the legal effect of securing a relative stability of standards of treatment
for this category of protected persons.

Article 60(5) of the Vienna Convention on the Law of Treaties seeks
to reject, in a very broad manner, the application of the condition
of reciprocity or *inadimplenti* rule to humanitarian law.[77] The effect of
the *inadimplenti* rule on the application of humanitarian law would be

---

l'objet de mesure de réciprocité': Alexandre-Charles Kiss, *Répertoire de la pratique
française en matière de droit international public* (Paris: CNRS, 1962) I, 106; Lassa
Oppenheim, *International Law*, Hersch Lauterpacht ed., 7th edn (London: Longmans,
1952) II, 562 n. 3; Campiglio, *Il principio*, at 114–16.

[75] See Ian Brownlie, *Principles of Public International Law*, 5th edn (Oxford: Clarendon,
1998) 526–30.

[76] Arts. 10(3), 30, 45–6, 63–4, 1929 Geneva Convention on Prisoners of War; Arts. 23, 25,
51, 82, 87–8, 99, 102, 106, 108, 1949 Third Geneva Convention.

[77] An early draft of what eventually became Protocol I contained a provision expressly
rejecting the application of the condition of reciprocity to the Geneva Conventions,
so that compliance could be suspended not as reciprocity but solely as reprisals: Art.
15, *Draft Rules for the Limitation of the Dangers Incurred by the Civilian Population in Time of
War*, 1st edn (Geneva: ICRC, 1956), *quoted in* Kalshoven, *Belligerent Reprisals*, at 279.

devastating. Unlike reprisals, which involve temporary suspension due to mutual violation of the norm, the condition of reciprocity means that the breached rule ceases to be mandatory, at least until the belligerents formally or informally agree to resume its application.[78] Reservations to the 1925 Geneva Gases Protocol, whereby the Protocol ceases *ipso facto* to be binding in case of a violation, graphically illustrate this danger.[79] For this reason, the condition of reciprocity has not been applied since the end of the First World War even in situations where rules apparently have been suspended or abandoned during an armed conflict. For instance, rules governing submarine warfare which prohibited the sinking of enemy merchant ships prior to placing the ship's crew and papers in a place of safety were largely ignored by both sides during the Second World War.[80] Although it refused to hold Admiral Dönitz responsible for breaches of the 1936 Protocol because of similar British and American behaviour at a later date, the International Military Tribunal at Nuremberg did not rely on the *inadimplenti* rule (nor, for that matter, on reprisals) but, on the contrary, seemed to find that the rules had remained fully in force.[81] In a somewhat similar

---

[78] See above, note 43, and accompanying text.

[79] The text of the reservations is *reprinted in* Schindler and Toman, *Laws of Armed Conflict*, at 121–7. See also para. 38(d), 1956 *US Field Manual 27–10* (as amended in 1976).

[80] Art. 3, 1907 Hague Convention VI; Art. 22, Treaty for the Limitation and Reduction of Naval Armament, 22 April 1930, *reprinted in* Schindler and Toman, *Laws of Armed Conflict*, at 881–2; Rule 2, *Procès-Verbal* Relating to the Rules on Submarine Warfare Set Forth in Part IV of the Treaty of London of 22 April 1930, 6 Nov. 1936, *reprinted in* Schindler and Toman, *Laws of Armed Conflict*, at 883–4. Disregard for the rules on naval warfare resulted from a mixture of outright violations of the norms and the fact that the sinking of enemy merchant ships was allowed if they resisted (which they were required to do, for instance, by the 1938 *British Handbook of Instructions*): Marjorie M. Whiteman, *Digest of International Law* (Washington: US Gov. Printing Office, 1968) X, 650–66; Edwin I. Nwogugu, 'Commentary on Treaties on Submarine Warfare', in Natalino Ronziti ed., *The Law of Naval Warfare* (Dordrecht: Nijhoff, 1988) 353, 357–60.

[81] *Judgment of the International Military Tribunal*, (1946) 1 IMT 171, 310–15; Robert W. Tucker, 50 *US Naval War College International Law Studies – The Law of War and Neutrality at Sea* (Washington DC: US Gov. Printing Office, 1955) 67 ('In reaching this decision the Tribunal did not thereby imply that the rules laid down in the 1936 London Protocol were to be considered as no longer binding upon belligerent warships in their behaviour towards enemy merchant vessels. There was no indication that, in the Tribunal's opinion, the ineffectiveness of the Protocol in regulating belligerent conduct had served to deprive it of its character as law. Indeed, the most reasonable interpretation of this particular aspect of the judgment rendered by the Nuremberg Tribunal is that the latter clearly assumed the continued validity of the 1936 London Protocol as it relates to inter-belligerent measures'). The IMT's rationale for not holding Dönitz responsible for breaching these binding rules, sometimes dubbed *tu quoque*, is discussed below, in chapter 5, pp. 227–35.

fashion, the US prosecutor in the *Hostages* case had argued that civilians 'had every right to rise and defend themselves by armed force because the Germans themselves so flagrantly violated the laws of war . . . If the occupying forces inaugurate a systematic program of terror, they cannot thereafter call the inhabitants to account for taking measures in self-defense.'[82] This is an argument based not on reprisals but on the reciprocity between the occupier's obligations towards the population (Arts. 42–56, 1907 Hague Regulations) and the latter's duty not to commit hostile acts, whereby civilians would be treated as privileged belligerents despite not meeting the traditional criteria associated with that status (Art. 1, 1907 Hague Regulations).[83] The US Military Tribunal, however, rejected this argument based on reciprocity, insisting instead on the population's duty to refrain from hostile acts and characterising the Germans' conduct as reprisals unjustified in the circumstances.[84]

The notion that conventional rules, usually agreed to in time of peace through arduous negotiations, could be indefinitely suspended or terminated during an armed conflict as a result of their violation, is inconsistent with the very purpose of humanitarian law, being the establishment of rules made to withstand the stresses of war and apply 'in all circumstances' (common Art. 1, 1949 Geneva Conventions and 1977 Protocol I). Indeed, as noted by one writer, 'no state seems to have openly argued a *legal* right to suspend the operation of the Geneva Conventions in whole or in part on the basis of a breach of the Geneva Conventions committed by the adversary'.[85] In curtailing the application of the *inadimplenti* rule to humanitarian conventions, Article 60(5) counters a certain tendency of belligerents to emancipate themselves (and each other) from rules which they find difficult to comply with.[86]

Some elements of humanitarian conventions do import into humanitarian law rules related to the condition of reciprocity. Article 19 of the 1949 Fourth Geneva Convention provides that the special protection against attacks given to civilian hospitals shall cease if the hospital is used to commit acts harmful to the enemy, for example if an artillery

---

[82] *US* v. *List et al.* (the *Hostages* trial), (1948) 11 USMT 757, 853 (Gen. Telford Taylor for the prosecution).

[83] See Kalshoven, *Belligerent Reprisals*, at 204–5 and 363.

[84] *Hostages* trial, at 1249.

[85] Allan Rosas, *The Legal Status of Prisoners of War* (Helsinki: Suomalainen Tiedeakademia, 1976) 112 (emphasis in the original).

[86] See Simma, *Das Reziprozitätselement*, at 105–6; Julius Stone, *Legal Control of International Conflict*, 2nd edn (London: Stevens & Sons, 1959) 355–6.

observation post is set up on top of the hospital.[87] In a similar fashion, Article 11(1) of the 1954 Hague Convention on Cultural Property provides that an object benefiting from special protection under the Convention becomes a legitimate target if it is used by a belligerent for military purposes. The scope of Article 11(1) is very narrow in that it applies only to objects under special protection. Indeed, it is closer in nature to reprisals than to the condition of reciprocity: it is limited in time, must stop when the illegal use for military purposes of the cultural object ceases, and must be preceded by a warning. As such, it stands as a special rule derogating from the general prohibition of reprisals and the rejection of reciprocity contained in Article 4(4)–(5) of the 1954 Hague Convention.[88] Far from implying that the condition of reciprocity generally applies to humanitarian conventions, then, the inclusion of special clauses providing for the exceptional application of reciprocity with respect to specific rules rather suggests that it does not apply in other cases.

One provision of Protocol I lends support to an interpretation of humanitarian norms as absolute obligations. According to Article 51(8), a belligerent's violation of the prohibition of using civilians to shield military targets (Art. 51(7)) 'shall not release the Parties to the conflict from their legal obligations' with respect to the civilian population and civilians, including the obligation to take precautionary measures provided for in Article 57'. The latter provision governs attacks which may be expected to cause injury to civilians. Because of the connection between these two obligations, it could be argued on the basis of reciprocity that

---

[87] 'Article 19   The protection to which civilian hospitals are entitled shall not cease unless they are used to commit, outside their humanitarian duties, acts harmful to the enemy. Protection may, however, cease only after due warning has been given, naming, in all appropriate cases, a reasonable time limit and after such warning has remained unheeded.
    The fact that sick or wounded members of the armed forces are nursed in these hospitals, or the presence of small arms and ammunition taken from such combatants which have not yet been handed to the proper service, shall not be considered to be acts harmful to the enemy.' See Pictet, IV, at 154–5.

[88] See Arts. 6 and 13 of the Second Protocol to the Hague Convention of 1954 for the Protection of Cultural Property in the Event of Armed Conflict, The Hague, 26 March 1999. See also Jirí Toman, *The Protection of Cultural Property in the Event of an Armed Conflict* (Paris: UNESCO/Dartmouth, 1996) 71–2; Jean de Breucker, 'Pour les vingt ans de la Convention de La Haye du 14 mai 1954 pour la protection des biens culturels', [1975] *Revue belge de droit international* 524, 535–6; Stanislaw E. Nahlik, 'La protection internationale des biens culturels en cas des conflits armés', (1967-I) 120 *Recueil des cours* 61, 127–8; Stanislaw E. Nahlik, 'Protection of Cultural Property', in UNESCO, *International Dimension of Humanitarian Law* (Dordrecht: Nijhoff, 1988) 203, 208–9.

the duty to refrain from attack which might cause injury to civilians is conditioned on the duty not to use the latter as a shield. A state's use of civilian shields could thus be argued to validate another state's attack on the shielding civilians. This is indeed the solution embodied in Article 11(1) of the 1954 Hague Convention on Cultural Property. Article 51(8) of Protocol I, however, explicitly rejects reciprocity in such a context, regardless of any direct adverse consequences on the state prevented from carrying out its attack on the enemy.[89]

The incompatibility of the condition of reciprocity with humanitarian law is also supported by the legal regime regulating denunciation of the 1949 Geneva Conventions and 1977 Additional Protocols. While suspension is not expressly considered by the Geneva Conventions and Protocols, there are provisions in each instrument governing the right of states parties to terminate the Conventions through denunciation (Arts. 63/62/142/158; Art. 99, Protocol I; Art. 24, Protocol II). Under these provisions, a denunciation of the Conventions or Protocols would produce no effect if the state is engaged in an armed conflict at the time or within a year of the denunciation. The rationale for this rule is similar to that precluding suspension in response to breaches by another party.[90] It follows that humanitarian conventions remain binding on both the denouncing state and other belligerents, despite a stated intent by one to abide by the conventions no longer.[91] If intentional and clear rejection of the binding force of a humanitarian convention produces no legal effect, then, *a fortiori*, no such effect should attach to a violation characterised as a *presumed* rejection. In this respect, Article 60(5) of the Vienna Convention seems to correspond to general principles of humanitarian law.[92]

---

[89] For example, during the 1990–1 Iraq-Kuwait crisis, Iraq was thought to have located a strategic communication centre in a residential neighbourhood of Baghdad, effectively preventing coalition forces from attacking it with indiscriminate bombing of the area. The centre was eventually destroyed using 'smart' bombs causing little damage to surrounding areas, in full compliance with Articles 51(8) and 57 of Protocol I. Tragically, the attack revealed that the centre was in reality used as a civilian shelter, and 200–300 civilians died in the air raid: Human Rights Watch, *Needless Deaths in the Gulf War* (New York: Human Rights Watch, 1991) 128–47; US Dept of Defense, *Report to Congress on the Conduct of the Persian Gulf War*, Appendix O 'The Role of the Law of War', *reprinted in* (1992) Int'l Leg. Mat. 612, 626–7.

[90] See CDDH/SR.47 para. 106, 7 *Off. Records* 35.

[91] Pilloud et al., *ICRC Commentary*, at 1108–10; Pictet, III, at 648.

[92] See Theodor Meron, *Human Rights in Internal Strife: Their International Protection* (Cambridge: Grotius, 1987) 11; Jean de Preux, 'The Geneva Conventions and Reciprocity', (1985) 244 *Int'l Rev. Red Cross* 25, 26–7. This is, of course, in addition to

The norm in paragraph 5 of Article 60 concerns not only multilateral conventions but also, as clearly indicated by the reference to paragraph 1, bilateral conventions of a humanitarian character. The *travaux préparatoires* reveal that the initial impetus for the Swiss amendment which brought about the inclusion of paragraph 5 was a concern over bilateral agreements to apply the Geneva Conventions or Protocol I to an armed conflict where one belligerent was not a party to those Conventions (common Art. 2(3); common Art. 3(3); Art. 96(2), Protocol I).[93] There is a measure of inconsistency in this respect between the Vienna Convention on the Law of Treaties and the humanitarian conventions. Under common Article 2(3) of the Geneva Conventions and Article 18(3) of the 1954 Hague Convention on Cultural Property, a party to the Conventions which agrees to apply the terms to a non-party belligerent must comply only as long as the enemy itself 'accepts *and applies* the provisions thereof'.[94] Protocol I retained the same wording as the 1949 Conventions regarding *ad hoc* agreements between a party state and a non-party state to apply the Conventions and Protocol (Art. 96(2)).[95] The inconsistency between the Vienna Convention on the Law of Treaties and the humanitarian conventions can be resolved by reinterpreting the latter to require solely the initial application of their terms rather than making compliance by the non-party a constant condition for the binding force of bilateral agreements. A more liberal interpretation conforms to the regime governing the application of the 1949 Conventions and Protocol I to national liberation struggles (Art. 96(3)), whereby liberation movements need only make a unilateral declaration addressed to the Swiss Government to render these instruments applicable. There is no requirement that the movement 'apply' the humanitarian conventions for them to be binding on the state party. It seems somewhat illogical to make application of the conventions subject to a stricter regime in the case of an inter-state war governed by common Article 2(3) and Article

---

the fact that many rules included in humanitarian conventions form part of customary law, and so would not be liable to suspension or termination following the *inadimplenti* rule (Art. 43, Vienna Convention on the Law of Treaties).

[93] *United Nations Conference on the Law of Treaties*, II, at 112 (remark by the representative of Switzerland).

[94] See above, note 7 and accompanying text.

[95] Although the draft of Art. 96 was presented by the ICRC as originating in both the 1949 Geneva Conventions and the Vienna Convention on the Law of Treaties, the *travaux préparatoires* do not reveal any discussion of the possible impact of Art. 60(5) of the Vienna Convention on the application of Art. 96(2) of Protocol I: CDDH/I/SR.67, para. 7, 9 *Off. Records* 355.

96(2) of Protocol I.[96] More generally, given that such agreements are in fact bilateralised forms of multilateral humanitarian conventions, rejection of the condition of reciprocity would seem warranted for reasons similar to those exposed in the previous paragraph.[97]

Apart from arrangements to apply the Geneva Conventions at large to an armed conflict, the Conventions encourage the signing of other agreements amongst belligerents on a variety of topics, from the appointment of a substitute to protecting powers to the conditions of captivity for prisoners of war (Arts. 6/6/6/7). The rejection of the condition of reciprocity with respect to this type of agreement raises distinct questions because the agreements often involve the undertaking by belligerents of obligations over and above those required by the Geneva Conventions, as Articles 6/6/6/7 specifically prohibit agreements detrimental to the rights of protected persons. Such agreements, for example the 1917 agreement between Britain and Germany providing that no reprisals should be taken against prisoners of war before the end of a four-week delay after a demand for redress,[98] seem unlikely to be complied with if violated by one or both sides. They do not represent the creation of new normative orders, which would involve the creation of absolute obligations, but rather the exchange of immediate benefits for each party, either directly to each state or through their nationals under the control of an enemy state.[99]

[96] See CDDH/I/SR.46, para. 73, 6 Off. Records 341 (remark by Israel).

[97] While this new interpretation conforms to the text and spirit of the Vienna Convention on the Law of Treaties, it may set unrealistic standards in the context of a conventional relationship as fragile as that of an ad hoc bilateral agreement to apply the Geneva Conventions and Protocol. An example of the difficulty is provided by the war in the former Yugoslavia, where an agreement by all six republics in November 1991 to apply humanitarian law 'seem[ed] to have been forgotten' following its repeated violation: Milan Sahović, 'International Humanitarian Law in the "Yugoslav War"', (1992) Jugoslenvska revija za medunarodno pravo 195, 213.

[98] See Oppenheim, International Law (1952) II, at 564 n. 3; von Kirchenheim, 'Kriegsgefangene', in Karl Strupp, Wörterbuch des Völkerrecht und der Diplomatie, 1st edn (Berlin: de Gruyter, 1924) I, 743, 748.

[99] Exceptionally, inter-belligerent agreements may in fact result in the creation of a public order normative system. For example, the majority of belligerents during the Second World War agreed, on the basis of reciprocity, to extend to civilian internees the regime of the 1929 Geneva Convention on Prisoners of War (Pictet, IV, at 65). Such a wide-ranging agreement – more unlikely since the post-Second World War development of conventional and customary humanitarian law – largely can be assimilated to agreements to apply the Geneva Conventions and Protocol under common Article 2(3) of the 1949 Geneva Conventions. Given the express condition of reciprocity in this example, however, the agreement would nevertheless have been liable to suspension or termination following its breach by other parties.

The reciprocal nature of another type of non-normative inter-belligerent agreement is expressly recognised by Article 60(7) of Protocol I. Under the provision, agreements setting up demilitarised zones automatically become void if violated by one party, such that 'the other Party [is] released from its obligations under the agreement'.[100] State practice suggests that the effect of the condition of reciprocity in such situations need not be automatic nullification, but rather can take the form of a *faculté* to suspend or terminate the agreement, in conformity with general rules applicable under the *inadimplenti* rule. Thus, for example, a demilitarised zone created in December 1943 by the German forces and Yugoslav partisans as a setting for future exchanges of prisoners of war was allegedly breached in January 1945 by the passage of a partisan group through the zone. The Germans nevertheless did not consider the agreement void, choosing instead to bomb the zone as a measure of reprisals but to continue to consider it a *bona fide* demilitarised zone.[101] There is little doubt, however, that the condition of reciprocity does apply to this type of agreement, despite the general rule found in Article 60(5) of the Vienna Convention on the Law of Treaties.

In the end, the effect of the rejection of the condition of reciprocity in human rights and humanitarian law found in Article 60(5) mirrors the relevance of reciprocity in the initial application of the norms. In human rights law, where reciprocity plays no significant role at the initial applicability stage, Article 60(5) affirms the unsuitability of the condition of reciprocity in the further application of human rights norms. In humanitarian law, on the contrary, reciprocity was only partially discarded as an element of initial applicability. The complete rejection of the condition of reciprocity with respect to humanitarian conventions in Article 60(5) is thus inconsistent with the general structure of humanitarian law as it now stands. As demonstrated by the previous discussion, the establishment of criteria as to which humanitarian provisions or agreements properly are covered by Article 60(5) is extremely difficult. The fusion of human rights and humanitarian law in Article 60 ultimately appears to have consequences unfortunate for humanitarian law. A more specific list of humanitarian provisions and agreements, shielded from the effect of the condition of reciprocity, would have proved more effective to protect individuals from the abusive suspension and termination of

---

[100] See Henri Meyrowitz, 'Die Repressalienverbote des I. Zusatzprotokolls zu den Genfer Abkommen vom 12. August 1949 und das Reziprozitätsprinzip', (1986) 28 *Neue Zeitschrift für Wehrrecht* 177, 186–8.

[101] Vladimir Dedijer, *On Military Conventions* (Lund: Gleerup, 1961) 113.

treaties. It is clear that reciprocity remains a powerful force in inducing continued compliance with humanitarian norms by belligerents, and there is some danger in proposing overly rigid rules which may remain dead letter rather than carefully crafting standards which stand a realistic chance of being applied in the field.[102]

[102] See Richard B. Baxter, 'Humanitarian Law or Humanitarian Politics? The 1974 Diplomatic Conference on Humanitarian Law', (1975) 16 *Harv. Int'l L J* 1, 16.

5   Sanction

There is a certain measure of overlap between the notions of application and sanction of norms in the international legal system where, owing to the lack of a central implementing authority, self-help still plays a critical role in enforcing law. Sanctions could broadly be defined as the set of rules available, following a breach, to force the resumption of compliance with the law, prevent further violations, or provide reparation. One form of sanction, state responsibility rules on countermeasures, is of particular interest with regard to reciprocity. Human rights law and humanitarian law differ quite markedly with regard to sanctions, mostly due to the greater institutionalisation of human rights. Countermeasures, examined in the first section of this chapter, are more closely associated with humanitarian law, in the form of belligerent reprisals, but nevertheless provide revealing insights concerning human rights law. The second section focuses on the humanitarian rule *tu quoque*, which represents one facet of individual responsibility involving elements of reciprocity.

Countermeasures

International law rules on state responsibility recognise as a general principle that any state is entitled to take countermeasures when its rights are being trenched upon by the actions of another state.[1] Countermeasures can take the form of the temporary suspension of

[1] *Case Concerning the Air Service Agreement of 27 March 1946 Between the United States of America and France*, (1978) 15 Rep. Int'l Arb. Awards 417, 443 para. 81; *Case Concerning the Gabcíkovo-Nagymaros Project (Hungary v. Slovakia)*, 25 Sept. 1997, paras. 82–7. See generally Denis Alland, *Justice privée et ordre juridique international – Etude théorique des contre-mesures en droit international public* (Paris: Pedone, 1994); Omer Yousif Elagab, *The Legality of Non-Forcible Counter-Measures in International Law* (Oxford: Clarendon, 1988);

some obligation otherwise binding on the state taking such measures. Countermeasures have played a critical role in the development and enforcement of humanitarian law, and also raise interesting issues in the context of human rights law.

BELLIGERENT REPRISALS

The institution of measures of reprisals pursuant to the law of war, known as 'belligerent reprisals', represents a relatively recent extension of the broader concept of reprisals, which dates back to medieval practices such as *lettres de marques* given to private individuals in peacetime.[2] As noted by one writer towards the end of the nineteenth century, belligerent reprisals, because they underline the normative nature of the law of war, represent progress. That is, upon violation by the enemy, the law of war is merely suspended, rather than wholly discarded.[3] The analysis here will aim not at a general exposition of the rules governing belligerent reprisals, which others have offered already in great detail,[4] but rather at ascertaining to what extent reprisals are grounded

Carlo Focarelli, *Le contromisure nel diritto internazionale* (Milan: Giuffrè, 1994); Linos-Alexandre Sicilianos, *Les réactions décentralisées à l'illicite* (Paris: LGDJ, 1990); Elizabeth Zoller, *Peacetime Unilateral Remedies: An Analysis of Countermeasures* (Dobbs Ferry: Transnational Publishers, 1984); James Crawford, 'Counter-Measures as Interim Measures', (1994) 5 *Eur. J Int'l L* 65, 66; Art. 30, Draft Articles on State Responsibility (Part I), [1979] 2:2 *YB Int'l L Com'n* 115 ('The wrongfulness of an act of a State not in conformity with an obligation of that State towards another State is precluded if the act constitutes a measure legitimate under international law against that other State, in consequence of an internationally wrongful act of that other State').

[2] See Evelyn Speyer Colbert, *Retaliation in International Law* (New York: King's Crown Press, 1948) 9–103; Remigiusz Bierzanek, 'Reprisals as a Means of Enforcing the Laws of Warfare: The Old and the New Law', in Antonio Cassese ed., *The New Humanitarian Law of Armed Conflict* (Naples: Ed. Scientifica, 1979) 232, 233–40; Yves de la Brière, 'Evolution de la doctrine et de la pratique en matière de représailles', (1928-II) 22 *Recueil des cours* 241, 251–70. So-called 'peacetime reprisals', measures involving recourse to force short of war, taken by states in response to a perceived infringement of their rights, are generally a much older institution of the *jus ad bellum* than that of belligerent reprisals in *jus in bello*.

[3] Henri Brocher, 'Les principes naturels du droit de la guerre (partie 3)', (1873) 5 *Revue générale de droit international et de législation comparée* 321, 349 ('Dans le principe, les représailles étaient inconnues, une fois que les hostilités avaient commencé, parce qu'alors le droit de la guerre autorisait ce qui aujourd'hui n'est possible que dans des conditions particulières. Elles sont donc le symptome d'un progrès, bien que de nouveaux progrès doivent amener leur diminution, peut-être même leur disparition').

[4] See especially Frits Kalshoven, *Belligerent Reprisals* (Leiden: Sijthoff, 1971); Christopher Greenwood, 'The Twilight of the Law of Belligerent Reprisals', (1989) 20 *Nether. YB Int'l L* 35–69 (also pub. in Michael Meyer ed., *Armed Conflict and the New Law*

in reciprocity and what impact, if any, human rights have on this institution of humanitarian law.

The modern law of belligerent reprisals remains clouded in uncertainty, and attempts to codify applicable standards authoritatively have failed owing to lack of agreement as to the precise nature of these standards, and disagreement over the desirability of providing an express legal basis for an institution which can hardly be considered compatible with the spirit of 'humanisation' found in the modern law of armed conflict. Instead of adopting standards to control resort to reprisals, the international community has favoured a piecemeal approach whereby reprisals are totally prohibited with respect to specifically protected classes of persons or objects.[5] Thus, reprisals against prisoners of war were first declared illegal in 1929 (Art. 2, 1929 Geneva Convention on Prisoners of War), a prohibition extended to the wounded, sick, shipwrecked and certain civilians in 1949 (Arts. 46/47/13/33), and later confirmed and expanded by Protocol I (Arts. 20, 51(6), 52(1), 53(c), 54(4), 55(2) and 56(4)). Article 4(4) of the 1954 Hague Convention on Cultural Property further forbids reprisals against cultural objects, while Protocol II to the 1981 UN Conventional Weapons Convention lays down a specific prohibition concerning the use of mines and booby-traps against civilians (Art. 3(2)).[6]

Where reprisals are still permitted, or when the conventions do not apply, two principles have come to be recognised as customary limitations to the resort to reprisals.[7] The first principle provides that reprisals must

(London: British Institute of International and Comparative Law, 1989) 227–50); Frits Kalshoven, 'Reprisals in the CDDH', in Robert J. Akkerman et al. eds., *Declarations of Principles – A Quest for Universal Peace* (Leiden: Sijthoff, 1977) 195–216; Frits Kalshoven, 'Belligerent Reprisals Revisited', (1990) 21 *Nether. YB Int'l L* 43; Stanislaw E. Nahlik, 'Le problème des représailles à la lumière des travaux de la conférence diplomatique sur le droit humanitaire', (1978) 82 *Revue générale de droit international public* 130–69; Ellery C. Stowell, 'Military Reprisals and the Laws of War', (1942) 36 *Am. J Int'l L* 643–50.

[5] One exception is Art. 11 of the 1954 Hague Convention on Cultural Property, providing for a limited right of reprisals in which are laid out the basic principles of the law of reprisals, although that term is nowhere used in the provision. See above, chapter 4, pp. 176–7.

[6] Protocol (II) on Prohibition or Restrictions on the Use of Mines, Booby Traps and Other Devices, to the 1981 UN Conventional Weapons Convention, *reprinted in* Dietrich Schindler and Jirí Toman, *The Laws of Armed Conflict*, 3rd edn (Dordrecht: Nijhoff, 1989) 185–6.

[7] See *Legality of the Threat or Use of Nuclear Weapons*, Advisory Opinion, [1996] ICJ Rep. para. 46; *The Prosecutor* v. *Kupreskić* (*Lasva Valley* case) (Judgment), 14 Jan. 2000, Case No. IT-95-16-T (Trial Chamber, ICTY) para. 535; 1958 *British Manual of Military Law*, paras. 646–8; 1992 *German Manual on Humanitarian Law*, para. 478; 1999 *Canadian War Manual*,

be the last option considered by a belligerent faced with a violation of humanitarian law by the enemy. It probably requires that a warning be given before measures of reprisals are implemented, so as to give the enemy the chance to resume compliance with humanitarian law. If other rapid and effective measures are available, for instance the International Fact-Finding Commission under Article 90 of Protocol I, they should be exhausted before resorting to reprisals.[8] The second principle requires that a resort to reprisals must not be unreasonably disproportionate to the original violation. For instance, the execution by German *Einsatzgruppen* of 2,100 hostages in retaliation for the killing of twenty-one German soldiers by partisans in occupied territories – in compliance with official guidelines directing that 50–100 hostages be shot for each German soldier killed – clearly was unreasonably disproportionate.[9] The question whether 'humanity' – and, by extension, human rights – is a third limitation to reprisals will be examined later in this section, following an analysis of (1) the function of reprisals and (2) the need to draw a distinction between 'Hague law' and 'Geneva law' when discussing this mode of sanction.

Function of belligerent reprisals

In the discussion of the condition of reciprocity in chapter 4, several differences between that rule and the institution of reprisals were underlined, so as to illustrate the fact that they constitute distinct legal mechanisms.[10] The analysis now turns to the question of whether, and to what extent, the institution of reprisals reflects the reciprocal nature of humanitarian law obligations. An examination of the function

---

s. 15–17; Erik Castrén, *The Present Law of War and Neutrality* (Helsinki: Suomalaisen Tiedeakatemian Toimituksia, 1954) 70; Kalshoven, *Belligerent Reprisals*, at 339–44; Lassa Oppenheim, *International Law*, Hersch Lauterpacht ed., 7th edn (London: Longmans, 1952) II, 142.

[8] See *Case Concerning the Air Service Agreement of 27 March 1946 Between the United States of America and France*, (1978) 15 Rep. Int'l Arb. Awards 417, 445–6 paras. 94–6. The validity of an obligation of prior resort to dispute settlement procedure in the wider context of countermeasures later became the subject of a debate within the ILC: Gaetano Arangio-Ruiz, 'Sixth Report on State Responsibility', UN Doc. A/CN.4/461 (1994); James Crawford, 'Third Report on State Responsibility', UN Doc. A/CN.4/507 (2000) paras. 355–60; 'Symposium on Counter-measures', (1994) 5 *Eur J. Int'l L* 20–119.

[9] *US v. Ohlendorf et al.* (the *Einsatzgruppen* trial), (1948) 15 Ann. Digest Rep. Pub. Int'l L Cases 565, 4 USMT 1, 493–4 (US Mil. Trib., Nuremberg); *In re Kappler* (the *Ardeatine Cave* trial), (1948) 15 Ann. Digest Rep. Pub. Int'l L Cases 471, 476 (Italian Mil. Trib., Rome).

[10] See the discussion in chapter 4, pp. 164–6.

of reprisals, as disclosed by the rules that govern them, can provide an indication as to whether they are instruments of pure retaliation, exercised in order to maintain the balance between belligerents as required by the principle of reciprocity, or whether reprisals have additional or altogether different purposes. Four possible functions may be assigned to sanctions: revenge, punishment, prevention and law enforcement.[11] There is much debate as to the nature and purpose of sanctions in international law generally,[12] but it is perhaps possible to derive from substantive rules of humanitarian law the main function of belligerent reprisals specifically.

Strong political and moral foundations exist for the view that reprisals are an instrument of revenge by a victim against the perpetrator of a breach of humanitarian law. It can hardly be denied that, in some cases, revenge acts as a trigger to a belligerent's decision to adopt measures of reprisals, which are then used politically for purely internal purposes. For instance, in the First World War, the council of the Yonne region, incensed at the German bombardment of French cities, demanded retaliation in kind against German cities.[13] Another example is the 18 October 1942 'Commando Order' which instructed military units to execute Allied commandos captured behind German lines, even if they were wearing their uniforms and otherwise had complied with the law of war. As this order was kept absolutely secret, and was not conditional on the prior commission of a crime by the Allies, it could claim no role as deterrent or punishment, at least in a legal sense. Its sole justification seems to be that of revenge against overly successful commando operations. As such, it could not be justified as a lawful measure of reprisals.[14] The vengeful purpose of reprisals is strictly relevant to the moral and political justification of such measures, and has no significant legal dimension.[15]

---

[11] See Laura Forlati Picchio, *La sanzione nel diritto internazionale* (Padua: CEDAM, 1974) 40; Gaetano Arangio-Ruiz, 'Third Report on State Responsibility', UN Doc. A/CN.4/440 (1991) para. 14.
[12] See e.g. the differing views of Anzilotti, Kelsen and Ago as to the existence and purpose of secondary norms governing sanctions, summarised by Benedetto Conforti, *Diritto internazionale*, 4th edn (Naples: Ed. Scientifica, 1992) 352–3; James Crawford, 'First Report on State Responsibility', UN Doc. A/CN.4/490 (1998) 232, paras. 12–18.
[13] A. Mérignhac and E. Lémonon, *Le droit des gens et la guerre de 1914–1918* (Paris: Sirey, 1921) I, 233 n. 1.
[14] The Commando Order is reproduced as Document 498-PS in (1946) 26 Int'l Mil. Trib. 100–1. See Kalshoven, *Belligerent Reprisals*, at 184–93.
[15] See Art. 28, *Instructions for the Government of Armies of the United States in the Field*, prepared by Francis Lieber, General Order No. 100, 24 April 1863 ('Retaliation will,

The second possible function of reprisals is that of punishment of the author of the violation of the law of war.[16] During an armed conflict, there is only a remote likelihood that the belligerent who is the victim of a breach of humanitarian law will be in a position to capture and try the individual author of the violation. Reprisals can thus be seen as the only available means to punish violators during an armed conflict.[17] There are, however, several problems with this construction of the purpose of reprisals. The first and most blatant is that reprisals are not directed specifically at the individual authors of the initial violation. Reprisals typically are taken in situations where the individuals personally responsible for the breach are either unknown or out of reach. The measures are aimed instead at other more vulnerable individuals or groups, who can be said to have a certain degree of solidarity with the presumed authors of the initial violation.[18] To construe reprisals as punishment would thus amount to collective punishment for the wrong committed by others, despite the absence of any demonstrated active or passive responsibility on the part of the target of measures of reprisals. It is to adopt a formal view of the state, or even the country, as a whole as the author of the initial violation. In the case of the occupied civilian population – which has been, more often than not, the target of reprisals – this runs directly contrary to the customary principle embodied in Article 50 of the 1907 Hague Regulations. The provision prohibits collective punishment for acts for which the population 'cannot be

therefore, never be resorted to as a measure of mere revenge'); 1956 *US Field Manual* 27–10, para. 497(d); 1999 *Canadian War Manual*, s. 15–14; Gaetano Arangio-Ruiz, 'Fourth Report on State Responsibility', UN Doc. A/CN.4/444/Add.1 (1992) paras. 3–4; Henri Meyrowitz, 'Die Repressalienverbote des I. Zusatzprotokolls zu den Genfer Abkommen vom 12. August 1949 und das Reziprozitätsprinzip', (1986) 28 *Neue Zeitschrift für Wehrrecht* 177, 178: 'Ebenso ist die Beizeichnung der Repressalien als *Vergeltungsmaßnahmen* zu verwerfen, weil dieses die Idee der Rache impliziriende oder suggerierende Wort mit dem legitimen Zweck des Repressalien nicht vereinbar ist' ('Nevertheless, the characterisation of reprisals as "*revenge*-measures" has been rejected, because the idea of revenge implied or suggested by the word is incompatible with the legitimate role of reprisals'). Emphasis in the original.

[16] See e.g. Antonio Cassese, 'On the Current Trends Towards Criminal Prosecution and Punishment of Breaches of International Humanitarian Law', (1998) 9 *Eur. J Int'l L* 2, 3.

[17] See 1958 *British Manual of Military Law*, para. 644.

[18] This passage is borrowed by the ICTY in the *Kupreskić* judgment, taken from an earlier published version of part of this work: *The Prosecutor v. Kupreskić (Lasva Valley* case) (Judgment), 14 Jan. 2000, Case No. IT-95-16-T (Trial Chamber, ICTY) para. 528; René Provost, 'Reciprocity in Human Rights and Humanitarian Law', (1995) 65 *Brit. YB Int'l L* 383, 416. See Castrén, *Present Law*, at 71; Wilhelm Wengler, 'La noción de sujeto de derecho internacional público examinada bajo el aspecto de algunos fenómenos políticos actuales', (1951) 3 *Revista española de derecho internacional* 831, 836.

regarded as jointly and severally responsible', a requirement wholly alien to the law of belligerent reprisals.[19] Reprisals viewed as punishment further appear inconsistent with the customary requirement of negotiations and the giving of warnings, and with the rule that reprisals must be stopped once the violation ceases. As noted by tribunals and writers, the confusion between collective punishment and reprisals is probably to blame for the mistaken perception that reprisals are, at least in part, punitive legal measures.[20] Belligerent reprisals are construed properly as forming part of rules on state responsibility, with no link to the issue of possible penal responsibility of the individual authors of the initial violation.[21]

A third possible function of reprisals is the prevention of further violations of humanitarian law. The question of the preventive nature of reprisals has arisen in the context of assessing the proportionality of measures taken. Some consider that the likelihood of further breaches constitutes a valid factor in the evaluation of proportional measures, while others insist that reprisals are fundamentally backward-looking and that the exceptional legality of acts otherwise prohibited by international law cannot rest on the mere speculation that future violation may take place.[22] Neither position is completely correct. On the one hand, if reprisals were wholly backward-looking, resting solely on the initial violation by the enemy belligerent, they would in fact constitute punitive actions, raising the problems discussed in the preceding paragraph. On the other hand, to allow a belligerent to factor apprehended violations into its reprisals would introduce to the law of war a dangerously subjective mechanism permitting the extension of lawful reprisals to a degree difficult to control. Further, such expanded reprisals could in theory lead the initial violator to take legal counter-reprisals in

[19] See 1958 British Manual of Military Law, para. 553; Kalshoven, Belligerent Reprisals, at 56-62.

[20] See In re Kappler (the Ardeatine Cave trial), (1948) 15 Ann. Digest Rep. Pub. Int'l L Cases 471, 477 (Italian Mil. Trib., Rome); Kalshoven, Belligerent Reprisals, at 38-40; Nahlik, 'Le problème', at 131; B. V. A. Röling, 'The Law of War and the National Jurisdiction since 1945', (1960-II) 100 Recueil des cours 329, 420. See generally Conforti, Diritto internazionale, at 361; Charles Cheney Hyde, International Law, 2nd edn (Boston: Little, Brown, 1947) III, 1843; Arangio-Ruiz, 'Fourth Report', UN Doc. A/CN.4/444/Add.1 (1992) paras. 3-4; Constantin Eustathiades, 'Les sujets de droit international et la responsabilité internationale – Nouvelles tendances', (1953-III) 84 Recueil des cours 397, 443.

[21] This is consistent with a rejection of the version of the rule tu quoque linking reprisals and penal responsibility: below, pp. 230-2.

[22] See e.g. Myres M. McDougal and Florentino P. Feliciano, Law and Minimum World Public Order (New Haven: Yale UP, 1961) 682.

answer to the measures of reprisals which corresponded to the merely apprehended breach. For example, the Forces françaises de l'intérieur (FFI) executed eighty German prisoners of war in September 1944 in response to the execution of eighty partisans by the Wehrmacht. Putting aside the prohibition of reprisals against prisoners of war, the notion of prevention might mean that, if the FFI had executed 160 prisoners rather than eighty on the basis of probable further executions, the German forces would have been in a position legally to execute a further eighty prisoners. The dangers involved in such a loosening of the rules governing belligerent reprisals become readily apparent.

Reprisals are forward-looking in that they aim to bring about a change of policy by the enemy belligerent with regard to the violation of a given rule of warfare (Beugezwang). But, at the same time, they are limited by the extent of the actual past breach committed by the enemy. There is no mathematical precision here, as exemplified by the unconvincing attempt to quantify the reprisal 'weight' of the bombing of German and English cities during the Second World War.[23] Of necessity, belligerents must be accorded a certain margin of appreciation. Nevertheless, and this brings us to the fourth and proper function of reprisals, the limitation does shed some light on the nature of reprisals as sanctions of humanitarian law, instruments designed to force compliance with law rather than concede to military necessity and thus undermine the obligatory character of the law.[24]

There have been suggestions that the initial violation must be imputable to the state targeted by reprisals.[25] Indeed, if the purpose of

[23] See Maximilian Czesany, Nie wieder Krieg gegen die Zivilbevölkerung: Eine völkerrechtliche Untersuchung des Luftkrieg 1939–1945 (Graz, 1961) 95–7, criticised by Kalshoven, Belligerent Reprisals, at 175–6. See more generally Case Concerning the Air Service Agreement of 27 March 1946 Between the United States of America and France, (1978) 15 Rep. Int'l Arb. Awards 417, 443–4 para. 83.

[24] See 1958 British Manual of Military Law, para. 642; 1999 Canadian Manual on the Law of Armed Conflict, s. 15–17(b) ('reprisals serve as law enforcement mechanism'); 1992 German Manual on Military Law, paras. 476 and 1206; Legge di guerra italiana del 1938, Art. 8(2); Castrén, Present Law, at 69–72 ('Reprisals belong to the small class of measures which enable warfare to be kept within legal limits and they may thus be said to be a kind of sanction for the laws of war' – ibid. at 69, emphasis in the original); Kalshoven, Belligerent Reprisals, at 37; Hans Kelsen, Principles of International Law (New York: Rinehart, 1952) 24–5.

[25] 1999 Canadian Manual on the Law of Armed Conflict, s. 15–17(a); Morris Greenspan, The Modern Law of Land Warfare (Los Angeles: U California Press, 1959) 410–11; Greenwood, 'Twilight of the Law', at 43; Françoise J. Hampson, 'Belligerent Reprisals and the 1977 Protocols to the Geneva Conventions of 1949', (1988) 37 Int'l & Comp. L Quart. 818, 822–3.

reprisals is to bring about a change of policy by the enemy, the latter must be sufficiently organised to adopt coherent policies. In the Italian *Ardeatine Cave* trial, the tribunal devoted considerable time to assessing whether the illegal attack against German troops in Rome which had triggered the retaliatory mass killings could be attributed directly or indirectly to the Italian state. In the court's view, reprisals could lawfully be ordered only if the Italian state had in fact directed the initial violation.[26] A Dutch court in the *Rauter* trial similarly concluded that reprisals could constitute a lawful response only to an act of the target state or its agents.[27] This is relevant to the present enquiry in that the conditioning of reprisals on the imputability of the initial violation to the targeted state could imply that reprisals indicate the reciprocal nature of the obligations of both states under humanitarian law.

A rigid requirement of imputability appears to be both inconsistent with the context in which belligerent reprisals take place and unsupported by state practice. In the *Ardeatine Cave* trial, for example, the Italian tribunal relied on organic links between the group having carried out the attack and the *Giunta militare*, the military arm of the Italian state. The very nature of resistance groups operating in occupied territory means, of course, that all such links must remain hidden from the enemy. Reprisals in such a situation are permissible only when police operations yield no result and the culprits remain unknown.[28] Keeping in mind the prohibition against torturing prisoners, there simply was no way for the German occupier to become intimately acquainted not only with the operating structure of the Italian resistance movement, but also with the specific links between the attackers and the state in that given case.[29] In view of the customary prohibition of collective

---

[26] *In re Kappler* (the *Ardeatine Cave* trial), (1948) 15 Ann. Digest Rep. Pub. Int'l L Cases 471, 473-5 (Italian Mil. Trib., Rome), a conclusion affirmed on appeal by the Italian Supreme Military Tribunal, [1953] *Rivista di diritto internazionale* 193, 197-9 ('L'inosservanza che legittima la rappresaglia del nemico deve essere effetto di azione o omissione imputabile allo stato, rispettivamente in contrasto con divieti o comandi del diritto internazionale', *ibid.*, at 198). British courts trying the German high command in Italy for the same crime did not seem to attach any importance to the question of imputability: *UK v. von Mackensen and Maelzer*, (1945) 8 L Rep. Trials War Crim. 1 (British Mil. Ct, Rome); *UK v. Kesselring*, (1947) 8 L Rep. Trials War Crim. 9 (British Mil. Ct, Venice).

[27] *The Netherlands v. Rauter*, (1949) 14 L Rep. Trials War Crim. 89, 131-2 (Spec. Ct Cass.).

[28] See Kalshoven, *Belligerent Reprisals*, at 235 ('Actually, this description of the perpetrators as "unknown partisans" was precisely the assumption at the root of the German retaliatory action'); 1958 *British Manual of Military Law*, para. 643.

[29] In this case, German authorities made no serious attempt to investigate the crime and ordered reprisals immediately, which was one of several reasons for which the reprisals were illegal.

punishment against the civilian population (Art. 50, 1907 Hague Regulations), it is hard to agree with the Italian tribunal's statement that if the
state were not involved, and the attack an action of private individuals,
then only the measure of collective punishment would be permissible.[30]
In the *Rauter* case, the Dutch government in exile had called for all-out
resistance by the civilian population, a call widely heeded by individuals and groups. In such a case, the question of imputability becomes
problematic, particularly from the perspective of commanders in the
field deciding whether to order reprisals.[31] At a structural level, a requirement of imputability seems inconsistent with the loose standard
of resistance groups 'belonging to a party to the conflict' in order to be
lawful combatants (Art. 4(A)(2), 1949 Third Geneva Convention).[32] Finally,
there are several examples of measures of reprisals aimed at states not
directly connected to the initial breach. For instance, the killing of US
prisoners of war by the Vietcong in response to a policy by the Republic
of South Vietnam of executing Vietcong prisoners was illegal by virtue
of the prohibition of reprisals against prisoners of war, but not by virtue
of the fact that it was directed against US rather than South Vietnamese
prisoners of war.[33]

The correct standard, then, is not one of strict imputability of the
initial breach to the enemy state. States are not the exclusive bearers

---

[30] The tribunal proposes an expansive interpretation of collective responsibility – which
may provide a legal basis for collective punishment – to justify its position: *In re
Kappler* (the *Ardeatine Cave* trial), (1948) 15 Ann. Digest Pub. Int'l L Cases 471, 478
(Italian Mil. Trib., Rome). This is also linked to the question of whether the civilian
population under occupation has a duty under the laws and customs of war not to
carry out acts of hostilities against the occupying forces: Roberto Ago, 'Nota sul caso
Kappler', [1953] *Rivista di diritto internazionale* 200, 206.

[31] See Röling, 'Law of War', at 423–6.

[32] Italian courts, in particular, have construed this requirement to be quite flexible:
Baffico v. Calleri, (1948) Ann. Digest Rep. Pub. Int'l L Cases 426 (App. Court, Torino);
Eric David, *Principes de droit des conflits armés* (Brussels: Bruylant, 1994) 355. This is
treated in more detail in chapter 2, pp. 90–3.

[33] Indeed the measures proved effective as pressure from the US put an end to the
executions. See Howard S. Levie, 'Maltreatment of Prisoners of War in Vietnam',
(1968) 48 *Boston UL Rev.* 323. One could also mention British Reprisals Orders,
initially taken against Germany as retaliation for its unrestricted submarine warfare,
but later extended to Italy and Japan without similar justifications: Kalshoven,
Belligerent Reprisals, at 156 (suggesting that the measures did not really constitute
reprisals but simply used German naval warfare violations as an excuse to impose
measures thought essential to the war effort by the British). On the other hand,
reprisals may not be directed at states in no way implicated in the conflict, as noted
in the arbitral award in the *Cysne* case, (1919) 2 Rep. Int'l Arb. Awards 1057, in which
the German sinking of a neutral ship in reprisal for British violations was judged
illegal. See 1999 *Canadian Manual on the Law of Armed Conflict*, s. 15–17(e); Sicilianos,
Réactions, at 82–7.

of obligations under the law of war, and individuals can perpetrate violations to which a belligerent can lawfully respond by way of reprisals. Both American and British field manuals in force during the Second World War considered that reprisals could be justified against illegal acts committed by individuals, as distinct from acts of the state.[34] The proper test is looser, relating to the solidarity between the target and the group whose policy is sought to be changed.[35] Thus, the US Military Tribunal in Nuremberg held in the *Einsatzgruppen* trial that solidarity could be geographic.[36] On this basis a belligerent cannot through reprisals target individuals several hundred kilometres away from where the illegal acts took place, because no connection can be presumed to exist between those individuals and the authors of the initial breach. It would be peculiar indeed to demand a strict legal link between the authors of the initial violation and the state in order to authorise measures directed against individuals in all likelihood innocent of any wrongdoing.[37] This grim fact underlines the function of reprisals as a lever to force a return to compliance with humanitarian law. It is an issue clearly distinct from that of whether a belligerent may incur international responsibility for the initial violation, for which it would be appropriate to question whether acts were indeed attributable to the state.[38]

---

[34] 1940 *US Field Manual 27–10*, para. 358(d) ('Illegal acts of warfare justifying reprisals may be committed by a government, by its military commanders, or by a community or individuals thereof, whom it is impossible to apprehend, try, and punish'); 1929 *British Manual of Military Law*, para. 453. The 1999 *Canadian Manual on the Law of Armed Conflict* (s. 15–17(a)) and 1956 *US Field Manual 27–10* (para. 497) no longer specifically mention individuals, although the 1958 *British Manual of Military Law* (para. 643) still does.

[35] See *The Prosecutor* v. *Kupreskić* (*Lasva Valley* case) (Judgment), 14 January 2000, Case No. IT-95-16-T (Trial Chamber, ICTY) para. 528; Greenspan, *Modern Law*, at 410–11 n. 35; Kalshoven, *Belligerent Reprisals*, at 28–9; A. R. Albrecht, 'War Reprisals in the War Crimes Trials and in the Geneva Conventions of 1949', (1953) 47 *Am. J Int'l L* 590, 595.

[36] *US* v. *Ohlendorf et al.* (the *Einsatzgruppen* trial), (1948) 15 Ann. Digest Rep. Pub. Int'l L Cases 656 (US Mil. Trib., Nuremberg). See Kalshoven, *Belligerent Reprisals*, at 230; Albrecht, 'War Reprisals', at 604.

[37] To borrow from Draper, it would be to make international law 'stern with human beings but very gentle with states which treat human beings inhumanely': G. I. A. D. Draper, 'The Relationship Between the Human Rights Regime and the Law of Armed Conflict', in *Proceedings of the International Conference on Humanitarian Law – San Remo, 24–27 Sept. 1970* (Grassi: Istituto Editoriale Ticinese, 1970) 141, 143.

[38] This is a reflection of the hybrid nature of international humanitarian law, imposing obligations on individuals, belligerent groups and states. Reliance by the ICTY in the *Tadić* judgment, for the purpose of determining whether individuals were 'in the hand of a party to the conflict', on the standard devised by the ICJ in the *Nicaragua* case in the context of state responsibility, raises similar issues: *The Prosecutor* v. *Delalić* (the '*Celebici*' case) (Appeals Judgment), 20 Feb. 2001, Case No.

Reciprocity of Hague law and Geneva law

In treaty law, reprisals are restricted exclusively by the Geneva Conventions and not by the older Hague Conventions.[39] In Protocol I, the seven specific prohibitions of reprisals can be found in Part II on Wounded, Sick and Shipwrecked (Art. 20) and Part IV on the Civilian Population (Arts. 51(6), 52(1), 53(c), 54(4), 55(2) and 56(4)). There are no such prohibitions to be found in Part III dealing with Methods and Means of Warfare, Combatant and Prisoner-of-War Status. This pattern of acceptability of reprisals, some have argued, reflects a fundamental difference between the two components of humanitarian law of armed conflict, that is 'Geneva law', or 'humanitarian law' proper, and 'Hague law', or combat regulation.[40] They further argue that 'Geneva law', being closer in nature to human rights, can evolve naturally to incorporate a general rejection of reprisals, while 'Hague law', under which an unanswered violation by one side may grant it a definite military advantage, cannot do away with effective reciprocity of its norms through measures of reprisals, and can only hope for a regulation of the conditions under which reprisals may be taken.[41]

IT-96-21-A (Appeals Chamber, ICTY) paras. 6–51; *The Prosecutor v. Tadić* (Appeals Judgment), 15 July 1999, Case No. IT-94-1-A (Appeals Chamber, ICTY) paras. 92–7; *Military and Paramilitary Activities in and Against Nicaragua (Nicaragua v. US)*, [1986] ICJ Rep. 14, 62–5; Crawford, 'First Report', UN Doc. A/CN.4/490 (1998) paras. 200–11; Theodor Meron, 'Classification of Armed Conflict in the Former Yugoslavia: *Nicaragua's Fallout*', (1998) 92 *Am. J Int'l L* 236–42. See also the discussion in chapter 2, pp. 90–3.

[39] Art. 50 of the 1907 Hague Regulations, on collective penalties against the civilian population, was intentionally not intended to govern belligerent reprisals: Edouard Rolin, 'Report to the Conference from the Second Commission on the Laws and Customs of War on Land', in James Brown Scott ed., *The Report of the Hague Conferences of 1899 and 1907* (Oxford: Clarendon, 1917) 137, 152; 1929 *British Manual of Military Law*, para. 452; Kalshoven, *Belligerent Reprisals*, at 56–62. As mentioned earlier, Art. 3(2) of Protocol II to the 1981 UN Conventional Weapons Convention also contains a prohibition of reprisals against civilians.

[40] Nahlik, 'Le problème', at 169.

[41] *Ibid.*, at 168–9; Joseph Kunz, *La problemática actual de las leyes de la guerra* (Universidad de Valladolid, 1955) 83–97 ('la observación de la leyes de la guerra, la protección de los soldados del beligerente legal y de la población civil dependen de la reciprocidad', *ibid.* at 96). The debate as to whether humanitarian law of armed conflict can indeed be divided into two distinct bodies of rules has been ongoing for some time, mostly with regard to the link between *jus ad bellum* and *jus in bello* and the equality of belligerents under the latter despite a breach of the peace by the initial aggressor. The International Court of Justice in its advisory opinion on the *Legality of the Threat or Use of Nuclear Weapons*, [1996] ICJ Rep. para. 75, suggested that this distinction is no longer warranted. See generally Aristidis Calogeropoulos-Stratis, *Droit humanitaire et droit de l'homme: La protection de la personne en conflits armés* (Geneva: Institut universitaire de hautes études internationales, 1980) 56–7; Henri Meyrowitz, *Le*

Leaving aside the relationship between these two allegedly distinct components of the humanitarian law of armed conflict, it is suggested that the distinction is misplaced in the specific context of reprisals. Even if 'Hague law' can be differentiated from 'Geneva law', the two are not watertight compartments. According to a generally accepted rule of the law of reprisals and, more generally, of countermeasures, the initial violation and the reprisals need not involve the same norm.[42] A breach of a 'Hague law' rule could lawfully trigger the suspension of a 'Geneva law' rule, given that the two must apply at the same time to similar situations. The 1956 *US Field Manual 27-10*, for example, indicates that mistreatment of prisoners of war by the enemy, a violation of 'Geneva law', could be answered by reprisals involving the use of dumdum bullets, a weapon normally prohibited under 'Hague law'.[43] This underlines the function of rules prohibiting reprisals in humanitarian law, that is, the shielding of specific individuals and groups from reprisals, regardless of the 'Hague' or 'Geneva' nature of the rule originally breached.

Undeniably, shielding civilians and other protected persons from reprisals by and large has the effect of ensuring that 'Geneva' rules are not suspended, given that most 'Geneva' norms apply specifically to these classes of individuals. Nevertheless, this is conceptually distinct from a declaration that reprisals play no part in 'Geneva law'. That is, 'purely humanitarian' rules can be suspended with respect to individuals who are not protected persons. In the regime of the 1949 Geneva Conventions, the class of non-protected persons which could be made legitimate targets of reprisals is extremely large, including civilians from a belligerent's own population as well as the populations of co-belligerents and neutral states (Art. 4, Fourth Geneva Convention). Protocol I considerably reduces the scope of potential targets of reprisals, by also prohibiting reprisals against all civilians (Art. 51(6)) and objects indispensable to the survival of the civilian population (Art. 54(4)). The ICTY Trial Chamber in the *Kupreskić* judgment suggests that this prohibition now forms part

principe de l'égalité des belligérents devant le droit de la guerre (Paris: Pedone, 1970) 130–40; Bruno Simma, *Das Reziprozitätselement im zutstandekommen völkerrechtlicher Verträge* (Berlin: Duncker & Humblot, 1972) 110–13; Institut de droit international, 'L'égalité d'application des règles du droit de la guerre aux parties à un conflit armé', (1963) 50:1 *Annuaire de l'Institut de droit international* 5–127; *ibid.*, vol. 50:2, at 306–56 and 376. Christopher Greenwood, 'The Relationship Between *Ius in Bellum* and *Ius ad Bello*', (1983) 9 *Rev. Int'l Studies* 221–34.

[42] 1956 *US Field Manual 27-10*, para. 497(e); 1958 *British Manual of Military Law*, para. 643; Albrecht, 'War Reprisals', at 600 n. 47. More generally, see above, chapter 4, pp. 165–6.

[43] 1956 *US Field Manual 27-10*, para. 497(a).

of customary law.[44] Any possible problems associated with widening the
class of individuals immune from reprisals concern the availability of
effective sanctions for a breach of humanitarian law, a matter not connected to the reciprocal or unilateral nature of the humanitarian law
of armed conflict.[45] Thus the fact that the prohibition of reprisals could
be said to stem from the 'Geneva law' provisions of humanitarian law
treaties does not indicate a greater relevance of reciprocity in 'Hague
law'.

The principle of humanity

Treaty and customary limitations as to who or what may be made the
object of reprisals are humanitarian limitations to that institution of the
law of war. The effect of Protocol I in this respect is to extend the protection against reprisals from individuals under the control of the belligerent, under the 1949 Geneva Conventions, to individuals not in the control of the belligerent and even those under the control of the enemy.[46]
This does not signal a fundamental change in the law of reprisals, but
simply the enlargement of the categories of persons against whom such
measures are unlawful. If certain categories of individuals can be re-
moved from the class of legitimate targets of reprisals on humanitarian
grounds, could the use of reprisals be limited in general by elementary
considerations of humanity? The question could also be framed so as
to evaluate the relevance of basic human rights norms to humanitarian
law, that is the degree to which both bodies of law are integrated in
the context of the legal regulation of belligerent reprisals. The practical
impact of a principle of humanity would be substantial if it rendered
illegal measures possibly falling into 'loopholes' of humanitarian rules
governing belligerent reprisals.

Several writers mention the principle of humanity as a limit on the
measures available as reprisals.[47] Often mentioned in support of this

---

[44] *The Prosecutor* v. *Kupreskić* (*Lasva Valley* case) (Judgment), 14 Jan. 2000, Case No.
IT-95-16-T (Trial Chamber, ICTY) paras. 531–6.

[45] This was one of the reasons leading the United States to reject ratification of
Protocol I: Abraham D. Sofaer, 'Agora: The US Decision not to Ratify Protocol I to the
Geneva Convention on the Protection of War Victims', (1988) 82 *Am. J Int'l L* 784, 785.

[46] Greenwood, 'Twilight of the Law', at 59–60.

[47] See e.g. Castrén, *Present Law*, at 70–1; Andrea de Guttry, *Le rappresaglie non
comportanti la coercizione militare nel diritto internazionale* (Milan: Giuffré, 1985) 273;
Flavia Lattanzi, *Garanzie dei diritti dell'uomo nel diritto internazionale generale* (Milan:
Giuffrè, 1983) 295–9; Mérignhac and Lémonon, *Droit des gens*, I, at 228–30 (although
Mérignhac and Lémonon later find that military necessity may lead to the justified

position is the resolution adopted in 1934 by the Institut de droit international, stating in Article 6 that 'l'Etat autorisé à user de représailles est tenu d'observer les conditions suivantes:...(4) S'abstenir de toute mesure de représailles qui serait contraire aux lois de l'humanité et aux exigences de la conscience publique.'[48] The text was explicitly derived from the Martens clause, understood as a general statement of the minimal conditions of humanity applicable to all acts of warfare, including reprisals.[49] Indeed, the inclusion of the Martens clause in all major humanitarian law conventions perhaps provides the strongest support for a principle of humanity that would limit belligerent reprisals. Another important source, Article 86 of the *Oxford Manual* adopted in 1880 by the Institut de droit international, provides that reprisals 'must conform in all cases to the laws of humanity and morality'.[50]

Many of the statements most often cited in support of the existence of a principle of humanity, such as the Award in the *Naulilaa* arbitration[51] or the 1934 resolution of the Institut de droit international, relate to reprisals in times of peace. Although peacetime and belligerent reprisals share a number of basic principles, the existence of a principle of humanity in the former does not necessarily imply its existence with respect to the latter. Peacetime reprisals are unfriendly measures, falling short of war, taken by one state against another, and are now probably rendered obsolete given universal adherence to Article 2(4) of the UN Charter.[52] Recourse to peacetime reprisals was regulated by *jus ad*

taking of any measure, however inhuman: *ibid.*, at 235–7 and 246); Arangio-Ruiz, 'Third Report', UN Doc. A/CN.4/440 (1991) 16–17; Denise Bindschedler-Robert, 'A Reconsideration of the Law of Armed Conflict', in Carnegie Endowment for International Peace, *Report of the Conference on Contemporary Problems of the Law of Armed Conflict, Geneva: 15–20 Sept. 1969* (New York: Carnegie Endowment, 1971) 1, 59; Giorgio Sacerdoti, 'A proposito del caso *Priebke*: La responsabilità per l'esecuzione di ordini illegitimi costituenti crimini di guerra', (1997) 80 *Rivista di diritto internazionale* 130, 139–40.

[48] See both the resolution and the report by Nicolas Politis, 'Le régime des représailles en temps de paix', (1934) 38 *Annuaire de l'Institut de droit international* 1–166 and 708–11.

[49] *Ibid.*, at 20. On the Martens clause generally, see Shigeki Miyazaki, 'The Martens Clause in International Humanitarian Law', in Christophe Swinarski ed., *Studies and Essays on International Humanitarian Law and Red Cross Principles in Honour of Jean Pictet* (Geneva/The Hague: Nijhoff, 1984) 433–44.

[50] 'Manuel des lois de la guerre sur terre', (1881–2) 5 *Annuaire de l'Institut de droit international* 156–74, *translated in* Dietrich Schindler and Jiří Toman, *The Laws of Armed Conflict*, 3rd edn (Dordrecht: Nijhoff, 1989) 48.

[51] (1928) 2 Rep. Int'l Arb. Awards 1012, 1026.

[52] The matter is still being debated. See *Legality of the Threat or Use of Nuclear Weapons*, Advisory Opinion, [1996] ICJ Rep. para. 46; Christiane Alibert, *Du droit de se faire justice*

bellum but, where they were permitted by international law, their nature and extent was not governed directly by *jus in bello*.[53] Given that peacetime reprisals were meant to be an institution less extreme than war, it is not surprising to find support for their limitation by a principle of humanity encompassing the most basic elements of the law of war. Without such a limit on peacetime reprisals, they might lawfully exceed in barbarity the horrors of war.[54] In the context of belligerent reprisals adopted during an armed conflict, to which the law of war does apply, the purpose of a principle of humanity is quite different.

The case-law generated by the Second World War provides little guidance as to the validity of limits on belligerent reprisals derived from a principle of humanity. The question of reprisals was often linked to the treatment of hostages, even though the two are distinct aspects of the law of war.[55] The reprisal killing of innocent persons, more or less chosen at random, without any form of trial or indeed any requirement of guilt, can safely be characterised as a clear infringement of the most minimal humanitarian principle. And yet, in American, British and Italian war crimes trials, military tribunals agreed with the statement that the execution of innocent civilians could, in some extreme cases and under specific conditions, constitute lawful reprisals, while that possibility was rejected by Belgian and Dutch courts.[56] It is revealing that,

dans la société internationale depuis 1945 (Paris: LGDJ, 1983); Ian Brownlie, *International Law and the Use of Force by States* (Oxford: Clarendon, 1963) 110 ff. and 281–2; Lattanzi, *Garanzie*, at 273–9; Arangio-Ruiz, 'Third Report', UN Doc. A/CN.4/440 (1991) para. 97; Jean-Claude Venezia, 'La notion de représaille en droit international public', (1960) 64 *Revue générale de droit international public* 465, 494.

[53] See Oppenheim, *International Law* (1952) II, at 135–44; Jorge Pueyo Losa, 'El derecho de las represalias en tiempo de paz: Condiciones de ejercicios', (1988) 40 *Revista española de derecho internacional* 9–40.

[54] The *Corfu Channel* case, [1949] ICJ Rep. 4, 22 ('elementary considerations of humanity, even more exacting in peace than in war'); Alfred Verdross, *Völkerrecht*, 5th edn (Vienna: Springer-Verlag, 1964) 426 ('Diese Schranke ergibt sich aus der Erwägung, daß die Friedensrepressalie ein milderes Mittel als der Krieg ist, so daß auch für sie jene Verbote gelten müssen, die im Kriege bestehen').

[55] *In re Kappler* (the Ardeatine Cave trial), (1948) 15 Ann. Digest Rep. Pub. Int'l L Cases 471, 477 (Italian Mil. Trib., Rome). Distinct treatment is given in the 1949 Fourth Geneva Convention to reprisals (Art. 33) and hostages (Art. 34).

[56] Which found reprisals in the form of execution justified in some cases: the *Ardeatine Cave* trial, *ibid.*; *US v. List et al.* (the *Hostages* trial), (1948) 8 L Rep. Trials War Crim. 34 (US Mil. Trib., Nuremberg); *US v. von Leeb* (*High Command* trial), (1948) 12 L Rep. Trials War Crim. 1 (US Mil. Trib., Nuremberg); *UK v. von Mackensen and Maelzer*, (1945) 8 L Rep. Trials War Crim. 1 (British Mil. Ct, Rome); *UK v. Kesselring*, (1947) 8 L Rep. Trials War Crim. 9 (British Mil. Ct, Venice). Reprisals killing is never justified: *Belgium v. Falkenhausen*, (1951) 31 *Revue de droit pénal et de criminologie* 863 (Conseil de guerre de

in the proposed regulation of belligerent reprisals brought forward by a French amendment at the 1977 Geneva Conference, no principle of humanitarian limitation was included.[57] Past practice is thus decidedly uncertain as to the existence of a legal principle of humanity which would restrict lawful reprisals.

The principle of humanity poses a dilemma in the context of belligerent reprisals. On the one hand, if it is irrelevant to the law of belligerent reprisals, then it would seem that there is no limit to what a state can lawfully do to the, albeit shrinking, class of non-protected persons and objects. On the other hand, if this principle operates as a legal standard restricting reprisals to the breach of 'non-humanitarian' rules, then it has the effect of depriving the practice of much of its effectiveness.[58] Given that the law of war is already said to be the product of a compromise between military necessity and considerations of humanity, the breach of its minimal rules will more often than not violate a broad principle of humanity.[59] While several clear norms attach to the most fundamental protection provided by humanitarian law, such as the illegality of weapons causing unnecessary suffering or the prohibition of torture, very little guidance is provided by the relevant humanitarian conventions or past state practice in warfare as to which rules might constitute the nucleus of a principle of humanity.

The ICJ in the *Nicaragua* case read common Article 3 of the 1949 Geneva Conventions as embodying 'elementary considerations of humanity' applicable to all armed conflicts.[60] Even if the Court had not intended to address the problem of belligerent reprisals, the pronouncement does hint at an innovative solution to the elusive content of the principle of humanity. The prohibition 'at any time and in any place whatsoever' of

Bruxelles, 2ème chambre); *The Netherlands v. Heinemann*, (1946) 13 Ann. Digest Rep. Pub. Int'l L Cases 395–7 (Neth. Spec. Ct Cass.); *In re 'Silbertanne' Murders*, (1946) 13 Ann. Digest Rep. Pub. Int'l L Cases 397–8 (Neth. Spec. Ct Cass.); *The Netherlands v. Rauter*, (1949) 14 L Rep. Trials War Crim. 89 (Neth. Spec. Ct Cass.) (it is not altogether clear whether Dutch courts rejected reprisals killing as distinct from the execution of hostages: Kalshoven, *Belligerent Reprisals*, at 254).

[57] CDDH/I/221/Rev.1, 3 *Off. Records* 324. The amendment is discussed in Kalshoven, 'Belligerent Reprisals Revisited', at 203–5, and Nahlik, 'Le problème', at 151–65.

[58] Castrén, *Present Law*, at 70–1 (suggesting that the principle would only prevent 'acts which are particularly offensive to human thinking', without specifying what those acts might be).

[59] Kalshoven, *Belligerent Reprisals*, at 43.

[60] *Military and Paramilitary Activities in and Against Nicaragua (Nicaragua v. USA)*, [1986] ICJ Rep. 14, 114. Art. 75 of Protocol I can be seen as an expanded version of these minimal norms, and could thus be considered as a further expression of elementary considerations of humanity. See El Kouhene, *Les garanties fondamentales*, at 103–7.

murder, torture, discrimination, taking of hostages and denial of due
process laid out in Article 3 would put an end to the most objectionable
forms of reprisals, leaving only 'benign' measures such as, for instance,
the destruction of private property.

An interesting feature of this solution is that it provides a degree
of harmonisation between non-derogable human rights and elementary
considerations of humanity, most importantly with respect to the protection against murder and torture.[61] A clash between the often irreconcilable norms of human rights law and humanitarian law is thus
avoided in that human rights norms are not understood to proscribe
actions necessarily permitted by the law of war, such as the collateral
killing of innocent civilians (Art. 51(5)(b), Protocol I). That no such clash
was intended is made clear, in the case of the European Convention, by
the exception to the right to life found in 'death resulting from lawful
acts of war' (Art. 15(2)). Similar exceptions are implied in all other major
human rights instruments.[62] Significance must be accorded to the adoption by the international community of human rights norms meant to
apply even in times of war – or more euphemistically, in the case of
the Civil and Political Rights Covenant, 'public emergency threatening
the life of the nation'.[63] There is no doubt that non-derogable human

[61] See *Abella v. Argentina (La Tablada* case), Rep. No. 55/97, Case No. 11,137, OAS Doc.
OEA/Ser.L/V/II.97 doc. 38 (1997) para. 158 n. 19 (Inter-Am. Com'n Hum. Rts). The most
important treaty provisions on non-derogable rights are: Art. 4(2), International
Covenant on Civil and Political Rights; Art. 15(2), European Convention on Human
Rights; Art. 27(2), American Convention on Human Rights. See Calogeropoulos-Stratis,
Droit humanitaire, at 139–65; Denise Plattner, 'International Humanitarian Law and
Inalienable or Non-derogable Human Rights', in Daniel Prémont ed., *Non-derogable
Rights and States of Emergency* (Brussels: Bruylant, 1996) 349–63. See the discussion in
chapter 7, pp. 332–7.
[62] With respect to Art. 6 of the International Covenant on Civil and Political Rights, see:
Legality of the Threat or Use of Nuclear Weapons, Advisory Opinion, [1996] ICJ Rep. para.
25; UN Secretary-General, 'Respect for Human Rights in Armed Conflicts', UN Doc.
A/8052 (1970) 104; and generally, Human Rights Committee, 'General Comment 6
(16) (Article 6)', [1982] YB Hum. Rts Com'tee 382–3. For an application of the right to life
as guaranteed by Art. 1 of the American Declaration on the Rights and Duties of Man
to acts of war, in this case the invasion of Grenada by the United States, see David
Weissbrodt and Beth Andrus, 'The Right to Life During Armed Conflict: *Disabled Peoples
International v. United States*', (1988) 29 *Harv. Int'l LJ* 59–83 (referring to an application
judged admissible by the Inter-American Commission on Human Rights, but later
withdrawn: Case No. 9213 (USA), OAS Doc. OEA/Ser.L/V/II.91 doc. 7 rev. (1 March 1996)).
[63] The *travaux préparatoires* of the Political Covenant leave no doubt that war is covered
by the expression 'public emergencies threatening the life of the nation'. The use of
the term 'war' was avoided because 'it was felt that the Covenant should not
envisage, even by implication, the possibility of war', as war is prohibited by Art. 2(4)
of the UN Charter: UN Doc. A/2929 (1955) Pt II ch. 5 para. 39; Thomas Buergenthal,

rights were intended by the drafters to be binding even in wartime, as protection alongside the often more detailed protections provided for by the 1949 Geneva Conventions.[64] Deriving a principle of humanity from non-derogable human rights, however, requires more than their simple applicability to armed conflicts. Humanitarian law norms are also applicable to belligerent relations, and yet they can be suspended by way of reprisals. Similarly, violation of non-derogable human rights in the form of reprisals could find its justification not in the existence of an armed conflict or a state of emergency, but in an earlier violation committed by the enemy. Adoption of these non-derogable human rights norms thus does not necessarily create a core of 'intransgressible' minimal humanitarian norms applicable even to measures of reprisals taken pursuant to the law of war.[65]

The progressive development of a principle of humanity restricting reprisals is related to the enlargement in Protocol I of the class of individuals protected from reprisals. Both phenomena are symptomatic of a slow but profound transformation of humanitarian law under the pervasive influence of human rights, a transformation that underlies the fact that belligerent reprisals and individual rights are fundamentally inconsistent legal concepts.[66] That is, reprisals rest on a theory of collective

'To Respect and to Ensure: State Obligations and Permissible Derogations', in Louis Henkin ed., The International Bill of Rights (New York: Columbia UP, 1981) 72, 79. For the American Convention on Human Rights, see Inter-American Commission on Human Rights, Report No. 26/97, Case No. 11,142 (Colombia), 30 Sept. 1997, para. 135.

[64] Jaime Oráa, Human Rights in States of Emergency in International Law (Oxford: Clarendon, 1992) 91, writes, after his thorough analysis of the travaux préparatoires of the Political Covenant, that '[t]he fact that the derogation clause covers the situation of war, which in principle is the gravest emergency threatening the life of the nation, seemed to have pushed the drafters of the Covenant to adopt a cautious and restrictive approach to the list of non-derogable rights. The case of war seems always to have been in the mind of the drafters when assessing the possibility of accepting any other right.'

[65] Legality of the Threat or Use of Nuclear Weapons, Advisory Opinion, [1996] ICJ Rep. para. 79; The Prosecutor v. Delalić (the 'Celebici' case) (Appeals Judgment), 20 Feb. 2001, Case No. IT-96-21-A (Appeals Chamber, ICTY) para. 149. This is connected to the question of whether non-derogable human rights may be suspended as countermeasures for other human rights violations, discussed below, at pp. 219–21.

[66] This passage is borrowed by the ICTY in the Kupreskić judgment, taken from a published earlier version of part of this work: The Prosecutor v. Kupreskić (Lasva Valley case) (Judgment), 14 Jan. 2000, Case No. IT-95-16-T (Trial Chamber, ICTY) para. 529; Provost, 'Reciprocity', at 427. See Hampson, 'Belligerent Reprisals', at 140; Frits Kalshoven, 'Human Rights, the Law of Armed Conflict, and Reprisals', in Proceedings of the International Conference on Humanitarian Law – San Remo, 24–27 Sept. 1970, at 175, 177.

solidarity in the enforcement of the laws of war, in which the individual is completely subsumed into a group. As a member of a group connected to those violating the law, the individual can logically become the target of sanctions. Human rights, while not necessarily rejecting the relevance of a person's connection to community, conceptualise the individual in an essentially atomistic fashion. By protecting a certain class of people from reprisals, the Geneva Conventions and Protocol I attempt not to preserve groups, but indirectly to protect individuals. The legality of most reprisals, then, with their necessary disregard for the innocence and integrity of the victims of the measures, will slowly come to an end as human rights norms progressively take on the universal and concrete character they were designed to possess.

COUNTERMEASURES AND HUMAN RIGHTS

The law of war is a system which predates the rejection of the use of force as a legitimate means of settling international disputes. It is therefore not surprising that self-help measures like belligerent reprisals historically have formed an integral part of humanitarian law. Positive international human rights norms, on the contrary, largely came into being after the inception of the United Nations Charter, in the wake of a movement seeking to reject the use of force in international relations. The relevance of self-help to human rights law was thus much more doubtful right from the outset. In part for this reason, the acceptability and nature of countermeasures taken in response to the violation of human rights raise issues only partially similar to those with respect to belligerent reprisals. The first issue is that of the identity of states which may lawfully adopt countermeasures. This is a problem largely confined to human rights law, but with some echoes in humanitarian law. On the contrary, the issue of identifying norms that may not be suspended by way of countermeasures is central to both human rights and humanitarian law. Given that the analysis here centres on reciprocity, the focus will be on the legality of suspending human rights as countermeasures in response to earlier human rights violations, and not on either the possibility of suspending the performance of human rights obligations in response to other breaches of international law, or that of other types of countermeasures in reaction to human rights violations. In particular, the legality of humanitarian intervention in response to human rights violations will not be considered here.

Who may adopt countermeasures?

Disregard for obligations under the law of war during an armed conflict by either an individual or a state generally produces immediate harm to the enemy belligerent. The international legal relationship involved provides a clear legal basis for a reaction by that belligerent. The existence and nature of the relationships amongst states created by human rights law are not quite so clear, and the effect on third states of the breach of human rights norms has been the subject of much debate.

It is interesting to note, before turning to that debate, that the indirect impact of a breach of humanitarian law has received scant attention, despite the fact that some new humanitarian norms found in Protocol I operate in a fashion very similar to human rights law. That is, they accord a measure of protection to a state's own nationals as well as to nationals of co-belligerents, both classes of individuals who were not protected persons under the 1949 Geneva Conventions. It would thus be possible for a belligerent to breach humanitarian law obligations in a purely internal manner, for instance by taking hostages from amongst its nationals who are members of a specific religious group (Art. 75(1) and (2)(c), Protocol I). Is an enemy state then justified in taking belligerent reprisals in response to that violation? Could neutral states consider themselves injured by the breach and adopt non-forcible countermeasures? These questions have attracted little attention in the context of humanitarian law.[67] And yet the parallels between human rights and this type of new humanitarian norm suggest that the answer given in a human rights context to the question of who is an injured state might be relevant to humanitarian law.

The impact on third states of a violation of human rights is not necessarily uniform. Various relationships between those states and the breach may be envisaged. First, and most clearly affected, is a state whose nationals are the victims of a breach of human rights by another state. While no agreement has been reached amongst states as to the exact nature of the human rights which provide an international minimum

---

[67] See Stefania Bariatti, *L'azione internazionale dello stato a tutela di non cittadini* (Milan: Giuffrè, 1993) 127–31; Lassa Oppenheim, *International Law*, Hersch Lauterpacht ed., 8th edn (London: Longmans, 1955) I, 308; Paolo Benvenuti, 'Ensuring Observance of International Humanitarian Law: Functions, Extent and Limits of the Obligation of Third States to Ensure Respect of International Humanitarian Law', (1989–90) *YB Int'l Inst. Humanitarian L* 27, 45–7; Dietrich Schindler, 'Die *erga omnes*-Wirkung des humanitären Völkerrecht', in Ulrich Byerlin et al. eds., *Recht zwischen Umbruch und Bewahrung: Völkerrecht, Europarecht, Staatsrecht. Festschrift für Rudolf Bernhardt* (Berlin: Springer, 1995) 207–10.

standard governing the treatment of aliens, there is an emerging consensus that such a minimum standard does exist and that it includes the
most important human rights now recognised by international law.[68]
Injury to aliens classically has been construed as injury to the state of
nationality itself, with the right to obtain reparation accruing directly to
that state.[69] Having been injured, then, the state of nationality can take
countermeasures against the offending state according to general international law. Short of such direct claims based on nationality, states in
the past sometimes have sought to rely on ethnic, religious and cultural
links to foreign nationals to justify their adoption of countermeasures
against the victimising state in order to end human rights violations. For
instance, Vietnam's intervention in Cambodia was partially presented
as a reaction to the mistreatment of members of the half-million-strong
ethnic Vietnamese minority by the Khmer Rouge. Further, as noted in the
earlier analysis of the effect of Article 60(3) of the Vienna Convention on
the Law of Treaties on states 'specifically affected', a breach of human
rights norms may have an economic impact on one or more third states,
providing them with some justification for adopting countermeasures.[70]

In perhaps most cases, the victims of violations of human rights
have no special links to any other country, and the illegal acts have no

[68] The clearest evidence of this emerging consensus is the 1985 UN Declaration of the
Rights of Individuals not Citizens of the Country in Which They Live, UN GA Res. 144
(XL), UN GAOR, 40th Sess., Supp. No. 53 (1985). See also *Restatement (Third) of the Foreign
Relations Law of the United States* (St Paul: American Law Institute, 1987) 41, para.
711(a); Baroness Elles, 'The Problem of the Applicability of Existing International
Provisions for the Protection of Human Rights to Individuals who are not Nationals
of the Country in which they Live', UN Doc. E/CN.4/Sub.2/392/Rev.1 (1982); F. V. García
Amador, 'Second Report on the Responsibility of the State for Injuries Caused in its
Territory to the Person or Property of Aliens', [1957] 2 *YB Int'l L Com'n* 104, 112–13;
'Harvard Draft Convention for Injuries to Aliens', (1961) 55 *Am. J Int'l L* 548–84. The
direct applicability of most human rights norms to aliens is already provided by
international instruments, calling into question the continued need for a separate
set of substantive rules governing the treatment of aliens. It is possible that the law
on injuries to aliens is called to evolve from substantive norms to merely rules
determining which sanctions are available to the state of nationality. See Ugo Villani,
'I diritti degli stranieri negli atti internazionali sui diritti dell'uomo', (1987) 99 *Studi
senesi* 105, 127–8.

[69] *Mavrommatis Palestine Concessions Case* (Jurisdiction), (1924) PCIJ Reports, Ser. A No. 2, at
12; *Advisory Opinion on Reparation for Injuries Suffered in the Service of the United Nations*,
[1949] ICJ Rep. 174, 184.

[70] See above, pp. 167–9. On the classification of the impact of breaches of obligations
erga omnes on third states and their consequent right to react, see Paolo Picone,
'Obblighi reciproci e obblighi *erga omnes* degli stati nel campo della protezione
internazionale dell'ambiente marino dall'inquinamento', in Vicenzo Starace ed.,
Diritto internazionale e protezione dell'ambiente marino (Milan: Giuffrè, 1983) 58–67 and
82–9.

direct impact beyond the borders of the offending state. In such cases, the violation of international law is purely internal, and there are no specifically affected third states. It does not necessarily follow, however, that there are no 'injured' states entitled to react. The idea that 'indirectly injured' or 'differently interested' states may take action to force a state to comply with its obligations is not new. As early as the seventeenth century, Grotius suggested that religious persecution by a state against its own citizens could justify intervention by other states.[71] The development of the concept of obligations *erga omnes* by the ICJ in the *Barcelona Traction* case centred not so much on the theoretical underpinnings of various kinds of obligations in the international legal order, but on the identity of states entitled to institute proceedings in the International Court with respect to a violation of international law. In the judgment, the critical issue was whether Belgium had standing to present a case on behalf of the Belgian shareholders of a Canadian corporation. The Court found that it did not, introducing as a contrast to rules on the treatment of aliens the concept of obligations *erga omnes*, such as basic human rights, in the protection of which 'all States can be said to have a legal interest'.[72] The Court's holding thus went beyond the limited jurisdictional question with which it was presented, and clearly was intended to reject its earlier position in the 1966 *South West Africa Cases (Second Phase)*, which had dismissed, for lack of standing, a claim by Ethiopia and Liberia against South Africa.[73]

---

[71] Hugo Grotius, *De jure belli ac pacis libri tres* (1625), James Brown Scott ed. (Oxford: Clarendon, 1925) II, bk 3 ch. 20 para. 40; Peter Pavel Remec, *The Position of the Individual in International Law According to Grotius and Vattel* (The Hague: Nijhoff, 1960) 208–18; Michael Akehurst, 'Reprisals by Third States', (1970) 44 *Brit. YB Int'l L* 1.

[72] *Barcelona Traction, Light and Power Co. Ltd (Belgium v. Spain)*, [1970] ICJ Rep. 3, 32. In this passage the ICJ mentions the 'basic rights of the human person', and there were doubts expressed as to whether this indicated that not all human rights generated obligations *erga omnes*. These doubts seem to have been resolved in the last few years in favour of the rejection of such a distinction, to consider all human rights *erga omnes*. See Theodor Meron, *Human Rights and Humanitarian Norms as Customary Law* (Oxford: Clarendon, 1989) 192–201; Oscar Schachter, *International Law in Theory and Practice* (Dordrecht: Nijhoff, 1991) 208–12; Yoram Dinstein, 'The *Erga Omnes* Applicability of Human Rights', (1992) 30 *Archiv des Völkerrecht* 16, 17; Art. 1, 'Resolution on the Protection of Human Rights and the Principle of Non-intervention in Internal Affairs of the State', (1989) 63:2 *Annuaire de l'Institut de droit international* 341, 343. *Contra* Maurizio Ragazzi, *The Concept of International Obligations Erga Omnes* (Oxford: Clarendon, 1997) 131–6, adopting a much more cautious approach.

[73] *South West Africa Cases (Second Phase) (Ethiopia v. South Africa; Liberia v. South Africa)*, [1966] ICJ Rep. 6, 47; Jonathan Charney, 'Third State Remedies in International Law',

The legal interest of every state in the enforcement of obligations *erga omnes* is in fact their defining characteristic.[74] It reflects not only the importance but also the nature of human rights norms, the prime function of which is the granting of rights to individuals rather than to states.[75] Because individuals, under general international law, are not granted adequate standing to protect their own rights, states are given the right to act both on behalf of individuals and in the interest of the international community as a whole.[76] State rights in the human rights system should be understood as secondary to those of individuals. They exist only because of the unavailability of effective mechanisms at the international level permitting individuals to act on their own behalf. If effective remedies were put at the disposal of individuals – a regime admittedly far from reality at present – the justification for corresponding state rights would be significantly reduced. This pertains to a deeper and slower transformation of the structure of the international legal system involving the gradual erosion of state sovereignty.[77]

The principle that all 'indirectly injured' or 'interested' states may take action following the violation of human rights norms has been

(1989) 10 *Mich. J Int'l L* 57, 70; Schindler, 'Die *erga omnes*-Wirkung', at 205–7. The matter is, however, still not free of confusion, as illustrated by the remarks of Judge Oda in his declaration in the *Application of the Convention on the Prevention and Punishment of the Crime of Genocide (Bosnia & Herzegovina v. Yugoslavia (Serbia & Montenegro))*, Preliminary Objections, 11 July 1996, para. 4, where he seems to deny that any state may react to the breach of an obligation *erga omnes*.

[74] Lattanzi, *Garanzie*, at 129; Crawford, 'First Report', 232 para. 22; Christian Dominicé, 'La contrainte entre Etats à l'appui des droits de l'homme', in *Hacia un nuevo orden internacional y europeo – estudios en homenaje al profesor Don Manuel Díos de Velasco* (Madrid: Tecnos, 1993) 261, 263; Pierre-Marie Dupuy, 'Observations sur la pratique récente des "sanctions" de l'illicite', (1983) 87 *Revue générale de droit international public* 505, 536; D. W. Greig, 'Reciprocity, Proportionality, and the Law of Treaties', (1994) 34 *Va. J Int'l L* 295, 304–5; José Juste Ruiz, 'Las obligaciones "erga omnes" en derecho internacional público', in *Estudios de derecho internacional: homenaje al profesor Miaja de la Muela* (Madrid: Tecnos, 1979) I, 228; Paolo Picone, 'Nazioni Unite e obblighi "erga omnes"', (1993) 48 *Comunità internazionale* 709, 713.

[75] See Sir Gerald Fitzmaurice, 'Second Report on the Law of Treaties', [1957] 2 *YB Int'l L Com'n* 54, 125.

[76] See Lattanzi, *Garanzie*, at 130; Giuseppe Barile, 'The Protection of Human Rights in Article 60 Paragraph 5 of the Vienna Convention on the Law of Treaties', in *International Law at the Time of its Codification: Essays in Honour of Roberto Ago* (Milan: Giuffré, 1987) II, 4–5; Giuseppe Barile, 'Obligationes *erga omnes* e individui nel diritto internazionale umanitario', (1985) 68 *Rivista di diritto internazionale* 5, 7; Institut de droit international, 'Resolution on the Protection of Human Rights and Non-intervention', at 245 (Dinstein).

[77] This also goes back to earlier comments on the passage from reciprocity to equality, coinciding with the gradual institutionalisation of the international legal system: see the Introduction to Part II.

echoed in several forums. First, several international and regional human rights conventions provide that all states parties may activate enforcement mechanisms, thus recognising the impact on their interests
of a violation purely internal to one state.[78] The *Greek* case, in which
Denmark, Sweden, Norway and the Netherlands claimed that Greece
had defaulted on its obligations under the European Convention on
Human Rights, constitutes a good, if rare, example.[79] In the context of
customary law, successive acts of the (then) Conference on Security and
Co-operation in Europe have acknowledged and indeed encouraged actions which would constitute intervention by third states in the internal
affairs of a state, following the violation of human rights standards.[80]
The idea that a state's treatment of its nationals falls within the reserved
domain of that state was forcefully refuted by the Institut de droit international in its 1989 Resolution on the Protection of Human Rights
and the Principle of Non-intervention in Internal Affairs of States, which
provides in Article 2:[81]

A State acting in breach of its obligation in the sphere of human rights cannot
evade its international responsibility by claiming that such matters are essentially within its domestic jurisdiction.
    . . . States, *acting individually or collectively*, are entitled to take diplomatic, eco-
nomic and other measures towards any other State which has violated the
obligations set forth in Article 1 [i.e. human rights as derived from the UN
Charter and the Universal Declaration of Human Rights]. [Emphasis added.]

---

[78] See Art. 41, International Covenant on Civil and Political Rights; Art. 11,
    International Convention on the Elimination of All Forms of Racial Discrimination;
    Art. 33, European Convention on Human Rights; Art. 45, American Convention on
    Human Rights; Art. 47, African Charter on Human and Peoples' Rights. See Bariatti,
    L'azione internazionale, at 131–53.
[79] *Denmark, Norway, Sweden and the Netherlands v. Greece*, Appl. 3321/67, 3322/67, 3323/67
    and 3344/67, [1968] YB Eur. Conv. Hum. Rts 730.
[80] Human Dimension of the CSCE, in the Concluding Document of the Vienna Meeting
    on the Follow-up to the Conference, *reprinted in* Ian Brownlie ed., *Basic Documents on
    Human Rights*, 3rd edn (Oxford: Clarendon, 1992) 450–3. See generally Arie Bloed and
    Pieter van Dijk eds., *The Human Dimension of the Helsinki Process* (Dordrecht: Nijhoff,
    1991); Arie Bloed and Pieter van Dijk eds., *Essays on Human Rights in the Helsinki Process*
    (Dordrecht: Nijhoff, 1985); Emmanuel Decaux and Linos-Alexandre Sicilianos eds., *La
    dimension humanitaire de la Conférence de sécurité et coopération en Europe* (Paris:
    Montchrestien, 1993); Gaetano Arangio-Ruiz, 'Droits de l'homme et non-intervention:
    Helsinki, Belgrade et Madrid', (1980) 35 *Comunità internazionale* 453; Gaetano
    Arangio-Ruiz, 'Human Rights and Non Intervention in the Helsinki Final Act',
    (1978-IV) 162 *Recueil des cours* 195.
[81] Institut de droit international, 'Resolution on the Protection of Human Rights and
    Non-intervention', at 343–4.

Further support for the existence of the right of third states to react to an 'internal' violation of human rights in another country can be derived from the work of the International Law Commission on state responsibility. From its discussion of the legal consequences of breaches of international law, the ILC concluded in its 1996 Draft Articles that, under existing law, an injured state included,

if the right infringed by the act of a State arises from a multilateral treaty or from a rule of customary international law, any other State party to the multilateral treaty or bound by the relevant rule of customary international law, if it is established that:... (iii) the right has been established or is established for the protection of human rights and fundamental freedoms.[82]

This was echoed in the 1996 Draft Articles by the legal consequences of international crimes, a concept which covers the 'serious breach on a widespread scale of an international obligation of essential importance for safeguarding the human being' (Art. 19, ILC Draft). According to the ILC, all states have an obligation 'to cooperate with other States in the application of measures designed to eliminate the consequence of the crime' (Art. 53(c), ILC Draft), which includes not only collective responses through international organisations but also individual action.[83] The US Restatement Third echoed the right of any state to take action pursuant to the breach of customary or treaty human rights, regardless of the nationality of the individual victim.[84] The ILC later modulated part of these conclusions, finding a difference between the concepts of 'injured state', which it would limit to those whose rights are directly affected by a breach, and 'interested states', which include third states who are only indirectly affected by

[82] Art. 40(2)(e)(iii) (originally numbered 5(2)(e)(iii)), 'Draft Article on State Responsibility (Part 2)', [1985] 2:2 YB Int'l L Com'n 25. See Willem Riphagen 'Preliminary Report on the Content, Form and Degree of State Responsibility', [1980] 2:1 YB Int'l L Com'n 107, 120–9, and Riphagen's commentary on Art. 5, [1985] 2:1 YB Int'l L Com'n 8 para. 21. This is consistent with a resolution adopted by the European Parliament on 20 April 1994, 128 Off. J Eur. Com'n. 226, whereby 'the protection of human rights may justify humanitarian intervention, whether military force is used or not' (para. 4).

[83] International Law Commission, 'Report to the General Assembly on the Work of its 48th Session', UN Doc. A/51/10 (1996), at 170 (Art. 53, comm. 3); Bruno Simma, 'From Bilateralism to Community Interest in International Law', (1994-VI) 250 Recueil des cours 217, 313–21.

[84] Restatement, 41, at paras. 703(2) and 901 and accompanying reporters' notes. See also Olivier Corten and Pierre Klein, Droit d'ingérence ou obligation de réaction?, 2nd edn (Brussels: Bruylant, 1996) 107–24; Jaroslav Zourek, 'Le respect des droits de l'homme et des libertés fondamentales constitut-il une affaire interne de l'Etat?', in Estudios de derecho internacional, at 603–25.

the violation of obligations *erga omnes* or *erga omnes partes*. The ILC still acknowledged that third states were entitled to adopt countermeasures in reaction to serious violations of human rights, but only at the request of the 'injured' state, if there was one. If no state is directly 'injured', as will most often be the case for human rights violations, then all interested states can adopt countermeasures. Ultimately, the ILC could not sufficiently ground this provision in state practice, and the 2001 Articles are limited to a savings clause (Art. 54).[85]

Practice offers some limited instances of states adopting countermeasures in reaction to the violation of human rights by a foreign state against its own population. For example, in the wake of the brutal killing of eighty-five youths by members of Bokassa's personal guard in the Central African Republic, France decided to suspend two international agreements on military and financial cooperation.[86] France was in that following the example set by the United States in 1978 in reaction to massive human rights violations by Idi Amin Dada's regime, when it adopted the Uganda Embargo Act in a manner contrary to the terms of the GATT.[87] Similarly, the United States suspended the 1972 US–Polish Air Transport Agreement in the wake of the Polish Government's crackdown against the Solidarity union, in a manner contrary to the terms of that treaty.[88] The Netherlands in December 1982 suspended a development cooperation agreement with Suriname in reaction to the massive violation of human rights in that country associated with a coup.[89] Several states, including Australia, Canada, New Zealand and

---

[85] See Arts. 41, 49 and 54, 2000 Draft Articles on State Responsibility: UN Doc. A/CN.4/L.600 (2000); James Crawford, 'Third Report on State Responsibility', UN Doc. A/CN.4/507 (2000) paras. 109–14; International Law Commission, 'Report to the General Assembly on the Work of its 53rd Session', UN Doc. A/56/10 (2001) pp. 349–55. Note that the concept of crimes of states, long a contentious issue, has been eliminated from the latest draft.

[86] Charles Rousseau, 'Chronique des faits internationaux', (1980) 84 *Revue générale de droit international public* 361–4.

[87] See Sicilianos, *Réactions*, at 156; A. H. Talkington, 'International Trade: Uganda Trade Embargo', (1979) 20 *Harv. J Int'l L* 206–13.

[88] Marian Nash Leich, 'Contemporary Practice of the United States Relating to International Law', (1982) 76 *Am. J Int'l L* 379–81.

[89] Although the Dutch Government also referred to a fundamental change of circumstances. See Hans-Heinrich Lindemann, 'Die Auswirkungen des Menschenrechtsverletzungen in Surinam auf die Vertragbeziehungen zwischen die Niederlanden und Surinam', [1984] *Zeitschrift für ausländische öffentliches Recht und Völkerrecht* 64, 81–8; R. C. R. Siekmann, 'Netherlands State Practice for the Parliamentary Year 1983–1984', (1984) 15 *Nether. YB Int'l L* 321.

the United States, adopted countermeasures against South Africa during the 1980s in reaction to the apartheid regime.[90] Countermeasures were later adopted by the United States, the EEC and Belgium in response to, respectively, the 1989 Tiananmen Square repression in China, human rights violations in Romania and the 1990 army rampage in Zaire.[91] More recently, in 1998, the European Community adopted regulations banning flights to and from Yugoslavia following human rights abuses in Kosovo, which required some European states to suspend air transport agreements with Yugoslavia in violation of their terms.[92] Political realities of international relations have meant that states have shown extreme caution in choosing to react to human rights violations to which they have no direct connection.[93]

Although some still question the legality of countermeasures by third states in reaction to human rights violations, practice, codification efforts and writers seem increasingly in agreement that such reactions necessarily flow from the *erga omnes* character of human rights norms.[94] The debate has shifted partly to consideration of the nature of norms which may lawfully be disregarded in order to pressure the delinquent state to resume compliance with human rights.[95]

---

[90] 'Comprehensive Anti-Apartheid Act (USA)', (1987) Int'l Leg. Mat. 78; Alland, *Justice privée*, at 365; Charles Rousseau, 'Chronique des faits internationaux', (1986) 90 *Revue générale de droit international public* 945–51.

[91] See Bariatti, *L'azione internazionale*, at 117 n. 33; Charles Rousseau, 'Chronique des faits internationaux', (1990) 94 *Revue générale de droit international public* 484 and 1051. To this could be added sanctions by Australia, Canada, Japan and Norway as well as the suspension of contracts with Iran by the European Community following the hostage-taking at the US embassy in Tehran, although the EEC and some states seem to have considered this as primarily a breach of diplomatic immunities: Menno Kamminga, *Inter-State Accountability for Human Rights Violations* (Philadelphia: U Pennsylvania Press, 1992) 161–3; Lattanzi, *Garanzie*, at 494.

[92] EC Regulations 1295/98 and 1901/98; 'UK Materials on International Law', (1998) 69 *Brit. YB Int'l L* 580–1.

[93] See Kamminga, *Inter-State Accountability*, at 7. This mirrors the extreme caution shown by states in their use of inter-state petitions under the various human rights conventions.

[94] Crawford, 'Third Report', paras. 397–405.

[95] See Lattanzi, *Garanzie*, at 316–24; Meron, *Human Rights and Humanitarian Norms*, at 233–6. Another question still unresolved today is the role of regional and international organisations in authorising or coordinating states' responses to infringement of obligations *erga omnes*: de Guttry, *Le rappresaglie*, at 290–3 and 298; D. N. Hutchinson, 'Solidarity and Breaches of Multilateral Treaties', (1988) 59 *Brit. YB Int'l L* 151, 202–13; Institut de droit international, 'Resolution on the Protection of Human Rights and Non-intervention', at 249 (Arangio-Ruiz); Karin Oellers-Frahm, 'Comment: The *Erga Omnes* Applicability of Human Rights', (1992) 30 *Archiv des*

Turning back to the parallel issue in humanitarian law regarding the lawful responses to internal violations directed against a state's own population during an armed conflict, the insights offered by a study of human rights shed some light. As in human rights law, violations may have *erga omnes* effects, such that all states party to the same treaty or bound by the same customary rule are entitled to consider themselves injured by the breach. The state at war with the perpetrator may respond by way of belligerent reprisals, for instance the use of a weapon normally prohibited, given that humanitarian law leaves each belligerent a wide margin of discretion to choose which measure of reprisal to adopt. For example, the persecution by Iraq of its Kurdish minority during the 1980-8 Iran–Iraq war, including the use of poison gases, could have been answered by Iran through the use of poison gases in combat. Countermeasures by third states are more problematic, however, because they lie at the intersection of the law of war and the law of neutrality. Any countermeasures directed against the perpetrator or its nationals could very well be considered hostile and thus jeopardise the neutrality of the state adopting such measures.[96] For example, unilateral countermeasures adopted by a neutral state against one of the belligerents in the armed conflict in the former Yugoslavia would in all likelihood have been regarded by that belligerent as support for its enemy. In situations of internal armed conflicts, countermeasures may also be construed by the state as an intervention aimed at aiding the rebels. In this respect, the rights of third states in relation to the *erga omnes* character of humanitarian law and their duty to 'ensure respect' of its rules stand in contrast to duties they hold as neutrals.[97] Perhaps not surprisingly, state practice seems to

Völkerrecht 28, 34–5; Picone, 'Obblighi reciproci', at 77–9; K. Sachariew, 'State Responsibility for Multilateral Treaty Violations: Identifying the "Injured State" and its Legal Status', (1988) 35 *Nether. Int'l L Rev.* 273, 282–5.

[96] This is even more so in the scheme proposed by the ILC in its 2000 Draft Articles, whereby countermeasures adopted by 'interested' states must have been requested by the 'injured' state, if there is one: see above, note 85 and accompanying text. For violations of humanitarian law, unlike those relating to human rights, there will very often be an 'injured' state, i.e. one of the belligerents. It seems likely that countermeasures adopted by third states 'at the request' of one of the belligerents would be considered hostile by the other party to an armed conflict.

[97] See Oppenheim, *International Law* (1952) II, at 673–84; Benvenuti, 'Ensuring Observance', at 33; Schindler, 'Die *erga omnes*-Wirkung', at 207; Dietrich Schindler, 'Transformations in the Law of Neutrality Since 1945', in Astrid Delissen and Gerard Tanja eds., *Humanitarian Law of Armed Conflict: Challenges Ahead – Essays in Honour of*

reveal no instance of third states adopting countermeasures in reaction to violations of humanitarian law.[98]

Similar considerations apply in the context of the widespread violation of human rights norms by a belligerent during an armed conflict: all states to which the same norm applies are indirectly injured, but the danger exists that countermeasures taken by non-belligerent states will be seen as hostile acts. The emergence of norms *erga omnes* in international humanitarian law would effect a transformation of the concept of neutrality, carving out an exception to the principle of non-intervention in the conflict by third states. In a fashion similar to the removal of human rights from the reserved domain of states, the *erga omnes* character of humanitarian norms would put compliance with humanitarian law squarely within the legitimate concern of third states.

Suspension of human rights obligations as a countermeasure

The exploration of the meaning and implications of reciprocity in human rights law will be limited to the legality of suspending performance of *human rights* obligations as a reaction to an infringement of the same or other human rights. Thus countermeasures involving other norms, such as the suspension of commercial or military agreements

---

Frits Kalshoven (Dordrecht: Nijhoff, 1991) 367. A right of third states to take countermeasures is suggested by paragraph 11 of Part II of the Declaration adopted by the plenary session of the International Conference for the Protection of War Victims, Geneva, 30 August–1 September 1993, reading: 'We affirm our responsibility, in accordance with Article 1 common to the Geneva Conventions, to respect and ensure respect for international humanitarian law in order to protect the victims of war. We urge all States to make every effort to:... 11. Ensure the effectiveness of international humanitarian law and take resolute action, in accordance with that law, against States bearing responsibility for violations of international humanitarian law with a view of terminating such violations', *reprinted in* (1993) 51 *Int'l Com'n of Jurists Rev.* 58. Likewise, a 1999 Berlin resolution of the Institut de droit international suggests that states may react 'collectively or individually' to violations of humanitarian law, although the specific reference to 'countermeasures' in earlier drafts was eventually eliminated: Institut de droit international, 'Resolution on the Application of International Humanitarian Law and Fundamental Human Rights, in Armed Conflicts in which Non-State Entities are Parties', (1999) 68:2 *Annuaire de l'Institut de droit international* 282 and 395.

[98] See Umesh Palwankar, 'Measures Available to States for Fulfilling their Obligation to Ensure Respect for International Humanitarian Law', (1994) 298 *Int'l Rev. Red Cross* 9–25, where the author seems to assume a right to adopt countermeasures in reaction to violations of humanitarian law, but refers to state practice consisting exclusively in countermeasures in reaction to illegal uses of force in a manner contrary to Art. 2(4) of the UN Charter.

mentioned earlier as examples of state practice, will not be considered. Similarly, humanitarian intervention, the most extreme state response to human rights violation in that it breaches the prohibition of the use of force, falls beyond the scope of the enquiry.

Scenarios

Two scenarios can be envisaged, with respect to which distinct arguments can be advanced to support the legality of a retaliatory suspension of human rights. The first scenario relies on the concept of solidarity between the target of countermeasures and the perpetrator of the initial violation. Solidarity is understood to be a minimal requirement for the legitimacy of countermeasures. Thus, a state could not justify suspending the human rights of its own nationals in response to an infringement of human rights in another country, because no solidarity exists between the former state's population and the foreign state which committed the initial breach. It can be argued, on the contrary, that the links between a violating state and its own nationals might justify countermeasures by third states in the form of suspension of certain specific human rights, at least those of individuals associated with the regime violating human rights. Indeed, there is support in both state practice and doctrinal writings for the proposition that a state is generally entitled to take countermeasures against nationals of another state, usually in the form of the freezing or taking of private property in response to any type of violation of international law.[99] For example, the United Kingdom froze all private assets of Egyptian nationals during the 1956 Suez crisis, and those of Argentinians during the 1982 Falklands war, as did the United States of Iranians in 1980.[100] There have also been a limited number of controversial instances in which states have

[99] Oppenheim, *International Law* (1952) II, at 139–40 ('The persons of officials, and even of private citizens, of the delinquent State are possible objects of reprisals'); *Restatement*, 41 para. 905 reporter's note 2; Zoller, *Peacetime Unilateral Remedies*, at 101–2; Derek W. Bowett, 'Economic Coercion and Reprisals by States', (1972) 13 *Va. J Int'l L* 1, 10 ('States taking reprisals have always regarded nationals of the delinquent State as permissible objects of reprisals and in many situations they are the only available objects').

[100] Elagab, *Legality*, at 108; Sicilianos, *Réactions*, at 358–60. There would be a progression towards the immunity of foreign individuals and their property, in part linked to the evolving status of a customary human right to property. See de Guttry, *Le rappresaglie*, at 274–80 (movement to limit takings of private property); Elagab, *Legality*, at 104–11 (private property now immune from reprisals); *Restatement*, para. 712 and comment (f); Edwin Borchard, 'Reprisals on Private Property', (1936) 30 *Am. J Int'l L* 108–13; Rosalyn Higgins, 'The Taking of Property by the State: Recent Developments in

responded in kind against foreign nationals when the state of nationality had committed a human rights violation. For example, in June 1967,
the Government of the Ivory Coast seized three citizens of Equatorial
Guinea as they made an unscheduled landing in that country because,
according to the Ivorian Government, Guinea was illegally holding several of its own citizens. The Ivory Coast agreed to release the Guineans
three months later, only after Equatorial Guinea had yielded and freed
the detained Ivorians.[101] Examples could perhaps also include the administrative harassment of Iranian students in the United States during
the hostage crisis, which was clearly a retaliatory and discriminatory
practice.[102] The questionable legality of countermeasures corresponding
to this first scenario is examined in the ensuing discussion.

The second possible scenario diverges from the first in that the legality
of countermeasures rests not on the existence of solidarity, but rather
on an identity, between the target of the countermeasures and the author of the initial breach. In other words, countermeasures are aimed
directly at the author of the violation of human rights. In most cases, of
course, the specific individuals responsible for the infringement will be
beyond the legal or physical reach of the state seeking to force compliance with international law. If the individuals are within reach, however,
the question arises as to whether and to what extent a third state may
adopt countermeasures affecting their human rights.[103] For example,
could a state prevent one of its own citizens from re-entering his or her
home country – an action normally prohibited by Article 12(4) of the International Covenant on Civil and Political Rights – in response to that
individual's participation in the ongoing systematic violation of human
rights in another country? Apart from situations where the responsible

International Law', (1982-III) 176 Recueil des cours 259, 279–97 and 355–75; Schachter,
International Law, at 194–6.
[101] See de Guttry, Le rappresaglie, at 80–3; P. Chandrasekhara Rao, 'The Detention of
Guinean Nationals in the Ivory Coast. Issues of International Immunities', (1967)
Indian J Int'l L 397–405; Charles Rousseau, 'Chronique des faits internationaux', (1967)
38 Revue générale de droit international public 1070.
[102] Schachter, International Law, at 194–5.
[103] Kalshoven, 'Human Rights', at 180 raises a related question by asking whether the
kidnapping of government officials by opposition groups in order to obtain the
release of political prisoners could ever be justified as countermeasures. He does not
offer any answer to his question. The rejection of an exception for the hostage-taking
of 'non-innocent' individuals by national liberation movements in the 1979
International Hostages Convention militates against the legality of such measures:
Wil D. Verwey, 'The Hostages Convention and National Liberation Movements', (1981)
75 Am. J Int'l. L 69–92.

individuals are accessible, countermeasures are often too blunt an instrument for targeting one person or a small group with any precision. This is especially the case if the countermeasures take the form of the suspension of human rights.

The emergence of so-called 'third-generation' collective rights brought a new element to countermeasures related to human rights. It is conceivable that collective rights could effectively be suspended in response to a serious breach committed by that very collectivity. National liberation movements fighting in pursuit of their right to self-determination can be taken as an example. If the right to self-determination is construed as creating a positive duty on the part of third states to recognise or otherwise help the national liberation movement, then the United Kingdom could justify its policy of not recognising movements resorting to terrorism as countermeasures in response to human rights violations.[104] More generally, a people represented by a body involved in the massive or systematic violation of human rights, such as seems to be the case of the Palestinian Authority,[105] could be denied its right to exercise self-determination by other states acting unilaterally.

Given the rarity of state practice corresponding to either of the two scenarios sketched above, the foregoing analysis is not offered in the guise of a *lex lata* analysis of this type of countermeasure, but rather as a theoretical exploration of the place of reciprocity in the articulation of an eventual rejection of suspending human rights as a countermeasure. Not surprisingly, a number of objections can be raised against the legitimacy and legality of countermeasures which infringe human rights standards derived from either customary or conventional law.

Discrimination

If we look first at the human rights themselves, it is possible that the adoption of countermeasures in either of the above scenarios would breach specific norms. Given that, under both scenarios, the measures are directed against citizens of another state, two separate questions arise: first, to what extent do aliens enjoy human rights under customary and conventional law and, secondly, is discrimination based on nationality permissible?

---

[104] See Parliamentary Debates (Commons), vol. 998, col. 739 (10 Feb. 1981).
[105] See e.g. 'The State of Human Rights in Palestine', (May 1997) 3 *Palestinian Human Rights Monitor* 1–24 (available at http://www.lebnet.com/phrmg).

In response to the first point, human rights are generally granted without any distinction based on nationality. Thus states must uphold human rights standards with respect to all individuals under their control, regardless of whether they are citizens, nationals of other states which may or may not be party to the particular human rights convention, or stateless individuals. Only a small number of rights are reserved to citizens, including democratic rights and the right to enter one's own country, or to aliens, such as the protection against mass expulsion and expulsion without due process.[106] Countermeasures involve the suspension of human rights to which aliens are entitled, anything falling short of that constituting mere retortion measures not prohibited by international law.[107]

A state, in suspending the basic human rights of the citizens of a given country, adopts a stance that differentiates on the basis of nationality. For example, the administrative harassment of Iranian students in the United States during the hostage crisis was clearly based on their nationality.[108] This brings up the second question of whether this is unjustified discrimination under human rights law. All major human rights instruments prohibit discrimination on the basis of, among other criteria, race, birth, and national, ethnic or social origins.[109] None contains a prohibition of discrimination on grounds of nationality or citizenship.[110] On the contrary, Article 1(2) of the International Convention on the Elimination of All Forms of Racial Discrimination specifies that the Convention does not apply to distinctions made between citizens and non-citizens.[111] The *travaux préparatoires* of the Universal Declaration and the Political Covenant reveal unambiguously that the

---

[106] See Villani, 'I diritti', at 105–28, and generally above, chapter 1, pp. 18–24.

[107] Arango-Ruiz, 'Third Report', UN Doc. A/CN.4/440 (1991) para. 27.

[108] See Schachter, *International Law*, at 194–5.

[109] Art. 2(1), Universal Declaration of Human Rights; Art. 2(2), International Covenant on Economic, Social and Cultural Rights; Art. 2(1), International Covenant on Civil and Political Rights; Art. 1(1), International Convention on the Elimination of All Forms of Racial Discrimination; Art. 14, European Convention on Human Rights; Art. 1(1), American Convention on Human Rights; Art. 2, African Charter on Human and Peoples' Rights.

[110] Three exceptions are the ILO Convention on Maternity Protection (Revised), 1952 (No. 103), the ILO Plantations Convention, 1958 (No. 110) and the International Convention on the Protection of All Migrant Workers and Members of Their Families, UN Doc. A/45/49 (1990). See Elles, 'Problem of the Applicability', UN Doc. E/CN.4/Sub.2/392/Rev.1 (1982), at 37.

[111] See Nathan Lerner, *The UN Convention on the Elimination of All Forms of Racial Discrimination*, 2nd edn (Alphen aan den Rijn/Rockville, Md.: Sijthoff/Noordhoff, 1980) 29–30.

reference to 'national origins' in those instruments was meant to proscribe distinctions between citizens born in the country and citizens who
had been naturalised, and not between nationals and aliens.[112] This is
supported, *a contrario*, by Article 16 of the Universal Declaration which
exceptionally prohibits discrimination based on nationality with respect
to the right to marry. On the other hand, the presence of Article 16 of the
European Convention, providing a special right to discriminate against
aliens by restricting their permissible political activity, would seem to
presuppose that discrimination against aliens is normally impermissible
under the European Convention.[113]

The Inter-American Court of Human Rights encountered this issue
when, in its *Advisory Opinion on a Proposed Amendment to the Naturalization
Provisions of the Constitution of Costa Rica*, it considered the legality of a constitutional provision whereby immigrants from specified hispanophone
countries were naturalised faster than other classes of immigrants.[114]
The Court applied Article 1(1) of the American Convention without so
much as pausing to remark that discrimination on the basis of nationality is not one of the listed grounds of prohibited discrimination.[115]
The Court eventually found the distinct treatment justified in the circumstances, in an opinion not altogether clear as to any general illegality of discrimination on the basis of nationality under the American
Convention.

The UN Human Rights Committee has also addressed the issue by
noting, in its general commentary on the position of aliens under the
Political Covenant, that:[116]

[112] See UN Doc. E/CN.4/Sub.2/SR.5 at 2–12; UN Doc. A/2929 (1952), ch. 4 paras. 180–2;
Albert Verdoodt, *Naissance et signification de la Déclaration universelle des droits de l'homme*
(Louvain: Nauwelaerts, 1964) 88 and 95; Elles, 'Problem of the Applicability', UN Doc.
E/CN.4/Sub.2/392/Rev.1 (1982), at 37; Villani, 'I diritti', at 107–9; David Weissbrodt,
'The Rights of Non-Citizens', UN Doc. E/CN.4/Sub.2/1999/7.

[113] See P. van Dijk and G. J. H. van Hoof, *Theory and Practice of the European Convention on
Human Rights*, 3rd edn (The Hague: Kluwer, 1998), at 747; Karl Doehring,
'Non-Discrimination and Equal Treatment Under the European Human Rights
Convention and the West German Constitution with Particular Reference to
Discrimination Against Aliens', (1970) 18 *Am. J Comp. L* 305, 315; Villani, 'I diritti', at
110–11. Note that in *Bouchelkia* v. *France*, Judgment of 29 Jan. 1997, the European
Court discussed the rights of aliens under the Convention but no argument based on
discrimination seems to have been raised.

[114] I/A Court HR, *Proposed Amendment to the Naturalization Provisions of the Constitution of
Costa Rica*, Advisory Opinion OC-4/84 of 19 Jan. 1984, Ser. A No. 4, paras. 52–63.

[115] See Daniel O'Donnell, *Protección internacional de los derechos humanos* (Lima: Comisión
andina de juristas, 1988) 387–8.

[116] UN Hum. Rts Com'tee, 'General Comment 15 (27) (The Position of Aliens Under the
Covenant)', UN Doc. CCPR/C/21/Add.5/Rev.1 (1986), GAOR 41st Sess., Supp. No. 40,
at 117–19.

1. In general, the rights set forth in the Covenant apply to everyone irrespective of reciprocity, and irrespective of his or her nationality or statelessness.
2. Thus, the general rule is that each one of the rights of the Covenant must be guaranteed without discrimination between citizens and aliens.

Despite the apparent logic, however, the second clause does not necessarily follow from the first. Entitlement to human rights is of course not limited to nationals of any given state, but applies to all individuals, including aliens, within the jurisdiction of a state.[117] That being said, aliens can enjoy rights and yet still be the object of discrimination in the application of those rights. For example, restrictions on the right of foreign citizens of a given nationality to travel to sensitive areas for reasons of national security do not deny these individuals their general liberty of movement (Art. 12, Political Covenant), but they nevertheless discriminate on the basis of nationality.

The Human Rights Committee had the opportunity to discuss this type of discrimination further in *Gueye v. France*.[118] In that case, the petitioner complained of a French law which froze the pensions of Senegalese veterans who had served in the French armed forces before independence, while continuing to index the pensions of veterans of French nationality. After noting that nationality was not one of the grounds listed in Article 26, the Committee stated that:[119]

Under article 26, discrimination in the equal protection of the law is prohibited on any grounds such as race, colour, sex, language, religion, political or other opinion, national or social origins, property, birth, or other status. There has been a differentiation by reference to nationality acquired upon independence. In the Committee's opinion, this falls within the reference to 'other status' in the second sentence of article 26.

The views of the Human Rights Committee and Inter-American Commission on Human Rights thus seem to signal an emerging consensus as to the unlawful character of unjustifiable discrimination based on nationality in international human rights instruments.

Whether or not countermeasures in the form of the suspension of aliens' human rights would constitute unlawful discrimination is, in any case, not necessarily as significant as some seem to suggest.[120] Even

---

[117] See the discussion above, chapter 1, pp. 18–26.
[118] *Ibrahim Gueye et al. v. France*, Comm. No. 196/1985 (3 April 1989), *reprinted in* 'Report of the Human Rights Committee to the General Assembly', GAOR 44th Sess., Supp. No. 40, at 189–95.
[119] *Ibid.*, at 193 para. 9.4.
[120] See Elagab, *Legality*, at 110–11; *Restatement*, 41 para. 905 reporter's note 2; Fatsah Ouguergouz, 'L'absence de clause de dérogation dans certains traités relatifs aux droits de l'homme: Les réponses du droit international général', (1994) 98 *Revue*

if such countermeasures were indeed discriminatory, it would simply mean that they involve not only a primary infringement of basic human rights, but also a secondary breach of the prohibition against discrimination. There is nothing in the law of countermeasures preventing a state from reacting to a violation by suspending multiple norms, inasmuch as the reaction is globally proportional to the initial violation. The issue of discrimination therefore does not provide a decisive answer to the question of the legality of human rights countermeasures.[121]

Standards developed in the context of human rights and the treatment of aliens have addressed the specific question of whether minimal norms may be suspended against foreign nationals as a countermeasure against their state. One position, taken by the US Restatement Third, holds that, under the law governing the treatment of aliens, a state may not suspend through countermeasures either human rights norms or minimum protections provided to aliens.[122] As such, human rights and rules relating to aliens would provide a rigid limit to the means available to a state under general international law in the adoption of countermeasures. An alternative position allows the state a greater power to suspend lawfully the rights of aliens. According to this view, in which the law on the treatment of aliens is largely collapsed into human rights law, not all rights are considered non-suspendible. Rather, there exists a core of rights that cannot be suspended, consisting of customary, *jus cogens* norms and those the breach of which would result in gross violations. Other norms, however, such as the emerging right to property, could be lawfully suspended.[123] This corresponds to a broader argument whereby no all-encompassing prohibition of countermeasures

générale de droit international public 289, 301; Claude Rucz, 'Les mesures unilatérales de protection des droits de l'homme devant l'Institut de droit international', [1992] Annuaire français de droit international 579, 620–1.

[121] Carlo Focarelli, 'Le contromisure pacifiche e la nozione di obblighi *erga omnes*', (1993) 76 Rivista di diritto internazionale 52, 858.

[122] Restatement, 41 para. 711 comment (q) and para. 905 comment (b) and reporter's note 2.

[123] The possibility of suspending property rights could be seen as the result of the as yet uncertain normative status of that 'right' under international law: above, note 100. See Conforti, Diritto internazionale, at 359–61 (for whom the state may perhaps have the right to suspend basic rights of aliens if it constitutes reprisals in kind);, Arangio-Ruiz, 'Third Report', UN Doc. A/CN.4/440 (1991) paras. 111–12; Focarelli, 'Le contromisure pacifiche', at 854–8; Oscar Schachter, International Law in Theory and Practice (Dordrecht: Nijhoff, 1991) 179–80 (distinguishing between non-suspendible human rights and suspendible privileges allowed aliens on the basis of reciprocity, such as the right to attend school).

can be derived from human rights law; instead, only the suspension of a limited number of norms is proscribed. Rules governing the treatment of aliens and human rights law become at that point so intimately intertwined that it is virtually impossible to identify a prohibition of the suspension of individual rights stemming distinctively from rules regarding aliens.

Self-contained regime

In the context of multilateral agreements on the protection of human rights, some writers have suggested that rights are derogable only in cases of emergency threatening the life of the nation, and in no other situations.[124] This perspective construes human rights instruments as self-contained regimes, in which the reaction to any breach must find its justification strictly within the given instrument. The notion of a self-contained regime was used by the ICJ in the *Hostages* case to reject an argument put forward by Iran to the effect that the taking of hostages was justified by US intrusion in Iranian internal affairs.[125] The Court found that, as a self-contained regime, the law of diplomatic immunities could in no case be suspended in response to a breach of other types of international obligation. If human rights law is similarly viewed as a self-contained regime, then ratification of human rights conventions implies a tacit renunciation of resort to means not expressly provided for in the conventions.[126]

The very concept of self-contained systems has been subject to challenge, even in cases where treaty provisions clearly prevent states from resorting to measures outside the treaty.[127] Although the matter is still

---

[124] See de Guttry, *Le rappresaglie*, at 271–2; Arangio-Ruiz, 'Third Report', UN Doc. A/CN.4/440 (1991) para. 106; Siracusa Principle 1, 'No limitations or grounds for applying them to rights guaranteed by the Covenant [on Civil and Political Rights] are permitted other than those contained in the terms of the Covenant itself': 'The Siracusa Principles on the Limitation and Derogation Provisions in the International Covenant on Civil and Political Rights', (1985) 7 *Hum. Rts Quart.* 3, 4.

[125] *Case Concerning United States Diplomatic and Consular Staff in Tehran (United States v. Iran)*, [1980] ICJ Rep. 3, 40.

[126] This is also linked to the question of discrimination, as derogation clauses of the International Covenant on Civil and Political Rights (Art. 4(1)) and of the American Convention on Human Rights (Art. 27(1)) prohibit discriminatory derogation measures.

[127] For example, the EEC Treaty has been construed by the EC Court of Justice as prohibiting self-help measures among state parties, a decision criticised by some as

debated, human rights conventions generally have not been regarded as self-contained regimes, and do not include provisions barring recourse to means outside the conventions to sanction their violation.[128] Indeed, any form of countermeasures taken by third states, including the suspension of commercial or other agreements – which has generally been regarded as lawful – would appear to be inconsistent with a construction of human rights as a self-contained regime. Generally speaking, the mechanisms set up by human rights conventions are simply too weak to stand on their own, and need the support of external mechanisms such as countermeasures.[129]

While it is clear that the suspension of human rights at a time when no emergency threatens the life of the nation would be illegal, that illegality itself constitutes the defining characteristic of countermeasures. For non-derogable human rights to be understood as a barrier limiting countermeasures, it would have to be shown that the principle of non-derogation was intended to cover countermeasures as well as states of emergency. Provisions allowing for the suspension of some human rights norms during times of emergency are not framed in a way which excludes other valid grounds of derogation. In other words, they are not general statements of the non-derogability of human rights. The derogation provisions are simply permissive, providing that in times of war

depriving a state of any means of sanctioning a state's refusal to abide by the Court's final decision: Alland, *Justice privée*, at 278–91; Benedetto Conforti, *International Law and the Role of Domestic Legal Systems* (Dordrecht: Nijhoff, 1993) 193; Arangio-Ruiz, 'Fourth Report', UN Doc. A/CN.4/444/Add.1 (1992) para. 98; Bruno Simma, 'Self-Contained Regimes', (1985) 16 *Nether. YB Int'l L.* 111, 123–9.

[128] See André de Hoogh, *Obligations* Erga Omnes *and International Crimes* (The Hague: Kluwer Law International, 1996) 254–5; Kamminga, *Inter-State Accountability*, at 179–83; *Restatement*, 41 para. 703(1) comment (a) reporter's note 2; Arangio-Ruiz, 'Fourth Report', UN Doc. A/CN.4/444/Add.1 (1992) paras. 97–127; Arangio-Ruiz, 'Third Report', UN Doc. A/CN.4/440 (1991) 45–6 paras. 84–5; Jochen Frowein, 'Reactions by Not-directly Affected States to Breaches of Public International Law', (1994-IV) 248 *Recueil des cours* 345, 400; Jochen Frowein, 'Die Verpflichtungen *erga omnes* in Völkerrecht und ihre Durchsetzung', in Rudolf Bernhardt et al. eds., *Festschrift für Herman Mosler* (Berlin: Springer, 1983) 255–7; Willem Riphagen, 'Fourth Report on the Content, Form and Degree of State Responsibility', [1983] 2:1 *YB Int'l L Com'n* 3, 15; Simma, 'Self-Contained Regimes', at 129–35. One limited exception is the European Convention on Human Rights whereby state parties agree not to petition other bodies to resolve disputes arising out of the interpretation of the Convention (Art. 55): J. E. S. Fawcett, *The Application of the European Convention on Human Rights*, 2nd edn (Oxford: Clarendon, 1987) 398. Conversely, Art. 44 of the Political Covenant specifically envisages the possibility of states 'having recourse to other procedures for settling a dispute'.

[129] See Meron, *Human Rights and Humanitarian Norms*, at 229–33.

or other emergency threatening the life of the nation, the state 'may take measures derogating from its obligations'.[130] Even non-derogable rights are not declared to be such at large. Rather, the treaty provisions state that no derogation to these rights is permitted 'under this provision'. The possibility of suspension through countermeasures is thus not directly covered by non-derogation provisions.

Jus cogens

Despite some resistance to a classification of human rights norms according to their importance, there is a recurring tendency to distinguish between more or less basic rights.[131] In the context of the suspension of human rights as countermeasures, both *jus cogens* and *erga omnes* norms have been considered as possible lists of human rights not amenable to suspension by way of countermeasures. It is generally accepted that *jus cogens* norms impose limits on a state's response to a violation of international law on the part of another state.[132] Indeed, the ILC, in its Article 50(1)(d) (formerly Art. 50(e)) on State Responsibility, mentions *jus cogens* norms as a limit to lawful countermeasures.[133] The fact that peremptory norms cannot be suspended by agreement of the states concerned (Art. 53, Vienna Convention on the Law of Treaties) *a fortiori* implies that derogation cannot legally stem from the unilateral response of a state to the breach of another.[134] Not all human rights can be considered *jus cogens* norms, however, and thus this is only a partial answer to the question of the legality of suspending human rights as a reprisal measure.[135]

[130] Art. 4(1), International Covenant on Civil and Political Rights; Art. 15(1), European Convention on Human Rights; Art. 27(1), American Convention on Human Rights. Such a principle is suggested in Siracusa Principle 58, providing that 'These rights are not derogable under any conditions': 'Siracusa Principles', at 10.
[131] See e.g. Theodor Meron, 'On a Hierarchy of International Human Rights', (1986) 80 *Am. J Int'l L* 1; Prosper Weil, 'Vers une normativité relative en droit international?', (1982) 86 *Revue générale de droit international public* 5.
[132] See Conforti, *Diritto internazionale*, at 359; Elagab, *Legality*, at 96–9; Arangio-Ruiz, 'Third Report', UN Doc. A/CN.4/440 (1991) 24 para. 119; Focarelli, 'Le contromisure pacifiche', at 855 and 858.
[133] 2001 ILC Draft, at 14; Crawford, 'Third Report', UN Doc. A/CN.4/507 (2000) paras. 342–3; International Law Commission, 'Report of the International Law Commission on the Work of its 46th Session', UN Doc. A/49/10 (1994) 366 n. 362 (former Art. 14(e)); Arangio-Ruiz, 'Fourth Report', UN Doc. A/CN.4/444/Add.1 (1992) para. 96.
[134] See Meron, 'Hierarchy', at 19–20; Sicilianos, *Réactions*, at 344.
[135] See *Restatement*, 41 para. 702 comment (n); Meron, *Human Rights and Humanitarian Norms*, at 237–8; ILC, 'Summary Record of the Thirty-Fifth Session', [1983] 1 *YB Int'l L*

Human rights as a whole, on the other hand, are generally considered to generate *erga omnes* or *erga omnes partes* obligations for states.[136] The suspension of the individual human rights of aliens in response to an initial breach cannot be directed solely and effectively against the offending state. Of necessity, all other states bound by the customary or conventional norm at stake will be indirectly injured by the countermeasures just as they were by the initial violation to which the countermeasures constitute a response. In theory, therefore, a state taking this type of measure is liable in turn to become the target of international sanctions.[137] No distinction can be drawn in this respect between the first and second scenarios envisaged earlier, because countermeasures aimed directly at the individual or collective authors of the initial breach will affect all states in the same way as would countermeasures directed against 'innocent' aliens.

State responsibility

The protracted work of the International Law Commission on questions of state responsibility also provides extensive reflection on this question. In the initial work of the ILC on the limitations to the means available to a state in response to a violation of international law, under the guidance of Riphagen as Special Rapporteur, no special reference was made to human rights. Draft Article 4 simply referred to peremptory norms as a limit to lawful countermeasures.[138] It was clear in the mind of Riphagen, however, that human rights were not considered derogable by way of countermeasures:

> Com'n 1, 144 para. 35 (McCaffrey); Alland, *Justice privée*, at 270–1; *The Prosecutor v. Furundžija* (Judgment), 10 Dec. 1998, Case No. IT-95-17/1-T (Trial Chamber, ICTY) 55 para. 144.
>
> [136] See ILC, 'Report on the 52nd Session', para. 123. See generally the discussion in chapter 3, pp. 133–5.
>
> [137] ILC, 'Report on the 48th Session', at 158 (Art. 47 comm. 8); de Guttry, *Le rappresaglie*, at 303; Sir Gerald Fitzmaurice, 'The General Principles of International Law Considered from the Standpoint of the Rule of Law', (1957-II) 92 *Recueil des cours* 5; Lattanzi, *Garanzie*, at 305 and 314; Meron, *Human Rights and Humanitarian Norms*, at 239; Arangio-Ruiz, 'Third Report', UN Doc. A/CN.4/440 (1991) para. 121; J. Delbrück, 'International Economic Sanctions and Third States', (1992) 30 *Archiv des Völkerrecht* 86, 95–6; Giorgio Gaja, 'Obligations *Erga Omnes*, International Crimes and *Jus Cogens*: A Tentative Analysis of Three Related Concepts', in Joseph Weiler, Antonio Cassese and Marina Spinedi eds., *International Crimes of States – A Critical Analysis of the ILC's Draft Article 19 on State Responsibility* (Berlin: De Gruyter, 1989) 151, 156.
>
> [138] Willem Riphagen, 'Third Report on the Content, Form and Degree of State Responsibility', [1982] 2:1 *YB Int'l L Com'n* 22, 47 para. 148; Willem Riphagen, 'Fifth Report on the Content, Form and Degree of State Responsibility', [1984] 2:1 *YB Int'l L Com'n* 1, 4.

There are several obligations the breach of which is not considered an 'international crime' by the international community as a whole, but which are nevertheless of such a peremptory character that their breach can never be justified as a countermeasure against an internationally wrongful act. *Thus, obviously, a violation of internationally protected human rights in one State cannot justify a violation of those rights in another state.*[139] [Emphasis added.]

The omission of human rights and the resulting uncertainty were largely remedied by Draft Article 11(1)(c) which prohibited the suspension of human rights entrenched in multilateral conventions.[140] As noted by Meron, however, the drafting of this new provision seemed to exclude human rights norms stemming from bilateral conventions and, more importantly, from customary law.[141] A later version, Draft Article 14(c)(i), stated that '[a]n injured State shall not resort, by way of countermeasures, to...any conduct which is not in conformity with the rules of international law on the protection of fundamental human rights', thus finally embodying a general principle shielding human rights from suspension by way of countermeasures.[142] With the expansion in the Draft Article of the prohibition of countermeasures to human rights protected by all sources, however, came a substantive restriction by way of reference to '*fundamental* human rights'. In his third report, Arangio-Ruiz suggests that protection against suspension does not extend to all human rights, and offers as an example the right to property.[143] This is maintained in Article 50(d) (formerly Art. 14(d)) adopted by the ILC in 1996, prohibiting as countermeasures 'any conduct which derogates from *basic* human rights'.[144] Article 50(1)(b) adopted by the ILC in 2001 reverts to the previous formulation of 'fundamental human rights'.[145]

[139] Riphagen, 'Preliminary Report', [1980] 2:1 YB Int'l L Com'n 107, 127 para. 91. See also Riphagen, 'Fourth Report', [1983] 2:1 YB Int'l L Com'n 3, 17 para. 89.
[140] Riphagen, 'Fourth Report', at 16–19 paras. 84–100; Riphagen, 'Fifth Report', at 3–4.
[141] See Meron, *Human Rights and Humanitarian Norms*, at 237–8.
[142] Arangio-Ruiz, 'Fourth Report', UN Doc. A/CN.4/444/Add.1 (1992) paras. 80 and 96; Arangio-Ruiz, 'Third Report', UN Doc. A/CN.4/440 (1991) paras. 111–12.
[143] Arangio-Ruiz, 'Third Report', UN Doc. A/CN.4/440 (1991) paras. 111–12.
[144] ILC, 'Report on the 46th Session', at 366 n. 362. This is also the formulation used by Judge Vereschetin in his Dissenting Opinion in the *Case Concerning the Gabcíkovo-Nagymaros Project (Hungary v. Slovakia)*, 25 Sept. 1997. Note that this and other provisions detailing the regime of countermeasures in the ILC Draft was debated to the end: 'Report of the International Law Commission on the Work of its 54th Session', UN Doc. A/54/10 (1999) paras. 426–52; James Crawford, 'Second Report on State Responsibility', UN Doc. A/CN.4/498/Add.4 (1999) paras. 357–92.
[145] 2001 ILC Draft Articles, at 14. See ILC, 'Report on the 52nd Session', paras. 122 and 326.

Whether described as 'basic' or 'fundamental', the question thus remains open as to which rights are considered so important that they are immune to possible countermeasures. These expressions have been criticised by states and by members of the ILC as too vague and, for some, too broad.[146] Consensus is limited but usually centres on a very short list which includes the right to life, protection against torture and slavery, and sometimes due process guarantees and the prohibition of racial discrimination.[147]

Conclusion

Countermeasures involving the suspension of human rights norms have found little approval in state practice. In several instances where countermeasures of an essentially economic nature were perceived as a potential threat to the basic rights of individuals, special steps were taken to ensure that no such effect was produced. For example, in the French countermeasures against Bokassa following the assassination of eighty-five youths by his personal guard, as well as in the British countermeasures against Argentina following the invasion of the Falkland Islands, exceptions were written into the measures so as to spare the living, educational and medical needs of individual aliens.[148] The detention of aliens as a form of countermeasures by the Ivory Coast in 1967 should thus be seen as an exception rather than the rule.[149]

At a general level, the notion of enforcing human rights law through disregard for its norms seems incompatible with the rationale, indeed the *raison d'être*, of that body of law. As noted by Lattanzi, there is a degree of absurdity in violating human rights in order to foster respect for them.[150] This criticism goes beyond the context of human

[146] ILC, 'Report on the 52nd Session'; Crawford, 'Third Report', UN Doc. A/CN.4/507 (2000) paras. 317 and 351.

[147] See Arangio-Ruiz, 'Fourth Report', UN Doc. A/CN.4/444/Add.1 (1992) paras. 80-1; de Hoogh, *Obligations*, at 261-2; Francisco Villagrán Kramer, 'Retorsión y represalias por violaciones a los derechos humanos', in *Hector Gros Espiell Amicorum Liber* (Brussels: Bruylant, 1997) II, 1765, 1790-1. As mentioned earlier (above, note 100), some consider violations of property rights lawful only if they are temporary and reversible.

[148] See Elagab, *Legality*, at 110; Arangio-Ruiz, 'Fourth Report', UN Doc. A/CN.4/444/Add.1 (1992) para. 79.

[149] See above, note 101 and accompanying text.

[150] Lattanzi, *Garanzie*, at 294 ('L'idoneità della violazione di norme umanitarie a porsi come garanzia dei diritti dell'uomo risulta della stressa *ratio*: la tutela, che queste norme attuano, di interessi individuali rende *assurda* una reazione alla lesione di tali interessi con una violazione che li leda a sua volta.' Emphasis in the original). See also Akehurst, 'Reprisals', at 11 n. 1; Institut de droit international, 'Protection of Human Rights and the Principle of Non-Intervention in the Domestic Concerns of States', (1989) 63:1 *Annuaire de l'Institut de droit international* 431 (Lalive).

rights law to apply to the law of countermeasures as a whole, including belligerent reprisals. Further, the infliction of what amounts to punishment upon individuals usually innocent of any wrongdoing, all in the name of the rule of law, may well appear irreconcilable with the concept of law itself.[151] This has a special poignancy in the field of human rights, designed to prevent the imposition by the state on defenceless individuals of exactly this type of injustice.[152] The argument loses some of its force in the second scenario envisaged earlier, where countermeasures are visited upon the actual authors of the initial violation rather than on innocent individuals. Nevertheless, a mechanism that would permit infringements of human rights to be echoed by further infringements would undoubtedly undermine the structure of human rights as a body of compulsory norms limiting the actions of the state.

The characterisation of human rights norms as 'unilateral', absolute obligations is a further indicator of the inappropriateness of countermeasures in the field. Article 60(5) of the Vienna Convention on the Law of Treaties, although dealing with the treaty rule *inadimplenti non est adimplendum* rather than countermeasures, supports this understanding of the nature of human rights obligations.[153] Under that provision, treaty rules that protect the human person are declared non-suspendible even if violated by another state. In the development and acceptance of human rights standards, there is no strict *quid pro quo* between states whereby consideration for the undertaking of an obligation is given in the form of a similar undertaking by other states.[154] Nevertheless, the rejection of suspension of certain norms under the *inadimplenti* rule does imply that, *a fortiori*, countermeasures should not derogate from norms unconnected to the one initially violated.

---

[151] This could be said to be true, up to a point, of all countermeasures. See e.g. Lori Fisler Damrosch, 'The Civilian Impact of Economic Sanctions', in Lori Fisler Damrosch ed., *Enforcing Restraint – Collective Intervention in Internal Conflicts* (New York: Council on Foreign Relations, 1993) 274–315.

[152] See Kalshoven, 'Human Rights', at 181 (whose suggestion for an answer to the question of the legality of countermeasures in the field of human rights is limited to a statement of the principle that innocents should not suffer for the deeds of others); Rucz, 'Les mesures unilatérales', at 620–1; ILC, 'Summary Records of the Second Part of its Seventeenth Session', [1996] 1:1 YB Int'l L Com'n 66 (Sir Humphrey Waldock) para. 23.

[153] See Barile, 'Protection of Human Rights', at 4; Barile, '*Obligationes erga omnes*', at 8–9; Picone, 'Obblighi reciproci', at 34; Rucz, 'Les mesures unilatérales', at 619–20; Schachter, *International Law*, at 180. On the distinction between countermeasures and *inadimplenti non est adimplendum*, see chapter 4, pp. 164–6.

[154] See the discussion in chapter 3, pp. 133–5.

In the end, despite broad declarations that, as a matter of principle, human rights cannot lawfully be suspended in response to the violation of similar norms by another state, it proves far from easy to derive a specific rule to that effect from existing international standards.[155] Doctrinal writings, *opinio juris* and state practice remain vague as to the basis of such a prohibition. Indeed, analysis of the legitimacy rather than legality of human rights countermeasures perhaps offers the firmest elements of a principle prohibiting the suspension of human rights as a form of countermeasures. Such considerations of legitimacy, in light of the rationale of human rights law, militate in favour of an absolute ban on countermeasures in the form of suspension of human rights, including not only so-called 'fundamental' or 'basic' rights – in any case difficult to define – but all widely accepted human rights. Such an absolute ban, however, appears as a debated idea at this stage, not yet embodied in a rule of general international law.

The difficulty in articulating a limit to peacetime countermeasures which infringe on human rights underscores the challenge posed by the elaboration of a corresponding principle of humanity governing belligerent reprisals under humanitarian law. Logically, any basic right protected against belligerent reprisals in wartime should enjoy a similar immunity from suspension in the course of peacetime countermeasures,[156] as belligerent reprisals represent the outer confines of a body of law issued from a compromise between humanitarian principles and the necessities of warfare. The two classes of non-suspendible norms need not correspond, however, and a larger bundle of rights will likely be protected under human rights law.

The availability of countermeasures in human rights and humanitarian law must mirror the degree to which reciprocity permeates norms in these two areas. More specifically, the taking of countermeasures is legitimate only when they affect norms embodying a relationship of immediate reciprocity. Human rights are *erga omnes* norms in which community

---

[155] The Institut de droit international, in the course of its work on the protection of human rights and the principle of non-intervention, considered several proposed provisions specifically condemning the suspension of human rights as a countermeasure, but eventually omitted the point from the final text of its resolution: Institut de droit international, 'Protection', at 379 (Draft Art. 7) and 391 (Draft Art. 5(3)); 'Resolution on the Protection of Human Rights and the Principle of Non-intervention in Internal Affairs of the State', (1989) 63:2 *Annuaire de l'Institut de droit international* 341, 345 (Dinstein; Art. 4(3) of the Resolution).

[156] See Daniel O'Donnell, 'Commentary by the Rapporteur on Derogation', (1985) 7 *Hum. Rts Quart.* 23, 31.

interests clearly predominate and which accordingly embody diffuse rather than immediate reciprocity. The very nature of these norms as diffusely reciprocal leads to the rejection of any possible suspension on the basis of countermeasures, regardless of whether the targets of such measures are the authors of the initial violations. Conversely, there are few norms in humanitarian law which are significantly disconnected from state interest to centre on community interests. The web of relations created by humanitarian law is grounded in immediate reciprocity. Save for these few *erga omnes* norms identified as forming elementary considerations of humanity, humanitarian law appears structurally predisposed for, indeed predicated upon, the possibility that countermeasures will be available.

Individual responsibility: the rule *tu quoque*

The gradual narrowing of the ambit of legitimate belligerent reprisals in the course of the twentieth century was paralleled by greater reliance on individual penal responsibility as a sanction of humanitarian law violations. One limited and disputed concept relating to individual penal responsibility for the violation of the humanitarian law of armed conflict draws on a broad principle of reciprocity. According to the rule, termed *tu quoque*, an individual's responsibility for grave breaches of humanitarian law could be limited by similar breaches committed by the enemy belligerent. This section briefly examines the basis and validity of the concept.

The humanitarian law of armed conflict applies equally to all belligerents in times of war. Basic notions of equality and fairness direct that an act be considered a war crime regardless of the nationality of the perpetrator. This can pose problems when, as after the Second World War, one side, by reason of its victory in the field, oversees the allocation of criminal responsibility for grave breaches of humanitarian law. A source of constant concern for the four powers which drafted the Statute of the International Military Tribunal was that the crimes defined therein should be illegal not only for Axis nationals but also for individuals of any nationality, despite the fact that the jurisdiction of the Tribunal was limited to nationals of Germany and her allies.[157]

---

[157] See Robert H. Jackson, *International Conference on Military Trials (London 1945)* (Washington DC: US Gov. Printing Office, 1949) 330 (Jackson), 333 (Trainin), 361, 394 (Jackson) and 416 (Nikitchenko); *In re Paul Burghoff*, (1949) 16 Ann. Digest Rep. Pub. Int'l L Cases 551–2 (Neth. Spec. Ct Cass.); Röling, 'Law of War', at 393.

No belligerent has a monopoly on the commission of war crimes. Given that certain actions are necessarily illegal for both sides in the conflict, what is the impact on individual responsibility of the fact that the crime imputed to an accused has also been carried out by his accusers and judges? There are five distinct possibilities, all of which have either occurred or been discussed in state practice: (1) the act is no longer considered illegal by the victorious side; (2) no charges may be laid against enemy persons for this type of crime; (3) the fact that the prosecuting belligerent has also committed the offence may offer a valid defence; (4) the accused may be found guilty of the offence but not sentenced for it; and (5) no relevance is attached to the enemy violations, whether they have been prosecuted or not, and the accused is convicted and sentenced for the war crime. The first four of these alternatives are applications of the rule *tu quoque*, and are grounded in one way or another in the principle of reciprocity. The last refuses the rule *tu quoque*, and indeed represents the rejection of the application of reciprocity to the context of war criminality.

1. Under the first alternative, the act earlier regarded as illegal but committed by several or all belligerents during the instant armed conflict is no longer considered a war crime. This phenomenon occurred during the Second World War in the course of the preparation of the prosecution of war criminals by the United Nations War Crimes Commission. In a report of 2 December 1942, a sub-committee of the Commission noted that it had to omit some war crimes from its list, 'as these refer to acts which, in the present war, the forces of the United Nations have themselves been obliged to commit'.[158] The dangers of such an attitude towards the definition of war crimes are clearly illustrated by the remark of von der Heydte:[159] 'Indeed, if full application of the rule *tu quoque* was accepted, the simple breach of an international law norm by one belligerent during a war would suspend it for the duration of the conflict. All of the law of war could be abolished in this way' (translation). Acceptance of this application of the rule *tu quoque* is a throwback to a primitive construction of the law

---

[158] Quoted in Röling, 'Law of War', at 391.

[159] Friedrich von der Heydte, 'Exposé préliminaire sur le problème que pose l'existence des armes de destruction massive et la distinction entre les objectifs militaires et non militaires en général', (1967) 52:2 *Annuaire de l'Institut de droit international* 73, 90 ('En effet, si l'on acceptait l'application intégrale de la règle *tu quoque*, il suffirait qu'au cours d'une guerre un Etat belligérent viole une norme de Droit international pour que cette norme n'ait plus de valeur durant toute la durée de la guerre. Tout le droit de la guerre pourrait alors être aboli de cette manière').

of war, based on absolute reciprocity, which more or less corresponds to a no-first-use agreement. It is completely at odds with the rejection of absolute reciprocity in the application of humanitarian law of armed conflict examined earlier, even at the time of the work of the War Crimes Commission.

Another, more limited, construction of this application of the rule *tu quoque* is indirectly suggested by Hersch Lauterpacht in his argument that the uncertainty of a given rule on warfare militates against the prosecution of individuals having violated that rule.[160] The principle of legality requires that a crime be sufficiently recognised as such at the time of its commission in order for criminal liability to be imposed pursuant to international law.[161] If both belligerent states adopt a policy openly at variance with a rule on the conduct of war which was generally recognised as valid before the start of the armed conflict, then sufficient uncertainty as to the continued validity of the rule may be created so as to block the criminal prosecution of individual violators. It is important to note that each belligerent must present its policy as independently legal, rather than as justified reprisals in response to earlier breaches by the enemy, given that the latter interpretation would constitute an affirmation of the validity of the violated rule.[162]

This construction exemplifies the principle of reciprocity in the context of the development, rather than application, of humanitarian law of armed conflict. It was applied in the *High Command* trial, where the US Military Tribunal noted that:[163] 'It is no defense in the view of this Tribunal to assert that international crimes were committed by an adversary, but as evidence given to the interpretation of what constituted accepted use of prisoners of war under International Law, such evidence is pertinent.' This does not necessarily imply that the rule has been discarded, but it does prevent the prosecution of individuals as a result of the uncertain state of the law. It would be both unjust and hypocritical for a belligerent, on the one hand, to justify its own conduct as legal under the laws of war and, on the other, to label similar behaviour by the

---

[160] Hersch Lauterpacht, 'The Law of Nations and the Punishment of War Crimes', (1944) 21 *British YB Int'l L* 58, 74–5.
[161] See *The Prosecutor v. Delalić* (the *'Celebici'* case) (Appeals Judgment), 20 Feb. 2001, Case No. IT-96-21-A (Appeals Chamber, ICTY) paras. 153–81; *The Prosecutor v. Aleksovski* (Appeals Judgment), 24 March 2000, Case No. IT-95-14/1-A (Appeals Chamber, ICTY) para. 126.
[162] See Kunz, *La problemática actual*, at 115–17.
[163] *US v. von Leeb et al.* (the *High Command* trial), (1948) 12 L Rep. Trials War Crim. 1, 88 (US Mil. Trib., Nuremberg).

enemy illegal and thus prosecute the responsible individuals. This represents a very narrow exception, as belligerent states usually present their actions as either fully valid according to the law or as reprisals against enemy violations. One example is that of unrestricted submarine warfare, adopted as a matter of policy by all sides during the Second World War despite the fact that it apparently ran contrary to the 1936 London Protocol.[164] The version of *tu quoque* described here would have justified a decision not to commence war crimes proceedings based on that ground. The relentless bombing of civilian targets in enemy cities during the same war, for which no one was prosecuted although the practice contravened a norm generally accepted before the war, provides another example.[165]

2. The second possible application of the rule *tu quoque* is that of a procedural block preventing a state which has violated the law of war from prosecuting enemy individuals for the same actions. There are two strands to this argument. The first concerns only cases where the prosecuting state's breach cannot be justified as reprisals. We are then in the presence of a true violation of the same rule by both sides, which according to some authors generates a sort of estoppel, that is, a procedural block preventing a state from validly prosecuting that particular war crime.[166] The important difference between this and the first application of the rule *tu quoque* outlined above is that no doubt exists here as to the illegality of the conduct. The reprisals and counter-reprisals involving the shackling of prisoners of war by the Germans, British and Canadians in 1942, for which no one was apparently charged, provides an illustration. All these measures contravened the binding 1929 Geneva Convention on Prisoners of War, which forbade the shackling of prisoners and prohibited the taking of any reprisals against them. In the second strand, the taking of reprisals, even if legitimate, also constitutes a procedural

---

[164] *Judgment of the International Military Tribunal*, (1946) 1 IMT 171, 313; 13 IMT 255 ff. (British documents on naval warfare); 17 IMT 378–80 (Admiral Nimitz on US naval warfare tactics). There were in fact charges laid against Dönitz and Raeder on that count at the IMT trial at Nuremberg: see below, pp. 232–3.

[165] See Kalshoven, *Belligerent Reprisals*, at 161–78; Telford Taylor, *Final Report to the Secretary General of the Army on the Nuernberg War Crimes Trials Under Control Council Law No. 10* (Washington DC: US Gov. Printing Office, 1949) 65 ('If the first badly bombed cities – Warsaw, Rotterdam, Belgrade, and London – suffered at the hands of the Germans and not the Allies, nonetheless the ruins of German and Japanese cities were not the result of reprisals but of deliberate policy, and bore witness that aerial bombardment of cities and factories has become a recognized part of warfare as carried out by all nations').

[166] See Kalshoven, *Belligerent Reprisals*, at 364–5; Hampson, 'Belligerent Reprisals', at 820.

block preventing a belligerent from charging its enemies with a war crime. One rationale offered for this rule is that the reprisals constitute a sanction of the initial breach by the would-be prosecuting state, so that further sanctions of the same violation are not justified.[167] Neither of these two strands appears to have a sound legal basis.

With respect to the suggested incompatibility between reprisals and the prosecution of war crimes found in the second strand, it is a mistake to view these two responses to violations of the law of war as similar types of sanction. They work through different means and achieve different ends. Reprisals, on the one hand, aim to bring about the change of a policy in breach of humanitarian law via the imposition of normally prohibited measures against individuals not connected to the violation. The prosecution of war crimes, on the other hand, seeks to punish the actual perpetrators of past breaches in order to achieve justice and deter others from committing such actions in the future. They are both sanctions in that they are grounded in a violation of international law, but their functions are completely different.[168] This application of the rule *tu quoque* in fact denies the existence of a legal regime governing belligerent reprisals, in that it fails to characterise reprisals as sanctions seeking to uphold humanitarian law, and wrongly considers them equivalent to any other breach of the law.

More generally, and this applies equally to both strands, this second application of the rule disregards the *erga omnes* dimension of parts of humanitarian law and instead envisages humanitarian law exclusively as a narrow bilateral exchange of rights and obligations.[169] Under the terms of Articles 49/50/129/146 of the 1949 Geneva Conventions, each state party to the Conventions is under an active duty to repress grave breaches either by prosecuting war criminals or by extraditing them to another state party ready to do so.[170] Even according to the construction of *tu quoque* as a procedural block, the effect of a state's own breach is limited to that particular state's ability to prosecute war crimes. Other states are in a position, or more accurately under an obligation, to punish the war criminals. Given this clear duty on the part of all states, there seems to be no reason for a special rule regarding a belligerent

---

[167] See Kalshoven, *Belligerent Reprisals*, at 214 n. 3, citing M. W. Mouton, *Oorlogsmisdrijsven en het internationale recht* (The Hague: Stols, 1947) 442; Lauterpacht, 'Punishment of War Crimes', at 77.
[168] See Kalshoven, *Belligerent Reprisals*, at 370–1. On the rationale for war crimes prosecution, see above, chapter 2, pp. 103–6.
[169] See above, chapter 3, pp. 136–40.   [170] See Pictet, IV, at 592–3.

which commits similar offences. The correct response to such a situation is rather that the state must punish its own war criminals as well as the enemy's.

3. The third application of the rule *tu quoque* provides that the commission of similar war crimes by the enemy offers a valid defence to an accused. Like *tu quoque* as estoppel, this is an argument resting on a purely reciprocal construction of obligations created by humanitarian law of armed conflict. Although *tu quoque* was raised as a defence in war crimes trials following the Second World War, it was universally rejected. The US Military Tribunal in the *High Command* trial stated very clearly that '[u]nder general principles of law, an accused does not exculpate himself from a crime by showing that another has committed a similar crime, either before or after the commission of the crime by the accused'.[171] There is in fact no support either in state practice or in the opinions of writers for the validity of such a defence.[172]

4. The fourth application of the rule *tu quoque* goes not to the guilt of the accused but rather shields them from being held responsible for their crimes. The conceptual distinction between this and the preceding application lies in the absence of any principle of substantive reciprocity. The effects are nevertheless largely the same from the point of view of the obligatory character of humanitarian law. This particular version of the rule *tu quoque* finds its most serious support in the judgment of the International Military Tribunal. In a passage discussing the conduct of Admiral Dönitz, the Tribunal found the accused guilty of unrestricted submarine warfare for the sinking of neutral ships and failing to rescue their crews. It concluded, however, that in view of similar British and American practices before and after the German crimes, directed against Germany as well as Japan, 'the sentence of Dönitz is not assessed on the ground of his breaches of international law of submarine warfare'.[173] This is a perplexing result, and one may wonder why, from a policy point of view, Dönitz was ever accused of this crime. The laying of charges by the Allies was a statement of the illegality of the conduct, inconsistent

---

[171] *US v. von Leeb et al.* (the *High Command* trial), (1948) 12 L Rep. Trials War Crim. 1, 64 (US Mil. Trib., Nuremberg). See also Carnegie Endowment for International Peace, *Report of the Conference on Contemporary Problems of the Law of Armed Conflict, Geneva: 15–20 Sept. 1969* (New York: Carnegie Endowment, 1971) 116–17 (Poltorak and Draper); Röling, 'Law of War', at 392; 'Final Report of the Commission of Experts Established Pursuant to Security Council Resolution 780', UN Doc. S/1994/674 (23 May 1994) 18 para. 63.

[172] This passage is borrowed by the ICTY in the *Kupreskić* Judgment, taken from a published earlier version of part of this work: *The Prosecutor v. Kupreskić (Lasva Valley* case) (Judgment), 14 Jan. 2000, Case No. IT-95-16-T (Trial Chamber, ICTY) para. 516; Provost, 'Reciprocity', at 450.

[173] *Judgment of the International Military Tribunal,* (1946) 1 IMT 171, 313.

with earlier Allied behaviour implying the legality of the tactic.[174] This inconsistency forced its way into the Court's judgment, considerations of fairness leading it to reject individual responsibility despite the guilt of the accused. In fact, the situation properly should have fallen within the first application of *tu quoque*, given the consensus among belligerents that rules considered valid before the war were impracticable and ought to be abandoned.[175]

The proposition that no responsibility should be assigned for war crimes committed by both sides is difficult to reconcile with the very notion of prosecution of war criminals. In the context of grave breaches of humanitarian law, individual guilt without responsibility seems by and large pointless. The criminalisation of the law of war has as its purposes punishment and deterrence, both of which are neutralised by this application of the rule *tu quoque*.[176] Given that all armies, even those of states most closely associated with the development and promotion of humanitarian law, have had episodes of war criminality, this version of *tu quoque* gravely threatens to undermine the whole edifice of the law of war. If taken seriously, it would imply, for instance, that Germans found guilty of the murder of French prisoners of war could be convicted but not sentenced, because French forces themselves have executed German prisoners of war in what certainly constituted a criminal exercise of reprisals.[177] In a more current setting, individuals accused of various war crimes committed in the context of 'ethnic cleansing' programmes in the former Yugoslavia could avoid any sentence, even if found guilty by the ICTY, because no one belligerent has had exclusivity

---

[174] Taylor, *Final Report*, at 85 ('No one has been indicted before the Nuernberg Military Tribunals unless, in my judgment, there appeared to be substantial evidence of criminal conduct under accepted principles of international law'). Taylor also termed 'unwise' the decision by the British prosecution team to lay charges before the IMT against Dönitz and Raeder for violating the law of submarine warfare: *ibid.*, at 65; Bradley Smith, *Reaching Judgment at Nuremberg* (New York: Basic Books, 1977) 247–65; William Fenrick, 'The Exclusion Zone in the Law of Warfare', (1986) 24 *Can. YB Int'l L* 91, 101–5.

[175] Echoes of this application of the rule *tu quoque* can be found in the *High Command* trial, where the US Military Tribunal mentioned that, if similar action by the enemy does not provide justification for criminal behaviour, it can constitute a mitigating circumstance relevant at the sentencing stage: Kurt Heinze and Karl Schilling, *Die Rechtsprechung der Nürnberger Militärtribunale* (Bonn: Girardet, 1952) 125 paras. 611–12 (quoting mimeographed pages 10,002 and 10,147 of the original records).

[176] See chapter 2, pp. 103–6.

[177] This refers to the execution of forty German prisoners of war by the French *Forces françaises de l'intérieur* in Annecy in September 1944: ICRC, *Report of the International Committee of the Red Cross on its Activities During the Second World War* (Geneva: ICRC, 1949) I, 519–23; Kalshoven, *Belligerent Reprisals*, at 193–200.

over these practices.[178] Such a consequence is not only absurd, but also incompatible with basic principles of criminal and humanitarian law.

The International Military Tribunal itself was not wholly consistent in its application of this version of *tu quoque*. One of the most serious war crimes – as distinct from crimes against humanity – listed in the indictment at Nuremberg was the illegal killing in Katyn of 14,500 Polish officers who initially had been taken prisoners of war by Soviet forces in the September 1939 invasion of Poland, and who allegedly were executed by the Germans upon their takeover of Eastern Poland in 1941. The evidence presented to the Tribunal by the Soviet prosecutor, in charge of crimes against prisoners of war, left so much to be desired that the crime is not mentioned at all in the judgment. The implication of this silence, supported by much of the evidence available at the time, is that some members of the IMT concluded that the Soviet forces in fact had carried out the executions themselves, a conclusion much later confirmed as true by the USSR.[179] The Tribunal nevertheless condemned and sentenced several of the German accused for the execution of Allied prisoners of war, refusing to apply the rule *tu quoque* in this case although it had been pleaded specifically by the defence.[180] The anomaly can be explained by political considerations – the Tribunal was after all not in this sense impartial, being made up of the former enemies of the accused who probably did not care to emphasise the illegality of their own policies.[181] The judgment of the IMT further appears contradictory in its conviction of Admiral Dönitz for the establishment of operational zones within which ships would be sunk without warning, despite evidence that the United States had used exclusion zones in the Pacific.[182]

The fourth application of the rule *tu quoque*, shielding guilty individuals from incurring any criminal responsibility for their war crimes, must in the end be rejected as legally unsound.

---

[178] See 'Report of the Commission of Experts', UN Doc. S/1994/674 (1994), at 36 para. 147.
[179] Only in 1990 did the USSR admit that it had in fact carried out the executions: 'Soviets Admit Blame in Massacre of Polish Officers in World War II', *New York Times*, 13 April 1990, p. A1, col. 4. See generally *The Crime of Katyn – Facts and Documents* (London: Polish Cultural Foundation, 1965) for a collection of evidence from various sources, including a 1952 US House of Representatives Select Committee Report on the Events in Katyn. For evidence presented by both prosecution and defence in Nuremberg, see 7 IMT 425–8; 8 IMT 178–83; 15 IMT 289–92; 17 IMT 274–371; Telford Taylor, *The Anatomy of the Nuremberg Trials – A Personal Memoir* (New York: Knopf, 1992) 466–72.
[180] 17 IMT 539–45.   [181] See Simma, 'Reciprocity', at 403.
[182] See Howard Levie, *Terrorism in War – The Law of War Crimes* (Dobbs Ferry: Oceana, 1993) 66–7 and 525.

5. We are thus left with the fifth alternative, being that the consequences of the commission during an armed conflict of war crimes
similar to those attributed to the enemy must be the prosecution and
sentencing of individuals from *all* sides. This point was put clearly by
the Dutch Special Court of Cassation in the *Burghoff* trial, where the
accused was charged with executing civilian hostages. He pleaded that
both American and British field manuals permitted such a practice, and
that he should therefore not be found guilty. The Court answered that:[183]

Instances of the application by the American forces of [paragraph 358(d) of the
1940 *US Field Manual 27-10*] are not known to the Court, but the only possible
conclusion in the light of Article 6(b) of the London Charter [of the International Military Tribunal – declaring the killing of hostages to be a war crime]
would be that, if such instances had occurred, they would have been a war
crime.

A similar argument was made by the defence in the *Kupreskić* case before
the ICTY, where the accused Bosnian Croats sought to introduce evidence
that Bosnian Muslims had carried out large-scale crimes against Croats.
The Trial Chamber deemed the evidence irrelevant, noting broadly that
'the *tu quoque* defence has no place in contemporary international humanitarian law'.[184] The acceptance by the International Military Tribunal
of a role for reciprocity in the sentencing of war criminals should in the
end be rejected.

The relevance of reciprocity to individual penal responsibility, in the
form of the *tu quoque* rule, thus appears extremely limited. Its sole valid
application relates to the unfairness of criminal responsibility in situations where the binding force of a rule in transition is openly challenged
by both or all belligerent states. In general, however, the rule *tu quoque*
is rejected so that the unilateral character of applicable humanitarian
law obligations is confirmed.

---

[183] *In re Paul Burghoff*, (1949) 16 Ann. Digest Rep. Pub. Int'l L Cases 551, 552 (Neth. Spec.
Ct Cass.); Röling, 'Law of War', at 393. Execution of hostages was permitted by para.
358(d) of the 1940 *US Field Manual 27–10*, and by para. 458 of the 1936 *British Manual
of Military Law*. The use of hostages by the Allies is discussed in August von Knieriem,
Nürnberg – Rechtliche und menschliche Probleme (Stuttgart: Klett, 1953) 412–13. On a
related point, see the Dissenting Opinion of Vice-President Weeramantry in the *Case
Concerning Application of the Convention on the Prevention and Punishment of the Crime of
Genocide (Bosnia & Herzegovina v. Yugoslavia)*, Counter-claims Order, 17 Dec. 1997.
[184] *The Prosecutor v. Kupreskić (Lasva Valley* case) (Judgment), 14 Jan. 2000, Case No.
IT-95-16-T (Trial Chamber, ICTY) para. 511. See also *The Prosecutor v. Kupreskić (Lasva
Valley* case) (Decision on Defence Motion to Summon Witness), 8 Feb. 1999, Case No.
IT-95-16-T (Trial Chamber, ICTY) at 3; *The Prosecutor v. Kupreskić (Lasva Valley* case)
(Decision on Evidence of the Good Character of the Accused and the Defence of *Tu
Quoque*), 17 Feb. 1999, Case No. IT-95-16-T (Trial Chamber, ICTY) at 4.

Conclusion to Part II

The analysis of the role of reciprocity in the development, application and sanction of human rights and humanitarian law paints a complex picture, reciprocity permeating both bodies of law and yet playing out differently in each field. Broad statements that reject reciprocity in human rights law altogether, or that insist on the essentially reciprocal nature of humanitarian law, must be considered unsound. The fact that immediate reciprocity plays a much more prominent role in humanitarian law has a significant impact at every stage of the life of these norms. Greater relevance for immediate reciprocity in humanitarian law goes hand in hand with the bilateralisable character of many humanitarian obligations. Human rights, on the contrary, generate substantive obligations which are almost exclusively non-bilateralisable and which correspond to systemic reciprocity. Despite this fundamental difference, both systems contain norms which, by their nature, are of interest to the international community as a whole. Thus the *erga omnes* character of human rights obligations has been much discussed, while the consequences of characterising humanitarian law obligations in a similar way requires further attention.

Human rights and humanitarian law have enjoyed tremendous development since the end of the Second World War, and the shifting role of reciprocity stands as witness to their currently unsettled status. In the largely decentralised legal systems that they represent, reciprocity plays an essential role in generating compliance with norms. It is an element important not only to the creation, application and sanction of human rights and humanitarian law, but also, more broadly, to the overall stability of these legal systems. Over-enthusiastic attempts to strip these systems completely of any element of reciprocity are risky, given that international mechanisms for enforcing *erga omnes* obligations have not yet been established or widely accepted. Without international institutions to replace immediate reciprocity, there is a real danger that the norms could be hijacked by powerful states and used as instruments serving their own foreign policy aims. This is equally true of humanitarian law and human rights, despite the greater institutionalisation of human rights at the regional and universal levels, because neither is construed as a self-contained regime limiting recourse to measures outside established mechanisms. Reciprocity, in the end, is Janus-faced.[1] Its positive side inspires moderation and compliance while its

---

[1] See Bruno Simma, *Das Reziprozitätselement in zustandekommen völkerrechtlicher Verträge* (Berlin: Duncher & Humblot, 1972) 106.

negative side limits application and allows for the reverberation of violations.

The preceding analysis has shown that there are close links between immediate and systemic reciprocity, and that each form of reciprocity can contribute in a positive and a negative fashion to human rights and humanitarian law. Despite broad statements pronouncing the total abandonment of immediate reciprocity in these two fields, it seems not only unlikely but probably undesirable to jettison it completely.[2] The movement from immediate to systemic reciprocity is not a one-way street, and institutional weaknesses in centralised systems may mean that states will revert to mechanisms which embody immediate reciprocity. Further, it is clear that neither human rights nor humanitarian law is a perfect regime in which systemic reciprocity can effectively protect all fundamental interests of participants. There is thus some legitimate space for immediate reciprocity alongside systemic reciprocity, with the weaker centralisation of humanitarian law translating into the need for a much greater reliance on immediate reciprocity.

Having examined and compared in turn the normative structure and one of the grounding principles of human rights and humanitarian law, the question remains as to the manner in which the principles embodied in these two legal systems are translated into standards to be concretely applied and enforced by states, intergovernmental and non-governmental organisations, as well as individuals. The lofty goals written into the constitutions of human rights and humanitarian law can only hope to become realities if efficient mechanisms, institutional or not, have been devised to oversee the implementation of these international norms. Once again, as will be seen in the next Part, the answer given for each legal system will be influenced by the degree to which it is driven by reciprocity. As Brunnée and Toope note, 'in a system that is reciprocally generated, issues of interpretation occupy a "sensitive, central position" in the legal imagination', adding that 'interpretative acts occur throughout the legal system, and involve many different actors'.[3] The level of institutionalisation and the penetration of immediate or systemic reciprocity are the two parameters which will determine how the interpretative challenge is met. If there are institutions, they will

[2] For an example, see *The Prosecutor* v. *Kupreskić* (*Lasva Valley* case) (Judgment), 14 Jan. 2000, Case No. IT-95-16-T (Trial Chamber, ICTY) para. 530.

[3] Jutta Brunnée and Stephen Toope, 'International Law and Constructivism: Elements of an Interactional Theory of International Law', (2000) 39 *Colum. J Transnat'l L* 19, 52; Lon Fuller, *The Morality of Law*, rev. edn (New Haven: Yale UP, 1969) 55, 91 and 176.

typically wield significant, although not exclusive, interpretative powers. If there are few or no institutions, norms embodying immediate reciprocity will often in effect give interpretative powers to agents directly involved in a dispute. In the case of human rights, there is a greater degree of institutionalisation matched by systemic reciprocity, whereas in humanitarian law there is a more limited institutionalisation but a more significant space for immediate reciprocity, which suggests that the interpretative dynamic in these two fields will be significantly different.

PART III • APPLICATION: LAW AND FACTS

'When *I* use a word,' Humpty Dumpty said in a rather scornful tone, 'it means just what I choose it to mean – neither more nor less.' 'The question is,' said Alice, 'whether you *can* make words mean so many different things.' 'The question is,' said Humpty Dumpty, 'which is to be the master – that's all.'

Lewis Carroll, *Through the Looking Glass* (1872)

Introduction

In what later became a standard defence tactic, the accused in the *Tadić* case before the ICTY argued that, at the time of the alleged war crimes, there was no armed conflict or that the conflict was of internal rather than international character.[1] The attractiveness of such a defence lies in its devastating effect on the prosecution, challenging the very applicability of rules which are said to have been violated by the accused. Of necessity, then, one of the Tribunal's first and most difficult tasks has been to characterise the various phases of the confrontations in that region as international or internal armed conflicts or as mere internal disturbances. In Bosnia-Herzegovina, for example, this involves determining *inter alia* when Bosnia became an independent state, the nature and duration of involvement in the conflict on the part of Croatia and the Federal Republic of Yugoslavia (Serbia and Montenegro), the intensity of hostilities between the government and Bosnian Serb and Croat rebels, the effect of the proclamation of an independent Serbian Republic of Bosnia-Herzegovina (*Republika Srpska*), the timing of Bosnia's succession to the Geneva Conventions and Protocols, and the effect of Security Council Resolution 808 (1993). It seems that the conflicts swung from international to internal several times during the period after January 1991 and that, in some situations, several conflicts overlapped in the same area.[2]

---

[1] See *The Prosecutor v. Tadić* (Opinion and Judgment), 7 May 1997, Case No. IT-94-1-T (Trial Chamber II, ICTY); *The Prosecutor v. Tadić* (Decision on the Defence Motion for Interlocutory Appeal on Jurisdiction), 2 Oct. 1995, Case No IT-94-1-AR72 (Appeals Chamber, ICTY). See also *The Prosecutor v. Furundžija* (Judgment), 10 Dec. 1998, Case No. IT-95-17/1-T (Trial Chamber, ICTY) 21–5 paras. 51–60; *The Prosecutor v. Delalić, Mucić, Delić and Landzo* (the '*Celebici*' case) (Appeals Judgment), 20 Feb. 2001, Case No. IT-96-21-A (Appeals Chamber, ICTY) 4–16 paras. 6–51; *The Prosecutor v. Akayesu* (Judgment), 2 Sept. 1998, Case No. ICTR-96-4-T (Trial Chamber I, ICTR) 124–6; *The Prosecutor v. Rajić* (Review of the Indictment Pursuant to Rule 61), 13 Sept. 1996, Case No. IT-95-12-R61 (Trial Chamber II, ICTY).

[2] See *Tadić* (Judgment) paras. 561–71; *Tadić* (Interlocutory Appeal) 35–8 paras. 66–70; *The Prosecutor v. Kordić* (Judgment), 26 Feb. 2001, Case No. IT-95-14/2-T (Trial Chamber, ICTY) paras. 73–8; *Rajić* (Rule 61) 7–18 paras. 7–32. Several writers underlined the difficulty of the task: William Fenrick, 'In the Field with UNCOE: Investigating Atrocities in the Territory of the Former Yugoslavia', (1995) 34 *Revue de droit militaire et du droit de la guerre* 33, 37–45; 'Final Report of the Commission of Experts Established Pursuant to Security Council Resolution 780 (1992)', UN Doc. S/1994/674 Annex (27 May 1994) paras. 42–54; Christopher Greenwood, 'International Humanitarian Law and the *Tadić* Case', (1996) 7 *Eur. J Int'l L* 265, 269–75; Bosko Jakovljević, 'Agreements for the Implementation of International Humanitarian Law in the Armed Conflict in Former Yugoslavia', in Sonja Biserko ed., *Yugoslavia: Collapse, War, Crime* (Belgrade: Center for Anti-War Action, 1993) 161, 182–4; Theodor Meron, 'Classification of Armed Conflict in the Former Yugoslavia: *Nicaragua's* Fallout', (1998) 92 *Am. J Int'l L* 236–42. See also

The same fundamental need for characterisation exists in human rights law with respect to the suspension of basic guarantees in case of war or other emergency threatening the life of the nation. For instance, Ireland and Great Britain have held opposite views with respect to the existence of a state of emergency in Northern Ireland, as a consequence of the activities of various paramilitary groups in the area. When the question was put to the European Court of Human Rights on a number of occasions, it acknowledged the difficulty of characterising the situation in Northern Ireland, and relied heavily on the finding of the territorial state, the United Kingdom.[3]

Both of these cases are exceptional in that an international judicial body was available to dispose of this and other questions. In the vast majority of situations, no international body will be available to provide an authoritative and binding characterisation, and other actors such as states and organisations will be faced with the need to proceed to their own characterisation of armed conflicts and states of emergency. In humanitarian and human rights law, indeterminacies in the field of application *ratione materiae* threaten the applicability of the law in whole or in large part. The nature, conditions and author of the required act of characterisation will play a critical role in the effective realisation of the standards contained in human rights and humanitarian law.

Indeterminacy and the need for characterisation are of course not peculiar to human rights and humanitarian law. It is a difficulty to a degree inherent in all legal norms. Indeed, as noted by Bilder, 'nations often seek to preserve broad flexibility in their agreement through the deliberate use of very general, equivocal, or ambiguous language'.[4] Such norms have a fluid content, or open texture, and an act of classification of the fact, action, institution or legal relationship will be needed in every case in order to determine which legal regime is applicable.[5] The same

Eric David, 'Le Tribunal pénal international pour l'ex-Yougoslavie', [1992] 2 *Revue belge de droit international* 565, 570–2; Karin Oellers-Frahm, 'Das Statut des Internationalen Strafgerichtshofs zur Verfolgung von Kriegsverbrechen im ehemaligen Jugoslawien', (1994) 54 *Zeitschrift für ausländisches öffentliches Recht und Völkerrecht* 416, 422.

3 See 'Lawless' case (Merits), Eur. Ct Hum. Rts, Ser. A 1960–1 at 56; *Ireland v. United Kingdom*, (1978) Eur. Ct Hum. Rts, Ser. A vol. 3 at 78–82; *Brannigan and McBride v. United Kingdom* (A/258-B), (1993) 17 Eur. Hum. Rts Rep. 539, 569–70 (Eur. Ct Hum. Rts).

4 Richard Bilder, *Managing the Risks of International Agreements* (Madison: U Wis. Press, 1981) 37.

5 See generally Thomas Franck, *The Power of Legitimacy Among Nations* (New York: Oxford UP, 1990) 50–66; H. L. A. Hart, *The Concept of Law* (Oxford: Clarendon, 1961) 121–32; Martti Koskenniemi, *From Apology to Utopia – The Structure of International Legal Argument* (Helsinki: Lakimiesliiton Kustannus, 1989) 22–3; Bin Cheng, 'Flight from Justiciable to

is true of facts, which may be objectively determinable but still require more than a passive assessment by an agent. Legally relevant facts are ascertainable only through the lens of an appropriate norm. Facts such as intention or emergency threatening the life of the nation are by their nature somewhat fuzzy and call for an active act of characterisation by an agent. The operation of characterisation is very close to interpretation, the latter seeking to clarify law in reference to a set of facts, and the former the classification of facts in reference to some legal norms. The two operations appear necessarily interconnected. There is nothing automatic in characterisation, even in cases where both facts and law are clear and undisputed. It is a creative 'construction' of an undoubtedly political nature.[6] For example, the United Kingdom insisted that municipal law applied in Rhodesia, while the United Nations thought international law obtained, without any necessary disagreement as to the facts or content of either set of rules.[7] Much of the debate between the 'declaratory' and 'constitutive' theories of state recognition can be expressed in terms of normative indeterminacy and the clash of factual characterisations.[8]

Because of the tendency to manipulate facts and law in order to achieve a desired result, the identity, jurisdiction and authority of the characterising agent will be of critical importance. In centralised legal systems, such as municipal legal systems, conflicting characterisations among actors may be resolved by unilaterally or jointly submitting the dispute to a neutral, often governmental, third party. In a decentralised system such as the international legal system, there is no principle requiring parties which disagree on the character of a situation to submit their dispute to a third party. As mentioned above, jurisdictions such as the ICTY and European Court of Human Rights are unusual. The dilemma of possible disagreement as to the existence of an armed

Auto-interpretative International Law', in *Liber Amicorum Elie van Bogaert* (Antwerp: Kluwer, 1985) 1–18; Leo Gross, 'States as Organs of International Law and the Problem of Autointerpretation', in George Lipsky ed., *Law and Politics in the World Community. Essays on Hans Kelsen's Pure Theory of Law and Related Problems in International Law* (Berkeley: U Calif. Press, 1953) 59–88; Jean J. A. Salmon, 'Some Observations on Characterization in Public International Law', in Antonio Cassese ed., *UN Law/ Fundamental Rights* (Alphen aan den Rijn: Sijthoff & Noordhoff, 1979) 3–21; Jean J. A. Salmon, 'Les faits dans l'application du droit international', (1982-II) 175 *Recueil des cours* 257.

[6] See Hans Kelsen, *General Theory of Law and the State* (Cambridge, Mass.: Harvard UP, 1946) 135–6 and 221–2; Salmon, 'Les faits dans l'application', at 385–7.

[7] Salmon, 'Some Observations on Characterization', at 8–9.

[8] See Koskenniemi, *From Apology to Utopia*, at 236–45.

conflict or a state of emergency is thus but one particular instance of a broader difficulty of international law, one which seems perhaps to challenge the very juridical nature of the international legal system.[9] International law can maintain a valid claim to legal normativity and deny that judicial action is the unique paradigm of legal interpretation and characterisation, by affirming that these tasks can validly be performed by a variety of actors in the international legal system.[10] The analysis will seek to determine whether characterisations of armed conflict and state of emergency raise identical problems, or whether different patterns emerge which would suggest distinct models for resolving inconsistencies.

In human rights as well as in humanitarian law, initial characterisation plays a key role, because the classification of a given situation as a state of emergency or an armed conflict may render one or the other legal system nearly or totally inapplicable.[11] The only exception concerns the small number of human rights from which no derogation is permitted even in time of war or state of emergency. These apply at all times independently of any act of characterisation by the state or any other agent. Non-derogable rights, however, provide only a restricted core of fundamental protection for the individual, leaving out many other essential rights such as freedom from arbitrary detention and freedom of expression. There are important variations among human rights treaties as to which rights are non-derogable, with longer (e.g. American Convention on Human Rights) and shorter (e.g. Covenant on Civil and Political Rights) lists. Further, several human rights conventions, like the International Covenant on Economic, Social and Cultural Rights, the Convention on the Rights of the Child and the African Charter on Human and Peoples' Rights, do not include a provision dealing with emergency derogation, creating much uncertainty as to the possibility and extent of permissible derogation during a state of emergency.[12]

---

[9] See Gross, 'States as Organs', at 73–4 (with reference to Kelsen's analysis).

[10] See Lon Fuller, *The Morality of Law*, rev. edn (New Haven: Yale UP, 1969) 55 and 176.

[11] For example, during the Vietnam war, both North and South Vietnam were party to the 1949 Geneva Conventions, but the North considered the conflict an internal war while the South viewed it as a war of aggression waged by the North. See Dietrich Schindler, 'The Different Types of Armed Conflicts According to the Geneva Conventions and Protocols', (1979-II) 163 *Recueil des cours* 117, 127.

[12] See '[First] Interim Report of the Committee on the Enforcement of Human Rights Law', in International Law Association, *Report of the 62nd Conference, Seoul, 24–30 August 1986* (London: ILA, 1987) 108, 140–1 (with respect to derogation under ILO

Indeterminacy in human rights and humanitarian law is by no means limited to broad issues of applicability. There is a sliding scale of indeterminacy in both legal systems from the very general to the very specific, from the easily ascertainable from abroad to the perceptible only by way of on-the-spot investigation. The scale ends with the need to characterise specific measures with respect to identified individuals, for instance 'who is a privileged belligerent?' or 'is a measure strictly required by the state of emergency?'. A distinction may be drawn between procedures aiming at the global characterisation of a situation as an armed conflict or a state of emergency, and other procedures directed at the enforcement of rules deemed applicable to a given set of facts, although it is conceded that initial characterisation forms part of the enforcement process. One distinctive element is that characterisation going to the initial applicability of human rights or humanitarian law can be performed more easily from abroad, without on-site investigation, than enforcement of specific rules.[13] As we will see, this may imply that some bodies unsuited to performing enforcement tasks can properly characterise a situation as an armed conflict or a state of emergency. More generally, arguments of inapplicability erect a facade of legitimacy providing blanket justification in a manner dangerous for the integrity of the legal systems created by human rights and humanitarian law, while enforcement procedures generally come closer to a case-by-case evaluation of each action taken by the state or other actors.

A first obstacle to a comparison of the characterisation of situations as armed conflicts and states of emergency is that in the first case the decision goes to the applicability of humanitarian law while in the second it goes to the inapplicability of human rights. This results from the fact that human rights law is generally applicable at all times, while humanitarian law is exceptional, applying only in a limited set of circumstances. The difference may be more apparent than real, however, because of the ease with which many governments resort to states of emergency as well as the phenomenon of institutionalisation of states of

conventions); Fatsah Ouguergouz, 'L'absence de clause de dérogation dans certains traités relatifs aux droits de l'homme: Les réponses du droit international général', (1994) 98 *Revue générale de droit international public* 289–334.

[13] See Inter-American Commission on Human Rights, 'Third Report on the Situation of Human Rights in Colombia', OAS Doc. OEA/Ser.L/V/II doc. 102 (1999) Ch. IV, para. 15; René-Jean Wilhelm, 'Problèmes relatifs à la protection de la personne humaine par le droit international dans les conflits armés ne présentant pas un caractère international', (1972-III) 137 *Recueil des cours* 316, 341.

emergency in several countries.[14] In situations where a problem arises, that is when the state has sought to justify its actions by declaring a state of emergency, the decision will also be one concerning the applicability of norms, or more precisely the permissibility of derogation.[15]

This Part explores the nature and effect of characterisation by various agents as to the applicability of human rights and humanitarian law to situations of armed conflict or state of emergency. The degree of indeterminacy of a norm conditions the need for procedural mechanisms aimed at the resolution of that indeterminacy, because indeterminate norms support a wider spectrum of apparently justified results. Clearer standards generate fewer debates, although there are limits to aspirations of clarity.[16] As such, it is a flight of fancy to suggest that any norm could be so clear or 'objective' as to be wholly independent of the subjective judgment of actors called to apply it.[17] Conversely, international norms may be vague because the facts out of which they grew were difficult to characterise.[18] Accordingly, chapter 6 briefly discusses standards applicable in armed conflicts and states of emergency and attempts to identify areas of indeterminacy. No systematic exposition of the law is intended, nor is a substantive comparison of the concepts of armed conflict and state of emergency, although the discussion will ineluctably touch on these elements. Chapter 7 examines the nature and effect of characterisation by various agents interested in the application of human rights and humanitarian law, and attempts to sketch a methodology to resolve the possible inconsistencies among these various assessments of facts and law.

---

[14] Latin America provides numerous examples of both practices. See e.g. with respect to Chile: Inter-American Commission on Human Rights, 'Report on the Situation of Human Rights in Chile', OAS Doc. OEA/Ser.L/V/II/66, doc. 17 (27 Sept. 1985); UN Human Rights Commission, Res. 1985/47 (1985).

[15] See below, pp. 217–18.

[16] See Franck, Power, at 60.

[17] See e.g. The Prosecutor v. Musema (Judgment), 27 Jan. 2000, ICTR-96-13-T (Trial Chamber, ICTR) para. 252; The Prosecutor v. Rutaganda, (Judgment), 6 Dec. 1999, ICTR-96-3-T (Trial Chamber, ICTR) para. 94.

[18] See James Brierly, The Law of Nations, Humphrey Waldock ed., 6th edn (Oxford: Oxford UP, 1963) 76 ('The difficulty of formulating the rules of international law with precision is a necessary consequence of the kind of evidence upon which we have to rely in order to establish them').

6 Areas of legal indeterminacy

> A specious clarity can be more damaging than an open-ended vagueness
> Lon Fuller, *The Morality of Law* (1969)

Even though norms might have an open texture, they nevertheless possess a core meaning and a penumbra which will not accommodate any and all possible applications. Some characterisations will have to be considered unreasonable in order to uphold the normative nature of a rule.[1] Clearly, the concepts of reasonableness and good faith will set parameters, even if ill-defined, restricting the ambit of legitimate characterisations.[2] Indeterminate norms, however, will accommodate a diversity of characterisations which cannot be labelled unreasonable or in bad faith. It is within that sphere of legitimate diversity that the thorniest problems of characterisation arise. It is therefore important, before passing on to the study of the relative effect of characterisation, to examine the degree of indeterminacy of the relevant rules. The overview of applicable standards centres first on the various categories of armed conflicts and their particular legal regimes, and secondly on the elements which have been found to lawfully justify derogation from human rights norms during a state of emergency.

Humanitarian law of armed conflict

Five different types of situations are differentiated under the humanitarian law of armed conflict, the last one of which, internal disturbances

---

[1] See Thomas Franck, *The Power of Legitimacy Among Nations* (New York: Oxford UP, 1990) 55–7; Jean J. A. Salmon, 'Le fait dans l'application du droit international', (1982-II) 175 *Recueil des cours* 257, 277.

[2] See generally Olivier Corten, *L'utilisation du 'raisonnable' par le juge international* (Brussels: Bruylant, 1997); Thomas Franck, *Fairness in International Law* (Oxford: Clarendon, 1995).

and tensions, falls outside the reach of that law. The four others, which will be examined successively, consist of (1) inter-state armed conflicts, (2) national liberation armed conflicts, (3) non-international armed conflicts as defined under the 1977 Additional Protocol II, and (4) internal armed conflicts as defined under common Article 3 of the 1949 Geneva Conventions.

INTER-STATE ARMED CONFLICTS

The notion of 'international armed conflict' evolved as a separate concept from 'war' only recently, through the adoption after the Second World War of the UN Charter and the 1949 Geneva Conventions. Previously, the law of war applied only in situations of 'war', defined by Oppenheim as 'a contention between two or more states through their armed forces for the purpose of overpowering each other and imposing such conditions of peace as the victor pleases'.[3] The notion of war was thus quite limited and excluded not only civil wars and measures short of war, such as peacetime reprisals, but also conflicts which belligerents did not view as war despite large-scale fighting between armed forces of several states. For example, the Boxer Expedition by various Western states in 1900–1 to quell a rebellion threatening the lives of their nationals in China was never considered a 'war', although thousands of soldiers participated in combat operations resulting in a large number of dead and wounded. It does not seem that the law of war was considered applicable, and indeed there reportedly were episodes of pillage, rape, destruction and refusal of quarters by the expeditionary forces.[4]

The inadequacy of a unique definition of war in international law became progressively clearer as the number and sophistication of norms regulating the use of force grew during the last century. The characterisation of a situation as 'war' has an impact on (1) the application of humanitarian law of armed conflict, or *jus in bello*, (2) the non-hostile

---

[3] Lassa Oppenheim, *International Law*, Hersch Lauterpacht ed., 7th edn (London: Longmans, 1952) II, 202. See also Yoram Dinstein, *War, Aggression and Self-Defense*, 2nd edn (Cambridge: Cambridge UP, 1992) 3–20; Joseph L. Kunz, *Kriegsrecht und Neutralitätsrecht* (Vienna: Springer, 1935) 4–11; Emer de Vattel, *Le droit des gens ou principes de la loi naturelle*, James Brown Scott ed. (Washington: Carnegie, 1916, 1st edn 1758) III, sec. 1–4 ('war is that state in which nations, under the authority of their respective government, prosecute their right by force'); Louis Delbez, 'La notion juridique de guerre', (1953) 57 *Revue générale de droit international public* 177, 178–200 (defining war as 'une lutte armée entre états, voulue par l'un d'entre eux au moins, et entreprise en vue de défendre un intérêt national' – at 178).

[4] See Fritz Grob, *The Reality of War and Peace* (New Haven: Yale UP, 1949) 64–79.

relations between belligerents, such as diplomatic relations and treaties in force, (3) relations with third states, by application of the law of neutrality, and (4) the belligerents' obligations towards the international community under the *jus ad bellum*, by effect of the Briand–Kellogg Pact and the UN Charter.[5] Each of these categories contains norms linked by their relation to war, but they nevertheless serve different purposes and call for distinct thresholds of applicability.

There is a clear need for different criteria for the applicability of, on the one hand, humanitarian law and, on the other, rules governing the effect of war on treaties.[6] This in fact has been so for quite some time. For instance, Italy was during 1915–16 at war only with Austria-Hungary, but some German divisions were fighting alongside Austro-Hungarian troops against Italy. Although neither Italy nor Germany considered itself in a state of war against the other, there was no disagreement as to the applicability of the 1906 Geneva Convention and 1907 Hague Conventions.[7] With the prohibition of war in international law by way of the Briand–Kellogg Pact and the League of Nations Covenant (Arts. 12–16), there was an even greater incentive not to admit to being in a state of war with another country. Thus, in the 1931–3 Sino-Japanese conflict, despite wide-scale fighting, both belligerents denied that there was a 'war' within the meaning of Article 16 of the League of Nations Covenant. The United States, France and Germany agreed with this characterisation for their own political reasons. Japan and China nevertheless considered that the Geneva and Hague Conventions were applicable to this 'non-war'.[8] Even prior to the Second World War, then, the notion of war with regard to the applicability of *jus in bello* was distinctly wider than a possible global definition of war in general international law.[9]

---

[5] See Ian Brownlie, *International Law and the Use of Force by States* (Oxford: Clarendon, 1963) 402–9; Christopher Greenwood, 'The Concept of War in Modern International Law', (1987) 36 *Int'l & Comp. L Quart.* 283, 294–5.

[6] See Grob, *Reality*, at 189. But see Werner Meng, 'War', in Rudolf Bernhardt ed., [Instalment] 4 *Encyclopedia of Public International Law* (Amsterdam: North-Holland, 1982) 282–90.

[7] Grob, *Reality*, at 79–81 and 217–18.

[8] Brownlie, *International Law*, at 386–8; Grob, *Reality*, at 140–61 and 208–16. Other examples could include the 1937–41 Sino-Japanese conflict, the 1935 Italo-Ethiopian conflict, the 1951–3 Korean war, the 1982 Falklands war, etc. See Julius Stone, *Legal Control of International Conflict*, 2nd edn (London: Stevens & Sons, 1959) 311 n. 79; Greenwood, 'Concept of War', at 293.

[9] On the present (ir)relevance of the notion of war in other areas of international law, see Dietrich Schindler, 'State of War, Belligerency, Armed Conflict', in Antonio Cassese ed., *The New Humanitarian Law of Armed Conflict* (Naples: Ed. Scientifica, 1979) 3–20.

The adoption in the 1949 Geneva Conventions of the concept of 'armed conflict' was meant to reflect the growing obsolescence of the notion of war as the threshold of applicability of humanitarian law. The operative provision consists of the first two paragraphs of common Article 2:

In addition to the provisions which shall be implemented in peace-time, the present Convention shall apply to all cases of declared war or of any other armed conflict which may arise between two or more of the High Contracting Parties, even if the state of war is not recognized by one of them.

The Convention shall also apply to all cases of partial or total occupation of the territory of a High Contracting Party, even if the said occupation meets with no armed resistance.

Article 2 is completed by Articles 5/4/5/6, specifying that the Conventions apply from the outset of any conflict or from the date of capture of individuals until the general close of military operations, the end of occupation, or the final repatriation of protected persons. The threshold of applicability is clearly intended to be very low, and to include all situations where humanitarian law may provide some protection to the victims of military operations. The most limited and brief clashes, such as the one between Mexico and the United States in 1916 involving 250 soldiers and lasting for thirty minutes, or the shooting down of a US plane over Lebanon by Syria in 1980, as well as measures constituting 'resort to force short of war' such as reprisals or intervention, would probably constitute armed conflicts governed by humanitarian law.[10] Apart from rather vague statements that humanitarian law of armed conflict, including the customary rules embodied in the 1907 Hague Conventions, applies 'in any case',[11] there are practically no objective elements agreed

[10] Grob, *Reality*, at 217–18; (1988) 82 *ASIL Proc.* 602–3 and 609–11. See *The Prosecutor v. Delalić, Mucić, Delić and Landzo* (the '*Celebici*' case) (Judgment), 16 Nov. 1998, Case No. IT-96-21-T (Trial Chamber, ICTY) 79 para. 208; Christopher Greenwood, 'Scope of Application of Humanitarian Law', in Dieter Fleck ed., *The Handbook of Humanitarian Law in Armed Conflict* (Oxford: Oxford UP, 1995) 39–51; Karl Joseph Partsch, 'Armed Conflict', in Rudolf Bernhardt ed., [Instalment] 3 *Encyclopedia of Public International Law* (Amsterdam: North-Holland, 1982) 25, 26. Note, however, the British declaration on signature of Protocol I, stating 'in relation to Article 1, that the term "armed conflict" of itself and in its context implies a certain level of intensity of military operations which must be present before the Conventions or the Protocol are to apply to any given situation': *reprinted in* Dietrich Schindler and Jirí Toman, *The Laws of Armed Conflict*, 3rd edn (Dordrecht: Nijhoff, 1989) 717. If the declaration was meant to cover all armed conflicts mentioned in Article 1 of Protocol I, and not only national liberation conflicts in Article 1(4), it would raise the threshold of applicability of humanitarian law so as to exclude inter-state conflict of a low intensity. The statement was not repeated when the UK ratified Protocol I in January 1998.

[11] Delbez, 'La notion juridique', at 207; Greenwood, 'Concept of War', at 295.

upon as necessary to the existence of an international armed conflict. The Appeals Chamber of the ICTY added little to this when it stated in the *Tadić* case that 'an [international] armed conflict exists whenever there is a resort to armed force between States',[12] although its later discussion of the conditions for the internationalisation of an internal armed conflict revealed the complexity of this facet of the issue.[13]

One clarification brought about by the inception of the 1949 Fourth Geneva Convention concerns belligerent occupation. The applicability of the laws of war to military occupation not preceded by any clash of arms was problematic until the adoption of Article 6.[14] Before and during the Second World War, there had been several instances in which German troops occupied foreign territory without the slightest resistance on the part of the occupied state. Cases include Austria in 1938, Czechoslovakia in 1938–9 and Denmark in 1940. In the *IG Farben* trial and the *Ministries* trial, two US Military Tribunals took opposite views as to the existence of a war between Germany and Austria and Czechoslovakia, the first finding that the 1907 Hague Convention IV did not apply,[15] the second that it did.[16] Polish courts concluded that neither German nor Soviet forces were occupiers entitled to the benefit of the 1907 Hague Regulations, the first because their invasion of Poland was 'criminal', the second because they were 'allied' troops.[17] Under Article 6 of the 1949 Fourth Geneva Convention, there is little doubt that these cases would be considered to constitute military occupation.[18] Roberts suggests four criteria which can help identify military occupation: (1) a military presence

---

[12] See *The Prosecutor* v. *Tadić* (Decision on the Defence Motion for Interlocutory Appeal on Jurisdiction), 2 Oct. 1995, Case No. IT-94-1-AR72 (Appeals Chamber, ICTY) at 37 para. 70; *The Prosecutor* v. *Tadić* (Opinion and Judgment), 7 May 1997, Case No. IT-94-1-T (Trial Chamber II, ICTY) paras. 569–71.

[13] *The Prosecutor* v. *Tadić* (Appeals Judgment), 15 July 1999, Case No. IT-94-1-A (Appeals Chamber, ICTY) paras. 68–171. This is discussed above, in chapter 2, pp. 91–3.

[14] The governing provision was Art. 42 of the 1907 Hague Regulation ('Territory is considered occupied when it is actually placed under the authority of the hostile army. The occupation extends only to the territory where such authority has been established and can be exercised').

[15] *US* v. *Krauch et al.* (*IG Farben* trial), (1948) 10 L Rep. Trials War Crim. 1, 42 (US Mil. Trib., Nuremberg).

[16] *US* v. *Weizsaecker et al.* (*Ministries* trial), (1949) 16 Ann. Digest Rep. Pub. Int'l L Cases 344, 347 (US Mil. Trib., Nuremberg).

[17] *In re Greiser*, (1946) 13 Ann. Digest Rep. Pub. Int'l L Cases 387, 388 (Supreme Nat'l Trib., Poland); *N v. B*, (1948) 24 Int'l L Rep. 941–3 (Supreme Court, Poland); *Jacub L v. Teofil B*, (1946) 26 Int'l L Rep. 730, 731 (Supreme Court, Poland).

[18] See Jean Pictet ed., *The Geneva Conventions of 12 August 1949 – Commentary on the IV Geneva Convention Relative to the Protection of Civilian Persons in Times of War* (Geneva: ICRC, 1958) 59–60.

in a territory not fully sanctioned by valid agreement; (2) the military
force has displaced the local public order and government; (3) there is
a difference in nationality, allegiance or interests between the occupier
and the population; and (4) emergency rules are needed to protect the
civilian population.[19]

Despite the apparent simplification and lowering of the threshold
of applicability of humanitarian law, nagging indeterminacies still
plague the characterisation of a conflict as an inter-state armed conflict.
Protocol I, apart from Article 1(4) dealing with national liberation conflicts, did nothing to reduce the vagueness of the concept.[20] The illegality
of the use of force in international relations since 1945 has meant that
inter-state armed conflicts, close to traditional international wars, have
become rarer. They have been replaced by other types of conflicts, in
which states other than the one on whose territory the fighting is taking place are more or less directly involved. The conflicts in Vietnam and
Afghanistan provide two examples of situations the characterisation of
which proved difficult and controversial. In the case of Vietnam, the Republic of South Vietnam and the United States characterised the conflict
as international, resulting from the armed aggression from the North.
North Vietnam viewed the conflict as an internal war in the South between Vietcong fighters and the Saigon government, in which it had
no involvement except to defend itself from US attacks in the North.[21]
In the case of Afghanistan, the Soviet Union's position was that it was
assisting the Government of Afghanistan in quelling a rebellion by bandits. The ICRC was of the opinion that the hostilities were at least at the
level of an internal armed conflict. Many other states and the United
Nations considered that there existed an international armed conflict between Afghanistan and the USSR.[22] In a more recent setting, the shifting

[19] Adam Roberts, 'What is Military Occupation?', (1984) 55 Brit. YB Int'l L 249–305
(although no clear distinction is made between 'military' and 'belligerent'
occupations).
[20] Yves Sandoz, 'La place des Protocoles additionnels aux Conventions de Genève du 12
août 1949 dans le droit humanitaire', (1979) 12 Revue des droits de l'homme 135, 140.
[21] See Louis Henkin, How Nations Behave, 2nd edn (New York: Columbia UP, 1979) 306–8;
Katia Boustany, 'La qualification des conflits en droit international public et le
maintien de la paix', (1989–90) 6 Revue québécoise de droit international 38, 46–7; Tom J.
Farer, 'Humanitarian Law and Armed Conflict: Towards the Definition of
"International Armed Conflict"', (1971) 71 Colum. L Rev. 37, 57–60.
[22] See Hans-Peter Gasser, 'Internationalized Non-international Armed Conflicts: Case
Studies of Afghanistan, Kampuchea and Lebanon', (1983) 33 Am. UL Rev. 145, 148–52;
Michael Reisman and James Silk, 'Which Law Applies to the Afghan Conflict?', (1988)
82 Am. J Int'l L 459–96.

nature of the various armed conflicts in the former Yugoslavia demands characterisation in order to decide which set of rules was applicable to each stage of the conflict. That this is a difficult task is shown by the differing opinions offered in the *Tadić* case as to the degree of foreign intervention needed to transform an internal conflict into an international one.[23]

NATIONAL LIBERATION ARMED CONFLICTS

Throughout the decolonisation period following the Second World War, the nature of national liberation struggles was a matter of great debate. Under the impetus of developing and Eastern Bloc states, the UN General Assembly on several occasions during the 1960s and 1970s affirmed the legitimacy of national liberation struggles taking place in territories in Africa under the control of South Africa, Portugal and the United Kingdom, and called for these powers to apply or ensure application of the 1949 Geneva Conventions to these situations.[24] In December 1973, the General Assembly adopted Resolution 3103 (XXVIII), a more general, nearly legislative resolution on the legal status of combatants engaged in national liberation struggles against colonial and alien domination and racist regimes. Its operative paragraph 3 lays down the principle that such conflicts 'are to be regarded as international armed conflicts in the sense of the 1949 Geneva Conventions'.[25] The aim was to remove national liberation armed conflicts from the ambit of common Article 3 of the Geneva Conventions, and create a new category of conflicts assimilable to inter-state armed conflicts.

---

[23] *The Prosecutor* v. *Tadić* (Appeals Judgment), 15 July 1999, Case No. IT-94-1-A (Appeals Chamber, ICTY) paras. 92–7; *The Prosecutor* v. *Tadić* (Opinion and Judgment), 7 May 1997, Case No. IT-94-1-T (Trial Chamber II, ICTY) para. 588; *ibid.* (Separate and Dissenting Opinion of Judge McDonald). See also *The Prosecutor* v. *Kordić* (Judgment), 26 Feb. 2001, Case No. IT-95-14/2-T (Trial Chamber, ICTY) paras. 80–146; Eric David, 'Le Tribunal pénal international pour l'ex-Yougoslavie', [1992] 2 *Revue belge de droit international* 565, 570; William Fenrick, 'In the Field with UNCOE: Investigating Atrocities in the Territory of the Former Yugoslavia', (1995) 34 *Revue de droit militaire et du droit de la guerre* 8–13.

[24] See e.g. General Assembly Resolutions 2383 (XXIII), 2395 (XXIII), 2508 (XXIV), 2547A (XXIV), 2621 (XXV), 2652 (XXV), 2678 (XXV), 2707 (XXV), 2795 (XXVI), 2796 (XXVI), 2871 (XXVI). See Georges Abi-Saab, 'Wars of National Liberation in the Geneva Conventions and Protocols', (1979-IV) 165 *Recueil des cours* 357, 373; Konrad Ginther, 'Liberation Movements', in Bernhardt, [Instalment] 3, at 245, 248.

[25] *Reprinted in* Schindler and Toman, *Laws of Armed Conflict*, at 602–3. See Gérard Cahin and Demis Çarkaçi, 'Les guerres de libération nationale et le droit international', [1976] *Annuaire du Tiers-Monde* 34–56; Gérard Petit, 'Les mouvements de libération nationale et le droit', [1976] *Annuaire du Tiers-Monde* 56–75.

The 1974–7 Geneva Conference was convened in part to deal with the problem of the classification of national liberation armed conflicts, as underlined by the fact that one of the first acts of the Conference was to adopt Resolution 3(I), inviting national liberation movements recognised by regional intergovernmental organisations to participate in the Conference.[26] After much acrimonious debate during the whole duration of the Conference as to the desirability and feasibility of classifying national liberation struggles as international armed conflicts, Articles 1(4) and 96(3) were adopted with only Israel voting against, although there was significant abstention from Western states:[27]

Article 1 . . .

3. This Protocol, which supplements the Geneva Conventions of 12 August 1949 for the protection of war victims, shall apply in the situations referred to in Article 2 common to those Conventions.

4. The situations referred to in the preceding paragraph include armed conflicts in which peoples are fighting against colonial domination and alien occupation and against racist regimes in the exercise of their right of self-determination, as enshrined in the Charter of the United Nations and the Declaration on Principles of International Law concerning Friendly Relations and Co-operation among States in accordance with the Charter of the United Nations.

Article 96 . . .

3. The authority representing a people engaged against a High Contracting Party in an armed conflict of the type referred to in Article 1, paragraph 4, may undertake to apply the Conventions and this Protocol in relation to that conflict by means of a unilateral declaration addressed to the depositary. Such declaration shall, upon its receipt by the depositary, have in relation to that conflict the following effects:

(a) the Conventions and this Protocol are brought into force for the said authority as a Party to the conflict with immediate effect;

(b) the said authority assumes the same rights and obligations as those which have been assumed by a High Contracting Party to the Conventions and this Protocol; and

---

[26] CDDH/SR.3 para. 48. The following were represented at the Conference: the ANC (South Africa), ANCZ (Zimbabwe), FNLA (Angola), FRELIMO (Mozambique), MPLA (Angola), PLO (Palestine), PAC (South Africa), SPUP (Seychelles), SWAPO (South West Africa), ZANU and ZAPU (Zimbabwe). See Richard B. Baxter, 'Humanitarian Law or Humanitarian Politics? The 1974 Diplomatic Conference on Humanitarian Law', (1975) 16 *Harv. Int'l LJ* 1, 9–11.

[27] Art. 1 was adopted in the Plenary Conference by a vote of eighty-seven in favour, one against and eleven abstaining: CDDH/SR.36, 6 *Off. Records* 40–1. Art. 96 was adopted by a vote of ninety-three in favour, one against and two abstaining: CDDH/SR.46 para. 76, 6 *Off. Records* 354.

(c) the Conventions and this Protocol are equally binding upon all Parties to the conflict.[28]

From the text of these provisions can be derived several criteria for the applicability of Protocol I and the 1949 Geneva Conventions to national liberation armed conflicts. These criteria attach first to the type of struggle, and second to the nature of the national liberation movement. National liberation struggles to which rules governing international armed conflicts are applicable must, first, involve a conflict by a people against colonial domination, alien occupation or a racist regime and, second, be in furtherance of that people's right to self-determination. It should be noted at the outset that the notion of 'alien occupation' corresponds to that of 'alien domination' in the UN Declaration on Friendly Relations. It is wider than belligerent occupation as understood in common Article 3 of the 1949 Geneva Conventions, and clearly includes cases such as Namibia, the Western Sahara, or the territories occupied by Israel, which constitute disputable or borderline situations under Article 3.[29]

There is no absolute identity between the notions of self-determination as understood in general international law and national liberation armed conflicts under humanitarian law. In other words, not all peoples fighting to uphold their right to self-determination will be eligible for national liberation movement status and benefit from the protections applicable to an international armed conflict. Only conflicts waged against colonial domination and alien occupation and racist regimes, and not other wars of liberation fought against oppressive regimes on purely political, social or religious grounds, are considered national liberation armed conflicts. Struggles aimed at the partition of a state are generally not authorised by the 1970 Declaration on Friendly Relations, except when the state itself is a plural state and violates the right to self-determination by not according equal and non-discriminatory access to the government.[30] In cases such as Eritrea,

---

[28] A similar provision is found in Art. 7(4) of the 1980 UN Conventional Weapons Convention.

[29] See Abi-Saab, 'Wars of National Liberation' (1979), at 394–6; Christina Murray, 'The Status of the ANC and SWAPO Under International Humanitarian Law', (1983) 100 *South Afr. LJ* 402, 404; Dietrich Schindler, 'The Different Types of Armed Conflicts According to the Geneva Conventions and Protocols', (1979-II) 163 *Recueil des cours* 117, 138.

[30] 'Nothing in the foregoing paragraph shall be construed as authorizing or encouraging any action which would dismember or impair, totally or in part, the territorial integrity or political unity of sovereign and independent States conducting

Biafra (1967–70), Bangladesh (1971), Kurdistan or Kosovo, the struggles may meet the conditions of the Declaration on Friendly Relations as the state can be said to have trenched on the right to equal access to government. Nevertheless, as the oppressive regimes cannot properly be labelled racist, alien or colonial, liberation struggles such as these cannot constitute national liberation armed conflicts as understood under Article 1(4) of Protocol I, and do not call for application of rules governing international armed conflicts.[31] Thus, the characterisation of a state as colonial, alien or racist is a key element of the applicability of humanitarian law to this type of conflict.

In order for the rules governing international armed conflict to apply to national liberation armed conflicts, the authority representing the people in their struggle for self-determination must make a declaration under Article 96(3) of Protocol I, undertaking to apply the Protocol and 1949 Geneva Conventions. Apart from the mechanical and objectively ascertainable transmission of the undertaking to the depository – the Swiss Government – , the eligibility of the authority making the declaration is subjected to further conditions stemming from Article 96(3) and other provisions of the Protocol. First, the authority must be representative of the people. Some have suggested that the mere existence of an armed conflict over a prolonged period of time is probative testimony of the representative character of the national liberation movement because such movements can only survive if supported by the population.[32]

themselves in compliance with the principle of equal rights and self-determination of peoples as described above and thus possessed of a government representing the whole people belonging to the territory without discrimination as to race, creed, or colour': 1970 Declaration on Principles of International Law Concerning Friendly Relations and Co-operation Among States in Accordance with the Charter of the United Nations, General Assembly Res. 2625 (XXV).

[31] See Abi-Saab, 'Wars of National Libration' (1979), at 396–8; Schindler, 'Different Types of Armed Conflicts', at 136–8. The Australian delegation suggested at the Geneva Conference that the wording of Art. 1(4) ('The situations referred to in the preceding paragraph *include* armed conflicts which peoples are fighting . . . ') is not exhaustive and could cover other types of liberation struggles: CDDH/I/SR.22 para. 14. Although a wider application of more elaborate humanitarian norms is always desirable, it seems that the word 'include' is used here because 'armed conflict' under the Protocol and Conventions covers not only national liberation conflicts but also inter-state conflicts. In view of the difficulty and partial success in reaching consensus on the extension of Protocol I to national liberation wars, it seems unlikely that an open door to the applicability of Protocol I to unspecified types of armed conflict was intended by the use of the word 'include'.

[32] See Abi-Saab, 'Wars of National Liberation' (1979), at 413; Fatsah Ouguergouz, 'Guerres de libération nationale en droit humanitaire: Quelques clarifications', in Frits Kalshoven and Yves Sandoz eds., *Implementation of International Humanitarian Law* (Dordrecht: Nijhoff, 1989) 333, 346.

Past events have shown, however, that rebel groups sometimes have survived for many years by coercing the population into giving them support, for instance the Shining Path in Peru, or by receiving substantial support from third states, such as the US-backed *Contras* in Nicaragua. The possibility that several authorities seek to represent a people, as happened in Angola with the FNLA, MPLA and UNITA, can also create problems with regard to representativeness.[33]

A second element attaching to the nature of the authority making a declaration under Article 96(3) is that the national liberation movement which undertakes to apply Protocol I and the Geneva Conventions must possess the characteristics of armed forces as described in Article 43 of the Protocol.[34] The liberation movement must thus be an organised force under responsible command, equipped with an internal disciplinary system charged with, *inter alia*, enforcing compliance with humanitarian law.[35] Only a movement with the institutional capacity to carry out its undertaking to apply the Protocol and Conventions is accorded the standing to wage a national liberation conflict calling for the applicability of rules governing international armed conflicts. The degree of organisation and control exercised over the troops by the command of the liberation movement are likely to be highly subjective and controversial matters. In some cases, the lack of control of an authority is demonstrated by its inability to enforce agreements signed with the enemy effectively. Very often, however, there will be no such clear evidence of the degree of organisation or disorganisation of the national liberation movement, and even a neutral and objective observer – to say nothing of the state itself – will often be hard pressed to make a determination of the eligibility of the movement.

A third element connected to the eligibility of groups for the status of national liberation movement is the necessity or effect of recognition by a regional intergovernmental organisation. Like many of the standards attaching to the legal regime governing national liberation armed conflicts, this element issues from UN practice with respect to participation by liberation movements in the activities of the organisation. Starting in the early 1970s, various UN bodies have invited national liberation

---

[33] Although not acting pursuant to Protocol I, it is interesting to note that the Organization of African Unity has in the past recognised several national liberation movements for one country, for example in Zimbabwe.

[34] See Claude Pilloud et al., *Commentary on the Additional Protocols of 8 June 1977 to the Geneva Conventions of 12 August 1949* (Geneva: Nijhoff, 1987) 55 (hereinafter *ICRC Commentary*).

[35] This is discussed in greater detail in chapter 1, pp. 34–6.

movements to participate as observers in discussions touching on their interests. The issue was first raised in the UN Economic Committee for Africa, where it was resolved to invite movements recognised by the regional organisations in Africa, that is the Organization of African Unity (OAU) and the League of Arab States (LAS). The practice gradually spread to the General Assembly and other UN bodies and specialised agencies.[36]

At the Geneva Conference, Turkey presented an amendment in line with UN practice, whereby Article 1(4) of Protocol I would apply only to liberation movements 'recognized by the regional intergovernmental organization concerned'.[37] The *travaux préparatoires* reveal little of the history of this amendment, but it was never adopted by the First Committee. Nevertheless, when Article 1(4) was voted on at the end of the Conference, Turkey and several other states declared that its application was linked to recognition of the movements by regional organisations.[38] The United Kingdom at signature, and South Korea and Belgium upon ratification, made declarations that recognition by regional organisations 'is to be regarded as necessary' under Article 96(3) of Protocol I.[39] Many writers, however, point to the rejection of the Turkish amendment at the Conference as evidence that such a condition cannot be read into the terms of Protocol I. They argue that recognition of national liberation movements by regional organisations creates a presumption or at least provides some evidence of the eligibility of the movement under Articles 1(4) and 96(3).[40] This is the route taken by Canada in ratifying Protocol I, declaring in a statement of understanding about Article 96(3) that 'the fact that such authority has or has not been recognised as such by an appropriate regional intergovernmental

---

[36] See e.g. General Assembly Resolution 47/29 (1992), 'Observer Status of National Liberation Movements Recognized by the Organization of African Unity and/or by the League of Arab States', UN Doc. A/RES/47/29 (25 Nov. 1992). See generally Claude Lazarus, 'Le statut des mouvements de liberation nationale à l'Organisation des Nations Unies', [1974] *Annuaire français de droit international* 173–200.

[37] CDDH/I/42, 14 March 1974.

[38] Plenary Meeting, 23 May 1977, CDDH/SR.36 para. 121 (Turkey); CDDH/SR.36 Annex, Explanation of vote by Indonesia; Plenary Meeting, 31 May 1977, CDDH/SR.46 Annex, 6 *Off. Records* 341, Explanation of vote by Mauritania and Turkey; Meeting of Committee I, 26 April 1977, CDDH/I/SR.68, 9 *Off. Records* 369, paras. 5 (Indonesia), 15 (Turkey) and 30 (Zaire).

[39] See para. 4 of the South Korean declaration, para. 7 of the Belgian declaration and para. h of the British declaration, *reprinted in* Schindler and Toman, *Laws of Armed Conflict*, at 707–8, 713 and 717. The UK did not mention this element when ratifying Protocol I in January 1998.

[40] See Abi-Saab, 'Wars of National Liberation' (1979), at 408–9; Schindler, 'Different Types of Armed Conflicts', at 142; Ouguergouz, 'Guerres de libération nationale', at 343.

organization is relevant'.[41] Another factor inconsistent with mandatory recognition by regional organisations is that there are many areas of the world not covered by any such organisations.[42] For instance, there was no regional organisation to grant recognition to FRETILIN fighting in East Timor.

Two further elements sometimes have been presented as conditions to the applicability of Protocol I to national liberation armed conflict – first, that the conflict be of an intensity no lower than internal conflicts covered by Protocol II, and second, that the liberation movement exercise control over some part of national territory. The minimum intensity requirement finds its most serious support in a declaration made by the United Kingdom at signature.[43] It has been sharply criticised because it lacks any foundation in the text of Protocol I, and because it introduces a concept of minimal intensity in the context of international armed conflicts, something which has clearly been rejected by customary international law up to now.[44] Territorial control is a condition found in Article 1 of Protocol II, and one which formed part of the now obsolete practice of recognition of belligerency under the laws and customs of war. Writers have rejected this element as inappropriate in the context of modern guerrilla warfare, in which liberation movements often as a matter of tactical advantage do not seek to attach themselves to any specific area. Examples of liberation movements recognised by regional organisations without any control over national territory include the ANC and the PLO. Further, national liberation struggles are grounded in the right of people to self-determination, so that the movements derive their status not from *de facto* control of territory but rather from their representativeness of the people as a whole.[45] In any case, the notions of minimum intensity and territorial control are both extremely fuzzy concepts, to be applied to very fluid sets of facts, underscoring the importance of the act of characterisation.[46]

[41] [1991] 2 Can. Treaty Ser. 182.
[42] See Sandoz, 'La place des Protocoles additionnels', at 139.
[43] See para. (a) of the UK declaration, *reprinted in* Schindler and Toman, *Laws of Armed Conflict*, at 717.
[44] See Abi-Saab, 'Wars of National Liberation' (1979), at 413–14; Ouguergouz, 'Guerres de libération nationale', at 345; Schindler, 'Different Types of Armed Conflicts', at 139–40.
[45] See Pilloud et al., *ICRC Commentary*, at 55; Abi-Saab, 'Wars of National Liberation' (1979), at 410–12; Ouguergouz, 'Guerres de libération nationale', at 344; Schindler, 'State of War', at 6–7.
[46] See Jean J. A. Salmon, 'Some Observations on Characterization in Public International Law', in Antonio Cassese ed., *UN Law/Fundamental Rights* (Alphen aan den Rijn: Sijthoff & Noordhoff, 1979) 3, 5.

The norms defining the conditions of applicability of humanitarian law to national liberation armed conflicts were the object of biting criticism, mostly from Western states, during and after the 1974–7 Geneva Conference. The most serious and recurring criticism was that the norms were simply too vague to provide any real guidance as to their application to real situations. The Federal Republic of Germany did not vote for Article 1(4) because, in its opinion, the provision contained no criteria of a fundamentally legal character, while Italy commented that national liberation conflicts were 'indefinable from the point of view of objective elements'.[47] While these condemnations of the concept of national liberation conflicts appear overstated in view of the preceding discussion, there is nevertheless a significant degree of indeterminacy in the criteria governing the applicability of humanitarian law in such armed conflicts. There is no denying that these rules cannot become applicable 'automatically'. Intervention by an agent is required to characterise the factual and legal nature of the situation. The debate as to the impact of recognition of national liberation movements by regional organisations represents a partial recognition of the critical role of characterisation in this context, but it can be broadened to apply to all other aspects of the application of humanitarian law to this type of conflict.

NON-INTERNATIONAL ARMED CONFLICTS UNDER PROTOCOL II

The regulation of non-international armed conflicts by Protocol II is intimately linked to the regime set up by common Article 3 of the 1949 Geneva Conventions. Indeed, the initial goal of the ICRC in its work leading to the 1974–7 Geneva Conference was to proceed to a revision of Article 3 rather than to create a wholly distinct set of rules. During the two conferences of government experts in 1971 and 1972, however, two contradictory tendencies emerged. For some, the field of application of humanitarian rules governing non-international armed conflicts should be expanded to cover more situations, or at least clarified so as to

---

[47] Plenary Meeting, 23 May 1977, CDDH/SR.36 para. 77 (Italy); CDDH/SR.36 Annex, Explanation of vote by the Federal Republic of Germany. See also Meeting of Committee I, 12 March 1974, CDDH/I/SR.4 para. 10 (Ireland); 25 March 1974, CDDH/I/SR.14. Statements by Canada and the UK to the effect that Art. 96(3) applies only to a national liberation movement 'which is truly such a movement' or which 'genuinely fulfils the criteria' do not do anything to resolve the indeterminacy: Plenary Meeting, 31 May 1977, CDDH/SR.46 Annex, 6 *Off. Records* 361, Explanations of vote by Canada and the UK.

increase their chances of being applied, even at the price of renouncing the expansion of the content of such rules. For others, a narrower field of application was deemed preferable because it would permit the elaboration of a more extensive regime of regulation of non-international armed conflicts. The solution eventually agreed upon was to create two regimes, one – Article 3 – wider in scope but narrower in content, the other – Protocol II – of more limited applicability but containing detailed rules.[48] By definition, then, all conflicts to which Protocol II is applicable are also governed by common Article 3.[49]

The field of application of Protocol II is set out by Article 1, providing:

Article 1 – Material field of application
1. This Protocol, which develops and supplements Article 3 common to the Geneva Conventions of 12 August 1949 without modifying its existing conditions of application, shall apply to all armed conflicts which are not covered by Article 1 of the Protocol Additional to the Geneva Conventions of 12 August 1949, and relating to the Protection of Victims of International Armed Conflicts (Protocol I) and which take place in the territory of a High Contracting Party between its armed forces and dissident armed forces or other organized armed groups which, under responsible command, exercise such control over a part of its territory as to enable them to carry out sustained and concerted military operations and to implement this Protocol.
2. This Protocol shall not apply to situations of internal disturbances and tensions, such as riots, isolated and sporadic acts of violence and other acts of a similar nature, as not being armed conflicts.

The second paragraph marks the lower threshold beneath which the Protocol does not apply. It constitutes not an exception to the definition of conflict covered in paragraph 1 but rather a somewhat redundant description of the negative of the conditions listed in the previous paragraph. Thus, 'isolated and sporadic' stand in contrast to 'sustained and concerted'. By definition, situations not meeting the 'sustained and

---

[48] See ICRC, *Report of the Work of the Conference of Government Experts on the Reaffirmation and Development of International Humanitarian Law of Armed Conflicts, Geneva, 24 May–12 June 1971* (Geneva: ICRC, 1971) 34–6; ICRC, *Report of the Work of the Conference of Government Experts on the Reaffirmation and Development of International Humanitarian Law of Armed Conflicts – Second Session, Geneva, 3 May–3 June 1972* (Geneva: ICRC, 1972) I, 68–9 paras. 2.54–.64; René-Jean Wilhelm, 'Problèmes relatifs à la protection de la personne humaine par le droit international dans les conflits armés ne présentant pas un caractère international', (1972-III) 137 *Recueil des cours* 316, 344–50. Similar tensions were also present at the 1949 Geneva Conference: II-B *Final Record* 76.
[49] See *The Prosecutor v. Musema* (Judgment), 27 Jan. 2000, ICTR-96-13-T (Trial Chamber, ICTR) para. 252; *The Prosecutor v. Rutaganda* (Judgment), 6 Dec. 1999, ICTR-96-3-T (Trial Chamber, ICTR) para. 94.

concerted' conditions listed in paragraph 1 constitute situations not covered by Protocol II. These situations may, however, be governed by common Article 3. The analysis must therefore be framed not as delineating the border between internal disturbances and tensions and non-international armed conflicts, but rather as defining armed conflicts under paragraph 1.[50]

Four closely interconnected conditions for the applicability of Protocol II to a non-international conflict can be extracted from the text of paragraph 1. First, the conflict must involve the state and its armed forces. Although the use by a state of its armed forces does not in itself indicate the existence of an armed conflict, as the other conditions listed in the article must also be present, the quelling of disturbances by a government without intervention by the armed forces cannot constitute a conflict within the meaning of Article 1(1). Further, military operations involving several non-state groups but not the country's armed forces are not covered by Protocol II. The possibility that a conflict of sufficient intensity to warrant application of humanitarian law might take place without the state being involved was deemed academic at the Geneva Conference, despite the opinion of the ICRC which had been involved in several such conflicts.[51] The conflict in Lebanon up to 1983, for example, involved the PLO and other Lebanese armed groups but not the Lebanese state, conclusively showing that high-intensity conflicts can take place without the state's involvement in situations where the state is either too weak or simply non-existent.[52]

A second condition, attaching to the nature of the group fighting the state, requires a degree of organisation and the presence of a responsible command. Without a minimally organised structure, the group will not be in a position to carry out sustained and concerted military operations, exercise control over part of national territory, or to implement the provisions of the Protocol. The ICTR in *Musema* noted that there was no requirement that the group's structure mirror the hierarchical organisation found in most armies.[53]

The element of organisation overlaps to a certain extent with the third condition requiring that the belligerent group be able to carry

---

[50] See Mohammed El Kouhene, *Les garanties fondamentales de la personne en droit humanitaire et droits de l'homme* (Dordrecht: Nijhoff, 1986) 78–81; Pilloud et al., *ICRC Commentary*, at 1354–5.

[51] Pilloud et al., *ICRC Commentary*, at 1351.

[52] See Boustany, 'La qualification des conflits', at 42–3.

[53] *The Prosecutor* v. *Musema* (Judgment), 27 Jan. 2000, ICTR-96-13-T (Trial Chamber, ICTR) para. 257.

out sustained and concerted military operations. This underlines both the collective character of armed conflicts, in contrast to the isolated and sporadic acts mentioned in paragraph 2 of Article 1, and the fact that hostilities involving the use of weapons must be occurring in order for the conflict to be regulated by humanitarian law. The 'sustained' and 'concerted' criteria were adopted instead of those of intensity and duration of military operations. The latter were thought too subjective and specific, a state being able to deny easily that the conflict possessed such characteristics. Interestingly, it was thought that a vaguer criterion in this context would hamper possible state attempts to deny that the group met this condition. Indeterminacy is here considered as a desirable quality for the legal norm.[54]

Finally, the fourth condition states that the rebel group must exercise control over part of national territory. This is seen by the ICTR in the *Musema* judgment as equivalent to the 'domination' of some territory by the insurgents.[55] This requirement, based on the recognition of belligerency under the laws and customs of war, had been abandoned during the preparatory expert conferences because of the perceived reluctance of states to admit to the loss of control over part of their territory during an internal strife. For instance, France acknowledged in 1956 that common Article 3 of the Geneva Conventions was applicable to the Algerian war, but never conceded that it did not control the Algerian territory in its entirety.[56] As mentioned in the context of national liberation armed conflicts, the notion of 'control' over territory is in itself very fuzzy and consequently difficult to apply. The condition nevertheless resurfaced at the 1974–7 Geneva Conference as states felt that it constituted a necessary facet of the rebel group's ability to carry out sustained and concerted military operations and also to implement

---

[54] See ICRC, *1972 Conference of Experts*, at 68 paras. 2.54–.59; Pilloud et al., *ICRC Commentary*, at 1353; Wilhelm, 'Problèmes relatifs', at 347–9; Charles Zorgbibe, 'De la théorie classique de la reconnaissance de belligérance à l'Article 3 des Conventions de Genève', in *Droit humanitaire et conflits armés – Actes du colloque du 28 au 30 janvier 1970, Université libre de Bruxelles* (Brussels: Ed. U de Bruxelles, 1976) 83, 91.

[55] *The Prosecutor v. Musema* (Judgment), 27 Jan. 2000, ICTR-96-13-T (Trial Chamber, ICTR) para. 258.

[56] See Wilhelm, 'Problèmes relatifs', at 338. Section 1808(2) Note 6 of the *Canadian Forces Law of Armed Conflict Manual (Second Draft)* (Ottawa: Dept. Nat'l Defence, 1984) went so far as to demand that the insurgent organisation be established in a fixed known place, or practically the establishment of the seat of a provisional government. That element was dropped from the final version of the Manual adopted in 1999: Judge Advocate General, *The Law of Armed Conflict at the Operational and Tactical Level* B-GG-005-027/AF-020 (Ottawa: Dept Nat'l Defence, 1999) s. 17–14 (hereinafter *1999 Canadian War Manual*).

humanitarian rules contained in Protocol II.[57] As noted in relation to national liberation armed conflicts, territorial control may in reality not be sought by an insurgent group using guerrilla warfare tactics. Guatemala provides a recent example where, despite the fact that insurgents carried out sustained and concerted military operations, no part of the national territory was under their control, making Protocol II inapplicable to the conflict.[58]

The global effect of all these conditions is to curtail Protocol II's field of application severely. In defending the idea of state sovereignty in the context of non-international armed conflicts, governments in effect have required that the belligerent party possess all the characteristics of a state – organisation, population and territory – before accepting any role for international humanitarian law.[59] Only the rather rare 'classic' civil war scenarios such as the 1936–9 Spanish civil war, the war in El Salvador during the 1980s or perhaps the recent conflict in Bosnia-Herzegovina will meet these stringent conditions. Protocol II can be considered a regression, given that it requires basically the same conditions as did recognition of belligerency, but without triggering the full application of all humanitarian rules for international armed conflicts. The key difference is that while recognition of belligerency depended on the state's characterisation of the conflict, Protocol II presents the applicability criteria as objectively ascertainable.[60] In other words, the Protocol leaves open the issue of who is to make the determinative characterisation of the situation.

INTERNAL ARMED CONFLICTS UNDER COMMON ARTICLE 3

As mentioned earlier, the debate at the 1974–7 Geneva Conference as to the most desirable route to expand humanitarian regulation of internal strife resulted in the creation of a regime distinct from common Article 3 of the 1949 Geneva Conventions, of narrower applicability but broader content. Presumably, then, the field of application of common Article 3

---

[57] Pilloud et al., *ICRC Commentary*, at 1352.

[58] See Adama Dieng, 'La mise en oeuvre du droit international humanitaire: Les infractions et les sanctions, ou quand la pratique désavoue les textes', in *Law in Humanitarian Crises – How Can International Humanitarian Law be Made Effective in Armed Conflict?* (Luxembourg: European Communities, 1995) I, 311, 340.

[59] El Kouhene, *Les garanties fondamentales*, at 76.

[60] See *The Prosecutor v. Musema* (Judgment), 27 Jan. 2000, ICTR-96-13-T (Trial Chamber, ICTR) paras. 252 and 255; *The Prosecutor v. Rutaganda* (Judgment), 6 Dec 1999, ICTR-96-3-T (Trial Chamber, ICTR) para. 94.

is wider than that of Protocol II, and covers situations which would not be classified as armed conflict under the Protocol. This is far from certain, however, as the relation between the scope of Article 3 and that of Protocol II was not clearly articulated at the Geneva Conference, apart from a statement in Article 1(1) of the Protocol to the effect that it 'develops and supplements Article 3...without modifying its existing conditions of application'. We must therefore turn to Article 3 itself for clues as to its field of application.

Common Article 3 was one of the most heatedly debated provisions at the 1949 Geneva Conference. It was at the time of its inception far from a simple codification of accepted international law, as there was no clear principle that all internal armed conflicts were matters of international concern.[61] The ICRC draft presented at the 1949 Conference simply proposed that the Conventions be applicable to both sides in case of an armed conflict not of an international character, but no consensus could be found in support of that principle. A Working Party of the Special Committee of the Joint Committee was created to prepare proposals defining and limiting the types of internal situations to which the Conventions would be applicable.[62] No agreement could be reached and eventually an alternative solution was adopted, narrowing not the field of application of Article 3 but rather its normative content, limiting rules applicable in internal armed conflict to a bare minimum.[63]

Although none of the proposals defining non-international armed conflict attracted sufficient consensus, the ICRC commentary on the Conventions lists them as 'convenient criteria' to determine whether there exists a non-international armed conflict.[64] They include: explicit or implicit recognition of belligerency or insurgency by the state or by the UN; organisation of the insurgent forces under a responsible command exercising control over a determined area of national territory in which the group has the means to respect and ensure respect of the Conventions; existence of a civil insurgent authority possessing the

---

[61] The supra-national dimension of the Spanish civil war certainly was the main influence on the internationalisation of civil strife. See II-B *Final Record* 9–15, 40–8, 75–9, 82–4, 90, 93–5 and 97–102; Geoffrey Best, *War and Law Since 1945* (Oxford: Oxford UP, 1994) 168–79; D. Elder, 'The Historical Background of Common Article 3 of the Geneva Conventions of 1949', (1979) 11 *Case W Res. J Int'l L* 37; Farer, 'Humanitarian Law', at 43–8.

[62] II-B *Final Record* 46–7.

[63] The same approach was incorporated into Art. 19 of the 1954 Hague Convention on Cultural Property.

[64] Pictet, IV, at 35–6.

characteristics of a state, exercising *de facto* authority over a population and territory; acceptance by the insurgent of the rules of the Geneva Conventions; and use of military force by the state to try to quell the insurgency.[65]

The criteria put forward by the ICRC in its commentary, however convenient, can be seriously misleading. The criteria were elaborated in the context of an attempt to define armed conflict not of an international character to which the Conventions as a whole would be applicable. A decision was made at the Conference not to make the Conventions applicable to a narrow type of internal conflict, but rather to adopt a widely applicable but substantively limited regime. There is therefore no justification for the adoption of the elements of a restrictive definition of internal armed conflict in the context of Article 3. Indeed, it seems illogical to list as relevant criteria that the insurgents possess an organisation enabling them to respect and ensure respect for the Conventions and that the insurgent authority agree to be bound by the Conventions, when the Conventions are not applicable to internal conflicts under Article 3. State recognition of belligerency or insurgency is also problematic, given that under the traditional laws and customs of war it leads to the full application of rules regulating armed conflict, and not merely the basic elements listed in Article 3.[66]

Farer notes that the only assured thing about the notion of internal armed conflict in common Article 3 is that no one can say with assurance what it means.[67] Although the text of Article 3 is extremely open-ended, it does refer to 'armed conflicts', so that a minimum intensity requirement was certainly intended. Conflicts imply the presence of military operations on the part of both sides. The non-applicability of the provision to internal disturbances and tensions was one element

---

[65] See: II-B *Final Record* 121; Farer, 'Humanitarian Law', at 48. The criteria were quoted with approval by the ICTR in *The Prosecutor* v. *Akayesu* (Judgment), 2 Sept. 1998, Case No. ICTR-96-4-T (Trial Chamber I, ICTR) 124–5. The same were applied by the Cour militaire de Bruxelles in *Ministère public et Centre pour l'égalité des chances et la lutte contre le racisme* v. *C ... et B ...* , Judgment of 17 Dec. 1997, [1998] *Journal des tribunaux* 286, 289, to deny the applicability of common Art. 3 to Somalia in 1993 and thus acquit Belgian peacekeepers of accusations of war crimes against civilians.

[66] As noted by Ford, 'the advantage of not giving any definition at all is that the risk of giving too narrow a definition is avoided': W. J. Ford, 'Resistance Movements and International Law', (1967–8) 79 *Int'l Rev. Red Cross* 515, 517. The ICRC commentary does add that these conditions are not indispensable, given that few states would argue for a right to torture or mutilate bandits, and that states should observe these minimum rules at all times: Pictet, IV, at 36.

[67] Farer, 'Humanitarian Law', at 43.

agreed upon at the 1949 Geneva Conference.[68] Closely linked to the element of intensity is the requirement that the insurgent group be organised under responsible command. Without minimal organisation and command structure, the group would not possess the ability to implement the basic humanitarian rules contained in Article 3. The ICTY in the *Tadić* case identified these two elements, minimum intensity of the conflict and organisation of the parties, as the key criteria signalling the existence of an internal armed conflict.[69]

The need for the state to grant some form of recognition to the insurgents does not follow from the text or the spirit of the provision. Recognition is an essentially discretionary power of the state, hardly compatible with the obligatory application of humanitarian law.[70] Contrary to Protocol II, the state does not have to be involved in any way for Article 3 to apply. Internal strife involving several non-governmental factions, such as the ones which occurred in Lebanon or Somalia, is covered by Article 3.[71] Finally, control of a determined portion of national territory by the insurgents is not a necessary condition for the application of Article 3. Territorial control was an element of the recognition of belligerency, built on the notion of a full application of the laws and customs of war when the insurgent side could be assimilated in a large measure to a state-like entity.[72] Instances of internal armed conflict

---

[68] See Schindler, 'Different Types of Armed Conflicts', at 146; Wilhelm, 'Problèmes relatifs', at 352; Charles Zorgbibe, 'Le caractère armé des conflits', in *Droit humanitaire et conflits armés*, at 93, 94–9.

[69] *The Prosecutor v. Tadić* (Decision on the Defence Motion for Interlocutory Appeal on Jurisdiction), 2 Oct. 1995, Case No. IT-94-1-AR72 (Appeals Chamber, ICTY) 37–8 para. 70; *The Prosecutor v. Tadić* (Opinion and Judgment), 7 May 1997, Case No. IT-94-1-T (Trial Chamber II, ICTY) para. 564.

[70] El Kouhene, *Les garanties fondamentales*, at 73; Victor Duculesco, 'Effet de la reconnaissance de l'état de belligérance par les tiers, y compris les organisations internationales, sur le statut juridique des conflits armés à caractère non-international', (1975) 79 *Revue générale de droit international public* 125, 140; Partsch, 'Armed Conflict', at 26. Lauterpacht argued for the development of a duty on the part of the state to grant belligerent or insurgent recognition: Hersch Lauterpacht, *Recognition in International Law* (Cambridge: Cambridge UP, 1948) 175–6 and 240–6; Wilhelm, 'Problèmes relatifs', at 326.

[71] *Tadić* (Interlocutory Appeal), at 37 para. 70 ('an armed conflict exists whenever there is a resort to armed force between States or protracted armed violence between governmental authorities and organised armed groups or between such groups within a State'). See Michael B. Akehurst, 'Civil War', in Rudolf Bernhardt ed., [Instalment] 3 *Encyclopedia of Public International Law* (Amsterdam: North-Holland, 1982) 88; Michael Bothe, 'Völkerrechtliche Aspekte des Angola Konflikts', (1977) 37 *Zeitschrift für ausländische öffentliches Recht und Völkerrecht* 572, 588–92.

[72] See Wilhelm, 'Problèmes relatifs', at 320.

involving large-scale military operations but not fixed territorial bases, for example the first phase of the Algerian conflict or of the Vietnam war, reveal that there is no necessary correlation between intensity and control of territory.[73] If the insurgents do control part of the national territory, as the Bosnian Serbs did in the *Republika Srpska*, it will simply make it harder to dispute that an internal armed conflict is indeed taking place, in addition possibly to calling for the application of Protocol II.[74]

The vagueness in the conditions of applicability of Article 3 has meant that the provision was applied in a rather discretionary way by states. Article 3 was deemed applicable by the concerned state in Guatemala (1954 and 1994), Algeria (after 1956), Lebanon (1958), Yemen (1962–7), the Dominican Republic (1965), Vietnam (after 1965), Nigeria (1967–70), Chile (1971), Uruguay (1972) and the Portuguese territories in Africa after 1974. On the other hand, in a few of many examples, the concerned state refused to apply it in Kenya (1954), Cyprus (1955), Algeria (before 1956), Malaysia (1956), Indochina (1957–65), Northern Ireland (from 1971), the Philippines (from 1972), Afghanistan (from 1981), El Salvador (after 1983) and Chechnya (1994–5).[75] The uncertain state of the law is partly due to the unsettled nature of the criteria governing the applicability of Article 3, but also to the absence of discussion of the effect of divergent characterisations by the state, the insurgent group and other agents.

There are some clearly identifiable areas of indeterminacy in the applicability criteria of each of the four categories of armed conflict governed by international humanitarian law. This is compounded to some degree by the distinction introduced in Article 8(2)(f) of the ICC Statute between short and protracted internal armed conflicts, a distinction which does not mirror that between Protocol II and common

[73] See El Kouhene, *Les garanties fondamentales*, at 75 n. 165.
[74] In *Tadić* (Judgment) at para. 564, the Trial Chamber noted that the 'Bosnian Serb forces occupied and operated from a determinate, if not definite, territory'.
[75] See Eric David, *Principes de droit des conflits armés* (Brussels: Bruylant, 1994) 113–14; El Kouhene, *Les garanties fondamentales*, at 74–9; Heather A. Wilson, *International Law and the Use of Force by National Liberation Movements* (Oxford: Clarendon, 1988) 124–5; Dieng, 'La mise en oeuvre', at 339–40; Tarcisio Gazzini, 'Consideration of the Conflict in Chechnya', (1996) 17 *Hum. Rts LJ* 93; David Forsythe, 'Legal Management of Internal War: The 1977 Protocol on Non-international Armed Conflicts', (1978) 72 *Am. J Int'l L* 272, 275–6; Reisman and Silk, 'Afghan Conflict', at 479; Howard J. Taubenfeld, 'The Applicability of the Laws of War in Civil War', in John Norton Moore ed., *Law and Civil War in the Modern World* (Baltimore: Johns Hopkins Press, 1974) 499, 509–12; Examination by the UN Human Rights Committee of periodic reports by El Salvador and Afghanistan: UN Doc. CCPR/C/SR.485 para. 5 (1983); CCPR/C/SR.608 para. 25 (1985).

Article 3. The jurisprudence of the ICTY and ICTR and the ICC Statute have eliminated some differences among the regimes associated with each category of armed conflict, for example the expansion of war criminality to all types of conflicts; fundamental differences remain, however, making it as essential as ever to characterise situations of armed conflict. The indeterminacy of norms and the multiplication of categories of armed conflict have made it more critical than ever to take a closer look at the identity of the authors of characterisations of a situation as an armed conflict and the effects of such multiple characterisations under humanitarian law.

State of emergency under human rights law

The three most important human rights conventions, as well as some other human rights instruments, contain provisions allowing for derogation from the majority of fundamental rights during a state of emergency.[76] The availability of derogation from all but a few rights has also been considered implied in some instruments not explicitly providing for such a possibility, for example in the labour conventions adopted under the aegis of the ILO and under customary human rights.[77]

---

[76] Art. 4, International Covenant on Civil and Political Rights; Art. 15, European Convention on Human Rights; Art. 27, American Convention on Human Rights; Art. 30, European Social Charter, 18 Oct. 1961, *reprinted in* Ian Brownlie ed., *Basic Documents on Human Rights*, 3rd edn (Oxford: Clarendon, 1992) 363. The concept of state of emergency was created in the French Law of 8 July 1791, providing that individual rights entrenched in the Declaration of the Rights of Man and the Citizen could be suspended in times of war: Daniel Hugo Martin, 'La protección de los derechos humanos frente a la suspención de los garantías constitucionales o "estado de sitio"', OAS Doc. OEA/Ser.L/V/II.15, doc. 12 (1966), in *The Organization of American States and Human Rights* (Washington DC: OAS, 1972) 122, 124.

[77] See Jaime Oráa, *Human Rights in States of Emergency in International Law* (Oxford: Clarendon, 1992) 54; '[First] Interim Report of the Committee on the Enforcement of Human Rights Law', in International Law Association, *Report of the 62nd Conference, Seoul, 24–30 August 1986* (London: ILA, 1987) 108, 140–1; Fatsah Ouguergouz, 'L'absence de clause de dérogation dans certains traités relatifs aux droits de l'homme: Les réponses du droit international général', (1994) 98 *Revue générale de droit international public* 289–334. The Inter-American Commission on Human Rights applied the rules governing states of emergency to Chile and Paraguay despite the fact that neither country is a party to the American Convention on Human Rights: Inter-American Commission on Human Rights, 'Report on the Situation of Human Rights in Chile' (1974) 212; I/A CHR, 'Report on the Situation of Human Rights in Paraguay' (1978) 14; [1974] *Ann. Rep. I/A Com'n Hum. Rts* 36. Note, however, the refusal by the African Commission on Human and Peoples' Rights to find an implied emergency derogation clause in the African Charter: *Commission nationale des droits de l'homme et des libertés v. Chad*, Comm. 74/92, 11 Oct. 1995, para. 21, *reprinted in* (1997) 18 *Hum. Rts LJ* 34.

Resort to derogation regimes turns on a characterisation of a situation as a state of emergency, performed primarily by the state, but possibly also by other actors concerned with compliance with human rights, for instance other states or international organisations. The risk of conflicting characterisations thus exists in human rights law as it does in humanitarian law. The ensuing discussion will focus on *de jure* states of emergency, that is instances in which the state has proceeded to characterise the situation as such, and not on the serious problems raised by *de facto* states of emergency, in which the state does not acknowledge that special circumstances exist. *De facto* states of emergency are problems of enforcement rather than applicability, because the state does not challenge the relevant and binding nature of human rights norms, but rather maintains that they have not been trenched upon.[78] *De jure* states of emergency can be particularly pernicious because they rely on a 'loophole' of human rights law, the legitimacy of which is not discussed – nor approved – here, legally condoning violations of individual rights by the state. Likewise, the list of non-derogable rights varies from treaty to treaty, meaning that under some regimes individuals are legally better protected than under some others. Such variations are extremely significant but leave untouched the question of how to control derogation in cases where a treaty does explicitly or implicitly permit it.

Some of the bodies overseeing the enforcement of human rights instruments have developed criteria attempting to delineate the limits of what may properly be labelled a state of emergency. The evolution of these criteria was originally guided by the European Commission and Court of Human Rights, for reasons owing to the earlier inception of the European Convention and creation of enforcement organs. The Inter-American Commission on Human Rights has added to that body of law since the 1960s, while the UN Human Rights Committee has yet to develop criteria of its own or state its agreement with the criteria issued from the work of the other two institutions. Given the similarity of norms found in the three conventions, it seems likely that the criteria will be broadly applicable to all of them.[79]

---

[78] For instance, the Turkish Government did not declare a state of emergency in Cyprus after its 1974 invasion of the northern part of the island, although the facts would certainly have supported such a characterisation. As a result, the European Convention is unquestionably fully applicable in the Turkish Cypriot territory: ILA, 'First Report', at 163 n. 13.

[79] See Dominic McGoldrick, *The Human Rights Committee* (Oxford: Clarendon, 1991) 303; Daniel O'Donnell, *Protección internacional de los derechos humanos* (Lima: Comisión andina

There are four general criteria identifying a situation which may properly be characterised as a state of emergency. These criteria must be
distinguished from other elements attaching not to the nature of the
situation but to the lawfulness of measures adopted by the state, for instance the conditions of proportionality, non-discrimination or respect
for other international obligations of the state.[80]

The first identifying feature of a state of emergency is that, as indicated by its very name, it relates to an exceptional situation of an essentially temporary character. This was problematic in a certain number of
Latin American countries, in which the Inter-American Commission on
Human Rights found that the state of emergency had been institutionalised or even constitutionalised, as done for example in the Chilean
Constitution of 1980.[81] The situation in Northern Ireland over the last
three decades can also be seen as a quasi-permanent state of emergency,
although the notice of derogation was withdrawn by the United Kingdom between August 1984 and December 1988.[82] Situations of a permanent or quasi-permanent character, such as the low level of economic
development, should not by themselves provide sufficient ground for a
declaration of a state of emergency.[83]

A second criterion stems from the use of the word 'threaten' in the
provisions governing states of emergency in all three human rights
treaties. It underscores the necessarily imminent character of the
situation. In other words, the danger to the community must be highly
probable in order to justify derogations from human rights. 'Imminent'
does not mean 'actual', however, and a potentiality is sufficient. This
is supported by Article 30 (Part V) of the Appendix to the European
Social Charter, specifying that 'the term "in time of war or other public

de juristas, 1988) 399. As discussed below, there is no absolute identity between the
norms in the three human rights conventions, so that some of the finer details of the
European Convention, for example, might not be totally transposable to the American
Convention.

[80] The distinction is not clearly drawn, for instance, in the ILA's first report on states of
emergency. 'First Report', at 115. Other elements attaching not to the definition of the
state of emergency but to the mechanisms by which the state may invoke such an
emergency, for example public proclamation by the state and notification to the
appropriate human rights body, also fall beyond the scope of the present study.

[81] See Inter-American Commission on Human Rights, 'Report on the Situation of Human
Rights in Chile', OAS Doc. OEA/Ser.L/V/II/66, doc. 17 (27 Sept. 1985).

[82] See *Brannigan and McBride* v. *United Kingdom* (A/258-B), (1993) 17 Eur. Hum. Rts Rep. 539,
570 (Op. of the Court) and 591–3 (Diss. Op. Makarczy). One could also mention the
state of emergency in Zambia between 1964 and 1991.

[83] Guy Tremblay, 'Les situations d'urgence qui permettent en droit international de
suspendre les droits de l'homme', (1977) 18 *Cahiers de droit* 3, 20.

emergency" shall be so understood as to cover also the *threat* of war'.[84]
Assessment of what constitutes an imminent threat to the state is a
highly subjective operation, compounded by the fact that the non-
realisation of the danger does not necessarily deny the prior existence
of a real and serious threat justifying the declaration of a state of
emergency.[85] The identity of the author of the characterisation becomes
in that context crucial, often leading to calls for greater deference to
the state's evaluation on the part of human rights bodies.

Thirdly, in a manner reminiscent of the elements differentiating
armed conflict from internal disturbances in humanitarian law, there is
a collective side to an emergency threatening the life of the nation.
Unlike humanitarian law, however, human rights norms concerning
states of emergency do not consider the collective or organised *source*
of the emergency, but rather its collective *effect* on the community and
the state. As a declaration of state of emergency indiscriminately affects
the rights of all individuals, and not only of those possibly at the source
of the emergency, the latter must have a magnitude sufficient to affect
the community as a whole. This does not imply that emergencies limited
to a portion of national territory cannot lawfully create a state of emergency, but rather that a limited emergency must be answered with a
circumscribed state of emergency. For example, if acts of terrorism were
limited to the territory of Northern Ireland, then a state of emergency
in the United Kingdom as a whole would not be justified.[86]

The fourth and final criterion is perhaps the most fundamental,
attaching to the nature of the emergency as a threat to the life of the
nation. In this respect, the exception is wider under the American Convention on Human Rights than under the European Convention and
the Political Covenant, defining a state of emergency as a threat to
the 'independence or security of a State Party', while the two other
instruments speak of a threat to the 'life of the nation'.[87] As noted by

[84] Emphasis in the original. See *The Greek Case*, (1969) 12 YB Eur. Conv. Hum. Rts 71–2
paras. 152–4 (Eur. Com'n Hum. Rts).

[85] Rusen Ergec, *Les droits de l'homme à l'épreuve des circonstances exceptionnelles. Etude sur
l'article 15 de la Convention européenne des droits de l'homme* (Brussels: Bruylant/U de
Bruxelles, 1987) 148–50.

[86] See Aristidis Calogeropoulos-Stratis, *Droit humanitaire et droits de l'homme: La protection
de la personne en conflits armés* (Geneva: Institut universitaire de hautes études
internationales, 1980) 81; 'The Siracusa Principles on the Limitation and Derogation
Provisions in the International Covenant on Civil and Political Rights', (1985) 7 *Hum.
Rts Quart.* 3, 9 (Principle 51); Ronald St J. Macdonald, 'Derogations under Article 15 of
the European Convention on Human Rights', (1997) 36 *Colum. J Transnat'l L* 225, 239–40.

[87] Calogeropoulos-Stratis, *Droit humanitaire*, at 84; Ergec, *Droits de l'homme*, at 136.

some members of the European Commission of Human Rights in the 'Lawless' case, a threat to the life of the nation does not refer merely to the possible disintegration of the state following total war or like situations, but also to a less extreme crisis threatening 'the organised life of the community which composes the State'.[88] It implies that the ordinary mechanisms of the state are overwhelmed by the emergency, and that the continued stability of the community is jeopardised in a fundamental way.[89]

The nature of the emergencies which may cause a state of emergency is extremely varied, from war to natural disasters, perhaps even including acute economic crisis.[90] In *Iversen v. Norway*, the Norwegian Government argued that the limited number of dentists in outlying areas of the country created an emergency situation affecting the life of the community, justifying a derogation under Article 15. Although the argument was not addressed by the majority of the European Commission of Human Rights, two members did accept the validity of the claim.[91] Principle 27 of the Siracusa Principles even includes a threat to public morals as a possible cause of a state of emergency.[92] New kinds of threats develop constantly, for example drug trafficking, which has become one of the leading justifications for states of emergency in Latin America in the last few years.[93] Few restrictions as to the nature of the emergency can in fact be found in the work of human rights bodies, an acknowledgment of the unforeseeable and versatile character of emergencies.

As an eminently indeterminate notion, the state of emergency lends itself easily to abuse by states anxious to provide a facade of legality for the perpetration of human rights violations in their country. Particularly in the Latin American context, it has served perhaps more as a tool to breach human rights than as an instrument to protect democracy

---

[88] 'Lawless' case, (1959) Ser. B 1960–1, at 81–2 (Eur. Com'n Hum. Rts).

[89] Ergec, *Droits de l'homme*, at 137–8.

[90] See O'Donnell, *Protección internacional*, at 399; ILA, 'First Report', at 113; Macdonald, 'Derogations', at 235–7; Nicole Questiaux, 'Study of the Implication for Human Rights of Recent Developments on Situations known as States of Siege or Emergency', UN Doc. E/CN.4/Sub.2/1982/15 (1982) para. 28.

[91] (1963) 6 YB Eur. Conv. Hum. Rts 279, 328–30; Tremblay, 'Situations d'urgence', at 20–1.

[92] 'Siracusa Principles', at 6.

[93] For example, the state of emergency declared by Bolivia on 26 August 1986. See ILA, 'Second Interim Report of the Committee on the Enforcement of Human Rights Law', in International Law Association, *Report of the 63rd Conference, Warsaw, 21–27 August 1988* (London: ILA, 1988) 129, 154 n. 131.

and political stability.[94] A resolution – or at least reduction – of the indeterminacy at the normative level, by way of more specific criteria delineating precisely what constitutes a state of emergency, seems hardly compatible with the exceptional nature of emergency situations, by definition adverse to systematic treatment.[95] An overly specific definition of the state of emergency is more likely to be imperfect and lead to the violation of the derogation regime than to bring a solution to the problem. Perhaps for this reason, discussions on the control of derogation under states of emergency has tended to focus on the identity of the agent performing the characterisation of the situation, be it the state, specialised agencies or political bodies. As human rights impose on the state obligations *erga omnes* the application of which is a matter of concern for the international community as a whole, there is a possibility of overlapping and even conflicting characterisations, and consequently a need to examine the validity and relative legal effect of these characterisations.

Human rights and humanitarian law constitute two wholly independent systems, allowing for the possibility of concurrent application to the same situation or, less happily, of the inapplicability of both systems. This results not only from the essentially constitutive effect of characterisation of a situation as a state of emergency, whereby much depends on the state's evaluation of the situation, but also from a normative gap between the concepts of armed conflict and state of emergency. There is no link between the notions, so that a situation in which derogation from human rights is permissible does not necessarily call for the application of humanitarian law. As noted earlier, the concept of state of emergency in human rights law explicitly includes a threat of war, to which humanitarian law is not applicable. This has led to the development of minimum humanitarian standards which would fill the gap.[96] Conversely, an armed conflict can be of limited scope and importance,

---

[94] O'Donnell, *Protección internacional*, at 397.

[95] Ergec, *Droits de l'homme*, at 135 ('Les situations exceptionnelles comportent un degré d'imprévisibilité rebelle à toute systématisation circonstanciée').

[96] See Human Rights Commission, Resolution 1997/21; 'Declaration of Minimum Humanitarian Standards', UN Doc. E/CN.4/1996/80; UN Secretary-General, 'Report on Minimum Humanitarian Standards', UN Doc. E/CN.4/1998/87, and follow-up reports E/CN.4/1999/92, E/CN.4/2000/94 and E/CN.4/2001/91; Calogeropoulos-Stratis, *Droit humanitaire*, at 96; Ergec, *Droits de l'homme*, at 126; P. van Dijk and G. J. H. van Hoof, *Theory and Practice of the European Convention on Human Rights*, 3rd edn (The Hague: Kluwer, 1998) 735; Christina M. Cerna, 'Human Rights in Armed Conflict: Implementation of International Humanitarian Norms by Regional Intergovernmental

for instance a border incident, and not constitute an emergency threatening the life of the nation. In such a case, both human rights and humanitarian law would be fully applicable.

Human rights and humanitarian law are connected by the reference in human rights derogation provisions to 'other obligations under international law', which include humanitarian law, and the protection of the right to life 'except in respect of deaths resulting from lawful acts of war'. It follows that the legality of certain acts committed during a state of emergency which is also an armed conflict will have to be assessed according to humanitarian law, even from within the perspective of the application of human rights law.[97] That being said, the distinct thresholds for states of emergency and armed conflict remain disconnected, and the conclusion as to one does not necessarily affect the other.

Despite efforts by writers and international bodies to develop sets of norms defining as precisely as possible the concepts of armed conflict and state of emergency, indeterminacies remain important in both human rights and humanitarian law, leaving a wide margin of appreciation to assess facts and law. The indeterminacy of these rules, however, does not necessarily imply that the state or other agents are at liberty to block the application of human rights or humanitarian law. Indeterminacy simply means that, where a situation falls within the significant grey zone in the definitions of armed conflict and state of emergency, several reasonable conclusions as to its nature may in good faith be derived from norms and facts. Conflicts may arise from these multiple lawful characterisations. Ideally, a mechanism should then intervene to resolve the indeterminacy and provide a definitive answer as to the nature of the situation. Such mechanisms are commonly used in conjunction with extremely indeterminate norms, for instance the Security Council's power

Human Rights Bodies', in Kalshoven and Sandoz, *Implementation*, at 31, 56 (arguing that minimum humanitarian law norms apply in all cases of state of emergency); Peter Kooijmans, 'In the Shadowland Between Civil War and Civil Strife: Some Reflections on the Standard-Setting Process', in Astrid Delissen and Gerard Tanja eds., *Humanitarian Law of Armed Conflict: Challenges Ahead – Essays in Honour of Frits Kalshoven* (Dordrecht: Nijhoff, 1991) 225; Theodor Meron, 'On the Inadequate Reach of Humanitarian and Human Rights Law and the Need for a New Instrument', (1983) 77 *Am. J Int'l L* 589–606; Hernán Montealegre, 'The Compatibility of a State Party's Derogations under Human Rights Instruments with its Obligations under Protocol II and Common Article 3', (1983) 33 *Am. UL Rev.* 41, 43–4.

[97] See ICJ, *Advisory Opinion on the Legality of the Threat or Use of Nuclear Weapons*, 8 July 1996, para. 25; Inter-American Commission on Human Rights, 'Third Report on the Situation of Human Rights in Colombia', OAS Doc. OEA/Ser. L/V/II doc. 102 (1999) Ch. IV, para. 12. This is discussed below, in chapter 7, pp. 332–7.

to determine the existence of a threat to international peace and security under Chapter VII of the United Nations Charter. In human rights and humanitarian law, however, few mechanisms are given a broad competence to label situations as armed conflicts or states of emergency. The relative effect of characterisations by various actors must be assessed, in order to determine whether there is a hierarchy among these divergent opinions, or whether another type of solution must be found. This in turn will inform the wider analysis of the similarities of solutions found in applying the concepts of armed conflict and state of emergency in humanitarian law and human rights.

7   Legal effect of characterisation

In considering the indeterminacy of the definitions of armed conflict and state of emergency, human rights law may appear to stand at an advantage with respect to humanitarian law because it is *lex generalis* applicable at all times, save in situations where a state of emergency is shown to exist, when it can be largely suspended. Humanitarian law, on the contrary, is *lex specialis*, requiring characterisation of a situation as an armed conflict before becoming applicable.[1] The distinction is somewhat formalistic in the context of the fluid application of both human rights and humanitarian law, merely offering a rebuttable presumption mostly relevant in case of review of the state's characterisation before a judicial body. In the ordinary application of the law, the existence of a legal presumption will have little effect on a state's power to characterise a situation as an armed conflict or a state of emergency.

Despite some inroads over the last few decades, the whole edifice of international law remains built on and around the state. Considerations of state sovereignty mean that each state may make a preliminary appreciation for itself of any situation of fact or law in all areas of international law, including human rights and humanitarian law.[2] Application by the state of somewhat indeterminate norms to often ambiguous facts cannot be totally discretionary, as this would contradict the postulated normative and mandatory nature of international law. There are necessarily

---

[1] See Aristidis Calogeropoulos-Stratis, *Droit humanitaire et droits de l'homme: La protection de la personne en conflits armés* (Geneva: Institut universitaire de hautes études internationales, 1980) 190; Thomas Fleiner-Gerster and Michael A. Meyer, 'New Developments in Humanitarian Law: A Challenge to the Concept of Sovereignty', (1985) 34 *Int'l & Comp. L Quart.* 267, 280.

[2] See *Case Concerning the Air Service Agreement of 27 March 1946 Between the United States of America and France*, (1978) 15 Rep. Int'l Arb. Awards 417 para. 81; *Lake Lanoux Award (France v. Spain)*, (1957) 12 Rep. Int'l Arb. Awards 101, 132.

some limits to the state's power to characterise. These can be found either in the norms themselves, in broad principles of reasonableness or good faith, or in concurrent or superior powers of characterisation by other agents. Many writers have noted that therein lies the key to the application of human rights as well as humanitarian law.[3] This is relevant not only to the institutionalised review of state characterisation, exclusive to the human rights system, but also to parallel characterisation by other agents for distinct purposes. For instance, third states may adopt countermeasures in reaction to the serious violation of human rights in another state.[4] Who, of the allegedly violating state, the third state or other international agent, is to judge of the existence of a state of emergency which may justify the violations? Similarly, the occurrence of an armed conflict has legal implications under humanitarian law for non-belligerent states, so that other international agents may perform acts of characterisation which do not necessarily correspond to that of the belligerent state or of the rebel movement. It is clear that the choice of the relevant characterising agent is of critical importance.

Four different types of characterisations can be identified with respect to the applicability of human rights and humanitarian law, being characterisations performed (1) by the state or the rebel movement ('self-characterisation'), (2) by third states, (3) by political organs of international or regional organisations, and (4) by independent bodies. The purpose of this analysis is not to articulate the web of relations between the different characterisations fully, but more modestly to contribute to a reflection on the legal nature and effect of each type of intervention in the context of these two legal systems.

Self-characterisation

'Self-characterisation' covers situations in which the classification of the situation as an armed conflict, state of emergency or simple disturbance affects in a direct and important way the obligations of the

---

[3] See UN Secretary-General, 'Report on Minimum Humanitarian Standards', UN Doc. E/CN.4/1998/87 paras. 40–1; Theodor Meron, *Human Rights in Internal Strife: Their International Protection* (Cambridge: Grotius, 1987) 163; Jaime Oráa, *Human Rights in States of Emergency in International Law* (Oxford: Clarendon, 1992) 42 (quoting Waldock); Joan F. Hartman, 'Derogation from Human Rights Treaties in Public Emergencies', (1981) 22 *Harv. Int'l LJ* 1, 36; Yves Sandoz, 'Réflexion sur la mise en oeuvre du droit international humanitaire et sur le rôle du Comité international de la Croix-Rouge en ex-Yougoslavie', [1993] *Revue suisse de droit international et européen* 461, 462.
[4] See chapter 5, pp. 201–11.

agent performing the act of characterisation. It is dubbed here 'self-characterisation' because the agent is not exterior to, but rather an active participant in, the situation under examination. It covers characterisation of either a state of emergency by the state on whose territory it is occurring, or an armed conflict by one of the belligerents, possibly including insurgent or national liberation movements.

HUMANITARIAN LAW

Under traditional laws and customs of war, a state faced with insurgency on its territory was at liberty to grant the rebels recognition of belligerency or insurgency in cases in which the rebels met certain conditions, close to those developed under Article 1 of Protocol II. The effect of recognition, which necessarily implied the characterisation by the state of the situation as an internal armed conflict, was to make the laws and customs of war as a whole applicable to the conflict. Writers were generally of the opinion that the power of recognition of belligerency or insurgency was purely discretionary.[5] The same principle obtained with respect to international armed conflicts. War could only take place if one of the belligerent states deemed it so. Limited – and sometimes not so limited – incidents could take place involving the use of force by states, without any state of war. For example, as mentioned earlier, the Boxer Expedition by several Western states in China in 1900–1 was not a war, despite fighting involving thousands of troops on both sides.[6]

Recognition of belligerency became obsolete over the course of the twentieth century, with no state practice after the Second World War and only limited instances prior to the war. The concept was replaced

---

[5] See Mohammed El Kouhene, *Les garanties fondamentales de la personne en droit humanitaire et droits de l'homme* (Dordrecht: Nijhoff, 1986) 72; Hersch Lauterpacht, *Recognition in International Law* (Cambridge: Cambridge UP, 1948) 240–6 (arguing that there is a duty to grant recognition); Michael B. Akehurst, 'Civil War', in Rudolf Bernhardt ed., [Instalment] 3 *Encyclopedia of Public International Law* (Amsterdam: North-Holland, 1982) 92; René-Jean Wilhelm, 'Problèmes relatifs à la protection de la personne humaine par le droit international dans les conflits armés ne présentant pas un caractère international', (1972-III) 137 *Recueil des cours* 316, 326; Charles Zorgbibe, 'De la théorie classique de la reconnaissance de belligérance à l'Article 3 des Convertions de Genève', in *Droit humanitaire et conflits armés – Actes du colloque du 28 au 30 janvier 1970, Université libre de Bruxelles* (Brussels: Ed. U de Bruxelles, 1976) 84.

[6] See above, p. 248. See also Erik Castrén, *The Present Law of War and Neutrality* (Helsinki: Suomalaisen Tiedeakatemian Toimituksia, 1954) 33 ('the characterization of armed action as war is made by the conflicting parties themselves, or rather by one of them').

with the adoption of common Article 3 of the 1949 Geneva Conventions and, more recently, the two 1977 Additional Protocols, in which recognition by the state in the classic sense plays no role. Likewise, the replacement of the notion of 'war' by that of 'armed conflict' in the 1949 Geneva Conventions lowered the applicability threshold so much that humanitarian norms should apply as soon as an armed conflict factually takes place.[7] No mention is made under any of the relevant provisions of who is to be the judge, or characterising agent, of the existence of one or the other type of armed conflict. Some have argued that since the state's power of appreciation is not curtailed, it subsists in the new norms, so that the state is the sole agent empowered to assess whether the conditions of applicability of humanitarian law have been met.[8] Thus, at the 1977 Geneva Conference, Colombia proposed an amendment specifying that only the state on whose territory an internal armed conflict took place could determine whether the conditions listed in Article 1(1) of Protocol II had been met. The amendment was eventually withdrawn, but Colombia and other states maintained that the provision as drafted left intact the state's exclusive power to assess whether its conditions were fulfilled in any given situation.[9] On the other hand, the fact that the amendment was not adopted at the Geneva Conference can be taken as an implicit rejection of the principle it embodies.[10] The debate could be extended to cover all types of armed conflicts.

Norms developed after the Second World War effected a fundamental change in the conditions of applicability of humanitarian law. Whereas norms under the older laws and customs of war depended at least in part on state recognition of belligerency or of the existence of a state of war, the Geneva Conventions and Protocols, and in their stride new customary rules, contain norms which are intended to apply automatically.

---

[7] See Dietrich Schindler, 'State of War, Belligerency, Armed Conflict', in Antonio Cassese ed., *The New Humanitarian Law of Armed Conflict* (Naples: Ed. Scientifica, 1979) 5-6.

[8] See Peter Kooijmans, 'In the Shadowland Between Civil War and Civil Strife: Some Reflections on the Standard-Setting Process', in Astrid Delissen and Gerard Tanja eds., *Humanitarian Law of Armed Conflict: Challenges Ahead – Essays in Honour of Frits Kalshoven* (Dordrecht: Nijhoff, 1991) 228 and 233.

[9] Plenary Meeting, CDDH/SR.49, 7 *Off. Records* 66-83 (Colombia, Brazil, Saudi Arabia, Philippines); CDDH/SR.56, at 239 (Chile); ICRC, *Report of the Work of the Conference of Government Experts on the Reaffirmation and Development of International Humanitarian Law of Armed Conflicts, Geneva, 24 May-12 June 1971* (Geneva: ICRC, 1971) 42 para. 203.

[10] See El Kouhene, *Les garanties fondamentales*, at 75; Dietrich Schindler, 'The Different Types of Armed Conflicts According to the Geneva Conventions and Protocols', (1979-II) 163 *Recueil des cours* 117, 148.

This is not to say that no act of characterisation is required, but rather it is argued that the applicable nature of humanitarian law finds its source in the norms themselves and not in the intervening act of recognition or characterisation. In other words, state characterisation has a declaratory rather than constitutive function.[11]

On the broad question of whether the state has an exclusive right to assess whether the elements defining an armed conflict are present in a given situation, the state generally can proceed to unilateral characterisation only with respect to discretionary powers. These include, for example, recognition of governments, the establishment of diplomatic relations or diplomatic protection of nationals abroad.[12] Even these powers are not without some parameters which limit their discretionary character. Application of humanitarian law to situations of armed conflict, on the contrary, is not a discretionary power. Customary norms, as well as the Geneva Conventions and Protocols, create a binding obligation for states to apply certain basic rules to all armed conflicts. A state cannot lawfully decide that, regardless of the fact that a conflict meeting the conditions of applicability of humanitarian law is occurring, it will not apply that body of law.[13] This is consistent with the declaratory rather than constitutive function of characterisation in this context. The ICJ in the *Asylum* case noted with respect to the right of a state to make a qualification of any offence committed by a refugee that 'a unilateral competence to qualify...involves a derogation from the equal rights of qualification which, in the absence of any contrary rule, must be attributed to each of the states concerned'.[14] In the context of humanitarian law, this equal right of other states to qualify or characterise the situation as an armed conflict is left untouched, so that the belligerent state's characterisation 'can only be, legally, *provisional and not definitive*'.[15]

---

[11] Wilhelm, 'Problèmes relatifs', at 326 and 333. As mentioned earlier, some have challenged that position.

[12] Jean J. A. Salmon, 'Some Observations on Characterization in Public International Law', in Antonio Cassese ed., *UN Law/Fundamental Rights* (Alphen aan den Rijn: Sijthoff & Noordhoff, 1979) 12; Jean J. A. Salmon, 'Les faits dans l'application du droit international', (1982-II) 175 *Recueil des cours* 257, 369–70.

[13] See Institut de droit international, 'Resolution on the Application of International Humanitarian Law and Fundamental Human Rights, in Armed Conflicts in which Non-State Entities are Parties', Art. V, (1999) 68-II *Annuaire de l'Institut de droit international* 395.

[14] The *Asylum* case, [1950] ICJ Rep. 274–5. See also Salmon, 'Some Observations on Characterization', at 12–13.

[15] Salmon, 'Some Observations on Characterization', at 12 (emphasis in the original). Similarly, the International Military Tribunal rejected an argument that Germany

The standing of national liberation movements under Protocol I and, to an even greater degree, insurgent groups in non-international armed conflicts to characterise a conflict is problematic. There have been several instances in the past of rebel groups or national liberation movements declaring their willingness to apply the 1949 Geneva Conventions and thus characterising their operations as an armed conflict, despite the fact that the state in question refused to acknowledge the existence of anything more than internal disturbances. Examples include the hostilities in Algeria, Angola, Cuba, Namibia, Nicaragua, Nigeria, Rwanda, Western Sahara, Yemen and Zimbabwe.[16] The belligerent state and other states have rarely attached any weight to such characterisations in the context of humanitarian law.[17]

National liberation armed conflicts rest, in a certain measure, on self-characterisation by the liberation movement. It must seek to represent the people in its struggle and undertake to apply the Conventions and Protocol before these can become applicable. As the characterisation of a national liberation armed conflict rests on the people's right to

alone had the power to make a conclusive determination of whether it could invade Denmark and Norway as a measure of self-defence: International Military Tribunal, *Trial of the Major War Criminals* (Nuremberg: IMT, 1947) I, 208.

[16] See *The Prosecutor v. Akayesu* (Judgment), 2 Sept. 1998, Case No. ICTR-96-4-T (Trial Chamber I, ICTR) para. 627; Julio A. Barberis, 'Nouvelles questions concernant la personnalité juridique internationale', (1983-I) 179 *Recueil des cours* 145, 255–8; David Forsythe, 'Legal Management of Internal War: The 1977 Protocol on Non-international Armed Conflicts', (1978) 72 *Am. J Int'l L* 272, 275–6; Christina Murray, 'The Status of the ANC and SWAPO Under International Humanitarian Law', (1983) 100 *South Afr. LJ* 402, 405; Denise Plattner, 'La portée juridique des déclarations de respect du droit international humanitaire qui émanent de mouvements en lutte dans un conflit armé', (1984–5) 18 *Revue belge de droit international* 298 n. 2; Wilhelm, 'Problèmes relatifs', at 330. For example, the 15 July 1981 declaration by SWAPO read: 'It intends to respect and be guided by the rules of the four Geneva Conventions of 12 August 1949 for the protection of the victims of armed conflicts and the 1977 Additional Protocol relating to the protection of victims of international armed conflicts (Protocol I)' (quoted in Plattner, 'La portée juridique', at 304).

[17] Even in cases of partition and the creation of a separate state, which would internationalise the conflict, much seems to turn on the established state's response. Compare, for example, the reaction of Nigeria to the Biafran secession in 1967, refusing to recognise both the secession and the application of humanitarian law, and that of Yugoslavia to the partition of the state, implicitly recognising partition in the new 1992 Constitution of 'Yugoslavia' and accepting the application of the Geneva Conventions and Protocol: Eric David, 'Le Tribunal pénal international pour l'ex-Yougoslavie', [1992] 2 *Revue belge de droit international* 565, 571; Victor Duculesco, 'Effet de la reconnaissance de l'état de belligérance par les tiers, y compris les organisations internationales, sur le statut juridique des conflits armés à caractère non-international', (1975) 79 *Revue générale de droit international public* 125, 149.

self-determination, an act of self-characterisation by the liberation movement is required before the conflict can properly be said to fall under
Article 1(4) of Protocol I. This act is evidenced by a declaration under
Article 96(3) of the Protocol. The same probably applies to internal armed
conflicts, as a state is unlikely to label hostilities as armed conflict if the
insurgents do not at least make a claim of that nature. Conversely, because the characterisation of a situation as an armed conflict constitutes
an implicit acknowledgment of the success of their campaign, insurgent
groups will rarely oppose it.[18] Finally, there is the possibility of an armed
conflict without involvement of the state on whose territory it is taking
place, either because the government is too weak or because it no longer
exists. In such situations, seen for instance in Lebanon and Somalia, the
various insurgent groups are left as the only possible self-characterising
agents.

What effect do these statements from insurgent and national liberation movements have on the legal nature of the situation? National
liberation movements and other insurgent groups are not sovereign entities in international law, but they are recognised as having a limited
personality by the text of the Geneva Conventions and Protocols. The
extent of this personality is a reflection of the rights and obligations
of the movements under international law.[19] Under Protocol I, national
liberation movements are given the power to make humanitarian law
applicable for both parties by way of a unilateral declaration (Art. 96(3)),
subject of course to the state's prior ratification of the treaty. Some have
suggested that, by application of the principle of effectivities, groups in
situations not covered by Protocol I could make unilateral declarations
which have a binding legal effect, at least for themselves.[20] A power to

[18] Even if both parties agree that the situation is an armed conflict, there can be
disputes as to the specific nature of that conflict. Often, a government will label a
conflict as an exterior invasion while the insurgents insist that it is actually a civil
war. In Vietnam, for example, South Vietnam and the United States viewed the
conflict as an invasion from the North, while the National Liberation Front of
Vietnam (Vietcong) insisted on the internal character of its struggle. The reverse
occurred in Afghanistan, where the rebels considered the war an invasion from the
USSR while the Afghan Government labelled the situation at most a
non-international armed conflict. See above, chapter 6, pp. 252–3.
[19] See *Reparation for Injuries Suffered in the Service of the United Nations* case, [1949] ICJ
Rep. 174, 178; P. H. Kooijmans, 'The Security Council and Non-State Entities as Parties
to Conflicts', in K. Wellens ed., *International Law: Theory and Practice* (Dordrecht: Kluwer,
1998) 333, 338–9; Wilhelm Wengler, 'La noción de sujeto de derecho internacional
público examinada bajo el aspecto de algunos fenómenos políticos actuales', (1951)
3 *Revista española de derecho internacional* 831, 842–4.
[20] See *The Prosecutor v. Kayishema and Ruzindana* (Judgment), 21 May 1999, Case No.

determine the existence of an armed conflict can certainly be deduced from the power to render humanitarian law applicable to such a conflict, implying that characterisation by insurgent and national liberation movements will have some legal effect. Of course, this power of characterisation is no more exclusive to the insurgent groups than it is to the state. Self-characterisations by insurgents are unlikely to be accepted as authoritative.[21] Nevertheless, statements by such movements should not be brushed aside as mere attempts to generate political support, without any genuine legal effect.

HUMAN RIGHTS

A fundamental difference between problems of characterisation in the context of human rights and those in humanitarian law lies in the fact that, at least at the initial state of the emergency threatening the life or security of the nation, there is only one possible characterising agent present and aware of the facts, that is, the state. Self-characterisation thus forms an integral part of the concept of state of emergency. This is not surprising, given that the state is all at once the potential victim of the unfurling emergency and the author of actions which would normally trench on the basic rights protected by human rights law. In this respect, the power of derogation in exceptional circumstances is the rule of human rights law most intimately connected to the notion of sovereignty, in that it permits the state to act to preserve the existence, or at least stability, of the nation.[22]

As a mechanism designed to protect the nation-state more than individual rights, indeed sacrificing these rights at the altar of state sovereignty, the decision not to declare a state of emergency would appear as an essentially discretionary power of the state. That is not to

ICTR-95-1-T (Trial Chamber, ICTR) para. 157; Plattner, 'La portée juridique', at 312–19. On the legal effects of unilateral acts, see *Nuclear Test* cases (*Australia* v. *France*; *New Zealand* v. *France*), [1974] ICJ Rep. 253 para. 43; Victor Rodríguez Cedeño, 'Third Report on Unilateral Acts of States', UN Doc. A/CN.4/505 (2000).

[21] This is reflected in the Canadian declaration with respect to Article 96(3) upon ratification of Protocol II: 'It is the understanding of the Government of Canada that the making of a unilateral declaration does not, in itself, validate the credentials of the person or persons making such a declaration and that States are entitled to satisfy themselves as to whether in fact the makers of such declaration constitute an authority referred to in Article 96': [1991] 2 Can. Treaty Ser. 182.

[22] Rusen Ergec, *Les droit de l'homme à l'épreuve des circonstances exceptionnelles. Etude sur l'article 15 de la Convention européenne des droits de l'homme* (Brussels: Bruylant/U de Bruxelles, 1987) 325.

say that no legal norms govern the invocation of the derogation provisions, but rather that it is up to the state to decide whether it wishes to adopt special measures to protect itself.[23] This suggests that when the state chooses not to characterise a situation as a state of emergency, its assessment of the situation should be final, and the full range of human rights norms considered entirely applicable in the state's territory. This was the position adopted by the European Commission of Human Rights in *Cyprus v. Turkey (1975)* and *McVeigh v. United Kingdom*, noting that it would not raise *proprio motu* the possible application of Article 15 of the European Convention.[24] The UN Human Rights Committee initially adopted the contrary position, stating in its views in *Ramirez v. Uruguay* that it would assess the existence of a state of emergency under Article 4 of the Covenant on Civil and Political Rights even if the state had not invoked it.[25] During more recent reviews of periodic reports, however, the Committee seems to have moved to a position whereby only an officially proclaimed state of emergency could justify derogations under Article 4, falling in line with the position of the European Commission of Human Rights.[26]

---

[23] See 'Lawless' case, Eur. Com'n Hum. Rts, Ser. B 1960–1, at 314; *Ireland v. UK*, (1978) Eur. Ct Hum. Rts, Ser. A vol. 25, at 78–9; *Brannigan and McBride v. United Kingdom* (A/253-B), (1993) 17 Eur. Hum. Rts Rep. 539, 569 para. 43 (Eur. Ct Hum. Rts); Human Rights Committee, UN Doc. CCPR/C/SR.224 para. 47 (Lallah); SR.284 para. 34 (Aguilar); SR.421 para. 38 (Graefrath). For example, no state of emergency was declared by the Government of Cyprus after the Turkish invasion in 1974, nor in the Falklands by Argentina during the 1982 conflict with Britain (making the islands the only part of Argentine territory not under a state of emergency), nor by the Russian Federation in Chechnya in 1994–5: ILA, '[First] Interim Report of the Committee on the Enforcement of Human Rights Law', in ILA, *Report of the 62nd Conference, Seoul, 24–30 August 1986* (London: ILA, 1987) 163 n. 13; Tarcisio Gazzini, 'Consideration of the Conflict in Chechnya', (1996) 17 *Hum. Rts LJ* 93, 104. It is understood that at some level human rights are dependent on internal stability, but there is no necessary nexus between the two. For example, wide-scale protests and civil disobedience for democracy in the Philippines in the 1980s could have been construed as a threat to the stability of the state, despite the fact that its eventual result was to bring about democracy and increase respect for human rights.

[24] *Cyprus v. Turkey*, Appl. 6780/74 and 6950/75, (1975) 4 Eur. Hum. Rts Rep. 482, 556 para. 527; *McVeigh v. UK*, Appl. 8022/77, 25 Decisions and Reports 15.

[25] Comm. 4/1977, UN Doc. A/35/40 at 121 para. 17, *reprinted in Selected Decisions of the Human Rights Committee Under the Optional Protocol of the International Covenant on Civil and Political Rights*, UN Sales No. E.89.XIV.1, I at 49.

[26] See 'Report of the Human Rights Committee on the Work of its 48th Session', UN Doc. A/51/40 (1996) para. 349 (dealing with Peru); Review of the Periodic Report of Nigeria, UN Doc. CCPR/C/SR/1505 (1996) paras. 66 (Lallah) and 71 (Aguilar Urbina); Comments on the Report of the Russian Federation, UN Doc. CCPR/C/79/Add.54 (1995) para. 27.

If the state does characterise a situation as a state of emergency, the conditions under which this may be done are no longer discretionary but subject to the legal requirements discussed in chapter 6.[27] The state, as the agent primarily involved in and concerned by the emergency, will necessarily perform the initial characterisation. The question then arises as to the effect of this characterisation on other agents. Although the issue has been discussed mostly in the context of the work of human rights bodies such as the Inter-American and European Courts and Commissions on Human Rights and the Human Rights Committee, the matter also concerns other states and the political organs of international or regional organisations, which may take action in response to violations of human rights. Broadly speaking, the state's characterisation may be ascribed three different effects. First, the declaration of a state of emergency by the state could be considered as a simple fact, and other agents could then objectively assess for themselves whether the conditions have been met for invoking special powers of derogation, based on all the facts available at the time of their own analysis. Second, the state's characterisation could be granted a measure of deference, and the existence of a state of emergency may be challenged only if the facts cannot reasonably support the state's conclusion. This is known as the 'margin of appreciation' approach. Third, a subjective approach may be adopted, whereby the state's action is given total deference.[28]

To start with the last option, the subjective approach, in which the declaration of a state of emergency is seen as pertaining solely to state sovereignty, has been rejected universally. It was pleaded by Ireland in the 'Lawless' case before the European Court of Human Rights, where it argued that 'it was for a Government, and for that Government alone, to determine when a state of emergency existed'.[29] The argument has

---

[27] See chapter 6, pp. 269–76. See also Guy Tremblay, 'Les situations d'urgence qui permettent en droit international de suspendre les droits de l'homme', (1977) 18 *Cahiers de droit* 3, 18; *Silva v. Uruguay*, (1981) *Selected Decisions of the Human Rights Committee* 65, in which the Committee articulates well the idea that '[a]lthough the sovereign right of a State Party to declare a state of emergency is not questioned, yet... a State, by merely invoking the existence of exceptional circumstances, cannot evade the obligations which it has undertaken by ratifying the Covenant'.

[28] Oráa, *Human Rights*, at 45; Joan F. Hartman, 'Working Paper for the Committee of Experts on the Article 4 Derogation Provision', (1985) 7 *Hum. Rts Quart.* 89, 125.

[29] 'Lawless' case, Ser. B 1960–1, at 77. See also Alexandre-Charles Kiss, 'Les fonctions du Secrétaire-général du Conseil de l'Europe comme dépositaire des Conventions européennes', [1956] *Annuaire français de droit international* 680, 685 ('l'article 15 laisse à chaque Etat le droit discrétionnaire d'apprécier s'il y a lieu de se prévaloir du droit de dérogation'); Elihu Lauterpacht, 'The Contemporary Practice of the United

been used in a variety of fora where the state's characterisation could be challenged.[30] The proposition was rejected clearly by both the European Commission and Court in 'Lawless', a holding repeated in Ireland v. United Kingdom, Brannigan and McBride v. United Kingdom and Askoy v. Turkey.[31] A position of total deference to the state in this respect appears incompatible with the erga omnes nature of obligations imposed on the state by human rights law, whereby derogations are matters affecting the public order created by the conventional and customary human rights norms.[32]

The second approach, titled 'margin of appreciation', was primarily developed by the European Commission and Court of Human Rights with respect to Article 15 of the European Convention. Upon rejection of an absolute discretion of the state in deciding whether the conditions for declaring a state of emergency had been met, the Commission and Court found that they could not ignore completely the state's appreciation of the situation. In the 'Lawless' case, Waldock as president of the Commission noted that the rationale for a 'margin of appreciation' approach was the nature of the task of characterisation in the context of an emergency threatening the life of the nation, being 'essentially a delicate problem of appreciating complex factors and of balancing conflicting considerations of the public interests'.[33] The Court in Ireland v. United Kingdom noted that the government concerned, being continuously and directly in contact with the situation in all its historical,

Kingdom in the Field of International Law', (1956) 5 Int'l & Comp. L Quart. 405, 433–4 ('it is arguable that the determination by the British Government that the situation in Cyprus is one of "public emergency threatening the life of the nation"... is a matter within their sole jurisdiction').

[30] See e.g. the declaration made by the Chilean representative before the UN Human Rights Commission to the effect that the decision to derogate from certain norms under Article 4 of the International Covenant on Civil and Political Rights was 'an internal act of that State', and that other state parties to the treaty 'were not entitled to change, object to, or derogate from what the State concerned had decided': UN Doc. E/CN.4/SR.1272 (1974) 76. This position has received support from Australia (E/CN.4/SR.617 (1981) para. 50), Costa Rica (ibid., para. 47), Colombia (A/C.3/31/SR.58 (1976) para. 5), Ecuador (ibid., para. 26) and Paraguay (A/C.3/31/SR.54 (1976) para. 17). See Menno Kamminga, Inter-State Accountability for Human Rights Violations (Philadelphia: U Pennsylvania Press, 1992) 122–3.

[31] 'Lawless' case (Merits), Eur. Ct Hum. Rts, Ser. A 1960–1, at 56 para. 28; Ireland v. UK, (1978) Eur. Ct Hum. Rts, Ser. A vol. 25, at 78–82; Brannigan and McBride v. United Kingdom (A/253-B), (1993) 17 Eur. Hum. Rts Rep. 539, 569 para. 43 (Eur. Ct Hum. Rts); Askoy v. Turkey, (1996) 23 Eur. Hum. Rts Rep. 553, 586–7 (Eur. Ct Hum. Rts).

[32] P. van Dijk and G. J. H. van Hoof, Theory and Practice of the European Convention on Human Rights, 3rd edn (The Hague: Kluwer, 1998) 731–5.

[33] 'Lawless' case, Ser. B, at 408.

economic, social, political and strategic dimensions, is in a better
position than any other agent to assess whether the emergency has
reached a level warranting the declaration of a state of emergency.[34] The
state's characterisation will therefore be left untouched if it is found to
be reasonable within a margin of appreciation. The notion of a 'margin'
of appreciation is eminently vague, and perhaps variable. The case-law
of the European Commission and Court of Human Rights contains no
indication of the breadth of this margin, apart from the statement in
Ireland v. *United Kingdom* that it is 'wide' and the remark of Waldock
in *'Lawless'* that being 'on the margin' is enough.[35] Good or bad faith
on the part of the government, although not expressly presented as a
relevant factor, seems to have the effect of narrowing the margin, as indicated by the stricter stand of the European Commission in the *Greek* case
with respect to the declaration of a state of emergency by the colonels'
regime.[36] Neither the Inter-American Court of Human Rights nor the Human Rights Committee has adopted ostensibly a margin of appreciation
approach.[37]

The margin of appreciation approach has come under heavy criticism
in the last few years as overly deferential to the state's characterisation.
Many writers argue that human rights bodies such as the Inter-American
Commission on Human Rights and the Human Rights Committee should
refrain from adopting the jurisprudence of the organs of the European
Convention on Human Rights, and move closer to an objective approach. Siracusa Principle 63, which provides that 'the provisions of the

[34] *Ireland* v. *UK*, Ser. A, at 79; *Brannigan and McBride* v. *UK*, at 569 para. 43; *Askoy* v. *Turkey*, at 587 para. 68; Ergec, *Droits de l'homme*, at 361.

[35] *Ireland* v. *UK*, Ser. A, at 79; *'Lawless'* case, Ser. B, at 408; Ergec, *Droits de l'homme*, at 363–4; W. J. Ganshof Van Der Meersch, 'Le respect des droits fondamentaux de l'homme, condition exigée de droit des Etats européens', [1983] *Revue de droit international et de droit comparé* 10, 25; Rosalyn Higgins, 'Derogations Under Human Rights Treaties', (1976–7) 48 *Brit. YB Int'l L* 281, 297–300; Michael Hutchinson, 'The Margin of Appreciation Doctrine in the European Court of Human Rights', (1999) 48 *Int'l & Comp. L Quart.* 638–50. Compare with the remark by Tarnopolski during the Human Rights Committee's review of a periodic report by Chile to the effect that the state has considerable latitude in characterising a state of emergency: UN Doc. CDDH/C/SR.128 para. 40.

[36] See Ergec, *Droits de l'homme*, at 368; Oráa, *Human Rights*, at 45; Ronald St J. Macdonald, 'Derogations under Article 15 of the European Convention on Human Rights', (1997) 36 *Colum. J Transnat'l L* 225, 248–9.

[37] See Dominic McGoldrick, *The Human Rights Committee* (Oxford: Clarendon, 1991) 305; David Harris, 'Regional Protection of Human Rights: The Inter-American Achievement', in David Harris and Stephen Livingstone eds., *The Inter-American System of Human Rights* (Oxford: Oxford UP, 1998) 1, 12.

Covenant allowing for certain derogations in a public emergency are to be interpreted restrictively',[38] is intended as a rejection of the margin theory in the context of the Political Covenant.[39] Likewise the guidelines for bodies monitoring human rights during a state of emergency, adopted by the International Law Association in 1990, provide in paragraph 8 that:[40] 'In contentious cases arising out of both inter-state and individual applications, the treaty implementing body should not extend a broad "margin of appreciation" to the derogating state *but should make an objective determination whether a public emergency as defined in the treaty actually existed . . .* ' (emphasis added). Because a genuine emergency threatening the life of the nation must, by definition, involve events of a magnitude sufficient to threaten to destabilise the state, it can be argued that its existence can be perceived just as easily from outside the country. The need for direct and continuous contact with the situation is perhaps more relevant to the evaluation of which measures are needed to deal with the emergency than to the assessment of whether an emergency exists.

Despite calls for an objective determination under the last approach, it seems unlikely that the state's appreciation of the facts will be overlooked altogether. The Siracusa and ILA proposals are symptomatic of a desire to narrow the deference to the state's characterisation considerably, to curb the repeated abuse of derogations in certain countries, but not to deny the sovereign right of states to be the judges of what constitutes an emergency threatening the life of their nation.[41] The state must after all effect the initial characterisation and declare a state of emergency. This approach, lying somewhere between the margin of appreciation and the objective approach on the spectrum of deference to the state's characterisation, seems to best reconcile the necessary consideration of state sovereignty and the public order dimension of the invocation of special powers to derogate from human rights during a state of emergency.

---

[38] 'The Siracusa Principles on the Limitation and Derogation Provisions in the International Coverant on Civil and Political Rights', (1985) 7 *Hum. Rts Quart.* 3, 10. Principle 57 rejects total deference for the state's appreciation with regard to the strict proportionality of the measures to the emergency: *ibid.*, at 9.

[39] Daniel O'Donnell, 'Commentary by the Rapporteur on Derogation', (1985) 7 *Hum. Rts Quart.* 23, 29.

[40] 'Final Report on Monitoring States of Emergency: Guidelines for Bodies Monitoring Respect for Human Rights During States of Emergency', in International Law Association, *Report of the 64th Conference, Queensland, 20–25 August 1990* (London: ILA, 1991) 228, 233.

[41] See Hartman, 'Working Paper', at 125; O'Donnell, 'Commentary', at 30.

CONCLUSION

A crucial problem common to both humanitarian law and human rights with respect to applicability of their norms is that so much turns on self-characterisation. More often than not, the state will simply disregard all relevant legal criteria and rely on strictly political considerations to officially label a situation as an armed conflict or a state of emergency. The problem is particularly acute in situations of state of emergency, and perhaps non-international armed conflict, because there is only one international agent present to characterise the facts. For example, Draper notes that the refusal by France and the United Kingdom to apply common Article 3 in Algeria, Kenya, Malaya and Cyprus had been 'determined by political considerations and not by any objective assessment of the facts'.[42] In international armed conflicts, the possibility of differing opinions as to the nature of the hostilities by two agents naturally tends to internationalise the debate on characterisation, with some chance that the most humanitarian interpretation of the situation will be favoured. This occurred, for instance, during the Vietnam war, in which the United States initially applied the 1949 Geneva Conventions to Vietcong fighters as well as North Vietnamese regulars, while the latter refused to consider the war an international armed conflict. Both characterisations reflected political considerations, the US claiming the war to consist in the invasion of the South by the North, the Vietcong and North Vietnam considering it to be the struggle of the people of the South against an oppressive regime and its ally.[43] The Geneva Conventions were eventually applied by all sides, at least informally. Reliance on non-legal criteria to characterise situations under human rights and humanitarian law owes much to the fact that internal judicial review of the characterisation is rarely available while the state of emergency or armed conflict is still ongoing.[44]

[42] G. I. A. D. Draper, *The Red Cross Conventions* (London: Stevens, 1958) 15 n. 47. Fleiner-Gerster and Meyer go so far as to suggest that the decision to apply Article 3 usually rests on non-humanitarian grounds: Fleiner-Gerster and Meyer, 'New Developments', at 274.

[43] See Heather A. Wilson, *International Law and the Use of Force by National Liberation Movements* (Oxford: Clarendon, 1988) 125; Tom J. Farer, 'Humanitarian Law and Armed Conflict: Towards the Definition of "International Armed Conflict"', (1971) 71 *Colum. L Rev.* 37, 58–9.

[44] See, for states of emergency, Ergec, *Droits de l'homme*, at 321–45; Imtiaz Omar, *Rights, Emergencies, and Judicial Reviews* (Dordrecht: Kluwer, 1995); International Commission of Jurists, *States of Emergency, their Impact on Human Rights* (Geneva: ICJ, 1983) 434–7; G. J. Alexander, 'The Illusory Protection of Human Rights by National Courts During

Reluctance by states to admit the applicability of human rights and humanitarian law norms to a given situation does not necessarily imply that they can indeed prevent it. It is unwarranted to suggest that because actual compliance with humanitarian law remains conditional on characterisation of the situation by the state, it is in fact if not in law optional.[45] The Israeli representative at the 1977 Geneva Conference erred in the same way when he criticised Article 1(4) of Protocol I because it 'had within it a built-in non-applicability clause, since a party would have to admit that it was either racist, alien or colonial – definitions which no state would ever admit to'.[46] The ICTR in the *Akayesu* case noted in this respect:

It should be stressed that the ascertainment of the intensity of a non-international conflict does not depend on the subjective judgment of the parties to the conflict... If the application of international humanitarian law depended solely on the discretionary judgment of the parties to the conflict, in most cases there would be a tendency for the conflict to be minimized by the parties thereto.[47]

It is undeniable that, when a state refuses to acknowledge the applicability of either human rights or humanitarian law norms, it is often in a *de facto* position to prevent their enforcement. The previous discussion has shown, however, that the state does not have exclusive or ultimate powers of characterisation, and that other agents may proceed to their own assessment of the situation. From a legal standpoint, the state cannot effectively prevent a situation from acquiring the status of armed conflict or artificially maintain it as a state of emergency. Thus, any characterisation by the state will be at its own risk. Once the equal validity of characterisation by other agents is recognised, there may be some pressure put on the state to revise its opinion, in addition to effects

Periods of Public Emergency', (1984) 5 *Hum. Rts LJ* 1–65; P. R. Gandhi, 'The Human Rights Committee and Derogation in Public Emergencies', (1989) 32 *German YB Int'l L* 323, 347–9. For armed conflicts, see Edward K. Kwakwa, *The International Law of Armed Conflict: Personal and Material Field of Application* (Dordrecht: Nijhoff, 1992) 74 and 80; Wilson, *International Law*, at 126. Israel remains somewhat of an exception in this respect: *Tsemel* v. *Ministry of Defense (Israel)*, (1983) 37:3 Piskei Din 365–80 (Israel Supreme Ct), *translated in* (1984) 1 *Palestinian YB Int'l L* 164–74 (reviewing the question of whether the territories are 'occupied' within the meaning of the Hague and Geneva Conventions).

[45] 'Report on Minimum Humanitarian Standards', UN Doc. E/CN.4/1998/87 para. 79; Calogeropoulos-Stratis, *Droit humanitaire*, at 94.

[46] Plenary Meeting, 23 May 1977, CDDH/SR.36 para. 61.

[47] *The Prosecutor* v. *Akayesu* (Judgment), 2 Sept. 1998, Case No. ICTR-96-4-T (Trial Chamber I, ICTR) para. 603.

of the existence of an armed conflict or state of emergency occurring outside the jurisdiction of the state.[48]

Third states

Human rights and humanitarian law impose on the state some obligations *erga omnes* in the application of which all states have a legal interest in the name of the international community. As discussed earlier, the ICJ in the *Asylum* case stated the principle that all interested states have a concurrent right to qualify facts unless an exclusive right is granted to one state by treaty or customary law. Neither human rights nor humanitarian law contains an exclusive devolution of the right to characterise situations as armed conflicts or states of emergency, opening the door to concurrent characterisation by any other state, given that all states have a legal interest in the application of human rights and humanitarian law.

Under the now probably obsolete rules on recognition of belligerence in civil wars, third states were entitled to grant recognition to the insurgents, regardless of the position adopted by the concerned state, if certain conditions were met.[49] During the Spanish civil war, for instance, the official Spanish administration formed by the Republicans never granted belligerent recognition to the insurgent Nationalist forces under Franco. Nevertheless, the United Kingdom acknowledged the fact that Nationalist forces were the *de facto* government of a part of the Spanish territory and granted them consequent belligerent rights.[50]

---

[48] On the broader issue of autointerpretation and its limits, see Denis Alland, *Justice privée et ordre juridique international – Etude théorique des contre-mesures en droit international public* (Paris: Pedone, 1994) 107–25; Bin Cheng, 'Flight from Justiciable to Auto-interpretative International Law', in *Liber Amicorum Elie van Bogaert* (Antwerp: Kluwer, 1985); Leo Gross, 'States as Organs of International Law and the Problem of Autointerpretation', in George Lipsky ed., *Law and Politics in the World Community. Essays on Hans Kelsen's Pure Theory of Law and Related Problems in International Law* (Berkeley: U Calif. Press, 1953) 59, 74–87.

[49] See Institut de droit international, 'Droits et devoirs des puissances étrangères, au cas de mouvement insurrectionnel, envers les gouvernements établis et reconnus qui sont aux prises avec l'insurrection', (1900) 18 *Annuaire de l'Institut de droit international* 227 (Art. 8); H. Lauterpacht, *Recognition*, at 176; James Garner, 'Recognition of Belligerency', (1938) 32 *Am. J Int'l L* 106, 112; Abdelmadjid Belkherroubi, 'Essai sur une théorie juridique des mouvements de libération nationale', [1972] *Revue égyptienne de droit international* 20, 23–4.

[50] Among other things, the laws passed by the insurgents rather than by the official government were deemed to be in force in proceedings before British courts: H. Lauterpacht, *Recognition*, at 272–4. See also Fritz Grob, *The Reality of War and Peace* (New Haven: Yale UP, 1949) 204.

In contemporary humanitarian law, the right of non-warring states to make their own assessment of the facts and decide for themselves whether the situation amounts to an armed conflict warranting the application of humanitarian law follows naturally from a conclusion that the belligerent states do not have an exclusive right of characterisation. Writers, such as Castrén, who find that the belligerent state does have an exclusive right naturally reject any foundation for a right of third states to characterise armed conflicts.[51] The rationale offered for this position is that the belligerent states are best positioned to evaluate the facts, and that characterisation by third states may conflict with that of the belligerents and bring confusion as to the applicable norms. The practice of states in past armed conflicts indicates that they have not felt bound by the characterisation of the belligerent parties, but rather have proceeded to their own evaluation of the facts.[52] In this respect, the position of the belligerents is not ignored but simply considered as one relevant probative element. For example, many states considered that the hostilities in Afghanistan starting in 1979 constituted an international armed conflict between Afghanistan and the USSR, while Afghanistan maintained that it was simply quelling internal disturbances with the help of Soviet forces.[53] The United States and the United Kingdom (speaking for the European Union) condemned the 1992 expulsion of 400 Palestinians by Israel as a violation of the 1949 Fourth Geneva Convention, despite the Israeli contention that the Convention was not applicable.[54]

States have proceeded to independent characterisations of facts even in situations of civil strife, in which the intrusion in the 'internationalised' internal affairs of the state is greatest. An example is provided by a note from the Swiss Legal Adviser with regard to the armed conflict in El Salvador. In his note, the Legal Adviser proceeded to an objective determination of the nature of the hostilities in El Salvador which in no way deferred to the appreciation of the situation by the parties to the conflict, to conclude that Protocol II was indeed applicable.[55] In national

---

[51] Castrén, *Present Law*, at 35.

[52] See Ian Brownlie, *International Law and the Use of Force by States* (Oxford: Clarendon, 1963) 410; Zorgbibe, 'De la théorie', at 87.

[53] See Michael Reisman and James Silk, 'Which Law Applies to the Afghan Conflict?', (1988) 82 *Am. J Int'l L* 459.

[54] Clyde Haberman, 'Israel Expels 400 From Occupied Lands', *NY Times*, 18 Dec. 1992, at A1; 'UN Security Council Votes on the Situation in the Occupied Territory', *US Dept State Dispatch*, 20 Jan. 1993, at 54.

[55] Lucius Caflisch, 'Pratique suisse relative au droit international en 1986', (1987) 43 *Annuaire suisse de droit international* 185-7.

liberation armed conflicts, as pointed out by the Israeli delegate at the 1977 Geneva Conference, it is unlikely that the state concerned will admit to being racist, colonial or alien, or that the liberation movement is representative of the people and thus capable of making a declaration under Article 96(3) of Protocol I. Other states may proceed to these characterisations however, and many have done so in the past. The PLO, for example, had been given recognition by a large number of states – including Austria, Greece and the USSR – as the representative of the Palestinian people in the territories occupied by Israel, even before the emergence of the Palestinian Authority in the wake of the Oslo Accords.[56]

Relevant state practice in the field of human rights is limited but hints at a similar attitude of third states confronted with declarations of states of emergency in other states. It is interesting to note in this respect that the International Covenant on Civil and Political Rights (Art. 4(3)) and the American Convention on Human Rights (Art. 27(3)) require the derogating state to give notice of its derogation to other High Contracting Parties, through the Secretary-General of the concerned organisation. Reactions by other states thus seem not only envisaged but also encouraged. When the facts have not seemed to support a reasonable evaluation of the situation as posing a threat to the life of the nation, third states have sometimes openly stated their disagreement with the declaration of a state of emergency and called for the state concerned to lift it. For example, the United States condemned the imposition of a state of siege in Poland following the crackdown on the Solidarity Union, and imposed countermeasures in order to pressure the Polish Government into lifting the state of siege.[57] There are few instances in state practice of third parties adopting such a clear characterisation at variance with that of the state concerned.

Characterisation by third states under human rights and humanitarian law shares many of the same problems marring self-characterisation. Most importantly, it seems commonly made on the basis of purely political considerations, with only lip service paid to the legal criteria attaching to the characterisation of a situation as an armed conflict or a state of emergency. In humanitarian law, High Contracting Parties have a duty to 'ensure respect' of the 1949 Geneva Conventions, which

[56] See Lassa Oppenheim, *International Law*, Robert Jennings and Arthur Watts eds., 9th edn (Harlow, UK: Longman, 1992) I, 164.
[57] Marian Nash Leich, 'Contemporary Practice of the United States Relating to International Law', (1982) 76 *Am. J Int'l L* 379–81. See the discussion in chapter 5, pp. 201–11.

may be construed as a duty to call for the application of humanitarian norms by other states if, in the opinion of the High Contracting Party, hostilities amount to an armed conflict. States have in fact made such calls in cases where they sought to support one or the other side to the hostilities.[58] Similarly, in human rights, third states have made calls for compliance in instances where criticism of the government concerned was considered desirable, such as in the case of the US–Polish dispute. In other cases, the likelihood that an act of characterisation would be considered by the concerned state as an interference in its internal affairs has had a chilling effect on third states, often discouraging clear challenges to disputable characterisations.[59]

In a manner similar to self-characterisation by the concerned state, characterisation by a third state binds only that state, and not the concerned state or any other agent.[60] That is of course not to deny that the characterisation can have significant effects at both the national and international levels. A government finding that a state of emergency was wrongly declared can adopt peaceful countermeasures to incite the concerned state to resume full compliance with human rights norms, as the United States did in suspending the 1972 US–Polish Air Service Agreement. In humanitarian law, a finding that an international armed conflict is taking place in the former Yugoslavia, for example, has given Austria, Denmark, Germany and Switzerland jurisdiction under Articles 49/50/129/146 of the Geneva Conventions and Article 86 of Protocol I to try individuals in their hands for serious violations of the Conventions and Protocol committed in former Yugoslavia.[61]

There have been some suggestions in favour of according greater weight to characterisation by third states in humanitarian law. At the expert conference preceding the 1977 Geneva Conference, one proposed solution to the problem of self-characterisation in internal strife was that recognition of belligerency by several other states would act as evidence that the hostilities warranted application of humanitarian law.[62]

---

[58] Wilhelm, 'Problèmes relatifs', at 337.

[59] See Charles Zorgbibe, 'Le caractère armé des conflits', in Droit humanitaire et conflits armés – Actes du colloque du 28 au 30 janvier 1970, Université libre de Bruxelles (Brussels: Ed. U de Bruxelles, 1976) 93, 99.

[60] See Lassa Oppenheim, International Law, Hersch Lauterpacht ed., 7th edn (London: Longmans, 1952) II, 209; Duculesco, 'Effet de la reconnaissance', at 130; Krzysztof Skubiszewski, 'Peace and War', in Bernhardt, [Instalment] 4, at 74, 75.

[61] For cases tried by national courts pursuant to these provisions, see YB Int'l Human. L (from 1998) and the ICRC database on humanitarian law at www.icrc.org/ihl-nat.

[62] See El Kouhene, Les garanties fondamentales, at 74 n. 162; Forsythe, 'Legal Management', at 286–9.

The proposition was not taken up by the conference. Some writers have argued that even under existing law, recognition of a national liberation movement by a number of states would constitute evidence of its capacity under Protocol I, on which the depositary could rely to accept a notification under Article 96(3).[63] In all likelihood, as Article 1(4) has yet to be applied for the first time, the depositary state would adopt a neutral position similar to the stance it took in the past when national liberation movements or unrecognised governments tried to ratify the 1949 Geneva Conventions. When the Provisional Government of the Algerian Republic tried to ratify the Conventions in 1960, for example, the Swiss Government simply transmitted the document to the High Contracting Parties with a note to the effect that it was thus expressing no opinion as to the capacity of the Provisional Government to ratify the Conventions.[64]

Acts of characterisation by third states are possible and can produce legal effects in and outside the jurisdiction of the characterising state. This does not solve the problem of the reluctance of the state directly concerned with the state of emergency or armed conflict, however, because the principle of equal sovereignty of states directs that the concurrent characterisations are equally authoritative, leaving the state in factual control of the application of human rights and humanitarian law on its territory. In a manner similar to the concerned states themselves, third states perform these characterisations at their own risk, and may incur responsibility if their assessment is later proven wrong by the binding decision of an international or arbitral body.

Political organs of intergovernmental organisations

CHARACTERISATION BY POLITICAL BODIES

Political organs of international and regional organisations sometimes express opinions amounting to characterisation of specific situations as armed conflicts or states of emergency. The basis for such an intervention in the application of human rights and humanitarian law is in

---

[63] Duculesco, 'Effet de la reconnaissance', at 130; Schindler, 'Different Types of Armed Conflicts', at 144.

[64] See Michel Veuthey, *Guérilla et droit humanitaire* (Geneva: Institut Henri-Dunant, 1976) 49. To the same effect with respect to the PLO 'ratification' of the Geneva Conventions and Protocols in 1989, see the Swiss Government's letter of transmittal to High Contracting Parties: (1989) 5 *Palestinian YB Int'l L* 328–32.

some cases expressly provided for in international conventions, as example being the role of the Committee of Ministers of the Council of Europe under Article 32 of the unamended European Convention on Human Rights. It can also simply rest on the general powers of the political body, as in the case of the UN General Assembly. Amongst the bodies which have been active in describing events as armed conflicts or states of emergency in specific countries, the most significant practice stems from the UN General Assembly, the Security Council and Human Rights Commission, the political organs of the Council of Europe and the Organization of African Unity. There is a very significant discrepancy between the volumes of practice in human rights and humanitarian law, with far fewer examples of characterisation relating to states of emergency than to the existence of armed conflicts.

The General Assembly of the UN has been quite active since the latter part of the 1960s in labelling certain situations as armed conflicts and calling for the application of the relevant humanitarian law norms. The Assembly at one time or another has characterised every type of armed conflict and used, in a selective fashion, the full range of humanitarian regimes available. It has labelled as inter-state armed conflicts or military occupation, in direct contradiction of the concerned state's characterisation of the hostilities, the recent conflict in Afghanistan, the Iraq–Kuwait war, and the occupation by Israel of the Golan Heights and other territories.[65]

The General Assembly periodically has turned its attention to national liberation struggles, deeming them to be international armed conflicts even before the adoption of Protocol I. It has thus qualified as international conflicts, and called for the full application of the 1949 Geneva Conventions, the conflicts in Southern Rhodesia, Angola, Mozambique and Guinea-Bissau.[66] Since the adoption of Protocol I, it has designated

[65] On Afghanistan, see General Assembly Resolutions 40/137 (13 Dec. 1985), 46/136 (17 Dec. 1991) and 47/141 (18 Dec. 1992) ('Noting with deep concern that a situation of armed conflict persists in Afghanistan'). On Israel, see e.g. General Assembly Resolutions 36/147F (16 Dec. 1981); 36/226B (17 Dec. 1981); 47/63, 47/64, 47/70 (11 Dec. 1992); 51/135 (20 Feb. 1997); 52/65 (20 Feb. 1998); 54/77 (22 Feb. 2000) and 55/131 (28 Feb. 2001). On Kuwait, see General Assembly Resolution 46/135 (17 Dec. 1991). See generally David Weissbrodt, 'The Role of International Organizations in the Implementation of Human Rights and Humanitarian Law in Situations of Armed Conflict', (1988) 21 *Vanderbilt J Int'l L* 313, 325–31.
[66] See e.g. General Assembly Res. 2383 (XXIII) para. 13 (Southern Rhodesia); 2395 (XXIII) para. 12 (Angola, Mozambique, Guinea-Bissau); 2508 (XXIV) para. 11 (Southern Rhodesia/Zimbabwe); 2547A (XXIV) (various territories); 2652 (XXV) para. 11 (Southern Rhodesia); 2678 (XXV) para. 11 (Namibia); 2707 (XXV) para. 6 (Angola,

several conflicts as falling within the definition of Article 1(4), involving a struggle by a people against a racist, colonial or alien regime in furtherance of its right to self-determination. For example, the Assembly had called repeatedly for the application of Protocol I in the national liberation conflict in Namibia.[67] With respect to the recognition of national liberation movements, the General Assembly has adopted the practice of relying on the recognition of liberation movements by the Organization of African Unity or by the League of Arab States in order to grant them observer status.[68] As mentioned earlier, the practice originated in the Economic Commission for Africa in the early 1970s, and there never has been in the General Assembly a discussion of the wisdom or legal basis of such a delegation of powers to regional organisations.[69] In the specific context of the application of humanitarian law, the General Assembly has labelled as national liberation movements which are the 'sole representative of the people' not only SWAPO for Namibia, as recognised by the OAU, but also the Frente POLISARIO in the Western Sahara and FRETILIN in East Timor, two movements not recognised by any regional organisations.[70] The General Assembly also has expressed negative opinions about the representative character of a national

Mozambique, Guinea-Bissau); 2795 (XXVI) para. 7 (Angola, Mozambique, Guinea-Bissau); 2796 (XXVI) para. 10 (Southern Rhodesia); 2871 (XXVI) para. 8 (Namibia); 3111 (XXVIII) (Namibia).

[67] See General Assembly Res. 41/39A (20 Nov. 1986), where in para. 75 the Assembly 'Declares that the liberation struggle in Namibia is a conflict of an international character in terms of article 1, paragraph 4, of Additional Protocol I to the Geneva Conventions of 12 August 1949, and, in this regard, demands that the Conventions and Additional Protocol be applied by South Africa'. See also General Assembly Res. 41/35A (10 Nov. 1986) para. 8; Res. 39/50A (12 Dec. 1984) para. 66.

[68] See General Assembly Res. 35/167 (15 Dec. 1980); 37/104 (16 Dec. 1982); 41/71 (3 Dec. 1986); 43/160B (9 Dec. 1988); 45/37 (28 Nov. 1990); 47/29 (25 Nov. 1992). The practice has been adopted by other UN agencies and bodies, including the Committee Against Apartheid, ICAO, ILO, UNESCO, UNDP, UNIDO and WHO: (1981) 38 YBUN 168–9; Oppenheim, International Law (1992) I, at 164 n. 12; 'Legal Opinion Prepared for the Under-Secretary-General's Office for Inter-Agency Affairs and Co-ordination', [1974] UN Jur. YB 149–56.

[69] See Lazarus, 'Le statut', at 182. There was a debate in the UN Council for Namibia as to the desirability of relying on OAU recognition of national liberation movements for granting observer status, with some members seeking to admit as observers SWANU and SWANUF, in addition to SWAPO, the movement recognised by the OAU. The Council eventually recognised only SWAPO: ibid., at 183.

[70] See, for SWAPO, General Assembly Res. 40/97A (13 Dec. 1985), 41/39A (20 Nov. 1986) para. 10, 41/101 (4 Dec. 1986) para. 27; for the Frente POLISARIO, General Assembly Res. 34/37 (21 Nov. 1979), 35/19 (11 Nov. 1980); and for FRETILIN, General Assembly Res. 36/50 (24 Nov. 81).

liberation movement, for example calling UNITA a band of 'armed criminal bandits'.[71]

Finally, the General Assembly has characterised as non-international armed conflicts a number of internal hostilities which the state did not consider to be more than internal tensions and disturbances. Thus the Assembly has called on the Government of Burma (Myanmar) to apply common Article 3 of the 1949 Geneva Conventions to the civil strife in that country.[72] It has called for the application of both common Article 3 and Protocol II in the internal armed conflicts in El Salvador and the Sudan.[73]

With respect to the application of human rights, in contrast, there is much less General Assembly practice challenging the state's characterisation of a given situation as a state of emergency. One specific instance concerns the entrenchment of a state of siege in the Chilean Constitution. The General Assembly called for its lifting at numerous times over several years in the 1980s.[74]

The UN Security Council has been much more subdued in its characterisation of specific situations as armed conflicts calling for the application of humanitarian law. It has limited its action in this respect to inter-state armed conflicts, not dealing at all with either national liberation armed struggles or internal conflicts. The secession of Bangladesh provides a case in point, with no reaction from the Security Council to the massive violations of humanitarian law until the conflict expanded to include India, at which point the Council called for full observance

---

[71] General Assembly Res. 41/35A (10 Nov. 1986) para. 12. See also General Assembly Res. 46/87 (16 Dec. 1991) para. 20, speaking of 'externally supported armed terrorists' in Mozambique.

[72] General Assembly Res. 47/144 (18 Dec. 1992) para. 10; 51/117 (5 March 1997) para. 15. Burma (Myanmar) acceded to the 1949 Geneva Conventions only in 1992, being one of the last states not party to the Conventions.

[73] General Assembly Res. 36/155 (16 Dec. 1981); 37/185 (17 Dec. 1982) para. 2; 38/101 (16 Dec. 1983); 39/119 (14 Dec. 1984) para. 9; 40/139 (13 Dec. 1985) ('*Considering* that there is an armed conflict of a non-international character in El Salvador in which the government of that country and the insurgent forces are under an obligation to apply the minimum standards of protection of human rights and humanitarian treatment provided for in article 3 common to the Geneva Conventions of 1949 and in Additional Protocol II thereto, of 1977'); 47/142 (18 Dec. 1992) para. 4; 51/112 (5 March 1997) para. 9 (calling for the application of the Additional Protocol despite the fact that Sudan is not a party thereto). See also General Assembly Res. 38/100 (16 Dec. 1983); 39/120 (14 Dec. 1984); 40/140 (13 Dec. 1985), labelling hostilities in Guatemala as 'an armed conflict not of an international character'.

[74] General Assembly Res. 39/121 (14 Dec. 1984) para. 6; 41/161 (4 Dec. 1986) para. 9(a); 42/147 (7 Dec. 1987) para. 10(b); 43/158 (8 Dec. 1988).

of the 1949 Geneva Conventions.[75] The Security Council called for com-
pliance with the 1925 Geneva Protocol on Chemical and Bacteriological
Warfare and 'other laws of armed conflict' in the context of the 1980–8
Iran–Iraq war.[76] On several occasions, the Council reminded Israel that
its occupation of the Golan Heights and other territories under its con-
trol since 1967 constituted military occupation governed by the 1949
Fourth Geneva Convention, despite the Israeli position that the Geneva
Conventions are not applicable.[77] Similarly, rejecting a claim made by
Iraq in August 1990 to the effect that it had annexed Kuwait, the Secu-
rity Council in Resolution 670 (1990) stated its opinion that the Fourth
Geneva Convention applied fully to the Iraqi occupation of Kuwait.[78]
More recently, it affirmed the applicability of the 1949 Geneva Conventions to the hostilities taking place in the territory of the former
Yugoslavia.[79] In addition to these relatively specific characterisations of
armed conflicts, the Security Council in many other cases has called for
compliance with 'applicable rules of international humanitarian law'
without specifying the nature of these rules or the character of the
conflict.[80] Once again, as with the General Assembly, there is a marked
difference between the practice of the Security Council in the area of
humanitarian law and that relating to human rights, with the Council

[75] See Security Council Res. 307 (1971); Christiane Bourloyannis, 'The Security Council
of the United Nations and the Implementation of International Humanitarian Law',
(1992) 20 *Denver J Int'l L & Pol'y* 335, 340–52; Stephen Schwebel, 'The Roles of the
Security Council and the International Court of Justice in the Application of
International Humanitarian Law', (1995) 27 *NYU J Int'l L & Pol'y* 731, 752. One limited
exception could be the Council's invitation to representatives of African national
liberation movements to participate in its special session in Addis Ababa in 1972,
although the representatives were heard in a purely personal capacity: Belkherroubi,
'Essai', at 28.
[76] See Security Council Res. 582 (1986) and 598 (1987).
[77] See Security Council Res. 465 (1980), 471 (1980), 497 (1981), 540 (1983), 672 (1990), 681
(1990), 726 (1992), 799 (1992) and 904 (1994) ('Reaffirming its relevant resolutions,
which affirmed the applicability of the Fourth Geneva Convention of 12 August 1949
to the territories occupied by Israel in June 1967, including Jerusalem'). In 1951, the
Security Council found that, contrary to the claim by Arab neighbours of Israel, no
state of war existed between these states (Res. S/2322, 1 Sept. 1951), but this was
relevant more to *jus ad bellum* and neutrality laws than to *jus in bello*. See Christopher
Greenwood, 'The Concept of War in Modern International Law', (1987) 20 *Nether. YB
Int'l L* 35, 287–8.
[78] Security Council Res. 670 (1990) para. 13. See also Security Council Res. 674 (1990).
[79] Security Council Res. 764 (1992) para. 10.
[80] See e.g. Security Council Res. 788 (1992) para. 5 (Liberia); 794 (1992) (Somalia); 804
(1993) para. 10 (Angola); 814 (1993) (Somalia); 853 (1993) para. 11 (Azerbaijan); 864
(1993) para. 15; 941 (1994) para. 1 (Bosnia-Herzegovina); 993 (1994) (Georgia); 1193 and
1214 (1998) (Afghanistan); 1234 (1999) (Congo–Zaire).

abstaining from characterising situations as not constituting a state of emergency.[81]

The UN Human Rights Commission is a political body constituted of the representatives of states and not, like the Human Rights Committee, of individuals sitting in their private capacity.[82] Under the 1503 Procedure, it has extensive powers to investigate and report on the application of human rights in any state, not dependent on the state's consent or even its membership in the UN.[83] It has reported on a growing number of situations of armed conflict and states of emergency, sometimes expressly characterising the facts as one or the other and expressing its opinion as to the applicability of humanitarian law or human rights. In the field of humanitarian law, for example, it has labelled hostilities in El Salvador as an internal armed conflict and called for the application of common Article 3 and Protocol II.[84] Recent resolutions have been directed to the application of humanitarian law in Kuwait, Yugoslavia, Burma (Myanmar), the Sudan and Uganda, marking a greater awareness of the Commission of the relevance of humanitarian law to its work.[85] In the field of human rights, a working group of the Commission has contradicted the legality of a declaration of state of emergency in Chile and in Bolivia.[86] The Commission itself has adopted

[81] One limited example is the call made on 13 June 1986 by the Security Council President, in the Council's name, for South Africa to end its state of emergency. See Kamminga, *Inter-State Accountability*, at 123 n. 237.

[82] See generally H. Tolley, *The United Nations Commission on Human Rights* (Boulder: Westview Press, 1987).

[83] ILA, 'First Report', at 122.

[84] Res. 1983/100 and 1984/120, and the reports of the Special Representative, UN Doc. A/40/818 (1985) paras. 166–76; UN Doc. E/CN.4/1986/22 (1986) paras. 145–73. See also, on the nature of hostilities in Afghanistan, Res. 1991/78 and the report of Special Rapporteur Felix Ermacora, E/CN.4/1986/24 (1986) paras. 70, 100 and 119; on the applicability of the 1907 Hague Convention IV and 1949 Fourth Geneva Convention to the Golan Heights and other territories occupied by Israel, see Res. 1983/2, 1995/2, 1998/62.

[85] Res. 1991/67 (Kuwait); Res. 1992/S-1/1, 1994/72 (Yugoslavia); Res. 1994/85, 1998/63 (Myanmar); Res. 1998/67 (Sudan); Res. 1998/75 (Uganda). See Michael Dennis, 'The Fifty-Second Session of the UN Commission on Human Rights', (1997) 91 *Am. J Int'l L.* 167, 168.

[86] 'Report of the Ad Hoc Working Group on the Situation of Human Rights in Chile', UN Doc. E/CN.4/1310 (1979) 103 ('continued application in Chile of the state of siege was not justified'); 'Study by the Special Envoy Héctor Gros Espiell on the Human Rights Situation in Bolivia', UN Doc. E/CN.4/1500 (1981) paras. 121–2; Hartman, 'Derogation', at 40–4. See generally Joan Fitzpatrick, *Human Rights in Crisis – The International System for Protecting Rights During States of Emergency* (Philadelphia: Pennsylvania UP, 1994) 116–51; ILA, 'First Report', at 124–33.

resolutions recommending the end of states of emergency in Chile (Res. 1983/38) and Paraguay (Res. 1984/46). The Sub-Commission on Human Rights (previously the Sub-Commission on the Prevention of Discrimination and Protection of Minorities) has devoted much attention to states of emergency since the early 1980s. In addition to the more theoretical report prepared by Nicole Questiaux in 1982,[87] the Sub-Commission has appointed a special rapporteur, Leandro Despouy, to draw up a list of countries in which a state of emergency had occurred since January 1985.[88] The Sub-Commission also occasionally has adopted resolutions declaring humanitarian law applicable to a given situation, for instance in the territories occupied by Israel.[89]

The Statute of the Council of Europe declares in Article 1(c) that one of the purposes of the organisation is the protection and development of human rights. The Parliamentary Assembly has relied on this to affirm the soundness of its interests in the implementation of the European Convention on Human Rights.[90] The Committee of Ministers, for its part, was expressly given powers under the European Convention (Arts. 32 and 54, prior to Protocol 11). These two bodies have not been very active with respect to the characterisation of situations as states of emergency under Article 15 of the European Convention. The Parliamentary Assembly did show great interest in the status of human rights in Greece and Turkey during states of emergency in those countries in 1967 and 1980, sending observers to report on the extent and legality of derogations. The Assembly, however, refrained from expressing any opinion as to the validity of the states' characterisations of the emergency as a threat to the life of the nation.[91] In a report on Assembly action regarding a 1984 Maltese law in breach of Article 10 of the Convention, the rapporteur of the Political Affairs Committee, relying on principles of separation of powers, took a narrow view of the Assembly's power to act towards the promotion of human rights, but singled out states of emergency as an exception: 'When there exists in a member country of the Council of

---

[87] Nicole Questiaux, 'Study of the Implication for Human Rights of Recent Developments on Situations known as States of Siege or Emergency', UN Doc. E/CN.4/Sub.2/1982/15 (1982).

[88] See 'List of States which Have Proclaimed or Continued a State of Emergency', UN Doc. E/CN.4/Sub.2/1999/31.

[89] Para. 3 of Res. 1989/5, UN Doc. E/CN.4/Sub.2/1989/L.11/Add.1 at 6.

[90] Ergec, Droits de l'homme, at 338; ILA, 'First Report', at 153–4.

[91] Ergec, Droits de l'homme, at 339–41; Howard D. Coleman, 'Greece and the Council of Europe: The International Legal Protection of Human Rights by the Political Process', (1972) Israel YB Hum. Rts 121–41; Dimitris C. Constas, 'The "Turkish Affair": A Test Case for the Council of Europe', (1982) 2 Legal Issues of Eur. Integration 69–87.

Europe a situation similar to that of Greece in 1967 or of Turkey in 1980, clearly the Assembly must decide and act on the basis of this article.'[92] Probably because of the wide powers of the Commission and Court of Human Rights in the European human rights system, the Assembly and Committee have not felt the need to intervene and characterise situations directly.[93]

The Organization of African Unity occupies a special place in any discussion of characterisation in humanitarian law because it is the only organisation to possess a permanent specialised agency whose work centres on the recognition and support of national liberation movements. The Committee for the Coordination of the Liberation of Africa, or Liberation Committee, was established in 1963 by the OAU with the specific aim of funding and coordinating the struggles of national liberation movements in Africa. It does not directly seek to contribute to the enforcement of humanitarian law, but, as discussed earlier, the recognition of liberation movements by a regional organisation can have an indirect effect on the applicability of Protocol I by establishing that the movement is representative of the people fighting for self-determination (Art. 96(3)).

The OAU Liberation Committee has granted recognition to thirteen different movements in Africa, relying on a set of criteria reflecting the purposes of the organisation's action: the movement must be representative of the entire people, be militarily and politically organised, and carry out effective military operations.[94] The territorial integrity of members of the OAU is a primordial consideration, so that movements which

[92] Political Affairs Committee, 'Opinion on the "Foreign Interference Act" of Malta', Council of Europe Doc. 5337 (21 Jan. 1985) at 4. The article mentioned is Article 3 of the Statute of the Council of Europe. In another report on the same matter, the rapporteur of the Legal Affairs Committee adopted a position generally supporting the powers of the Assembly to act to enforce human rights: Legal Affairs Committee, 'Report on the Foreign Interference Act and the Human Rights Situation in Malta', Council of Europe Doc. 5325 (19 Dec. 1984). See Ergec, *Droits de l'homme*, at 339.

[93] The Assembly has instead taken the indirect route of calling for High Contracting Parties to file inter-state applications with the European Commission of Human Rights. This was done in the cases of Greece and Turkey: Ass. Res. 346 (1967); Ergec, *Droits de l'homme*, at 18–23; Coleman, 'Greece', at 124; Constas, 'Turkish Affair', at 77–8 and 81. Despite some statutory support since 1991, OAS political bodies have been reluctant to act to protect overthrown democratic governments, situations which are often combined with states of emergency: Joan Fitzpatrick, 'States of Emergency in the Inter-American System', in Harris and Livingstone, *Inter-American System*, at 271, 272–3.

[94] See Oppenheim, *International Law* (1992), I, at 163 n. 6; Wilson, *International Law*, at 145; Konrad Ginther, 'Liberation Movements', in Rudolf Bernhardt ed., [Instalment] 3 *Encyclopedia of Public International Law* (Amsterdam: North-Holland, 1982) 245, 246–7;

posed a threat of partition, such as those in Biafra, Katanga, Eritrea or
the Sudan, have not been given recognition. Further, how systematically
these criteria were being applied by the Liberation Committee is a matter open to debate, as it recognised several national liberation movements not actively engaged in military operations, for instance MOLI-
NACO in the Comoros or SPUP in the Seychelles.[95] The Committee seems
to have been dormant for a number of years. As for the League of Arab
States, it does not have a body comparable to the Liberation Committee
of the OAU, and has recognised only one national liberation movement,
being the PLO as representative of the people of Palestine.[96]

Political bodies thus do express opinions, often with clear reference
to applicable standards, as to the legal character of a specific situation
as an armed conflict, calling for the application of a set of humanitarian
rules, or, more infrequently, as an improper state of emergency, rejecting
the lawfulness of human rights derogations. The question then arises as
to the nature and legal effect of this type of resolution in the context
of human rights and humanitarian law.

NATURE AND EFFECT OF CHARACTERISATION

Resolutions or other decisions of political organs of international organisations occasionally were considered as a possible answer to the difficulties raised by the need for an active act of characterisation declaring
human rights or humanitarian law fully applicable to a given situation.
This section first reviews the potential sources of such a power for political bodies, then turns to an evaluation of the effect of this type of
statement on the applicability of human rights and humanitarian law.

At the 1949 Geneva Conference, it was suggested in the discussions
surrounding common Article 3 that a situation would automatically be
considered a non-international armed conflict if it had been labelled
by the UN General Assembly or Security Council as a threat to international peace and security under Chapter VII of the UN Charter.[97]

Lazarus, 'Le statut', at 179–80. The OAU has recognised PAIGC, FRELIMO, MPLA, FNLA
and UNITA (in Portuguese territories); SWAPO (Namibia); ZAPU and ZANU (Southern
Rhodesia); ANC and PAC (South Africa); MOLINACO (Comoros); SPUP (Seychelles) and
FLCS (French Afars & Issas): Lazarus, 'Le statut', at 180 n. 51.
[95] Wilson, *International Law*, at 143–4; Lazarus, *Le statut*, at 181.
[96] See Ginther, 'Liberation Movements', at 247. To this limited list of examples could be
added the recognition of the FMLN in El Salvador by the Andean Pact States:
Barberis, 'Nouvelles questions', at 240.
[97] II-B *Final Record* 121; Jean Pictet ed., *The Geneva Conventions of 12 August
1949 – Commentary on the IV Geneva Convention Relative to the Protection of Civilian Persons
in Times of War* (Geneva: ICRC, 1958) 35.

The need for characterisation abated somewhat when the idea of a full application of the Conventions to internal conflicts was abandoned, and the suggested role of the UN was discarded. The same idea resurfaced in the two conferences of government experts preceding the 1977 Geneva Conference. There, it was proposed that the problem surrounding the positive identification of non-international and national liberation armed conflicts could be solved by using the UN General Assembly as a judge of whether hostilities were more than internal disturbances and tensions or whether they involved a struggle by a people against colonial domination, alien occupation or a racist regime.[98] It was objected that the UN, and primarily the Security Council, has a limited power to determine the existence of a threat to or breach of international peace, and no power to declare humanitarian law applicable to an armed conflict of any type.[99] The Special Representative of the Secretary-General pointed out that, apart from Chapter VII, the UN Charter sets as one of the purposes of the Organisation the promotion of both peace and the self-determination of peoples (Arts. 1(3) and 55–6, UN Charter), leaving a door open to characterisation of various situations as armed conflicts.[100] Despite the recognition of the importance of the problem, a provision dealing specifically with characterisation by the UN was rejected at the expert conference, owing mainly to the fear of long delays, the political nature of the UN process, and the factual complication of armed conflicts, particularly internal conflicts.[101]

Article 89 of Protocol I could perhaps be interpreted as opening the door to UN intervention in the form of characterisation. Initially proposed as a provision subjecting the taking of belligerent reprisals to control by the Security Council, the article was diluted to the point of containing an exceedingly vague exhortation for states to cooperate with the UN in case of 'serious violations' of the Protocol or Conventions.[102] The notion of 'serious violations' is wider than grave breaches and, according to the ICRC's commentary on the Protocol, would include

[98] See El Kouhene, *Les garanties fondamentales*, at 74 n. 162.

[99] ICRC, *1971 Conference of Experts*, at 42 para. 201.

[100] *Ibid.*, paras. 207–8. Already in 1970 the Secretary-General had suggested the creation of a permanent UN body charged with the enforcement of international humanitarian law and, specifically, of the characterisation of situations as armed conflicts of one type or another: UN Secretary-General, 'Respect for Human Rights in Armed Conflicts', UN Doc. A/8052 (1970) paras. 246–7.

[101] See Wilhelm, 'Problèmes relatifs', at 343 (referring to the 1971 Conference of Experts).

[102] '*Article 89 – Co-operation* In situations of serious violations of the Conventions or of this Protocol, the High Contracting Parties undertake to act jointly or individually, in co-operation with the United Nations and in conformity with the United Nations Charter.' On the concept of 'serious violations', see below, pp. 328–30.

global violations of the Protocol and Conventions such as the unjustified refusal to admit that a situation constitutes an armed conflict. The
ICRC suggests that one type of UN action possible in the context of a
serious violation would be the adoption of resolutions requiring the application of the Protocol or Conventions to specific hostilities.[103] Several
states abstained from voting in favour of Article 89 because of its overly
vague and imprecise wording, also expressing serious misgivings about
giving the UN a power to react to serious violations of humanitarian
law.[104] While one may feel sympathy for the ICRC's attempt to make the
most of this failed attempt to regulate resort to belligerent reprisals, it
is unjustified to find in a call to 'cooperate' with the UN the creation
of a duty to submit to its characterisation of situations as armed conflicts. Even if we admit that the 1977 Conference could have granted
additional powers to the Security Council or General Assembly, by a
sort of *dédoublement fonctionnel*, it did not do so in adopting Article 89 of
Protocol I. The UN may rely on its specific powers under the UN Charter
to heed the call of Article 89 to cooperate in repressing serious violations
of humanitarian law, as the Security Council did, for example, in calling
on states to gather evidence of violations of humanitarian law by Iraq
in Kuwait or in creating the International Criminal Tribunals for former
Yugoslavia and Rwanda.[105] This power is to be contrasted, for example,
with the specific competence given to the Security Council by Article
V(5) of the ENMOD Convention, whereby state parties undertake to as-
sist a victim state if the Council concludes that the Convention has been
violated.[106]

---

[103] Claude Pilloud et al., *Commentary on the Additional Protocols of 8 June 1977 to the Geneva
Conventions of 12 August 1949* (Geneva: Nijhoff, 1987) 1033–4. See Dietrich Schindler,
'Die *erga omnes*-Wirkung des humanitären Völkerrecht', in Ulrich Beyerlin et al. eds.,
*Recht zwischen Umbruch und Bewahrung: Völkerrecht, Europarecht, Staatsrecht. Festschrift für
Rudolf Bernhardt* (Berlin: Springer, 1995) 199, 200.

[104] Meeting of Committee I, 16 May 1977, CDDH/I/SR.73, 9 *Off. Records* 435 (remarks by
Canada); Plenary Meeting, CDDH/SR.46 and Annex, 6 *Off. Records* 341 and 361 (remarks
by Italy and others).

[105] See *The Prosecutor* v. *Tadić* (Decision on the Defence Motion for Interlocutory Appeal on
Jurisdiction), 2 Oct. 1995, Case No. IT-94-1-AR72 (Appeals Chamber, ICTY) at 52 para.
93; Bourloyannis, 'Security Council', at 349. A somewhat similar provision is found in
Art. XII(4) of the 1993 Chemical Weapons Convention: Adam Roberts, 'The Laws of
War: Problems of Implementation in Contemporary Conflict', in *Law in Humanitarian
Crises – How Can International Humanitarian Law be Made Effective in Armed Conflict?*
(Luxembourg: European Communities, 1995) I, 13, 44–5 (also in (1995) 6 *Duke J Int'l &
Comp. L* 11).

[106] Convention on the Prohibition of Military or Any Other Hostile Use of Environmental
Modification Techniques, General Assembly Res. 31/72 (10 Dec. 1976), Art. V(5).

In the end, no consensus could be found at the 1977 Conference in favour of a provision clarifying the effect of the many resolutions adopted by various political organs of the UN characterising hostilities as armed conflicts and declaring the applicability of the Geneva Conventions or Protocols.

The conference discussions and treaty provisions touching on the relevance of characterisation by UN political bodies in humanitarian law constitute the most extensive consideration of the role of such bodies in the classification of factual situations under either human rights or humanitarian law. Still in humanitarian law, recognition of national liberation movements by regional organisations was contemplated as a possible condition of application of Protocol I but, ultimately, no such provision was included.[107]

In human rights law, political bodies generally are given no role to play in the enforcement of norms. One significant exception was Article 32 of the European Convention on Human Rights (prior to the entry into force of Protocol 11), giving the Committee of Ministers the power to determine if a violation of the Convention had taken place.[108] The scope of the Committee's power was not substantively limited, so that a resolution finding a breach of Article 15 because no state of emergency existed in a given country would have fallen squarely within the purview of Article 32. The Committee was generally extremely reluctant to use what it itself acknowledged were quasi-judicial powers, especially in the politically charged context of an alleged breach of Article 15 of the European Convention.[109] This function of the Committee of Ministers was eliminated with the entry into force of Protocol 11 in November 1998. No other human rights instrument provides for the intervention of political bodies in the determination of a violation of state of emergency provisions or any other human rights norm.[110] Several non-treaty bodies,

---

[107] See above, chapter 6, pp. 257–9.

[108] Another, more limited, function entrusted in the Committee is the supervision of the execution of the judgments of the European Court of Human Rights (Art. 46(2)). See Andrew Drzemczewski, 'Decisions on the Merits: By the Committee of Ministers', in R. St J. Macdonald et al. eds., *The European System for the Protection of Human Rights* (Dordrecht: Nijhoff, 1993) 733–54; Caroline Ravaud, 'The Committee of Ministers', in Macdonald, *European System*, at 645–55.

[109] See Arthur Henri Robertson, *Human Rights in Europe* (Manchester: Manchester UP, 1977) 242–5.

[110] Under the African Charter on Human and Peoples' Rights, the Assembly of Heads of State and Government is given a controlling role in the investigation of violations of the Charter (Art. 58) but, as there is no provision allowing for derogation in time of emergency, its intervention to review the state's characterisation of a situation as a

such as the UN Security Council, General Assembly and Commission on Human Rights, do have broad powers which can lead them to discuss the existence of a state of emergency or armed conflict.

Some writers, drawing on the general powers of political bodies and their status as an embodiment of the community of states, conclude that, despite the lack of a specific provision in most of the relevant instruments, characterisation by these bodies does have binding force on states.[111] Political, legal and institutional elements combine to refute this position.

In addressing the issue of whether a given situation ought to be considered an armed conflict or a state of emergency for the purposes of the applicability of humanitarian law or human rights, political organs of international organisations such as the UN General Assembly and Parliamentary Assembly of the Council of Europe may rely on a variety of political and legal considerations. The same is true of declarations by the OAU or by the General Assembly that a national liberation movement is representative of a people or that hostilities constitute an armed conflict.[112] In the context of state recognition, this political factor explains the fact that recognition of states or governments by the UN does not imply their recognition by the member states or an obligation to

state of emergency seems unlikely. See Fatsah Ouguergouz, *La Charte africaine des droits de l'homme et des peuples – Une approche juridique des droits de l'homme entre tradition et modernité* (Geneva: Presses Universitaires de France, 1993) 278–80 and 357–8. As discussed in chapter 6, pp. 269–70, the African Commission, for its part, has concluded that the African Charter does not allow formal derogation in case of a state of emergency.

[111] See Eric David, *Principes de droit des conflits armés* (Brussels: Bruylant, 1994) 108; David, 'Le Tribunal pénal international', at 571; Duculesco, 'Effet de la reconnaissance', at 144–5; Helmut Freudenschuss, 'Legal and Political Aspects of the Recognition of National Liberation Movements', (1982) 11 *Millennium: J Int'l Stud.* 115, 122; UN Secretary-General, 'Respect for Human Rights in Armed Conflicts', UN Doc. A/8052 (1970) 65–8 paras. 205–14; Zorgbibe, 'Le caractère armé', at 100. Even the Institut de droit international, in a resolution adopted at its Berlin session in August 1999, seems to leave open a window for characterisation by political bodies, depending on the meaning given to the word 'impartial': Institut de droit international, 'Resolution', at 397 (Art. IX 'Should the State concerned claim that no internal armed conflict has broken out, the authorisation [should be] given to the United Nations or any other competent regional or international organisation to establish impartially whether international humanitarian law is applicable').

[112] This is evidenced, for example, by the fact that the OAU has not granted recognition to any national liberation movements fighting against member states, despite the fact that they met all other conditions. See Wilson, *International Law*, at 141–3; Georges Abi-Saab, 'Wars of National Liberation in the Geneva Conventions and Protocols', (1979-IV) 165 *Recueil des cours* 357, 408–9; Ginther, 'Liberation Movements', at 247; Schindler, 'Different Types of Armed Conflicts', at 143.

do so.[113] Thus Arab states could cohabit with Israel at the UN while not recognising the existence of that state. Similarly, recognition of a national liberation movement as representative of a people by the General Assembly does not bind member states with respect to the application of Article 1(4) of Protocol I. For instance, the United Kingdom and Australia have clearly rejected the General Assembly's repeated recognition of SWAPO as the movement representing the Namibian people.[114] The same obtains for characterisation by the General Assembly of a situation as an armed conflict to which humanitarian law is applicable.

The Assembly, in invoking humanitarian law, cannot determine in a binding manner whether that body of norms is legally applicable to the facts, but rather uses the Geneva Conventions and Protocols as sources of the most elementary considerations of humanity to which all governments should feel morally bound in all situations.[115] In human rights law, a determination by the Assembly that no state of emergency exists in a country would also be in the nature of a moral or political call for the state to abide fully by its international obligations. Simply put, legal and political mechanisms at the international level have different, even if sometimes overlapping, implications for states.[116] Thus, for example, the fact that the General Assembly held at one point that 'Zionism is racism' does not imply that Israel should legally be considered a racist regime for the purposes of Article 1(4) of Protocol I, as declared by the PLO representative at the 1977 Geneva Conference.[117] This is not to underestimate the value of a determination by the Assembly that a state should feel compelled to apply the Conventions or Protocols, as it is by no means evident, considering the general underdevelopment of the international legal system, that political mechanisms are generally less effective than legal ones.

[113] See Secretary-General, 'Memorandum on the Legal Aspects of the Problem of Representation in the United Nations', UN Doc. S/1446 (8 March 1950), reprinted in (1950) 4 Int'l Org. 356, 359; Oppenheim, International Law (1992) I, at 177–8.
[114] Parl. Deb. (Lords), vol. 405, col. 564 (19 Feb. 1980); Parl. Deb. (Commons), vol. 414, col. 749 (3 Nov. 1980); Sen. Deb. (Austral.) 1980, vol. 84, at 168 (20 Feb. 1980). See Oppenheim, International Law (1992) I, at 164; Stefan Talmon, 'Recognition of Governments: An Analysis of the New British Policy and Practice', (1992) 63 Brit. YB Int'l L 231, 253.
[115] Theo C. van Boven, 'Reliance on Norms of Humanitarian Law by United Nations Organs', in Astrid Delissen and Gerard Tanja eds., Humanitarian Law of Armed Conflict: Challenges Ahead – Essays in Honour of Frits Kalshoven (Dordrecht: Nijhoff, 1991) 502.
[116] See Ergec, Droits de l'homme, at 343.
[117] Plenary Meeting, 23 May 1977, CDDH/SR.36 para. 114; General Assembly Res. 3379 (XXX).

These remarks on the political character of the decisions of the General Assembly equally apply to the Security Council. Its decisions are also of a political nature, even though they may incorporate considerations of international law, as clearly shown by the existence of an unequal right of veto. As such, Security Council resolutions should not be considered legal opinions of the existence of an armed conflict binding on all states under Article 25 of the UN Charter.[118] Arangio-Ruiz's comment regarding the inappropriateness of relying on the General Assembly or Security Council to determine the commission of an international crime is equally applicable to the problem of characterisation. He points out that neither body is adequate for the task because of the highly discretionary nature of their decisions, the lack of uniform criteria to be applied in similar situations, the absence of a duty to motivate decisions on the basis of international law, and the unavailability of review mechanisms.[119] It would be an exaggeration to say that the Security Council and General Assembly ignore international law completely in their decision-making; they both fulfil political functions within the international legal order rather than making legal decisions in accordance with international law.[120]

One element specific to the Security Council lies in its power under Article 39 of the UN Charter to determine the existence of a threat to, or breach of, international peace or an act of aggression. As noted at the 1971 Conference of Government Experts, the determination of the existence of such a threat and the characterisation of a situation as an armed conflict or a state of emergency do not necessarily coincide. Past threats to international peace have included severe human rights violations which did not involve armed hostilities, international or internal, such as the events in Haiti leading to the adoption of Resolution 841 (1993). The *Lockerbie (Provisional Measures)*, *Lockerbie (Admissibility)* and *Application of the Genocide Convention (Provisional Measures)* decisions by the ICJ raise the question of whether there are any limits on the Security Council's discretion to assess what constitutes a threat to international peace and security, and then order any measure that it deems appropriate

---

[118] See Hans Kelsen, *The Law of the United Nations* (New York: Praeger, 1950) 476–7; Monique Chemillier-Gendreau, 'Rapport sur la fonction idéologique du droit international', [1974] *Annales de la Faculté de droit et de sciences économiques de Reims* 221, 228.

[119] Gaetano Arangio-Ruiz, 'Seventh Report on State Responsibility', UN Doc. A/CN.4/466 (1995) 36 para. 97.

[120] See Rosalyn Higgins, 'The Place of International Law in the Settlement of Disputes by the Security Council', (1970) 64 *Am. J Int'l L* 1, 14–15.

including the application of the Geneva Conventions or Protocols.[121] For instance the Security Council in Resolution 670 (1990), acting expressly under Chapter VII, declared that the Iraqi invasion and occupation of Kuwait was governed by the Geneva Conventions. The normative source of a binding decision of this kind lies entirely in Chapter VII of the UN Charter, and not in international humanitarian law. Chapter VII here is the sword allowing the Security Council to cut right through the Gordian knot of characterisation. Any decision by the Security Council based on provisions other than Chapter VII of the Charter will have no obligatory effect on either the state(s) concerned or third states.

The ICJ discussed the nature of the decision-making process of both General Assembly and Security Council in its 1948 advisory opinion on the *Admission of a State to the United Nations*.[122] The question centred on whether member states, in voting for or against admission of a state to the UN, could take into consideration elements other than those listed in Article 4 of the UN Charter, including purely political elements. The Court split sharply by a vote of nine to six. The majority found that, despite their nature as political bodies, the General Assembly and Security Council were entrusted a quasi-judicial function by the Charter, and thus were under an obligation to refrain from considering elements not included in the necessary and sufficient conditions listed in Article 4.[123] The dissenters strongly disagreed, stating that the Assembly and Council were perfectly entitled to rely on political factors in making political decisions such as whether to admit new states as members of the UN.[124]

---

[121] *Questions of Interpretation and Application of the 1971 Montreal Convention Arising from the Aerial Incident at Lockerbie (Libyan Arab Jamahiriya v. United Kingdom; Libyan Arab Jamahiriya v. United States of America), Provisional Measures, Order of 14 April 1992,* [1992] ICJ Rep. 3 and 114; *ibid., Admissibility, Judgment of 27 Feb. 1998; Application of the Convention on the Prevention and Punishment of the Crime of Genocide (Bosnia & Herzegovina v. Yugoslavia (Serbia & Montenegro)), Provisional Measures, Order of 13 Sept. 1993,* [1993] ICJ Rep. 325; *ibid.,* Separate Opinion of Judge E. Lauterpacht, at 439 para. 99; Vera Gowlland-Debbas, 'The Relationship Between the International Court of Justice and the Security Council in Light of the *Lockerbie* Case', (1994) 88 *Am. J Int'l L* 643–77; Salmon, 'Some Observations on Characterization', at 15; Skubiszewski, 'Peace and War', at 75.

[122] [1947–8] ICJ Rep. 57.

[123] *Ibid.,* at 64 ('The political character of an organ cannot release it from the observance of the treaty provisions established by the Charter when they constitute limitations on its powers or criteria for its judgment...There is therefore no conflict between the function of the political organs, on the one hand, and the exhaustive character of the prescribed conditions, on the other').

[124] *Ibid.,* at 85 (Joint Dissenting Opinion by Judges Basdevant, Winiarski, Sir Arnold McNair and Read) ('The main function of a political organ is to examine questions in their political aspects, which means examining them from every point of view. It

Even if the validity of the more restrictive majority position is granted, it would apply only to functions specifically devolved to these bodies, and not to acts performed under their general powers. In other words if, in matters such as the admission of new members or termination of mandates by the General Assembly, or the declaration of the existence of threat to or breach of the peace by the Security Council, these bodies are so limited, they are not so when characterising a situation as a state of emergency or an armed conflict. In executing the latter, political bodies at the UN perform a political task to which should not attach effects similar to characterisation by a judicial body. As noted by the ICJ in the *Nicaragua (Jurisdiction and Admissibility)* case, these two functions are 'separate but complementary'.[125] The question of the characterisation of situations under human rights and humanitarian law thus does not raise problems similar to those posed by the *Lockerbie* and *Application of the Genocide Convention* cases.

In Resolution 808 (1993) on the creation of the ICTY, the UN Security Council refers explicitly to norms traditionally considered to be applicable only in international armed conflicts, posing the question of whether the Tribunal has any competence to examine violations of norms governing internal conflicts and opening a Pandora's box of characterisation of each specific conflict examined by that body.[126] In the *Tadić* appeal on jurisdiction, the Prosecutor had argued that the Security Council had characterised, in a binding manner, the entire web of conflicts in the former Yugoslavia as international. The same argument was made

follows that the Members of such an organ who are responsible for forming its decisions must consider questions from every aspect, and, in consequence, are legally entitled to base their arguments and their vote upon political considerations'). See also Salmon, 'Some Observations on Characterization', at 14.

[125] *Military and Paramilitary Activities in and Against Nicaragua (Nicaragua v. US), Jurisdiction and Admissibility*, [1984] ICJ Rep. 392, at 435 ('The [UN Security] Council has functions of a political nature assigned to it, whereas the Court exercises purely judicial functions with respect to the same events. Both organs can therefore perform their separate but complementary functions'). See also Judge Schwebel's dissent on the merits in the same case, [1986] ICJ Rep. 290 ('In short, the Security Council is a political organ which acts for political reasons. It may take legal considerations into account, but, unlike a court, it is not bound to apply them').

[126] The Secretary-General's 'Report Pursuant to Security Council Resolution 808 (1993)' notes with respect to para. 1 of the Resolution limiting the Tribunal's jurisdiction to events occurring after 1 January 1991 that 'no judgment as to the international or internal character of the conflict is being exercised': UN Doc. S/25704 (3 May 1993), *reprinted in* 32 Int'l Leg. Mat. 1159, para. 62. See Theodor Meron, 'Classification of Armed Conflict in the Former Yugoslavia: *Nicaragua*'s Fallout', (1998) 92 *Am. J Int'l L* 236, 238.

by the defence in the appeal in the *Celebici* case. The Appeals Chamber rejected that position, finding that the Council had not made any binding characterisation, leaving the matter to be decided judicially. It was therefore up to the Tribunal to determine the nature of the various conflicts in the region.[127] The ICTR in the *Akayesu* case came to an identical conclusion with respect to the character of the situation in Rwanda.[128] Because the ICTY and ICTR are both subsidiary organs of the Security Council, they are in a particular position with respect to any characterisation by the latter. Indeed, as the ICTR Statute illustrates, the Council can consider a conflict as internal and limit the Tribunal's jurisdiction to the administration of the violations of norms applicable to internal conflicts. This limitation of the Tribunal's competence should not be taken as extending its binding effect beyond the Tribunal itself, however, leaving states to proceed to their characterisation of the Rwanda conflicts and, if the facts were reasonably to bear it, consider the conflict as international.

The Human Rights Commission, as a political body, suffers from the same limitations with respect to the application of human rights and humanitarian law. The overtly political nature of the work of the Commission has been reflected not only in its application of norms but also in its selective choice of concerns, with the result that some situations where the state's characterisation was very questionable have escaped scrutiny, including those in Argentina, Cyprus, Cambodia, Poland and China.[129] Further, the essentially *ad hoc* procedure of the Human Rights Commission means that much depends on the personality of the rapporteur or working group assigned to examine a given case.[130]

---

[127] See *The Prosecutor v. Tadić* (Decision on the Defence Motion for Interlocutory Appeal on Jurisdiction), 2 Oct. 1995, Case No. IT-94-1-AR72 (Appeals Chamber, ICTY) 42–3 para. 76; *The Prosecutor v. Delalić, Mucić, Delić and Landzo* (the *Celebici* case) (Appeals Judgment), 20 Feb. 2001, Case No. IT-96-21-A (Appeals Chamber, ICTY) paras. 130 and 135; Christopher Greenwood, 'International Humanitarian Law and the *Tadić* Case', (1996) 7 *Eur. J Int'l L* 265, 270–1; Marco Sassòli, 'La première décision de la Chambre d'appel dans l'affaire *Tadić*', [1996] *Revue générale de droit international public* 120–1.

[128] *The Prosecutor v. Akayesu* (Judgment), 2 Sept. 1998, Case No. ICTR-96-4-T (Trial Chamber I, ICTR) paras. 604–5.

[129] For instance, in the case of China, a draft resolution was presented at the Commission following the imposition of martial law, but was never brought to vote: UN Doc. E/CN.4/1990/L.47 (1990). See Fitzpatrick, *Human Rights in Crisis*, at 148–51; ILA, 'First Report', at 123 and 132–3; van Boven, 'Reliance on Norms of Humanitarian Law', at 495, 500.

[130] See Fitzpatrick, *Human Rights in Crisis*, at 126–7. One study concludes that '[p]ractice concerning the applicability of international humanitarian law, including when it comes to dealing with admittedly sensitive and sometimes complex issues such as

As for the Sub-Commission, its work has focused more on the cataloguing of states of emergency than on providing an independent evaluation of the adequacy of the state's characterisation of specific situations.

The only complete fusion of political and legal mechanisms in the characterisation of situations as states of emergency or armed conflicts was the role played by the Committee of Ministers under the European Convention on Human Rights prior to 1998. As noted earlier, Article 32 of the Convention operated a complete *dédoublement fonctionnel* with respect to the Committee, to give it true quasi-judicial functions in addition to its more usual political ones. When fulfilling quasi-judicial functions, the Committee in principle ceased to be a political body and, in a manner similar to the role of the UN General Assembly as envisaged in the majority opinion in the *Admission to the United Nations* decision, it had to behave as such. The Committee indeed adopted special procedural rules applicable to proceedings under Article 32, in an attempt to bring its own decision-making process in line with the requirements of the European Convention.[131] Whether the Committee of Ministers was indeed capable of successfully transforming itself at will into a quasi-judicial body was open to question. Its role under the European Convention was the object of intense criticism, and indeed this possible intrusion by a political body into the legal characterisation of a situation as a state of emergency was eliminated by the entry into force of Protocol 11 to the Convention in late 1998.[132]

whether a situation qualifies as an armed conflict and, if so, whether it is domestic or international in character, has unfortunately been somewhat inconsistent and, on occasion, frankly questionable': Daniel O'Donnell, 'Trends in the Application of International Humanitarian Law by United Nations Human Rights Mechanisms', (1998) 324 *Int'l Rev. Red Cross* 481, 497. For example, one special rapporteur on Chile did not proceed to assess the existence of a state of emergency because it had been institutionalised in the Constitution: UN Doc. E/CN.4/1986/2 (1986) para. 145.

[131] See Drzemczewski, 'Decisions on the Merits', at 750–4.

[132] Only the Committee's limited role in the enforcement of decisions by the European Court of Human Rights remains. Protocol 11 is reprinted in (1994) 15 *Hum. Rts LJ* 104–7. This constitutes an implicit rejection of an argument advanced by van Dijk and van Hoof to the effect that whether a state of emergency exists in a country is an essentially political question, which courts are not equipped to answer. They suggested that the characterisation of a situation as a state of emergency be systematically referred to the Committee of Ministers: P. van Dijk and G. J. H. van Hoof, *Theory and Practice of the European Convention on Human Rights*, 1st edn (Deventer: Kluwer, 1984) 470–2 (an argument not repeated in later editions of the same work). As noted by some writers, this would have the effect of emptying the norm of any legal content: Ergec, *Droits de l'homme*, at 385–6; Wilhelm Wengler, *Der Begriff des*

At a very general level, the quasi-judicial and law-making functions of political organs of international organisations are intimately linked. Applications of an existing set of rules to particular facts inevitably result in the creation of a new, more specific rule, following the model of common law development in Anglo-American law.[133] As Kelsen put it, '[a]uthentic interpretation, whether general or individual, is a law-creating act'.[134] As long as there is resistance to considering the resolutions of political organs as creating positive law, and not merely aspirational 'soft law', the same resolutions cannot be accepted as being legally binding on states in the case at hand. Characterisation by political organs is thus 'soft characterisation', not in itself binding on member states.

Independent bodies

Other types of supra-national bodies concerned with the enforcement of, or more widely the compliance with, norms of human rights and humanitarian law have been confronted with the need to characterise situations as a state of emergency or an armed conflict. The bodies whose work is discussed in this section differ greatly in status and structure, but share the common feature that they are not directly controlled by state interests.

Given the much higher degree of institutionalisation of human rights law, it is not surprising that bodies operating in that area of law have developed a practice considerably more important than those in the field of humanitarian law. This suggests *a priori* that the cross-pollination

politischen im internationalen Recht (Tübingen: Mohr, 1956) 60 ('Vom Recht her gesehen ist ein Missbrauch der Rechtsnorm, wenn man sie als bindend verkündet, aber ihre objektive richtige Anwendung im Einzelfall durch eine unabhängige Instanz mit der Behauptung, es handeln sich um eine politische Entscheidung, hindern will').

[133] See Oscar Schachter, 'The Quasi-Judicial Role of the Security Council and the General Assembly', (1965) 58 *Am. J Int'l L* 960–6; Salmon, 'Le fait dans l'application', at 325–6. It thus seems difficult to follow Castañeda in his assertion that the General Assembly can make binding determination of 'facts' which exist objectively as a condition to which the rule attaches legal consequences in the form of obligations for the state: Jorge Castañeda, *Legal Effect of United Nations Resolutions* (New York: Columbia UP, 1969) 118–19 and 131–2. Facts become conditions because they are legally defined (Martti Koskenniemi, *From Apology to Utopia – The Structure of International Legal Argument* (Helsinki: Lakimiesliiton Kustannus, 1989) 466–7). Every finding by an organ that a situation meets the legal definition of a fact constitutes a refinement of, and thus a change to, this legal definition. This is so despite the fact that the doctrine of *stare decisis* is inapplicable to this type of decision.

[134] Kelsen, *Law of the UN*, at xv.

316 APPLICATION: LAW AND FACTS

with respect to characterisation by this type of body will primarily be one originating in human rights law and benefiting humanitarian law. The creation of the ICTY, ICTR and ICC nevertheless indicates that these issues will also be dealt with by specialised international bodies in the humanitarian law field.

HUMAN RIGHTS

The various bodies created within the framework of universal and regional human rights instruments are given general competence to enforce human rights, with no special reference in the text of the conventions to the problem of characterisation.[135] They thus had to determine the extent of their competence in this respect, faced with at least some state claims that recourse to emergency derogation is a sovereign, political act, and therefore not reviewable.[136] Few trends emerge from an analysis of the activities of the various specialised bodies, apart from a general inclination to reject state claims regarding the political and non-reviewable nature of a declaration of a state of emergency.

The European Commission and Court of Human Rights have from the very beginning of their activities expressed clearly a willingness to go beyond a state's characterisation of a situation as a state of emergency, and make their own assessment of the existence of an emergency threatening the life of the nation. Thus in the *First Cyprus* case in 1956, the Commission stated its opinion that nothing in the Convention prevented it from reviewing derogation under Article 15.[137] Later decisions by both the Commission and the Court in '*Lawless*', *Ireland* v. *UK*, and recently *Brannigan and McBride* v. *UK* and *Askoy* v. *Turkey*, confirmed the power of the human rights bodies to proceed to their own global characterisation of a situation as constituting or not a state of emergency.[138] Indeed in the *Greek* case, the Commission did find that there was no

---

[135] There was a suggestion put forward by the Belgian delegation during the *travaux préparatoires* of the International Covenant on Civil and Political Rights to create a summary procedure to assess the legality of derogations based on a state of emergency, but this was not followed up: E/CN.4/528 paras. 79–86 (1951); Hartman, 'Working Paper', at 130.

[136] See above, pp. 286–7.

[137] (1956) 1 YB Eur. Com'n Hum. Rts 174–6; Ergec, *Droits de l'homme*, at 329.

[138] '*Lawless*' case, (1960–1) Eur. Com'n Hum. Rts, Ser. B, at 334; *Ireland* v. *UK*, (1978) Eur. Ct Hum. Rts, Ser. A, vol. 3, at 78–82; *Brannigan and McBride* v. *United Kingdom* (A/253-B), (1993) 17 Eur. Hum. Rts Rep. 539, 569–70 (Eur. Ct Hum. Rts); *Askoy* v. *Turkey*, (1996) 23 Eur. Hum. Rts Rep. 553, 586–7 (Eur. Ct Hum. Rts).

justifiable state of emergency under Article 15.[139] Tagged onto this clear statement of its power, however, is the doctrine of 'margin of appreciation' providing that the Commission and Court cannot proceed to a purely objective assessment of the situation, but can intervene only if the state's characterisation falls outside of this margin. As discussed in the context of the effect of the state's characterisation, the doctrine of 'margin of appreciation' has been the target of criticism for its vagueness and its general deference to the derogating state.[140] Although the jurisprudence of the organs of the European Convention on the character of a state of emergency under Article 15 is quite limited, these organs have not adopted a policy of systematically reviewing the validity of state characterisations of emergencies threatening the life of the nation.[141] In the 1993 decisions by the Commission and Court in the *Brannigan and McBride* case, however, both bodies proceeded to make their own assessment of the existence of a state of emergency despite the fact that this point was not challenged by the parties.[142] This perhaps signals a move towards more systematically reviewing the state's characterisation of the situation each time Article 15 is invoked.

The UN Human Rights Committee so far has adopted a two-tier approach in its review of characterisations by states under Article 4 of the International Covenant on Civil and Political Rights. Questions relating to derogations under a state of emergency have been brought to the attention of the Committee pursuant to two distinct jurisdictions. First, the Committee has been called on to assess the existence of states of emergency in the context of states' periodic reports required under Article 40 of the Covenant. The Committee had been divided as to its power to question the existence of a state of emergency in this context. This was in fact but one facet of a wider debate within the Committee regarding its powers under Article 40, more specifically the power to make general comments directed at individual states.[143] The Human Rights Committee in 1992 finally resolved the debate by adopting a

---

[139] (1969) 12 *YB Eur. Conv. Hum. Rts* 71–6 and 100.
[140] See above, pp. 287–9.
[141] Subrata Roy Chowdhury, *Rule of Law in a State of Emergency* (London: Pinter, 1989) 67; ILA, 'First Report', at 149–50.
[142] *Brannigan and McBride*, at 556–7 para. 45 (Commission) and 570 para. 47. Non-governmental organisations intervening in the case did contest the existence of a state of emergency.
[143] See McGoldrick, *Human Rights Committee*, at 89–92; ILA, 'First Report', at 117–18; 'Siracusa Principle 71', at 13.

318 APPLICATION: LAW AND FACTS

decision authorising 'comments of the Committee as a whole' directed at specific states, to be drafted in the wake of its review of the state's periodic report.[144] In addition, the Committee since April 1991 has had a policy of requesting special reports under Article 40(1)(b) of the Covenant from states experiencing an emergency, not necessarily limited to cases of *de jure* derogations under Article 4. This can even be done between sessions by the Chair of the Committee.[145] These broader powers, however, have not resulted in critical reviews of the existence of states of emergency under Article 4 of the Covenant.[146] The Committee's very limited fact-finding capabilities are clearly an obstacle difficult to overcome in this respect. The problem is compounded by the fact that states do not always indicate in their periodic reports that emergency measures have been resorted to in their country, thus preventing any scrutiny of the issue unless the Committee is indirectly made aware of the state of emergency and requests further details.[147] To this day, there has been no frank review of characterisation of states of emergency under Article 40, although the Committee's expression of 'deep concern' in its 1998 review of Israel's periodic report is the most implicitly critical yet.[148]

---

[144] 'Report of the Human Rights Committee', UN Doc. A/47/40 (1992); UN Doc. CCPR/C/79 (1992).

[145] Special emergency reports have been requested from Iraq (1991), Yugoslavia (1991), Peru (1992), Bosnia-Herzegovina, Croatia and the Federal Republic of Yugoslavia (1992), Angola and Burundi (1993), Haiti and Rwanda (1994): 'Report of the Human Rights Committee on the Work of its 51st Session', UN Doc. A/50/40 (1995) paras. 36–9. Later reports of the Committee do not mention requesting emergency reports but are limited to a mention of states having invoked Art. 4. See e.g. 'Report of the Human Rights Committee on the Work of its 56th Session', UN Doc. A/55/40 (2000) 12–13.

[146] See Fitzpatrick, *Human Rights in Crisis*, at 96. At its most incisive, the Committee 'expresses concern' over questionable states of emergency, without really challenging their validity. See e.g. the Committee's comment on the reports by Egypt, Zambia and Colombia, UN Doc. CCPR/C/79/Add.23 (1993) para. 9, CCPR/C/79/Add.62 (1996) para. 11, 'Report of the Human Rights Committee on the Work of its 53rd Session', UN Doc. A/52/40 (1997) para. 288.

[147] For instance in periodic reports by Lebanon (UN Doc. CCPR/C/SR.442–4, SR.446 (1983)), Afghanistan (UN Doc. CCPR/C/SR.603, SR.604, SR.608 (1985)) and Zambia (UN Doc. CCPR/C/SR.772, SR.776); Fitzpatrick, *Human Rights in Crisis*, at 85; ILA, 'First Report', at 117; ILA, 'Second Interim Report of the Committee on the Enforcement of Human Rights Law', in ILA, *Report of the 63rd Conference, Warsaw, 21–27 August 1988* (London: ILA, 1988) 129, 133–4.

[148] UN Doc. CCPR/C/79/Add.93 (1998) para. 11 ('The Committee expresses its deep concern at the continued state of emergency prevailing in Israel, which has been in effect since independence. It recommends that the Government review the necessity for the continued renewal of the state of emergency with a view to limiting as far as possible its scope and territorial applicability and the associated derogation of rights'). See McGoldrick, *Human Rights Committee*, at 305; Hartman, 'Derogation', at 40.

The Human Rights Committee is also presented with the question of the legitimacy of states of emergency in individual communications under the Optional Protocol to the Political Covenant. There, the consensus among the members of the Committee has been much more favourable to a relatively interventionist stance. The position of the Committee on this point has been an evolving one, starting from a narrower interpretation of its powers leading it to review the legality and proportionality of measures rather than the state's characterisation of a public emergency, to a clear statement in *Landinelli Silva v. Uruguay* that it falls squarely within its functions to assess the very existence of a state of emergency. In that case, where the notice of derogation required by Article 4(3) had been sent by Uruguay to the Secretary-General, the Committee expressed the view that:[149]

Although the sovereign right of a State party to declare a state of emergency is not questioned, yet, in the specific context of the present communication, the Human Rights Committee is of the opinion that a State, by merely invoking the existence of exceptional circumstances, cannot evade the obligations it has undertaken by ratifying the Covenant... It is the function of the Human Rights Committee, acting under the Optional Protocol, to see to it that States party live up to their commitment under the Covenant. In order to assess whether a situation of the kind described in article 4(1) of the Covenant exists in the country concerned, it needs full and comprehensive information. *If the respondent Government does not furnish the required justification itself, as it is required to do under article 4(2) of the Optional Protocol and article 4(3) of the Covenant, the Human Rights Committee cannot conclude that valid reasons exist to legitimize a departure from the normal legal regime prescribed by the Covenant.* [Emphasis added.]

The competence of the Committee under the Optional Protocol to review the state's characterisation of a public emergency is thus clearly stated. The extent of this power, however, remains unclear. In particular, it has not been decided whether the doctrine of 'margin of appreciation' developed by the European Commission and Court of Human Rights will

There have been comments by individual members of the Human Rights Committee expressing doubts as to the validity of a state of emergency, for example in the review of the Uruguayan and Peruvian periodic reports: UN Doc. CCPR/C/SR.357 (1982), CCPR/C/SR.1520 (1996) para. 30 (Aguilar Urbina).

[149] *Landinelli Silva et al. v. Uruguay*, Comm. 43/1978, UN Doc. A/36/40 (1981) at 130 para. 8.3, *reprinted in Selected Decisions*, UN Sales No. E.89.XIV.1, at 66. See also McGoldrick, *Human Rights Committee*, at 312–13; Daniel O'Donnell, *Protección internacional de los derechos humanos* (Lima: Comisión andina de juristas, 1988) 401–2; Oráa, *Human Rights*, at 48–51.

be adopted, or whether the Human Rights Committee intends to proceed to its own, objective characterisation of the situation.[150] After its firm statement in *Landinelli Silva*, the Committee has always shied away from a direct assessment of the state's characterisation of the situation as an emergency threatening the life of the nation.[151] Generally speaking, then, the very lopsided acceptance of the Optional Protocol and the Committee's unwillingness to review state characterisation of emergencies under Article 40 result in a less than satisfactory monitoring mechanism of derogation under Article 4 of the Covenant on Civil and Political Rights.[152]

The experience of the Inter-American Commission on Human Rights with respect to characterisation of emergencies has followed a pattern opposite to that of the Human Rights Committee. The Inter-American Commission has been active in reviewing the existence of a state of emergency in country reports rather than in individual communications.[153] As early as 1968, the Commission expressed its opinion that there was no incompatibility between an international control of derogations under Article 27 of the American Convention on Human Rights and the principle of non-intervention in the internal affairs of the state.[154] Despite this bold statement, the Commission only progressively came to adopt a practice of questioning the state's characterisation of the situation as a threat to its independence or security. Initially, for example in its 1981 reports on Bolivia and Colombia, the Commission centred on whether the specific measures adopted were necessary and proportional.[155] In the 1983 Misquito report and in another report on Nicaragua in 1987, the Commission did expressly address the issue of whether there were valid grounds to declare a state of emergency, finding in the affirmative in

---

[150] Although individual members have publicly stated their opinions on the subject. See McGoldrick, *Human Rights Committee*, at 305 and 315–16.

[151] See the review of decisions in Fitzpatrick, *Human Rights in Crisis*, at 101–2.

[152] The possibility of inter-state complaints under Art. 41 of the Covenant has not been addressed, given the lack of state practice.

[153] On individual petitions, see Fitzpatrick, *Human Rights in Crisis*, at 185–8.

[154] 'Resolution on the Protection of Human Rights in Connection with the Suspension of Constitutional Guarantees or "State of Siege"', OAS Doc. OEA/Ser.L/V/II.19, doc. 32 (1968); Oráa, *Human Rights*, at 53.

[155] 'Report on the Situation of Human Rights in Bolivia', OAS Doc. OEA/Ser.L/V/II.53, doc. 6 (1981) 23; 'Report on the Situation of Human Rights in the Republic of Colombia', OAS Doc. OEA/Ser.L/V/II.53, doc. 22 (1981) 221. See O'Donnell, *Protección internacional*, at 402; Christina M. Cerna, 'Human Rights in Armed Conflict: Implementation of International Humanitarian Norms by Regional Intergovernmental Human Rights Bodies', in Frits Kalshoven and Yves Sandoz eds., *Implementation of International Humanitarian Law* (Dordrecht: Nijhoff, 1989) 31, 49.

both cases.[156] Finally, and more critically, the Inter-American Commission noted in its 1987 report on Paraguay that the absence of any serious social incidents in the previous seven years contradicted the state's characterisation of the situation as an emergency, concluding that no proper state of emergency existed pursuant to Article 27 of the American Convention.[157] Similar conclusions were reached in later reports.[158] There thus seems to be a willingness on the part of the Inter-American Commission on Human Rights to review state characterisation of emergency situations directly in the course of its country reports. This is an important development because the Inter-American Commission, unlike its UN and European equivalents, can independently initiate such a review mechanism. There is no legal barrier preventing the Commission from adopting a policy of systematically assessing state characterisations of situations as states of emergency.[159] Indeed, the Commission in its 1996 annual report indicates that one of the four criteria it uses to determine whether a state should be the object of a country report is whether a state of emergency was declared in the country.[160]

Mention can also be made of the limited experience of specialised bodies of the International Labour Organization (ILO) in reviewing the existence of a state of emergency. Most ILO conventions do not contain specific provisions allowing for exceptional derogations in times of emergency threatening the life or security of the nation. The ILO faced the issue when a complaint was filed against Greece in June 1968 alleging the breach of Conventions Nos. 87 and 98.[161] The Greek Government objected to the ILO Commission of Inquiry that its international

---

[156] 'Report on the Situation of Human Rights of a Segment of the Nicaraguan Population of Misquito Origin', OAS Doc. OEA/Ser.L/V/II.62, doc. 10, rev. 3 (1983) 116; 'Report on the Situation of Human Rights in Nicaragua', [1987] Inter-Am. YB Hum. Rts 452, 470 ('Facts that are a matter of public knowledge show, in the Commission's view, that the Nicaraguan Government is facing a threat to State security and that such a threat now exists'); O'Donnell, Protección internacional, at 402; Cerna, 'Human Rights', at 50–1; ILA, 'Second Report', at 138.

[157] 'Report on the Situation of Human Rights in Paraguay', [1987] Inter-Am. YB Hum. Rts 516, 556.

[158] See, for example, Recommendation No. 2, 'Report on the Situation of Human Rights in Colombia', OAS Doc. OEA/Ser.L/VIII.84 (1993).

[159] See O'Donnell, Protección internacional, at 403; ILA, 'First Report', at 144. More immediate limitations would probably stem from the Inter-American Commission's limited budget and staff.

[160] Inter-American Commission on Human Rights, '1996 Annual Report', available at http://www.oea.org/.

[161] (1971) 54:2 ILO Off. Bull. (Spec. Suppl.) 1. For earlier examples of control of emergency derogations by the ILO Committee of Experts and Conference Committee, and in particular the derogation by Czechoslovakia in 1955, see E. A. Landy, The Effectiveness

obligations under ILO conventions were subject to suspension when the state was of the opinion that an emergency had arisen. The Commission of Inquiry, although accepting the principle of derogation in times of emergency, rejected the Greek argument of total deference towards the state's appreciation:[162]

> If a plea of emergency is to be treated in international law as a legal concept there similarly has to be appraisal by an impartial authority at the international level. It is for this reason that international tribunals and supervisory organs, when seized of such a plea, have invariably made an independent determination of whether the circumstances justified the claim, and have not allowed the state concerned to be the sole judge of the issue.

While the reference to the 'invariable' practice of international bodies might be overstated, the Commission's perception of its own power to review the state's characterisation is clear. In the case against Greece, the Commission eventually concluded that no evidence of the existence of a state of emergency had been adduced, and thus that the Greek Government's plea of emergency could not be accepted.[163] In a 1983 case concerning Poland, another Commission of Inquiry similarly determined that the characterisation of the situation as a state of emergency was unsupported by the evidence, and rejected the Polish Government's plea.[164]

The practice of specialised bodies in the field of human rights with respect to the characterisation of a situation as a state of emergency is somewhat disappointing. Of all intervenors on the international scene having a possible input in the characterisation of a given situation, they present the most guarantees as to objectivity and competence. The difficulty stems from the fact that, often, the broader powers exercised by specialised bodies are in non-judicial settings. For instance, the Inter-American Commission on Human Rights in its country reports and

---

of International Supervision – Thirty Years of ILO Experience (London/Dobbs Ferry: Stevens & Sons/Oceana, 1966) 149–50.

[162] (1971) 54:2 ILO Off. Bull. (Spec. Suppl.) 1, para. 111.

[163] Ibid., para. 112. The case is discussed in ILA, 'First Report', at 140–2.

[164] (1984) 67 ILO Off. Bull. (Ser. B) (Spec. Suppl.) paras. 479–81. On the other hand, the ILO Committee on Freedom of Association seems to have adopted a hands-off policy, deeming declarations of states of emergency to be purely political and non-reviewable decisions: 197th Report, Case No. 930 (Turkey), (1979) 62:3 ILO Off. Bull. (Ser. B) 152–3; ILA, 'First Report', at n. 209. See also the critique of Burma's derogation in the 'Report on Forced Labour in Myanmar (Burma)', 2 July 1998, paras. 212 and 471 (applying the express derogation provision in Art. 2(2)(c) of the 1930 Forced Labour Convention).

the Human Rights Committee in its review of periodic state reports do not perceive themselves to be acting judicially. In one case, the Human Rights Committee even forcefully denied that it was sitting in judgment of a state presenting a report, holding its purpose to be the promotion of 'a fruitful and necessary dialogue'.[165] Even the European Commission and Court of Human Rights have been the target of justified criticism for a 'margin of appreciation' doctrine showing too much deference to the state in the context of a state of emergency. It remains to be seen whether the ratification of the European Convention by states in Central and Eastern Europe will lead the European Court of Human Rights to reconsider the breadth of the 'margin of appreciation' doctrine. As noted by Judge Martens in *Brannigan and McBride* v. *UK*, this doctrine was developed at a time when states parties to the Convention were united by a history of democracy and a strong commitment to human rights.[166] A broader range of states parties will bring these bodies closer to the situation in which the Inter-American Commission on Human Rights and the Human Rights Committee find themselves, perhaps leading to a reconsideration of the validity or scope of the 'margin of appreciation' doctrine.

If, as suggested by McGoldrick, the state's response to a public emergency is an acid test of its commitment to human rights,[167] the specialised bodies' response is an acid test of their perceived legitimacy. Because it touches on the very integrity of the state, the review of emergency derogation is one of the issues most intrusive on state sovereignty. At the same time, however, it represents the best mechanism in the existing international legal system to provide the world community with a neutral characterisation of a given situation as a valid or invalid state of emergency.

HUMANITARIAN LAW

In the field of humanitarian law, international judicial bodies have sometimes been given the opportunity to characterise armed conflicts. The International Court of Justice in the *Nicaragua* v. *United States* case, for

---

[165] 'Report of the Human Rights Committee', UN Doc. A/38/40 (1982) para. 239 (members of the Human Rights Committee 'expressed their indignation at an article . . . depicting the Committee as a tribunal'); Chowdhury, *Rule of Law*, at 83 n. 213. For the Inter-American Commission on Human Rights, see ILA, 'First Report', at 144–5.

[166] *Brannigan and McBride* v. *United Kingdom* (A/253-B), (1993) 17 Eur. Hum. Rts Rep. 539, 590–1 (Eur. Ct Hum. Rts, Martens J conc.).

[167] See McGoldrick, *Human Rights Committee*, at 301.

example, did find that a non-international armed conflict was ongoing in the territory of Nicaragua.[168] Similarly, Judge Kreća in his dissent in the *Genocide Convention Application (Bosnia-Herzegovina v. Yugoslavia)* case found the conflict in Bosnia-Herzegovina to be of a mixed character, an issue which the Court may revisit at the merits stage.[169] Such interventions by the ICJ, however desirable because of their impartial and binding nature, are unlikely to be more than exceptions because of the limited acceptance of the Court's jurisdiction. The problem is similar for the International Criminal Court: its power to try grave breaches and serious violations of humanitarian law certainly implies the power to characterise a situation as an armed conflict of one kind or another. The optional and complementary nature of its jurisdiction, however, makes it quite improbable that the ICC will provide more than an occasional solution to the all-too-frequent problem of characterisation. Finally, *ad hoc* bodies such as the ICTY and ICTR have a jurisdiction which is strictly limited to situations and acts within narrowly defined parameters.[170] Within these parameters, they provide a fully satisfactory solution to the problem of characterisation, but unfortunately their jurisdiction is dwarfed by the magnitude and generality of the difficulty.

Two other independent bodies are the most likely candidates for an active role in characterising a situation as an armed conflict of one type or the other: the International Committee of the Red Cross (ICRC) and the International Fact-Finding Commission.

The ICRC is of course not an international organisation but rather a hybrid body, formed by private individuals but given a measure of international legal personality by its recognition in the Geneva Conventions and Protocols.[171] The role specifically envisaged for the ICRC by these instruments is one of protection and assistance to the victims of armed

---

[168] *Military and Paramilitary Activities in and Against Nicaragua (Nicaragua v. USA)*, [1986] ICJ Rep. 14, 114. See Meron, *Human Rights in Internal Strife*, at 162; Oppenheim, *International Law* (1992) I, at 167.

[169] Dissenting Opinion of Judge *ad hoc* Kreća, *Application of the Convention on the Prevention and Punishment of the Crime of Genocide (Bosnia & Herzegovina v. Yugoslavia (Serbia & Montenegro))*, Preliminary Objections, 11 July 1996, para. 100.

[170] See, for instance, Art. 1 of the Statute of the International Criminal Tribunal for Rwanda, giving the Tribunal power to prosecute persons for crimes committed between 1 January and 31 December 1994 in Rwanda or by Rwandans in neighbouring states: UN Doc. S/RES/955 (1994) Annex.

[171] See Julio A. Barberis, 'El Comité internacional de la Cruz Roja como sujeto de derecho internacional', in Christophe Swinarski ed., *Studies and Essays on International Humanitarian Law and Red Cross Principles in Honour of Jean Pictet* (Geneva/The Hague: Nijhoff, 1984) 635; Christian Dominicé, 'La personnalité juridique du CICR', in *ibid.*, at 663–72; Paul Reuter, 'La personnalité juridique du CICR', in *ibid.*, at 783–92.

conflicts.[172] No provision of the Geneva Conventions and Protocols expressly assigns any role to the ICRC with respect to the characterisation of a situation as an armed conflict. Such a provision was envisaged at the 1971 and 1972 Conferences of Government Experts, during which suggestions were made to include in Protocol I an article giving the ICRC power or discretion to determine in a non-binding manner that an armed conflict was taking place in a given territory.[173] The ICRC actually opposed these suggestions, which were never pursued further.[174]

In the regular course of its work, the ICRC is called upon to assess, for its own purposes, which type of situation is occurring within the targeted country. The decision to ask for compliance with the Third Geneva Convention, for instance, must rest on the characterisation of the hostilities as an international armed conflict. In that respect, the ICRC is no more bound by the unilateral characterisations of the belligerents than are third states or international organisations. The practice of the ICRC is to assess independently the situation in each theatre in which it intervenes, but in a purely internal manner.[175] On that basis, if its own characterisation does not accord with that of the belligerents, the ICRC's preferred approach is to initiate a private dialogue with the authorities concerned, in the hope of bringing about greater compliance with humanitarian law.

The ICRC has publicly expressed opinions as to the legal basis of its intervention. For instance, at the request of the International Red

---

[172] See Arts. 9–11 and 23, First Geneva Convention; Arts. 3 and 9–11, Second Geneva Convention; Arts. 3, 9–11, 56 and 72–81, Third Geneva Convention; Arts. 3, 10–12, 14, 30, 59, 61, 63, 76, 96, 102, 104, 108–9, 111, 140 and 142–3, Fourth Geneva Convention; Arts. 3, 5–6, 33, 78, 81 and 97, Protocol I.

[173] Amendment CE/COM/II/61, ICRC, *Report of the Work of the Conference of Government Experts on the Reaffirmation and Development of International Humanitarian Law of Armed Conflicts – Second Session, Geneva, 3 May–3 June 1972* (Geneva: ICRC, 1972) II, 44; I, 94 paras. 2.293–4; ICRC, *1971 Conference of Experts*, at 43 para. 215; UN Secretary-General, 'Respect for Human Rights in Armed Conflicts', UN Doc. A/8052 (1970) 49–50 paras. 158–61.

[174] See ICRC, *1971 Conference of Experts*, at 42 para. 195; Wilhelm, 'Problèmes relatifs', at 342. Perhaps surprisingly, the head of the ICRC Legal Division expressed the opinion that '[c]ompte-tenu des tâches qui lui sont confiées par les Conventions de Genève et par son mandat reconnu internationalement, le CICR a sans doute la compétence de qualifier juridiquement les conflits armés, sans qu'il soit obligé de l'exercer': Toni Pfanner, 'Le rôle du Comité international de la Croix-Rouge dans la mise en oeuvre du droit international humanitaire', in *Law in Humanitarian Crises – How Can International Humanitarian Law be Made Effective in Armed Conflict?* (Luxembourg: European Communities, 1995) I, 177, 207–8.

[175] See François Bugnion, *Le Comité international de la Croix-Rouge et la protection des victimes de la guerre* (Geneva: ICRC, 1994) 460–2 and generally the ICRC Annual Reports.

Cross Conference, the ICRC opined that common Article 3 applied in Afghanistan, Ogaden and the Western Sahara.[176] In relation to other episodes, such as the Iran–Iraq conflict, the invasion of Kuwait by Iraq, or in Bosnia-Herzegovina, the ICRC has called for compliance with humanitarian norms, impliedly qualifying the situation as an armed conflict.[177] Nevertheless, the general policy of the ICRC is to abstain from openly characterising situations in which it intervenes. As put by its president, Alexander Hay, 'the primary interest of the ICRC is the protection of victims, and not to provide a legal definition of a conflict situation, or to specify the status of persons to be protected. Besides, the ICRC is perfectly aware that it has neither the competence nor the power to impose its views in these matters.'[178] Thus, for example, the ICRC asked to visit prisoners in Kenya in 1957 and in Afghanistan in 1979 without specifically referring to their status as prisoners of war or to the nature of events occurring in these countries.[179] The ICRC visits political prisoners in peacetime as well as in wartime, and provides relief in a wide array of natural and artificial crises, so that its mere presence in any given context cannot be taken in itself as a characterisation of the situation as an armed conflict. For the ICRC, the fact that its intervention is

---

[176] See Weissbrodt, 'Role of International Organizations', at 343. But see Hans-Peter Gasser, 'Internationalized Non-international Armed Conflicts: Case Studies of Afghanistan, Kampuchea and Lebanon', (1983) 33 *Am. UL Rev.* 145, 151 and 156, where the author, then head of the ICRC Legal Division, insists that the references to humanitarian law in Afghanistan and other conflicts were not a legal characterisation by the ICRC.

[177] See David, *Principes*, at 499–500. Again, these are not clearly presented as legal opinions classifying the situations. The ICRC did characterise the 1990–1 Iraq–Kuwait conflict as an international armed conflict, at the request of national Red Cross/Crescent societies. It specified, however, that its statement was only 'provisional' and 'should not be considered as the official position of the International Committee of the Red Cross': ICRC Outline of Legal Aspects of the Conflict in the Middle East, 21 January 1991, reprinted in Walter Kalin, *Human Rights in Times of Occupation: The Case of Kuwait* (Berne: Law Books Europe, 1994) 155.

[178] Alexander Hay, 'The ICRC and the World Today', (1982) 226 *Int'l Rev. Red Cross* 12, 14. See also Meron, *Human Rights in Internal Strife*, at 44 and 161–3; Donald Tansley, *Final Report: An Agenda for Red Cross* (Geneva: ICRC, 1975) 70–1; Olivier Dürr, 'Humanitarian Law of Armed Conflict: Problems of Applicability', (1987) 24 *J Peace Res.* 263, 271–2; David Forsythe, 'Choices More Ethical than Legal: The International Committee of the Red Cross', (1993) 7 *Ethics & Int'l Aff.* 131, 137; ICRC, 'Action by the International Committee of the Red Cross in the Event of Breaches of International Humanitarian Law', (1981) 221 *Int'l Rev. Red Cross* 76, 77; Marco Sassòli, 'Mise en oeuvre du droit international humanitaire et du droit international des droits de l'homme', (1987) 43 *Annuaire suisse de droit international* 24, 29.

[179] See David Forsythe, 'Human Rights and the International Committee of the Red Cross', (1990) 12 *Hum. Rts Quart.* 265, 272; Zorgbibe, 'Le caractère armé', at 91 and 101.

not an implied or express act of characterisation is seen as essential to its function of assistance, which it considers to be largely incompatible with one aiming to enforce the application of humanitarian law.[180] Even when directly involved in the negotiation of agreements relating to the application of humanitarian law, for instance in the context of the conflicts in the former Yugoslavia, the ICRC has insisted on the need to reach an agreement acceptable to all parties rather than trying to impose its own legal characterisation of the situation.[181] Despite all this, the ICRC's intervention has been seen by some as necessarily indicative of the nature of a conflict. In the *Tadić* case, the Appeals Chamber of the ICTY found that the Red Cross's involvement in the negotiation of the agreements mentioned earlier clearly represented an implied characterisation on which the Tribunal could rely to buffer its conclusions as to the nature of the conflict.[182] The temptation to rely on characterisation by the ICRC is all the greater given that its neutrality and impartiality are increasingly being recognised in international law, above and beyond common Articles 9/9/9/10 of the Geneva Conventions.[183] There may be some danger in this position, both because it runs counter to the ICRC's intention and because the primary concern of the ICRC and other impartial humanitarian organisations is the protection of victims, and not an assessment of the legality of the belligerents' behaviour.[184] It seems somewhat paradoxical

---

[180] See ICRC, *1971 Conference of Experts*, at 43 para. 213; Bugnion, *CICR*, at 1101–9; ICRC, 'Action', at 80; Wilhelm, 'Problèmes relatifs', at 327.

[181] See Sandoz, 'Réflexion', at 462–70.

[182] *The Prosecutor* v. *Tadić* (Decision on the Defence Motion for Interlocutory Appeal on Jurisdiction), 2 Oct. 1995, Case No. IT-94-1-AR72 (Appeals Chamber, ICTY), 40 para. 73 ('On account of the unanimously recognized authority, competence and impartiality of the ICRC, as well as its statutory mission to promote and supervise respect for international humanitarian law, it is inconceivable that, even if there were some doubts as to the nature of the conflict, the ICRC would promote and endorse an agreement contrary to a basic provision of the Geneva Conventions. The conclusion is therefore warranted that the ICRC regarded the conflicts governed by the agreement in question as internal'). Compare this to the more measured position adopted in *The Prosecutor* v. *Blaskić* (Judgment), 3 March 2000, Case No. IT-95-14-T (Trial Chamber, ICTY) paras. 80–2, in which the Tribunal refuses to see in these agreements a conviction by the ICRC that the conflicts were internal.

[183] See *The Prosecutor* v. *Simić et al.* (Decision on the Prosecution Motion Under Rule 73 for a Ruling Concerning the Testimony of a Witness), 27 July 1999, Case No. IT-95-9-PT (Trial Chamber, ICTY).

[184] See Sassòli, a member of the ICRC Legal Division, 'Mise en oeuvre', at 52–3 ('le CICR a une approche plus pratique que juridique. Comme "on ne peut se faire à la fois champion de la justice et de la charité" [Jean Pictet], le CICR a choisi de secourir les victimes plutôt que de porter des jugements ... Dans cet esprit, le CICR n'entre pas

that the very qualities which make the ICRC an attractive agent of characterisation – its neutrality and impartiality – could be jeopardised by an insistence on attaching unwanted legal consequences to its actions; in effect, it would amount to forcing the ICRC to 'testify' at a time when its immunity from enforced testimony is being recognised.[185]

The International Fact-Finding Commission, the first permanent international body entrusted specifically with the implementation of humanitarian law, was established by Article 90 of Protocol I. The Commission came to life in June 1991, a few months after Canada became the twentieth state to make a declaration accepting the Commission's competence.[186] Under the terms of Article 90(2)(c)(i), the Commission is competent to enquire into any allegation of a 'grave breach as defined in the Conventions and this Protocol or other serious violation of the Conventions or of this Protocol' committed by a state party which has accepted the competence of the Commission. While the concept of 'grave breaches' is precisely defined in the Conventions and Protocol I (Arts. 50/51/130/147; Arts. 11(4) and 85, Protocol I), that of 'serious violations' appeared for the first time in Protocol I, without any clear indication as to what its content might be.[187] It is clear from the phrasing of the provision that 'serious violations' are a wider concept than 'grave breaches'. The ICRC in its commentary on Protocol I suggests that 'serious violations' include, *inter alia*, 'global' violations of the Conventions and Protocol which can be described as improper characterisations of a

---

dans des querelles juridiques stériles lorsque l'applicabilité du droit humanitaire est contestée'). See also Dürr, 'Humanitarian Law', at 271; David Forsythe, 'Who Guards the Guardians?: Third Parties and the Law of Armed Conflict', (1976) 70 *Am. J Int'l L* 41, 59–60.

[185] See *Simić* (Decision on the Prosecution Motion Under Rule 73 for a Ruling Concerning the Testimony of a Witness), 27 July 1999, Case No. IT-95-9-PT (Trial Chamber, ICTY); Preparatory Commission for an International Criminal Court, 'Rules of Procedure and Evidence', UN Doc. PCNICC/2000/1, Rule 73(4)–(6).

[186] See Sylvain Vité, *Les procédures internationales d'établissement des faits dans la mise en oeuvre du droit international humanitaire* (Brussels: Bruylant, 1999); Dieter Fleck, 'Die internationale Ermittlungskommission: Probleme und Perspektiven einer neuen Einrichtung des humanitären Völkerrecht', in Horst Schötter and Bernd Hoffman eds., *Die Genfer Zusatzprotokolle: Commentare und Analysen* (Bonn: Osang, 1993) 258; Françoise Hampson, 'Fact-Finding and the International Fact-Finding Commission', in Hazel Fox and Michael Meyer eds., *Armed Conflict and the New Law – Effecting Compliance* (London: British Institute of International and Comparative Law, 1993) II, 53; Erich Kussbach, 'The International Humanitarian Fact-Finding Commission', (1994) 43 *Int'l & Comp. L Quart.* 174, 175.

[187] The expression is also used in Art. 89 of Protocol I, again without definition. The *travaux préparatoires* of both Arts. 89 and 90 do not shed any light in this respect.

situation so as to deny the applicability of humanitarian law.[188] Others have suggested that while grave breaches are offences attributable both to the individual perpetrator and to the state, incurring individual responsibility as envisaged in the Conventions and Protocol, serious violations are actions exclusively imputable to the state, for which there would be no individual responsibility.[189] This is also consistent with an interpretation of 'serious violations' as including improper characterisation, given that this is a collective rather than individual act.

The Appeals Chamber of the ICTY has offered a broad interpretation of the concept of 'serious violations' of humanitarian law in the *Tadić* case. Reflecting on the breadth of its jurisdiction under Article 3 of its Statute, the Appeals Chamber found that the 'power to prosecute persons violating the laws and customs of war' covered all violations of the Geneva Conventions not explicitly designated as 'grave breaches'. In consideration of the numerous references to 'serious violations of international humanitarian law' in the ICTY Statute, the Chamber concluded that all 'non-grave breaches' of the Geneva Conventions and Protocol could be labelled 'serious violations' of those instruments, thereafter linking this to the reference to 'serious violations' in Article 89 of Protocol I.[190] The net effect of this interpretative exercise is to give broad meaning to the concept of serious violations, and in turn provide the basis for extending the jurisdiction of the International Fact-Finding Commission under Article 90 of Protocol I to cover all violations of the Geneva Conventions and Protocol I, including global violations in the form of an improper characterisation of an armed conflict.

Even admitting the reasonable conclusion that 'serious violation' should be read to include the question of characterisation, three elements combine to undermine the potential contribution of the International Fact-Finding Commission in this respect.

First, the Commission's competence does not extend to cover violations of Protocol II (Article 90(2)(c)(i), Protocol I), nor does the narrowly defined notion of 'grave breach' include the violation of common

[188] Pilloud et al., *ICRC Commentary*, at 1033; Hampson, 'Fact-Finding', at 76–7; Kussbach, 'Fact-Finding Commission', at 178.

[189] Meeting of Committee I, 14 May 1976, CDDH/I/SR.58, 9 *Off. Records* 223, para. 42 (New Zealand); Kussbach, 'Fact-Finding Commission', at 177.

[190] *The Prosecutor v. Tadić* (Decision on the Defence Motion for Interlocutory Appeal on Jurisdiction), 2 Oct. 1995, Case No. IT-94-1-AR72 (Appeals Chamber, ICTY), 48–52 paras. 86–93. See also *The Prosecutor v. Akayesu* (Judgment), 2 Sept. 1998, Case No. ICTR-96-4-T (Trial Chamber I, ICTR) paras. 611–17.

Article 3 of the 1949 Geneva Conventions.[191] Thus, the application of humanitarian law in non-international armed conflicts, in which disagreements as to characterisation are most frequent, at first sight seems excluded from the Commission's general competence under Article 90(2)(c). Article 90(2)(d), however, in referring to 'other situations' – as opposed to 'grave breach' and 'serious violation' (in Art. 90(2)(c)(i)) – and 'Parties to the conflict' – as opposed to 'High Contracting Parties' (in Art. 90(2)(a)) – opens a door through which the Commission could construe its competence as including non-international armed conflicts.[192] The opening is quite narrow, however, in that it subjects the Commission's competence to the consent of the other parties to the conflict. Alternatively, the concept of 'serious violations' in Article 90(2)(c)(i) could be construed in accordance with Security Council Resolution 955 (1994) on the establishment of an International Criminal Tribunal for Rwanda, to include violations of common Article 3 of the Geneva Conventions.[193] The Appeals Chamber of the ICTY in *Tadić* concurred, concluding that violations of common Article 3 of the Geneva Conventions should indeed be considered as 'serious violations'.[194] With the support of these new developments, the Commission could interpret its general competence to cover violations of common Article 3 and, more generally, non-international armed conflicts, although not violations of Protocol II.[195]

The second element pertains to the power to initiate an enquiry. After protracted discussions at the Geneva Conference, the idea that the Commission could initiate an enquiry *proprio motu* was rejected by a majority of states. Under the terms of Article 90(2), the procedure is necessarily inter-state or, at most, inter-belligerent. An enquiry can be started either at the request of any state, not necessarily a party to the conflict, having accepted the Commission's competence with respect to a

---

[191] *Tadić* (Interlocutory Appeal), at 46 para. 81.

[192] The Commission already has stated its agreement with this position: David, *Principes*, at 518.

[193] Article 4 of the Statute of the International Criminal Tribunal for Rwanda provides that the latter has jurisdiction for 'serious violations of Article 3 common to the Geneva Conventions . . . and of Protocol II': UN Doc. S/RES/955 (1994) Annex. See the discussion of the extension of individual penal responsibility for war crimes committed in internal conflict in chapter 2, pp. 103–10.

[194] *Tadić* (Interlocutory Appeal), at 70 para. 134.

[195] Violations of Protocol II cannot be successfully included in the general competence of the Commission even with this broad interpretation of the notion of 'serious violations', because Art. 90(2)(c)(i) speaks of a 'serious violation of the Conventions or of this Protocol' and not of Protocol II.

similarly obligated state (Art. 90(2)(a)), or at the request of a party to the conflict if all other parties concerned agree (Art. 90(2)(d)).[196] Given the marked reluctance of states to use inter-state complaint mechanisms where available, and especially with respect to the jurisdiction of human rights bodies,[197] it appears unlikely that states not involved in the conflict would present the necessary petition to the Commission. This is especially problematic in non-international armed conflicts and in national liberation armed conflicts, where the concerned state would probably consider, albeit incorrectly, that the petition is an intrusion into its internal affairs.[198] Only in the case of an international conflict in which the parties have already accepted the Commission's competence is it at all likely that the latter will be given the chance to act.

The third element hindering a significant role for the Fact-Finding Commission in the characterisation of armed conflict is the nature of its function. It is not a tribunal, and does not judge of the legality of the parties' conduct.[199] Its task is simply to assess the factual situation and report it to the parties 'with such recommendations as it may deem appropriate' (Art. 90(5)(a), Protocol I). Findings of fact of course cannot be completely detached from the law, if only in the evaluation of which facts are significant. Further, the Commission will have to determine whether there appears to be *prima facie* evidence of a grave breach or serious violation.[200] Nevertheless, the fact-finding function of the Commission will probably limit its power to seek firm conclusions as to the legal character of the situation. It is at this stage rather difficult to determine how strongly worded these recommendations can be, since the Commission has never been called upon to perform its function. Much will depend on its interpretation of its own jurisdiction under Article 90 of Protocol I. As shown by the experience of the Human Rights

---

[196] Nothing in the provision excludes national liberation movements or insurgent groups from the definition of 'Party to the conflict', allowing for the possibility of an investigation being initiated at the request of one of these non-state actors, still with the consent of the state and all other parties concerned. See David, *Principes*, at 516–17.

[197] See Ergec, *Droits de l'homme*, at 381; Hartman, 'Working Paper', at 122; Tremblay, 'Situations d'urgence', at 15.

[198] The dynamic is quite similar to that of third states adopting countermeasures in reaction to violations of humanitarian law. See chapter 5, pp. 210–11.

[199] See Pilloud et al., *ICRC Commentary*, at 1045–6; Kussbach, 'Fact-Finding Commission', at 176 and 183–4.

[200] Kussbach, 'Fact-Finding Commission', at 177 (suggesting that the discretion of the Commission would be wider with respect to 'serious violations' than with respect to grave breaches because the former are not defined in the Conventions and Protocol).

Committee, even non-binding recommendations by a neutral and impartial body such as the Commission can be effective in alerting the world community and thus pressuring the state to acknowledge the applicability of humanitarian law. This potential impact of the Commission's findings and recommendations is hampered, however, by the fact that they cannot be made public by the Commission unless so requested by all parties to the conflict (Art. 90(5)(c), Protocol I). Parties to the conflict, on the other hand, are free to release the Commission's report.[201]

The International Fact-Finding Commission is still at the development stage, and it is too early to predict the significance of its possible contribution to solving the problem of characterisation of armed conflicts. Nevertheless, the low rate of acceptance by states parties of the Commission's competence, standing in 2001 at 59 of 159 parties, and the serious limitations imposed on that competence by Article 90 of Protocol I, suggest that this contribution may well be rather limited.

Some have suggested that human rights bodies could be used to control compliance with humanitarian law.[202] The competence of regional and universal human rights bodies is of course limited to the enforcement of the human rights entrenched in the relevant conventions, so that these bodies cannot simply expand their jurisdiction to cover the application of humanitarian law.[203] The European Convention on Human Rights does contain one window through which the European Court could examine the applicability of humanitarian law. Article 15(1) specifies that no derogation from the right to life (Art. 2) is permissible 'except in respect of death resulting from lawful acts of war'. This means that, in cases where the state concerned has declared a state of emergency, the Court may be called upon to decide whether a killing

---

[201] In case of petition by a High Contracting Party not involved in the conflict, the wording of the provision suggests that that state would not be entitled to publicise the Commission's findings without the agreement of all parties to the conflict.

[202] See Cerna, 'Human Rights'; Françoise J. Hampson, 'Using International Human Rights Machinery to Enforce the International Law of Armed Conflict', (1992) 31 Revue de droit pénal militaire et de droit de la guerre 119–42.

[203] See Arts. 40–1, International Covenant on Civil and Political Rights; Art. 1, Optional Protocol to the International Covenant on Civil and Political Rights; Arts. 33–4, European Convention on Human Rights; Arts. 44–5, American Convention on Human Rights (but see Art. 41 which refers more widely to 'matters of human rights'); Arts. 46–59, African Charter on Human and Peoples' Rights. Interestingly, the 1987 European Convention for the Prevention of Torture and Inhuman or Degrading Treatment or Punishment provides in Art. 17(3) that 'The [European] Committee [on the Prevention of Torture] shall not visit places which representatives or delegates of protecting powers or the International Committee of the Red Cross effectively visit on a regular basis by virtue of the Geneva Conventions [and] Protocols.'

was justified according to humanitarian law. This necessarily implies a prior characterisation by the European Court of the situation as an armed conflict.

More widely, the limitation found in the Covenant on Civil and Political Rights (Art. 4(1)), the American Convention on Human Rights (Art. 27(1)) and the European Convention (Art. 15(1)) whereby emergency measures must comply with 'other obligations under international law' includes compliance with applicable humanitarian law.[204] The ICJ in its 1996 *Advisory Opinion on the Legality of the Threat or Use of Nuclear Weapons* found that, with respect to a violation during an armed conflict of the non-derogable right to life entrenched in Article 6 of the International Covenant on Civil and Political Rights, the determination of whether that deprivation was arbitrary or not must be made exclusively by reference to applicable rules of humanitarian law.[205] A similar need to refer to the laws of war with respect to the right to life was seen as implied in the American Convention by the Inter-American Commission on Human Rights.[206] Determining whether humanitarian law creates obligations applicable in the context of the emergency will therefore require the human rights monitoring body to characterise the situation as either an armed conflict of one type or another, or as disturbances not calling for the application of humanitarian law. It is thus possible that various human rights bodies could be called upon to characterise armed conflicts.[207]

In *Cyprus v. Turkey*, the majority of the European Commission addressed this point and concluded that, since Turkey had not declared a state of emergency, all norms were fully applicable, so that there was no need to examine the applicability of humanitarian law.[208] In their dissent, Judges Sperduti and Trechsel adopted a much broader

---

[204] See e.g. 'Siracusa Principle 67', at 11.

[205] ICJ, *Advisory Opinion on the Legality of the Threat or Use of Nuclear Weapons*, 8 July 1996, [1996] ICJ Rep. 66, para. 25.

[206] *Abella et al. v. Argentina* ('*La Tablada*' case), Rep. No. 55/97, Case No. 11,137, OAS Doc. OEA/Ser.L/V/II.95 doc. 7 at 271 (1997) para. 161; *Avila v. Colombia*, Rep. No. 26/97, Case No. 11,142, OAS Doc. OEA/Ser.L/V/II.95 doc. 7 at 444 (1997) para. 173.

[207] Because Art. 38 of the Convention on the Rights of the Child incorporates humanitarian law by reference, the Committee on the Rights of the Child may be in a privileged position to assess the applicability of humanitarian law. References to humanitarian law by the Committee have been rather general so far. See e.g. 'Concluding Observation of the Committee on the Rights of the Child: Uganda', UN Doc. CRC/C/15/Add.80 (1997) paras. 19 and 34; *ibid*.: 'Georgia', UN Doc. CRC/C/97 (2000) paras. 134–5; *ibid*.: 'Sierra Leone', UN Doc. CRC/C/94 (2000) paras. 185–90.

[208] *Cyprus v. Turkey* (Appl. 6780/74 and 6950/75), (1976) 4 Eur. Hum. Rts Rep. 482, 556 para. 528.

position, holding that humanitarian law generally marks the limits
of derogations 'strictly required by the exigencies of the situations'
(Art. 15(1), European Convention), so that an action in compliance with
humanitarian law will constitute a permissible derogation from human rights law.[209] This interpretation of humanitarian law as supplementary to human rights law is problematic, because the threshold
of protection afforded by humanitarian law is not systematically lower
than that of human rights law. Some interests are actually more fully
protected under humanitarian law in wartime than under human rights
law in peacetime (e.g. protection against medical experimentation) while
some human rights have no equivalents at all in humanitarian law (e.g.
prohibition of preventive detention).[210] The European Commission and
Court were presented with other opportunities to explore this question in cases dealing with Cyprus and south-east Turkey, but declined to
do so.[211]

The decision of the Inter-American Commission on Human Rights in
the 1997 'La Tablada' case provides the first instance where a human
rights body has relied squarely on humanitarian law.[212] The petition
related to an armed confrontation in January 1989 between Argentine
armed forces and a group of individuals who had seized part of an army
base. The Commission noted that:

Thus, when reviewing the legality of derogation measures taken by a State Party
to the American Convention by virtue of the existence of an armed conflict
to which both the American Convention and humanitarian law apply,
the Commission should not resolve this question solely by reference to the text of
Article 27 of the American Convention. Rather, it must also determine whether
the rights affected by these measures are similarly guaranteed under applicable
humanitarian law treaties. If it finds that the rights in question are not subject to suspension under these humanitarian law instruments, the Commission

[209] Ibid., Diss. Op. Sperduti and Trechsel, at 564 paras. 6–7 ('It follows that respect for
[the 1907 Hague Convention Regulations and the 1949 Fourth Geneva Convention] by
a High Contracting Party during the military occupation of the territory of another
state will in principle assure that that High Contracting Party will not go beyond the
limits of the right of derogation conferred on it by Art. 15 of the Convention'). This is
explored by Hampson, 'Using International Human Rights Machinery', at 123–35.
[210] See Yoram Dinstein, 'Human Rights in Armed Conflict: International Humanitarian
Law', in Theodor Meron ed., Human Rights in International Law: Legal and Policy Issues
(Oxford: Clarendon, 1984) II, 345, 351–4.
[211] See Aisling Reidy, 'The Approach of the European Commission and Court of Human
Rights to International Humanitarian Law', (1998) 324 Int'l Rev. Red Cross 513–29.
[212] Abella et al. v. Argentina ('La Tablada' case), Rep. No. 55/97, Case No. 11,137, OAS Doc.
OEA/Ser.L/V/II.95 doc. 7 at 271 (1997).

should conclude that these derogation measures are in violation of the State Parties' obligations under both the American Convention and the humanitarian law treaties concerned.[213]

Unlike the dissenters in the *Cyprus* v. *Turkey* decision of the European Commission, this position does not necessarily equate lawful acts of war and permissible derogations under human rights instruments. The Commission in the '*La Tablada*' case characterised the armed clash as an internal conflict calling for the application of common Article 3, but concluded that there had been no violation of humanitarian law.[214] The Commission adopted a similar approach in *Avila* v. *Colombia*, also decided in 1997, where it decided to apply humanitarian law despite the fact that no petitioner had invoked it, and over the objections of the Colombian state which had argued that the Commission was not competent to do so.[215]

The Inter-American Commission went one step further in its 1999 opinion in *Coard* v. *United States*, which dealt with the incarceration of Grenadian nationals by US armed forces during the American military takeover of Grenada in October 1983.[216] Because the United States is not a party to the American Convention on Human Rights, the Commission was acting pursuant to its mandate under the OAS Charter, interpreted as incorporating the American Declaration on the Rights and Duties of Man. That instrument does not contain a derogation provision similar to Article 27 of the American Convention with its reference to 'other obligations under international law', which had been the bridge used by the Commission in '*La Tablada*' and *Avila* to link human rights and humanitarian law. Over the strenuous objections of the United States, which argued that the Commission was lacking both jurisdiction and specialised expertise to apply humanitarian law, the latter concluded that the American Declaration must be interpreted within the overall framework of the legal system, including humanitarian law norms.[217]

---

213 *Ibid.*, para. 170. Indeed, in addition to Article 27 of the American Convention, the Commission found that it had a broad competence to apply humanitarian law on the basis of the similarities between human rights and humanitarian law, and by reference to Articles 25, 29(b) and 64 of the American Convention.

214 *Ibid.*, paras. 327–8.

215 *Avila* v. *Colombia*, Rep. No. 26/97, Case No. 11,142, OAS Doc. OEA/Ser.L/V/II.95 doc. 7 at 444 (1997) paras. 169–70.

216 *Coard* v. *United States*, Rep. No. 109/99, Case No. 10,951 (1999).

217 *Ibid.*, paras. 38–42 ('As a general matter, while the Commission may find it necessary to look to the applicable rules of international humanitarian law when interpreting and applying the norms of the Inter-American human rights system, where those

The Commission thereafter proceeded to characterise the conflict as international, calling for the application of the Fourth Geneva Convention. It concluded that delays between arrest and judicial supervision were inconsistent with Article 78 of the Fourth Geneva Convention and, as a result, constituted arbitrary detention within the meaning of Articles I and XXV of the American Declaration. This very progressive stance is not limited to the context of individual petitions, as illustrated by the 1999 'Third Report on the Situation of Human Rights in Colombia', in which the Commission makes extensive and direct use of humanitarian law, to the point where the greater part of the report is concerned with the application of humanitarian law rather than human rights law.[218]

As these cases illustrate, the significant parallels between the two legal systems suggest that in some respects humanitarian law could prove useful in determining which human rights derogations are strictly required by the state of emergency. There is clearly a need for a greater articulation of the substantive relationship between human rights and humanitarian law in situations combining a state of emergency and an armed conflict, an issue falling outside the scope of the present enquiry.[219]

Human rights bodies need to be cautious in labelling a situation an armed conflict, because it could be taken by the state concerned as a political justification for its policies violating human rights.[220] For this reason, the Inter-American Commission on Human Rights initially had refrained from discussing the applicability of common Article 3 of the 1949 Geneva Conventions to emergency situations, despite a call by the General Assembly of the Organization of American States to address the question of the violation of human rights by non-governmental groups.[221] It is clear that, as a matter of law, the state of emergency and armed conflict remain independent concepts, so that an impartial

bodies of law provide levels of protection which are distinct, the Commission is bound by its Charter-based mandate to give effect to the normative standard which best safeguards the rights of the individual' – para. 42).

[218] Inter-American Commission on Human Rights, 'Third Report on the Situation of Human Rights in Colombia', OAS Doc. OEA/Ser.L/V/II doc. 102 (1999).

[219] See Denise Plattner, 'International Humanitarian Law and Inalienable or Non-derogable Human Rights', in Daniel Prémont ed., *Non-derogable Rights and States of Emergency* (Brussels: Bruylant, 1996) 349–63.

[220] See *Avila v. Colombia*, Rep. No. 26/97, Case No. 11,142, OAS Doc. OEA/Ser.L/V/II.95 doc. 7 at 444 (1997) para. 168 (discussing the state's invocation of humanitarian law as a 'defence').

[221] OAS General Assembly Resolution (XX-0/90); Inter-American Commission on Human Rights, 'Groups of Armed Irregulars and Human Rights', [1990–1] *Ann. Rep. Inter-Am. Com'n Hum. Rts* 504–14.

characterisation of a situation as an armed conflict should not in itself be taken as a leave to derogate.

Independent bodies active in the fields of human rights and humanitarian law offer the most promising solution to the problem of characterisation of situations as states of emergency or armed conflicts, because they are both impartial in their nature and legal in their approach. They suffer from serious limitations, however, related to the breadth of their powers and acceptance of their competence in the case of humanitarian law, and to a narrow interpretation of their own jurisdiction in the case of human rights law. Because of these limitations, characterisation by independent bodies does not provide a simple and definitive answer to the problem, but merely contributes one piece to the puzzle of the definition of armed conflicts or states of emergency.

Conclusion to Part III

The characterisation of situations as armed conflicts under humanitarian law and as states of emergency under human rights law raises, at a basic level, the same problem: how to assess the legal character of these situations in the presence of characterisations which are often numerous, usually contradictory, and sometimes legally unfounded? The difficulty is one that affects international law as a whole, leading states to rely on their own appreciation of whether there has been a material breach of a treaty before suspending it, whether a norm has been violated before adopting countermeasures, or whether there has been an armed attack before acting in self-defence.[1] That being said, the fact that indeterminacy affects all of international law does not mean that a universal solution can be found. As this entire book has sought to show, different areas of international law will have distinct normative dynamics, calling for a modulated response to the challenge of indeterminacy. Thus a number of significant differences between characterisation of situations under human rights and humanitarian law have emerged in the course of the preceding analysis. These differences stem from both the context of application and the nature of norms in human rights and humanitarian law.

First, characterisation of a situation as an armed conflict necessarily implies the possibility of competing autoqualifications by the various belligerents. Even in the case of an internal conflict, international law grants insurgents a measure of functional sovereignty whereby they are entitled to make a valid legal characterisation of the conflict. There will therefore be a 'dialogue' on international norms between these two or more actors holding possibly divergent views on the nature of the situation. In human rights, on the contrary, the declaration of a state of emergency implies a unilateral act by the government of the nation whose life or security is threatened. During a state of emergency, there is no other international actor and, therefore, no competing autoqualification.[2]

---

[1] See Denis Alland, *Justice privée et ordre juridique international – Etude théorique des contre-mesures en droit international public* (Paris: Pedone, 1994) 107–20; Leo Gross, 'States as Organs of International Law and the Problem of Autointerpretation', in George Lipshy ed., *Law and Politics in the World Community* (Berkeley: U Calif. Press, 1953) 59, 80–1.

[2] This is related to Hans Kelsen's proposition that only state parties to a controversy could autoqualify it. In an armed conflict, there would thus be two autoqualifications while that can be so in human rights only by reliance on the *erga omnes* nature of the norms. See Hans Kelsen, *Peace Through Law* (Chapel Hill: U North Carolina, 1944) 13–14; Gross, 'States as Organs', at 72–3.

Intervention by any type of third party, be it a state, an international organisation or an independent body, appears less intrusive in the context of a dialogue – or dispute – between various actors, than in the context of a unilateral act, challenged directly by the intervention of a third party. This is reflected in the conclusion that, if the state may perhaps enjoys a 'margin of appreciation' in the characterisation of a state of emergency, no such principle is warranted in the qualification of an armed conflict under humanitarian law, even for internal armed conflicts.

The differences in the very nature of the events covered by the concepts of state of emergency and armed conflict have a significant impact on the role of characterisation in human rights and humanitarian law. From the point of view of perceptibility, sustained and concerted military operations are likely to be more easily 'visible' from abroad than an emergency threatening the life of the nation, which need not necessarily be public in order to be real. But there is more: whereas armed hostilities in themselves are the trigger for application of humanitarian norms, leading agents to enquire whether such hostilities are indeed taking place, an emergency can lawfully trigger derogation from human rights norms even if it merely poses a threat to the life or security of the nation or government, leading agents to enquire not simply whether the emergency is taking place but also whether the state's assessment of the possible future impact of this emergency does indeed pose such a threat. In other words, competing characterisations in humanitarian law relate to facts whereas, in human rights, they relate to the appreciation of the possible impact of such facts. The more speculative nature of the state of emergency seems to indicate that legitimate divergent opinions are more likely, lessening the weight of competing characterisations and again justifying a certain 'margin of appreciation'.

There is a paradox in that the state of emergency, as a political exception to the human rights regime, is usually given a more formal legal review than the armed conflict, which is meant to be a factual classification free from political elements. This is largely due to the fact that human rights law is institutionalised to a greater degree than humanitarian law. In many countries, there is one and sometimes even two overlapping systems providing for an international review of derogations to human rights in situations of emergencies. Some have suggested that the very existence of such mechanisms has an impact on the quality of legal norms, transforming them from auto-interpretative to justiciable, and reducing the likelihood of spurious characterisations.[3] If this

---

[3] See Bin Cheng, 'Flight from Justiciable to Auto-interpretative International Law', in *Liber Amicorum Elie van Bogaert* (Antwerp: Kluwer, 1985) 1, 16–17.

obtained in all areas of the world, we could conclude that the problem of characterisation of states of emergency is less significant than that of armed conflict, despite the shortcomings noted in the study of reviewing bodies. Unfortunately this is not so, and the optional nature of competence of review bodies combined with the lack of regional human rights systems in many parts of the world means that the problem of characterisation of emergencies is alive and well in many of the areas where violations are rampant. Examples include Bangladesh, Ghana, India, Malaysia, Somalia and the Sudan.[4] In these areas, the applicability of human rights and humanitarian law appears equally fragile.

States, armed insurgents, third states, political organs and independent bodies all concurrently perform active acts of characterisation. When recourse to an independent body offering guarantees of neutrality and legality is impossible, a straightforward application of the doctrine of sovereignty would lead to the conclusion that each one of these characterisations remains valid within its respective sphere of authority. Thus, the concerned state could safely refuse to apply humanitarian law or derogate from human rights; third states and political organs of international organisations could adopt measures within their competence to give effect to their own characterisation. These positions would of course be taken at their own risks, with the rather theoretical possibility of being proven wrong by an eventual judicial decision. Such a disjointed application of human rights and humanitarian law, largely subjecting it to the concerned state's whim, does not appear to reflect adequately the very nature of these legal systems as imposing binding universal norms.

An alternative approach to the legal characterisation of factual situations centres on consensus-building, in a manner similar to the creation process of customary international law. There are, in fact, close links between the processes of creation and application of international law, because each interpretation of a given norm on the basis of a new fact pattern fosters a new variation of that norm. This is the reason why the PCIJ in the 1923 *Jaworzina* case found that 'it is an established principle that the right of giving an authoritative interpretation of a legal rule belongs solely to the person or body who has the power to modify or suppress it'.[5] Building on the interconnection of interpretation and

---

[4] See International Commission of Jurists, *States of Emergency, their Impact on Human Rights* (Geneva: ICJ, 1983) 453.

[5] *Advisory Opinion Regarding the Delimitation of the Polish–Czechoslovakian Frontier (Question of Jaworzina)*, (1923) Ser. B No. 8 at 37. See Kelsen, *The Law of the United Nations* (New York: Praeger, 1950) xv; Gross, 'States as Organs', at 81.

characterisation, we can posit that if the international community has the power to create legal norms by consensus, then it should also be seen to have the power to interpret norms authoritatively and characterise facts by consensus.[6]

Under such an approach, applicable most clearly when binding review by an independent body is unavailable, the totality of opinions as to the legal character of a situation would be taken into consideration. Until a consensus is reached, any agent, state or other, may at its own risk characterise situations for its own purposes. When, however, a consensus has emerged among participants, taking into account their representativeness, neutrality and impartiality, that global opinion acquires an obligatory character for all agents. This builds on a phenomenon already in existence, whereby actors rely on previous acts of characterisation to support their own conclusion. For instance the Swiss Government, in support of its characterisation of the conflict in El Salvador as a non-international armed conflict to which Protocol II was applicable, relied on resolutions by the UN General Assembly, the Economic and Social Council and the Human Rights Commission, in addition to the position of the Government of El Salvador.[7] Interestingly the ICTY itself, in the *Tadić* interlocutory appeal, supported its characterisation of the armed conflict in Bosnia-Herzegovina by referring to the positions of the warring parties, the ICRC, the Security Council and third states in the proceedings of the Security Council.[8] It is suggested

---

[6] Somewhat similar solutions have been suggested in the field of state recognition. See Philip Jessup, *A Modern Law of Nations* (New York: Macmillan, 1948) 43–51; Martti Koskenniemi, *From Apology to Utopia* (Helsinki: Lakimiesliiton Kustannus, 1989) 242–3; Ian Brownlie, 'Recognition in Theory and Practice', in Ronald St J. Macdonald and Douglas Johnston eds., *The Structure and Process of International Law* (Dordrecht: Nijhoff, 1983) 627, 630–4. Fundamental differences between recognition and characterisation of situations under human rights and humanitarian law include the greater indeterminacy of legal standards governing recognition, the inexistence of a state duty to recognise, and the fact that statehood is a relational concept, necessarily granting recognition at least a partly constitutive effect.

[7] See Lucius Caflisch, 'Pratique suisse relative au droit international en 1986', (1987) 43 *Annuaire suisse de droit international* 185, 187. See also Michel Veuthey, 'Assessing Humanitarian Law', in Thomas Weiss and Larry Minear eds., *Humanitarianism Across Borders – Sustaining Civilians in Times of War* (Boulder: Lynne Rienner, 1993) 125, 131.

[8] *The Prosecutor v. Tadić* (Decision on the Defence Motion for Interlocutory Appeal on Jurisdiction), 2 Oct. 1995, Case No. IT-94-1-AR72 (Appeals Chamber, ICTY), at 39–44 paras. 72–8. This approach reflects a vision of international law not purely based on state consent; in particular, it is consistent with a narrow version of the persistent objector rule with respect to the creation or interpretation of norms, whereas such objection may succeed only during the emergence of the norm, and not after it has grown to be generally accepted. See Jonathan Charney, 'The Persistent Objector Rule

that converging factual qualifications coalesce to form an authoritative characterisation, a process distinct from an approach which simply considers other characterisations as evidence of the legal nature of a situation.[9]

This approach based on consensus-building among international actors brings us back to the differing dynamics of characterisation of situations as states of emergency and armed conflicts under human rights and humanitarian law noted earlier. The conclusion that multiple interventions by third parties are more intrusive, and therefore less likely, in the context of human rights than in humanitarian law means that consensus-building offers less of a solution for the challenges posed by states of emergency. Indeed, this echoes the dominant implementation patterns already present in each area of law, with humanitarian law traditionally turning to third-party intervention (the protecting powers system) while human rights has fostered a more institutional approach (review bodies such as the Human Rights Committee). This may help explain why the reverse patterns which can be found in treaty law, for example the International Fact-Finding Commission for humanitarian law and inter-state petition mechanisms for human rights, have generated little or no state practice and, ultimately, offered no viable solution.

and the Development of Customary International Law', [1985] *Brit. YB Int'l L* 1–24. The same goes for the particular weight given by the ICJ to state practice and *opinio juris* from 'specifically affected' states: *North Sea Continental Shelf* case *(FRG v. Denmark; FRG v. Netherlands)*, [1969] ICJ Rep. 3, para. 73.

[9] Such as the approach adopted by Taft J in the *Tinoco Arbitration (Great Britain v. Costa Rica)*, (1923) 1 Rep. Int'l Arb. Awards 369, 381, with respect to recognition of governments.

General conclusion

Both human rights and humanitarian law are fields which have witnessed change at an accelerated pace in the last decade. The aim of this book has not been to attempt to overlay tidiness and coherence within and between these two fields, but rather to identify some of the forces at work in human rights and humanitarian law to provide a greater comprehension of ongoing transitions. More specifically, given the similarity of their fundamental purpose, the protection of basic interests of the individual, the analysis has sought to assess the closeness of the humanitarian law regime to that of human rights law. Because human rights have permeated every area of international law including, without the slightest possible doubt, humanitarian law, the question arises as to whether the difference between these two fields is mostly semantic and contextual. If there is indeed a specificity to each regime, should it be celebrated and highlighted or deplored and downplayed?

The differences between human rights and humanitarian law go far beyond an acknowledgment that one applies more readily to situations of political stability and the other to times of armed conflict. The vastly distinct power dynamics at work in war and peace have led to opposite conceptualisations of the individual vis-à-vis those wielding power over that individual. Through various institutions of humanitarian law, the main picture of the individual that emerges is that of a person necessarily and dialectically connected to a designated state or group. As such, with few exceptions, the position of an individual in relation to a power-holder cannot be established without considering the nature of the relation between the state or group to which the individual belongs and the state or group exercising power over him or her. This is to be contrasted with the position of the individual in the vast majority of human rights norms: the individual holds most rights regardless of any association or link to a given state or group, with the corresponding state obligations applying *erga omnes*. The different contexts in which human rights and humanitarian law are applied are not therefore mere externalities restricting or facilitating the application of these norms, but rather powerful forces shaping every aspect of these systems, including their normative frameworks, the place of reciprocity as a grounding principle, and the manner in which factual and legal indeterminacies are resolved.

The distinctive normative thrusts of human rights and humanitarian law are reflections both of their context of application and the resulting conceptualisation of the individual. A stable political situation is a founding premiss of human rights law whereby, in the absence of any emergency threatening the life of the nation, it may be reasonably expected that individuals can use institutional mechanisms such as the judicial system effectively to protect their own interests.[1] The individual being the central and isolated holder of these rights, all individuals ought to benefit from the same guarantees, resulting in the broadest possible entitlement for these rights.

Humanitarian law, by contrast, is posited on the existence of an armed conflict which will trigger, more often than not, a breakdown of order and institutions. In such a context, it is broadly futile to empower individuals by granting them rights upon which they will be unable to act. Armed conflicts also imply the clash of collective interests, illustrated by the fact that isolated troubles do not call for applicability of these norms. Individuals in such a context necessarily become identified with a community, and it is this broader identity which shapes the legal regime aimed at protecting them. Given that the protection most needed crosses the boundaries between hostile communities, for instance protecting the occupied civilian population against abuses of the occupying forces, the granting of rights to the community itself will usually be largely as ineffective as the granting of rights to the individual. For example, granting rights to the occupied population's state as against the occupier is unlikely to be sufficient given the enmity between them. This explains why humanitarian law, while providing protection which dovetails that afforded by international standards on the treatment of aliens, does not adopt the latter's model of granting a derivative right of action to the state of nationality as a central

---

[1] While judicial supervision is still required during an emergency, practice has shown that both external constraints on, and self-restraint by, courts in such situations limit their role.

theme. Instead, humanitarian standards are directed squarely at those wielding power over persons in need of protection, by way of individual obligations reflecting public order requirements. Reliance on powerless victims or collectivities (states or groups) thus becomes purely secondary.

We have seen that the normative framework of human rights and humanitarian law is marked by the centrality of, respectively, rights and obligations of individuals. Given that individual human rights-holders in times of political stability are not always in a position to act effectively to redress violations, could the normative framework of humanitarian law be taken as a source of inspiration in the development of human rights law? In other words, could we envisage a human rights system imposing obligations on individuals? As demonstrated by the African Charter on Human and Peoples' Rights, such a proposition is neither legally nor conceptually impossible. Its potential benefits include lifting the state veil to render state agents more responsible for their behaviour, and acting as a tool to bring within the fold of human rights law the very significant problem of violations of basic rights by non-state actors. Such a model, however, stands at odds with the normative framework of human rights, the thrust of which centres on individual rights against abuses originating in the state. More significantly, the introduction of individual obligations in a rights-based system raises the spectre that rights and obligations may become tied, so that states may allege disrespect of obligations as an excuse to disregard basic rights. Such a possibility does not exist with individual obligations under humanitarian law because there are no corresponding individual rights. A more promising avenue borrows the notion of individual responsibility from humanitarian law, but refuses to ground it in individual obligations. Instead, the state veil could be lifted for egregious violations of human rights such that the specific state agent is held personally responsible. This would, in effect, constitute individual responsibility for state violations, similar to that found with respect to crimes against peace. Further, it would contribute to compliance with non-derogable human rights during a state of emergency, when the normal recourse to enforce rights may well not be available to the individual. As for violations of human rights by non-state actors, the approach developed by the Inter-American Court on Human Rights in the *Velásquez-Rodríguez* case, whereby a broader interpretation of the state's duty to ensure rights includes protection against private violations of basic rights, seems more consistent with the structure of human rights law.

The same picture emerges when looking at the respective role of reciprocity as a grounding principle of human rights and humanitarian law. In human rights, the relation between the individual and the state exercising control is disconnected from any inter-state component. In particular, the links, such as nationality, which the individual may have with other states, and the links which the state may have with other states, for instance as parties to the same international convention, are largely irrelevant to the content and exercise of rights. Thus, any reservation or violation by other states bound by the same norm will leave untouched the relation between the state and the individuals under its control.

In humanitarian law, on the contrary, the hybrid nature of the individual's place as well as the interconnection among the obligations of the various belligerents vis-à-vis each other and protected persons results in a much more complex place for reciprocity. There are structural links built into humanitarian law which connect the relations between groups or states to those between states and individuals under their control. This is so even under the more flexible construction of the nationality of protected persons found in ICTY cases. The reciprocity between states embodied in older humanitarian norms, for example the fact that two belligerents are bound by the 1949 Geneva Conventions, limits the need for reciprocity in the state's obligations with respect to individuals under its control. Thus the fact that a regular military unit systematically violates the laws and customs of war does not allow the enemy state to consider itself no longer bound to comply with humanitarian norms, even with respect to that particular unit (with the limited exception of belligerent reprisals analysed in chapter 4). The same goes for the occupying power's duties towards the civilian population, a relation in which reciprocity plays no significant role.

When the reciprocal nature of humanitarian law obligations between the groups is less certain, however, then it is introduced as an element of the relation between the bearer of duties and the person benefiting from the norms, again underscoring the interconnection between the two sets of relations. This explains, for instance, the explicit requirement that groups of irregulars 'conduct their operations in accordance with the laws and customs of war' (Arts. 13(2)–(6)/13(2)–(6)/4(A)(2)–(6), First, Second and Third Geneva Conventions), as their connection to a party to the conflict is less well established. A limited number of humanitarian norms escapes this pattern, setting minimum requirements of humanity which ought to be complied with in all situations. Those norms, found in common Article 3 of the 1949 Geneva Conventions, Part II of the Fourth Geneva Convention, and in Protocol II, impose obligations *erga omnes* on belligerents vis-à-vis non-combatants which, as in human rights law, are completely disconnected from any relation which these non-combatants may have with an insurgent group, the enemy state or any other collectivity.

Protocol I departs from this model in two distinct ways. First, it combines the regulation of inter-state and national liberation conflicts, and, second, it adopts an approach to some protective standards which is partly inspired by human rights. In seeking to incorporate into one single regime the regulation of inter-state and national liberation armed conflicts, Protocol I assimilates the national liberation movement to a state-like belligerent able to 'ratify' the Protocol and Conventions (Art. 96(3), Protocol I). The reciprocity of obligations between the state and insurgent belligerents, however, could not be fully analogised to inter-state relations, thus triggering the introduction in the Protocol of an element of reciprocity to the relation between duty-holders and the beneficiaries of the norms. Legitimate belligerents are thus defined as those who comply with the rules of humanitarian law (Art. 43(1), Protocol I), in a fashion similar to irregular combatants under the 1949 Geneva Conventions. This element of reciprocity seems appropriate when the conflict involves a national liberation movement. Its apparent extension to all regular armed forces in an international armed conflict, a situation in which a stable reciprocal relation exists at the state level, stands at odds with the approach embodied in the majority of humanitarian law norms. Protocol I also expands on what was an exceptional phenomenon in the older humanitarian norms, that is the creation of obligations towards individuals conceived atomistically. The Protocol abandons the concept of 'protected persons' in favour of the more all-encompassing one of 'civilians' (Part IV), whereby protection is granted on a model, closer to human rights law, in which links between the individuals and groups or states are not relevant. Contrary to the 1949 Geneva Conventions, this approach is adopted in Protocol I with respect to all norms protecting fundamental interests of civilians.

The changing place of reciprocity in the interconnected web of relations embodied in most humanitarian norms, especially those predating the two 1977 Protocols, has a direct impact on the means available to sanction violations of these norms. In this, once again, human rights and humanitarian law appear to follow significantly different patterns.

In humanitarian law, the link between the obligations of belligerents towards individuals under their control and other belligerents meant that sanctions were initially left in the hands of the interested state. Violations of the laws and customs of war were thus countered by reprisals by the enemy belligerent, and individual authors of war crimes were tried and punished either by their own state or, more likely, by the enemy state. The hybrid nature of humanitarian obligations, as well as the existence of some obligations which relate to individuals regardless of their link to any other group or state, permitted the expansion of that model to broaden the class of states able to participate in the sanction of their violation. The duty of all parties to the 1949 Geneva Conventions and Protocol I to try or extradite authors of grave breaches constitutes a reflection of this phenomenon, as does the creation of an International Criminal Court with jurisdiction to try war crimes. The move in more recent instruments towards a greater place for humanitarian obligations *erga omnes* opens the door to decentralised sanction measures by all states bound by the same norm, but the lack of significant state practice in prosecuting grave breaches as well as the experience of decentralised sanctions in human rights law show that this is an avenue unlikely to generate concrete results. In fact, despite the broader inclusion of states entitled to react to violations of humanitarian law, sanctions are most likely to come from states having a direct interest in the violation.

Because human rights standards are *erga omnes*, no state can normally be said to be specifically affected by the vast majority of violations, begging the question of the identity of the actor most likely to intervene to sanction such violations. The refusal of states to rely on the *erga omnes* nature of human rights in order to take unilateral countermeasures or to use the treaty inter-state petition mechanisms is somewhat offset by the granting of rights and standing to individuals themselves, although this is the case usually only with treaty norms and remains purely optional. Proposals such as that by the ILC of a crime of 'serious and systematic violations of human rights' to which would attach a duty of *aut dedere aut judicare* seem unlikely to contribute significantly to greater compliance with human rights, given the lack of concrete results of a similar obligation under humanitarian law in which individual responsibility is central. Efforts to expand the jurisdiction of human rights bodies to hear individual petitions seem a more promising avenue.

Finally, differences of context influence the resolution of legal indeterminacies in the characterisation of factual situations as armed conflicts or states of emergency. The significant inter-state component of obligations under humanitarian law results in competing autoqualifications by the various belligerent states or groups. Human rights law, on the contrary, imposes obligations which are essentially *erga omnes* and thus does not lead to multiple autoqualifications. Only the state on whose territory an emergency is taking place will be in a position to proceed to a self-characterisation of the situation. Other characterisations must necessarily rely on the *erga omnes* nature of human rights norms, a weaker basis as demonstrated by the 'margin of appreciation' given to the concerned state.

The overall result still remains a 'crazy quilt of norms',[2] with inconsistent standards of protection for individuals in at least five categories of legal situations. The expansion of lists of non-derogable human rights brings only a partial solution to that difficulty, even though they embody norms which remain applicable in all situations. One lesson to draw from the analysis is that a rights-based approach will not likely be the most effective in bringing needed protection to individuals during periods of armed conflict. There is room for considerable improvement of humanitarian norms, and in particular the expansion of absolute obligations centred on the individual construed in an atomistic fashion, detached from any links to a state or group. In this respect, the recent developments brought about by the creation of the ICTY, ICTR and ICC must be considered as highly positive. With the statutes of the ICTR and ICC, and in decisions of the ICTY, norms of customary humanitarian law have been expanded to cover internal armed conflict in a much more comprehensive fashion. Unlike older humanitarian treaties, customary norms tend to impose absolute obligations on belligerents, in some ways providing a better protection for individuals. In this, customary norms have largely overtaken even the more recent humanitarian treaties such as the 1977 Protocol II and, in some respects, the proposed declaration of minimum humanitarian standards.[3]

The analysis has shown significant differences between human rights and humanitarian law. More tellingly, it has demonstrated that each displays a peculiar normative richness and resilience likely to be weakened, if anything, by oversimplistic or overenthusiastic attempts to recast one in terms of the other. Thus, while there is indeed space for

---

[2] Theodor Meron, 'Classification of Armed Conflict in the Former Yugoslavia: *Nicaragua's* Fallout', (1998) 92 *Am. J Int'l L* 236, 238.

[3] See UN Secretary-General, 'Report on Minimum Humanitarian Standards', UN Doc. E/CN.4/1998/87; Turku Declaration, UN Doc. E/CN.4/1995/116.

enlightened cross-pollination and better integration of human rights and humanitarian law, each performs a task for which it is better suited than the other, and the fundamentals of each system remain partly incompatible with that of the other. In particular, there is a limit to which an atomistic construction of the individual ought to be adopted into humanitarian law, a system the hybrid construction of which reflects the reality that, in times of armed conflict, the individual will very often carry the label of friend or foe. Humanitarian law recognises and incorporates that reality in an approach that mingles individual and collective interests, one which seems more likely to bring about concrete protection for the individual in armed conflict than its human rights counterpart. Each system teaches us hard and unpleasant lessons about human behaviour in war and in peace. Each also captures the human potential for learning and hands us tools to attempt to bring about change. Both are lessons which we must go on learning again and again.

Bibliography

Abi-Saab, Georges, 'Wars of National Liberation and the Laws of War', (1972)
    3 *Annales d'études internationales* 102
    'Wars of National Liberation in the Geneva Conventions and Protocols',
    (1979-IV) 165 *Recueil des cours* 357
    'The Specificities of Humanitarian Law', in Christophe Swinarski ed., *Studies
    and Essays on International Humanitarian Law and Red Cross Principles in Honour
    of Jean Pictet* (Geneva/The Hague: ICRC/Nijhoff, 1984) 365
Acevedo, Domingo E., 'The Haitian Crisis and the OAS Response: A Test of the
    Effectiveness in Protecting Democracy', in Lori Fisler Damsrosch ed.,
    Enforcing Restraint – Collective Intervention in Internal Conflicts (New York:
    Council on Foreign Relations, 1993) 119
Ago, Roberto, 'Nota sul caso Kappler', [1953] *Rivista di diritto internazionale* 200
Akehurst, Michael, 'Reprisals by Third States', (1970) 44 *Brit. YB Int'l L* 1
    'Civil War', in Rudolf Bernhardt ed., [Instalment] 3 *Encyclopedia of Public
    International Law* (Amsterdam: North-Holland, 1982) 88
    A Modern Introduction to International Law (London: Routledge, 1987)
Albrecht, A. R., 'War Reprisals in the War Crimes Trials and in the Geneva
    Conventions of 1949', (1953) 47 *Am. J Int'l L* 590
Aldrich, George H., 'Establishing Legal Norms Through Multilateral
    Negotiations – The Laws of War', (1977) 9 *Case W Res. J Int'l L* 9
Alexander, G. J., 'The Illusory Protection of Human Rights by National Courts
    During Periods of Public Emergency', (1984) 5 *Hum. Rts LJ* 1
Alibert, Christiane, *Du droit de se faire justice dans la société internationale depuis
    1945* (Paris: LGDJ, 1983)
Alkema, Evert Albert, 'The Third-Party Applicability or "Drittwirkung" of the
    European Convention on Human Rights', in Franz Matscher and Herbert
    Petzold eds., *Protecting Human Rights: The European Dimension*, 2nd edn
    (Cologne: Karl Heymanns, 1990) 33
Alland, Denis, *Justice privée et ordre juridique international – Etude théorique des
    contre-mesures en droit international public* (Paris: Pedone, 1994)

Alston, Philip, 'Implementing Children's Rights: The Case of Child Labour',
(1989) 58 Nordic J Int'l L 35

Ambos, Kai, 'Impunity and International Criminal Law – A Case Study
on Colombia, Peru, Bolivia, Chile and Argentina', (1997) 18 Hum.
Rts LJ 1

American Red Cross, 'The Sixth Annual American Red Cross–Washington
College of Law Conference on International Humanitarian Law: A
Workshop on Customary International Law and the 1977 Protocols
Additional to the 1949 Geneva Conventions', (1987) 2 Am. UJ Int'l L &
Pol'y 415

Annacker, Claudia, Die Durchsetzung von erga omnes Verpflichtungen vor dem
internationalen Gerichtshof (Hamburg: Kovac, 1994)

Anzilotti, Dionisio, 'L'azione individuale contraria al diritto internazionale', in
Opere di Dionisio Anzilotti (Padua: CEDAM, 1956) II:1, 210

Arangio-Ruiz, Gaetano, 'Human Rights and Non Intervention in the Helsinki
Final Act', (1978-IV) 162 Recueil des cours 195

'Droits de l'homme et non-intervention: Helsinki, Belgrade et Madrid', (1980)
35 Comunità internazionale 453

Atlam, Hazem, 'National Liberation Movements and International
Responsibility', in Marina Spinedi and Bruno Simma eds., United Nations
Codification of State Responsibility (New York: Oceana, 1987) 35

Bailey, Sydney D., Prohibitions and Restraints in War (London: Oxford UP, 1972)

Bank, Roland, 'Der Fall Pinochet: Aufbruch zu neuen Ufern bei der Verfolgung
von Menschenrechtsverletzungen', (1999) 59 Zeitschrift für auslandisches
öffentliches Recht und Völkerrecht 677

Baratta, Roberto, 'Le riserve incompatibili con l'art. 64 della Convenzione
Europea dei diritti dell'uomo', (1992) 75 Rivista di diritto internazionale
288

Barberis, Julio A., 'Nouvelles questions concernant la personnalité juridique
internationale', (1983-I) 179 Recueil des cours 145

'El Comité internacional de la Cruz Roja como sujeto de derecho
internacional', in Christophe Swinarski ed., Studies and Essays on
International Humanitarian Law and Red Cross Principles in Honour of Jean Pictet
(Geneva/The Hague: Nijhoff, 1984) 635

Bariatti, Stefania, L'azione internazionale dello stato a tutela di non cittadini (Milan:
Giuffrè, 1993)

Barile, Giuseppe, 'Obligationes erga omnes e individui nel diritto internazionale
umanitario', (1985) 68 Rivista di diritto internazionale 5

'The Protection of Human Rights in Article 60 Paragraph 5 of the Vienna
Convention on the Law of Treaties', in International Law at the Time of its
Codification: Essays in Honour of Roberto Ago (Milan: Giuffrè, 1987) II, 3

Bassiouni, M. Cherif, 'The Proscribing Function of International Criminal Law
in the Process of International Protection of Human Rights', (1982) 9 Yale J
World Public Order 193

Crimes Against Humanity in International Criminal Law (The Hague: Nijhoff, 1992)

ed., *International Criminal Law* (Dobbs Ferry: International Publishers, 1987) I

Bassiouni, Cherif and Edward Wise, *Aut Dedere Aut Judicare – The Duty to Extradite or Prosecute in International Law* (Dordrecht: Nijhoff, 1995)

Baxter, Richard, '*Jus in Bello Interno*: The Present and Future Law', in J. Moore ed., *Law and Civil War in the Modern World* (Baltimore: Johns Hopkins, 1974) 518

'Humanitarian Law or Humanitarian Politics? The 1974 Diplomatic Conference on Humanitarian Law', (1975) 16 *Harv. Int'l LJ* 1

Becker, Howard, *Man in Reciprocity* (New York: Prager, 1956)

Belkherroubi, Abdelmadjid, 'Essai sur une théorie juridique des mouvements de libération nationale', [1972] *Revue égyptienne de droit international* 20

Bello, Emmanuel, 'The African Charter on Human and Peoples' Rights', (1985-V) 194 *Recueil des cours* 13

Benvenuti, Paolo, 'Ensuring Observance of International Humanitarian Law: Functions, Extent and Limits of the Obligation of Third States to Ensure Respect of International Humanitarian Law', [1989–90] *YB Int'l Inst. Humanitarian L* 27

Berderman, David, 'Historic Analogues of the UN Compensation Commission', in Richard Lillich ed., *The United Nations Compensation Commission* (Irvington NY: Transnational, 1995) 257

Bernard, Montague, 'The Growth of Law and Usages of War', in *Oxford Essays* (London: Parker, 1856) 88

Bernhardt, Rudolf, 'The International Enforcement of Human Rights: General Report', in Rudolf Bernhardt and John Anthony Jolowicz eds., *International Enforcement of Human Rights* (Berlin: Springer-Verlag, 1987) 143

Bernhardt, Rudolf and John Anthony Jolowicz eds., *International Enforcement of Human Rights* (Berlin: Springer-Verlag, 1987)

Best, Geoffrey, 'The Restraint of War in Historical and Philosophical Perspectives', in Astrid Delissen and Gerard Tanja eds., *Humanitarian Law of Armed Conflicts – Challenges Ahead* (Dordrecht: Nijhoff, 1990) 3

War and Law Since 1945 (Oxford: Oxford UP, 1994)

Bewes, Wyndham A., 'Reciprocity in the Enjoyment of Civil Rights', (1918) 3 *Transact. Grotius Soc.* 133

Bierzanek, Remigiusz, 'Le statut juridique des partisans et des mouvements de résistance armées: Evolution historique et aspects actuels', in Vladimir Ibler ed., *Mélanges offerts à Juraj Andrassy* (The Hague: Nijhoff, 1968) 54

'Reprisals as a Means of Enforcing the Laws of Warfare: The Old and the New Law', in Antonio Cassese ed., *The New Humanitarian Law of Armed Conflict* (Naples: Ed. Scientifica, 1979) 232

Bilder, Richard, *Managing the Risks of International Agreements* (Madison: U Wis. Press, 1981)

Bindschedler-Robert, Denise, 'A Reconsideration of the Law of Armed Conflict', in Carnegie Endowment for International Peace, *Report of the Conference on Contemporary Problems of the Law of Armed Conflict, Geneva: 15–20 Sept. 1969* (New York: Carnegie Endowment, 1971) 1

Blakesley, Christopher, 'Jurisdiction, Definition of Crimes and Triggering Mechanisms', (1997) 13 *Nouvelles études pénales* 177

Blaustein, Albert, Roger Clark and Jay Sigler eds., *Human Rights Sourcebook* (New York: Paragon, 1987)

Blishchenko, Igor, 'Responsibility in Breaches of International Humanitarian Law', in UNESCO, *International Dimensions of Humanitarian Law* (Dordrecht: Nijhoff, 1988) 283

Bloed, Arie ed., *The Conference on Security and Co-operation in Europe* (Dordrecht: Nijhoff, 1993)

Bloed, Arie and Pieter van Dijk eds., *Essays on Human Rights in the Helsinki Process* (Dordrecht: Nijhoff, 1985)

The Human Dimension of the Helsinki Process (Dordrecht: Nijhoff, 1991)

Bogaïewsky, P., 'Les secours aux militaires malades et blessés avant le XIXème siècle', (1903) 10 *Revue générale de droit international public* 202

Boissier, Pierre, *L'épée et la balance* (Geneva: Labor et Fides, 1953)

Boling, David, 'Mass Rape, Enforced Prostitution, and the Japanese Imperial Army: Japan Eschews International Legal Responsibility?', (1995) 32 *Colum. J Transnat'l L* 532

Bollecker-Stern, Brigitte, *Le préjudice dans la théorie de la responsabilité internationale* (Paris: Pedone, 1973)

Borchard, Edwin, 'Reprisals on Private Property', (1936) 30 *Am. J Int'l L* 108

Bosly, 'Responsabilité des Etats parties à un conflit quant à l'application du droit humanitaire', (1973) 12:2 *Revue de droit pénal militaire et de droit de la guerre* 207

Bossuyt, Marc J., 'The Direct Applicability of International Instruments on Human Rights', (1980) 15 *Revue belge de droit international* 317

Guide to the 'Travaux Préparatoires' of the International Covenant on Civil and Political Rights (Dordrecht: Nijhoff, 1987)

Bothe, Michael, 'Völkerrechtliche Aspekte des Angola Konflikts', (1977) 37 *Zeitschrift für ausländische öffentliches Recht und Völkerrecht* 572

'The Role of Municipal Law in the Implementation of International Humanitarian Law', in Christophe Swinarski ed., *Studies and Essays on International Humanitarian Law and Red Cross Principles in Honour of Jean Pictet* (Geneva/The Hague: ICRC/Nijhoff, 1984) 301

Bothe, Michael, Peter Macalister-Smith and Thomas Kurzidem eds., *National Implementation of International Humanitarian Law* (The Hague: Nijhoff, 1990)

Bourloyannis, Christiane, 'The Security Council of the United Nations and the Implementation of International Humanitarian Law', (1992) 20 *Denver J Int'l L & Pol'y* 335

Boustany, Katia, 'La qualification des conflits en droit international public et le maintien de la paix', (1989–90) 6 *Revue québécoise de droit international* 38

Bowett, Derek W., 'Economic Coercion and Reprisals by States', (1972) 13 *Va. J Int'l L* 1

Bretton, P., 'La mise en oeuvre des Protocoles additionnels de 1977 aux Conventions de Genève de 1949', (1979) *Revue de droit public et de la science politique en France et à l'étranger* 379

Brierly, James, *The Law of Nations*, Humphrey Waldock ed., 6th edn (Oxford: Oxford UP, 1963)

Briggs, Herbert W., 'Unilateral Denunciation of Treaties: The Vienna Convention and the International Court of Justice', (1974) 68 *Am. J Int'l L* 51

British Manual of Military Law, Hugh Godley ed., 6th edn (London: HMSO, 1914)

Brocher, Henri, 'Les principes naturels du droit de la guerre (parties 1–2)', (1872) 4 *Revue générale de droit international et de législation comparée* 1 and 381

'Les principes naturels du droit de la guerre (parties 3–4)', (1873) 5 *Revue générale de droit international et de législation comparée* 321 and 566

Brossard, Jacques, 'Le droit du peuple québécois de disposer de lui-même au regard du droit international', (1977) 15 *Can. YB Int'l L* 84

Brownlie, Ian, *International Law and the Use of Force by States* (Oxford: Clarendon, 1963)

'Recognition in Theory and Practice', in Ronald St J. Macdonald and Douglas Johnston eds., *The Structure and Process of International Law* (Dordrecht: Nijhoff, 1983) 627

System of the Law of Nations: State Responsibility (Oxford: Clarendon, 1983)

Principles of Public International Law, 5th edn (Oxford: Clarendon, 1998)

ed., *Basic Documents on Human Rights*, 3rd edn (Oxford: Clarendon, 1992)

Brunnée, Jutta and Stephen Toope, 'International Law and Constructivism: Elements of an Interactional Theory of International Law', (2000) 39 *Colum. J Transnat'l L* 19

Buergenthal, Thomas, 'To Respect and to Ensure: State Obligations and Permissible Derogations', in Louis Henkin ed., *The International Bill of Rights* (New York: Columbia UP, 1981)

'The Advisory Practice of the Inter-American Human Rights Court', (1985) 79 *Am. J Int'l L* 1

'Self-executing and Non-self-executing Treaties in National and International Law', (1992-IV) 235 *Recueil des cours* 303

Bugnion, François, *Le Comité international de la Croix-Rouge et la protection des victimes de la guerre* (Geneva: ICRC, 1994)

Burgos, Hernan S., 'The Application of International Humanitarian Law as Compared to Human Rights Law in Situations Qualified as Internal Armed Conflict, Internal Disturbances and Tensions, or Public Emergency, With Special Reference to War Crimes and Political Crimes', in Frits Kalshoven and Yves Sandoz eds., *Implementation of International Humanitarian Law* (Dordrecht: Nijhoff, 1989) 1

Caflisch, Lucius, 'Pratique suisse relative au droit international en 1986', (1987) 43 *Annuaire suisse de droit international* 185

Cahin, Gérard and Demis Çarkaçi, 'Les guerres de libération nationale et le droit international', [1976] *Annuaire du Tiers-Monde* 34

Calò, Emanuele, *Il principio di reciprocità* (Milan: Giuffrè, 1993)

Calogeropoulos-Stratis, Aristidis, *Droit humanitaire et droits de l'homme: La protection de la personne en conflits armés* (Geneva: Institut universitaire de hautes études internationales, 1980)

Campiglio, Cristina, 'Profili internazionali della questione del Québec', (1991) 74 *Rivista di diritto internazionale* 73

Il principio di reciprocità nel diritto dei trattati (Padua: CEDAM, 1995)

Canadian Armed Forces, *The Law of Armed Conflict at the Operational and Tactical Level (B-GG-005-027/AF-020)* (Ottawa: Judge Advocate General, 1999)

Canadian Forces Law of Armed Conflict Manual (Second Draft) (Ottawa: Dept Nat'l Defence, 1984)

Capotorti, Francesco, 'L'extinction et la suspension des traités', (1971-III) 134 *Recueil des cours* 417

'Incidenza della condizione di straniero sui diritti dell'uomo internazionalmente protteti', in *Studi in onore di Giuseppe Sperduti* (Milan: Giuffrè, 1984) 143

Carbonneau, Thomas E., 'The Convergence of the Law of State Responsibility for Injuries to Aliens and International Human Rights Norms in the Revised Restatement', (1984) 25 *Va. J Int'l L* 99

Carnahan, Bruce, 'Customary Law and Additional Protocol I to the Geneva Conventions for Protection of War Victims: Future Direction in Light of the US Decision not to Ratify', (1989) 81 *ASIL Proc.* 26

Carnahan, Burrus C., '*In re Medina*: Are the 1949 Geneva Conventions Self-Executing?', (1987) 26 *Air Force L Rev.* 123

Cassese, Antonio, 'The Geneva Protocols of 1977 on the Humanitarian Law of Armed Conflict and Customary International Law', (1984) 3 *UCLA Pac. Basin LJ* 55

'Modern Constitutions and International Law', (1985-III) 185 *Recueil des cours* 331

'On the Current Trends Towards Criminal Prosecution and Punishment of Breaches of International Humanitarian Law', (1998) 9 *Eur. J Int'l L* 2

ed., *The New Humanitarian Law of Armed Conflict – Proceedings of the 1976 and 1977 Conferences* (Naples: Ed. Scientifica, 1980)

Cassin, René, 'L'homme, sujet de droit international, et la protection des droits de l'homme dans la société universelle', in *La technique et les principes du droit public – Etudes en l'honneur de Georges Scelle* (Paris: LGDJ, 1950) I, 67

'De la place faite aux devoirs de l'individu dans la Déclaration universelle des droits de l'homme', in *Mélanges Poly Modinos – Problèmes des droits de l'homme et de l'unification européenne* (Paris: Pedone, 1968) 479

Castañeda, Jorge, *Legal Effect of United Nations Resolutions* (New York: Columbia UP, 1969)

Castrén, Erik, *The Present Law of War and Neutrality* (Helsinki: Suomalaisen Tiedeakatemian Toimituksia, 1954)

Cerna, Christina M., 'Human Rights in Armed Conflict: Implementation of International Humanitarian Norms by Regional Intergovernmental Human Rights Bodies', in Frits Kalshoven and Yves Sandoz eds., *Implementation of International Humanitarian Law* (Dordrecht: Nijhoff, 1989) 31

'The Inter-American Court of Human Rights', in Mark Janis ed., *International Courts for the Twenty-First Century* (Dordrecht: Nijhoff, 1992) 117

Chandrasekhara Rao, P., 'The Detention of Guinean Nationals in the Ivory Coast. Issues of International Immunities', [1967] *Indian J Int'l L* 397

Charney, Jonathan, 'The Persistent Objector Rule and the Development of Customary International Law', [1985] *Brit. YB Int'l L* 1

'Third State Remedies in International Law', (1989) 10 *Mich. J Int'l L* 57

Chemillier-Gendreau, Monique, 'Rapport sur la fonction idéologique du droit international', [1974] *Annales de la Faculté de droit et de sciences économiques de Reims* 221

Cheng, Bin, 'Flight from Justiciable to Auto-interpretative International Law', in *Liber Amicorum Elie van Bogaert* (Antwerp: Kluwer, 1985) 1

Chowdhury, Subrata Roy, *Rule of Law in a State of Emergency* (London: Pinter, 1989)

Clapham, Andrew, '*Drittwirkung* and the European Convention of Human Rights', in R. St J. Macdonald et al. eds., *The European System for the Protection of Human Rights* (Dordrecht: Nijhoff, 1993) 163

Human Rights in the Private Sphere (Oxford: Oxford UP, 1993)

Coccia, Massimo, 'Reservations to Multilateral Treaties on Human Rights', (1985) 15 *Cal. W Int'l LJ* 1

Cohen-Jonathan, Gérard, 'Les réserves à la Convention européenne des droits de l'homme (à propos de l'arrêt Bélilos du 29 avril 1988)', [1989] *Revue générale de droit international public* 273

Colbert, Evelyn Speyer, *Retaliation in International Law* (New York: King's Crown Press, 1948)

Colby, Elbridge, 'War Crimes', (1924–5) 23 *Mich. L Rev.* 482

Coleman, Howard D., 'Greece and the Council of Europe: The International Legal Protection of Human Rights by the Political Process', (1972) 2 *Israel YB Hum. Rts* 121

Combacau, Jean and Serge Sur, *Droit international public*, 2nd edn (Paris: Domat, 1995)

Commission on Wartime Relocation and Internment of Civilians, *Personal Justice Denied* (Washington: US Gov. Printing Office, 1982)

Condorelli, Luigi and Laurence Boisson de Chazournes, 'Quelques remarques à propos de l'obligation des Etats de "respecter et faire respecter" le droit international humanitaire "en toutes circonstances"', in Christophe Swinarski ed., *Studies and Essays on International Humanitarian Law and Red Cross Principles in Honour of Jean Pictet* (Geneva/The Hague: ICRC/Nijhoff, 1984) 17

'Common Article 1 of the Geneva Conventions Revisited: Protecting Collective Interest', (2000) 837 *Int'l Rev. Red Cross* 67

Conforti, Benedetto, *Diritto internazionale*, 4th edn (Naples: Ed. Scientifica, 1992)

International Law and the Role of Domestic Legal Systems (Dordrecht: Nijhoff, 1993)

Constas, Dimitris C., 'The "Turkish Affair": A Test Case for the Council of Europe', (1982) 2 *Legal Issues of Eur. Integration* 69

Corten, Olivier, *L'utilisation du 'raisonnable' par le juge international* (Brussels: Bruylant, 1997)

Corten, Olivier and Pierre Klein, *Droit d'ingérence ou obligation de réaction?*, 2nd edn (Brussels: Bruylant, 1996)

Coursier, Henri, 'Les éléments essentiels du respect de la personne humaine dans la Convention de Genève du 12 août 1949, relative à la protection des personnes civiles en temps de guerre', [1950] *Revue internationale de la Croix-Rouge* 354–69

'Definition du droit humanitaire', [1955] *AFDI* 223

'L'évolution du droit international humanitaire', (1960-I) 99 *Recueil des cours* 357

Craven, Matthew, *The International Covenant on Economic, Social and Cultural Rights* (Oxford: Clarendon, 1995)

'Legal Differentiation and the Concept of the Human Rights Treaty in International Law', (2000) 11 *Eur. J Int'l L* 489

Crawford, James, 'Counter-Measures as Interim Measures', (1994) 5 *Eur. J Int'l L* 65

The Crime of Katyn – Facts and Documents (London: Polish Cultural Foundation, 1965)

Crook, John R., 'The United Nations Compensation Commission: A New Structure to Enforce State Responsibility', (1993) 87 *Am. J Int'l L* 144

'The UNCC and Its Critics: Is Iraq Entitled to Judicial Due Process?', in Richard Lillich ed., *The United Nations Compensation Commission* (Irvington, NY: Transnational, 1995) 77

Czesany, Maximilian, *Nie wieder Krieg gegen die Zivilbevölkerung: Eine völkerrechtliche Untersuchung des Luftkrieg 1939–1945* (Graz, 1961)

Daes, Erica-Irene A., 'Freedom of the Individual Under Law: The Individual's Duties to the Community and the Limitations on Human Rights and Freedoms Under Article 29 of the Universal Declaration of Human Rights', UN Sales No. E.89.XIV.4 (1990)

'Status of the Individual and Contemporary International Law: Promotion, Protection and Restoration of Human Rights at the National, Regional and International Levels', UN Sales No. E.91.XIV.3 (1992)

Daniel, J., *Le problème du châtiment des crimes de guerre d'après les enseignements de la deuxième guerre mondiale* (Cairo: Schindler, 1946)

Daniel, José, 'The Vienna Convention of 1969 on the Law of Treaties and Humanitarian Law', (1972) 136 *Int'l Rev. Red Cross* 367

d'Argent, Pierre, 'Le fonds et la Commission de compensation des Nations Unies', [1992] 2 *Revue belge de droit international* 484

David, Eric, 'Le Tribunal pénal international pour l'ex-Yougoslavie', [1992] 2 *Revue belge de droit international* 565

Principes de droit des conflits armés (Brussels: Bruylant, 1994)

de Breucker, Jean, 'Pour les vingt ans de la Convention de La Haye du 14 mai 1954 pour la protection des biens culturels', [1975] *Revue belge de droit international* 524

de Guttry, Andrea, *Le rappresaglie non comportanti la coercizione militare nel diritto internazionale* (Milan: Giuffrè, 1985)

de Hoogh, André, *Obligations* Erga Omnes *and International Crimes* (The Hague: Kluwer Law International, 1996)

de la Brière, Yves, 'Evolution de la doctrine et de la pratique en matière de représailles', (1928-II) 22 *Recueil des cours* 241

de la Pradelle, Paul de Geouffre, 'Jus cogens et Conventions humanitaires', (1968) 18 *Ann. de droit int'l médical* 9

de Preux, Jean, 'The Geneva Conventions and Reciprocity', (1985) 244 *Int'l Rev. Red Cross* 25

de Vattel, Emer, *Le droit des gens ou principes de la loi naturelle*, James Brown Scott ed. (Washington: Carnegie, 1916, 1st edn 1758) III

Decaux, Emmanuel, *La réciprocité en droit international* (Paris: LGDJ, 1980)

Decaux, Emmanuel and Linos-Alexandre Sicilianos eds., *La dimension humanitaire de la Conférence de sécurité et coopération en Europe* (Paris: Montchrestien, 1993)

Dedijer, Vladimir, *On Military Conventions* (Lund: Gleerup, 1961)

Dekker, Ige F., 'Criminal Responsibilities and the Gulf War of 1980–88. The Crime of Aggression', in Ige Dekker and Harry Post eds., *The Gulf War of 1980–1988: The Iran–Iraq War in International Legal Perspectives* (The Hague: Nijhoff, 1992)

Delbez, Louis, 'La notion juridique de guerre', (1953) 57 *Revue générale de droit international public* 177

Delbrück, J., 'International Economic Sanctions and Third States', (1992) 30 *Archiv des Völkerrecht* 86

Dennis, Michael, 'The Fifty-Second Session of the UN Commission on Human Rights', (1997) 91 *Am. J Int'l L* 167

'The Fifty-Fourth Session of the UN Commission on Human Rights', (1999) 93 *Am. J Int'l L* 246

'The Fifty-Fifth Session of the UN Commission on Human Rights', (2000) 94 *Am. J Int'l L* 189

Detter de Lupis, Ingrid, *The Law of War* (Cambridge: Cambridge UP, 1987)

Dieng, Adama, 'La mise en oeuvre du droit international humanitaire: Les infractions et les sanctions, ou quand la pratique désavoue les textes', in *Law in Humanitarian Crises – How Can International Humanitarian Law be Made Effective in Armed Conflict?* (Luxembourg: European Communities, 1995) I, 311

Dinstein, Yoram, *The Defense of 'Obedience to Superior Order' in International Law* (Leiden: Sijthoff, 1965)

'Human Rights in Armed Conflict: International Humanitarian Law', in Theodor Meron ed., *Human Rights in International Law: Legal and Policy Issues* (Oxford: Clarendon, 1984) II, 345

'International Criminal Law', (1985) 20 *Israel L Rev.* 206

'The Distinction Between Unlawful Combatants and War Criminals', in Yoram Dinstein ed., *International Law at a Time of Perplexity – Essays in Honour of Shabtai Rosenne* (Dordrecht: Nijhoff, 1989) 105

'The *Erga Omnes* Applicability of Human Rights', (1992) 30 *Archiv des Völkerrecht* 16

War, Aggression and Self-Defense, 2nd edn (Cambridge: Cambridge UP, 1992)

Doehring, Karl, 'Non-discrimination and Equal Treatment Under the European Human Rights Convention and the West German Constitution with Particular Reference to Discrimination Against Aliens', (1970) 18 *Am. J Comp. L* 305

Domb, Fania, 'Supervision of the Observance of International Humanitarian Law', (1978) 8 *Israel YB Hum. Rts* 178

Dominicé, Christian, 'La personnalité juridique du CICR', in Christophe Swinarski ed., *Studies and Essays on International Humanitarian Law and Red Cross Principles in Honour of Jean Pictet* (Geneva/The Hague: ICRC/Nijhoff, 1984) 663

'La contrainte entre Etats à l'appui des droits de l'homme', in *Hacia un nuevo orden internacional y europeo – Estudios en homenaje al profesor Don Manuel Díos de Velasco* (Madrid: Tecnos, 1993) 261

Donnedieu de Vabres, Henri, 'Le procès de Nuremberg devant les principes modernes du droit pénal international', (1947-I) 70 *Recueil des cours* 477

Donnelly, Jack, *Universal Human Rights in Theory and Practice* (Ithaca: Cornell UP, 1989)

Doswald-Beck, L. and S. Vites, 'International Humanitarian Law and Human Rights', (1993) *Int'l Rev. Red Cross* 99

Draper, G. I. A. D., *The Red Cross Conventions* (London: Stevens, 1958)

'The Relationship Between the Human Rights Regime and the Law of Armed Conflict', in *Proceedings of the International Conference on Humanitarian Law* (Grassi: Istituto Editoriale Ticinese, 1970) 141

'Rules Governing the Conduct of Hostilities – The Laws of War and their Enforcement', in *United States Naval War College, Readings in International Law 1969–1970* (Washington DC: US Gov. Printing Office, 1970) 380

'The Modern Pattern of War Criminality', (1976) 6 *Israel YB Hum. Rts* 9

'The Implementation and Enforcement of the Geneva Conventions of 1949 and of the Two Additional Protocols of 1977', (1979) 164 *Recueil des cours* 1

Drzemczewski, Andrew, *European Human Rights Convention in Domestic Law* (Oxford: Clarendon, 1983)

'Decisions on the Merits: By the Committee of Ministers', in R. St J. Macdonald et al. eds., *The European System for the Protection of Human Rights* (Dordrecht: Nijhoff, 1993) 733

Dubois, Olivier, 'Meeting of Experts on Committees or Other Bodies for the National Implementation of International Humanitarian Law, Geneva, 23–25 October 1996', (1997) 317 *Int'l Rev. Red Cross* 187

Duculesco, Victor, 'Effet de la reconnaissance de l'état de belligérance par les tiers, y compris les organisations internationales, sur le statut juridique des conflits armés à caractère non-international', (1975) 79 *Revue générale de droit international public* 125

Dugard, John, 'SWAPO: The *Jus ad Bellum* and the *Jus in Bello*', (1976) 93 *S Afr. LJ* 144

Dupuy, Pierre-Marie, 'Observations sur la pratique récente des "sanctions" de l'illicite', (1983) 87 *Revue générale de droit international public* 505

Droit international public (Paris: Dalloz, 1996)

Dürr, Olivier, 'Humanitarian Law of Armed Conflict: Problems of Applicability', (1987) 24 *J Peace Res.* 263

Eide, Asbjorn, 'The Law of War and Human Rights – Differences and Convergences', in Christophe Swinarski ed., *Studies and Essays on International Humanitarian Law and Red Cross Principles in Honour of Jean Pictet* (Geneva/The Hague: ICRC/Nijhoff, 1984) 675

Eissen, Marc-André, 'La Convention européenne des droits de l'homme et les obligations de l'individu: Une mise à jour', in *René Cassin Amicorum Discipulorumque Liber* (Paris: Pedone, 1971) III, 151

El Kouhene, Mohammed, *Les garanties fondamentales de la personne en droit humanitaire et droits de l'homme* (Dordrecht: Nijhoff, 1986)

Elagab, Omer Yousif, *The Legality of Non-Forcible Counter-Measures in International Law* (Oxford: Clarendon, 1988)

Elder, D., 'The Historical Background of Common Article 3 of the Geneva Conventions of 1949', (1979) 11 *Case W Res. J Int'l L* 37

Ergec, Rusen, *Les droits de l'homme à l'épreuve des circonstances exceptionnelles. Etude sur l'article 15 de la Convention européenne des droits de l'homme* (Brussels: Bruylant/Université de Bruxelles, 1987)

Ermacora, Felix, 'Über die völkerrechtliche Verantwortlichkeit für Menschenrechtsverletzungen', in H. Miehsler ed., *Ius Humanitaris: Festschrift für Alfred Verdross* (Berlin: Duncker & Humblot, 1980) 357

Espersen, Ole, 'Human Rights and Relations Between Individuals', in *René Cassin Amicorum Discipulorumque Liber* (Paris: Pedone, 1971) III, 177

Eustathiades, Constantin, 'Les sujets de droit international et la responsabilité internationale – Nouvelles tendances', (1953-III) 84 *Recueil des cours* 397

Falk, Richard, 'Son My: War Crimes and Individual Responsibility', in Falk ed., *The Vietnam War and International Law* (Princeton: Princeton UP, 1972) III, 327

Farer, Tom J., 'Humanitarian Law and Armed Conflict: Towards the Definition of "International Armed Conflict"', (1971) 71 *Colum. L Rev.* 37

'The Laws of War 25 Years After Nuremberg', (1971) 358 *Int'l Conciliation* 47

Fawcett, J. E. S., *The Application of the European Convention on Human Rights*, 2nd edn (Oxford: Clarendon, 1987)

Feldmann, D. I., 'International Personality', (1985) 191 *Recueil des cours* 343

Fenrick, William, 'The Exclusion Zone in the Law of Warfare', (1986) 24 *Can. YB Int'l L* 91

'In the Field with UNCOE: Investigating Atrocities in the Territory of the Former Yugoslavia', (1995) 34 *Revue de droit militaire et du droit de la guerre* 33

Fisler Damrosch, Lori, 'The Civilian Impact of Economic Sanctions', in Lori Fisler Damrosch ed., *Enforcing Restraint – Collective Intervention in Internal Conflicts* (New York: Council on Foreign Relations, 1993) 274

Fitzmaurice, Sir Gerald, 'Reservations to Multilateral Conventions', [1953] *Int'l & Comp. L Quart.* 1

'The General Principles of International Law Considered from the Standpoint of the Rule of Law', (1957-II) 92 *Recueil des cours* 5

Fitzpatrick, Joan, *Human Rights in Crisis – The International System for Protecting Rights During States of Emergency* (Philadelphia: Pennsylvania UP, 1994)

'States of Emergency in the Inter-American System', in David Harris and Stephen Livingstone eds., *The Inter-American System of Human Rights* (Oxford: Oxford UP, 1998) 1

Flauss, Jean F., 'Le droit à un recours effectif: L'article 13 de la Convention européenne des droits de l'homme dans la jurisprudence de la Commission et de la Cour', in Gérald-A. Beaudoin ed., *Vues canadiennes et européennes des droits de la personne* (Drummondville: Yvon Blais, 1989) 258

Fleck, Dieter, 'Die internationale Ermittlungskommission: Probleme und Perspektiven einer neuen Einrichtung des humanitären Völkerrecht', in Horst Schötter and Bernd Hoffman eds., *Die Genfer Zusatzprotokolle. Commentare und Analysen* (Bonn: Osang, 1993) 258

ed., *The Handbook of Humanitarian Law in Armed Conflict* (Oxford: Oxford UP, 1995)

Fleiner-Gerster, Thomas and Michael A. Meyer, 'New Developments in Humanitarian Law: A Challenge to the Concept of Sovereignty', (1985) 34 *Int'l & Comp. L Quart.* 267

Focarelli, Carlo, 'La reciprocità nel trattamento degli stranieri in Italia come forma di ritorsione o rappresaglia', (1989) 72 *Rivista di diritto internazionale* 825

'Le contromisure pacifiche e la nozione di obblighi *erga omnes*', (1993) 76 *Rivista di diritto internazionale* 52

Le contromisure nel diritto internazionale (Milan: Giuffrè, 1994)

Foot, M. R. D., *Resistance*, 2nd edn (London: Granada, 1978)

Ford, W. J., 'Resistance Movements and International Law', (1967–8) 79 *Int'l Rev. Red Cross* 515

Forde, M., 'Non-governmental Interference with Human Rights', (1985) 56 *Brit. YB Int'l L* 253

Forlati Picchio, Laura, *La sanzione nel diritto internazionale* (Padua: CEDAM, 1974)

Forsythe, David, 'Who Guards the Guardians?: Third Parties and the Law of Armed Conflict', (1976) 70 *Am. J Int'l L* 41

Humanitarian Politics: The International Committee of the Red Cross (Baltimore: Johns Hopkins UP, 1977)

'Legal Management of Internal War: The 1977 Protocol on Non-international Armed Conflicts', (1978) 72 *Am. J Int'l L* 272

'Human Rights and the International Committee of the Red Cross', (1990) 12 *Hum. Rts Quart.* 265

'Choices More Ethical than Legal: The International Committee of the Red Cross', (1993) 7 *Ethics & Int'l Aff.* 131

Fox, Hazel, 'Reparations and State Responsibility: Claims Against Iraq Arising out of the Invasion and Occupation of Kuwait', in Peter Rowe ed., *The Gulf War 1990–1991 in International and English Law* (London: Routledge, 1992) 261

Fraenkel, Ernst, *Military Occupation and the Rule of Law – Occupation Government in the Rhineland 1918–23* (London: Oxford UP, 1944)

Françillon, Jacques, 'Crimes de guerre, crimes contre l'humanité', (1993) 410 *Juris-Classeurs de droit international*

Franck, Thomas, *The Power of Legitimacy Among Nations* (New York: Oxford UP, 1990)

Fairness in International Law (Oxford: Clarendon, 1995)

Freeman, Alwyn, 'Responsibility of States for Unlawful Acts of their Armed Forces', (1955-II) 88 *Recueil des cours* 267

Freudenschuss, Helmut, 'Legal and Political Aspects of the Recognition of National Liberation Movements', (1982) 11 *Millennium: J Int'l Stud.* 115

Friedmann, Wolfgang, *The Changing Structure of International Law* (London: Stevens & Sons, 1964)

Frigessi di Rattalma, Marco, *Nazione Unite e danni derivanti dalla guerra del Golfo* (Milan: Giuffrè, 1995)

'Le régime de la responsabilité internationale institué par le Conseil d'administration de la Commission de compensation des Nations Unies', (1997) 101 *Revue générale de droit international public* 44

Frowein, Jochen, 'Die Verpflichtungen *erga omnes* im Völkerrecht und ihre Durchsetzung', in Rudolf Bernhardt et al. eds., *Völkerrecht als Rechtsordnung, internationale Gerichtsbarkeit, Menschenrechte: Festschrift für Herman Mosler* (Berlin: Springer, 1983) 243

'Reactions by Not-directly Affected States to Breaches of Public International Law', (1994-IV) 248 *Recueil des cours* 345

Fuller, Lon, *The Morality of Law*, rev. edn (New Haven: Yale UP, 1969)

Gaja, Giorgio, 'Obligations *Erga Omnes*, International Crimes and *Jus Cogens*: A Tentative Analysis of Three Related Concepts', in Joseph Weiler, Antonio Cassese and Marina Spinedi eds., *International Crimes of States – A Critical Analysis of the ILC's Draft Article 19 on State Responsibility* (Berlin: de Gruyter, 1989) 151

Gandhi, P. R., 'The Human Rights Committee and Derogation in Public Emergencies', (1989) 32 *German YB Int'l L* 323

Ganshof Van Der Meersch, W. J., 'Le respect des droits fondamentaux de l'homme, condition exigée de droit des Etats européens', [1983] *Revue de droit international et de droit comparé* 10

García Amador, F. V., 'Le sujet passif de la responsabilité et la capacité d'être demandeur en droit international', (1956) 34 *Revue de droit international, des sciences diplomatiques et politiques* 266

Garner, James W., *International Law and the World War* (London: Longmans, Green, 1920) II

'Punishment of Offenders Against the Laws and Customs of War', (1920) 14 *Am. J Int'l L* 70

'Recognition of Belligerency', (1938) 32 *Am. J Int'l L* 106

Gasser, Hans-Peter, 'Internationalized Non-international Armed Conflicts: Case Studies of Afghanistan, Kampuchea and Lebanon', (1983) 33 *Am. UL Rev.* 145

'Ensuring Respect for the Geneva Conventions and Protocols: The Role of Third States and the United Nations', in Hazel Fox and Michael Meyer eds., *Armed Conflict and the New Law – Effecting Compliance* (London: British Institute of International and Comparative Law, 1993) II, 15

Gazzini, Tarcisio, 'Consideration of the Conflict in Chechnya', (1996) 17 *Hum. Rts LJ* 93

Giegerich, Thomas, 'Vorbehalte zu Menschenrechtsabkommen: Zulässigkeit, Gultigkeit und Prufungskompetenzen von Vertragsgremien', (1995) 55 *Zeitschrift für ausländisches öffentliches Recht und Völkerrecht* 712

Ginsburg, George and Vladimir Kudriavtev eds., *The Nuremberg Trials and International Law* (Dordrecht: Nijhoff, 1990)

Ginther, Konrad, 'Liberation Movements', in Rudolf Bernhardt ed., [Instalment] 3 *Encyclopedia of Public International Law* (Amsterdam: North-Holland, 1982) 245

Giraud, E., *Le respect des droits de l'homme dans la guerre internationale et la guerre civile* (Paris: LGDG, 1958)

Golsong, Héribert, 'Implementation of International Protection of Human Rights', (1963-III) *Recueil des cours* 1

'Les réserves aux instruments internationaux pour la protection des droits de l'homme', in *Les clauses échappatoires en matière d'instruments relatifs aux droits de l'homme* (Brussels/Louvain-La-Neuve: Bruylant/Cabay, 1982) 23

Gomaa, Mohammed, *Suspension or Termination of Treaties on Ground of Breach* (Dordrecht: Nijhoff, 1996)

Gouldner, Alvin, 'The Norm of Reciprocity: A Preliminary Statement', (1960) 25 *Am. Sociol. Rev.* 161

Gowlland-Debbas, Vera, 'The Relationship Between the International Court of Justice and the Security Council in Light of the *Lockerbie* Case', (1994) 88 *Am. J Int'l L* 643

Graefrath, Bernard, 'Iraqi Reparations and the Security Council', (1995) 55 *Zeitschrift für ausländisches öffentliches Recht und Völkerrecht* 1

Gray, C., *Judicial Remedies in International Law* (Oxford: Clarendon, 1987)

Green, Leslie C., *Superior Orders in National and International Law* (Leiden: Sijthoff, 1976)

'Canadian Law, War Crimes, and Crimes Against Humanity', (1988) 59 *Brit. YB Int'l L* 217

'International Criminal Law and the Protection of Human Rights', in Bin Cheng and E. D. Brown eds., *Contemporary Problems of International Law: Essays in Honor of Georg Schwarzenberger* (London: Stevens, 1988) 116

'The Intersection of Human Rights and International Criminal Law', in Irwin Cotler and Pearl Eliadis eds., *International Human Rights – Theory and Practice* (Montreal: Canadian Human Rights Foundation, 1993) 231

Greenspan, Morris, *The Modern Law of Land Warfare* (Los Angeles: U Calif. Press, 1959)

'The Protection of Human Rights in Times of Warfare', (1970) 1 *Isr. YB Hum. Rts* 228

Greenwood, Christopher, 'The Relationship Between *Ius ad Bellum* and *Ius ad Bello*', (1983) 9 *Rev. Int'l Studies* 221

'The Concept of War in Modern International Law', (1987) 36 *Int'l & Comp. L Quart.* 283

'The Twilight of the Law of Belligerent Reprisals', (1989) 20 *Nether. YB Int'l L* 35

'Scope of Application of Humanitarian Law', in Dieter Fleck ed., *The Handbook of Humanitarian Law in Armed Conflict* (Oxford: Oxford UP, 1995) 39

'International Humanitarian Law and the *Tadić* Case', (1996) 7 *Eur. J Int'l L* 265

'Rights at the Frontier – Protecting the Individual in Time of War', in *Law at the Centre – The Institute of Advanced Legal Studies at Fifty* (Dordrecht: Kluwer, 1999) 277

Greig, D. W., 'The Underlying Principles of International Humanitarian Law',
    (1985) 9 *Austr. YB Int'l L* 46
    'Reciprocity, Proportionality, and the Law of Treaties', (1994) 34 *Va. J Int'l L*
    295
Grevy, R., 'La répression des crimes de guerre en droit belge', [1947-8] *Revue de
    droit pénal et de criminologie* 806
Grob, Fritz, *The Reality of War and Peace* (New Haven: Yale UP, 1949)
Gros Espiell, Héctor, *La Convención americana y la Convención europea de derechos
    humanos - Analysis comparativo* (Santiago: Ed. juridica de Chile, 1991)
Gross, Leo, 'States as Organs of International Law and the Problem of
    Autointerpretation', in George Lipsky ed., *Law and Politics in the World
    Community. Essays on Hans Kelsen's Pure Theory of Law and Related Problems in
    International Law* (Berkeley: U Calif. Press, 1953) 59
Grotius, Hugo, *De jure belli ac pacis libri tres (1625)*, James Brown Scott ed.
    (Oxford: Clarendon, 1925) II, bk 3
Halleck, H. W., *International Law* (New York: Van Nostrand, 1861)
Hampson, Françoise J., 'Belligerent Reprisals and the 1977 Protocols to the
    Geneva Conventions of 1949', (1988) 37 *Int'l & Comp. L Quart.* 818
    'Human Rights Law and Humanitarian Law: Two Coins or Two Sides of the
    Same Coin?', (1991) 1 *Bull. Hum. Rts* 46
    'Using International Human Rights Machinery to Enforce the International
    Law of Armed Conflict', (1992) 31 *Revue de droit pénal militaire et de droit de la
    guerre* 119
    'Fact-Finding and the International Fact-Finding Commission', in Hazel Fox
    and Michael Meyer eds., *Armed Conflict and the New Law - Effecting Compliance*
    (London: British Institute of International and Comparative Law, 1993)
    II, 53
Hannum, Hurst ed., *A Guide to Human Rights Practice*, 3rd edn (Philadelphia:
    U Penn. Press, 1999)
Harris, David J., *Cases and Materials on International Law*, 4th edn (London: Sweet
    & Maxwell, 1991)
    'Regional Protection of Human Rights: The Inter-American Achievement', in
    David Harris and Stephen Livingstone eds., *The Inter-American System of
    Human Rights* (Oxford: Oxford UP, 1998) 1
Hart, H. L. A., *The Concept of Law* (Oxford: Clarendon, 1961)
Hartman, Joan F., 'Derogation from Human Rights Treaties in Public
    Emergencies', (1981) 22 *Harv. Int'l LJ* 1
    'Working Paper for the Committee of Experts on the Article 4 Derogation
    Provision', (1985) 7 *Hum. Rts Quart.* 89
Hassan, Farooq, 'The Theoretical Basis of Punishment in International Criminal
    Law', (1983) 15 *Case W Res. J Int'l L* 39
Hay, Alexander, 'The ICRC and the World Today', (1982) 226 *Int'l Rev. Red Cross* 12

Heinze, Kurt and Karl Schilling, *Die Rechtsprechung der Nürnberger Militärtribunale* (Bonn: Girardet, 1952)

Henkin, Louis, *How Nations Behave*, 2nd edn (New York: Columbia UP, 1979)

'International Human Rights as "Rights"', (1979) 1 *Cardozo L Rev.* 425

Herzog, J. B., 'Les principes juridiques de la répression des crimes de guerre', (1946) 61 *Revue pénale suisse/Schweizerische Zeitschrift für Strafrecht* 285

Higgins, A. Pearce, *War and the Private Citizen* (London: King & Son, 1912)

Higgins, Rosalyn, 'The Place of International Law in the Settlement of Disputes by the Security Council', (1970) 64 *Am. J Int'l L* 1

'Derogations Under Human Rights Treaties', (1976–7) 48 *Brit. YB Int'l L* 281

'Conceptual Thinking About the Individual in International Law', (1978) 24 *New York L School L Rev.* 11

'The Taking of Property by the State: Recent Developments in International Law', (1982-III) 176 *Recueil des cours* 259

Problems and Process – International Law and How We Use It (Oxford: Clarendon, 1994)

Hodos, *Die Allbeteiligungsklausel als eine Erscheinungsform Kriegsrechtlicher Gegenseitigkeit* (diss., Innsbruck, 1947)

Hohefeld, Wesley, 'Fundamental Legal Conceptions as Applied in Judicial Reasoning', (1913) 23 *Yale LJ* 16

Horn, Frank, *Reservations and Interpretative Declarations to Multilateral Treaties* (Amsterdam: North-Holland, 1988)

Hudson, Edward G., 'The Status of Persons of Japanese Ancestry in the United States and Canada During World War II: A Tragedy in Three Parts, (1977) 18 *Cahiers de droit* 61

Human Rights Watch, *The Philippines: Violations of the Laws of War by Both Sides* (New York: Human Rights Watch, 1990)

Needless Deaths in the Gulf War (New York: Human Rights Watch, 1991)

The Sri Lankan Conflict and Standards of Humanitarian Law (New York: Human Rights Watch, 1992)

World Report 1993 (New York: Human Rights Watch, 1992)

Hutchinson, D. N., 'Solidarity and Breaches of Multilateral Treaties', (1988) 59 *Brit. YB Int'l L* 151

Hutchinson, Michael, 'The Margin of Appreciation Doctrine in the European Court of Human Rights', (1999) 48 *Int'l & Comp. L Quart.* 638

Hyde, Charles C., 'Japanese Executions of American Aviators', (1943) 27 *Am. J Int'l L* 480

International Law, 2nd edn (Boston: Little, Brown, 1947) III

Hyndman, Patricia, 'The Exploitation of Child Workers in South and South East Asia', (1989) 58 *Nordic J Int'l L* 94

ICRC, *Report of the International Committee of the Red Cross on its Activities During the Second World War* (Geneva: ICRC, 1949) I

Report of the Work of the Conference of Government Experts on the Reaffirmation and Development of International Humanitarian Law of Armed Conflicts (Geneva: ICRC, 1971)

Report of the Work of the Conference of Government Experts on the Reaffirmation and Development of International Humanitarian Law of Armed Conflicts – Second Session (Geneva: ICRC, 1972) I

'Action by the International Committee of the Red Cross in the Event of Breaches of International Humanitarian Law', (1981) 221 *Int'l Rev. Red Cross* 76

ILA, '[First] Interim Report of the Committee on the Enforcement of Human Rights Law', in International Law Association, *Report of the 62nd Conference, Seoul, 24–30 August 1986* (London: ILA, 1987) 108

'Second Interim Report of the Committee on the Enforcement of Human Rights Law', in International Law Association, *Report of the 63rd Conference, Warsaw, 21–27 August 1988* (London: ILA, 1988) 129

'Final Report on Monitoring States of Emergency: Guidelines for Bodies Monitoring Respect for Human Rights During States of Emergency', in International Law Association, *Report of the 64th Conference, Queensland, 20–25 August 1990* (London: ILA, 1991) 228

'Final Report on the Status of the Universal Declaration of Human Rights in National and International Law', in International Law Association, *Report of the 66th Conference, Buenos Aires, 1994* (London: ILA, 1994) 525

Imbert, Pierre-Henri, *Les réserves aux traités multilatéraux* (Paris: Pedone, 1978)

'Reservations and Human Rights Conventions', (1981) 6 *Hum. Rts Rev.* 28

'Les réserves à la Convention européenne des droits de l'homme', (1983) 87 *Revue générale de droit international public* 580

Institut de droit international, 'Droits et devoirs des puissances étrangères, au cas de mouvement insurrectionnel, envers les gouvernements établis et reconnus qui sont aux prises avec l'insurrection', (1900) 18 *Annuaire de l'Institut de droit international* 227

'L'égalité d'application des règles du droit de la guerre aux parties à un conflit armé', (1963) 50:1 *Annuaire de l'Institut de droit international* 5

'Protection of Human Rights and the Principle of Non-Intervention in the Domestic Concerns of States', (1989) 63:1 *Annuaire de l'Institut de droit international* 431

'Resolution on the Application of International Humanitarian Law and Fundamental Human Rights in Armed Conflicts in which Non-State Entities are Parties', (1999) 68:2 *Annuaire de l'Institut de droit international* 395

International Commission of Jurists, *States of Emergency, their Impact on Human Rights* (Geneva: ICJ, 1983)

Iwasawa, Yuji, 'The Doctrine of Self-executing Treaties in the United States: A Critical Analysis', (1986) 26 *Va. J Int'l L* 627

'The Relationship Between International Law and Municipal Law: Japanese Experiences', (1993) 64 Brit. YB Int'l L 333

Jackson, Robert H., International Conference on Military Trials (London, 1945) (Washington DC: US Gov. Printing Office, 1949)

Jakovljević, Bosko, 'Human Rights Accorded by International Humanitarian Law', (1991) 1 Bull. Hum. Rts 25

'Agreements for the Implementation of International Humanitarian Law in the Armed Conflict in Former Yugoslavia', in Sonja Biserko ed., Yugoslavia: Collapse, War, Crime (Belgrade: Center for Anti-War Action, 1993) 161

Jessup, Philip, A Modern Law of Nations (New York: Macmillan, 1948)

Jiménez de Aréchaga, Eduardo, 'La Convención interamericana de derechos humanos como derecho interno', (1989) 7 Revista del Instituto interamericano de derechos humanos 25

Junod, Marcel, Le troisième combattant (Geneva: ICRC, 1989)

Juste Ruiz, José, 'Las obligaciones "erga omnes" en derecho internacional público', in Estudios de derecho internacional: Homenaje al profesor Miaja de la Muela (Madrid: Tecnos, 1979) I, 219

Kalin, Walter, Human Rights in Times of Occupation: The Case of Kuwait (Berne: Law Books Europe, 1994)

Kalshoven, Frits, 'Human Rights, the Law of Armed Conflict, and Reprisals', in Proceedings of the International Conference on Humanitarian Law (Grassi: Istituto Editoriale Ticinese, 1970) 175

Belligerent Reprisals (Leiden: Sijthoff, 1971)

'Reaffirmation and Development of International Humanitarian Law Applicable in Armed Conflict: The Diplomatic Conference, Geneva, 1974–77', (1977) 8 Netherlands YB Int'l L 107

'Reprisals in the CDDH', in Robert J. Akkerman et al. eds., Declarations of Principles – A Quest for Universal Peace (Leiden: Sijthoff, 1977) 195

Constraints on the Waging of War (Dordrecht: Nijhoff, 1987)

'Belligerent Reprisals Revisited', (1990) 21 Nether. YB Int'l L 43

'State Responsibility for Warlike Acts of the Armed Forces', (1991) 40 Int'l & Comp. L Quart. 827

Kamminga, Menno, Inter-State Accountability for Human Rights Violations (Philadelphia: U Penn. Press, 1992)

Karagiannis, Syméon, 'L'aménagement des droits de l'homme outre-mer: La clause des "nécessités locales" de la convention européenne', [1995] 1 Revue belge de droit international 224

Kelsen, Hans, 'Théorie générale du droit international public – Problèmes choisis', (1932-IV) 42 Recueil des cours 116

'Collective and Individual Responsibility in International Law with Particular Regard to the Punishment of War Criminals', (1943) 31 Cal. L Rev. 530

Peace Through Law (Chapel Hill: U North Carolina, 1944)

General Theory of Law and the State (Cambridge, Mass.: Harvard UP, 1946)
'Collective and Individual Responsibility for Acts of State in International Law', (1948) 1 *Jewish YB Int'l L* 226
The Law of the United Nations (New York: Praeger, 1950)
Principles of International Law (New York: Rinehart, 1952)
Keohane, Robert, 'Reciprocity in International Relations', (1986) 40 *Int'l Org.* 1
Kingsbury, Benedict, 'Claims by Non-State Groups in International Law', (1992) 25 *Cornell Int'l LJ* 481
Kirgis, Frederic L., 'Some Lingering Questions About Article 60 of the Vienna Convention on the Law of Treaties', (1989) 22 *Cornell Int'l LJ* 549
Kiss, Alexandre-Charles, 'Les fonctions du Secrétaire-général du Conseil de l'Europe comme dépositaire des Conventions européennes', [1956] *Annuaire français de droit international* 680
Répertoire de la pratique française en matière de droit international public (Paris: CNRS, 1962) I
'La protection des droits de l'homme dans les rapports entre personnes privées en droit international public', in *René Cassin Amicorum Discipulorumque Liber* (Paris: Pedone, 1971) III, 215
'Permissible Limitations on Rights', in Louis Henkin ed., *The International Bill of Rights* (New York: Columbia UP, 1981) 290
Kokott, Juliane, 'No Impunity for Human Rights Violations in the Americas', (1993) 14 *Hum. Rts LJ* 153
Komarow, Gary, 'Individual Responsibility Under International Law: The Nuremberg Principles in Domestic Legal Systems', (1980) 29 *Int. & Comp. L Quart.* 21
Kooijmans, Peter, 'In the Shadowland Between Civil War and Civil Strife: Some Reflections on the Standard-Setting Process', in Astrid Delissen and Gerard Tanja eds., *Humanitarian Law of Armed Conflict: Challenges Ahead – Essays in Honour of Frits Kalshoven* (Dordrecht: Nijhoff, 1991) 225
'The Security Council and Non-State Entities as Parties to Conflicts', in K. Wellens ed., *International Law: Theory and Practice* (Dordrecht: Kluwer, 1998) 333
Kornblum, Elizabeth, 'A Comparison of Self-evaluating State Reporting Systems', (1995) 305 *Int'l Rev. Red Cross* 137
Koskenniemi, Martti, *From Apology to Utopia – The Structure of International Legal Argument* (Helsinki: Lakimiesliiton Kustannus, 1989)
Kramer, Francisco Villagrán, 'Retorsión y represalias por violaciones a los derechos humanos', in *Hector Gros Espiell Amicorum Liber* (Brussels: Bruylant, 1997) II, 1765
Kunstle, David, '*Kadić v. Karadzić*: Do Private Individuals Have Enforceable Rights and Obligations Under the Alien Torts Claims Act?', (1996) 6 *Duke J Comp. & Int'l L* 319
Kunz, Joseph L., *Kriegsrecht und Neutralitätsrecht* (Vienna: Springer, 1935)

La problemática actual de las leyes de la guerra (Valladolid: Universidad de Valladolid, 1955)

Kussbach, Erich, 'The International Humanitarian Fact-Finding Commission', (1994) 43 *Int'l & Comp. L Quart.* 174

Kwakwa, Edward K., *The International Law of Armed Conflict: Personal and Material Field of Application* (Dordrecht: Nijhoff, 1992)

Landy, E. A., *The Effectiveness of International Supervision – Thirty Years of ILO Experience* (London/Dobbs Ferry: Stevens & Sons/Oceana, 1996)

Lattanzi, Flavia, *Garanzie dei diritti dell'uomo nel diritto internazionale generale* (Milan: Giuffrè, 1983)

'La competenze delle jurisdizioni di stati "terzi" a ricercare e processare i responsabili dei crimini nell'ex-Iugoslavia a nel Ruanda', (1995) 78 *Rivista di diritto internazionale* 707

Lauterpacht, Elihu, 'The Contemporary Practice of the United Kingdom in the Field of International Law', (1956) 5 *Int'l & Comp. L Quart.* 405

Lauterpacht, Hersch, 'The Law of Nations and the Punishment of War Crimes', (1944) 21 *British YB Int'l L* 58

'The Subjects of the Law of Nations – 1', (1947) 63 *L Quart. Rev.* 438

Recognition in International Law (Cambridge: Cambridge UP, 1948)

'The Subjects of the Law of Nations – 2', (1948) 64 *L Quart. Rev.* 97

International Law and Human Rights (London: Stevens & Sons, 1950)

Lazarus, Claude, 'Le statut des mouvements de libération nationale à l'Organisation des Nations Unies', [1974] *Annuaire français de droit international* 173

Lenhoff, Arthur, 'Reciprocity: The Legal Aspect of a Perennial Idea', (1954–5) 49 *Northwestern ULJ* 617

Lerner, Nathan, *The UN Convention on the Elimination of All Forms of Racial Discrimination*, 2nd edn (Alphen aan den Rijn/Rockville, Md.: Sijthoff/Noordhoff, 1980)

Levasseur, Georges and Roger Merle, 'L'état des législations internes au regard des obligations contenues dans les conventions internationales de droit humanitaire', in *Droit humanitaire et conflits armés – Colloque des 28, 29 et 30 janvier 1970, Université libre de Bruxelles* (Brussels: Editions de l'Université de Bruxelles, 1976) 219

Levie, Howard S., 'Maltreatment of Prisoners of War in Vietnam', (1968) 48 *Boston UL Rev.* 323

Protection of War Victims: Protocol I to the 1949 Geneva Conventions (Dobbs Ferry, NY: Oceana, 1979)

Terrorism in War – The Law of War Crimes (Dobbs Ferry: Oceana, 1993)

Levrat, Nicolas, 'Les conséquences de l'engagement pris par les Hautes Parties contractantes de "faire respecter" les conventions humanitaires', in Frits Kalshoven and Yves Sandoz eds., *Implementation of International Humanitarian Law* (Dordrecht: Nijhoff, 1989) 263

Lijnzaad, Liesbeth, *Reservations to UN Human Rights Treaties – Ratify or Ruin?* (Dordrecht: Nijhoff, 1995)

Lillich, Richard B., 'Duties of States Regarding the Human Rights of Aliens', (1978-III) 161 *Recueil des cours* 329

The Human Rights of Aliens in Contemporary International Law (Manchester: Manchester UP, 1984)

'Invoking International Human Rights Law in Domestic Courts', (1985) 54 *Cin. L Rev.* 367

Lillich, Richard B. et al., 'Claims Against Iraq: The UN Compensation Commission and Other Remedies', (1992) 86 *Am. Soc. Int'l L Proc.* 477

Lillich, Richard B. and Hurst Hannum eds., *International Human Rights – Problems of Law, Policy and Practice* (Boston: Little, Brown, 1995)

Lindemann, Hans-Heinrich, 'Die Auswirkungen des Menschenrechtsverletzungen in Surinam auf die Vertragbeziehungen zwischen die Niederlanden und Surinam', (1984) *Zeitschrift für ausländische öffentliches Recht und Völkerrecht* 64

Macdonald, Ronald St J., 'Derogations under Article 15 of the European Convention on Human Rights', (1997) 36 *Colum. J Transnat'l L* 225

Maison, Rafaëlle, 'Les premiers cas d'application des dispositions pénales des Conventions de Genève par les juridictions internes', (1995) 6 *Eur. J Int'l L* 260

Majoros, F., 'Le régime de la réciprocité dans la Convention de Vienne et les réserves dans les Conventions de la Haye', (1974) *Journal du droit international* 73

Malintoppi, Antonio, 'L'elemento della reciprocità nel trattamento delle missioni diplomatiche', (1956) 39 *Rivista di diritto internazionale* 532

Mallison, W. Thomas and Sally V. Mallison, 'The Juridical Status of Privileged Combatants Under the Geneva Protocol of 1977 Concerning International Conflicts', (1978) 42:2 *L & Contemp. Problems* 4

Maresca, Adolfo, *La protezione internazionale dei combatenti e dei civili* (Milan: Giuffrè, 1965)

Il diritto dei trattati (Milan: Giuffrè, 1971)

Marks, Stephen, 'Emerging Human Rights: A New Generation for the 1980s?', (1981) 33 *Rutgers L Rev.* 435

Marshall, Patricia F., 'Violence Against Women in Canada by Non-State Actors: The State and Women's Human Rights', in Kathleen E. Mahoney and Paul Mahoney eds., *Human Rights in the Twenty-First Century – A Global Challenge* (Dordrecht: Nijhoff, 1993) 319

Martin, Daniel Hugo, 'La protección de los derechos humanos frente a la suspención de los garantías constitucionales o "estado de sitio"', in *The Organization of American States and Human Rights* (Washington: OAS, 1972) 122

Maunoir, Jean-Pierre, *La répression des crimes de guerre devant les tribunaux français et alliés* (Geneva: Editions médecine et hygiène, 1956)

Mbaya, Etienne-Richard, 'Symétrie entre droits et devoirs dans la Charte africaine des droits de l'homme', (1987) 168 *Le Supplément – Revue d'éthique et de théologie morale* 35

Mbaye, Kéba, *Les droits de l'homme en Afrique* (Paris: Pedone, 1992)

McCoubrey, Hilaire, *International Humanitarian Law* (Hants: Dartmouth, 1990)

McDougal, Myres M., *Studies in World Public Order* (New Haven: Yale UP, 1960)

McDougal, Myres M. and Florentino P. Feliciano, *Law and Minimum World Public Order* (New Haven: Yale UP, 1961)

McDougal, Myres, Harold Lassel and Lung-chu Chen, 'The Protection of Aliens from Discrimination and World Public Order: Responsibility of States Conjoined with Human Rights', (1976) 70 *Am. J Int'l L* 432

McGoldrick, Dominic, *The Human Rights Committee* (Oxford: Clarendon, 1991)

McNair, Lord, *The Law of Treaties*, 2nd edn (Oxford: Clarendon, 1961)

Meng, Werner, 'War', in Rudolf Bernhardt ed., [Instalment] 4 *Encyclopedia of Public International Law* (Amsterdam: North-Holland, 1982) 282

Mérignhac, A., 'De la sanction des infractions aux droit des gens commises au cours de la guerre européenne par les Empires du centre', (1917) 24 *Revue générale de droit international public* 5

Mérignhac, A. and E. Lémonon, *Le droit des gens et la guerre de 1914–1918* (Paris: Sirey, 1921) I

Meron, Theodor, 'On the Inadequate Reach of Humanitarian and Human Rights Law and the Need for a New Instrument', (1983) 77 *Am. J Int'l L* 589

'On a Hierarchy of International Human Rights', (1986) 80 *Am. J Int'l L* 1

Human Rights in Internal Strife: Their International Protection (Cambridge: Grotius, 1987)

'*Lex Lata*: Is there Already a Differentiated Regime of State Responsibility in the Geneva Conventions?', in J. Weiler, A. Cassese and M. Spinedi eds., *International Crimes of States* (Berlin and New York: De Gruyter, 1989) 225

Human Rights and Humanitarian Norms as Customary Law (Oxford: Clarendon, 1989)

'State Responsibility for Violation of Human Rights', (1989) 83 *Am. J Int'l L* 372

'The Protection of the Human Person Under Human Rights Law and Humanitarian Law', (1991) 1 *Bull. Hum. Rts* 33

'International Criminalization of Internal Atrocities', (1995) 89 *Am. J Int'l L* 554

'Classification of Armed Conflict in the Former Yugoslavia: *Nicaragua's* Fallout', (1998) 92 *Am. J Int'l L* 236

'Is International Law Moving Towards Criminalization?', (1998) 9 *Eur. J Int'l L* 18

'The Humanization of Humanitarian Law', (1999) 94 *Am. J Int'l L* 239

Meron, Theodor and Allan Rosas, 'A Declaration of Minimum Humanitarian Standards', (1991) 85 *Am. J Int'l L* 375

Mertens, Pierre, *Le droit de recours effectif devant les instances nationales en cas de violation d'un droit de l'homme* (Brussels: Université Libre de Bruxelles, 1973)

Meyrowitz, Henri, *La répression par les tribunaux allemands des crimes contre l'humanité et de l'appartenance à une organisation criminelle en application de la loi no. 10 du Conseil de contrôle allié* (Paris: LGDJ, 1960)

'Le statut des saboteurs dans le droit de la guerre', (1966) 5 *Revue de droit pénal militaire et de droit de la guerre* 121

'Le droit de la guerre dans le conflit vietnamien', [1967] *Annuaire français de droit international* 153

Le principe de l'égalité des belligérents devant le droit de la guerre (Paris: Pedone, 1970)

'Le droit de la guerre et les droits de l'homme', (1972) 88 *Revue de droit public et de la science politique en France et à l'étranger* 1059

'La guérilla et le droit de la guerre, problèmes principaux', in *Droit humanitaire et conflits armés – Actes du colloque du 28 au 30 janvier 1970, Université libre de Bruxelles* (Brussels: Ed. Université de Bruxelles, 1976) 185

'Réflexions sur le fondement du droit de la guerre', in Christophe Swinarski ed., *Studies and Essays on International Humanitarian Law and Red Cross Principles in Honour of Jean Pictet* (Geneva/The Hague: ICRC/Nijhoff, 1984) 419

'Die Repressalienverbote des I. Zusatzprotokolls zu den Genfer Abkommen vom 12. August 1949 und das Reziprozitätsprinzip', (1986) 28 *Neue Zeitschrift für Wehrrecht* 177

Migliazza, Alessandro, 'L'évolution de la réglementation de la guerre à la lumière de la sauvegarde des droits de l'homme', (1972-III) 137 *Recueil des cours* 142

Miyazaki, Shigeki, 'The Application of the New Humanitarian Law', (1980) 217 *Int'l Rev. Red Cross* 184

'The Martens Clause in International Humanitarian Law', in Christophe Swinarski ed., *Studies and Essays on International Humanitarian Law and Red Cross Principles in Honour of Jean Pictet* (Geneva/The Hague: ICRC/Nijhoff, 1984) 433

Montealegre, Hernán, 'The Compatibility of a State Party's Derogations under Human Rights Instruments with its Obligations under Protocol II and Common Article 3', (1983) 33 *Am. UL Rev.* 41

Morellet, Jean, 'La notion de réciprocité dans les traités de travail et les conventions internationales de travail', [1931] *Revue de droit international privé* 643

Morgan, J. H., *The War Book of the German General Staff* (Kriegsbrauch in Landkriege) (London: Murray, 1915)

Morgenstern, Felice, 'Validity of the Acts of the Belligerent Occupant', (1951) 28 *Brit. YB Int'l L* 291

Morsink, Johannes, 'World War Two and the Universal Declaration', (1993) 15 *Hum. Rts Quart.* 357

Mosler, H., *The International Society as a Legal Community* (Alphen aan den Rijn and Germantown, Md: Sijthoff & Noordhoff, 1980)

Mouton, M. W., *Oorlogsmisdrijsven en het internationale recht* (The Hague: Stols, 1947)

Mullins, Claud, *The Leipzig Trials* (London: Witherby, 1921)

Murray, Christina, 'The Status of the ANC and SWAPO Under International Humanitarian Law', (1983) 100 *South Afr. LJ* 402

Mutua, Makau wa, 'The Banjul Charter and the African Cultural Fingerprint: An Evaluation of the Language of Duties', (1995) 35 *Va. J Int'l L* 339

Nahlik, Stanislaw E., 'La protection internationale des biens culturels en cas des conflits armés', (1967-I) 120 *Recueil des cours* 61

'Droit dit "de Genève" et droit dit "de la Haye": Unicité ou dualité?', [1978] *Annuaire français de droit international* 9

'Le problème des représailles à la lumière des travaux de la conférence diplomatique sur le droit humanitaire', (1978) 82 *Revue générale de droit international public* 130

'Protection of Cultural Property', in UNESCO, *International Dimensions of Humanitarian Law* (Dordrecht: Nijhoff, 1988) 203

Nash Leich, Marian, 'Contemporary Practice of the United States Relating to International Law', (1982) 76 *Am. J Int'l L* 379

Nørgaard, Carl, *The Position of the Individual in International Law* (Copenhagen: Munksgaard, 1962)

Nowak, Manfred, *CCPR Commentary* (Kehl: Engel, 1993)

Nwogugu, Edwin I., 'Commentary on Treaties on Submarine Warfare', in Natalino Ronziti ed., *The Law of Naval Warfare* (Dordrecht: Nijhoff, 1988) 353

Nys, Ernest, *Le droit international: Les principes, les théories, les faits*, new edn (Brussels: Weissenbruch, 1912) III

O'Donnell, Daniel, 'Commentary by the Rapporteur on Derogation', (1985) 7 *Hum. Rts Quart.* 23

Protección internacional de los derechos humanos (Lima: Comisión andina de juristas, 1988)

'Trends in the Application of International Humanitarian Law by United Nations Human Rights Mechanisms', (1998) 324 *Int'l Rev. Red Cross* 481

Obradović, Konstantin, 'Le "conflit yougoslave" et le problème de la responsabilité des Etats parties aux Conventions humanitaires quant à la mise en oeuvre', (1992) *Jugoslenvska revija za međunarodno pravo* 222

Oellers-Frahm, Karin, 'Comment: The *Erga Omnes* Applicability of Human Rights', (1992) 30 *Archiv des Völkerrecht* 28

'Das Statut des internationalen Strafgerichtshofs zur Verfolgung von Kriegsverbrechen im ehemaligen Jugoslawien', (1994) 54 *Zeitschrift für ausländisches öffentliches Recht und Völkerrecht* 416

Omar, Imtiaz, *Rights, Emergencies, and Judicial Reviews* (Dordrecht: Kluwer, 1995)

Oppenheim, Lassa, *International Law*, Ronald Roxburgh ed., 3rd edn (London: Longmans, 1921) II

  International Law, Hersch Lauterpacht ed., 7th edn (London: Longmans, 1952) II

  International Law, Hersch Lauterpacht ed., 8th edn (London: Longmans, 1955) I

  International Law, Robert Jennings and Arthur Watts eds., 9th edn (Harlow, UK: Longmans, 1992) I

Oráa, Jaime, *Human Rights in States of Emergency in International Law* (Oxford: Clarendon, 1992)

Orentlicher, Diane, 'Settling Accounts: The Duty to Prosecute Human Rights Violations of a Prior Regime', (1991) 100 *Yale LJ* 2539

Ouguergouz, Fatsah, 'Guerres de libération nationale en droit humanitaire: Quelques clarifications', in Frits Kalshoven and Yves Sandoz eds., *Implementation of International Humanitarian Law* (Dordrecht: Nijhoff, 1989) 333

  La Charte africaine des droits de l'homme et des peuples – Une approche juridique des droits de l'homme entre tradition et modernité (Geneva: Presses Universitaires de France, 1993)

  'L'absence de clause de dérogation dans certains traités relatifs aux droits de l'homme: Les réponses du droit international général', (1994) 98 *Revue générale de droit international public* 289

Palwankar, Umesh, 'Measures Available to States for Fulfilling their Obligation to Ensure Respect for International Humanitarian Law', (1994) 298 *Int'l Rev. Red Cross* 9

Paoli, Jules, 'Contribution à l'études des crimes de guerre et des crimes contre l'humanité en droit pénal international', (1941–5) *Revue générale de droit international public* 129

Paolillo, Felipe, 'Reclamaciones colectivas internacionales: El caso de los damnificados por la crisis del Golfo', in Manuel Rama-Montaldo ed., *El derecho internacional en un mundo en transformación – Liber Amicorum en homenaje al profesor Eduardo Jiménez de Aréchaga* (Montevideo: FCU, 1994) 545

Partsch, Karl Joseph, 'Armed Conflict', in Rudolf Bernhardt ed., [Instalment] 3 *Encyclopedia of Public International Law* (Amsterdam: North-Holland, 1982) 25–8

  'Human Rights and Humanitarian Law', in Rudolf Bernhardt ed., [Instalment] 8 *Encyclopedia of Public International Law* (Amsterdam: North-Holland, 1985) 292

Patrnogic, Jovica, 'Les droits de l'homme et les conflits armés', in *Proceedings of the International Conference on Humanitarian Law* (Grassi: Istituto Editoriale Ticinese, 1970) 165

Paust, Jordan, 'The Other Side of Rights: Private Duties Under Human Rights Law', (1992) 5 *Harv. Hum. Rts J* 51

Pavel Remec, Peter, *The Position of the Individual in International Law According to Grotius and Vattel* (The Hague: Nijhoff, 1960)

Pérez González, Manuel, 'Consideraciones sobre la aplicación del derecho internacional humanitario, con especial referencia a su aplicación en el orden interno', in *Héctor Gros Espiell Amicorum Liber* (Brussels: Bruylant, 1997) II

Peters, Paul, 'Commentary on the Draft Code of Crimes – Article 21', (1993) 11 *Nouvelles études pénales* 249

Petit, Gérard, 'Les mouvements de libération nationale et le droit', [1976] *Annuaire du Tiers-Monde* 56

Pettiti, Louis-Edmond et al. eds., *La Convention Européenne des droits de l'homme* (Paris: Economica, 1995)

Pfanner, Toni, 'Le rôle du Comité international de la Croix-Rouge dans la mise en oeuvre du droit international humanitaire', in *Law in Humanitarian Crises – How Can International Humanitarian Law be Made Effective in Armed Conflict?* (Luxembourg: European Communities, 1995) I, 177

Picone, Paolo, 'Obblighi reciproci e obblighi *erga omnes* degli stati nel campo della protezione internazionale dell'ambiente marino dall'inquinamento', in Vincenzo Starace ed., *Diritto internazionale e protezione dell'ambiente marino* (Milan: Giuffrè, 1983) 15

'Nazioni Unite e obblighi "erga omnes"', (1993) 48 *Comunità internazionale* 709

Pictet, Jean ed., *The Geneva Conventions of 12 August 1949 – Commentary on the IV Geneva Convention Relative to the Protection of Civilian Persons in Times of War* (Geneva: ICRC, 1958)

ed., *The Geneva Conventions of 12 August 1949 – Commentary on the III Geneva Convention Relative to the Treatment of Prisoners of War* (Geneva: ICRC, 1960)

Pilloud, Claude, 'La Déclaration universelle des droits de l'homme et les Conventions internationales protégeant les victimes de la guerre', [1949] *Revue internationale de la Croix-Rouge* 252

'Les réserves aux Conventions de Genève de 1949', [1957] *Revue internationale de la Croix-Rouge* 409

'Reservations and the 1949 Geneva Conventions', (1965) *Int'l Rev. Red Cross* 315

'Reservations and the 1949 Geneva Conventions (1)', (1976) 180 *Int'l Rev. Red Cross* 107

'Reservations and the 1949 Geneva Conventions (2)', (1976) 181 *Int'l Rev. Red Cross* 163

Pilloud, Claude et al., *Commentary on the Additional Protocols of 8 June 1977 to the Geneva Conventions of 12 August 1949* (Geneva: Nijhoff, 1987)

Pinto, Mónica, 'Responsabilidad internacional por la violación de los derechos humanos y los entes no estatales' in *Hector Gros Espiell Amicorum Liber* (Brussels: Bruylant, 1997) II, 1155

Pisillo Mazzeschi, Riccardo, *Risoluzione e sospensione dei trattati per inadempimento* (Milan: Giuffrè, 1984)

'Termination and Suspension of Treaties for Breach in the Work of the ILC', in Marina Spinedi and Bruno Simma eds., *The UN Codification of State Responsibility* (New York: Oceana, 1987) 57

Plattner, Denise, 'La portée juridique des déclarations de respect du droit international humanitaire qui émanent de mouvements en lutte dans un conflit armé', (1984–5) 18 *Revue belge de droit international* 298

'The Penal Repression of Violations of International Humanitarian Law Applicable in Non-international Armed Conflicts', (1990) 30 *Int'l Rev. Red Cross* 409

'International Humanitarian Law and Inalienable or Non-derogable Human Rights', in Daniel Prémont ed., *Non-derogable Rights and States of Emergency* (Brussels: Bruylant, 1996) 349

Politi, Mauro, 'The Establishment of an International Criminal Court at a Crossroad: Issues and Prospects After the First Session of the Preparatory Committee', (1997) 13 *Nouvelles études pénales* 115

Politis, Nicolas, 'Le régime des représailles en temps de paix', (1934) 38 *Annuaire de l'Institut de droit international* 1 and 708

Provost, René, 'Emergency Judicial Relief for Human Rights Violations in Canada and Argentina', (1992) 29 *U Miami Inter-Am. L Rev.* 693

'Starvation as a Weapon: Legal Implications of the United Nations Food Blockade Against Iraq and Kuwait', (1992) 30 *Colum. J Transnat'l L* 577

'Reciprocity in Human Rights and Humanitarian Law', (1995) 65 *Brit. YB Int'l L* 383

Pueyo Losa, Jorge, 'El derecho de las represalias en tiempo de paz: Condiciones de ejercicios', (1988) 40 *Revista española de derecho internacional* 9

Quentin-Baxter, R., 'Human Rights and Humanitarian Law – Confluence or Conflict?', (1985) 9 *Australian YB Int'l L* 94

Ragazzi, Maurizio, *The Concept of International Obligations Erga Omnes* (Oxford: Clarendon, 1997)

Rama Rao Pappu, S. S., 'Human Rights and Human Obligations: An East–West Perspective', (1982) 8 *Phil. & Soc. Action* 15

Ramcharan, B. G., 'State Responsibility for Violations of Human Rights', in Edith Brown Weiss ed., *Contemporary Problems of International Law: Essays in Honour of Georg Schwarzenberger* (London: Stevens & Son, 1988) 246

Ratner, Steven 'The Schizophrenias of International Criminal Law', (1998) 33 *Tex. Int'l LJ* 237

Ratner, Steven and Jason Abrams, *Accountability for Human Rights Atrocities in International Law* (Oxford: Oxford UP, 1997)

Ravaud, Caroline, 'The Committee of Ministers', in R. St J. Macdonald et al. eds., *The European System for the Protection of Human Rights* (Dordrecht: Nijhoff, 1993) 645

Raz, Joseph, 'Legal Rights', (1984) 4 *Ox. J Leg. Stud.* 1

Reidy, Aisling, 'The Approach of the European Commission and Court of Human Rights to International Humanitarian Law', (1998) 324 *Int'l Rev. Red Cross* 513

Reisman, Michael and Janet Koven Levit, 'Reflections on the Problem of Individual Responsibility for Violations of Human Rights', in Antonio Cançado Trindade ed., *The Modern World of Human Rights – Essays in Honour of Thomas Buergenthal* (San Jose, Costa Rica: Inter-American Institute for Human Rights, 1996) 419

Reisman, Michael and James Silk, 'Which Law Applies to the Afghan Conflict?', (1988) 82 *Am. J Int'l L* 459

Reisman, W. Michael and William K. Leitzau, 'Moving International Law from Theory to Practice: The Role of Military Manuals in Effectuating the Law of Armed Conflict', in Horace B. Robertson ed., 64 *US Naval War College International Law Studies, The Law of Naval Operations* (Newport, RI: Naval War Coll. Press, 1991) 1

Ress, Hans-Konrad, 'Die Zulässigkeit territorialer Beschränkungen bei der Anerkennung des Zuständigkeit des europäischen Gerichtshofs für Menschenrechte', (1996) 56 *Zeitschrift fur ausländisches öffentliches Recht und Völkerrecht* 427

Restatement (Third) of the Foreign Relations Law of the United States (St Paul: American Law Institute, 1987)

Reuter, Paul, 'La personnalité juridique du CICR', in Christophe Swinarski ed., *Studies and Essays on International Humanitarian Law and Red Cross Principles in Honour of Jean Pictet* (Geneva/The Hague: ICRC/Nijhoff, 1984) 783

Introduction to the Law of Treaties (London: Pinter, 1989)

Ricoeur, Paul ed., *Philosophical Foundations of Human Rights* (Paris: UNESCO, 1986)

Roberts, Adam, 'What is Military Occupation?', (1984) 55 *Brit. YB Int'l L* 249

'The Laws of War: Problems of Implementation in Contemporary Conflict', in *Law in Humanitarian Crises – How Can International Humanitarian Law be Made Effective in Armed Conflict?* (Luxembourg: European Communities, 1995) I, 13–82 (also in (1995) 6 *Duke J Int'l & Comp. L* 11)

Robertson, Arthur Henri, 'Human Rights as the Basis for International Humanitarian Law', in *Proceedings of the International Conference on Humanitarian Law* (Grassi: Istituto Editoriale Ticinese, 1970) 55

Human Rights in Europe (Manchester: Manchester UP, 1977)

'Humanitarian Law and Human Rights', in Christophe Swinarski ed., *Studies and Essays on International Humanitarian Law and Red Cross Principles in Honour of Jean Pictet* (Geneva/The Hague: ICRC/Nijhoff, 1984) 793

Rodley, Nigel S., 'Can Armed Opposition Groups Violate Human Rights?', in Kathleen E. Mahoney and Paul Mahoney eds., *Human Rights in the Twenty-First Century – A Global Challenge* (Dordrecht: Nijhoff, 1993) 297

Roht-Arriaza, Naomi ed., *Impunity and Human Rights in International Law and Practice* (New York: Oxford UP, 1995)

Rolin, Albéric, *Le droit moderne de la guerre* (Brussels: Dewit, 1920) I

Rolin, Edouard, 'Report to the Conference from the Second Commission on the Laws and Customs of War on Land', in James Brown Scott ed., *The Report of the Hague Conferences of 1899 and 1907* (Oxford: Clarendon, 1917) 137

Röling, B. V. A., 'The Law of War and the National Jurisdiction since 1945', (1960-II) 100 *Recueil des cours* 329

Röling, B. V. A. and C. F. Rüter eds., *The Tokyo Judgment* (Amsterdam: UP Amsterdam, 1977) I

Rosas, Allan, *The Legal Status of Prisoners of War* (Helsinki: Suomalainen Tiedeakademia, 1976)

Rosenne, Shabtai, *Breach of Treaty* (Cambridge: Grotius, 1985)

Rousseau, Charles, 'Chronique des faits internationaux', (1980) 84 *Revue générale de droit international public* 361

'Chronique des faits internationaux', (1986) 90 *Revue générale de droit international public* 945

Rucz, Claude, 'Les mesures unilatérales de protection des droits de l'homme devant l'Institut de droit international', [1992] *Annuaire français de droit international* 579

Sacerdoti, Giorgio, 'A proposito del caso *Priebke*: La responsabilità per l'esecuzione di ordini illegitimi costituenti crimini di guerra', (1997) 80 *Rivista di diritto internationale* 130

Sachariew, K., 'State Responsibility for Multilateral Treaty Violations: Identifying the "Injured State" and its Legal Status', (1988) 35 *Nether Int'l L Rev.* 273

Sahović, Milan, 'International Humanitarian Law in the "Yugoslav War"', (1992) *Jugoslenvska revija za međunarodno pravo* 195

Salmon, Jean J. A., 'Some Observations on Characterization in Public International Law', in Antonio Cassese ed., *UN Law/Fundamental Rights* (Alphen aan den Rijn: Sijthoff & Noordhoff, 1979) 3

'Les faits dans l'application du droit international', (1982-II) 175 *Recueil des cours* 257

Sandoz, Yves, 'La place des Protocoles additionnels aux Conventions de Genève du 12 août 1949 dans le droit humanitaire', (1979) 12 *Revue des droits de l'homme* 135

'Unlawful Damage in Armed Conflicts and Redress Under International Humanitarian Law', (1982) 228 *Int'l Rev. Red Cross* 131

'Penal Aspects of Humanitarian Law', in M. Cherif Bassiouni ed., *International Criminal Law: Crimes* (Dobbs Ferry, NY: Transnational Publishers, 1986) I, 230

'Implementing International Humanitarian Law', in UNESCO, *International Dimensions of Humanitarian Law* (Dordrecht: Nijhoff, 1988) 259

'Réflexion sur la mise en oeuvre du droit international humanitaire et sur le rôle du Comité international de la Croix-Rouge en ex-Yougoslavie', [1993] *Revue suisse de droit international et européen* 461

Sassòli, Marco, 'The Status, Treatment, and Repatriation of Deserters under International Humanitarian Law', [1985] *YB Int'l Inst. Hum. L* 23

'Mise en oeuvre du droit international humanitaire et du droit international des droits de l'homme', (1987) 43 *Annuaire suisse de droit international* 24

'La première décision de la Chambre d'appel dans l'affaire *Tadić*', [1996] *Revue générale de droit international public* 120

Scelle, Georges, 'Règles générales du droit de la paix', (1933-IV) 46 *Recueil des cours* 327

Schachter, Oscar, 'The Quasi-judicial Role of the Security Council and the General Assembly', (1965) 58 *Am. J Int'l L* 960

'The Obligation to Implement the Covenant in Domestic Law', in Louis Henkin ed., *The International Bill of Rights* (New York: Columbia UP, 1981) 311

'International Law in Theory and Practice', (1982-V) 178 *Recueil des cours* 9

International Law in Theory and Practice (Dordrecht: Nijhoff, 1991)

Scharf, Michael, 'The Letter of the Law: The Scope of the International Legal Obligation to Prosecute Human Rights Crimes', (1996) 59 *L & Contemp. Prob.* 41

Schindler, Dietrich, 'The Different Types of Armed Conflicts According to the Geneva Conventions and Protocols', (1979-II) 163 *Recueil des cours* 117

'State of War, Belligerency, Armed Conflict', in Antonio Cassese ed., *The New Humanitarian Law of Armed Conflict* (Naples: Ed. Scientifica, 1979) 3

'Human Rights and Humanitarian Law: The Interrelationship of the Laws', (1982) 31 *Am. UL Rev.* 935

'Transformations in the Law of Neutrality Since 1945', in Astrid Delissen and Gerard Tanja eds., *Humanitarian Law of Armed Conflict: Challenges Ahead* – *Essays in Honour of Frits Kalshoven* (Dordrecht: Nijhoff, 1991) 367

'Die *erga omnes*-Wirkung des humanitären Völkerrecht', in Ulrich Byerlin et al. eds., *Recht zwischen Umbruch und Bewahrung: Völkerrecht, Europarecht, Staatsrecht. Festschrift für Rudolf Bernhardt* (Berlin: Springer, 1995)

Schindler, Dietrich and Jiří Toman, *The Laws of Armed Conflict*, 3rd edn (Dordrecht: Nijhoff, 1989)

Schneeberger, Ernst, 'Reciprocity as a Maxim of International Law', (1948) 37 *Georgetown LJ* 29

Schwarzenberger, Georg, '*Jus Pacis ac Belli*? Prolegomena to a Sociology of International Law', (1943) 37 *Am. J Int'l L* 460

The Frontiers of International Law (London: Stevens & Sons, 1962)

International Law as Applied by International Courts and Tribunals – *The Law of Armed Conflict* (London: Stevens & Sons, 1968) II

Schwebel, Stephen, 'The Roles of the Security Council and the International
    Court of Justice in the Application of International Humanitarian Law',
    (1995) 27 *NYU J Int'l L & Pol'y* 731
Schwelb, Egon, 'Termination or Suspension of the Operation of a Treaty as a
    Consequence of its Breach', (1967) 7 *Indian J Int'l L* 309
'The Law of Treaties and Human Rights', in Michael Reisman and Burns
    Weston eds., *Toward World Order and Human Dignity – Essays in Honor of Myres
    S. McDougal* (New York: Macmillan, 1976) 262 (also in (1973) 16 *Archiv des
    Völkerrecht* 1)
Sepulveda, Cesar, 'Interrelationship in the Implementation and Enforcement of
    Humanitarian Law and Human Rights', (1983) 33 *Am. UL Rev.* 117
Sereni, Angelo, *Diritto internazionale* (Milan: Giuffrè, 1965) IV
Shapira, Amos, 'Comment: The *Erga Omnes* Applicability of Human Rights',
    (1992) 30 *Archiv des Völkerrecht* 22
Shelton, Dinah, 'State Practice on Reservations to Human Rights Treaties',
    (1983) 1 *Can. Hum. Rts YB* 208
'State Responsibility for Aiding and Abetting Flagrant Violations of Human
    Rights', in D. Prémond ed., *Essays on the Concept of a 'Right to Life'* (Brussels:
    Bruylant, 1988) 222
Shestack, Jerome, 'The Jurisprudence of Human Rights', in Theodor Meron ed.,
    Human Rights in International Law: Legal and Policy Issues (Oxford: Clarendon,
    1984) II, 69
Shields Delessert, Christiane, *Release and Repatriation of Prisoners of War at the End
    of Active Hostilities* (Zurich: Schulthess Polygraphischer Verlag, 1977)
Sicilianos, Linos-Alexandre, *Les réactions décentralisées à l'illicite* (Paris: LGDJ, 1990)
'The Relationship Between Reprisals and Denunciation or Suspension of a
    Treaty', (1993) 4 *Eur. J Int'l L* 341
Siekmann, R. C. R., 'Netherlands State Practice for the Parliamentary Year
    1983–1984', (1984) 15 *Nether. YB Int'l L* 321
Simma, Bruno, 'Reflections on Article 60 of the Vienna Convention on the Law
    of Treaties and its Background in General International Law', (1970) 20
    Österreichische Zeitschrift für öffentliches Recht 5
Das Reziprozitätselement in der Entstehung des Völkergewohnheitsrecht (Munich:
    Fink, 1970)
Das Reziprozitätselement im zustandekommen völkerrechtlicher Verträge (Berlin:
    Duncker & Humblot, 1972)
'Reciprocity', in Rudolf Bernhardt ed., [Instalment] 7 *Encyclopedia of Public
    International Law* (Amsterdam: North-Holland, 1984) 400
'Self-Contained Regimes', (1985) 16 *Nether. YB Int'l L* 111
'From Bilateralism to Community Interest in International Law', (1994-VI)
    250 *Recueil des cours* 217
Simpson, Gerry, 'War Crimes: A Critical Introduction', in Timothy McCormack
    and Gerry Simpson eds., *The Law of War Crimes* (The Hague: Kluwer, 1997) 1

Sinclair, Sir Ian, *The Vienna Convention on the Law of Treaties*, 2nd edn (Manchester: Manchester UP, 1984)

Sinha, Bhek Pati, *Unilateral Denunciation of Treaty Because of Prior Violation of Obligations by Other Party* (The Hague: Nijhoff, 1966)

Siotis, Jean, *Le droit de la guerre et les conflits armés d'un caractère non-international* (Paris: LGDJ, 1958)

'The Siracusa Principles on the Limitation and Derogation Provisions in the International Covenant on Civil and Political Rights', (1985) 7 *Hum. Rts Quart.* 3

Skubiszewski, Krzysztof, 'Peace and War', in Rudolf Bernhardt ed., [Instalment] 4 *Encyclopedia of Public International Law* (Amsterdam: North-Holland, 1982) 74

Smart, Carol, *Feminism and the Power of Law* (London: Routledge, 1989)

Smith, Bradley, *Reaching Judgment at Nuremberg* (New York: Basic Books, 1977)

Sofaer, Abraham D., 'Agora: The US Decision not to Ratify Protocol I to the Geneva Convention on the Protection of War Victims', (1988) 82 *Am. J Int'l L* 784

Sohn, Louis B., 'The New International Law: Protecting the Rights of Individuals Rather than States', (1982) 32 *Am. UL Rev.* 1

Spaight, J. M., *War Rights on Land* (London: Macmillan, 1911)

Sperduti, Giuseppe, 'L'individu et le droit international', (1956-II) 90 *Recueil des cours* 727

'Responsibility of States for Activities of Private Law Persons', in Rudolf Bernhardt ed., [Instalment] 10 *Encyclopedia of Public International Law* (Amsterdam: North-Holland, 1987) 373

Spinedi, Marina, 'Implementation of International Humanitarian Law and Rules of International Law on State Responsibility for Illicit Acts', (1987) 261 *Int'l Rev. Red Cross* 668

Stern, Brigitte, 'Un système hybride: La procédure de règlement pour la réparation des dommages résultant de l'occupation illicite du Koweit par l'Irak', (1992) 37 *McGill LJ* 625

Stone, Julius, *Legal Control of International Conflict*, 2nd edn (London: Stevens & Sons, 1959)

Stowell, Ellery C., 'Military Reprisals and the Laws of War', (1942) 36 *Am J Int'l L* 643

Sund, H., 'Les criminels de guerre en Norvège et la répression de leurs délits', (1946–7) *Revue de droit pénal et de criminologie* 705

Sunga, Lyal, *Individual Responsibility in International Law for Serious Human Rights Violations* (Dordrecht: Nijhoff, 1992)

Suy, Erik, 'Droit des traités et droits de l'homme', in Rudolf Bernhardt et al. eds., *Völkerrecht als Rechtsordnung, internationale Gerichtsbarkeit, Menschenrechte: Festschrift für Herman Mosler* (Berlin: Springer, 1983) 935

Talkington, A. H., 'International Trade: Uganda Trade Embargo', (1979) 20 *Harv. J Int'l L* 206

Talmon, Stefan, 'Recognition of Governments: An Analysis of the New British Policy and Practice', (1992) 63 *Brit. YB Int'l L* 231

Tansley, Donald, *Final Report: An Agenda for Red Cross* (Geneva: ICRC, 1975)

Taubenfeld, Howard J., 'The Applicability of the Laws of War in Civil War', in John Norton Moore ed., *Law and Civil War in the Modern World* (Baltimore: Johns Hopkins Press, 1974) 499

Taylor, Charles, 'Human Rights: The Legal Culture', in Paul Ricoeur ed., *Philosophical Foundations of Human Rights* (Paris: UNESCO, 1968) 49

Taylor, Telford, *Final Report to the Secretary General of the Army on the Nuernberg War Crimes Trials Under Control Council Law No. 10* (Washington: US Gov. Printing Office, 1949)

   'Concept of Justice and the Law of War', (1974) 13 *Colum. J Trans. L* 189

   The Anatomy of the Nuremberg Trials – A Personal Memoir (New York: Knopf, 1992)

Tenekides, G., *L'individu dans l'ordre juridique international* (Paris: Pedone, 1933)

Thurnwald, Richard, *Economics in Primitive Communities* (London: Oxford UP, 1932)

Tolley, H., *The United Nations Commission on Human Rights* (Boulder: Westview Press, 1987)

Toman, Jiří, *The Protection of Cultural Property in the Event of an Armed Conflict* (Paris: UNESCO/Dartmouth, 1996)

Tomuschat, Christian, 'Grundpflichten des Individuums nach Völkerrecht', (1983) 21 *Archiv des Völkerrecht* 289

   'Crimes Against the Peace and Security of Mankind and the Recalcitrant Third State', in Yoram Dinstein and Mala Tabory eds., *War Crimes in International Law* (Dordrecht: Nijhoff, 1996) 41

   'Individual Reparations Claims in Instances of Grave Human Rights Violations: The Position Under General International Law', in Albrecht Randelzhofer and Christian Tomuschat eds., *State Responsibility and Human Rights* (The Hague: Nijhoff, 1999) 1

Tremblay, Guy, 'Les situations d'urgence qui permettent en droit international de suspendre les droits de l'homme', (1977) 18 *Cahiers de droit* 3

Tucker, Robert W., *50 US Naval War College International Law Studies – The Law of War and Neutrality at Sea* (Washington: US Gov. Printing Office, 1955)

Tunkin, Grigory, *Theory of International Law* (London: George Allen & Unwin, 1965)

Tushnet, Carl, 'An Essay on Rights', (1984) 62 *Tex. L Rev.* 1363

Umozurike, Oji, *The African Charter on Human and Peoples' Rights* (The Hague: Nijhoff, 1997)

Umozurike, U., 'The African Charter on Human and Peoples' Rights', (1983) 77 *Am. J Int'l L* 902

UN War Crimes Commission, *History of the United Nations War Crimes Commission and the Development of the Laws of War* (London: HMSO, 1948)

Urner, Paul, *Die Menschenrechte der Zivilperson im Krieg gemäss der Genfer Zivilkonvention von 1949* (Winterthur: Keller, 1956)

van Boven, Theo C., 'Reliance on Norms of Humanitarian Law by United Nations Organs', in Astrid Delissen and Gerard Tanja eds., *Humanitarian Law of Armed Conflict: Challenges Ahead – Essays in Honour of Frits Kalshoven* (Dordrecht: Nijhoff, 1991) 495

van Dijk, P. and G. J. H. van Hoof, *Theory and Practice of the European Convention on Human Rights*, 3rd edn (The Hague: Kluwer, 1998)

van Houtte, Hans, 'Mass Property Claim Resolution in a Post-War Society: The Commission for Real Property Claims in Bosnia and Herzegovina', (1999) 48 *Int'l & Comp. L Quart.* 625

Vasak, Karel, 'Proposition pour une Déclaration universelle des devoirs de l'homme, introduction et texte', (1987) 168 *Le supplément – Revue d'éthique et de théologie morale* 9

Vázquez, Carlos Manuel, 'The Four Doctrines of Self-executing Treaties', (1995) 89 *Am. J Int'l L* 695

Velu, Jacques, 'Les effets directs des instruments internationaux en matière de droits de l'homme', [1980] 2 *Revue belge de droit international* 293
Les effets directs des instruments internationaux en matière de droits de l'homme (Brussels: Swinnen, 1981)

Venezia, Jean-Claude, 'La notion de représaille en droit international public', (1960) 64 *Revue générale de droit international public* 465

Verdoodt, Albert, *Naissance et signification de la Déclaration universelle des droits de l'homme* (Louvain: Nauwelaerts, 1964)

Verdross, Alfred, 'Das neue italienische Kriegs- und Neutralitätsrecht', (1939) 19 *Zeitschrift für öffentliches Recht* 193
Völkerrecht, 5th edn (Vienna: Springer-Verlag, 1964) 425

Verhoeven, Joe, 'La notion d'applicabilité directe en droit international', (1980) 15 *Revue belge de droit international* 243

Verplaetse, Julian, 'The *Jus in Bello* and Military Operations in Korea 1950–53', (1963) 23 *Zeitschrift für ausländisches öffentliches Recht und Völkerrecht* 679

Verwey, Wil D., 'The Hostages Convention and National Liberation Movements', (1981) 75 *Am. J Int'l L* 69

Vescovi, Enrique, *Los recursos judiciales y además medios impugnativos en Iberoamérica* (Buenos Aires: Depalma, 1998)

Veuthey, Michel, *Guérilla et droit humanitaire* (Geneva: Institut Henri-Dunant, 1976)
'Assessing Humanitarian Law', in Thomas Weiss and Larry Minear eds., *Humanitarianism Across Borders – Sustaining Civilians in Times of War* (Boulder: Lynne Rienner, 1993) 125

Villani, Ugo, 'I diritti degli stranieri negli atti internazionali sui diritti dell'uomo', (1987) 99 *Studi senesi* 105

Villiger, Mark E., *Customary International Law and Treaties* (Dordrecht: Nijhoff, 1985) 274

Virally, Michel, 'Le principe de réciprocité dans le droit international contemporain', (1967-III) 122 *Recueil des cours* 1

Vité, Sylvain, *Les procédures internationales d'établissement des faits dans la mise en oeuvre du droit international humanitaire* (Brussels: Bruylant, 1999)

von der Heydte, Friedrich, 'Exposé préliminaire sur le problème que pose l'existence des armes de destruction massive et la distinction entre les objectifs militaires et non militaires en général', (1967) 52:2 *Annuaire de l'Institut de droit international* 73

von Glahn, Gerhard, 'The Protection of Human Rights in Times of Armed Conflicts', (1970) 1 *Isr. YB Hum. Rts* 208

von Kirchenheim, 'Kriegsgefangene', in Karl Strupp, *Wörterbuch des Völkerrecht und der Diplomatie*, 1st edn (Berlin: de Gruyter, 1924) I, 743

von Knieriem, August, *Nürnberg – Rechtliche und menschliche Probleme* (Stuttgart: Klett, 1953)

Waldron, Jeremy ed., *Theories of Rights* (Oxford: Oxford UP, 1984)

Weil, Prosper, 'Vers une normativité relative en droit international?', (1982) 86 *Revue générale de droit international public* 5

Weiss, P., 'Diplomatic Protection of Nationals and International Protection of Human Rights', (1971) 2–3 *Revue des droits de l'homme* 645

Weissbrodt, David, 'The Role of International Organizations in the Implementation of Human Rights and Humanitarian Law in Situations of Armed Conflict', (1988) 21 *Vanderbilt J Int'l L* 313

Weissbrodt, David and Beth Andrus, 'The Right to Life During Armed Conflict: *Disabled Peoples International v. United States*', (1988) 29 *Harv. Int'l LJ* 59

Weissbrodt, David and P. L. Hicks, 'Enforcement of Human Rights and Humanitarian Law in Belligerent Relations', (1993) *Int'l Rev. Red Cross* 129

Wells, Donald A., *Guide to the US Army Manuals* (Westport, Conn.: Greenwood, 1993)

Wengler, Wilhelm, 'La noción de sujeto de derecho internacional público examinada bajo el aspecto de algunos fenómenos políticos actuales', (1951) 3 *Revista española de derecho internacional* 831

Der Begriff des politischen im internationalen Recht (Tübingen: Mohr, 1956)

Völkerrecht (Berlin: Springer, 1964) II

Wexler, Leila Sadat, 'The Interpretation of the Nuremberg Principles by the French Court of Cassation: From *Touvier* to *Barbie* and Back Again', (1994) 32 *Colum. J Transnat'l L* 289

Whiteman, Marjorie M., *Digest of International Law* (Washington: US Gov. Printing Office, 1968) X

Wilhelm, René-Jean, 'Le caractère des droits accordés à l'individu dans les Conventions de Genève', [1950] *Revue internationale de la Croix-Rouge* 561

'Problèmes relatifs à la protection de la personne humaine par le droit international dans les conflits armés ne présentant pas un caractère international', (1972-III) 137 *Recueil des cours* 316

Willis, James F., *Prologue to Nuremberg: The Politics and Diplomacy of Punishing War Criminals of the First World War* (Westport, Conn.: Greenwood, 1982)

Wilson, Heather A., *International Law and the Use of Force by National Liberation Movements* (Oxford: Clarendon, 1988)

Wise, 'International Crimes and Domestic Criminal Jurisdiction', (1989) 38 *DePaul L Rev.* 923

Wolf, 'ILO Experience in the Implementation of Human Rights', (1975) 10 *J Int'l L & Econ.* 599

Wright, Quincy, 'International Law and Guilt by Association', (1949) 43 *Am. J Int'l L* 746

Zayas, Alfred M. de, *The Wehrmacht War Crime Bureau 1939–1945* (U Nebraska Press, 1989)

Zoller, Elizabeth, *Peacetime Unilateral Remedies: An Analysis of Countermeasures* (Dobbs Ferry, NY: Transnational Publishers, 1984) 3

Zorgbibe, Charles, 'De la théorie classique de la reconnaissance de belligérance à l'Article 3 des Conventions de Genève', in *Droit humanitaire et conflits armés – Actes du colloque du 28 au 30 janvier 1970, Université libre de Bruxelles* (Brussels: Ed. Université de Bruxelles, 1976) 83

'Le caractère armé des conflits', in *Droit humanitaire et conflits armés – Actes du colloque du 28 au 30 janvier 1970, Université libre de Bruxelles* (Brussels: Ed. Université de Bruxelles, 1976) 93

Zourek, Jaroslav, 'Le respect des droits de l'homme et des libertés fondamentales constitut-il une affaire interne de l'Etat?', in *Estudios de derecho internacional: Homenaje al profesor Miaja de la Muela* (Madrid: Tecnos, 1979) I, 603

Index

Non-combatants
see also Civilians
enemy states, relationships, 7–8
Fourth Geneva Convention (1949),
158, 347
Geneva Conventions (1949), 347
hostile acts, 31, 37
individual obligations, 78
Protocol II (1977), 347
status jeopardised, 158
violations, 78, 79–89
Non-derogable provisions
American Convention on Human
Rights (1969), 244
characterisation, 244
International Covenant on Civil and
Political Rights (1966), 244, 333
reservations, 141, 142, 199–200
suspension, 220–1
Non-international armed conflict *see*
Internal armed conflict
Normative frameworks
conclusions, 54–6, 98–102, 116–17
conditionality, 34–42
deconstructive approach, 13–14
internal armed conflict, 94–8
introduction, 13–15
obligations, 57–102
procedural capacity, 42–56
responsibility, 57, 102–15
rights, 17–42
Norms
application *see* Application of norms
human rights *see* Human rights
humanitarian *see* Humanitarian law
jus cogens, 124, 142, 218, 221
object and purpose, 133–40
self-executing, 23–4, 32
North Vietnam
Third Geneva Convention (1949), 148
Vietnam War, 30, 148, 252, 290
Northern Ireland, 242, 268, 271, 272
Norway, 273
Nuremberg trials
IMT *see* International Military Tribunal
(IMT) (Nuremberg)
United States *see* US Military Tribunal
(Nuremberg)

Obligations
absolute, 176

erga omnes see Erga omnes
human rights, 58–75, 129, 147
humanitarian law, 13, 75–102, 147,
176
inadimplenti rule, 163, 166, 225
individuals *see* Individual obligations
insurgents, 78, 89, 97
internal armed conflict, 94–8
international law subjects, 13, 14
irregular armed forces, 78, 89, 90–8
normative frameworks, 57–102
rebel authorities, 97–8
reciprocity, 121–5, 147, 163
resistance groups, 97, 98
sanctions disassociated, 57–8
states *see* State obligations
synallagmatic, 122, 124
Occupying powers
alien domination, 255
Austria, 251
belligerent occupation, 255
Czechoslovakia, 251
death penalty, 149
diplomatic relations, 41
Fourth Geneva Convention (1949), 251
Hague Regulations (1907), 8, 175, 251
Israel, 3, 21, 23, 51, 56, 255, 297, 300,
302
military occupation, 251–2
occupied population
allegiance, 8
relations, 162
self-defence, 175
plundering/looting, 86, 87, 101, 102
reciprocity, 175
resistance *see* Resistance groups
Second World War, 251
Turkey/Cyprus, 19, 21, 333–4
Ogaden, 326
Oppenheim, Lassa, 248
Organization of African Unity (OAU)
African Charter on Human and Peoples'
Rights (1979), 128
Liberation Committee, 303, 304
national liberation movements, 258,
298, 303–4, 308
political bodies, 297, 303–4
territorial integrity, 303–4
Organization of American States (OAS), 65,
335, 336
Oslo Accords, 294

Books in the series

Principles of the institutional law of international organisations
C. F. Amerasinghe

Fragmentation and the international relations of micro-states
Jorri Duursma

The Polar regions and the development of international law
Donald R. Rothwell

Sovereignty over natural resources
Nico Schrijver

Ethics and authority in international law
Alfred P. Rubin

Religious liberty and international law in Europe
Malcolm D. Evans

Unjust enrichment
Hanoch Dagan

Trade and the environment
Damien Geradin

The changing international law of high seas fisheries
Francisco Orrego Vicuña

International organizations before national courts
August Reinisch

The right to property in commonwealth constitutions
Tom Allen

Trusts: A comparative study
Maurizio Lupoi

On civil procedure
J. A. Jolowicz

Good faith in European contract law
Reinhard Zimmerman and Simon Whittaker

Money laundering
Guy Stessens

International law in antiquity
David J. Bederman

The enforceability of promises in European contract law
James Gordley

International commercial arbitration and African states
Amazu A. Asouzu

The law of internal armed conflict
    Lindsay Moir

Diversity and self-determination in international law
    Karen Knop

Remedies against international organisations: basic issues
    Karel Wellens

International human rights and humanitarian law
    René Provost

Sharing transboundary resources: international law and optimal resource use
    Eyal Benvenisti

LaVergne, TN USA
01 September 2009
156659LV00012B/100/A